ECONOMIC ANNALS OF THE NINETEENTH CENTURY

1821–1830

Volume II

ECONOMIC ANNALS

OF THE

NINETEENTH CENTURY

1821–1830

Volume II

BY

WILLIAM SMART

M.A., D.PHIL., LL.D. : ADAM SMITH PROFESSOR OF POLITICAL ECONOMY
IN THE UNIVERSITY OF GLASGOW

REPRINTS OF ECONOMIC CLASSICS

Augustus M. Kelley, Bookseller
New York 1964

Library of Congress Catalogue Card Number
63 - 23520

PRINTED IN THE UNITED STATES OF AMERICA
by SENTRY PRESS, NEW YORK, N. Y. 10019

PUBLISHERS' NOTE

THIS second volume of "Economic Annals of the Nineteenth Century" was, except for the Index, in type, and
had been revised once and part of it twice before Professor
Smart's death on the 19th March, 1915.

PUBLISHER'S NOTE

CONTENTS

CHAPTER I

1821. CONTINUED DEPRESSION IN AGRICULTURE AND SLOW REVIVAL OF INDUSTRY

CHAPTER II

1821. THE FIRST VICTORY OF FREE TRADE : THE TIMBER DUTIES

Contents

CHAPTER III

1821. TAXATION AND FINANCE

CHAPTER IV

1821. THE UNEVENTFUL YEAR

CHAPTER V

1822. THE AGRICULTURAL AGITATION AGAINST TAXATION

Contents

CHAPTER VI

1822. THE BUDGET

CHAPTER VII

1822. THE STRUGGLE AGAINST RESUMPTION

CHAPTER VIII

1822. FIRST ALTERATION IN THE NAVIGATION ACTS

Contents

CHAPTER IX

1822.   PROTECTION AT HOME AND ABROAD

CHAPTER X

1822.   AGRICULTURE AND INDUSTRY : THE NEW CORN LAW

CHAPTER XI

1822.   ANOTHER UNEVENTFUL YEAR

Contents

CHAPTER XII

1823. THE PASSING AWAY OF AGRICULTURAL DISTRESS

CHAPTER XIII

1823. INDUSTRY : A QUIETLY PROSPEROUS YEAR

CHAPTER XIV

1823. ROBINSON'S FIRST BUDGET

CHAPTER XV

1823. TOWARDS FREE TRADE

Contents

Contents

CHAPTER XX

1824.   THE REPEAL OF THE COMBINATION LAWS

CHAPTER XXI

1824.   SOCIAL AND ECONOMIC

CHAPTER XXVI

1825. THE SPECULATIVE MANIA

CHAPTER XXVII

1825. AGRICULTURE : A THREATENED CHANGE IN THE CORN LAW

CHAPTER XXVIII

1825. LABOUR LEGISLATION : COMBINATION AND FACTORY ACTS

Contents

CHAPTER XXIX

1825. OTHER HAPPENINGS OF THE YEAR

CHAPTER XXX

1826. THE AFTERMATH

CHAPTER XXXI

1826. THE END OF THE ONE-POUND NOTES

Contents

CHAPTER XXXII

1826. THE BUDGET

CHAPTER XXXIII

1826. FREE TRADE ON ITS TRIAL

CHAPTER XXXIV

1826. THE CORN LAWS : JACOB'S REPORT

Contents

Contents

Contents

CHAPTER XLIII

1829. SUDDEN RELAPSE INTO DEEP DISTRESS

CHAPTER XLIV

1829. GOULBURN'S SECOND BUDGET

CHAPTER XLV

1829. THE PROGRESS OF FREE TRADE IDEAS

Contents

Contents

CHAPTER XLIX

1830. THE BUDGET : REDUCTION OF TAXATION : THEORY OF TAXATION

CHAPTER L

1830. THE FALL OF THE WELLINGTON ADMINISTRATION

CHAPTER I

1821. CONTINUED DEPRESSION IN AGRICULTURE AND SLOW REVIVAL OF INDUSTRY

IN 1821, the condition of agriculture was puzzling everybody. If Protection could have ensured prosperity, agriculture ought to have been prosperous : till the famine price of 80/- for wheat, and a proportionally high price for other grains, had been the home average for six weeks, the ports were absolutely shut against foreign produce. But, no matter whether crops were good or bad, whether prices were high or low, the cry of distress had never been stilled since the war, save for a brief eighteen months. At the moment, the country had just enjoyed what used to be considered the national blessing of an abundant and good quality harvest. It was only natural that prices should come down. But was not the Corn Law expressly designed to prevent low prices ? Had the farmers not been promised that a monopoly would always secure them something like 80/- ? [1] One would think that it had not occurred to anybody that a monopoly of supply will not ensure high prices, if the article produced is one for which the demand is limited, and if the supply is overabundant. But the agriculturists were now to be told that perhaps the monopoly itself was to blame.

At the opening of the session, the King's Speech spoke of the considerable improvements which had taken place within the last half year in several of the most important branches of commerce and manufacture, and of the abatement of distress in many of the manufacturing districts. Criticism was at once directed to the significant omission of any mention of the special depression of agriculture. The Prime Minister, somewhat lamely, defended it

Something wrong with agriculture.

---

[1] The average annual price of wheat since 1815 had been, successively, 78/6, 96/11, 86/3, 74/6, 67/10. Now, in the beginning of the year, it was 54/-.

on the ground that the agricultural depression arose from the low prices, and that the full explanation of the fall in prices was the abundance of the home production. If Liverpool thought this a "full explanation," others did not, and the issues were confused according as speakers looked at agriculture and industry generally as one interest or as two—as affected by a single cause or by distinct causes. The reason most confidently given was the late reform in the currency. And, whatever amount of truth there was in the one statement, or assumption, that the "too hasty" change from paper to gold had directly reduced prices by the contraction in the amount of that commodity in which all prices are named, or in the other, that the banks had contracted their accommodation and checked adventure and enterprise, there could be no doubt that the contraction had, for the time at least, injured the "productive classes" just as its expansion had injured the salaried classes. The point most dwelt on was the effect on the two agricultural classes. During the high prices, landowners, enjoying unprecedented rents, had not only launched into extravagant ways of living, but had burdened their estates with jointures, mortgages, rent-charges, etc., and found themselves unable to discharge these obligations when reduced rents were got in with difficulty. In the same confidence of continued high prices, the farmers had taken leases at rents which were not likely to be realised when prices were low, and had sunk capital, as well as labour, in farms which were now likely to be taken from them. And they also had adopted ways of life which, Cobbett roundly told them, were "not fitting."[1] The hardship was undoubted; the weakness of the

The currency to blame.

[1] "I am aware that there are above a hundred thousand farmers, with wives, sons, and daughters that would make up half a million of persons, and that each of these will long to cut my throat for what I am now going to say; but I nevertheless will say that it is an unnatural state of society, that it is a state of society tending to misery and confusion, in which farmers in general can lead a life at all resembling that of what is called a gentleman; a life including the circumstances of *Sir, Ma'am*, gig, musical instruments, parlour, bell to call servants, and some other things in the way of dress; but, above all things, *wine upon table after dinner.* I say, and I put my name to the saying, that is an unnatural and bad state of society in which farmers in general can even think of doing these things. The truth is that the business of the common farmer is a very plain sort of thing. It is learned by living and working upon a farm. There are very few labourers who have gone through all the grades of crow boy, shepherd's boy, plough-boy, ploughman, hedger, thresher, reaper and mower; very few labourers who have gone through all these and who are sober and in other respects morally endowed for the purpose, are deficient in point of capacity to conduct the affairs of an ordinary farm. Now here is not a sufficiency of mental endowment and of talent of any sort required to seem to merit any considerable portion of what is called

argument lay in the assumption that it was the change in the currency which had produced the low prices; and the extravagance of those who called for a repeal of the resumption of cash payments made reasonable people a little impatient of the real hardship.

The constant presentation of petitions—they amounted to 1,200 from the session of 1819 to that of 1821, the greatest number of petitions ever presented to Parliament on one subject, and all of them complaining of the principle and operation of the Corn Law of 1815 [1]—made it impossible longer to refuse parliamentary enquiry; and, after obtaining an assurance from Castlereagh that the Government, while convinced that the evils of the agricultural distress were dependent on causes beyond the control of the legislature, would give their cordial support, Gooch, the member for Suffolk, moved for a committee to enquire into the distress of the Agricultural Interest.[2] He intimated his own opinion that some further protection must be given against the importation of foreign produce if the country were not to degenerate into what our great enemy had called us, a *nation boutiquière*,[3] and trusted that "the gentlemen who usually opposed the agricultural interest, especially that individual amongst them who was so highly distinguished for his knowledge of political economy (Mr. Ricardo),[4] would permit the committee to see what good they could effect by their deliberations." Knatchbull, the member for Kent, who seconded, said that it was not the wish of the supporters of the motion to enter into any questions of political economy—for such discussion their habits were unfit. Farming had been a losing concern for three years; in 1820, the loss was almost ruinous. It was to be feared

Demand for parliamentary enquiry.

Knatchbull.

fortune. There are too many men in the world with sufficient capacity to conduct the affairs of a farm to permit farming, generally speaking, to be a *money-making occupation.* . . . To obtain a good living, and to rear up well a pretty large family is all that, in general, a farmer can expect. To attempt to make them gentlemen is to put everything out of place " (*Register*, June 28, 1823).

[1] Goderich in 1827; *Hansard*, xvii. 988.

[2] *Hansard*, iv. 360, 895, 1139.

[3] As a fact, Napoleon was not the author of the expression: " To found a great empire for the sole purpose of raising up a people of customers," said Adam Smith, " may at first sight appear a project fit only for a nation of shopkeepers. It is, however, a project altogether unfit for a nation of shopkeepers, but extremely fit for a nation whose government is influenced by shopkeepers " (iv. vii. iii.).

[4] Ricardo had said, in a debate in February, that the only remedy for agricultural distress was the repeal of the Corn Laws (*Hansard*, iv. 945).

that, if things went on as they were doing, the whole of the poorer
land would be thrown out of cultivation.[1] The causes, he thought,
were foreign import, the warehousing system, and the alteration
in the currency ; but the only remedies he hinted at were the
establishment of a correct mode of taking the averages, and a

Robinson. small advance in the importing price of oats. Robinson, the
President of the Board of Trade, not ashamed of having voted
against an enquiry in the past year, welcomed the proposal now,
but called attention to the fact, sometimes ignored, that further
protection had been given to agriculture since 1812 ; many other
articles of agricultural produce, cattle, sheep, and other live stock

Curwen. were now prohibited. Curwen accused Ministers of being ignorant
of the real extent of the distress ; if they had known it, they would
have seen it " their imperative duty long ago to have interposed
relief." One great cause was the " enormous taxation." " In the
most flourishing times, while taxation amounted to £80 millions,
the income of the whole empire could never be placed higher than
£400 millions. At present the income was only £300 millions ;
yet taxation was the same." He asked for " fair countervailing
duties "—a Polish landowner had told him that, " if the agriculturists of Poland received 8/- for their corn, they would not count
it bad ; but, if they received 12/-, they would consider themselves
completely remunerated. . . ."[2] There was a point at which it

[1] One notices an assumption very generally underlying the discussions,
that, to allow the poorer lands to go out of cultivation, was not to be thought
of : it was " madness beyond parallel "—and this quite independently of the
two more relevant considerations, that capital had been sunk in them, and
that they were needed to secure independence of the foreigner.   Curwen, for
instance, the member for Cumberland, who was the most pronounced adherent
of this doctrine, said : Some people thought it necessary that the inferior
grounds should go out of cultivation. This he expressly denied. " Every acre
in the country ought to be brought into cultivation ; for what was the evil
which the country at present endured above any other but want of employment ? " ; and he thought it enough to say that " the produce of our bad lands
generally supplied the consumption of the country for two months in the
year, and that was more than had ever been imported."   In justice to this
view, it might be suggested that, in these days, if the staple grains were
not grown, there were not, known or introduced into field cultivation, sufficient alternative uses to take up all the land, and thus a great part of the
" natural capital " of the country might lie unused. This, to those who had
a wholesome dread of " political economy," seemed almost a criminal waste
of what they considered " productive " capital because it would " grow
things."   In other words, they could not grasp the idea that land, like other
natural resources, may in certain circumstances be " worth nothing," and
indeed cost something to use. It is an idea not yet dead.

[2] A foreigner well acquainted with the corn trade of the North of Europe
at once pointed out that this was either misrepresentation or a mistake ; that

became even a duty to resist, and, if Government would not take care of the interests of those committed to their charge, men would feel that they had a right to take the preservation of those interests into their own hands. " Squire Western," the recognised champion _{Western.} of the agricultural interests, pleaded that the extra price of bread under Protection was to this country the price of security, and hoped that the protection would be " such as to keep in cultivation at least as much land as stood at present in that situation." Denis Browne, an Irish member, who did not scruple to say that the main cause of the distress was the want of protection against the produce of the Continent, would have prohibited the importation of foreign corn altogether, leaving it to the discretion of Parliament to decide when it was proper to remove the restriction.

Ricardo felt bound to say, as he had said before, that, in the present case, the interest of the landholders must necessarily be opposed to that of the consumers—and he reminded the House that he himself was not a " mercantile man," with a mercantile interest to serve, but a landed proprietor. He hoped that, while contending for the policy of Free Trade, he might not be supposed an advocate for unlimited free trade in corn : " there were circumstances attending that question which rendered it imperative upon the legislature to impose some shackles upon a trade which, more than any other, being once without restraint, speedily required them." As regards the countervailing duties which were urged by many, " if the agriculturists would show that they had any particular taxes to cope with which other producers had not, then, undoubtedly, they ought to have a countervailing duty to that amount ; and, not only so, but there ought to be a drawback upon exportation to that amount." [1] " The great principle upon which

Ricardo explains the Countervailing Duty.

---

the price in Poland, Russia and Galicia was equal to about 25/4 per quarter, and that this price could not pay the farmers there if they got the ground for nothing (*Farmer's Magazine*, p. 254).

[1] The argument is given in Ricardo's *Protection to Agriculture*. If taxation, he says, equally affected all producers, there would be no necessity for a protecting duty : no one, *e.g.* has ever yet suggested that such a duty would be necessary in the case of an Income Tax because, after the tax is imposed, all products are left of the same relative value. But a tax at home which falls on a particular commodity tends to raise the price of that commodity—otherwise the producer would no longer gain the ordinary profits—and, in this case, unless there is a corresponding duty on the similar article when introduced from abroad, he cannot raise his price, and is driven from his trade. To impose no duty is, in fact, to give a bounty to the foreigner. Now tithes, a portion of the poor rate, and one or two other taxes are peculiar taxation of this kind. If there were no foreign competition, the farmer would be able

they should go was this—to make the price of their corn approximate, as nearly as possible, to the price it bore in other countries." But they could not reach this great and true principle at one step. " Although a duty on the importation of corn would not be so wise a measure as the approach to that system which he had suggested as constituting the true principle of a corn trade, yet he did think that a permanent duty upon importation would be a much wiser measure than the sliding scale which some had proposed and advocated." He considered that the low price of corn was occasioned by too great a supply—however that came about—and was not the consequence of taxation. Ricardo then went on to answer some arguments adduced by the protectionists, but, unfortunately, the speech was very briefly, and, one fears, badly reported, and it might be unjust to Ricardo's great reputation to accept those answers as representing even the substance of what he said.[1]

The motion was agreed to, and the following Committee appointed: Gooch (chairman), Castlereagh, Robinson, Althorp, Bankes, Brougham, Huskisson, Knatchbull, Wortley, Baring, Parnell, Wodehouse, Western, Holme Sumner, Escourt, Bourne, Tremayne, Rowley, Calthorpe, Hunter Blair, Irving, Lethbridge, Littleton, Bridges, Calvert, Ricardo, Curwen, Denis Browne, Williams Wynn, and Foster.[2]

The Agricultural Committee's Report.　After sitting for fourteen weeks, and examining forty-two witnesses whose evidence covers 344 folio pages, the Committee reported on 18th June. The Report, which was credited to

to raise his prices correspondingly with the peculiar taxes. If there is foreign competition, it should be countervailed by a duty equivalent to them. In these circumstances, and for the same reason, a corresponding bounty must, on every principle of justice, be given.

[1] One thing he appears to have dwelt on with some insistence :—that, if capital was not employed in land, it would not lie idle, but would be employed in raising other forms of exchangeable wealth. And, as regards the cultivation of poor land, when people spoke of the capital employed on it, they generally forgot that, if such land went out of cultivation, the current wages and improvements, the manures, etc., would be so much capital saved.

[2] House of Commons' Journals, p. 146. I have quoted the very diverging opinions held by members of the Committee before they entered on their work, in order that the Report afterwards agreed to—which, among other things, certainly did not " avoid political economy "—should have its due weight. It is only fair to say, however, that the Protectionists ceased to attend, with the view of preventing the issue of a Report. Indeed, Althorp is said to have been the only member representing a large agricultural constituency who signed it. It was, then, either disingenuous or ignorant to describe the Report, as Villiers did in 1842, as a Report in favour of Free Trade drawn up by " a Committee of shrewd landowners carefully considering their own interests."

Huskisson—with what justice will appear later—began by admitting, frankly and with deep regret, that the complaints of the petitioners were founded on fact, in so far as they represented that, at the existing price of corn, the returns to an arable farmer were by no means adequate to his charges and outgoings, a considerable portion of which could be paid only out of capital.[1] It was a fair inference that, for a considerable part of the war period, the returns of farming capital somewhat exceeded the ordinary rate of profit, and that now they were considerably below it. This was, however, " a revulsion of the same nature (whatever might be its degree) as many which had occurred at different periods of our history," and its pressure had led in many instances to a diminution of rents, both for old leases and new, varying in degree according to the proportion in which such rents had been increased between 1793 and 1814. In mentioning rents, the Committee took occasion to say that this increase was largely owing to the bringing waste lands into cultivation by capitals permanently vested in improvements, made partly by owners, partly by tenants,[2] and that a further proportion of the increase was unquestionably to be ascribed to " the diminished value of our currency during a great part of that period." And to the restoration of the currency must be ascribed a proportion of the depression of prices. But the Committee were also satisfied that, in the present year, the price of corn had been further depressed by the general abundance and good quality of the last harvest in all articles of grain and pulse, more particularly in Ireland. The contention that prices were still being kept down by the very large importations of foreign grain before February 15, 1819, they dismissed by pointing to the very high prices, and the constant and brisk demand so long as the ports continued open in 1817 and 1818, from which it might be inferred that the greatest part of these importations was necessary, and was disposed of during these years.

Abundance must cause low prices.

[1] It was noted, however, that the pressure upon the farmer did not seem to have materially affected the retail businesses of the country towns ; the total consumption of dutiable articles, of cotton, of wool for home consumption, and of Yorkshire cloth, had increased in comparison with the average of the three years preceding. According to Curwen, however, such consumption was no evidence, " because people, though they could not afford them, were unable to shake off old habits " (*Hansard*, iv. 1148).

[2] The number of Enclosure Bills was 906 for the first decade of the century, and 771 for the second (only 187 for the third). Porter's calculation is that over 3 million acres were brought into cultivation from 1800 to 1819, and only 375,150 from 1820 to 1829 (*Progress of the Nation*, pp. 146, 154).

While it was scarcely necessary to remark that the growth of wheat had been greatly extended and improved since 1807, it was important to recall the fact that, in 1804 and 1814, there had been a similar depression of prices owing to large harvests and extension of tillage, similar pressure and uneasiness, similar difficulty in paying rents, and similar prophecies of agricultural ruin, and that the alarm had proved only temporary. In other commodities, too, the staple productions of other countries, there had been even a greater fall in prices due to reaction—the general derangement which the convulsions of the last thirty years had produced in all the relations of commerce, in the application of capital, and in the demand for labour—the influence of which was not yet spent and exhausted. And, so far as depression of prices was produced by redundant production, it admitted of no adequate remedy except what must arise from the progressive adjustment of the supply to the demand.

Fluctuations
inevitable : One consideration, however, had constantly to be borne in mind : namely, that the price of corn fluctuated more than that of other commodities in proportion to any excess or deficiency of the supply, because, as explained by Tooke—who was one of the witnesses— "the average quantity was sufficient for the supply of every individual ; all beyond that, was an absolute depression of the market for a great length of time, and a succession of even two or three abundant harvests must evidently produce an enormously inconvenient accumulation." [1] To apply this leading principle, the Committee would assume, as not far from the actual situation, that the annual growth of corn in the United Kingdom was, upon an average, about equal to the existing annual consumption, and that, with such an average crop, the 80/- importing price was fully sufficient to secure to the British grower the complete monopoly of the home market. their limit
under
monopoly. In that case, so long as he maintained this monopoly, fluctuations would range between a maximum of 80/- and the

[1] "When the quantity of corn at market, from a succession of good crops, is abundant, it falls in price, not in the same proportion as the quantity exceeds the ordinary demand, but very considerably more. The demand for corn, with a given population, must necessarily be limited ; and, although it may be, and undoubtedly is, true that, when it is abundant and cheap, the quantity consumed will be increased, yet it is equally certain that its aggregate value will be diminished. . . . This I think certain, that the aggregate value of an abundant crop will always be considerably less than the aggregate value of an average one ; and that the aggregate value of a very limited crop will be considerably greater than that of an average crop " (Ricardo, *Protection to Agriculture*).

minimum to which the price must be reduced by a very abundant harvest before it fell below the price in some foreign market, and could find a vent in exportation. And, if it were true, as Burke and Adam Smith said, that favourable and unfavourable seasons came in pretty large cycles of years, it suggested "how hazardous and embarrassing must be the situation of the grower of corn in a country where the lowest price which is considered to afford him a remuneration shall habitually and considerably exceed the prices of the remainder of the world; although, up to that price, he should be secured in the complete monopoly of that country."

But much misconception prevailed on the subject of "a remunerative price," and, particularly, in the application made of these words by those who represented it as a fixed amount of 80/- per quarter.[1] A remunerative price in 1815 might not be a remunerative price in 1821. If the country should require now for its annual consumption one-fifth more than it did in 1815, this would require increased tillage, and recourse to worse lands on which wheat could not be grown even at 80/- when no rent was paid. If, then, the policy of the State was to continue to the home grower the monopoly of the home market, it would, on this hypothesis, be necessary to raise the importing price beyond 80/-; the extra profit on the old lands would go first to occupying tenants and then to landlords, and, "after a new engagement, 80/- would no more be a remunerative price upon the richest land, paying the highest rent, than it would upon the poorest, paying no rent at all." [2]

The change in the value of our money, the Committee said boldly, was an advance of this kind in the importing and monopoly limit, and the result of every such advance, supposing prices not to undergo a corresponding rise in other countries, was bound to expose this country to greater and more grievous fluctuations in price, and the business of a farmer to greater uncertainty and hazard, according to the alternations of good or bad seasons. This was the part of

marginal note: "A remunerative price."

[1] For instance, I find the *Farmer's Magazine* in February saying: "The agriculturists are selling the produce of their industry at a fourth part at least below what the united wisdom of the nation considered absolutely necessary for their existence."

[2] This, of course, was pure Ricardo, and was repeated in a very fresh way in Section I. of *Protection to Agriculture* (1822). Cf. also his speech in 1820 (*Economic Annals, 1801-1820*, 733). Or, as the *Quarterly Review* put it in 1827: "The consumer was called upon to pay a price which would remunerate the capitalist for raising wheat where a rabbit could not find a blade of grass to conceal itself, and this, in its reaction, had the effect of raising the rent of every acre of land of superior quality throughout the United Kingdom" (p. 271).

the present system which required earnest and serious consideration.
The ruinously low prices of agricultural produce could not be
ascribed to any deficiency in the protecting power of the law.
Protection could not be carried further than monopoly, and this
monopoly had been enjoyed for nearly thirty months.[1] And, as
the harvests of 1818 and 1819 on the Continent were very abundant,
there was an accumulation of corn there at prices so low that no
relief in exportation could be looked for.[2]

Taking, therefore, as basis of all wise regulations, that the common
interest demanded a permanent and adequate supply of corn at
prices as steady as possible, and that steadiness of price must
depend on guarding, as much as legislative interference could
guard, against the effects of fluctuations of the seasons, the Committee went on to examine the practical operation of the existing
law with reference to these two points.

Effect of
absolute
prohibition
followed by
free entry.

The absolute prohibition of foreign grain up to a certain price,
and the unlimited competition beyond it, was likely to have the
effect of, at one time, reducing low prices lower than they would
probably have been under a state of Free Trade, at another, of
enhancing prices already perhaps too high ; on the one hand, it
deceived the grower with the false hope of a monopoly, on the other,
it created a sudden competition on the Continent which raised
prices against ourselves ; and it had, moreover, a direct tendency
to excite resentment and exclusion of our goods among other states.
This was evident when it was considered that a difference of twopence in the averages might open or shut the ports for three months
after the date of taking them,[3] whatever the state of our harvest,
and the necessities of our own people might be. This was well
illustrated by what had happened in August last, when the ports
were opened for oats ; there was an immediate rise of 30 per cent.
to 50 per cent. in the price at Hamburg ; an immense importation ;

---

[1] No foreign corn came in between February, 1819 and midsummer, 1822.

[2] In 1821, again, the price of corn throughout all Europe, it was said, seemed
to have fallen below its cost of production, and, in some parts of Germany,
the price was even below the cost of harvesting (*Memoir of Earl Spencer*,
p. 201).

[3] In 1818 a " fatal surplus " of 2d. in the average allowed the importation
of wheat during the entire summer. " It is a delusion to suppose," said Peel
in 1826, " that foreign corn is admitted directly the price of corn actually
reaches 80/-. That is not the law. The price must be regulated by a long
course of averages, so that corn might be, in fact, at 100/-, and yet the ports
could not be opened unless the average of a number of weeks would make
the price of it 80/-."

and a sudden fall in price here by which the importers lost much money—all this caused by the bringing in of the trifling quantity of under three-quarters of a million quarters as against a home consumption in Great Britain of nearly 30 millions.

When, then, they found, in the seventeen months between January 1816 and June 1817, the price of wheat varying from 53/1 to 112/7, and again, in the three months from June to September 1817, from 112/7 to 74/-, the Committee could not but ask themselves if there had been fluctuations so rapid and excessive in any other commodity, and if these fluctuations were not aggravated by some of the effects of the present law—the more particularly as such a system of absolute prohibition and unlimited competition had not the sanction of long usage, but was introduced only in 1815. For forty years before that date, the trade in corn with the Continent was open, and importation was allowed, at duties merely nominal or very moderate, when the price was above 63/-, with the necessary consequence that the general price at the shipping ports of the Continent had not, upon an average, been materially lower than the price in England except to the amount of the charges for transportation.

It was the more necessary to look back to those forty years of prosperity that the Committee thought it highly deserving of future consideration whether a trade in corn, constantly open to all nations of the world, and subject only to such a fixed duty as might compensate to the grower the loss of that encouragement which he received during the late war from the obstacles thrown in the way of free importation, and might thereby protect the capitals now vested in agriculture from an unequal competition in the home market, was not, as a permanent system, preferable. " It would be indispensable, for the just execution of this principle, that such duty should be calculated fairly to countervail the difference of expense, including the ordinary rate of profit, at which corn, in the present state of this country, could be grown and brought to market within the United Kingdom, compared with the expense, including also the ordinary rate of profit, of producing it in any of those countries from whence our principal supplies of foreign corn have usually been drawn, joined to the ordinary charges of conveying it from thence to our markets." [1]

Was the natural fluctuation not aggravated by the Corn Law ?

Suggestion of open trade with a fixed duty.

---

[1] It must have cost Ricardo a sore struggle to let this go out under his name, after the pains he had been at, on the institution of the Committee, to get the true principle and measure of compensatory or countervailing

But such an alteration was for future consideration only, the Committee being fully aware of the unfitness of the present moment for attempting any such change. Assuming, then, that Parliament would not now deem it expedient to abandon entirely the principle of the existing law, they went on to the possibility of modifying that law so as to remedy the inconvenience of the suddenness and irregularity with which foreign corn might be introduced on the opening of the ports.[1] This might, they conceived, be attained by the imposition of a fixed duty whenever, upon the opening of the ports, corn should be admissible for home consumption. But, if this suggestion were carried into effect, it would be necessary to revise the importing price and fix it at a lower rate; otherwise the effect would be to enhance the price—the last thing which they desired. If such a change should have the effect of checking extravagant speculation and excessive import, it would be equally beneficial to the grower and the consumer. It would apply some remedy for the evil so loudly complained of, and it would have " no tendency, either hastily or prematurely, to affect the principle upon which was rested that protection which the law now gave to the agricultural interest of the country."

It was not for them to specify any precise permanent duty for the protection of the British grower. At the same time, they inclined to the opinion that, having the inestimable public benefit of full and free competition within the home market, it might be difficult, if not impossible, putting rent out of the question, for the occupiers of some of the poorest and most expensive soils now under cultivation to bring their produce to market, in competition with the more fertile lands of the country, and especially of Ireland. They were anxious to suggest, then, as principle and basis of the

duty set down. But most such Reports are, and must be, a compromise, and loyalty to colleagues very often induces members to sit quiet under the assumption that they have agreed to something which they strenuously opposed *in camera*.

[1] The evil of this was now fully recognised. " The present Corn Law," said a correspondent of the *Farmer's Magazine*, " is more hostile to our cultivators than no law at all. It operates as a perpetual stimulus upon speculators to import excessive quantities of foreign grain, to be laid up in magazines, ready to drive the home produce out of the market. It appears that, when it suits these gentlemen's purpose, the ports may be opened by collusion as well as by the fair rise of prices; and thus, before our farmers can get their produce ready for sale, they find the markets forestalled and glutted with foreign grain." But the remedy still recommended was to give the home grower " more to come and go upon, by raising the importing price from 80/- to 90/-, and other grain in proportion " (p. 108).

trade in foreign corn, that the protecting duty should not be such as would aggravate to the occupiers of such soils the present difficulty of that competition. As to how far the " forced cultivation " of these inferior lands had been of advantage, they offered no opinion ; they had no difficulty, however, in stating that, " within the limits of the existing competition at home, the exertions of industry and the investment of capital in agriculture ought to be protected against any revulsion, but that the protection ought not to go further."

For the rest, they had, they said, abstained from urging " those general principles of freedom of trade which were now universally acknowledged to be sound and true in reference to the commerce of nations." If the wisdom of the House thought it right to endeavour to revert to those principles, so far as practicable, the prudence and justice of the House ought to take care, in that application, to spare vested interests, and " sometimes even to modify and limit that principle in reference to considerations of general polity connected with the institutions, or the safety, of the State." Whatever general suggestions they offered ought to be scrupulously examined with a due regard to two things ; the importance of securing the country, in case of war, from a state of dependence on foreign and possibly hostile countries for the subsistence of its population,[1] and, still more, the preservation to the landed interest of that weight, station, and ascendency, which it had enjoyed so long and so beneficially. *Guarding clauses.*

The remainder of the Report dealt with the general influence of taxation upon the state of the country—" desirous of correcting the mistaken opinion that the depression under which our agriculture now labours is, either exclusively or principally, to be attributed to taxation " ;[2] condemned the prayer for prohibitory protection of wheat by a fixed and permanent duty of 40/-, and of all *Other subjects.*

[1] " The nation which feeds you in peace can starve you in war " (Lord Kames).

[2] It was well pointed out that, during the war, the accumulation of national capital must have been large and progressive, and that while, if population only were taken into account, England was the most taxed portion of Europe, it might be doubted if it was not the least, if capital or income per head were the measure. The reminder was very necessary. Again and again, in future debates, occur comparisons of the burden of taxation, taking the amount of taxation per head in two countries—which, of itself, is fallacious enough—but, beyond that, taking no account of the comparative wealth per head. See a vigorous exposure of this in Lowe, *Present State of England*, 317.

the products of agriculture on the same footing;[1] defended the warehousing system [2]—" it has this great advantage that it places the
supply of our wants, to the extent of the quantity warehoused, out
of the reach of foreign states, putting it out of their power, in a
season of scarcity, to aggravate the pressure of these wants either
by prohibiting the export of corn or by imposing a heavy duty
upon that export ";—and admitted fully the injurious effect of the
restoration of the currency on several classes, " specially on those
who had engaged in speculative adventures, either of farming or
trade." This part, like all the Report, is well worthy of study
even by the modern reader, but two notable quotations must suffice.
(1) " Your Committee may entertain a doubt (a doubt, however,
which they wish to state with that diffidence which a subject so
extensive naturally imposes upon their judgment) whether the only
solid foundation of the flourishing state of agriculture is not laid
in abstaining as much as possible from interference, either by
protection or prohibition, with the application of capital in any
branch of industry." (2) " So far as the present depression in
the markets of agricultural produce is the effect of abundance
from our own growth, the inconvenience arises from a cause which
no legislative provision can alleviate ; so far as it is the result of

[1] George Webb Hall, the Secretary of the Board of Agriculture—the " distracted creature," as Cobbett called him, who had given it on evidence that
the greatest calamity which could befal this country would be to have wheat
for nothing—had laid before the Committee the monstrous proposal of a
permanent duty on wheat of 40/-, to be rigidly levied "whatever the price
might be," with a corresponding duty on all other grains, hides, tallow,
seeds, wool, flax, hemp, butter, cheese, poultry, fruit, ending with, " all things
the produce of the soil not enumerated, £38 per cent. *ad valorem.*" The
scheme was ventilated at county meetings all over the country, and resolutions
were passed in its favour. But for his rashness and incapacity, which injured
the petitioners both in and out of Parliament, said the *Farmer's Magazine*,
a graduated scale of duties, engrafted on the present system, might have been
obtained—say, a duty of 10/- to 15/- on wheat, when our prices were at 70/-,
falling a shilling a quarter as the prices rose. Anyone who reads the evidence
will agree as to the " rashness and incapacity." Cobbett did the good service
of heartily trouncing his scheme in a pamphlet entitled *The Farmer's Friend.*
Cf. my *Economic Annals of the Nineteenth Century, 1801-20*, 730.

[2] The usual argument against the warehousing system was, in Gooch's words,
that, the moment the price of corn rose to what was considered a fair remunerating price, the corn from the warehouses rushed to market ; the farmer was
panic-struck ; put his threshing machine to work ; his produce found a
glutted market ; the price quickly fell from 80/- to 60/- and 50/-, and all his
industry and labour were wasted. The evil was like the sword of Damocles.
The Committee, as will be seen, fully admitted the evil, but contended that
it was inherent in the system of alternate prohibition and unlimited competition, and would not be cured although the grain were stored on the other side
of the channel.

the increased value of our money, it is one not peculiar to the farmer, but which has been, and still is, experienced by many other classes of society." (But they were satisfied that the return to a fixed standard "was the only course which it was in the power of Parliament to adopt.")

The Report is given in full in *Hansard*, vol. v. Appendix, in the *Annual Register*, and also, with hostile comments, in the *Farmer's Magazine* (p. 325). "It is," said the *Annual Register*, "one of the most valuable documents ever laid before parliament. It is full of the soundest views ; and, at the same time that it admits abstract principles in all their extent, modifies them by due regard to the circumstances of the times. It is a pleasing monument of the rapid progress which enlarged notions on very abstract subjects have made, within the last few years, among that class of the community on whose opinions the improvement of our legislation and the excellence of our internal public economy chiefly depend." It was not, said the Editor of the *Farmer's Magazine*, a " mere milk and water production," as many represented, but a "very ominous document," inasmuch as it gave countenance to a fixed duty. "Does anyone think that this or any other Committee will ever recommend a duty of 40/- or the half of it ?—or that any duty at all would long be submitted to by the public when corn exceeded the present import rates ? The operation of a duty of only 10/- on wheat when our prices were above 80/-, with an additional duty of other 10/- probably on its export from the Baltic, would in a few weeks load the tables of parliament with petitions from every corner of the United Kingdom. With such prices, instead of imposing a duty, it would perhaps be thought expedient, as has been done before, to offer a bounty on import ; for it ought to be carefully attended to that 80/- now is a very different sum from what it was eight or ten years ago. Wheat is now as high at 80/- as it was in 1812 at 100/-." It would be, in fact, he said, " a first step and a very long one towards the repeal of all restrictions on the corn trade. The duty would necessarily be but a few shillings a quarter, and from this to a trade perfectly free, the transition was natural, and would not be far distant." And he used the prophetic words, " it will soon be found out, whenever the manufacturing classes choose to take up the matter, that, of all taxes, the most odious and oppressive is a tax, and a direct and obvious tax, on bread." He counselled the agricultural interests to be content with the Corn Law they had ; it had been carried by them in the

Opinions of the Report.

teeth of great opposition from the rest of the public, and it would
be very imprudent for them to be the first to call for its repeal.
" The labours of the Committee have ended, as was generally expected," said the *Glasgow Herald*, " in doing nothing. Their cure
for the present distress among farmers is like Sir Abel Handy's
plan for extinguishing a fire, ' perhaps it will go out of itself.' . . .
Indeed, the drawers-up of the Report, Mr. Huskisson and Mr.
Ricardo, appear fully more anxious to defend their own well-
known views in Political Economy than to look after the interests
of either landlord or tenant." [1]

Ricardo

     In a debate of the next year, Ricardo gave a very frank opinion
of it. He would say that the first part was as excellent a report
as had ever emanated from any Committee of the House—well
worthy of being placed beside the Bullion Report and that on the
Resumption of Cash Payments. It most justly pointed out two
great evils arising from the Corn Law ; first, the sudden deluge
with foreign corn when the price rose to 80/-, operating to bring
down prices at the very time when the short harvest ought to be
compensated by high prices ; second, that, in a season of plenty,
we habitually produced corn at an expense very considerably above
other countries, and so, when harvests were good on the Continent,
we could obtain no relief from exportation and were ruined by

on right
and wrong
countervailing
duties.

this abundance of produce. But another part of the Report was
totally incorrect. It spoke of countervailing duties, " not, as all
countervailing duties ought to be, imposts upon the importer in
order to subject him to all the burdens of the home grower of corn,
so that the taxes might fall equally on both grower and importer,
but as duties which should be equal to the additional expense of
growing corn in this country over other countries." Countervailing
duties on this principle would be sometimes 20/- and sometimes
30/- ; for there appeared to him to be no principle more clear than
that there could not be a fixed remunerating price in any country.
As population increased, and population went to poorer lands, the
price would continue to rise, and, on this wrong principle, no limit
could be affixed to the amount of the countervailing duties. He
could not conceive any system of duties more destructive to the
best interests of the country.[2] The only true policy was to allow

[1] 25th June.

[2] In the fourth edition of the *Protection to Agriculture*, Ricardo delivers a
striking and, for him, animated attack on this quite erroneous doctrine :
" Is it not in the highest degree absurd, first to pass a law, under the operation

us to go to the country where the article required was most easily and abundantly produced.

Or, as he said, in his *Protection to Agriculture*, the Report contained some excellent statements and reasonings on the subject. He could refer to it with confidence in support of the principles he was endeavouring to lay down as to the impolicy of protecting corn laws. Its arguments in favour of freedom of trade appeared to him unanswerable. But it must be confessed, he went on, that, in that same Report, recommendations were made utterly inconsistent with those principles. After condemning restrictions on trade, it recommended measures of permanent restriction ; after showing the evils resulting from prematurely taking poorer lands into cultivation, it countenanced a system which, at all sacrifices, was to keep them in tillage. " In principle, nothing so odious as monopoly and restriction ; in practice, nothing so salutary and desirable."

As Parliament rose on 11th July, the Report was not formally Reception by the landed classes. discussed during the Session. It did not, of course, please the landed classes. Ministers knew, it was said, before the Committee was appointed, whether they could do anything in favour of the farmer or not : it was only an insult to tell him that his case was desperate, and, in the same breath, to recommend only time and patience. It was the most unsatisfactory production he ever knew, said Lauderdale ; but, somewhat illogically, added, " it stated what was very true, and what was well known without a committee —that no remedy could be applied, and that nothing was to be done but to wait the effect of time."[1] The pervading influence

of which the necessity is created of cultivating poor lands, and then, having so cultivated them at a great expense, make that additional expense the ground for refusing ever to purchase corn from those who can afford to produce it at a cheaper price ? I can produce a quantity of cloth which affords me a remunerating price at £60, which I can sell to a foreign country, if I will pay out the proceeds in the purchase of thirty qrs. of wheat at £2 per qr. ; but I am refused permission to do so, and am obliged, by the operation of a law, to employ the capital which yielded me £60 in cloth in raising fifteen qrs. of wheat at £4 per qr. . . . If the principle recommended by the Committee were consistently followed, there is no commodity whatever which we can raise at home which we should ever import from abroad ; we should cultivate beetroot, and make our own sugar, and impose a duty on the importation of sugar equal to the difference of expense of growing sugar here and growing it in the East or West Indies. We should erect hothouses, raise our own grapes for the purpose of making wine, and protect the maker of wine by the same course of policy. Either the doctrine is untenable in the case of corn, or it is to be justified in all other cases."

[1] *Hansard,* v. 1506.

of Ricardo was not appreciated by those who could not understand
" the strange theory of Messrs. Malthus and Ricardo," which based
price on a cost of production on land where no rent was paid, and
they fatuously asked who ever heard of any such land. But the
more thoughtful among them recognised that Corn Bills and taxes
on wool were " not such matters of absolute wisdom or utility as
they were at one time supposed to be," and began to suspect
that insistence on a legislative remedy might land them where
they least desired. They seized eagerly on those parts of the
Report which admitted the bad effects on many classes of the
return to cash payments, and argued, with some plausibility, that
the main cause of the depression, *pace* the opinion of the Committee, was the too hasty return to a coin currency while the obligations of the country, public and private, contracted in a currency
greatly depreciated, remained still in force. And, in some respects,
it seemed to create a new hostility between the agricultural and
the manufacturing classes. Sir John Sinclair, *e.g.*, spoke of the
new doctrine promulgated by the partisans of foreign commerce
that, in order to send manufactured goods to foreign markets,
a large proportion of the territory of the country was to be
thrown waste or doomed for ever to remain in a state of barrenness.[1]

Agricultural
distress.

The King's Speech in July spoke of the " quiet and good order
which continued to prevail in those parts of the country which
were not long since in a state of agitation," but " deeply lamented
the distress to which the agricultural interests in many parts of
the kingdom were still subject." The circumstances of agriculture,
indeed, which were lamentable enough at the beginning of the year,
seemed to be going from bad to worse by the end of it. An exceedingly mild winter and a fair seed-time sent up the farmers' hopes
—" never perhaps did the earth bear a more abundant promise,"
said the English Monthly Report—but a cold summer damped,
and a rainy and late harvest extinguished them. " The corn lay
rotting in the fields and the farmers were unable to gather it." [2]

The harvest:
poor quality
and low
prices.

In quantity, indeed, the crop was a full one except in oats ; but,
in wheat and barley, much of the produce was greatly inferior.
The price of wheat, which had already fallen from 57/6 in the previous

[1] The conclusions and anticipations of this Report were suggestively compared with the existing condition of things in 1833 by the Select Committee
on Agriculture of that year. See the Report in *Annual Register*, 1833, 341.

[2] Colchester, iii. 241.

November to 54/- in January, went down to about 51/6 in May ;
rose to 54/- in August ; and, when the rain came, speculation ran
up the price for the moment to over 70/- in September. But,
as the poorness of the quality was realised, while large quantities
of the old crop were still coming forward, the price gradually fell,
till December closed with wheat under 47/-. The average price
of the year was 56/1.[1]

By considerate landlords, it appears, rents were largely remitted,
and, where they were not, only a fraction was collected. In Buckinghamshire, the number of sales under distress was greater than
ever known before. Everywhere we hear of the " settled gloom
of agriculture " ; of farmers looking forward to bankruptcy ; of Continued
matters coming to a crisis. And still the discussion raged as to puzzlement.
what was the cause of it all. " The too hasty return to a coin
currency " continued the favourite object of attack.[2] The warehousing system, too, was criticised ; merchants, it was said, could
not speculate in British grain when foreign grain, grown at half
the cost, might be let in at any moment. And all agriculturists,
of course, were agreed that taxation was the enemy.[3] Many,
indeed, continued to blame the foreign import, although the ports
had been closed now for two years—the enormous quantity imported before the ports closed in February of 1819, they argued,
had reduced the market to a state of depression from which it
seemed unable to rally. As a fact, there was some cause for this
complaint in regard to oats, inasmuch as the importing price had
been fixed lower than it should have been in proportion to
other prices, and in the previous August the ports were open to

---

[1] It should be noticed that, when I give the average annual price, it is taken
from the Customs Tariff Blue Book of 1897, which gives it in imperial quarters.
For the monthly prices I have to trust to the *Annual Register*, which usually
takes its figures from the returns of the twelve maritime districts determining
the importing price, where the quarter contains eight Winchester bushels. The
comparison, therefore, is not exact, and in some years I am not sure of the
Annual Register's figures, but, so far as possible, I compare like with like.

[2] " It was not till the following two or three years," says Tooke, " during
which wheat of the harvest of 1820 continued to appear in the markets,
that the exuberant produce of that season became known. Instead, therefore,
of seeking in the currency for the cause of the fall of price, it is a matter of
more difficulty to explain how and why the real and sufficient reason, namely,
the increase of quantity, did not sooner and more powerfully operate "
(*History of Prices*, ii. 83).

[3] The farmers were suffering, said Lord Nugent to a deputation, not because
their productions were too cheap, but because the means of producing them
were too dear.

oats for six weeks with "ruinous results." [1] But this did not apply to wheat and other grain ; and most people, indeed, had given up the idea that this particular distress had anything to do with the Corn Laws, and, while ascribing it vaguely to "want of demand," could not suggest any means of increasing the demand.

As to employment, it would seem that, during the year, the labourers were fully employed at wages which, though low, were adequate to living. One finds 18d. a day, or, at most, 20d. without victual, quoted.[2] In Dumfriesshire, we read significantly that thousands of Irish labourers, who used to swarm in that district in more prosperous times, had been obliged to return to their own

Increased imports from Ireland.

country from want of employment. But, in some quarters, Ireland itself was counted responsible for the distress. In Bristol, where land was being taken by good tenants at 30/- and 35/- which previously fetched 50/- and 60/-, the greatest evil, wrote a correspondent, was Irish import ; " not a tide flows without cargoes of pigs, corn of all sorts, and even mutton and beef, which these Paddies sell about 30 per cent. under the market prices." Tooke has noticed that, by this time, the imports of grain from Ireland had acquired an extension beyond all expectation ; in 1820 and 1821, the import of wheat alone was nearly a million quarters, whereas, in 1817, there was actually a balance of exports to Ireland.[3]

Manufactures improving.

Of the state of manufacturing industry, singularly little is to be gathered, except the general statement that the distress was passing. The few references in current literature seem to confirm the words of the King's Speech that considerable improvement had taken place in several of the most important branches. Operatives were in full employment, at good wages—more than doubled in some cases, it was said. The ordinary textiles,[4] both in Scotland and England, were busy, and silk in particular was making great

---

[1] Some said this was due to a " fraudulent average." At anyrate, the Committee of 1821 called it both " ill-timed and unnecessary."

[2] This was in Dumfriesshire ; see *Farmer's Magazine, passim.* But Sydney Smith writes in August : " The wretchedness of the poor in this part of the country (Taunton) is very affecting. The men are working for a shilling a day all the year round, and, if a man have only three children, he receives no relief from the parish."

[3] *History of Prices*, ii. 84.

[4] The annual Yorkshire cloth returns up to March showed a total increase of 1,116,000 yards (*Annual Register, Chron.* 76). In the same month, we read that the weaving in Paisley and the West of Scotland was busy—the situation of the weaver vastly more comfortable than it was two years before.

strides ; according to Lansdowne's statement in the House of Lords, our silk industry already exceeded that of France. In March, we read that the iron trade was in a very depressed state, and that the condition of Birmingham did not improve—in fact, grew worse, but this was quoted as an exception to the general revival. After the promise of the beginning, however, all that could be said of manufacturing for the later part of the year was that the improvement was maintained.

In the troubled state of so many continental and South American Foreign trade. markets, it could scarcely be expected that foreign trade would show much of an advance, and one reads with amusement the commercial article in *Blackwood* saying that, above all, it was to Africa that we should turn—to the vast territories opened up by the great river Niger ! The Official figures were :

Imports - - -	£30,837,000 as compared with	£32,471,000 in 1820
Exports of British produce and merchandise - -	40,832,000 ,,	38,393,000 ,,
Exports of foreign and colonial merchandise - -	10,629,000 ,,	10,556,000 ,,

The Real value of the British exports was £36,655,000, as compared with £36,423,000 in the preceding year.[1]

The number of vessels built and registered in the several ports of the United Kingdom was 585, representing 58,076 tons.

[1] For the meaning and difference of Official and Real Values, see *Economic Annals, 1801-1820*, 12.

CHAPTER II

1821. THE FIRST VICTORY OF FREE TRADE:
THE TIMBER DUTIES

ONE of the questions which will come up all through this volume is as to how far the Free Trade principles, so clearly laid down in the Merchants' Petition of 1820, and then adopted by the leading members both of the Ministry [1] and of the Opposition, had entered into the minds of those who guided the national policy in regard to foreign trade, and how far they were appreciated by those who carried on this trade.   I think we shall find that Free Trade, though considered as a doctrine theoretically sound, was still only in the academic stage.   As in Adam Smith's day, it was "Utopian." The circumstances were all against it, and the vested interests were overwhelming.   But this did not prevent it from being an ideal consummation or a theory which might be used as a principle of revision.   Meanwhile " a free trade " meant only an " open trade " —the repeal of prohibition or prohibitory duties.[2]

What a "free trade" meant in 1821.

The Government lost no time in showing that they had embraced the new policy.   Ten days after the opening of the session, the first step was taken by Thomas Wallace,[3] who had become Vice-

Wallace makes the first move.

[1] " With every sentiment and every principle contained in the Petition," said Liverpool, " he fully and unreservedly agreed, and, if he were then to form a commercial code, these were the principles on which he would establish it."

[2] The moderate protectionist argument of the day—that which stood against absolute Free Trade, but for " open trade," with duties sufficient to guard the national and vested interests, and for reciprocity treaties—may be seen in an article in the *Quarterly* of January.   The points dwelt on are : the difficulty of transferring labour and capital from industries that succumb—" it can hardly be expected that any material new openings for labour can at this day be discovered " ; the limitation of demand for our manufactures among less civilised countries, and the consequent export of specie ; the necessity of preserving naval pre-eminence ; and hostile tariffs.

[3] Wallace (1768-1844) seems to have left few marks in history beyond his

President of the Board of Trade in 1818, and was Chairman of the Foreign Trade Committee of 1820. The Report of that Committee had specifically recommended revision of the vast and complicated mass of legislation by which commerce was regulated, and some relaxation of the Navigation Laws.[1] Wallace, intimating that the motion was made by a member of the Government instead of being committed to the " better hands " of Baring, as an earnest of their intention to effect an alteration of the system, now moved for a Select Committee to consider of the means of maintaining and improving the foreign trade of the country. It was true, he said, that " some of the most important branches of our manufactures had considerably improved "—cotton manufacturers in England and Scotland were generally employed, and the same might be stated of the woollen manufacturers—but others were in a situation of very great, and, he feared, of increased depression. An enquiry was necessary, not only on account of the distress, but with reference to the commercial exertions which other countries were making. We no longer had the exclusive foreign trade which the protection of our fleets had given us during the war, and we were " labouring under burdens which pressed on the industry of no other country in Europe." The only way in which we could meet this was by " a full and complete revision of our commercial system. We must also get rid of that feeling of appropriation which exhibited itself in a disposition to produce everything necessary for our own consumption and to render ourselves independent of the world—no notion could be more absurd or mischievous." He indicated, as subjects for the enquiry, the state of the Navigation Laws—on which he proposed bringing in bills to carry into effect the recommendations of the Committee of 1820—and simplification and consolidation of the commercial laws. He was persuaded that trade prosperity could be gained " only by a recurrence, so far as was practicable, to the true principles of the commercial system." Baring, who had taken such an important part in the discussions of last session, agreed that it was " most desirable to examine how it happened that, in the sixth year of peace, not any amendment had evinced itself in the condition of the country ; " and the Committee was appointed.[2]

work. He was educated at Eton and Christchurch, where he was the associate of Liverpool and Canning ; M.P. for Grampound, 1790 ; subsequently refused to join Canning's Government in 1827, and was gazetted Baron Wallace in 1828.

[1] *Economic Annals, 1801-20*, 754.   [2] *Hansard*, iv. 425.

Report of his
Foreign Trade
Committee.

It is not a little interesting to find that the first duty to be reduced was one imposed in the interests, not of home producers, but of the Colonies, although a home interest had, incidentally, attached itself to the colonial.   Reporting on 9th March,[1] the Committee explained that, on account of the inconvenience of a continuance of suspense in respect of the system which Parliament might deem it expedient to adopt on the expiration of the existing provision on 25th March, they had confined their attention to the question of the Importation of Timber from the northern states of Europe and from the British colonies in North America.   The timber duties had two distinct objects ;—protection and encouragement of the wood trade in the colonies,[2] and revenue.   The first question was how far the public faith was committed to their continuance.   The beginning of the duties was in 1809.[3]   Previous to that date, our supply of timber, as well for domestic as for naval purposes, came almost exclusively from the north of Europe.   But, in that year, " the course of events had placed our relations with those states in a situation which gave rise to a well-founded apprehension lest the resources in that quarter might entirely cease to be available for the demands of this country."   A virtual exemption was then granted to the timber imported from our North American possessions, while large additions were successively made to the duty levied on timber from the north of Europe.[4]   The total duties on the latter now amounted to £3 5/- per load when imported in British ships.   It appeared that the actual protection, intended and avowed as such, amounted to £2 1/- per load, and this had led to the extension of the colonial timber trade " by the application of capital which, except for such inducement, would never have been so invested."   But the colonial exemption was

[1] The Report is given in full in the *Annual Register*, p. 486, and in Appendix to *Hansard*, v. xlix.

[2] Protection of the colonies had, of course, long been part of the national policy.   A tax on brandy, said David Hume, increases the sale of rum and supports our southern colonies.   But, generally, it took the shape of differential duties, on indigenous produce, between colonial and foreign producers ; seldom came directly into collision with the home producer ; and did not markedly prejudice the home consumers as the Timber Duties did.

[3] Before, and in, Adam Smith's time, a bounty had, indeed, been given on the export from the British American colonies, but it had not much effect.

[4] In 1810, on the guarantee of the Government that the preference would be such as to secure them freights from Canada, certain private shipowners undertook to supply British shipping for transport, and the European duties were doubled.   In 1813, 25 per cent. was added to them (M'Culloch, *Dictionary*, *ad verb*.).

originally temporary—only continued from time to time for limited periods—and had been studiously stated to be so. There was nothing, then, to preclude revision of the whole system.

The policy most advantageous to the country would be, of course, "to obtain timber of the best quality and at the lowest price without reference to the quarter from which it might be derived." The question, then, was how far this policy was infringed by the existing duties. On this head, they spoke definitely enough. The use of Baltic timber was now in great measure confined to the higher and more valuable description of buildings, and to purposes for which increased strength in bearing was necessary or desirable : the yellow pine of America—of which the great importation consisted—was, except for particular purposes, inferior owing to its supposed greater liability to dry-rot and comparative deficiency in strength and durability. But, so long as these high duties were imposed, it was obvious that a great proportion of wood of an inferior quality would be forced into consumption, both in avowed substitution for the superior timber and "in a fraudulent application of it when that of a superior kind had been contracted for, which, according to the evidence, if practised, could with difficulty be detected." It appeared, too, that the difference was such as to be prejudicial to the trade itself, and to bring into the market an excessive quantity of timber of a very inferior description, both in point of quality and preparation, and that some alteration of the duty, calculated to approximate the relative prices of the two classes of timber would be desirable, if only to confine the supply of the market to a more carefully selected and better prepared commodity.

Thus, concludes this part of the Report, "the amount of the duty levied on Baltic timber and the increased price which, under the operation of the duty, the American timber must have borne, may be considered as a bounty paid by the consumers of the United Kingdom for the benefit of the North American colonies and the support of the superfluous shipping in which the transport of their wood is said to afford the only employment." [1]

Coming to the other side of the question, the "prudential

Comparison of Baltic and Canadian timber.

Prudential considerations.

---

[1] The case for the colonies had meantime been strongly reiterated by Joseph Marryat, the chairman of Lloyds, in presenting a petition from New Brunswick. The merchants there, he said, depended exclusively upon the exportation of timber to Great Britain to make their remittances, and, if this came to an end, " all importation of British goods must cease." In Canada, the timber was estimated at half the exports of the province (*Hansard*, iv. 542). See also Marryat's speech in 1820 (*Economic Annals, 1801-1820*, 755).

considerations " were (1) the danger incident to want of competition, from the exclusion of colonial timber and from the reliance for our supplies on a single source ; (2) the possible failure of supply from the north of Europe in a moment of necessity ; (3) the maintenance and employment of our shipping ; (4) the effect that might be produced on the various interests connected with our American trade and on the capital embarked in the establishment for carrying it on. These considerations, said the Committee, were strong enough to forbid at present any recommendation tending entirely to take away the legislative protection hitherto enjoyed by the colonial trade. But, as the extent of that protection was admitted, on almost all hands, to exceed the necessary bounds, they had directed their attention to ascertain to what amount and in what mode that protection should be prospectively continued. The alteration proposed would not, they thought, be attended by the effect of depriving the colonies of their due participation in the benefits of the wood trade. But it would have a moderate and temporary tendency to reduce the imports from the colonies, and so far might, in the first instance and for

The shipping interest. a given period, affect the interests of the shipowners. As a fact, the interest of the shipowners was the one most concerned. Owing to the close of the war, a great amount of shipping had found employment in this colonial carrying—and, of late, the expectation of a change had greatly increased the amount of the imports. But, with all due regard to this, the Committee did' not think that every other consideration should be sacrificed to that one object, or that it was consistent with the public welfare that the care due to the interests of our merchants and manufacturers, and every regard to our foreign commercial relations, should be forgone for the purpose of supporting, by artificial means, a mercantile marine in a state of magnitude at which it had arrived from accidental causes alone, and which was neither conducive to the commercial prosperity nor essential to the political security of the nation, and in which (unless by the opening of new sources of employment or the extension of those existing) the regular trade of the country was incapable of maintaining it.

The degree in which the shipping interest might be affected by the change would depend, of course, on its influence in reducing the import of wood from the colonies. In estimating this, it had to be remembered that, for several purposes, American timber was as good as Baltic, and that, since 1809, the prejudice against it had been weakening. As regards British capital invested in saw-milling, etc., in the colonies—which the Committee put down at £150,000—it must again be remembered that the advantage given to the colonial trade, on which these establishments were founded, had already extended beyond the period on which those engaged in it had any right to calculate. To the Canadian proprietary, lastly, the principal value of the timber trade appeared to consist in the employment afforded to the persons concerned in agriculture and their servants during a certain period of the year, in conveying the wood from the places where it had been felled to the ports of export, the cutting and rafting being, in many instances, performed by axe-men coming from the United States for this purpose. " Within certain limits," they summed up, " the In justice to trade of the colonies of Great Britain has a just claim to encourage- ourselves, ment and support from the mother country, and to such claim your Committee are anxious to give full weight. It is not, however, a question whether this encouragement and support should be given or withholden ; but, admitting it to be due, to what extent it should be carried in justice to other interests which have also their peculiar claims to attention, and which are, in the opinion of your Committee, also deeply involved in this discussion. On the fair regard shown to foreign countries, the extent of our commerce with them may depend ; and, in providing with too much partiality for the interests connected with the trade to and from our American colonies, we may put in hazard still more extensive interests that are engaged in the export to those countries which are directly concerned in the timber trade (if not our foreign trade generally) by such a proof of deliberate preference of a principle of restriction as the rule of our commercial policy." On the colonial these lines, the Committee proceeded to recommend the reduction preference should be of the difference created by the duty from £3 5/- per load to £2 5/-, reduced. to be arranged by taking 10/- from the Baltic duty and imposing 10/- on the colonial one. They calculated that, " after providing for the ordinary difference in freight," this would leave a protection of 30/- per load in favour of the colonial timber.

The Committee concluded by a reference to the usual difficulty of reform—the vested interest. It had been their endeavour, they said, to the utmost of their power to conciliate the claims of adverse interests, and the contending considerations of policy that demanded their attention. " If what they propose falls far short of a recurrence to those sound principles by which all commerce ought to be regulated, they trust that it will appear to the House that they have proceeded as far as, under present circumstances, is consistent with an equitable regard to the protection due to extensive interests that have grown up under an established system, and which must be deeply affected by any material and sudden change to which that system is subjected."

In calling attention to the Report on 29th March,[1] and moving Resolutions in conformity with the recommendation, Wallace stated that, comparing 1803-06 with 1816-19, the reduction in the import of Baltic timber considerably exceeded one-half; and that the " enormous protection " given to the colonies doubled the prime cost of Baltic timber, and was equal to a tax of a million sterling. The shipping employed in carrying North American timber was the worst in the merchant service—in fact, shipping that was good for nothing else—but the shipowners were the only class who gave determined opposition to any attempt to repeal or modify the

This only a first step.

duties. The importance of the proposal, however, he said frankly, was not in itself—he did not regard it as having any great effect upon the state of our manufactures—but in its being " the first step in receding from a system detrimental to our commercial relations, and towards conciliating those foreign powers without whose goodwill the relations of mercantile intercourse could never be securely established."

Marryat opposes.

Marryat, who had been spokesman for the shipping interests in the debate of 1820, objected that the Report was in opposition to the evidence ; that it betrayed too great a leaning to the principles laid down by certain merchants—" the disciples of the new political economy "—in the petition of last Session. The whole condition of industry in England was artificial ; the heavy taxation to pay for the national debt entered into the price of labour, and made it impossible for us to maintain an equal competition with foreign nations ; we were pursuing a wrong course in attempting to increase the sale of our manufactures in Europe, for most of the powers were now manufacturing for themselves, and those which were not would only take from us what we could supply more cheaply than our neighbours. " The obvious tendency of a free trade is to make rich countries poor and poor countries rich ; because poor countries, where articles are cheap, will undersell rich countries where they are dear, until the inequality between them ceases "— a very proper system for those which are poor but not for those

[1] *Hansard*, iv. 1500.

which are rich. He proceeded to argue, with more force, that a reduction of the duty on corn and linens would be more to the purpose of conciliating foreign powers; the protection given to the landholders by the Corn Laws, for instance, was no less than £30 millions per annum. The colonies, as a fact, had been encouraged to engage in the trade by a specific pledge of a decided preference. Not to speak of destroying a branch of trade employing 17,500 seamen, the change would alienate Canada and make her an easy prey to the ambition of the United States, and the West Indies would follow; whereas, if we consulted the interests of our manufacturers, we should encourage the trade with the colonies in preference to that with foreign nations, " because foreigners only *may* deal with us but our colonies *must*." And, finally, this would diminish the protection and lower the value of British-grown timber, which already was selling at unremunerative prices. In later discussions, he fell back on the political argument, that ships, colonies, and commerce all went together, and that it was not safe to trust to the liberality of foreign powers to supply us with goods—of course quoting Adam Smith on the Navigation Acts.

All through the debates which followed, there was strong evidence of the extent to which Free Trade doctrines had now established themselves, in spite of Marryat's sneers at " our new school of political economists." Parnell, reverting to the principles which Parnell. he had abandoned in the Corn Law of 1815, said that no case had been made out for continuing such a benefit to the colonies even in its modified form—nothing said to justify a bounty to them which must amount to not less than £300,000 or £400,000 a year— and proposed the equalisation of all the duties by 1825. H. G. Bennet, in a speech which Ricardo pronounced full of the soundest Bennet. arguments, " wished to give his public aid to that great principle of free trade which alone could relieve the country from its present difficulties." The proposition now made by the Committee " went to prohibit the good article which was near at hand in those northern countries, for the sake of introducing one so bad that it would otherwise never find its way here "— all for the sake of saving the pockets of the Canadian lumbermen or those other lumbermen, the shipowners. " If the Report were now adopted, and a revision should be proposed three or four years hence after a greater portion of capital was engaged and a greater number of interests should have become dependent upon it, the answer would be that a full opportunity had

been afforded for consideration, and that, although country
gentlemen had neglected their duty and left the question to be
decided by merchants interested in it, it was too late to unsettle
Baring,   what had then been established." Baring looked upon lumbermen
as a "set of vagabonds who encouraged every species of profligacy among the agricultural settlers, and were the pests of the
colony : outside of this class, Canada was not particularly interested
in the present question, being, indeed, the most thriving part of
America in consequence of the monopoly it enjoyed with the West
and Ricardo. Indian islands." Ricardo said that there was a principle involved
of infinitely greater importance than the proposition immediately
under consideration. "They had been told that they ought to
go to the best and cheapest market, and also that the timber of
Norway and Russia was better and cheaper than that of America,
and yet they were recommended, as a practical measure, to take
the worst timber at the dearest rate." He would rather give the
£400,000 specifically and directly to the shipowners, for in that
case the capital given to them might be more usefully employed :
as it was, it was a total sacrifice of £400,000 a year—" as much
as if the ships engaged in the coasting trade should be obliged to
sail round the island in order to give employment to a greater
number." All the consumer had to consider was where he could
get the article he wanted cheapest : all the House had to consider
was how the people of England as a body could best employ their
capital and labour. Wrong notions of commercial policy had too
long prevailed ; and now that the country had begun to recognise
sounder principles, the sooner they acted upon them the better.
There were exceptions to be made in cases of very old established
arrangements, but this American trade was not one of those—it
was of new date, and mainly sprung out of a quarrel between England
and the Baltic powers. "It was contended that the interest of
the producer ought to be looked to as well as that of the consumer
in legislative principles. But the fact was that, in attending to
the interest of the consumer, protection was at the same time
extended to all other classes. The true way of encouraging production was to discover and open facilities to consumption."

The Bill based on the Resolutions met, of course, with strong
opposition from many interests and classes, and four divisions,
representing different views, were made upon it in Committee.
The chief   But the chief struggle was between those who thought that it did
struggle.   not go far enough in the direction of Free Trade and those who

thought that it was as much of a beginning as the circumstances warranted.[1] When it came to the Lords, Bathurst admitted that "the arrangement could not be satisfactory to those who went the length of thinking that no protection should be given to any trade, and that the true policy was to buy everything where it could be got best and cheapest." Few, however, he said, were fond of applying this doctrine in cases where it affected their own interests, and, indeed, to apply the doctrine to one particular article while all the others remained unchanged, would be unjust. Lauderdale, usually a protectionist, did not mince matters. It had been proved, he said, to the Committee that, of twenty-six frigates built of Canadian and Baltic wood, those built of European timber lasted more than double the time of those built of Canadian. He regarded the Bill as altogether a colonial job. It protected no interest except those of the proprietors of a number of old ships and of £150,000 of capital. After the statement of principles by the Government, it was curious that the first measure derived from those principles was one which placed the trade to which they were applied in a worse position than it stood in 1813.[2] Ellenborough, too, "certainly expected that Ministers would have acted with more firmness in this business. The effect of the Bill would be a premium to introduce the dry-rot into every building in the kingdom." All that Liverpool could say in defence was that they should consider, not whether the Bill did all that could be wished, but whether it did not put these matters on a better footing than they were before.[3]

Lauderdale and the "colonial job."

The Bill, however, was duly passed, and Lauderdale had to content himself with a very plain-spoken protest on the Journals, beginning, "Because, whilst the speeches in the House and the Reports of our Committees display to the public an enthusiastic admiration of the most sound and liberal principles of commercial legislation, it is with feelings of the deepest regret that I have seen this House agree to the commitment of a Bill which, instead of showing any disposition to liberality in our future commercial intercourse with foreign nations, will exhibit a specimen of our predilections for that illiberal, artificial, and restrictive system of regulation which has long disgraced our commercial codes ; under

[1] *Hansard*, v. 50, 264.
[2] Lauderdale had some authority as an economist from his *Inquiry into the Nature and Origins of Public Wealth*, published in 1804. The above, however, is almost his only appearance as a Free Trader.
[3] *Hansard*, v. 881.

all the circumstances of the case, more disgusting than the arrangement it is intended to correct." [1]

How the measure was received in Canada appears from a petition from the House of Lower Assembly in March of the following year. It was stated that, within the twelve months, wages, prices of produce of the soil, and value of landed property in that province had all diminished by one-half; that the exports had fallen from £800,000 to about £500,000, the imports from £1,300,000 to under £900,000, and the provincial revenue from £100,000 to less than £80,000. All these results, they said, were due to the acts of the British legislature, which had imposed a duty on their timber while lowering that on foreign timber, and had, besides, established a system of Corn Laws under which their corn had been excluded from British consumption since October 1820.[2] They represented that, if their produce was thus rendered of no value by the legislative measures of the Mother Country, while they were compelled to send their produce to her ports and prohibited from all commercial intercourse with every foreign power, they would be unable to provide their population with the articles of comfort and necessity which they had been in the habit of importing, or to raise a revenue; and they concluded by praying that their grain might be admitted into the home consumption of Great Britain. Marryat, in presenting the petition, said forcibly that, to require from the colonies a double monopoly—to bind them to take their supplies from England and to ship all the produce of their industry to England, while, at the same time, laws were passed to make that produce of no value, or prohibit it from home consumption altogether—was exercising an unexampled degree of arbitrary power over them, which, if continued, must soon devote them to absolute ruin.

John Bennet (of Wilts.), with equal reason, from the protectionist point of view, pointed out that it was at least as necessary to protect the English agriculturist as to relieve the Canadian corn grower;

and said that the Canadians had brought this upon themselves, as, when the home ports were open, large quantities of American grain had been sent to Canada and thence smuggled into England.

---

[1] *Hansard*, v. 884.

[2] Or, as the *Quebec Gazette* put it pithily: " While the statutes oblige us to buy and sell only in England, and have our goods carried in British ships, the Corn Laws practically direct that we shall not buy or sell at all. They admit our corn at 67/- instead of 80/-, but, by the late fall in price, both foreigners and we are excluded."

Ricardo thought the House bound to attend to the complaint. If we asserted the right to buy our timber wherever we pleased, " on that very principle " their corn ought to have access to our markets : the colonies ought not to be forced to purchase from us when they could be more conveniently supplied elsewhere. Sir Isaac Coffin thus early voiced a view which was to come into prominence much later. He said it would have been a good thing for this country if Canada had been sunk to the bottom of the sea ; it cost us £500,000 per annum, and did not make a return of 500 pence. It had been cheating this country out of £300,000 a year, by suffering great quantities of American timber to be sent down the St. Lawrence and brought to England as Canadian. Yet, after acting such a part, they now threw themselves on the House for support. The sooner the Governor was called home, and the Assembly and colony suffered to go to the devil, the better.[1]

This was the first victory for Free Trade, and it must be owned that it was a very little one. As W. Smith, the member for Norwich, said : " All persons must admit that the shipping interest was one of the most important branches for our commercial prosperity ; but it might still be a question whether it was wise to encourage it by sending ships ten times as far as was necessary for particular commodities."

A small victory.

The debates show how little statesmen could see ahead in the campaign now begun. The stoutest hearted was appalled at the wreck of existing interests which seemed inevitable if Free Trade were adopted as a policy even gradually to be introduced. I am inclined, all the same, to say that the debates showed a much fuller acceptance of the academic doctrine than appeared in after years, when statesmen came into grips with the strength and the validity, so far, of the vested interests argument. One feels some sympathy with Wallace himself when he said that, although he had frequently stated his opinion upon protecting duties generally, and was adverse to the system, he did not know how practically it could be done without.

Free Trade and the Vested Interest.

In February, the Committee of the Lords was reappointed and under the former limitations—" to enquire into the means of extending and securing the foreign trade of the country." [2] Lansdowne,

Report on the eastern trade.

[1] *Hansard*, vi. 1073. In 1831, we find it asserted, not only that much of the Canadian timber on which preference was given was really American, but that much timber was actually sent from the Baltic to Canada to gain the same advantage (*Hansard*, ii. 520).

[2] See *Economic Annals, 1801-20*, 750.

who again moved it, stated that the impediments which it was necessary to remove were, in the case of our foreign trade, the restrictions under which it laboured, and, in the case of our home trade, the taxes which it had to pay. The repeal of taxes belonged to the other House, but the restrictions on foreign trade, which had forced it into channels that were most unnatural and unproductive to the country, was the business of the House of Lords as well. The only difficulty was the carrying this into practice; the admission of the principle that restrictions on trade were injurious was easily obtained; but, the moment it was attempted to apply that principle, the various interests involved were in arms—merchants, shipowners, manufacturers, all put in their claims. And every interest was well supported in Parliament except that of the unfortunate consumers—nine-tenths of the population. "He knew there had been persons who had maintained that the various Acts of Parliament imposing restrictions had been the foundation of the commercial prosperity of the country; he, on the contrary, thought, as had been well said in another place by one whose alliance on the question he was glad to have, that the trade of the country had flourished in spite of them all." [1]

The Report, presented on 11th April, confined itself to the Asiatic trade (East Indies and China) and to the facilities which might be given, taking up those parts of it carried on by British merchants under licenses from the East India Company and from the Board of Control respectively, and that part which was carried on with the city of Canton by American merchants but might be carried on by British. "The Committee cannot conceal from themselves," they said, "that, in the present state of the law, no material benefit or facility to Free Trade in this quarter of the globe can be obtained without infringing, in a greater or less degree, upon the privileges vested in the East India Company, until the year 1834, when their present charter expires, and that their consent may be required to any measures which may be submitted for that purpose to the consideration of Parliament." But they put forward a few recommendations not intended, directly or indirectly, to affect the monopoly enjoyed by the Company of the home market, but calculated to procure for the British free trader an access to markets entirely new, or the means of fair competition with the foreign merchant in those which already existed. [2]

---

[1] *Hansard*, iv. 824.   [2] *Ibid.* v. 150; Appendix lxiii.

CHAPTER III

1821. TAXATION AND FINANCE

ONE who reads a little further in these *Annals*, and sees how great The attitude towards taxation. was the reduction of taxation within the next few years when Ministers were forced to give their mind to it, will find reason to wonder at the patience with which the nation was still, six years after, bearing so large a proportion of the burdens imposed by the war. In 1817, indeed, there was much agitation in Ireland for relief from the Salt, Leather, and House Taxes— which came to nothing—but, in Great Britain, as yet, not even political capital was made of a policy of retrenchment. Altogether some £18 millions of taxes had been taken off, including the Income Tax and the War Malt Duties ; while, in 1819, some £3 millions more had been imposed. But, by 1821, the feeling of the country against the continuance of this excessive taxation had grown very strong. The remission of any tax seemed so much gained for an overdue reform, and the attack on taxation was adopted as a policy—" the system adopted by the Opposition seemed to be that of taking a round at every tax in the hope that with some one they might be able to succeed."

First, however, came the suggestion of a new tax. In March, Proposal to tax fundholders. Curwen proposed the imposition of a duty on the Transfer of Stock, on the ground that a property " equal in amount to the whole real property of the united empire " was exempt from all share in the public burdens. Vansittart, the Chancellor of the Exchequer, reprobating, of course, such a breach of faith with the public creditor, met this subtlety very well by saying that Curwen appeared to confound the burden which the stockholder was bound to bear in conjunction with the rest of the community with the imposition of a specific and peculiar tax on the stockholder. For twenty years, the stockholder had submitted to the Property Tax without complaint; but, to a specific tax, he did, and justly did, object. The motion was negatived.[1]

The attack on the taxes began when Maberly, the member for Abingdon, proposed the reduction of all duties on Inhabited Houses and Windows by 50 per cent. The debate is interesting, not so much for the immediate proposal, as for the animated discussion on the maintenance of the Sinking Fund in its dilapidated state. On a previous occasion,[2] Maberly had stated his intention of endeavouring, on some future day, to reduce its system and management to a simpler and clearer detail than that which led the public to believe they had a sinking fund of £17 millions when the reality was only £2 millions, to meet a debt of nearly £900,000,000. Why not get rid of this delusive Sinking Fund altogether? asked Grenfell, and Baring agreed with him. Vansittart immediately replied that it was far wiser to persevere in the present system than, under the name of simplification, to unsettle the whole method with which public accountants were conversant. Philips retorted that the accounts of the Chancellor of the Exchequer were beyond all comprehension—a sentiment with which anyone who tries to understand the Finance Accounts will heartily agree. "If the motion had been to reduce the Sinking Fund," said Ricardo, "it would have met no opposition from him: he considered it a delusion which was encouraged, and made to amount to a certain sum, that Ministers might be enabled finally to lay their hands upon it and devote it to purposes of unnecessary expenditure." Taunted with saying that because Ministers were going to rob the Sinking Fund, he would willingly take it away himself, Ricardo replied that it was good policy, when one's purse was in danger, rather to spend the money oneself than allow it to be taken from him. Maberly's resolutions, of course, were negatived.[3]

The Sinking Fund.

The Malt Duty.

Of more importance was the determined attempt made by the landed members to secure some relief from the taxation which weighed directly upon their industry. In March, Western actually carried a motion against the Government to introduce a Bill for the repeal of the additional Malt Duty of 14d. per bushel imposed in 1819, and, in April, the Bill got to a second reading. Western's arguments were not so strong as his assertions, and Ministers had at least very good ground for the retention of the tax. The additional duty, calculated to yield something like a million and a quarter, was, it will be remembered, the leading feature of the new Sinking

[1] *Hansard*, iv. 1082.   [2] *Ibid.* iv. 299.   [3] *Ibid.* iv. 1100.

Fund scheme resolved upon in 1819—the chief of the taxes imposed to make up the £5,000,000 " clear surplus " of a Sinking Fund ; and, to repeal it almost before it had time to be tried, could be argued as giving up the hope of a Sinking Fund altogether. The weakness of the motion was, first, the uncertainty as to the real incidence of the tax—whether it fell on the landowners, or the farmers, or the brewers, or the consumers—and, second, the still greater uncertainty as to how that incidence would be affected by the repeal. Little, one notes, was said of the argument which afterwards carried the removal of the Agricultural Horse Tax, the inequality of the burden,[1] except that the tax bore more heavily on the small farmers, preventing many from growing barley at all and driving them to grow wheat.

Castlereagh, in an admirable speech, brought some order into the discussion by asking attention to three points : (1) Was the country in such a situation with regard to the public creditor, its revenue, its expenditure, as justified it in remitting any particular tax ? (2) Supposing it were, was the Malt Tax the particular one which ought to be remitted ? (3) Was there anything in the working of this tax that afforded a financial motive for repealing it ? All these points he answered in the negative. It was necessary to the public credit to have a surplus revenue of five millions. There was much more reason for repealing the Agricultural Horse Duty, or the Window Tax. No inconvenience or injury had arisen from its working ; it had not reduced the consumption of barley, and the price of beer had been twice reduced since June 1819 ; " it was not taxation but the price of produce that was the cause of the farmer's distress—it was proved that, if you could withdraw all taxation from his expenses, he would hardly be eased by such a reduction." He ended by saying that, " if the House should think fit to repeal the tax, he would not wish to continue a member of the Government of the country, whilst it was under the degraded situation of having a revenue only equal to its expenditure, and under the dangerous contingency of having that revenue even below it," and, on a division, the Bill was lost by 144 to 242.[2]

---

[1] Indeed, Huskisson expressly said that he did not think any objections could be made to its unequal operation.

[2] *Hansard*, iv. 1384 ; v. 6. The voting power of the agriculturists, Walpole calculates, was evidently about 150 : " the Ministry owed its defeat to its own supineness, and not to the strength of the country gentlemen " (*History of England*, ii. 29).

The Budget.   On 1st June, Vansittart introduced the Budget.[1] The principal features were a reduction of the total amount for the various services from £19,600,000 in 1820 to £18,000,000 ; a reduction of nearly £3 millions in the total expenses ; and the taking of a loan, from the Sinking Funds of Great Britain and of Ireland respectively, of £12,500,000 and £500,000.[2]

SUPPLY.

Army - - - - - - - - -	£8,750,000
Navy - - - - - - - - -	6,176,700
Ordnance - - - - - - - -	1,195,100
Miscellaneous - - - - - -	1,900,000
Interest and Sinking Fund on Exchequer Bills -	1,290,000
Reduction of Unfunded Debt - - - -	706,400
	£20,018,200

WAYS AND MEANS.

Annual Taxes - - - - - - -	£4,000,000
(Excise Duties), Tea Duties - - - -	1,500,000
Lottery - - - - - - - -	200,000
Old Stores - - - - - - -	163,400
Surplus of Indemnity payable by France - -	500,000
Exchequer Bills for Public Works repaid - -	125,000
Surplus of Ways and Means, 1820 - - -	81,630
Sinking Fund Loans - - - - - -	13,000,000
Bank of Ireland, increase of capital [3] - - -	461,539
	£20,031,569

Assuming that the general revenue would be the same as last year, he estimated the total at £55,011,000, and put the expenditure at £50,200,000. From these figures—and by juggling with the Sinking Fund—he made out that there would be an actual reduction of debt of nearly £4,000,000 : it was not likely that the clear £5,000,000 surplus could be obtained unless the revenue experienced a very considerable increase. And he " did not know that he had a right to hold out the expectation that any further material reductions would be made in the public expenditure." On the whole there was reason, he thought, to congratulate them-

Estimated
surplus of
£4 millions.

[1] *Hansard*, v. 1073. It remained a bad habit of the Chancellor of the Exchequer not to preface his estimates for the coming year by announcing how the past year's estimates had corresponded with the realisations. According to Porter, the total income of 1820 had been £54,282,958 ; the total expenditure £54,457,247, and the amount applied to reduction of debt £1,918,019.

[2] In 1819 £12,000,000 were " borrowed " from the Sinking Fund, and, in 1820, another £12,000,000 (*Economic Annals, 1801-20*, 687, 735).

[3] By permission of the House, the Bank of Ireland had increased its capital by £500,000 (Irish currency) (*Hansard*, v. 655).

selves on the state of affairs. If there had been, and still was, much distress, it must be remembered that there had been similar distress in most of the countries of Europe, and an extraordinary amount of it in the United States. This, at least, must be said, that England was the only country that had reduced its debt since the termination of the war, and the only one in which taxes to the amount of many millions had been repealed. A most striking illustration of the great internal resources of the country was that the deposits in the Savings Banks had progressively increased in every month—from £19,000 to £20,000 per week had regularly been paid into the Bank of England on their account—while the latest returns showed a greater progressive advance than had been previously known.

Of the Budget, there was little criticism. Ricardo, however, attacked the whole policy of the Sinking Fund. He confessed that he was one of those who thought a Sinking Fund very useless. He was, of course, favourable to such a fund in the abstract—there could hardly be any doubt of the soundness of the principle. But, after the experience from the time of Walpole, he never expected to see a Sinking Fund made applicable to the reduction of the debt. He, therefore, was rather disposed now to say, " Let us have no Sinking Fund ; let the money remain in the pockets of the people. When the Ministers want supplies, whether for carrying on a war or for any other purpose, let them come down to the House and ask for them, without having any such fund to resort to." Ministers were accustomed to tell the House that they must have a Sinking Fund to meet exigencies, to second the efforts of our armies, and to inspire the enemy with a salutary respect for us. But the legal and the original intention of the Sinking Fund was to pay off the National Debt . . . and, unfortunately, the people of England were at that moment much more in debt than they would have been if no such fund had been in existence.[1]

Although the agriculturists could not carry the repeal of the tax on Malt, they were successful as regards one where the amount was less and the argument stronger. The impost on Husbandry Horses, originally imposed by Pitt in the third year of the war, had been raised successively till it was now a considerable burden. Nothing was to be said for it in theory, and its incidence was

Ricardo on the Sinking Fund.

Husbandry Horse Tax repealed.

---

[1] A sound plain-spoken article on the fallacy of the Sinking Fund had appeared in the *Manchester Observer*, and was copied into other papers. It may be found in the *Glasgow Herald* of 22nd January.

grossly unequal; for instance, it scarcely affected grass lands, some of the richest in the kingdom. As a fact, its only defence was that it could not be avoided, and that, in the times of the high prices, agriculture " could stand it."

Curwen, whom we have met before as a leader among the farmers,[1] now attacked it as vexatious and unjust. " What farmer could conscientiously swear that he never used any of his agricultural horses for any other purpose than farming ? but, if he did not so swear, the horse otherwise used was charged as a saddle horse." Again, if " a farmer had four horses, three were charged at 17/- each as agricultural horses, and the fourth was set down as a saddle horse at 20/-, although it had never had a saddle upon its back, or anything more in that shape than a wisp of straw ; in addition to which 10/6 was charged for a groom." In the northern parts of the kingdom, seven horses were required for five in the southern : more horses were required—say for the carting of lime —where the waste lands were being taken in ; generally speaking, more horses were required on bad land than on good, and on heavy soils the tax amounted to 3 per cent. on the rent. Ricardo supported his motion, for the curious diplomatic reason of compelling the Government to strict economy ; as the Sinking Fund was at the moment " unproductive of one single good effect," he would, "abrogate every tax so long as any portion of that fund remained in existence." Vansittart replied that the repeal of an Act producing half a million of money was a serious thing. He took the tax as one " of which a particular class might complain," and, quite consistently from that point of view, described it as the opening of a general assault on the Consolidated Fund [2]—" an assault to be varied by every member according to the interests of his constituents or his own views of political economy "—and Huskisson supported him in this. But, as Brougham pointed out, the reason of the demand was, not that the tax weighed upon agriculture, but that it weighed unequally, and " most unequally upon the lands which were least able to bear it." In spite of Vansittart, Curwen's motion was carried, and, at the second reading, the Government withdrew

---

[1] *Economic Annals, 1801-20.* Curwen was author of a pamphlet, *Hints on Agricultural Subjects, and on the best means of Improving the Condition of the Labouring Classes,* 1809.

[2] The Consolidated Fund, it will be remembered, was the fund which received the great mass of the permanent taxes, such as Customs, Excise, Assessed Taxes, Stamps, Post Office and Land Tax : the largest charge on it was the interest on the National Debt.

their opposition—the Chancellor was now convinced, he said, that
the sense of the country was in favour of the repeal, and Londonderry looked on it as " a measure of sympathy," although he did
not expect any beneficial results from it. Lauderdale unkindly
remarked that the measure was resorted to only in consequence
of the disappointment created by the report of the Agricultural
Committee. No new tax was substituted.[1]

In this year, Joseph Hume, who had been out of Parliament for
six years, imbibing the doctrines of James Mill and Bentham, and
now returned as member for Aberdeen, played a part very like
what Brougham had done in former years—the part of a new
member constantly speaking and gradually conquering respect.[2]
In 1820, after his demand for enquiry as to the system on which
the revenue was collected had been defeated by the Government,
he brought forward a set of Resolutions on the subject, and accepted
Vansittart's proposal to refer them to a Select Committee.[3] The
Report, printed in June but not discussed in Parliament,[4] was a
triumph for Hume. It recommended that the Receivers-General
should be reduced from 66 (of whom only 28 performed even in
part their duties in person, the others acting by deputy) to 44 ;
that they should have fixed salaries instead of getting paid by a
poundage ; and that the collection should be managed as in the
excise, instead of the sums being left for, perhaps, six weeks at
the credit of the receivers' accounts with their own banks. During
the current session, at every presentation of the estimates, Hume
submitted the accounts of the various services to a minute examination, undeterred either by the ridicule of his opponents or by
his own occasional mistakes, and, long before the end of the Session,
he was recognised as " one of the most useful members of the
House." [5]

Finally, on a motion " to enforce the necessity of Economy and
Retrenchment in every department of the Public Expenditure,"

Hume becomes financial critic in chief.

---

[1] *Hansard*, iv. 1078 ; v. 42, 1184, 1201, 1505.

[2] *Economic Annals, 1801-20*, 712.   [3] *Hansard*, iv. 1401.

[4] The substance is given in *Annual Register*, chron. 101.

[5] Mackintosh, *Hansard*, iv. 1410.   Hume was well hit off by a squib of the
period :

> " Ward and Lord Palmerston always detest him at
> A dull unamusing debate on an estimate ;
> E'en Huskisson's best explanations he spurns,
> And is constantly calling for further returns.
> When papers are granted, he's never contented,
> But condemns them as vague before they're presented."

he submitted elaborate tables comparing the expenditure of "the golden year of 1792," with that of 1820, showing the progressive increase during the past four years, and exposing the very unsatisfactory nature of the public accounts.[1] The Resolutions founded on these were, indeed, defeated, but another set by Bankes, to much the same effect but saying more polite things about the Government, was passed.[2] It is some testimony to the place which Hume now occupied that, in consideration of his "zealous and indefatigable exertions to reduce the public expenditure and for the introduction of every practicable economy," he was presented with the thanks of the Common Council, and with the freedom of the city, "in a gold box, value a hundred guineas."

Resumption of gold coin payments. In this year, the Bank Restriction came to an end. By Peel's Bill of 1819, the Bank was bound to resume cash payments of notes on demand, in the legal coin of the realm, by 1st May, 1823. Till then, and after 1st February, 1820, gold payment could be demanded, but only in bars weighing 60 oz. and for large amounts, at a successively reduced rate.[3] In March, Vansittart [4] brought in a Bank Cash Payments Bill, giving the Bank the power of paying in gold coin from 1st May, 1821, if it thought fit. The reason of the proposal was that the Bank, in order to prepare for the resumption, had been making a drain on other countries for gold, and that this was unfavourable to commerce, as it restricted the circulation of these countries ; bullion instead of merchandise was imported in return for exported goods, and the accumulation of gold in the Bank was so rapid as to be inconvenient. On the third reading, when attention was called to the fact that, as the law stood, the Bank was not compelled to give small notes in exchange for large ones, a clause was added making it compulsory to pay either £1 notes or legal coin in exchange for the large notes.[5] Thus, after a period of twenty-four years and two months, cash payments were resumed in May.

It is interesting to note that, when the Bill was passing through

---

[1] The accounts were in such a state that it was impossible for any man, whatever industry he might possess, to come to an undisputed conclusion upon them. "In so simple a matter as the deficiency of the Consolidated Fund, there were three public accounts, all signed by the same person, all relating to the same period, and all differing in amounts. . . . As to the reduction of the debt, there was a difference of some millions between the Budget and the annual accounts."

[2] *Hansard*, v. 1345.   [3] *Economic Annals, 1801-20*, 679.

[4] *Hansard*, iv. 1315.   [5] *Ibid.* v. 203.

the Upper House, Lord King suggested the idea of a brassage on Brassage. the gold coin—not a seigniorage, but the taking out of each coin the exact expense of the coining. As it was, the regulations of the Mint made specie more convenient than bullion for sending abroad, and, with this and the melting down, we were kept coining for all Europe.[1] And the evil would grow, as gold was being brought here with more facility than to any other part of Europe, and there was a continual influx and reflux. While King said that brassage was the custom of every other country in Europe, Liverpool thought that the system was entirely new, and would require much consideration, and nothing came of the suggestion.[2]

In bringing in the Bill, Vansittart had given another reason for Forgery of the earlier issue of gold coin ; namely, that it must necessarily Notes. diminish the crime of forgery of notes.[3] The convictions of the previous six months showed that forgery was still increasing, and that Applegarth's invention of a note which would render imitation almost impossible was, if not a failure, not yet perfected.

In the meantime, this was being discussed in another connection. Mackintosh's Forgery Punishment Mitigation Bill, to abolish capital punishment for the crime, made an exception (along with wills, transfers of stock, marriage registers and licences) of the forgery of Bank of England notes, to which he subsequently added country notes.[4] Mackintosh defended the exception on the ground that such forgery had more mischievous consequences than others, seeing that notes passed through all hands, were taken by the ignorant

---

[1] The " twisting of straw for asses to eat," as Dudley North called it.

[2] *Hansard*, v. 495.

[3] *Ibid.* iv. 286. In this connection, it is suggestive to notice the proportion of the small notes to the others. The official statement of the circulation on 6th April is given as follows (*Annual Register*, 69) :

£1 and £2 notes - - - - - - -	£6,481,000
£5 notes - - - - - - - -	2,865,000
£10 ,. - - - - - - - -	3,249,000

Although not stated, the preponderance shows that this return included country bank notes, as a return of Bank of England notes in October showed only £2¾ millions of small notes as against £3 millions of £5 notes (*ibid.* 152). The convictions for forgery of Bank of England notes, which never reached sixty per year before 1816, rose in that year to 106 ; in 1818, to 227 ; and, in 1820, to 352 (*ibid.* 86). It is a curious sidelight on the place of the note in England that the Bank was said to be calling in the £5 notes as they had already done the £1 and £2, " thus leaving none of lower denomination than £10 " (*Glasgow Herald*, 15th October).

[4] In 1820, 154 persons were tried at the Old Bailey alone for uttering false notes, and, of these, forty-six suffered death.

and inconsiderate, and were received in moments of haste and inadvertence, and by persons who had neither leisure nor knowledge to detect the forgery. As the *Annual Register* remarked, this was to abandon his great principle that capital punishment was not so sure a means of repressing crime as were more merciful modes ; here the fear of death was allowed to be the best security. But, as the Bill did not pass, the matter was of less importance.[1]

Baring advocates a Double Standard.

The most interesting feature of the currency debates, however, was the unexpected breaking away of Baring from the principles for which he had fought under the Bullion Committee. On 8th February, in the course of a debate on the distress at Birmingham,[2] he said that he was convinced that a very considerable part of the distress arose from the nature of the currency, and went on to point out very clearly—as a warning of the danger of a departure from a proper standard—how the change had affected various classes. The departure had undoubtedly produced extravagance in public expenditure, and enormously increased the public debt. True, if corn was now 60/- instead of 80/-, and a man had no debt and was in receipt of an income of £60, he was in the same relative position, as regards corn, as when he had £80, and so with other commodities which had fallen in price. But, unfortunately, many farmers of small capital had been induced, by the rise in the prices of corn, to take farms under mortgages for a large portion of the price, and had not only lost all their property but were now in gaol. And the evil had extended to every kind of landed property. " It appeared to him that there was no difficulty whatever in reconciling the diminished consumption of which the manufacturers of Birmingham complained with the increased consumption of exciseable commodities. If £100 now would go as far as £120 or £130 did before, it was evident that the increased consumption of exciseable commodities arose from the increased means of the man of fixed income. . . . It was the drones in society whose means of enjoyment were increased, while the interests of all who were engaged in commercial and agricultural pursuits were depressed." The most serious subject of consideration was undoubtedly the expenditure of the country—how to bring back, as it were, the 80/- to the 60/- in our expenditure. Certain branches, of course, could not be reduced, such as soldiers' pay, retired allowances, and the like, in which it would be impossible to explain, to the persons to whom the reduction would apply, the necessity of the alteration. " This

[1] *Hansard*, v. 893, 999, 1099.   [2] *Ibid.* iv. 523.

was one of the great mischiefs of tampering with the currency of the country; for it was, in many instances, impossible to take back what had once been granted, when the pay became more than adequate to the services." But, although he considered that it would be highly inexpedient to tamper with the currency, he wished to hint at the course which he would wish to see adopted. He was desirous of giving the public creditor all that he was by law entitled to, but not to go beyond it. " If the House would hereafter grant him a Committee to facilitate the investigation of this subject, he would suggest the expediency of giving to the Bank the option of paying either in gold or silver, that the value of the two precious metals might be rendered more equal, and the present pound sterling, which was somewhat too high, relaxed. He wished, in fact, to relax a cord which was at present stretched somewhat too tightly." This could be done without the slightest injury to the public creditor.

This was more than Ricardo could listen to. He pointed out Ricardo condemns it. that the reduction of prices was not general and equal; the fall in corn was severe beyond measure, while there had been no fall in many other articles, or at any rate no fall in the least degree similar. He was surprised to find Baring making a statement from which, if correct, it must be inferred that the distresses began at the moment when the last change in the currency took place. Now if he looked back to the price of bullion in the flourishing year 1818, and compared it with the present price, it would be seen that the difference did not exceed 6 per cent. or 7 per cent. To this extent, other prices might have since been affected. ... And what increased his surprise at the view Baring had taken in tracing all our distress to a variation in the currency, was that when, a few years back, we had so much greater variations, we had no such distress. As to Baring's specific plan, it appeared to him to be a complete departure from the true and sound principles of currency. No currency could be of the same value perpetually, any more than other articles could always retain the same price. Gold bullion, however, was the commodity which varied the least, and, if a contract was made to pay £100 at a future period, the contract would be most faithfully performed by the payment of that sum in gold. But it might suit the purpose of the debtor to pay it in silver, whilst, by so doing, the creditor would sustain a loss. The two metals seldom long maintained the same proportion to each other. The price of the one might rise while that of the

other fell. . . . The relative value of the two metals had varied
since the act of Parliament ; but what was the cause of that variation ? It was this : the Bank being a timid body, seldom clinging
to the true principles of circulation, had taken alarm, and had
made great and unnecessary purchases of gold, although they found,
by experience, that no person applied to them for any. He almost
doubted whether a single bar had been demanded from them since
the commencement of the new plan.[1] If the Bank were enabled,
according to Baring's proposition, to pay in silver instead of gold,
they would now realise a profit equal to the difference between
4/11½ and 5/2. As soon as this profit should cease, the two
metals would have recovered their relative value, and then it would
be difficult to discover the value of Baring's proposition.

Bimetallism. Unmoved by Ricardo's condemnation, Baring, on 19th March,
reiterated his proposal formally—" the establishment of a double
standard, namely, of gold and silver." This, he said, " was no novel
proposition ; for, by the Act of 1774, silver was made a legal tender
to the amount of £25, and, for any sum above that, it was made a
legal tender by weight, according to an Act of 1790. Up till the
year 1790, then, there could be no doubt of the existence of a double
standard of value in the country." [2] There was no likelihood of
any material variation, he affirmed, between the price of gold and
silver if both were established as standards : the ordinary operation
of the money market would be a sufficient guarantee against it.
" In France, indeed, where the double standard had long existed,
one per mill. was the utmost variation that had, he understood,
ever appeared between the price of gold and silver." And, on
9th April, he moved for a Select Committee to report whether it
would be expedient to make any alteration in the Act 59 Geo. III.
c. 49, so as to alleviate the pressure which its operation was producing, and was likely to continue to produce, on the various
branches of public industry. Ricardo, reiterating his adherence
to the single gold standard, said that the evil of uncertainty and

---

[1] Only three ingots had been issued, said the *Annual Register.*

[2] When Vansittart denied this, Ricardo corrected him. " It was true that
£25 had been the utmost amount in the degraded currency of the country,
but a man might have gone to the Mint with his silver, and £100,000 might
be paid in silver of standard value. This, however, had never been any man's
interest. . . . The change in the relative value of the metals had taken
place between 1796 and 1798, and large quantities of silver had been carried
to the Mint, in order to profit by the state of the law. If Government had not
interfered, not a guinea would have been found in the country, and silver
would have been the standard " (*Hansard,* v. 137).

alarm could be got rid of only by Parliament being determined to adhere to the measure they had adopted. Such speculations coming from so great an authority were calculated to do much mischief. On a division, Baring received only 27 votes as against 141.[1]

[1] *Hansard*, iv. 1317 ; v. 91. The " mischief " suggested may be seen by the way in which the *Glasgow Herald* of 13th April translated Baring's proposal. Baring moved for a Select Committee, it said, " with a view, as he avowed, of introducing a measure to raise the nominal value of money to something like the point at which it stood when the majority of existing debts were contracted." And one is rather horrified to find Ward (afterwards Earl of Dudley) " pleased with the project " of " letting our currency down a peg or two," on the ground that silver was already cheaper in the market and was likely to go still lower ! (Letter lx.).

CHAPTER IV

1821. THE UNEVENTFUL YEAR

FOR many of the nations of Europe, 1821 was a year of storm and stress—of social and political ferment—of new wine bursting old bottles. The constitutions of Spain, the Sicilies, Piedmont, Portugal and Norway seemed to be in the melting pot. In the New World, many of the old colonies of the Peninsula threw off the yoke and became independent states. An inordinate space, accordingly, is given in the newspapers of the day to foreign affairs.

The Holy Alliance.

But all this little affected England except that it somewhat contracted her foreign markets. Only on one occasion did there seem some chance of becoming involved with the concerns of Europe —when the Holy Alliance, holding by the " eternal truth " that changes in legislation and administration ought only to emanate from those " whom God had rendered responsible for power," attacked the liberties, or at least the internal concerns, of Naples and Sicily. This was much resented here, and the popular indignation was powerfully voiced by Mackintosh. There were many debates in Parliament, and a good deal of criticism of the conduct of the Ministry—at least, thought many, a remonstrance might have been made to our dear allies. But this died down on the publication of a formal dispatch to His Majesty's ministers at foreign courts, to the effect that the King felt himself obliged to decline becoming a party to the measures in question, and the Government's attitude was approved.

While thus a year of notable events in the history of many countries, 1821 has a smaller place in our political annals than perhaps any since the beginning of the century, and general history would not suffer much if it were passed over in silence. The time of both Houses was taken up for weeks by the presentation of a flood of petitions in favour of the unhappy Queen, and with

endless wrangles as to what was to be done with her. There were
long debates on the Catholic Claims : in the Commons, Plunkett
carried his six Resolutions by a majority of four, when the intellectual preponderance in favour of Emancipation was strongly
marked ; and the Roman Catholic Disabilities Removal Bills were
passed—only to be thrown out in the Lords. Although more atten-
tion was given to Parliamentary Reform outside than in the House,[1] *Change of attitude towards*
Grampound was disfranchised, and the two seats given to the
county of York. Lambton, " the young Iulus of the fallen empire *parliamentary reform.*
of the Foxites "—in a speech which Canning privately pronounced
" quite perfect "—stood forward beside Russell as the champion
of reform.

The Government were now occupying a very uneasy position. *Position of the Government.*
They were only tolerated by the King—" it is one of the phenomena
of the present times," wrote Greville, " that the King should have
ministers whom he abuses and hates, and who entertain corresponding sentiments of aversion to him ; yet they defend all his
errors and follies, and he affords them constant countenance and
protection." Already very unpopular in many quarters on account
of their treatment of the Queen, they were falling out of favour
with everybody. Yet, though defeated on four important occasions,
the prospects of a change of ministry were no nearer ; " there is
an end for ever of all idea of the Whigs coming into power," wrote
Sydney Smith in February. " The Whigs," said the American
Minister, " are a party of leaders with no rank and file—accomplished men, but as aristocratic as the Tories : they have lost
their strong ground—the Reformers have taken it from them."
The only change in the Cabinet was that Canning, differing with
his colleagues, and determined to take no share in the proceedings
as to the Queen, resigned from the Board of Control ; though it
was expected that Peel might be induced to take his place, Peel
had no mind to involve himself in the unpopularity of Ministers,[2]
and Bragge Bathurst succeeded.

In 1819, as we saw,[3] Robert Owen's scheme, which he modestly *Owen's Plan.*

[1] " I never saw so great a change as to Reform in my life," wrote Hobhouse.
Harriet Martineau dates the continuous and successful agitation from this
year.

[2] " Peel has declined accepting office, but whether it is because he likes to
live retired with his pretty wife, or that he thinks the Ministry will not stand,
I know not " (Wilbraham, in the *Colchester Correspondence*, iii. 202). " With
a great fortune and domestic habits like his, I think the stormy sea of politics
can have little temptation for him," thought Croker.

[3] *Economic Annals, 1801-20*, 706.

described as " a Plan for relieving public distress and removing discontent by giving permanent productive employment to the poor and working classes, under arrangements which will essentially improve their character and ameliorate their condition, diminish the expenses of production and consumption, and create markets co-extensive with production," had been refused the compliment of a parliamentary enquiry. The Plan was, however, laid, by request, before a Committee of the county of Lanark in 1820, and was much quoted in the newspapers of the day.[1] His ideas and their practical working out were by this time attracting much attention—" the crowds of people who flock to New Lanark from all parts of the United Kingdom, the Continent, and America," says a contemporary, " engross nearly the whole of his time." In June of the current year, John Maxwell of Pollok, the member who had distinguished himself in the previous Session by condemning machinery as one of the great causes of the general distress, and now rather injured his cause by an irrelevant preface on " the unrepresented labourer of the British Empire who had drained his best veins for the House of Hanover, and now, with impaired force but unshaken fortitude, was working the vessel of the state out of that maelstrom into which a rash and ignorant pilot had steered it," moved for a Royal Commission to " visit New Lanark, to examine the condition and treatment of the working classes in that establishment, and to enquire into any further arrangements which Mr. Owen might propose for the benefit of labourers." Full recognition was given by many speakers to Owen's success at New Lanark, and Brougham, among others, was prepared to vote for

---

[1] The following quotation from it is characteristic : " The Romans and the Highlanders of Scotland appear to have been the only two nations which adopted a national dress on account of its utility." (He recommended that all the male children of the new villagers should be clothed in a similar garb.) " All other circumstances remaining the same, sexual delicacy and virtue will be found much higher in nations among whom the person, *from infancy,* is the most exposed than among those people who exclude from sight every part of the body except the eyes." (Under such arrangements, they would be better dressed, for all the acknowledged purposes of dress, at much less than a hundredth part of the labour, inconvenience, and expense now required.) " If your Reporter should be told that all this waste of thought, time, labour, and capital (on dress) is useful, inasmuch as it affords employment for the working classes, he replies that no waste of any of these valuable means can be of the slightest benefit to any class." It would be better to make them dig holes and fill them up again, than " suffer a large proportion of the working classes to be immured all their lives in unhealthy atmospheres, and toil at wretched employments, merely to render their fellow creatures weak and absurd both in body and mind."

the motion, but, in the end, Maxwell announced that he would not divide the House.[1]

In April, Michael Angelo Taylor brought in his Bill based on the recommendations of the Committee which reported in 1820,[2] " for giving greater facility in the prosecution and abatement of nuisances arising from furnaces used in the working of steam engines." Injury to health and deterioration of property were the grounds on which he based the measure, and he defended it by the assertion that it had been found quite practicable for engines to consume their own smoke. There was strong opposition from many who said that smoke consumption was quite illusory except at very great expense, and, in many cases, was quite impossible, and it was represented that opposition might be disarmed if Cornwall and perhaps some other mining counties wère exempted from the operation of the Bill. But Taylor said he would rather drop it altogether than make any exceptions, and the Bill passed both Houses as c. 41.[3]

Smoke prevention.

The Third Census of Great Britain—" which Parliament had so judiciously ordered for the benefit of the infant science of Political Economy," it was said—was taken on 28th May. It showed a total population of 14,391,631.[4] As the population was 12,596,803 in 1811, and 10,942,646 in 1801, this showed an increase of $14\frac{1}{4}$ per cent., as compared with an increase of about 15 per cent. for the previous decade. The increase of females was $15\frac{4}{5}$ per cent., as compared with 14 per cent. between 1801 and 1811, and the proportion of the sexes was 106 females to 100 males, as compared with 110 females at the two previous censuses. The important statement was made that one-third of the population of Great Britain was employed in raising subsistence for the other two-thirds; in 1811, the proportion had been slightly more than one-third.

The Census.

The separate totals were :

England	-	-	-	11,261,437,	an increase of 18 per cent.[5]
Wales	-	-	-	717,438,	,, $17\frac{1}{5}$,,
Scotland	-	-	-	2,093,456	,, $15\frac{9}{7}$,,
Army, Navy, etc.			-	319,300	

---

[1] *Hansard*, v. 1316.   [2] *Economic Annals, 1801-20*, 709, 737.

[3] *Hansard*, v. 441, 535, 654.

[4] In 1820, according to the *Annual Register,* the population of the eighty-six departments of France was 30,407,000. The *Edinburgh Magazine* for April gives it as 29,217,000.

[5] It is amusing to find Cobbett, in 1823, denouncing the Census returns as the biggest lie ever put in print, even in romance, on the ground that, as the

The most densely populated counties were :

In England—Middlesex	-	1,167,500, an increase of 19 per cent.
Lancaster	-	1,074,000,	,,	25	,,
West Riding		815,400,	,,	21	,,
In Scotland—Lanark	-	249,300,	,,	26	,,
Edinburgh		195,300,	,,	27	,,
Aberdeen	-	158,500,	,,	14	,,
Perth	-	141,800,	,,	2	,,

The populations of the chief cities were :

London - - - - - - - - -	1,274,800 [1]
Glasgow - - - - - - - - -	147,043
Edinburgh and Leith - - - - - -	138,235
Manchester and Salford - - - - - -	133,788
Liverpool - - - - - - - -	118,972
Birmingham - - - - - - - -	106,722

Census of Ireland.

The first census of Ireland, taken at the same time (but not regarded as satisfactory), gave Leinster 1,757,492 ; Munster, 1,935,612 ; Ulster, 1,998,494 ; Connaught, 1,110,229 : in all, 6,801,827. The population of Dublin was 238,201. It is interesting to note the calculation that the population of Ireland was 365 to the square mile, as against 210$\frac{4}{5}$ for England and Wales, and 86 for Scotland.

After the rising of Parliament, the newspapers are principally taken up with the Coronation—which was estimated for £100,000 and cost £230,000—with the King's visit to Ireland—"like a popular candidate come down upon an electioneering trip "—and with the death of the Queen, who had already outlived the brief popularity roused by chivalrous resentment at her trial.[2]

population in 1700 was not quite five millions, and, in 1801, was eight millions, the figures would mean that it took the country a hundred years to make five into eight, and only twenty years to make eight into eleven—a monstrous proposition, not to be believed on the oaths of 50,000 return makers ; the size of the churches alone was sufficient to convince any man of sound judgment that there had been a prodigious decrease ! In 1824, we find him asserting —without any proof—that four-fifths probably of the whole people of England, Scotland, and Ireland were landowners and their households, farmers and their labourers, and workmen and tradesmen connected with and dependent upon agriculture (*Register*, 49, 585).

[1] Alarm was sometimes expressed at the "monstrous overgrowth" of London. Cobbett called it the Wen, and would have had Peel stop the extension of buildings.

[2] When the news of Napoleon's death, in May, was brought to the King by Sir E. Nagle, in the words, " I have the pleasure to tell your Majesty that your bitterest enemy is dead," he replied eagerly, " No ! Is she, by Gad ? " (Moore's *Diary*, iii. 270).

The progress of invention by this third decade of the century is Steamboats. indicated most strikingly by the steady increase in the number and size of steam vessels. When Lord Albemarle was leaving for India in 1821, he wrote in his journal : " The driver (of the Greenwich stage) called my attention to a little steamboat wending its way down the Thames. It was the first I ever remember to have seen. There were, I believe, a few of these boats plying between the bridges, but it was thought a rash act for one of them to venture so near to the river's mouth. ' There's the things,' said my Jehu, ' that will ruin us coachmen.' " [1] But the records of Clyde sailings show that " steam packets " were regularly plying not only all down the estuary as far as Campbeltown, but to Belfast, Dublin, Liverpool, and Harwich—the woodcut represents a fearsome-looking paddle steamer, with a funnel about as long as the main-mast, vomiting out clouds of smoke. The *Majestic*, built by John Scott and Sons, Greenock, made her first run to Liverpool in twenty-four hours, including stoppages. She is described as " the most elegant as well as the largest vessel of this description hitherto built in Britain " ; 144 feet in length ; 39 in breadth ; of 345 tons burden ; driven by two engines of 50 horse-power each ; the cost, " little short of £14,000." [2] In the current year, the Postmaster-General introduced steamboats at Holyhead and Dover for the conveyance of the mails.[3] But shipping generally was still under sail, in the shape of sloops, brigs, and ships, generally from 170 to 350 tons, with a few East Indiamen of 600 to 750 tons for the Cape and New South Wales: the largest I have seen mentioned is one of 1,300 tons.

The new illuminant was being introduced into private houses. Gas. In December, Sydney Smith wrote from Lambton : "And here I ask what use of wealth so luxurious and delightful as to light your house with gas ? . . . How pitiful to submit to a farthing candle existence when science puts such intense gratification

---

[1] *Fifty Years of my Life*, ii. 148.

[2] Hobhouse was on board the *Majestic* in September 1823, when the pipe of one of the boilers burst six miles off Greenock and the boat stopped, and reflects that, if this had happened half-way, they might have been lost : " I cannot think after all that the steam-boats are or can be made secure in a heavy sea off a lee shore." This wonderful application of steam, he muses, " is yet perhaps only in its infancy " (*Recollections*, iii. 25).

[3] The Fifth Report of the Select Committee on the London and Holyhead Roads, Regulations for Conveying the Mails, 1822, gives a history of the progress of steam navigation from 1736.

within your reach.   Dear lady, spend all your fortune on a gas.
apparatus.''[1]

But every advance in the mechanical arts had to meet with the
opposition of the vested interest.   In February, for instance, we
find a petition, signed by 700 journeymen ropemakers of the
Metropolis, complaining of a machine called " The Devil," which,
with the assistance of six or seven men, did the work that formerly
occupied ninety-seven ; thus, it said, two-thirds of the workmen
previously employed were prevented from earning a living.   And
the work so done was, of course, stated to be so extremely imperfect
as to injure the character of the manufacture in foreign countries.
The only remedy which suggested itself to them, however, was to
place "the devil in more immediate connection with the Chancellor
of the Exchequer," and get a tax laid upon it.[2]

To locate the year. The year may be located by the frequent mention in newspapers
and diaries of Shelley, Byron, Wordsworth, Coleridge, Moore, Rogers,
Campbell, Southey, Lamb, De Quincey, and the " Author of Waver-
ley."   On the stage are Kean (still *facile princeps*), Charles Kemble,
Macready, Wallack, Cooper, Charles Mathews, Farren, Munden,
Liston, Elliston, Grimaldi, Miss Kelly, Miss Tree ; and, among
singers, Madame Vestris, Miss Stephens, Miss Wilson, and Braham.
Sir Humphry Davy has just become President of the Royal Society,
and Sir Thomas Lawrence is President of the Royal Academy.
The painters who draw attention are Haydon, Etty, Collins, Martin,
Landseer, Wilkie, Flaxman, and Turner.   Mrs. Fry is to be found
on her mission of mercy at Newgate, and the papers are full of the
brutal details of " The Fancy."

In general literature appeared Shelley's *Adonais*, Galt's *Annals
of the Parish*, Fenimore Cooper's *The Spy*, and *The Pirate*, of which
last, said Blackwood, "the author's name is as well known to me as
if he had put it on the title-page—none but himself can be his
parallel."   The growth of journalism is shown by the fact that,
in London, there appeared 16 daily, 8 bi-weekly, and 32 weekly
newspapers.[3]

Economic publications. In the literature of Political Economy, the more important are
James Mill's *Elements* ; Torrens' *Essay on the Production of Wealth* ;
the first volume of Chalmers' *Christian and Civic Economy of*

[1] *Memoir*, ii. 223.   [2] *Hansard*, iv. 579.

[3] " Scotland boasts but one original newspaper, the *Scotsman*, and has but
one subject, Political Economy," said the *Edinburgh* in May, 1823.

Large Towns; in German, Rau's *Ansichten über Volkswirthschaft.* The Political Economy Club was founded by Ricardo and others.

Among the book advertisements, I find the following less known : *Remarks on Some Fundamental Doctrines in Political Economy*, by John Craig, F.R.S.E. ; *Essays on Money, Exchanges, and Political Economy*, by Henry James, of Birmingham (1820) ; *A Few Doubts as to Opinions entertained on the Subjects of Population and Political Economy*, by P. Ravenstone, M.A. ; *Conversations on Political Economy, in a series of Dialogues*, by J. Pinsent ; *An Inquiry into those principles respecting the nature of Demand and the necessity of Consumption lately advocated by Mr. Malthus ; An Essay on the Political Economy of Nations, or a view of the Intercourse of Countries as influencing their Wealth ; Observations on certain verbal disputes in Political Economy, particularly relating to Value and to Demand and Supply ; Essays on the present false and unjust Standard of Value*, by the Rev. R. Cruttwell, LL.B. ; *An attempt to define some of the Principles of Political Economy*, by Thomas Smith.

MISCELLANEA.

A dandy, on a velocipede,
　I saw in a vision sweet,
Along the highway making speed,
　With his alternate feet.
Of a bright and celestial hue,
Gleam'd beauteously his blue surtout ;
While ivory buttons, in a row,
Showed like the winter's cavern'd snow,
Which the breezy North
Drives sweeping forth,
To lodge in the cave below :
Ontario's beaver, without demur,
To form his hat did lend its fur :
His frill was of the cambric fine,
And his neckcloth starch'd and aquiline ;
And oh, the eye with pleasure dwells
On his white jean indescribables :
And he throws the locks from his forehead fair,
And he pants, and pants, and pants for air.
　　　　　　Blackwood's Magazine, May, 135.

" We never remember so little change in fashion as has taken place during the last two or three years. The evening dress of our ladies is as nearly what it should be as it is in the nature of human imperfection to make it " (*Glasgow Herald*, 6th April).

"We understand that an exhibition of rather an extraordinary nature took place lately in the Metropolis of Scotland; no less than that of a Ball at which the gentlemen were arrayed in the full Highland costume of hose and kilt. . . . We understand that, bating the indelicacy of the thing, the Ball went off very well. . . . We really must say that nothing conveys to us a more ludicrous idea than kilted gentlemen figuring in the insipid monotony of a French quadrille " (*Morning Chronicle*, March).

CHAPTER V

1822. THE AGRICULTURAL AGITATION AGAINST TAXATION

THE organised and widespread agitation, carried on throughout the country in 1822 by means of public meetings and petitions, had so many effects, direct and indirect, on the Budget, that it seems advisable, at the risk of some repetition, to take them first and group them all together in a separate chapter.

By the month of May, some 500 petitions had been presented *The unholy* from the agricultural classes, and supported generally by the *alliance.* country gentlemen; the strange spectacle was presented of the classes dependent on land as owners and farmers, hitherto notorious for their conservatism, suddenly assuming the character of political agitators and joining hands with the Radicals.[1] As Sir Herbert Maxwell says, a generation of landlords had grown up with no other experience than that, come what might, agriculture was impregnable. But now the inevitable demand for reduction of rents had touched them on the raw—Cobbett kept reiterating that wheat could never again be more than 4/- a bushel on an average after 1823, and that rents would disappear by 1824—and, for once, they practically inscribed " our trade, our politics " on their banners. Most of the petitions, strangely enough, suggested Parliamentary Reform as the remedy.[2] Some boldly demanded the breaking of

---

[1] Walpole, *History of England*, ii. 30. Some very biting home truths on this untoward alliance were told by a Glasgow manufacturer, who wrote under the *nom de plume* of " Bandana " in the pages of *Blackwood* in October and November.

[2] This is not, perhaps, so strange as it seems, except that the landowners for the moment lent it their countenance. The petitions, on the whole, are so many echoes of Cobbett's *Register*, and Cobbett's two texts were the evils of the taxes and the necessity of Parliamentary Reform to secure their removal. In justice to Cobbett, it must be said that his vehement attack on the taxation, immediately after the war at anyrate, was because it went so largely

faith with the national creditor—were the fundholders alone to receive their full pound of flesh while they bore no part of the universal distress ?   But nearly all agreed in attacking the " overwhelming and all-devouring taxation," as the Kent petition called it.   The conviction was expressed almost universally that excessive taxation was the chief—many said the sole—cause of the agricultural distress.   In short, while, in 1821, various causes were suggested, such as the contraction of the currency, foreign importation, the warehousing system, excessive taxation, and the one most dwelt on was the first of these—that the evil was low prices caused by Peel's Act [1]—the *mot d'ordre* of the agitation in the present year was one better understood and appreciated by the farmers,—the taxation.   It is the predominance of this rallying cry that forms the characteristic political feature of the year 1822.

The broad lines of the coming struggle emerged at the very beginning of the Session.   The King's Speech called for early attention to the depressed state of the agricultural interest.   Hume, in moving an amendment to the Address, asked the House to represent to His Majesty that excessive taxation, disproportionate to the reduced value of all property, was a principal cause of the distress, and to request that he would be pleased to direct such reductions in every branch of the public expenditure, from the highest to the lowest department, as would enable the House forthwith to deliver the people from a large portion of that burden which, in their present impoverished condition, pressed so heavily upon all classes.   He accused Ministers, among other things, of maintaining a system of accounts which concealed the truth instead of making a plain statement of debtor and creditor, and of retrenching by cutting down " labourers, carpenters, porters, and such persons " instead of, say, junior lords of the Admiralty, while the

The mot d'ordre.

Hume on economy.

to support " placemen, pensioners, and sinecures," instead of being a payment for " value received " in Government service.   He preached, in season and out of season, that the army was a useless expenditure and merely a danger to freedom at home—" the army, the barracks, the ordnance, secret service money, a high paid police, jobs, etc., these items stand the country in about £15 millions.   What do we want of these things ?   What are barracks for ? Nothing grows in them ; they produce nothing.   If we get rid of them, here are £15 millions cut off out of £53 millions of annual expenditure.   Now all these £15 millions are spent on nothing more or less than preventing a Reform.   It has no other object ; it can have no other object " (*Register*, February).

[1] " There appears to be no ground whatever for the assertion that the issues of the Bank of England were contracted by the operation of Peel's bill " (Tooke, *History of Prices*, ii. 110).

total expenditure increased and places were made for their relatives
and friends.[1] But the main object of his speech was to present a
formidable array of figures as to the expenditure, and he made no
attempt to establish a connection between the taxation and the
distress.[2]

To this Vansittart replied, rather loftily, that Hume should
have waited a little ; he would then have seen that the reductions
which the Government proposed would extend as well to the highest
as to the lowest official situations—although, indeed, no mere
reduction of taxation would affect the distress of the country ;[3]
and reiterated his old contention that Hume's plan, by involving
the destruction of the Sinking Fund, would shake public credit
and make it impossible to raise money, even at five or six per cent.
Ricardo agreed with everything that had fallen from Hume in
favour of economy and retrenchment ; but he could not vote with
him, he said, as he differed widely on the causes of the existing
agricultural distress. The real cause, it could not be denied, was
the low price of produce ; and, that taxation should be the cause of
low prices was so absurd[4] and so inconsistent with every principle
of political economy, that he could not assent for a moment to the
doctrine.

The debate was a heated one, and the issues were somewhat
obscured by the uncertainty as to what members were committed
to by either motion or amendment. The ground taken by many,
including most of the country members, was that it was not possible
to judge of Hume's mass of figures without consideration, and that
it was only fair to Ministers to wait till it was known what they had
to propose ; and, in the end, Hume's amendment was lost by
89 to 17.[5]

Without waiting, however, and affecting to believe that the
Chancellor of the Exchequer had practically asserted that, to lighten

Brougham on
taxation as
cause of the
distress,

---

[1] He quoted the will of a certain nobleman who left sums to certain members
of his family of from £200 to £500 a year, " until they should be better provided for by Government in some other manner ! "

[2] *Hansard,* vi. 47.

[3] " Gracious God ! " said Coke, "at a time when the people, from one end
of the country to the other, were complaining of distress, were they to be
told by a hard-hearted and callous Government, on the first day of the Session
too, that they were to meet with no relief " ; and this formed the text for much
ill-directed oratory.

[4] One connection suggested, more ingenious than convincing, was that, to
pay their taxes, the farmers were forced to sell their produce at unfavourable
times.

[5] *Hansard,* vi. 47.

the burdens of the people, would be a public evil, and that he would bring forward rather a budget of new taxes than a reduction of the old ones, Brougham, that formidable fighter, on 11th February, led another attack on the Government under the guise of a discussion on the Distressed State of the Country. It was a mistake, he said, to think of the distress either as local or as confined to the agricultural farmer. It was general, and the pressure was being felt even more by the stock than by the arable farmer. However it might be with foreign trade, where there were powerful stimulants to exertion and industry, to tell him that the manufacturers, to whom the internal market was of most importance, could be in a flourishing state when their chief customers were ruined, was to assert a contradiction in terms. He believed the word of those who told him that the demand of the agricultural interest for manufactured commodities was very much contracted, and that profits were very much reduced below the amount which characterised a period of even modern prosperity. For this, he went on, the finance of the Government was largely accountable. " If a man in private life, having an income of £10,000 a year, went on increasing his expenditure, till the interest of the debt that he incurred amounted to £5000 per annum ; and if he still continued to spend the sum which should be employed in liquidating that interest, so that he was compelled every quarter to borrow money to meet his creditor, that individual would be precisely in the same situation in which the country was placed." The huge expenditure still went on ; " we had been at peace for no less than six years, and yet the expenditure was only a million less than was required in the second year of the war." To defray this, there came huge taxation. This taxation increased prices, for those on whom the tax fell advanced the price to the immediate purchaser without much nicety, and this purchaser in turn advanced it to the consumer without much nicety, and so the augmentation went on in geometrical ratio. And this was the cause of the public distress. The country gentleman first paid by the increase of taxes ; he, next, paid as a consumer by the increased price of what he consumed ; he, lastly, paid as a producer, the expenses of cultivation having been raised. And of this taxation an undue share was borne by the agricultural classes. The remedy was to reduce it by every expedient, not by lopping off the salaries of petty clerks, and by consolidating a few clerkships in one to serve the dependent of some great man, but by beginning at the highest and going down

to the lowest salaries till every class of the State was included.
A very large proportion of the distress, indeed, might be ascribed
to the return to cash payments, which had increased the burden
of the taxation by £4 millions. But seeing they had returned to
cash payments, the only specific remedy was such a reduction of
taxes as might be suited to the change in the value of money.

The speech, which contained a good deal of vague threatenings
of the desperate measures which might be necessary if the landowners
of England were to continue permanently in the state, or in anything
like the state, in which they at present stood, was received with loud
cheers. "It is the fashion," said Creevey, "to praise Brougham's
speech more than it deserved—at least in my opinion. It was free
from faults, I admit, or very nearly so ; and that, I think, was its
principal merit." But, though a powerful party effort, the speech
was not what might have been expected from Brougham, and one
rather agrees with the *Annual Register* that it was very long and very
desultory ; "had it not been for some strains of bitter sarcasm,
one could scarcely have believed that it was the member for Winchelsea who was labouring with such parasitical zeal to flatter all
the prejudices of the country gentlemen, and who was even bold
enough to hint that, if the comfort of full purses could not be otherwise obtained for them, the true line of policy would be to plunder
the public creditor that they might be enriched." [1]

Ricardo weakened its effect very much by a calm reiteration —which
of his old statement, that taxation was not the cause of the present Ricardo
denies.
agricultural distress. "A country might be totally without taxes
and yet in the exact situation that England was at present. It
was consistent enough, in those who thought that the restoration
of the currency had made a change of 50 per cent. or 56 per cent.
in the value of money, and had consequently increased the actual
value of the taxes in that proportion, though their nominal amount
still remained the same, to say that taxation was the chief cause of
the distressed state of agriculture ; but it was impossible for those
who held that the restoration in the currency had not created anything like so great a change. If he were called on to declare
what he conceived the cause, he would repeat that it was the abundance of produce now in hand arising from the late plentiful
harvest, the quantity of land recently brought into cultivation,

[1] P. 98. The object of the speech, it seems agreed, was to feel the pulse of
the country gentlemen, and to ascertain how far they were likely to abandon
the Government.

the importation of corn from Ireland,[1] and various other causes
which it was not material for him at that time to mention. Indeed,
the House would deceive both itself and the country if it should
come to a resolution that taxation was the cause of the distresses
of the agricultural interest." He added that, on a future occasion,
he would explain why he thought that the alteration produced in
the value of money by the restoration of the currency had been
greatly over-stated, and would then endeavour to show that, if
proper measures had been taken at the time of passing Peel's Bill,
the resumption would have produced no greater effect on the price
of corn and other agricultural produce than a fall of five per cent.[2]
Brougham's motion was defeated by 212 to 108. It is notable
that, although Ricardo voted for it, none of the country gentlemen did.

Londonderry, replying to Brougham,

Four days later, Londonderry [3] took the unusual step of replying

[1] Tooke, as we saw, had already drawn attention to the imports of grain from
Ireland as at least a contributory cause of the distress of the British farmer.
If no alteration had been made in the corn trade with Ireland, said Huskisson
subsequently, probably the pressure of the glut might never have been felt
by the English grower. He himself had not allowed for the prolific powers of
the more fertile soils of that country ; he did not foresee that Ireland would
now be sending in an annual supply exceeding the average import of foreign
corn from all parts of the world before the change of 1806. (Peel gave the
figures : in 1820 1,425,000 qrs. had come from Ireland, and in the nine months
ending 10th October, 1821, no less than the amazing quantity of 1,502,000
—nearly double the quantity ever before imported from Ireland in one year,
Hansard, vi. 495). The existing depression, continued Huskisson, was the
result of an excess in both countries. The Corn Law of 1815 had been passed
under an impression of the inability of this country to raise corn enough for
its own consumption. Thus it had been the decided opinion of great authorities
that the import price of 80/- would be the minimum price of wheat in England,
and improvements were entered on, and lands let, on this assumption. But
now it was shown that the home produce exceeded the consumption, and two
or three productive harvests had led to the current depression (*Hansard*, vi.
424).

[2] Ricardo redeemed his promise later on when replying to Attwood. He
begged the House to recollect the state in which the currency stood in 1819.
At the time of the passing of the Bill, the difference between the paper currency
and gold was only 5 per cent. What he had then suggested was that measures
should be taken which, while they restored the value of the paper currency to
an equality with gold, and thus put an end to the depreciation, would make
any purchases of gold unnecessary. Under these measures, as there would
have been no additional demand for gold, there could have been no increase
in the value of that metal. But that suggestion was not followed, and the
purchases of gold had made a considerable change in its value. Undoubtedly,
as the hon. member contended, the burden of money taxation was increased
in proportion to the increase in the value of money, but it was at the utmost
about 10 per cent. (*Hansard*, vii. 392).

[3] Castlereagh had become Marquis of Londonderry in the previous year.

to Brougham, and, at the same time, adumbrating the Budget [1]—
as Huskisson said, it might be considered in the light of an
adjourned debate upon the nature and causes of the existing
distress. He maintained that he started from the same standpoint as Brougham, namely, that there was no kind or degree of
retrenchment, founded on sound and rational principles of political
economy and calculated to relieve people from the pressure of
taxation, which it was not the bounden duty of Parliament immediately to adopt. But he differed with him as to the universality
of the distress. With the exception of the iron trade, which had,
indeed, suffered some abatement of the rapidly progressive prosperity
which it had of late so eminently enjoyed, he asserted that the
manufacturing and commercial interests had undergone so favourable a change that, taking them generally, at no period in the
history of the country had they been in a condition of more healthful
though temperate prosperity. Although wages were certainly not
so high as they had been during the war—which was not altogether
to be regretted—they were adequate, and operatives were already
living in great comfort. " Throughout the manufacturing districts,
the manufacturers were now receiving the sum of twelve-pence,
where, during the recent period of actual distress, they received
eight-pence ; and, with that eight-pence, they could obtain as many
of the necessaries of life as would then have cost them twelve-pence ;
so that their condition was 100 per cent. better."

Brougham, he said, had created a real impression by stating denies the
that the consumption of malt was less by one-seventh than it had universality of
been thirty years before, and by assuming that the heavy taxation the distress ;
was the cause of the decrease. As a fact, the consumption in 1821
was the greatest since 1792, with the exception of one year (1797),
and that of 1822 promised to be much greater still. But there was
no necessary connection of this kind between the consumption and
taxation : " it appeared from the records that least malt was
consumed in those years in which there was least taxation upon it."
Even, however, had it been the case that the consumption of malt
had decreased, might it not be that the people were now drinking
other beverages ? A great change had taken place in the habits
of the people ; they were certainly less addicted to drinking strong
liquors than they were formerly. It was clear that tea had come
into more general use, and that a large class of individuals who
formerly drank beer now drank tea, not from being too poor to

[1] *Hansard*, vi. 350.

command the former, but from preferring the latter. The amount of tea consumed, on a mean of 1820 and 1821, was 22 million lbs., and, during the whole of the past thirty years, the duty, with little interruption, had been gradually increasing from 13 per cent. until it had reached 100 per cent. In short, the people of this "impoverished" country voluntarily incurred an annual charge of three millions sterling which they might avoid! [1] There had been not only an increase of comfort, but an increase of cleanliness; excise returns showed that the consumption of soap had nearly doubled in the past eight or ten years. The making of bricks for dwelling-houses had largely increased. So with other articles of consumption. Taken altogether, the excise—"that great barometer of consumption"—showed in the past year (exclusive of London) an increase of £1,400,000, or between 9 per cent. and 10 per cent.—which surely manifested a recovery diffused throughout the kingdom. He did not bring forward this to deny the existence of distress, but to show how powerful were the principles of resurrection and prosperity in the country; principles which, if the House would only support by encouraging public credit, would soon, by their natural progress, restore everything to a satisfactory state. The exports, too, of British and Irish produce and manufactures showed an increase of nearly £4½ millions over the preceding year, and of nearly £6 millions over the foregoing year. But what he was mainly concerned to contest was Brougham's assertion that, " by no other plan could an effectual relief be found for the distresses

---

[1] Brougham's answer to this would scarcely be believed. "The noble lord," he said, "in the excess of his sagacity, and with a wise and provident benevolence of heart, had found out that tea was an admirable substitute for that good wholesome old English beverage which was produced from malt. Now, against that substitute he had the strongest objection; he would ever contend that, whilst the great body of the people consumed tea instead of beer, they consumed an article which he believed was not so wholesome—which he knew was not so British—which he was sure, in whatever quantities it might be consumed, could give no relief to the British farmer." And he asked what classes of people this consumption benefited, except the agriculturists of China and English importers.

"Does the hon. and learned gentleman," asked Huskisson severely, "wish us to understand that the Chinese kindly make us a present of all the tea, and, still more kindly, deliver it free of expense in Leadenhall Street; and that no British industry is put in motion, either to provide the means of procuring this foreign article or to convey it to the shores of this country? Are we to take this as the hon. and learned gentleman's doctrine in respect to commerce with foreign States, and another sample of that political economy which the hon. and learned gentleman has attempted to palm off upon the good sense of the House of Commons, but which is, in fact, more worthy of a drunken mob in Palace-yard" (*Hansard*, vi. 402, 439).

of the country, but by pushing to its utmost extent the reduction
of taxation." While wishing as eagerly as he did for the repeal
of taxation, he took his position alongside Ricardo that, so far **agrees with Ricardo;**
from taxation being the only evil, he did not hesitate to assert
that, suppose we could sweep away the whole mass of our taxation
in a moment, our distress would still continue to press upon us—
in so small a degree did that distress originate in the operation of
taxation. He made a calculation to show that the total amount
of the taxes, direct and indirect, which could by any possibility
bear upon the farmer, considered in his double capacity of cultivator
and consumer, did not amount to more than one-seventh of his
rent. But even taking it at one-fifth of the rent, it was equal to
5 per cent. on the outgoings and incomings of the whole farm.
It was for Brougham to show how such a sum of 5 per cent. on the
value of the produce of the soil could have the effect of occasioning
or continuing the present distress. But to give this relief of 5 per
cent., the House must be prepared to sacrifice 14 or 15 millions of
revenue—which was too absurd a proposition to argue. "The
hon. and learned gentleman asserted the other evening that, if
the whole of the landlord's rent were surrendered to the farmer,
even that sacrifice would be insufficient for the farmer's relief. Is
it not, then, an insult to the common sense of the House to contend,
in the same breath, that the reduction of taxation, forming, as it
does, but a proportion of that rent, could be effectual or could even
materially contribute to relieve the farmer ? "

He then proceeded to state the views of the Government, as to **and adumbrates the Budget.**
the means which Parliament might most wisely apply for the
double purpose of relieving the present distress and securing the
general and permanent prosperity. First, there would be a reduction in Army, Navy and other estimates, amounting to £2,000,000.[1]
Then the accounts would show that they had now secured the
object of the resolution of 1819, a "clear, undisputed, available
surplus revenue" of £5,000,000 for the Sinking Fund. "The
question for you to decide is, will the interests of the country be
best consulted by sweeping away all this surplus revenue which
you have been at so much pains and have bestowed so much labour
to create ; and, by giving it at once to the people, under all the
hazards of such an act, even to the regular payment of the dividend
to the public creditor ; under all the inevitable depression of public

---

[1] Thus early was Vansittart's expectation of 1821 falsified, that no further
material reduction would be made in the public expenditure.

and private credit ; under the danger, or indeed the certainty, of suddenly impairing the resources of the country, public and private ; for the purpose of affording what, in point of fact would, after all, be a very limited relief to those who are now undergoing a temporary distress ? "

Conversion.

Next, they proposed to reduce the Navy 5 per cent. stock, amounting to £155 millions, to 4 per cent. ; taking the market prices of the four per cents. at 97, this conversion would effect an immediate saving of £1,400,000. This sum would be devoted to the reduction

The Malt Tax. of taxation ; and it seemed to them that, as the Malt Tax was one respecting which great anxieties seemed to exist, and as its reduction was considered (whether on sound principles or not) the surest means of affording relief to the agricultural interest, they could best utilise the sum to take off the duty of 1/- a bushel,[1] i.e. the new tax imposed in 1819, all but 2d. Further, conceiving that, consistently with the preservation of the present standard, happily restored, " much relief might be afforded to all money operations, and to none more so than those in which the landed interest were engaged, by somewhat increasing the floating debt of the country,"

£4 millions of Exchequer Bills. the Bank had consented to advance up to £4 millions on Exchequer Bills at 3 per cent. This would be an effective relief in itself, even if simply thrown into circulation through the supplies of the year, but the further question was whether something more should be done by lending it. A proposal had been made to advance the £4 millions to agricultural proprietors on security of mortgages, and to farmers on security of their produce ; and, if the Government at a former period had assisted the manufacturing and commercial classes by a loan of £5 millions in Exchequer Bills, he could not see for his part what should deter them now from rendering

[1] Londonderry's misgiving whether reducing the Malt Duty was the best means of helping the agricultural distress was justified when it became known that the brewers had avowed their intention of not reducing the price of beer by the farthing a pot which the reduction made possible. On the reporting of the Bill, Huskisson drew attention to the fact that a tax, remitted with the view of increasing the consumption of beer and giving indirectly some encouragement to the growers of barley—the price of which had been reduced to a degree which had no parallel for the last twenty or thirty years—had gone, to the amount of £800,000 or so, into the pockets of the brewers. " Either the brewers must at one time have been great losers, or they were now receiving a most disproportionate and most inordinate profit," and he called upon the House to prevent the intentions of the legislature from being frustrated in this way. But, subsequently, we gather from a speech of Fowell Buxton, himself a brewer, that the price of beer had been lowered by a halfpenny a pot. This, he said, was what the Government had expected ; " they had granted a farthing and they wanted a halfpenny " (Hansard, vi. 1187; vii. 331).

similar aid to the agricultural interest. But there was this difference ; that, in the former case, there was " great tangible property to be pledged " in a few hands ; and, after mature consideration, the Government were not prepared to recommend such
a loan. He suggested, however, that it might be advisable to make
advances to distressed parishes, to be used for corporate purposes,
on the security of the parochial rates, not to exceed the amount
of one year's assessment. Finally, he gave notice that he would
move the revival of the Agricultural Committee for the purpose
of enabling it to reconsider, and, by some practical measure, to
correct the admitted defects of the existing Corn Laws.[1]

Brougham, who came next, showed himself anything but careful of
his reputation. Instead of being in the philosophical dispassionate
vein which had won him his triumphs in the previous year, his speech
was in the worst style of party vituperation. Reckless of what he
said so long as he scored a point, it is difficult to see what he or his
party gained, and he laid himself open to a series of dignified and
reasoned counters by Huskisson.[2]

On 18th February, then, Londonderry moved that the Agricultural
Report of 1821, along with petitions on the subject, should be referred
to another Select Committee.[3] Gooch, goaded by criticism, gave some
interesting family history of the late Report. Although Chairman,
he confessed that to him it appeared worse than useless. The House
probably did not know by whom the Report had been drawn up.
He had not done it.[4] Even had his opinions been those of the right

---

[1] *Hansard*, vi. 350. " Such *hash*," writes Creevey, " was never delivered
by man. The folly of him—his speech as a composition in its *attempt* at style
and ornament and figures, and in its real vulgarity, bombast, and folly, was
such as, coming from a man of his order, with 30 years' Parliamentary experience, and with an audience quite at his devotion, was such as I say amounted
to a perfect miracle. . . . I thought I should have died with laughing when
he spoke gravely and handsomely of the increased *cleanliness* of the country
from the increased excise revenue of soap." This is Creevey at his worst.
The speech, whatever its defects, was a very fine one, and, in the matter of
taste, contrasted strongly with the reply of Brougham who, according to
Creevey, " played the devil with him " (*Papers*, ii. 34).

[2] He never heard a speech, said Huskisson, more abundant in mistaken
assertions, more fraught with erroneous principles and contradictory inferences,
more pregnant with alarm, mischief, and danger, or more calculated to mislead
the judgment by a delusive appeal to the prejudices and sufferings of the
people.

[3] *Hansard*, vi. 462.

[4] Probably no one thought that he had, but it is a little unusual for a Chairman to speak of the labours of his Committee as he did. A prohibitory duty,
it seems, was what he thought would be most beneficial to the farmer (*Hansard*,
vii. 142).

honourable gentleman who performed the task, he could not have executed it with that gentleman's talent. Still, the document, though admirably got up, had been considered by the country as a piece of mystification ; he was bound to confess that he thought it threw dust in the eyes it should have opened. The member indicated was, as most people knew, Huskisson ; and Wodehouse proceeded to the further suggestion that Huskisson was also the author of the Report of 1814, and quoted some passages in it which were in contradiction with that of 1821. Huskisson was thus forced to reveal the truth. He was *not*, he said, the author of the 1814 Report. It was the production of the Chairman (Parnell), and he had objected to the Bill which followed. Indeed, it was well known that, at a meeting of gentlemen previously held, he was almost the only one who had supported protecting duties instead of the fixed price of 80/-. But, although he had always understood that a Report was considered as the production of the whole of the Committee to which the subject discussed was referred, he would explain the facts as to the Report of 1821. Like others, he had proposed a series of resolutions. The Committee approved of them, and did him the honour to request that he would draw up a Report founded on them. He protested, but yielded under pressure. His draft was discussed paragraph by paragraph, and many altera-tions were made, in the propriety of which he did not concur— alterations affecting not only the wording but the principle. He thought, then, that he was not being treated fairly, when the authorship was attributed exclusively to him. He would be ready, indeed, to defend his own resolutions—although some persons had thought fit to call them stupid and contradictory. But, after being thus accused, the House would not be surprised if he declined attending the Committee on its reappointment. His principles were known and recorded, and, during future discussions, he would not be found to depart from them.

After a discursive debate, in which the Sinking Fund, the taxation, and the resumption were spoken to at great length, if not with great relevancy, the Committee was appointed. As will be seen from its membership, it was practically a reappointment.[1]

(margin note: Huskisson's share of the 1821 Report.*)*

---

[1] Londonderry (Chairman), Gooch, Robinson, Althorp, Bankes, Brougham, Huskisson (who, however, kept his promise of not attending), Knatchbull, Wortley, Baring, Parnell, Wodehouse, Western, Sumner, Estcourt, Bourne, Tremayne, Rowley, Calthorpe, Hunter Blair, Irving, Lethbridge, Littleton, Whitmore, Bridges, Calvert, Ricardo, Curwen, Browne, Frankland Lewis, Cranbourne, Binning, Lamb, Goulborn, Newport.

As if the Opposition were determined to give a lead to the Committee in their recommendations, Althorp, who up till now had made no great name for himself, raised the whole question again three days later.[1] He desired, he said, to get an expression of opinion from the House on Londonderry's proposals, and he felt himself called upon to state his own views of the policy which ought to be adopted. Althorp on the cause of the distress.

His account of the connection of taxation and distress was naïve enough. In 1792, the prices of agricultural produce had been the same as they were now, and the value of money, real and nominal, was the same, yet there had been no distress. The only difference between the two periods was the enormous load of taxation. There was, therefore, no mode of accounting for the present distress but by ascribing it to excessive taxation.[2] And the substance of his motion was that the reduction of taxation proposed by the Government was not sufficient to satisfy the just expectation of the people, and that the £5 millions surplus of the year should be diverted from the Sinking Fund to make further reductions. Lord John Russell, in supporting him, went the length of suggesting, by way of economy, that England should give up the expense of sending ambassadors to foreign courts, except, perhaps, to France.[3]

Ricardo did not speak in this debate, but Wolrych Whitmore, a member of the Agricultural Committee, made a speech which showed that he had been reading West's pamphlet—to which he referred—to some purpose.[4] The present distresses, he said, arose as a reaction from the extraordinary stimulus that agriculture had received during the course of the war. In any country which did Whitmore paraphrases West.

---

[1] *Hansard*, vi. 558.

[2] In addition to this curiously inconclusive argument, he did, indeed, venture the statement that " the price of labour was raised by the taxes on the necessaries of life," presumably meaning that this should have raised the price of produce but didn't—contrary to the effect of similar taxation on manufactures—but he safeguarded himself by saying that " it required much greater practice and knowledge of political economy than he possessed to make such statements sufficiently clear and intelligible," and he would only affirm again that " taxation was the real cause of the distressed state of agriculture."

[3] Russell, it would seem, stuck to his last of parliamentary reform, and did not take much part in other debates. His friends complained of his extreme taciturnity and his apparent indifference to what was said by others (Moore's *Memoirs*).

[4] Whitmore in this year published a *Letter on the Present State and Future Prospects of Agriculture*, which gained him much credit.

not export corn, the price had always a tendency to rise with the increase of population and with the expenditure of capital on the soil. Suppose £100 expended on ten acres of good land producing 20 quarters of wheat; the same money expended on inferior land would not produce so much, and the price must be increased, as the capital expended must be remunerated. Since 1792, there had been an increase of the population by 4,000,000. In ordinary course, corn would have been imported. But the war charges interposed an obstacle, and prices rose and rose. The consequence was that an extraordinary stimulus was given to the home cultivator. Enclosure Bills multiplied. Premiums were given for the best, not the cheapest, managed farms. Cultivation was carried on at an enormous and unprecedented expense. In the course of a few years, the production increased in every way beyond the consumption. We had more than we wanted, and the surplus fell back on the country. The remedy was " to retrograde from the point of agricultural eminence which we occupied, and to come to one more suited to the circumstances of the present situation." Such a change, it had been said, would be the ruin of the agricultural classes. As a fact it would only be the removal of the last layer of capital which had been applied to the land. It would, no doubt, throw considerable portions of land out of cultivation, but they would only be such as were forced into it during the period of the great stimulus. Rents, of course, would have to be reduced 20 per cent. or 30 per cent. or more. He had done so in his own case, and he thought it but natural he should, seeing (1) that the rents had been raised so high since 1792, and (2) that the state of the land had been so much ameliorated by enclosures and other circumstances : he personally was not inclined to complain on account of the reduction of rents. One is glad to notice that " the hon. member sat down amidst loud cheering." Althorp's motion was lost by 126 to 234.[1]

[1] If I may put his argument in the plainest language : A country which puts so much of its land under wheat as to be self sufficient in years of average harvests, and takes measures absolutely to prohibit the competition of foreign wheat in such years, must expect to be over supplied in years of abundant harvests. But as the demand for bread is limited by the capacity of the human stomach, a comparatively small increase in supply will drive prices very low. And, where the rents of farmers have been fixed for long terms of years on the calculation of average harvests and high prices, the low prices in abundant years will cause great disaster among them, and the disaster must spread to the landlord on the one hand, and to the labourer on the other. Reason, then, would dictate that the amount of land under wheat should be less than the consumption in an average year, and that the balance should be imported,

Still another debate on the subject took place in the House of Lords on 26th February,[1] when Liverpool vigorously defended the plans of the Government, dwelling on the signs of prosperity— the rapid increase of population, agricultural as well as manufacturing —the increase in the revenue—the position of the Savings Banks, where deposits had risen from £707,000 to £1,205,000 in the course of the past year—the increase of two or three millions in the British exports—the marked improvement in almost all branches of manu- facture with the exception of iron—and went on to argue that there was no foundation whatever for the opinion expressed in most of the petitions that the pressure on agriculture was the result of excessive taxation. It was, in fact, one of the greatest of delusions. There was similar distress in all the other countries of the world—France, for instance, for the first time had restricted the importation of foreign corn—and, in Switzerland at least, taxation was almost unknown.

He commented on the fact that the cry of *excessive* taxation was a new one. During the latter part of the war, agriculture, as well as commerce and manufacture, was in a most thriving state. But, since the war, some seventeen millions, or about a quarter of the whole taxation of the country, had been remitted. It was argued again that the state of the currency made the smaller sum a more grievous burden than was the heavier. But, taking the extreme and absurd assumption that the depreciation during the course of the war had been 25 per cent. instead of being so only during the last three years of it, the reduction of taxation had fully equalled the alteration. Again, if the revenue of 1792 was between 16 and 17 millions, while now it was 50 millions, had the wealth of the country not increased in at least as great a ratio ? In that case, the chief evil of taxation—its tendency to retard the growth of capital—had not been operative—and taxation must always be compared with wealth. Indeed, the increased ability of the country to bear increased taxation could not be doubted—it was proved by foreign trade, by the effect of enclosure bills, by the increased consumption of excisable articles—and he gave figures of the consumption of tea, candles, soap for domestic purposes, leather, bricks, in all of which the increase was greater than that of popula- tion Salt, however, he admitted, was an exception.

in order that, in abundant years, there should not be such a surplus as the country could not take off.

[1] *Hansard*, vi. 681.

Wanted a market.

Assuming that there was no wish to break faith with the public creditor, Liverpool went on to say that what the agriculturist really wanted was a market. This Parliament could not give. Indeed, one reason of the distress was that the Government had, during the war, by force of circumstances, made an annual demand for meat and other provisions to the amount of over £2,000,000, and that the demand did not now reach £200,000. Thus, the only possible relief was from the excess of the revenue, the £5 millions. " The annual income of Great Britain, after making allowance for the reduction of rents and the diminution of the profits of trade since the war, may be stated at from £250,000,000 to £280,000,000.[1] The annual public revenue is £50,000,000. The reduction of taxation, therefore, which some proposed, would amount to about a tenth of the existing taxation of the country, and to about a fiftieth of its income. This is the utmost extent to which the reduction of taxation can be carried. Does any man seriously believe that this would afford to the agriculturist a relief which would be an adequate substitute for that which he wants—a market for his produce ? " But even suppose it did, what must be set against

Defence of the Sinking Fund.

it ?—no less than the abandonment of the Sinking Fund. The immediate consequence of such a measure would be to raise the interest of money throughout the country ; and, if this were considered as a mere question of profit and loss, he could not conceive that the House would hesitate for a moment.

Liverpool then went over again the old arguments for the Sinking Fund, declaring, in spite of Hamilton, that a sinking fund should be continued even during a war—because of the moral effect produced. France had a sinking fund much greater in proportion to her debt than ours, and the sinking fund of America, it was estimated, would wholly redeem her debt in twenty years. He quoted with some indignation the statement from a petition lately presented that the lower prices were beneficial only to Jews and jobbers—the agricultural interest was not the only interest in Great Britain ; it was not even the most numerous interest. Was it not a material advantage to the other classes of the people to be

[1] Calculations of the National Income before Dudley Baxter laid the statistical foundation on which Giffen built must, of course, be taken with great reserve. At the Revolution, it was " commonly computed " at £43 millions. Arthur Young, in 1776, made it £100 millions. Pitt and Auckland's calculation of the entire income in 1798 was about £200 millions (*Economic Annals, 1801-20*, p. 31). Lowe, in 1822, estimated the taxable income of 1792 at £125 millions ; of 1806, at £170 millions ; of 1814, at £188 millions ; and the entire income of the country, in 1822, at £251 millions.

enabled to buy meat at fourpence a pound instead of eightpence, and the other necessaries of life in the same proportion ? No one could be blind to the fact that the low prices certainly benefited a great majority of the people—among others, the annuitants and the mortgagees, who were, during the war, the principal, and almost the only sufferers. He reiterated the opinion which he had already stated to the House, that the cause of agricultural distress was that The poor the war prices had forced into cultivation lands which in ordinary lands. times could not repay the capital expended on them.[1] Hence came over-production in times of peace. At the same time, prices had been affected by the enormous increase of corn from Ireland— which, indeed, now exceeded what, some years ago, was the common average importation of corn into this country from the whole of the continent. " And now the rich lands, in both parts of the United Kingdom, press on the poor lands, just as the rich settlements acquired, during the war, on the coast of South America, press upon some of our ancient but poorer colonies in the West Indies."

He finished by declaring that he was determined to stand or fall by the steady maintenance of an efficient Sinking Fund.

Again the Opposition insisted that the excessive taxation was, if not the cause of the distress, at least, as Lansdowne said, the great obstacle to recovery ; and the history of the Sinking Fund, its intention, its success, and its actual position were all keenly discussed and at great length, but little of importance was added.

But, as might be expected, the courageous reiteration by the Prime Minister that the remedy must come naturally from abandoning the cultivation of the poorer lands cost him the support of the country gentlemen. It was, said Lansdowne, " one of the most extraordinary doctrines, and must lead to the most extraordinary results, that could possibly be contemplated." And it did not fail to be twisted round into sinister interpretations, such as : " the new doctrine, promulgated by the partizans of foreign commerce, that, for the sake of sending goods to foreign countries, a large proportion of the territory of a country is either to be thrown waste or doomed for ever to a state of barrenness." [2]

Still the Opposition had no mind to wait on the Agricultural The Salt Committee's Report before pressing for further reductions, and, Duties.

[1] As the Duke of Buckingham put it, " the large quantity of poor land which God had never intended to produce wheat."

[2] Sinclair, *Address to Landowners and Farmers*.

in February, Calcraft [1.] began with a motion for the repeal of the Salt Tax. The excise duties, which amounted to only three half-pence per gallon in the reign of William and Mary, had been raised to 5/- per bushel in the reign of George II., to 10/- in 1798, and to 15/- in 1805. To say nothing of the injury done to the fisheries, and to agriculture, they were in effect a poll tax falling ten times more heavily on the poor than on the comfortable classes. They amounted, it had been calculated, to a burden on the labourer of from 20/- to 25/- per family—" no man ate salt at a less rate than 36 or 37 times the cost price." It was sometimes said that they were not in reality a burden on the poor, as the impost necessitated a rise in the wages of labour. This might be true as regarded the manufacturer, who could raise the price of his goods to the consumer. But the farmer could not. These taxes, too, formed a direct temptation to evasion and dishonesty—they were found the most fruitful source of crime and vice in Cheshire. Moreover, they tended to make the salt trade a monopoly of wealthy men ; a man who purchased £100 worth of salt had to advance £3,000 to the government—there were individuals in the trade who paid from £100,000 to £200,000 a year in duties. Calcraft, therefore, strengthening himself by the report from a committee in 1818, asked for a gradual reduction of the duties by 5/- a bushel per year, till the whole tax was extinguished. The duties were yielding £1,500,000 to the revenue ; surely the Sinking Fund would not be seriously prejudiced by being diminished by a third of that amount—particularly as the reduction would inevitably increase the consumption.

The Chancellor of the Exchequer's reply was, of course, a *non possumus*, and the Government took the ground that those who had voted for the maintenance of that *nominis umbra*,[2] the Sinking Fund, were precluded from asking for any further reduction of taxation in the meantime. On the other hand, it was urged that, as a measure of general relief, the repeal of the Salt Tax should come before that of the Malt Tax ; that it would greatly stimulate the fisheries [3]—which, in Holland, yielded ten millions to our one ;

---

[1] John Calcraft, the younger (1765-1831) ; Clerk of the Ordnance under the Greville Administration, 1806 ; M.P. for Wareham since 1818 ; a staunch Whig till, in 1822, he joined the Duke's Administration as Postmaster-General ; in 1831 reverted to his old faith and voted for Russell's Bill ; his mind unhinged by the reproaches of his friends, he committed suicide.

[2] The expression was Lord Normanby's.

[3] " That most lucrative of our commerce, with reference to which Dr. Franklin had said that every fish taken out of the sea was a piece of money."

that it did not involve breaking in on the Sinking Fund as the expenditure could easily be reduced by half a million. The Sinking Fund, argument, however, seemed to carry the day, and Calcraft's proposal was lost, though only by 169 to 165.[1]

Meanwhile the second Agricultural Committee had been sitting for six weeks. Londonderry, the Chairman, " manfully stood up for Huskisson's principles at the risk of offending some of his most zealous supporters," and the proceedings were conducted with much warmth and bad temper. The Committee took no fresh evidence, and all its time was occupied in preparing a Report which was presented on 1st April. It was short and practical—very different from that of 1821. Pointing out that the sales of wheat and oats for the past six months had very considerably exceeded the average of a similar period for the past twenty years, and that this " excess of supply over demand "—an expression at which, one would think, Ricardo must have winced—must continue the depression and increase the accumulation of stock, its attention was limited definitely to measures for affording some temporary relief. It dismissed, as too dangerous, the proposal that the Government should, by an issue of Exchequer Bills, buy and store a million's worth of corn ; as also the proposal for advancing loans to parishes on the credit of the rates ; but suggested—" although much less efficacious in its operation " than the first plan—advances to the amount of a million sterling by the Government on corn deposited ; recommended that the foreign grain under the King's lock might be ground into flour for the purpose of exportation ; reiterated the opinion that " protection could not be carried further than monopoly," and that the British grower had had three years of this monopoly ; emphasised the contention of last Report as to the " excessive inconvenience and impolicy of the existing system," to prove " how little reliance could be placed upon a regulation which contained an absolute prohibition up to a certain price and an unlimited competition beyond that " ; approved the imposition of a duty upon all foreign corn whenever, upon re-opening the ports, it should be admissible for home consumption, and the raising of the importing price of oats ; recommended that, if Parliament should decide to legislate during the current Session, after our wheat should have reached 80/-, " a lower price should be assumed for the future import, subject to a duty," naming 70/- as " not an improper limit," to be accompanied by a duty of from 12/- to 15/- between 70/- and 80/-, of 5/-

Marginal notes: Report of Second Agricultural Committee.

70/- named as importing price.

[1] *Hansard*, vi. 837.

between 80/- and 85/-, and of 1/- above 85/- ; and ended by saying that, " if the circumstances of this country should hereafter allow the trade in corn to be permanently settled upon a footing constantly open to all the world, but subject to such a fixed and uniform duty as might compensate to the British grower the difference of expense at which his corn could be raised and brought to market, together with the fair rate of profit upon the capital employed, compared with the cost of production and other charges attending upon corn grown and imported from abroad, such a system would, in many respects, be preferable to any modification of regulations depending upon average prices with an ascending and descending scale of duties." But the Committee " rather looked forward to such a system as fit to be kept in view for the ultimate tendency of our law than as practicable within any short or definite period." [1]

On 3rd April, on the presentation of a petition from distressed agriculturists of Wiltshire, a discussion arose prematurely on the Report. Western considered that the remedy proposed, of admitting corn at 70/-, was wholly objectionable, and would place the agriculturist even in a worse situation than before.

---

[1] The Report—credited to Bankes—is given in the *Annual Register*, p. 438 ; the *Edinburgh Annual Register*, 340 ; the *Farmer's Magazine*, p. 152 ; and *Hansard*, vi. 1406. Londonderry said that he never sat on a Committee engaged in the consideration of a difficult subject in which, after full delibera- tion, coincidence of opinion as to the object in view was more strongly marked. " We all felt that some measure was indispensably necessary, and that, under the difficult circumstances of the case, the adoption of the present proposition would be much safer than to leave the law on the subject as it now stands " (*Hansard*, vii. 188). One may not agree with Lord Grey that the Report was " utterly deficient in any character of wisdom and practicability " (*ibid.* 325). but it certainly was not such as one might expect from the composition of the Committee. Subsequently, however, on two occasions Ricardo explained why he had allowed it to go out without protest. " He had gone into that Com- mittee with the opinion that the agricultural classes were in a state of great and overwhelming distress—that any relief which could be held out to them, ought to be held out—and that he would give them such relief ; but on condition that he should, in his return, receive a pledge that some better measures of legislation would instantly be resorted to. He had been dis- posed to give the agriculturists everything they required. They had a prohibi- tion at present, and they could not have more. Indeed, he had been ready to adopt any proposition that the Committee might originate, so long as they expressed a willingness to propose some more salutary measures of legislation to the consideration of Parliament. The Committee had held out a hope to him that they would do what he advised ; they told him that they would insert something in their Report which would satisfy him upon that point. When he saw the Report and found that it contained no such clause as he had anticipated, the conditional assent that he had given to their propositions was immediately dissolved ; and he refused to concur in it because it contained nothing of the nature which he had hoped it would contain " (*ibid.* 459, cf. also vi. 1448).

It was impossible not to feel that an immense proportion of the present difficulties arose from the alteration in the currency. The House would be compelled to retrace its steps and take into consideration the Act of 1819. If nobody more competent would take it up, he would feel it his duty to call on the House to reconsider that Act. H. G. Bennet, indeed, went a step further. He was unwilling to embark again on the discussion of the resumption of cash payments. The only mode of relief was the reduction of taxation. He would say " Get rid of that juggler, the Sinking Fund, and give the people the five or six millions which it takes from them ; if that will not do, the first creditor is the plough : the gentlemen of England must not be stripped of their estates, the farmer must not be deprived of his pittance, and we must come to an accommodation with the public creditor." Though it might now seem bold to say so, he was sure that he would live to see that result.[1]

The Report was formally brought up for discussion on the 29th April, when Londonderry unfolded all the proposals of the Government.[2] Withdrawing the original one of advancing money to parishes on security of the parochial rates, they asked : (1) An advance of a million to agriculturists on security of British corn stored for that purpose ; (2) A vote of credit placing at the disposal of the Lord Lieutenant funds to make " local and appropriate advances " for mitigating the distress in Ireland ; (3) An additional vote of a million to be applied in the forwarding of public works in Ireland, " where there is the prospect of a profit which will indemnify the public for the advance " ; (4) To take from the Bank an advance of £4,000,000 on Exchequer Bills, with the double purpose (i) of providing for the above expenses as well as paying off the holders of the Navy five per cents. who dissented from the conversion, and (ii) of adding that amount to the general circulating medium, thereby producing " a general and important benefit to the country independent of any particular and individual advantage " ;[3] (5) To renew till the expiry of the Bank Charter, which would be extended for ten years, the Act expiring in 1825 which

Government proposals.

---

[1] *Hansard,* vi. 1434.   [2] *Ibid.* vii. 150.

[3] Ricardo had already given a very plain opinion as to this. It was a hazardous experiment. Four millions more could not be absorbed into the circulation of the country ; if they were added, it would afford a great inducement to export the gold, lower its value all over the world, and turn the foreign exchanges against us. He entreated the House to consider the matter well before they increased the existing currency by so large a sum (*Hansard,* vi. 483).

empowered country banks to issue notes under £5;[1] (6) To convert the "dead expense" of the naval and military pensions into an annuity of £2,800,000, running for 45 years; (7) To tie up the £5 millions of clear surplus to accumulate at compound interest until it amounted to a Sinking Fund of 1 per cent. on the whole capital of the debt—which would be effected in ten years, when the Sinking Fund would have risen to £7,400,000; (8) From the £2,200,000 saved by (6), to make further reductions in taxation; (9) To enable persons having foreign corn warehoused under the King's lock to grind it for re-exportation; (10) To bring in a new Corn Law according to the recommendations of the Agricultural Committee.

(1) and (9) withdrawn.

Of these proposals, the first—to advance Exchequer Bills to the amount of a million sterling whenever the average price of wheat should be under 60/-, upon such corn, the growth of the United Kingdom, as should be deposited in fit and proper warehouses— was withdrawn almost at once, to the deep disgust of many, although Western agreed that it would give no material relief, and said that "speculations of this sort ought not to be made with the public purse: if they were to take place at all, they ought to proceed from individuals and not from the Government."[2] It turned out that Londonderry had opposed the proposal in the Committee. All he could say for it now was that the farmers thought it might do good, and that, at any rate, it could do no harm. But, he said, "when I see the measure so tamely supported by some members of the Committee, and when I hear nothing in support of it from others who ought to regard it with parental feeling, I am not in any degree disposed to press it."[3] Subsequently, the ninth proposal, the grinding of foreign corn in bond for exportation, was also withdrawn on account of the strong opinion expressed against it—it would be fatal to agriculture, and "impossible to prevent foreign flour

---

[1] The reason given for this was that, in anticipation of the withdrawal of the small notes in 1825, the country bankers had been contracting their issues, and were likely to make some pressure upon gold to replace the notes—a useless hardship, as the people evidently preferred notes. (The accumulation of gold by the Bank to prepare for this was one of the reasons subsequently given for the speculation of 1824.) At the same time, Londonderry announced that negotiations had been entered on with the Bank for such a relaxation of their Charter as might enable individuals to establish private Banks, consisting of a greater number of partners than six, and so assimilate the country banks to those of Scotland. It was to induce the Bank to surrender this portion of its privileges that the charter was extended, and Ricardo solemnly protested against its renewal on any such insufficient grounds.

[2] *Hansard*, vii 198.   [3] *Ibid.* 364.

from being smuggled into home consumption "—although Ricardo
urged that, unless the agriculturists could show that injury would
arise to them from the adoption of the claim, Parliament should
not hesitate to give to the foreign importer the proposed relief.[1]
The fate of the other financial proposals will be more conveniently
discussed under the Budget.[2]

[1] *Hansard*, vii. 874.

[2] It was in one of the six sittings over this Report that Attwood made a
long attack on the Law of Diminishing Returns—that it was not the best
lands which were first, or the worst lands last, cultivated—that the order of
cultivation was determined by other circumstances—that land which now
yielded what had been called " no more than twelve bushels " had once
yielded only six, etc. Ricardo did not explain, as his followers would have
done, that all this was not incompatible with a " tendency " to diminishing
returns, but contented himself with stating the second part of his law : " it
was not that cultivators were always driven by the increase of population
to lands of inferior quality ; but that, from the additional demand for grain,
they might be driven to employ on land previously cultivated a second portion
of capital which did not produce as much as the first. On a still further
demand, a third portion might be employed which did not produce so much
as the second. . . . It was manifestly by the return on the last portion of
capital applied that the cost of production was determined " (*Hansard*, vii.
371 ; Cannan, *Theories of Production and Distribution*, 2nd ed. 167).

CHAPTER VI

1822. THE BUDGET

As we saw in last chapter, Londonderry had indicated that the saving from the conversion scheme would enable the Government to devote £1,400,000 to taking 1/- per bushel off Malt—that is, the extra excise imposed in 1819 all but 2d.

Repeal of the Salt Tax,

On 24th May, Vansittart [1] announced that, from the saving made by the Dead Weight Annuity, further reductions would be made. First in importance would be a practical repeal of the Salt Tax. Excusing himself, a little lamely, for opposing Calcraft's motion three months before, on the ground of "the general objection at that time to a remission of any taxes," he announced that, of the existing Salt Duty of 15/- per bushel, 13/- would be given up, leaving a duty of 2/-; this would have the convenience of equalising the tax with that existing in Ireland. The Scots duty of 6/- also would be reduced to 2/-. All allowances and drawbacks on salt for particular purposes would cease, with the single exception of the drawback on exportation to foreign parts; and the duty would in all cases be levied at the pit mouth, so that all the charges of management would be saved and the trade left entirely unfettered. This reduction would amount to £1,300,000. As the Irish people would get no benefit from this reduction, he would compensate them by the repeal of the Window Tax and the Hearth Duty. He

half the Leather Duty,

would also repeal the additional Leather Tax—the war tax imposed in 1812, amounting to one-half the whole duty—bringing the tax back to what it was in the reign of Queen Anne. Lastly, he would

and the Tonnage Duty.

repeal the Tonnage Duty on all ships clearing inwards and outwards. This would be a total reduction, in addition to the £1,400,000 on Malt, of £2 millions.

[1] *Hansard*, vii. 743.

Hume's reasonable objection was : " Why, for so small a part of the Salt Tax as 2/-, retain the expense of the whole system of collection and management ? " and he calculated that it would take £20,000 a year to collect the £200,000.[1] Curwen moved an amendment to repeal the whole tax : the only conceivable object of continuing 2/- of it was, he said, the patronage it gave to Ministers. Vansittart would not consent to give up a " contemptible remnant " which amounted to £200,000 ; if he did so, he must cancel his proposal to reduce the Leather Duty.   And he supported his case by a statement which showed how very different interests become dependent under a system of protection.   " The total repeal of the tax would materially interfere with the kelp trade, a trade which gave employment to 40,000 persons ; " and thus, said an Irish member (Martin), the whole of the West coast of Ireland would be deprived of the only market for their labour.   The amendment was lost, but only by 92 to 104.[2]

The equalisation of the Salt Duties over the three kingdoms was, however, met with very considerable clamour in Ireland. Under the protection afforded by getting salt 13/- cheaper, the Irish provision trade, the butter trade, the salt works, and the fisheries had prospered exceedingly.   The Dublin Chamber of Commerce declared that the reduction in England would mean the " total ruin " of all these trades.   Vansittart, acknowledging that, " unless the measure was taken with due preparation it would be ruinous to Ireland," consented that the change should not take effect till the 5th of January *proximo*.   In Scotland, also, there was dissatisfaction for the same reason ; and, to meet this, the entire Scots duty was ultimately removed—not without grumbling that England had got 13/- remission of taxation against Scotland's 6/-!   A countervailing duty of 2/- was imposed on Scots salt imported into England. *Criticism of the Salt reduction.*

The relief of one-half on Leather was very welcome   Hides and skins were almost the only articles on which additional burdens had not been laid since 1709 and 1711, till Vansittart incurred much obloquy by doubling the tax in 1812.   It was an obvious grievance of the consumer—as Brougham said, it was a poll tax which weighed most heavily on the wrong class.   In 1816 and

---

[1] Brougham confirmed this by pointing out that the expense of collecting £1½ millions of the salt revenue in England was £55,000, while the collection of £100,000 in Scotland cost £21,000 (*Hansard*, vii. 787).

[2] *Hansard*, vii. 1407.

1818, Althorp had tried to get it repealed, but without success.[1] But, although, like all such imposts, many vested interests had grown up round it, and the producers were much concerned at the reduction, no attempt was made to defend it now.[2]

Otherwise, the reductions were met with much gratitude and approbation. Ricardo, however, was one of the few exceptions to the chorus of praise : he thought Ministers had not dealt quite fairly by the House ; it looked to him as if they wished to induce the House to assent to those parts of their propositions which were bad under the cover of those parts which were good.

The Conversion. But over the other financial proposals brought forward by the Government, there was much debate. The Conversion scheme was carried out as follows. Of the funded debt, £153 millions, known as the Navy five per cents., stood at the market value of about £105 10/-. The value of the four per cents. was about £98. It was now proposed, following the precedent of Pelham's conversion of the four per cents., in 1749, that every holder of £100 in this 5 per cent. stock should receive in lieu of it £105 in a new four per cent. stock not redeemable before 1829. Those holders—but only those—who sent in a formal dissent would be paid off at par. It is a little difficult to believe that the very considerable amount of opposition to the proposed conversion was other than that dictated by party, or that the member who said that it was distinguished by "crookedness, trick, and artifice" believed, what he said,[3] but at anyrate a strong fight was made on its legality. The wording of the Act under which the money was borrowed bore that the five per cents. should be irredeemable till £25 millions either of three or of four per cents. had been paid off, and it was argued that the Sinking Fund purchases could not be held as satisfying that requirement. The objection, however, was overruled by the Solicitor-General and by the Lord Chancellor. Ricardo thought the plan very desirable and the terms extremely fair.[4]

The scheme itself was completely successful. About £150

---

[1] See *Economic Annals, 1801-20, passim.*

[2] By 1824, however, I find the reduction of the Leather Tax quoted as an instance of failure—it had not reduced the price of boots and shoes, collars and harness, by a penny, said the *Glasgow Herald* in September.

[3] Cobbett, with strange perversity, insisted that the conversion was, in fact, a reduction of a part of the interest of the debt : "they might call it what they liked, but it was giving the stockholders 16/- less out of every £5 than they had received before" (*Register*, March).

[4] *Hansard*, vi. 663.

millions of the whole £153 millions were converted. The dissentients—who numbered only 1373 (out of about 100,000) representing £2,600,000 of stock—were paid off. The interest of £150 millions at 5 per cent being £7,500,000, and that of £157 millions at 4 per cent. being £6,300,000, the saving to the country was about £1,230,000 a year. A question, however, rose out of the conversion which was angrily debated. One of the criticisms raised had been that it created about £7 millions of additional debt. Some astonishment was expressed when it was discovered that the Bank would, unless specifically prevented, charge its usual £300 per million on this sum—" for executing a bill," as Grenfell said, " which entailed upon them no additional trouble," and Ricardo supported a clause proposed by Hume that the Bank should not derive any profit from the management of the increased capital stock caused by this measure. But the clause was negatived.[1]

This was not the only occasion on which the Bank had to listen to some very plain speaking. On a request by Maberly for papers to show that the Bank of Ireland was receiving a very high rate of interest from the Government as compared with the Bank of England,[2] a director (Pearse) thought fit to take credit to the latter Bank for its general treatment and " most honest and honourable intentions," and, in passing, threw a jibe at Ricardo for having said that the directors had scarcely ability enough to perform the duties with which they were entrusted—for his part he preferred the opinion of proprietors of bank stock, who elected them annually, to all the theories of modern philosophers on the subject. Ricardo, nettled, re-stated that he should think it his duty to speak of the Bank as he thought and felt. He was willing at all times to give them full credit for honesty of intention ; but he could not help thinking that they had at different times involved the country in considerable difficulties. " He persisted in saying that the Bank Restriction Act of 1797 might have been unattended with detriment to the country had the directors known how to manage their own concerns upon true principles. But, not knowing this, they had issued a quantity of paper so large as to depreciate its own value ; and, to recover from that depreciation, the country had found it necessary to undergo a painful process, which had been the cause of a great part of the present distress. Ever since the year 1819, the Bank had committed a great error in its eagerness to provide gold. This error they specifically confessed when they offered to

Criticism of the Bank's conduct.

---

[1] *Hansard*, vi. 1013.　　　　　　　　[2] *Ibid*. vi. 992.

lend Government £4,000,000, for such an offer was a declaration that they had amassed more gold than was necessary, and had aggravated the very evils under which the country suffered. As to this loan, he viewed it with some degree of fear, because the directors had convinced him by their conduct that they did not know what they were about. If they thought they could issue either £4,000,000 of gold coin, or even of paper, without withdrawing the gold coin from circulation, they were mightily mistaken. He was quite sure that the currency could not absorb it, and that, accordingly, it must go abroad." Grenfell followed by saying that, although he gave the directors credit for having no personal interests to serve, they had adopted measures fatal to the interests of the country and productive of enormous profits to the Bank. Before 1797, the profits had never exceeded 7 per cent. Since then, thanks to the advantages arising from the Restriction Act, from the public balances, and from the high charge for the management of the public debt, the property of the Bank had improved to the enormous extent of £30 millions. They had never advanced a single sixpence without being very handsomely paid for it. And not one director had ever voted with him against the continuance of the restriction. " On the contrary, they had, one and all, up to the very last hour, fought hard to prevent the resumption of cash payments. It was therefore a mockery to say that the Bank of England had always shown an anxiety to resume its payments in specie." And, later on, Ricardo said that he would oppose to the utmost the renewal of the Bank Charter, because he was satisfied that every farthing made by the Bank ought to belong to the public : even if a paper currency were wanted, Ministers could accomplish the object more advantageously for the public without than with the assistance of the Bank of England.[1]

Small notes.   The fifth of the Government proposals, the renewal of the Act authorising the continued issue by country banks of notes under £5, passed without much opposition, except on the ground that it might lead to a new outbreak of forgery. It would seem that this Act continued also the issue of small notes by the Bank of England, and this was welcomed by many as " equal to a repeal of, or, to some extent, a counteraction of Peel's Bill," and as tending to throw an increased quantity of money into circulation.[2]

[1] *Hansard*, vii. 761.
[2] *Ibid.* vii. 1456, 1521, 1661. This Act, said Canning, hedged the £1 note with a divinity which was never supposed to belong to it before.

Much greater was the opposition to what Walpole calls "the worst of the many bad proposals with which Vansittart's term of office is associated," namely, to save £2,200,000 by changing the "dead expense" of £5,000,000 into an annuity of 45 years. This dead weight was an annual charge consisting of officers' pensions, retired allowances, pensions of the widows of officers, and the half pay, under the heads of army, navy, and ordnance. The sum, said Londonderry, on 29th April, "seemed to belong to our annual expenditure, but in fact had nothing to do with it," and it gave rise to the wrong idea that the national expenditure was 17 or 18 millions per annum, when, in fact, it did not exceed 12 or 13. It would be a great advantage if this could be separated from the general expenditure, and "treated as a debt incurred rather than a service to be provided." The proposal, then, was to enter into a contract with parties, who, in consideration of a fixed annual payment on the part of the public, would agree to supply such a sum in each year, as, upon calculation, might be required to pay the survivors the sums to which they were entitled. It would appear that, by granting a fixed annuity of £2,800,000 for 45 years, such a contract might be made. This would represent a saving of £2,200,000, and the attraction was that the greater part of this sum might be applied to further reduction of taxation.[1]

On 1st May, Vansittart further explained the plan, and asked meantime for an "approval of the general principle." It was a measure of so novel a nature that he did not feel himself justified in adopting it without the sanction of Parliament. It would exclude those pensions and allowances paid out of the Consolidated Fund, amounting to between £400,000 and £500,000 a year, as well as payments to the royal family, and to illustrious persons as matters of justice and bounty for high and meritorious services. It would also exclude all pensions upon the Civil List, and upon the $4\frac{1}{2}$ per cent. duties, because these were charged on limited funds belonging to the Crown. The annuitants to be provided for would be about 60,000, and the table on which he based his calculation was made out from the returns of the ages of 15,000 persons and was founded on the natural decrement of human life.

The debates upon this were very long, very able, and very subtle —and one is inclined to think highly of an assembly which could argue so well on either side, in a matter involving such command of the principles of finance. The matter may be put simply thus.

[1] *Hansard*, vii. 164.

its principle. If no such arrangement were made, the nation would be paying
now, to some 60,000 persons, annuities amounting to £5 millions.
As the pensionaries died off, this sum would annually diminish.
It would fall below £2,800,000 in sixteen years ; in the forty-fifth
year, it would be only £300,000 ; and, in the next year, would disappear altogether. In this case, the burden of the pensions—a
" public debt of gratitude and justice "—fell most heavily on the
present and bore with less and less weight on future years. But,
under the proposed arrangement, the burden would be equally
divided between the present and the future for forty-five years ;
that is to say, the present payers would pay less and the future
payers more. Concretely, in the first year the Government would
receive from the contractors £5 millions and would pay them
£2,800,000, and would therefore in effect borrow £2,200,000. About
the sixteenth year, they would receive just about as much as they
paid. In succeeding years, they would receive successively less
and pay more.

The defence of thus lightening the burden of the present at the
expense of the future was two-fold ; (1) the exceptionally embarrassed
state of the country at the moment, (2) that the " dead expense "
of the late war ought to be shared by the generation that came
after ; and its only tempting feature was the reduction of present
taxation promised. Huskisson, supporting it, said that the question
was " whether, under the present circumstances of the country,
after having, during a war of twenty-five years, taken upon themselves to raise about £230,000,000 of war taxes specially for the
benefit of posterity, they were not justified in throwing on that
posterity the small burden " under discussion.[1] Brougham, anticipating that the plan was so novel that contractors would require to
be tempted to take it in hand, put the " gross absurdity " of the
scheme thus : " They were taking £5 millions and putting it into
a chest in order that it might accumulate for the payment of a debt
at the end of a certain period. In one and the same moment, they
borrowed the same sum as they had in the chest, but at a great
disadvantage "—going into debt as lenders and as borrowers.
The only reasonable course, he concluded, was to take the money
from the Sinking Fund.[2]

It must be admitted that the position of the Government in this
regard was weakened by its former resolve to maintain the Sinking
Fund at all costs, for the principle embodied in the Sinking Fund

[1] *Hansard*, vii. 289.   [2] *Ibid.* 322.

was the very opposite of that embodied in the present scheme. As Hume put it : " This plan, of making a new loan for relieving the present distress and adding to the public debt by burdening posterity, was resorted to by the very Ministers who lately spoke so loudly about preserving inviolate a Sinking Fund of five millions that we might reduce the charge upon posterity." [1] And both Ricardo and Hume showed that, at the end of the forty-five years, the country would be in a worse situation by the new plan than by the old. In the end, Vansittart [2] announced that negotiations with capitalists to contract for the annuity had fallen through—

Modification of the scheme.

" there was a possibility, and even a probability, that there would be either great loss or extreme advantage to the parties contracting, and it seemed that the fear of grievous burden had operated to prevent contractors from making any offers "—but he proposed to carry out the wishes of Parliament in another mode ; namely, to place the annuity in the hands of trustees accountable to Parliament, charging the annuity on the Consolidated Fund. Thus the risk would fall upon the public. The mode in which the sums necessary to make the payments should be realised would be by the successive sale of the annuities placed at their disposal, by the dividends on the unsold annuities, or by the power reserved of issuing Exchequer Bills when it was thought that the annuities could not be brought to sale to advantage.[3]

But the opposition to the scheme was not yet done with. In June, Hume moved an amendment, as a more simple and honest way, to take from the Sinking Fund an annual sum equal to the amount of taxation to be remitted, towards relieving the distresses of the country, instead of raising money by loan or annuities as proposed by the Chancellor of the Exchequer. Ricardo supported him. Hume's plan, he said, was simple and easy to be effected, while the Chancellor's plan was neither more nor less than sending one set of commissioners into the market to sell stock, and another set into the market to buy stock, and, he added, even the Chancellor now understood that fact so fully that he was about to support a clause which would enable these two sets of commissioners to deal

---

[1] *Hansard*, vii. 291.   [2] *Ibid*. vii. 737.

[3] In other words, an annuity of £2,800,000 for forty-five years was vested in trustees, and the trustees were required from time to time to pay into the Treasury the sum required for the pensions. Obviously they could do so only by borrowing in the money market, and they were accordingly authorised either to raise money by Exchequer Bills or to sell portions of the annuity (Walpole, *History*, ii. 47).

with one another. The amendment, however, was lost [1] and the Bill passed on to the Upper House. There Lansdowne said that there " had hitherto been two modes of proceeding with respect to public burdens ; either to increase that which we bore ourselves in order to relieve posterity, or to remove the weight from our own shoulders and place it on those of posterity. It had been reserved for the noble earl to act upon both systems at once, by creating a Sinking Fund of £5 millions to extinguish so much of the National Debt, and, in the course of the same session, adding £2,800,000 to that debt." [2]   And Lord King moved a sarcastic preamble to the Bill : "Whereas an impatience of taxation, no less ignorant than irresistible, pervades all ranks of his Majesty's subjects, and it is highly expedient to afford some relief ; and, whereas the minimum of relief which will give satisfaction, and the least intelligible plan which can plausibly be stated, is that of extending the burden of the military and naval pensions over a longer period of time than the natural lives of the present annuitants, and defraying the expense of the first sixteen years by a series of annual loans— . . . therefore, be it enacted that a series of loans shall be raised in a circuitous manner, and that the Lords Commissioners of the Treasury shall have power to lend to themselves, and to borrow of themselves, and to conceal the whole transaction from themselves and from other ignorant and well-disposed persons," etc.[3]   But, spite of argument and ridicule, the Bill passed.

The Budget.   As consequence of the long debates on the Government proposals, the Budget was not brought in till 1st July, and, even then, Vansittart had to apologise that some of the services had not been voted.[4]

SUPPLY.

Army - - - - - - - - -	£7,925,000
Navy - - - - - - - - -	5,480,000
Ordnance - - - - - - - -	1,200,000
Miscellaneous - - - - - - -	1,700,000
Out-pensioners of Greenwich Hospital - - -	310,000
Interest on Exchequer Bills - - - -	1,200,000
Sinking Fund on Exchequer Bills - - -	290,000
Repayment of 5 per cent. holders - - -	2,801,000
Deficiency of Ways and Means, 1821 - - -	290,456
	£21,196,000

[1] *Hansard*, vii. 782.   [2] *Ibid.* 1322.
[3] *Ibid.* vii. 1396.   [4] *Ibid* vii. 1413.

WAYS AND MEANS.

Annual Taxes	£3,000,000
Tea Duties	1,500,000
Lottery	200,000
Old Stores	151,000
Repaid by Public Works Commissioner	110,000
Loan taken from the Sinking Fund	7,500,000
East India Co.	530,000
Payments on account of Half-pay Pensions, etc.	2,450,000
By Increase of Unfunded Debt	5,831,000
	£21,272,000 [1]

The only other attempt at further reduction of taxation was Window Tax. immediately after the Budget, when Hobhouse proposed the repeal of the Window Tax—" a species of property tax more odious and unpopular than any other impost." The £2½ millions it yielded might be got, he said, by reducing the " illusory Sinking Fund," and the proposal was made the occasion of again going over the old dispute as to the *nominis umbra*. Vansittart, naturally, considered that remission of taxes to the amount of £3½ millions in one year was enough, and the motion was negatived by 144 to 59.[2]

But, among the many demands for reducing taxation, one curious Proposed tax on Absentees. proposal in the opposite direction is interesting enough to deserve

[1] This figure, of course, thanks to the complicated system of book-keeping, did not represent the estimated *total* revenue of the year. According to Porter, the total income of 1821 had been £55,834,192 ; the total expenditure, £57,130,586 ; and the amount applied to reduction of debt, £4,104,457. On the assumption that the produce of the taxes would equal that of the previous year, Vansittart made out the total thus :

Customs	£10,743,000
Excise	26,156,000
Stamp Duty	6,637,000
Post Office	1,335,000
Assessed Taxes	7,385,000
Miscellaneous Taxes	380,000
Old Stores	151,000
One-fourth of the Annual Taxes and Tea Duties	1,220,000
	£54,000,000

This was (roughly) the basis on which he calculated that, at the end of the year, there would be a " clear surplus " for the Sinking Fund of £5 millions. But the figures given in the reported speech do not make it clear how he arrived at that sum, and there is no means of checking them, as Vansittart took the produce from April to April, while the public accounts are given as from January to January. But as Ricardo calculated the surplus at about a million, while Hume insisted that there was no surplus at all, I may be excused further attempt at accuracy.

[2] *Hansard*, vii. 1458.

mention. It was when a petition from Somersetshire was presented by Lethbridge, with the unusual clause that it prayed the House to impose an additional tax—which would supply an ample fund to allow of the repeal of other taxes—namely, one on Absentees. There were in Paris alone 10,000 British families, who, spending a guinea a day each, might be calculated to make up an expenditure of £18 millions a year. Boulogne, Calais, Tours, Bruges, Brussels, and almost all other cities of the Continent were filled with English. Half the men of property of Ireland, for instance, were absentees, and, as all taxes were on consumption, they all fell on the resident gentry. Ricardo at once pointed out that such a tax would be a direct encouragement to the absentees to remove their capitals as well as their persons. What surprised him most was that Lethbridge was at the very time proposing in the Agricultural Committee a resolution which would make all provisions dearer—a very direct inducement to people of small fortunes to quit the kingdom. If it were not for the Corn Laws, he said, England would be the cheapest country in the world, and capital would be attracted instead of withdrawn. And this latter would certainly be the case if we could once reduce the National Debt—a reduction which was quite possible by a fair contribution from all sorts of property, mercantile, landed, and funded. Hudson Gurney spoke for the free ingress and egress to and from the kingdom, but he would have equal laws for the poor as for the rich ; he referred to the laws at present enforced against the emigration of artizans, while there was no law to prevent a rich man removing his capital and establishing a manufactory abroad—" if a rich man might go abroad for convenience or amusement, surely the poor man should be allowed to go abroad for subsistence." Vansittart summed up that no plan of taxing absentees ever suggested had been shown to be practicable, and that, from calculations made, he did not believe that the proportion of taxes escaped by absentees abroad exceeded £5000 a year. Nothing, of course, came of the proposal.[1]

Roasted wheat. In last volume was noticed an extraordinary prosecution by the Excise of sellers of roasted wheat under the name of " breakfast powder "[2] In March of the present year, we find Lansdowne bringing up the matter as involving a very important constitutional question. In the House of Commons, later, Sir Robert Wilson asserted that a person had been imprisoned, in lieu of a fine of £60, for selling such grain, and, as was pointed out, this decision went

[1] *Hansard*, vii. 653.　　　　[2] *Economic Annals, 1801-20*, 735.

the monstrous length of saying that, if any person should discover a substitute for coffee, no matter how wholesome or economical, he would not be allowed to sell it. Pursuing the matter, Lansdowne brought out the facts as follows : The commissioners of Excise had thought themselves authorised by Act of Parliament to prosecute not merely persons charged with, or suspected of, frauds on the revenue, but also persons who were guilty of no fraud, nor of any fraudulent intention, but who only wished to do what every subject had a right to do ; namely, to sell articles of food not forbidden by the law. Moreover, they had laid down a distinction, which they had no right to do, that persons might roast wheat for their own use but that those who sold it were to be prosecuted. Liverpool admitted that he saw no reason for the prohibition, and no more is heard of the matter. But among the Acts of the year we find one (c. 53), " to regulate the manufacture and sale of scorched or roasted corn, peas, beans, or parsnips, and of cocoa paste, broma, and other mixtures of cocoa." [1]

[1] *Hansard*, vi. 992, 1310, 1400. In the *Parliamentary Review* of 1825, I find that " a cheap, wholesome, and not unpalatable substitute for coffee " had lately been introduced under the sanction of the legislature, p. 671.

CHAPTER VII

1822. THE STRUGGLE AGAINST RESUMPTION

Money and the low prices. ONE who remembers the long struggle after the war before the Government could be forced to decree the resumption of cash payments by the Bank, would scarcely expect to find the same Government, in 1822, standing firmly for the retention of the recovered standard against an angry schism of its own followers. But so it was. The modern reader, too, is puzzled what to make of the glib handling of an abstract theory by a party not usually remarkable for its acquaintance with economic science. That the contraction of the currency was the cause of the fall in prices was a doctrine tossed about, at the time, as if the very statement carried conviction. It would be assuming too much to think that many of those who made the assertion understood the theory of money—a theory always more easy to express mathematically than to demonstrate in the concrete. Possibly they thought they understood when they were told that it was " tightness of money " which accounted for the withdrawal of the old facilities of banking accommodation. When they found that they had to reduce the price of anything they wanted to sell before they could get a buyer, possibly they thought that it was because the buyer had not coins enough in his pocket to pay the proper price. One who has for years found the difficulty of getting students to understand the " quantity " theory is sceptical that it came by nature to distressed farmers and landowners.

Cobbett predicts lower prices. Perhaps the explanation is that " the most powerful voice in England " had said it.[1] Cobbett had now declared himself the ally

---

[1] Cobbett occupied a curious position at this time. He professed himself a free lance. As a rule, against the Government, he would as soon turn and rend the Opposition, and was generally the enemy of the established order in all departments. No extravagance was too great to support his theories. He said, for instance, that the war never raised the price of crop—it was only

of the agriculturists, and went about the country, from meeting to meeting, enlightening them as to what should be done. At a meeting in Huntingdon, in January, where his health was drunk with great professions of esteem, he took for text the " Noble Conduct of Earl Fitzwilliam." That nobleman, he understood, had called his tenants together ; told them that the price of grain had now touched the level of 1792 to 1795, and would not sink lower ; and that he thought it right to reduce the rents of his tenants to the standard of these years—that is by 35 per cent. to 45 per cent. It was, indeed, a noble act. Nevertheless it was useless. " If, indeed, the whole of the outlays of the farmers consisted of rent, then nothing could be more completely just than the voluntary offer of the noble Marquis, but—rents formed a comparatively small portion of the outlays of the farmer." And the Marquis' belief about prices was totally erroneous. Prices would fall far below those of 1793. " It is now universally acknowledged, except by Mr. Webb Hall and a few others, that it is the Bill of Mr. Peel that has brought down prices—in other words, the diminution in the quantity of circulating money. What will it do by the time that it shall go into its full effect in May, 1823, when the Bank of England notes will not longer be a legal tender ; when the country Banks will be

the paper money that did it ; that the present fall in grain prices " had not arisen from any peculiar circumstances in the seasons or connected with the crop, but from the change in the volume of the currency " ; and, with reasoning difficult to follow, asserted that the Irish potato famine itself arose from the resumption of cash payments. To the modern reader—at least to one who considers personalities, strong language and vulgarity always a weakness, and generally a mistake—the *Register* is very wearisome reading. How could any fair-minded person pay attention to a journalist who called "that name sanctified and immortalised in the memories of all good men," Wilberforce, a malignant, canting hypocrite ; Ricardo, " a stupid, bothering stock-dealer " ; Canning, " a haggis, a loathsome Scotch dish " ; and served up to his readers the most disgusting details of unnatural crimes ? Yet it is impossible not to see that his main ideas were taken, without acknowledgment as he complained, by politicians and statesmen, as well as by farmers and landowners. He seems to me to have had a morbid craving to be different from other men, posing as the one honest man in the nation, while no one quite believed in his honesty. With it all, his articles were constantly and largely quoted by the provincial press—sharing that honour with extracts from " the most infamous paper that was ever seen in the world—by name *John Bull*." This, however, was the man whom the *Edinburgh Review*, in May, called, of weekly journalists, " first in power and popularity," adding, " Certainly he has earned the latter : would that he abused the former less ! . . We once tried to cast this Antaeus to the ground, but the earth-born rose again and still staggers on, blind or one-eyed, to his remorseless, restless purpose,—sometimes running upon posts and pit-falls—sometimes shaking a country to its centre. It is best to say little about him and keep out of his way ; for he crushes, by his ponderous weight, whomsoever he falls upon ; and, what is worse, drags to cureless ruin whatever cause he lays his hands upon to support."

compelled to pay in gold ; and when the far greater part of these
Banks will of necessity have totally disappeared ? "

But, however it may be explained, certain it is that the cry
was raised loudly and insistently in 1822 by the friends of the agricultural interest, that the low prices of farm produce were due to
insufficiency of the circulating medium :—" No remedy will be
either immediate or effectual that does not include an extension
of the currency " ; " the resumption of cash payments appears
to have been a masterstroke of policy in favour of the fund-holders
and the monied interest."

Peel defends
his Bill.   As early as 18th February, Peel had found it necessary to make a
vigorous defence of his Bill, asking the House to remember the
circumstances of 1819—circumstances which presented a more
favourable opportunity for resuming cash payments than would
probably ever have occurred again.   " Had the system of paper
money continued, individuals never could have been satisfied with
a fixed high price for their commodities, as all the stimulus which
prevailed during the war arose, not from a fixed high price, but from
a continually rising price."   At that time, the argument against
resumption was that the pressure of the measure would be severely
felt on the revenue and on the manufacturing and commercial
interests ; nobody predicted similar consequences on the state
of the agricultural population.   Since then, the revenue had increased, commerce had extended, manufacture had become prosperous.   What was there in the measure that could cause depression
on agriculture alone ? [1]

But all this was disregarded.   On 5th March, in presenting a
petition fearing that " a great portion of the distress arose from the
return of cash payments," Scarlett (afterwards Lord Abinger) stated
the " fact as it was—that prices had been reduced by the increase
which that measure necessarily gave to the value of the currency " [2]
On 8th May, Wyvill said that only two courses were open to them—
the repeal of Peel's Bill, or the reduction of taxation; as the former
was not advisable, the only remedy was the reduction of taxation
by £20 millions ! [3]

Indeed, the Government had already given not a little occasion

[1] *Hansard*, vi. 491.
[2] *Ibid.* vi. 919. His chief argument, however, seemed to be that it could
be nothing else, as abundance of produce could not be the cause—unmoved
by Ricardo's question if abundance of supply of any commodity of limited
consumption did not always lower price.
[3] *Ibid.* vii. 423.

to this view. The fourth of the Government proposals, as we The misleading £4 millions. saw, was to take from the Bank an advance of £4 millions on the security of Exchequer Bills; and Londonderry, while entering a solemn and unqualified protest against shaking in the slightest degree the sound system of currency re-established and consecrated by Peel's Bill, said that much relief might be afforded to the industrious classes, and particularly to the landed interest, by increasing the floating debt of the country by that amount, and spoke, though rather vaguely, of the advantages of this extra sum finding its way into general circulation. The £4 millions would, among other things, go to pay off the dissentients to the Conversion scheme, and to carry out the proposals of advancing money to the agricultural interest if these were approved. But, he said subsequently, he would be prepared to urge Parliament, should all schemes of local application be abandoned, still to adopt measures by which the sum in question might "find its way into general circulation:" the object which the Government had in view was "in some degree to relieve the pressure upon the money circulation."[1]

Liverpool, in his speech of 26th February, was even more candid. Finding it impossible to induce the Bank, he said, to lower their discounts, they had borrowed the £4 millions "with the view of applying that sum, in some manner, to the relief of the country." Whether it could best be done by advances to parishes, or by advances for public works was a question. But "the chief object which His Majesty's Government have in view is, not so much the adoption of this or that particular measure, as the adoption of any measure which will have the effect of getting these £4 millions into general circulation." The sum, he said emphatically, was not wanted, for the supplies of the year, or for any Government service; it was only "to extend and quicken the general circulation."[2]

---

[1] *Hansard*, vi. 380; vii. 157.

[2] *Ibid.* vi. 715. It is perhaps worth noticing that Huskisson approved this, for a reason which may be found to have significance even yet. He took it as a kind of admission from the Bank that they had now more gold in their cellars than was required to ensure the cash payments, and more than was convenient for their own interest. It was not, however, that he expected the whole of the gold to remain in the country—he knew it could not—but " by diffusing itself generally, it would everywhere have a tendency to bring ease and life to the labouring markets of the world." And then followed the significant words : " What is most urgent is to stop the progress of depression. That once effected, speculation, which is now in a manner dormant, will revive, and it is in this view, more than by its actual amount, that this operation of the Bank seems to hold out a prospect of reviving confidence and hope " (*Hansard*, vi. 433).

Western's
attack. The matter was brought to a head by Western on 11th June.[1]
He proposed to prove that the Act of 1819 was " one of the most
impolitic and mischievous measures that was ever adopted in this
or any other country." Without underrating other causes, such as
taxes, want of protection, tithes, and poor rates, this was " the
irresistible cause of the general suffering." He called attention to
the very different effect produced by lowering or raising the standard
of money ; " morally speaking, the injustice and mischief were
less by lowering than by raising." One mischief was that the taxes
became more burdensome—say by 10 per cent. or 15 per cent.
" When they had deserted the ancient standard for twenty-two years
and were imposing taxes all that time in a depreciated currency,
they ought to have reflected " on this. Without entering on an
essay on the theory of money, he would say that the precious
metals were chosen as money because they were more invariable
in their value than other commodities. But they were not altogether invariable. Locke and Adam Smith had suggested that corn
was less variable. Then he went on to say, with reasoning difficult
to follow, that the increase in the price of commodities (during the
restriction) particularly in the price of wheat, arose " almost solely
from the alteration in the value of the currency." And what was
the effect of a diminished value of money ? The prosperity which
accompanied it was not fictitious : " the vast increase of credit
currency had had the effect of giving a great stimulus to industry
at a period when the produce of that industry could be most advantageously applied." He quoted Bacon on the advance of the country
in Elizabeth's reign, ascribing it to the gold and silver discoveries
in America, and Bacon's description he " felt to be an exact picture
of the actual effects experienced in this country during the restriction on the Bank." He turned then to the immense fluctuations
in the price of wheat during the past fifty years, and asserted that
the fall, say, from 125/- in 1812 to 50/- in 1821, was due to the
present scarcity in the currency and not to redundancy of corn.
" That it could not arise from a redundancy of corn, was evident
from this fact—that a corresponding reduction had taken place in
all other commodities, in most of which it was not pretended that
any redundancy had taken place." [2]

[1] *Hansard*, vii. 877.

[2] I should be glad to think that this summary does injustice to Western,
but I confess myself unable to follow the logic of his speech. He seems to me
to be struggling with ideas imperfectly grasped. He is always stating that he

What Western meant to be at, is not very clear.[1]　He wanted the standard "revised." But the only suggestion of method was in the words, "by the substitution of a system which should give to the products of industry of every description the same relative money price which they commanded during the suspension of cash payments, and secure a fair and reciprocal remuneration for the general industry of the country." The *Annual Register* translates this as : "His object was to obtain the sanction of the House to the establishment of a currency which should raise the price of wheat to 80/- per quarter and the wages of labour to 15/- a week." This may have been the impression produced by his speech, and, in some newspaper reports, the words are ascribed to him, though not in *Hansard*. But, however this may be, all that his motion bore was the request for a Committee to consider of the effects produced by the Act of 1819.

Huskisson, however, gave the speech the compliment of a long, lucid, and convincing reply, supplying Western, it seems to me, with the arguments he was only dimly conscious of advancing, and then crushing them with remorseless logic. He credited him, for instance, with advocating a constantly progressive depreciation of money as the great secret of public prosperity. This, he said, was the scheme of the famous Mr. Law [2]—a minister, said a French political writer of the day, far above all that the past age has known, that the present can conceive, or that the future will believe— if once adopted by any country, it must end as his scheme ended : you must either retrace your steps or the bubble must burst at last.

Huskisson replies.

is going to prove this and that, and, when one comes to the point, there is nothing but strong assertion. His views had already been embodied in an *Address to Landowners of the United Empire.*

[1] What was in the background of his mind, I have no doubt, was the Corn Rent, which he himself had adopted, and which several landowners were now introducing. The Marquis of Stafford, for instance, sent a circular round his tenantry in January, saying that, if the rent agreed on was £500 at a time when wheat was 80/-, and that rent was realised by the sale of 125 qrs., the rent in future would be 125 qrs. at the average price of the year (*e.g.* £410 for 1820, when wheat was 65/7). This seemed a very reasonable practical solution where rent was a speculation by the farmer on the value of one commodity whose amount, quality, and price, were all alike speculative, and where the landowner's share of the produce, in theory, was the whole of the surplus " over the ordinary profits of cultivation." But it was very far from indicating that corn was a better standard of value, for transactions generally, than gold.

[2] Ci gît cet Ecossois celèbre,
　　Ce calculateur sans égal,
　Qui, par les règles de l'algèbre,
　　A mis la France à l'Hôpital.

Western, he said, would lower the standard of the currency in, or
nearly in, the proportion of the difference between the average of
wheat taken for the period between 1797 and 1819 and the average
price between 1819 and the present year ; for instance, if the average
price in the latter case should be 45, and, in the former, 80 shillings,
he would provide that henceforth 45 shillings should pass for 80
shillings ; and consequently that, for every debt or contract now
existing, a tender in this proportion should be a payment in full.
" Admitting that a certain *quantum* of injustice has been done to
one class of the community during the suspension, and that now, by
its removal, a consequent degree of injury and hardship is inflicted
upon another, does it follow that we are either to perpetuate and
aggravate the first injustice, or that it is wise or practicable to
attempt to revise and readjust all the pecuniary transactions of
the last twenty-five years ? " Western, he said, always looked at
the hardship of the landowner who had encumbered his estate
during the depreciation, never at that of the man who had lent
his money before that event. Taking Western's hint as to corn
as an indication that he wanted to make corn the standard of
value, he credited him with laying down the principle that the
standard of value in every country should be that article which
formed the constant and most general food of its population. But,
on that principle, potatoes would be the standard in Ireland—a
novelty even in theory. " What a beautiful simplicity of system
and what facility it would afford to the settlement of all transactions
between the two parts of the same empire, to have a wheat standard
for the one and a potato standard for the other ! " Finally, he
repeated what he had said before, that the pressure due to the
resumption of cash payments was " the inevitable consequence
of having tampered with the currency." And, just as the House,
following Montague in a similar situation in 1696, thought it
necessary to lay down explicitly a general principle, so now he would
propose to amend Western's motion by substituting for it the very
resolution of 1696 ; " that this House will not alter the standard
of gold or silver, in fineness, weight, or denomination." [1]

[1] The question one has always to decide, in giving a short account of a great
speech like this, is, whether barely to summarise its line of argument, or to
quote at length its most memorable passages. In either case, I feel that considerable injustice is done to the speaker. The speech—" one of the most
remarkable financial addresses ever delivered in the House," Walpole calls
it—is given " in substance " in *Hansard*, vii. 897, and more at length in the
collected edition of Huskisson's *Speeches*, ii. 129.

Many of the subsequent speakers, like Bennett and Lord Archibald Hamilton—a little scared at their own temerity—announced that they would vote for Western's motion, considering that it did not pledge them to anything but enquiry, and generally were very anxious to show that they did not agree with his views. Ricardo, however, maintained that they were not justified in this course, as the declared object of the motion was to alter the standard ; and Peel implored such members to think what it would mean to commence, at this period of the Session, an enquiry introduced under such auspices. " Let them vote that which was proposed to them that night, and, to-morrow, every man of common sense would be trying to possess himself of every guinea in the country, that, when the Committee had closed their labours, he might be ready to profit by the new state of things." Could it be possible, he exclaimed, that such a motion was now to be brought forward, " after the House had stood pledged for seven or eight years to favour the earliest return to cash payments, and after all the concerns of the country had been, for so long a period, accommodating them-selves to the change." [1]   Attwood, however, had no such misgivings.[2] Attwood. He concluded a long and abstruse speech, the chief thesis of which was that, as Tooke's table of prices since 1818 showed that the chief commodities, iron, wool, cotton, etc. had fallen about as much as wheat—say 40 per cent.—it was thereby proved that " the old standard now re-established was incapable of sustaining any higher level of price than the present," by saying that the chief duty of the House was " to arrest the present measures ; to return to the circulation and to the standard of the war, or one approaching nearly to it ; and to establish finally our metal standard on that adjusted basis." [3]

[1] One of Peel's unanswered arguments was that, in Holland, where the cur-rency had never been altered, the prices of agricultural produce had suffered very much the same fall between 1818 and 1822. How, then, could it be said that the distress in this country could be due to nothing else but to the return to cash payments ?

[2] Attwood's speech against this " iniquitous measure," as he called Peel's Bill, was by far the ablest on Western's side, and, with all its wrongheadedness, almost deserved Brougham's eulogium of practical knowledge, logical acute-ness, and eloquence rarely combined on such a topic.

[3] His argument, that is to say, was that the fall in prices could be produced only by one of two causes ; either that the quantity of all commodities had been enormously increased, or that the quantity of money had diminished. But it was incredible that a great augmentation had suddenly taken place in the produce of all labour, that all industry had became suddenly more skilful and efficient, and the produce of all soil more abundant—we were not at the beginning of the golden age. It was therefore the quantity of money that had

Ricardo on the
premature
return to coin
payments.

Ricardo, in the course of a masterly speech supporting Huskisson and riddling Western's scheme, admitted that the conduct of the Bank in 1819, in accumulating so much gold to allow them to begin cash payments sooner than they needed to, had materially affected the public interests, and caused much distress that might have been avoided. But this was due, not to return to the old standard, but to the premature return to coin instead of payment in bullion as the Act contemplated and as he had advised; "That Bill he had always considered as an experiment to try whether a Bank could not be carried on with advantage to the general interests of the country upon the principle of not being called upon to pay their notes in coin but in bullion ; and he had not the least doubt, that, if the Bank had gone on wisely in their preliminary arrangements— if, in fact, they had done nothing but watch the exchanges and the price of gold, and had regulated their issues accordingly—the years 1819, 1820, 1821, and 1822 would have passed off so well with the working of the bullion part of the plan that Parliament would have continued it for a number of years beyond the time originally stipulated for its operation." He could ascribe the mistake of "making purchases for amply filled coffers " to nothing else than ignorance of the principles of currency.

Brougham again distinguished himself on the wrong side, apparently because it gave him the opportunity of criticising Peel for some statements of his to the effect that the state of the country as a whole was better than was said, and because any stick was good enough for beating the Government. In the end, happily, Western's motion was lost by 30 to 194. Huskisson's amendment was then put and agreed to.[1]

Western, however, reopened the question on 10th July, with eighteen lengthy resolutions. Ricardo was the first speaker against them, and, finally, they were negatived.[2]

been reduced. Tooke, on the other hand, who scouts any such connection between the prices and the state of the currency, sums up : " That the very great increase of the importations at the close of 1818, and the very high prices which then prevailed, and which could only be justified by the previous scarcity, led inevitably, supposing a perfectly uniform state of the currency, to a great fall of prices of 1819 : and that the continued abundance of supplies accounts fully for a low range, with a tendency to a continued fall, to the close of 1822 " (*History of Prices*, ii. 116).

[1] *Hansard*, vii. 877. The *Annual Register's* account of the debate (p. 108) is unusually full, clear, and accurate. Ricardo's speech on this occasion is the longest reported in *Hansard*. In it he used the words : "*Quantity regulates the value of everything*. This is true of corn, of currency, and of every other commodity, and more, perhaps, of currency than of anything else."

[2] *Ibid.* 1596.

CHAPTER VIII

1822. FIRST ALTERATION IN THE NAVIGATION ACTS

THE year 1822 is notable for the first formal amendment of those Acts of which Adam Smith said that, though some of them might have proceeded from national animosity, they were as wise as if they had all been dictated by the most deliberate wisdom. Whatever may be thought of this judgment, the Navigation Laws had served their day and generation, and were generally considered, even by the shipping interests of the country, to be hampering our growing foreign trade. The interests of navigation, as Wallace pointed out, had been all too well attended to. Everything, indeed, had been done to encourage commerce that was in the power of those who had legislated on the subject ; but, as the establishment of maritime power was deemed of much greater importance than the extension of trade, whenever there was an opposition between commerce and navigation, commerce was always obliged to give way, and made a sacrifice to the interests of navigation, whereas, it was easy to see, the only true foundation for a powerful marine was a great, flourishing and extensive commerce.

It may be as well to recall the fact that their broad principle was Principles of two-fold : to create and maintain a great mercantile marine, and these Acts. to prevent any one other nation from doing the same. The method used was to confine the importation of the products of foreign countries to British ships [1] or to ships of the producing country. By this, three things were gained : (1) the carrying trade of foreign countries which had shipping was divided out among them ; (2) countries which had no shipping of their own had to export their produce to us in British vessels ; (3) no third carrying power, such as Holland, could rival England in this trade.

[1] A British ship was defined as one where the owner, master, and three-fourths of the mariners were British subjects.

The beginning of these laws may be traced back at least to the reign of Richard II. Their leading intention was distinctly recognised in the time of Henry VII., and made quite explicit in the Act of Navigation of the Commonwealth. But what was proudly called the Charta Maritima of England was the 12th of Charles II., which regulated our navigation till 1783, under five heads :

(1) Fisheries : fish wanted for the consumption of Great Britain must be exclusively procured by British industry and imported in British ships.

(2) The coasting trade of Great Britain (afterwards extended to the United Kingdom) : this was confined to British shipping.

(3) The European trade : the rule laid down was that 28 " enumerated articles," including the most bulky—those which employed the greatest quantity of shipping—could be imported only in British ships or in ships of the country in which they were produced, proceeding directly from such country to this ; but any other article of European production could be imported from any port in Europe in ships of the other states of Europe except Holland (that is to say, Dutch ships could import nothing but Dutch goods into Great Britain).

(4) The trade with Asia, Africa and America : the rule was that the products of these three quarters of the globe could be imported only in British vessels.

(5) The trade with our Colonies : intercourse was confined strictly to the Mother Country. The colonies could not dispose of their produce otherwise than by sending it to this country and in British bottoms, and they were equally restricted from receiving any articles except from this country and in British bottoms.[1]

The Navigation Laws, it may be noted, laid no burden on foreign ships that came to export the produce of British industry. But, so far as such ships could not bring a cargo, they could not very well afford to take away a cargo.

Their hostility to Holland.   As everyone knows, these Acts were defended by Adam Smith on the ground that the defence of Great Britain depended very much upon the numbers of its sailors and shipping, and that defence was of much more importance than opulence. The hostility shown

---

[1] " This truly shopkeeper law," Adam Smith called it,—and the preamble justifies the expression. Some kinds of colonial produce, however, which might have interfered with British trade, were not admitted : these Englanc was " willing that the colonists should sell where they could—the farther oft the better—and upon that account proposed that their market should be confined to the countries south of Cape Finisterre."

to Holland is manifest when it is remembered that the Dutch were the only fishers in Europe who attempted to supply foreign nations with fish ; that they were the great carriers of Europe ; and that Holland was the great emporium for all European goods. In Adam Smith's view, " national animosity at that particular time aimed at the very same object which the most deliberate wisdom would have recommended, the diminution of the naval power of Holland, the only naval power which could endanger the security of England." After the lost American colonies became an independent nation, for a little time (between 1783 and 1787) every state of the Union established a different rule of commercial intercourse with this country dictated by peculiar hostility, but, in 1787, Congress laid down one uniform system. It was that all foreign ships trading to America should pay half a dollar—afterwards, one dollar—per ton duty beyond what was paid by the national ships, and, further, that all goods imported in such foreign ships should pay a duty of 10 per cent. over and above what was demanded on the same description of goods in American vessels. This system of taking a leaf out of our book was the cause of much deliberation and negotiation. In 1796, the ships of the United States were permitted to bring United States produce direct to Great Britain. But in 1815, after a long struggle to counteract the navigation system of America without further relaxing our own, this country found it necessary to adopt the system of Reciprocity ; Reciprocity namely, equality of all charges upon the ships belonging to either begins. country in the ports of the other, and a like equality of duty upon all articles the production of the one country imported into the other, whether such importation was made in the ships of the one or of the other.[1]

The legislation by which the Navigation Laws were altered in 1823 and 1825 has made the partial reform of 1822 almost forgotten. But this reform was sufficiently revolutionary to those brought up in the old ideas. We saw that, in the past year, Wallace obtained a Select Committee to which was remitted the state of the Navigation Laws generally, and that this Committee made a First Report recommending a modification of the Timber Duties, which, carried into effect in the same year, made the first breach in the Protective system. This, however, as Wallace had intimated, was only the " first step," and the next, and more important, was taken without

[1] The best statement of the aims and history of the Acts is in Huskisson's speech of 1826 (*Hansard*, xv. 1144 ; *Speeches*, iii. 1).

loss of time. Before the Session of 1821 ended, Wallace had acted on the further recommendations made by the 1820 Committee,[1] and had introduced five *pro forma* Bills for clearing, simplifying, and amending the Navigation Laws, as well as with a view to extending and improving our commercial intercourse with foreign nations, and the Bills were printed to give members an opportunity of weighing the subject.[2] He now, early in the session of 1822, brought forward three Bills on these lines.

Wallace's reforms.

The first (c. 41) was formal, merely repealing some 300 ancient, disused, and inconsistent statutes regarding the importation and exportation of goods, passed between the days of Edward III. and the Navigation Act of Charles II.

The second (c. 42) dealt with statutes passed during and since the reign of Charles II., cancelling some and consolidating others. Its chief effect was to repeal two famous clauses of the old Navigation Act : namely, Clause 3, which read that " no goods of the growth, product, or manufacture of Asia, Africa, or America shall be imported into England but in such ships as do truly belong to English people, and are navigated by a master and three fourths English mariners," and Clause 4, which enacted that " no goods or commodities of foreign growth, production, or manufacture, which shall be brought into England otherwise than in ships built and navigated as above, shall be shipped from any other place but the place of their growth, production, or manufacture, or from those ports where they can only be or usually have been brought," and also to repeal some special sections relating to the importation of goods from Russia, Turkey, the Levant, Spain, Portugal, the Western Isles, Madeira, and the Canaries.

These two were introductory to a third, which might be called the new Navigation Act (c. 43). It was entitled " an Act for the Encouragement of Navigation and Commerce, by regulating the Importation of Goods and Merchandise, so far as relates to the countries or places from whence, and the ships in which, such importation shall be made." [3] The great change made by this Act

[1] *Economic Annals, 1801-20*, 755.

[2] *Hansard*, v. 1289. If his speech on this occasion be compared with the speeches of Huskisson in 1826, it will be seen how closely Huskisson worked out Wallace's sketch.

[3] The principles of the new Navigation Act and its differences from the old one are given in detail in Wallace's speech of 20th May (*Hansard*, vii. 708). Brougham hailed the changes as a portion, though a very minute portion, of the improvements which had often been recommended from his side of the

was that it allowed foreign ships to bring goods from any port in
Europe where they happened to be, provided the ship belonged to
the port in question, and superseded the necessity of using circuitous
routes.   Other changes made were : to place Holland, on which,
as we saw, ancient rivalry had long placed peculiar restraints, in the
same position as the other states of Europe ; to permit British ships
to bring articles, the growth or produce of Asia, Africa, and America,
from any place in Europe (instead of only bringing them directly
from the place of growth or manufacture), but for exportation only ;
to permit goods of any country or place in America or the West
Indies, belonging to, or which had belonged to, Spain, to be imported
direct from the place of growth in ships of the country.   But no
importation was permitted in foreign ships from any port in America
or the West Indies where British ships were not admitted.

The three Bills, which " completed the revision of the Navigation
Law and the statutes relative to foreign trade," passed the second
reading in June.[1]   Liverpool succinctly put their substance thus :
Under the system of regulations now brought forward, the departure
was as little as possible from the old.   The great object of the
Navigation Act had been to give a preference to British shipping.
The chief exception to this policy in the past had been that all
European countries were allowed to transmit goods to this country
in their own ships, and, after 1786, the United States were put on
the same footing.   The change now made would extend the same
privilege to South America.   With regard to Asia, Africa, and
the colonial parts of America, the law would, generally speaking,
remain unaltered, and goods could be imported from these countries
only in British bottoms.   Foreign ships might, however, bring
goods, not for home consumption, but for exportation only.   They
might also, under certain conditions, bring from countries in Europe
articles not the produce or manufacture of those countries.   The
result of the whole of the arrangements was that the principle of
the Navigation Laws had been adhered to as closely as possible ;
keeping always in view the great object of rendering this country
the *entrepôt* of the merchandise of the world, and extending our
export trade.   The doctrine was no longer maintained that, to limit
the trade of other countries was advantageous to our own.   Indeed,

Substance of the new Navigation Acts.

House, and Ricardo considered it a happy omen that so many gentlemen were
now of opinion that our system admitted of improvement ; the only complaint he had against the Bill was that it did not go far enough.

[1] *Hansard,* vii. 1119.

precisely the contrary was the truth : any measure which tended
to increase the wealth of foreign nations was calculated to produce
an increase of our own, and the increase of the trade of foreign
countries offered the best security against the distress of our manufactures.

Colonial
Navigation
Acts.

Concurrently with these, the Colonial Trade Bill (c. 44), and
the West Indian and American Trade Bill (c. 45), were read a second
time, allowing a direct trade, both of export and import, between
the American and the West Indian colonies on the one hand, and
America (practically the United States), the foreign West Indies,
and other parts of the world, on the other—the great object being
to open a wider market to the West India planters by enabling them
to sell their produce directly to other markets than ours.[1]

All five Bills passed into law without much discussion or opposition. Their importance, says the *Annual Register* naïvely, was
that they marked the commencement of a new system, " this being
the first instance in which practical statesmen have professed to
act under the more liberal principles of Political Economy."

[1] The justification and principle of these last two Acts, and the provisions
which they replaced, are given in detail in Robinson's speech of 1st April
(*Hansard*, vi. 1414). In view of the further relaxation made in 1825, it is as
well to note the content and the limits of these Acts. They did not modify the
exclusive right of this country to supply the colonies with *manufactured*
goods. But, firstly, they permitted intercourse between any countries in
America and our colonies in the ships of these countries or in British ships.
The first of these Acts, however, required that the intercourse, at least as
regards the foreign vessel, should be direct from the colony to the country
to which the vessel belonged, and it limited very much the articles which could
be imported into the colonies according to schedules in which the articles were
enumerated. Secondly, they permitted a direct trade from the colonies, in
articles of their own growth or production, to the ports of foreign Europe ;
but this trade was confined to British ships, which might also carry from those
ports, direct to the colonies, certain enumerated articles of foreign growth.
(See Huskisson's speech in 1825, *Hansard*, xii. 1105.)

CHAPTER IX

1822. PROTECTION AT HOME AND ABROAD

But while in so many ways the more enlightened views regarding
foreign trade—the "fashionable views," as they were called by
some who wished to hesitate a doubt without committing themselves—were making headway, the old doctrine was now and then
re-asserted.

A very suggestive discussion was raised on 20th March on a frankly
protectionist proposition by Curwen in the interests of agriculture,
to impose a heavy duty on foreign Tallow.[1] The graziers, he said, Protection for
Tallow.
were suffering more than the growers of corn. Meat which formerly
sold for 10d. was now 3d. or 4d., and, in the metropolis—where
prices were highest—at not more than 7d. per lb. (This was the
price to the consumer, but the farmer received not more than $3\frac{1}{2}$d.
per lb., sinking the offal.) Russia, which produced altogether
40,000 tons of tallow, exported 30,000 or 35,000 of this to England.
While the English grazing farmer could not produce his tallow,
without feeding his cattle upon land equal in value to about 20/-
per acre, the Russian farmer produced his from lands worth not quite
1/- per acre, producing it too without any more labour or expense
than the trouble of slaughtering his beasts and boiling down the
fat, for these beasts were not valuable cattle like ours, but animals
merely raised and kept for the purpose of obtaining their tallow.
And, on the tallow thus produced, Russia imposed an export duty
of 8 per cent., and made us pay annually about £70,000—for what ?
—for permission to bring her tallow to our own markets, to put
down the produce of our own agriculturists. He would propose,
then, to impose a heavy duty of £20 per ton on foreign imported
tallow—about 15 per cent. on the value. The present duty was
most unfair ; it was only 10 per cent., while the duty on hemp was

---

[1] *Hansard,* vi. 1206.

35 per cent. : was there any just gradation of policy, he would ask, in taxing an article like hemp—of indispensable necessity to our most valuable service, and of which we ourselves were not growers but consumers only—at this high rate, and levying upon tallow—an article raised by ourselves—a duty almost nominal in comparison ? The effect of the duty proposed would be that the Russian grazing farmer, instead of getting 3¼d. would get only 2½d. per lb. This tax of 15 per cent., divided upon the whole quantity, foreign as well as home produced, would cause a rise in the price of tallow of about £5 per ton, and this would have the effect of increasing the yearly value of grazing lands by about £300,000. The consequence would be beneficial in another way. Spain took off her heavy duty on exported wool the moment she found that the right hon. gentleman opposite had placed a new duty on its importation.[1] Holland had done the same when the duties of foreign butter and cheese were imposed. Russia ought now to be made, through the same mode of proceeding, to take off her duty upon tallow. The new impost, he calculated, would yield £300,000 extra to the revenue. It would, indeed, raise the price of tallow, as he said, by about £5 per ton, but, to compensate for this, he would relieve the consumer by devoting the £300,000 to taking the duty off candles. Thus the farmer would be relieved without any burden being cast on the consumer.

Arguments against.   The arguments brought forward against the proposals were these : (1) It was unwise to irritate the Russian Government— it might lead to retaliation.   (2) If the imports from Russia were diminished, the exports to Russia must diminish proportionately. (3) The increase in the price of tallow would increase the duty on a ton of candles to £20, and more than counterbalance the repeal of the duty on candles, and a tax on candles was a tax " on labour itself," as the industrious mechanic worked many hours after his daily labour by candle light.   (4) The most active advocate of the tax (not Curwen) was greatly interested in the increase of the price of tallow.   (5) It was asserted that the new duty would not increase the price of tallow by more than £5 10/- a ton ; this would mean a protection to the British grazier of 3/- a head on the ox—a boon not worth having.   (6) The just complaint of foreigners, said Robinson, was that the trade of this country was so restricted that

---

[1] Spain, however, it was pointed out, had re-retaliated in a more serious way ; she immediately thereafter prohibited the import of our woollen manufactures.

all their ingenuity was required to get an article into this country
on profitable terms ; and now that one article was found on which
they could get a profit, the State was to step in and take it in the
shape of a tax ! If this was to be our rule of commercial policy,
we might as well have shut up shop at once.[1]

The whole proposal is interesting, as an early attempt at " a
scientific tariff " which would tax the foreigner, and profit home
industry, and not injure the consumer. The motion of course,
was negatived.

In Chapter VI., was noticed the outcry of Ireland at the Protection for
equalisation of the Salt Duties, which took away the protection Irish Butter.
given to the provision trade and the fisheries. On 20th June,
more protection was asked for Irish butter. The story is an interesting one as illustrating the ordinary course of any protection—as
the Duke of Somerset once said, " when medicine has been administered, it must be frequently continued." The monopoly
granted to grain farmers suggested to the Irish graziers in 1816
that they were equally entitled to a monopoly. This was not
granted, but, " on account of the peculiarly distressed state of the
butter trade in Ireland," the duty on foreign butter was raised from
5/1½d. per cwt. to 20/- when brought in British, and to 25/- when
brought in foreign vessels—avowedly " a just protection " against
Holland with its productive soil and nearness to English markets." [2]
And now, in 1822, this amount of protection was found inadequate
to protect the butter growers in Ireland. In spite of the duty, the
importation of Dutch butter had doubled within the past year.
The price of Irish butter had fallen from 80/- or 90/- to 45/- or 50/-.
The prospect threatened was that pasture land would be thrown
out of cultivation, and Ireland converted into " one great arable
farm," and that this in turn would add to the supply of corn and
reduce the already low prices. Whereupon it was gravely proposed
to add 10/- to the existing duties.

Much indignation was expressed among the English members
at this new demand to tax a necessary of life in England after so
much consideration had already been given to Irish interests—" it
seemed to be understood," said one, " that the people of England
were to pay everything and the people of Ireland nothing." At the

---

[1] Ricardo heard this argument with great pleasure, and hoped Robinson
would thereafter act upon it ; if it had hitherto been followed up, the right
hon. gentleman would never have proposed the duties upon cheese and
butter.

[2] *Economic Annals, 1801-20*, 483.

existing price, the duty was equal to 50 per cent. ; the new proposal
would make it 75 per cent., and give Ireland a complete monopoly—
all to support the " exorbitant rents " of Irish landlords. Robinson
pointed out that the fall in butter was only one case of the universal
fall in agricultural produce. Far from the importation of Irish
butter into England having decreased, it was greater for the past
two years than it had ever been. Butter was one of the few things
with which Holland—"the most taxed country in Europe, not
even excepting England," said Huskisson—could pay for her
British imports : we might as well declare at once that, on principle,
we would have no commercial intercourse with foreign states.
Ricardo said that the House was assailed on all sides for protecting
duties—one day by the butter trade, then by the dealers in tallow,
while the West India planters complained, and the shipping interest
demanded legislative interference. Instead of adding to the butter
duties, Parliament ought to be called on to get rid of this protecting
duty by degrees. Huskisson also protested ; the only effect of the
proposal would be, not to increase the use of Irish butter, but, by
raising the price of a bad article, to drive it altogether out of consumption. Spring Rice, on the other hand, raised the old cry that
the principles of political economy, however true in the abstract,
could not be applied to Ireland. Happily, the motion was negatived.[1]

The interest of this struggle, however, between the economists
and the adherents of the old faith is added to by something almost
like an inverted reflection on the Continent. During the times of
Protection, natural and governmental, England had risen to a height
of manufacturing greatness formerly unthought of. How this
struck the foreigner, and how it was interpreted by him, is seen in
the protectionist proposals of other countries. The point of contact
was that in France, in the Netherlands, and in Germany, there was
during the year the same agricultural distress as in England, accompanied by the same low prices both of corn and stock and by much
the same outcry as to foreign competition.

Protection in France,

Of late years France had been vacillating in her commercial
policy. In 1817, we find her giving a bounty on the export of cotton
yarns while lowering the duty on raw and thrown silk. In 1821,
on the other hand, she imposed a protective duty against our
hammered iron. A party was now working for free entrance of
corn from the Black Sea, while the majority were denouncing
"the fatal importation of foreign corn." The economists, who,

[1] *Hansard*, vii. 1210.

led by Ganilh, were now making themselves heard, urged a liberal system, in imitation of the example which England was now setting ; others advocated prohibition of competing manufactures, colonial preference, and navigation laws, contending that England was only forced into her new system by finding that other countries were adopting the old system on which she had built up her fortunes. " Let the system of prohibition," said Saint Cricq, the Director General of Customs, " be for an instant abolished. Then Odessa inundates us with her grain—England, with her steel, her hardware, her cottons, almost all the objects of daily use and convenience in which she possesses the same superiority over us which we have over her in the products of our soil and the objects of our industry. Bengal and Brazil can send us their sugars—the Americans, their tobacco, their cotton, and their salt fish, at a price much lower than our colonies can. Thus you would lose your agriculture, your manufactures, and your colonies. No person who understands the interests of our trade would consent to enter on the career of freedom."

In the Netherlands, the farmers complained bitterly of the Netherlands, " ruinous abundance," the consequence of excessive cultivation under the stimulus of high prices, followed by a couple of good harvests ; denounced the importation of foreign grain ; and called for a restrictive system similar to that adopted in England. In October, the King's Speech intimated a special enquiry into the interests of the farmers relative to those of the consumers.

But it was in Germany that the most notable results followed. Germany, The complaint there was not of the importation of foreign grain, but that other countries had shut their ports to German grain. Some of the South German states, such as Bavaria, Wurtemburg, Baden, and Hesse Darmstadt, now adopted a scheme long talked of—to favour free intercourse among themselves, and to make common reprisals against states which put restrictions on the import of German goods, beginning with France. The duty on French wines was raised from 5 florins to 20 ; on spirits, from 10 to 30 ; on jewellery, trinkets, perfumery, and porcelain, from 20 to 100 ; on olive oil, from $1\frac{2}{3}$ to 20 ; on colonial produce, from $3\frac{1}{2}$ to 5. They went on to propose favourable terms of intercourse between the Swiss cantons and the south of Germany on condition of Switzerland agreeing to take similar measures against France, but meantime this part of the attempt failed.

Russia imposed a greatly increased tariff on foreign commodities, Russia.

giving as reasons the necessity of protecting home industries and of pursuing towards others the same restrictive measures as adopted towards her. The tariff was particularly directed against Great Britain, woollens, hardware, etc., being totally excluded, and smuggling, of course, was carried on to a great extent. An interesting experiment was begun in the establishment of public granaries. To prevent the bad effects of local scarcity, an imperial ukase ordered that a corn magazine should be established in the capital of each province. The details are imperfect, but one gathers that advances were made by the Government against grain put in store, repayable in two years at 6 per cent., on the model of the recommendation rejected by our Agricultural Committee.

It would seem, then, that, just as Great Britain was relaxing her restrictive system, other countries were about to make it more difficult for her by introducing the principles which she had discarded.[1]

[1] *Annual Register, passim.*

CHAPTER X

1822. AGRICULTURE AND INDUSTRY: THE NEW CORN LAW

THE position which agriculture still held in the country may be recalled by a passage from Lansdowne's speech in the debate on the Address. While glad to hear from the King's Speech of the prosperity of manufactures and commerce, he said that he chiefly estimated the advantages of that prosperity for its influence in vivifying agriculture—the chief value of commercial prosperity was the influence it might have in stimulating to the cultivation of the soil. Agriculture, agreed Lord Liverpool, notwithstanding our important commerce and manufactures, " must still be considered the great source of our wealth and greatness." The modern student notices, with some surprise, that manufactures are seldom conceived of as goods which enter directly into the maintenance of life. It would not be far from the truth to say that they are spoken of, predominantly, either as tools and auxiliaries of agricultural pursuits, or as luxuries which might very well be dispensed with —and these are the principal aspects presented by those who defended the interests of the manufacturing classes as classes who made goods for sale to other countries in exchange for raw materials and tropical produce. Taking this view, it is not to be wondered at that the continued agricultural distress took up so much of the attention of Parliament.

The farmer's diary of the year, as given in his favourite organ,[1] is painful reading. In the early months, prices, both of grain and live stock, were still low and tending to sag. But while the Agricultural Committee was sitting, hopes were still high as to what Government might do—the feeling was that " some regulation should certainly be made in the importations of land produce,

Agriculture still our first industry.

---

[1] See *Farmer's Magazine, passim.*

even from Ireland." Something, too, was to be hoped from the
landlords—" at last term many proprietors have not realised a
tenth part of their rent rolls, and the payment of arrears is totally
out of the question." And had not one great landowner intimated
that one-third would be deducted from the rents of his arable
tenants, and 15 per cent. from the rents of sheep farms entered
on only three years ago ? [1]   But the competition for farms in some
parts of Scotland was as great as ever, and the lairds were conjured
not to take advantage of the " singular infatuation." Cobbett's
strong expression of opinion that prices would go still lower struck
a chill, and the suspicion that there was some deeper evil at work,
perhaps the currency, took hold of many with all the power of the
unknown.

The mild winter and the early spring were scarcely reassuring—
what if Heaven should again be mistakenly kind ?   " The general
question is, What is to become of us ? "   By summer, Western's
views had caught hold :   " gold is a bad standard of value " ;
Ricardo's views might have done great harm " if they had not
been powerfully met and refuted by—Sir John Sinclair " !   In the
midst of this confused dread, the " plain unsophisticated common
sense of Archibald Dunlop, Esq." supplies a comic interlude ; was
not his plan for " a free spirit trade and extended distillation,"
which would consume seven million gallons more of spirits, and
demand over 300,000 quarters of barley, " the most rational and
effectual remedy for the agricultural distress " ? [2]

[1] It was about this time that Western introduced his system of Corn Rents.
As explained by him in 1829, he reduced nearly all his rents into rents determined by the price of corn, calculated on the prices of the preceding half-
year. The farms which were let in 1814 were calculated at the rate of 80/-
per qr. on wheat ; but, when the price came down, he calculated by the
rule of three, and said—If 80/- give 100/-, what will 56/- or 50/- or 40/- give ?
When wheat went down to 40/-, his rents were down 50 per cent.   As a consequence, he had on his land in 1829 not an arrear of £100 (*Hansard*, xxii. 435).
Several other landlords, such as the Duke of Portland, adopted the same
plan.   In Scotland, Campbell of Blythswood, the Member for Glasgow, adopted
the principle of regulating his rents by fiars' prices, and a great proportion
of the landlords in Fife followed his example in the next year.   Many reductions, ranging from 15 per cent. to 40 per cent. were announced in the spring.
Among others, the Duke of Montrose took off 20 per cent. to 30 per cent. and
relinquished all arrears.   One of the most generous was the Duke of Buckingham, but the following from a newspaper in March hints at a *quid pro quo,*
" We understand that his Grace, the Duke of Buckingham, has signified to
his tradesmen in Buckingham that, in consequence of his Grace having reduced
his rents to his tenants, they must lower their prices one-third, or he will get
his articles from London."

[2] The two objections which might be urged to the scheme, it was said, were :
that the increase of distilling would be compensated by a proportional diminu-

By November, the blow had fallen. A dry summer resulted in A fifth good
harvest. an early and abundant harvest—the fifth in succession ; every crop, except in some places barley and oats, was good, wheat and potatoes being exceptionally fine. The price of wheat fell lower and lower. It had been a little over 50/- in the end of January. It was 34/- in the end of November. The mildness of the winter produced great plenty of beef and mutton, and the prices towards the end of the year fell to a very low level. Wool shared the same fate, in spite of the revival of the manufacture.[1] And, indeed, one may grant that, to the ordinary mind, the spectacle of abundant food for man and beast throwing the shadow of utter ruin on the greatest industry of the country, tempted to the thought that some malign power—perhaps the Government—must be thwarting the designs of Providence.[2]

tion of brewing—which was dismissed as absurd ; and that spirits were prejudicial to health—which could not be the case in a moist or damp atmosphere like ours. " The only persons who could reasonably complain of the alteration would be those interested in quack medicines, in hospitals, or in poor houses, to whom we may add the upholsterer and the grave digger."

[1] The other grains, however, rye, barley, oats, beans and peas all rose after harvest. It is suggestive to hear that, in spite of these circumstances, the breadth of land sown down in wheat kept every year increasing.

[2] The following passage from the *Farmer's Magazine*, p. 494, so clearly puts the resentful bewilderment of the classes most concerned that I quote it in full : " Oats, the staple commodity of this country (Scotland), are above a medium crop and the grain is of the best quality. Wheat is far above a medium crop. Potatoes were never so abundant. The orchards never yielded nearly such a crop, and seldom the half of this year's produce. The dairy gives a fair return and the butcher never had a more ample supply. All this is matter of thankfulness to the Bountiful Giver. But alas ! what is to become of the occupiers and even of the proprietors of land, under the present depreciation of farm produce ? In so far as prices are lowered by an abundant return, the farmer has no cause to complain. He may as well sell two pecks of meal at a shilling as one peck at 1/10. But, unfortunately, the prices of all sorts of farm produce have sunk below the fair proportion of increase. It was the intention of the legislature, when the Corn Laws were formerly under discussion, to render the markets steady : and, as near as possible, to have wheat at 40/- per boll and oatmeal at from 1/6 to 1/8 per peck, the lowest price at which they could be raised in Britain. Years of uncommon plenty might lower and those of scarcity might raise the price. The former could not injure the grower, and the latter was beyond human control. But, in so far as Parliament had the power, these were meant to be standard prices. Owing to defects in the law then enacted, and partly from circumstances not then obvious, as well as from a succession of productive seasons, the prices have fallen nearly one-half below the rates then contemplated, so that the occupiers of land are getting little more than half the prices which the legislature, the laird, and the tenant, all calculated upon about seven years ago ; and on the faith of which prices, four-fifths of the land in Scotland have been taken in lease." Having thus successfully reduced the argument to a *cul de sac*, the writer disappoints our expectation by saying that it would be " out of place to enquire into the

The wheat average for the year was 44/7, being the lowest average of any year since 1792 when it was 43/-, and the lowest till 1835 when it was 39/4.

Attack on the threshing machines. In this year, one notices in the newspapers several cases of a phenomenon which did not reappear till 1830. In Norfolk and Suffolk, in the spring, the threshing machine became the object of riotous attack, and this was accompanied by the firing of stacks and farm buildings. At one time, Cobbett had not minced matters in regard to the folly of this. In a letter to the Luddites, in November 1816, he asked why not as well destroy flails, or spades, or ploughs, which were but digging machines. The notion, he con-

Cobbett, who condemned it in 1816, tinued, of our labourers in agriculture is that threshing machines injure them, because, say they, if it were not for those machines we should have more work to do. This is a great error. For if, in consequence of using a machine to beat out his corn, the farmer does not expend so much money on that sort of labour, he has so much more money to expend on some other sort of labour. If he saves £20 a year in the article of threshing, he has that £20 a year to expend in draining, fencing, or some other kind of work; for, you will observe that he does not take the £20 and put it into a chest and lock it up, but lays it out in his business, and his business is to improve his land and to add to the quality and amount of his produce. Thus, in time, he is enabled to feed more mouths in consequence of his machine; and to buy, and cause others to buy more clothes than were bought before; and the skill of the mechanic tends to produce ease and power and happiness. The threshing machines employ women and children in a dry and comfortable barn while the men can be spared to go to work in the fields. Thus the weekly income of the labourer who has a large family is in many cases greatly augmented, and his life rendered so much the less miserable. " But this is a trifle compared with the great principle upon which I am arguing, and which is applicable to all manufactories as well as to farming; for, indeed, what is a farmer other than a Manufacturer of Corn and Cattle? " This was his language

condones it in 1822. in 1816. But now, commenting on the fact that the mail coach had passed seventeen fires in one night in Suffolk, while he condemned machine-breaking as a " crime," he minimised it by saying that the cause was more important than the phenomenon, and that

causes of that alteration of price, or how they can be remedied, if that be practicable," but hints that, at any rate, rents must be reduced by at least a third.

the cause was unsatisfied hunger. It will be interesting to see
what he said in 1830.

Meanwhile, following the recommendation of the Agricultural The new
Committee, a new Corn Law was passed.[1] Briefly, it came to this Corn Law.
that, till the home price, ascertained in the old way of averages,
reached 70/-, foreign grain should be entirely excluded. 70/- thus
took the place of 80/- as the prohibition limit. But when 70/-
was reached, the importation was no longer free, as it had been
after 80/-, but subject to a sliding scale of duties. When the price
was between 70/- and 80/-, the duty was 12/-; when between
80/- and 85/-, the duty fell to 5/-; and, above 85/-, only 1/- duty
was charged. Similar scales were fixed for other species of grain,
and the proportional price of oats, as recommended, was raised.
The colonial preference was in the same proportion as before—
59/- being substituted for 67/-. The change, however, was not
to take place till the ports were opened by an 80/- home price;
that is to say, the new Act was not to come into operation till then.
This provision, as Canning said afterwards, " stood as an outwork
to prevent the body of the law from being ever approached . . .
the consequence of which was, and still is (1827), that we live as
much now under the operation of the original prohibition of exclusion
up to 80/- as if the law of 1815 still continued unaltered." [2] Another
" outwork " was that, even after 80/- was reached, the duty for
the first three months was to be 17/-, and, only afterwards, 12/-.
But there was a special provision as regards grain warehoused before
13th May, on the ground that it had been stored on the faith of
free entry at 80/-. It—and it alone—could be taken out for home
consumption when the home price reached 70/-, subject to the
new duty of 12/- (plus an extra duty of 5/ for three months after
the opening of the ports). If the owners of the stored grain did
not care to avail themselves of this privilege, they could take it
out duty free when the ports were opened at 80/-. But grain
warehoused after 13th May would not be admitted for home consumption till the price reached 80/-.

Sir Thomas Lethbridge, the member for Somersetshire—who,
by the way, hoped that " the House would put down with all their
might and force the abominable theories of political economists "
—moved the forlorn hope of Webb Hall's fixed 40/- protecting
duty on wheat whatever should be the home price, and a corresponding duty on almost every species of agricultural produce

[1] *Hansard*, vii. 1504.　　　　　　　　[2] *Ibid.* xvi. 767.

down to apples and pears,[1] and got 23 supporters. Huskisson and
Althorp moved other proposals which were rejected. But the real
rival scheme was that of Ricardo.[2] He proposed that, when the
home price was 65/-, the foreign corn already warehoused should
be admitted on a payment of 15/-. But, when the home price
reached 70/-,[3] the trade should thenceforth be permanently free "
on payment of a duty of 20/- per qr., to be reduced by 1/- in each
successive year till it reached 10/-. To this was added a drawback
or bounty of 7/- per qr. on the exportation of wheat to foreign
countries. This plan, he admitted, was not adopted of choice, but
forced upon him reluctantly on account of the duties which now
existed. The farmers were " the most distressed class in the country
and the most cruelly used." When the prices rose in consequence
of a short harvest, and when the farmers ought to have compensation, corn was let in from all parts of the world. This great
evil was not remedied by Londonderry's scheme. If the price
rose to 85/-, foreign corn only required to pay a duty of 1/-,
and the poor farmer might be inundated. His plan, moreover,
would do what Londonderry's had no tendency to do—would attain
the ideal of approximating the price of grain in this and foreign
countries—" making the growing price in this country on a level
with that of other nations." If it were adopted, he thought it
impossible that the price of wheat could ever be materially higher
than that of foreign nations. The reason for fixing on 10/- was
that it appeared on evidence that the whole of the charges which
the farmer had to pay—principally tithes and poor rates—amounted
to about 10/- per qr.[4] " He implored them to recollect that they
were legislating for the happiness of millions, and that there was
no evil so intolerable as the high price of human food." His scheme,
however, was rejected by 218 to 25.

Ricardo
proposes a
fixed duty.

[1] Reverting to this proposal, Lethbridge said in 1827 that he was now
convinced that it would not have afforded just protection to the landed
interest (*Hansard*, xvi. 1069).

[2] *Hansard*, vii. 199, 455.

[3] The wording is ambiguous, but it seems that the condition of the home
price reaching 70/- held only in the existing circumstances ; after that price
had once been touched, only the 20/- falling to 10/- duty was to be imposed
whatever the home price was.

[4] In other words, he would agree to a protecting duty gradually diminishing
till the duty was equal to the peculiar burdens to which the farmer was liable
(*Hansard*, vi. 486). It is interesting to find the issue now raised between
Londonderry and Ricardo afterwards raised between Peel and Russell in 1842,
of which Walpole says, " the House might have almost contented itself with
reading the old debates of 1822 instead of discussing the issue in 1842 " (iv. 120).

It will be observed that, as the home average price never reached 80/- till 1828, when the Act was repealed, the law was completely inoperative as regards foreign wheat, although barley and oats came in in large amounts in 1824 and 1825. It is for this reason that I give less consideration to the long and interesting debates of 1822. In the circumstances, they are only of academic interest. The new law never operative.

The extreme irritation between the two parties, generated during these debates, may be seen by the angry scene on June 14th. A petition from the county of Kent was presented, complaining of agricultural distress and asking for parliamentary reform, with a rider tacked on calling on Parliament to make reduction in the interest of the National Debt. Knatchbull, the member for Kent, in presenting it, protested against this latter part of the petition being considered the expression of opinion of the freeholders of Kent, and put the blame of it on the great Whig leaders who had called the meeting, and had expressed no opinion regarding the rider. Russell was surprised to hear that a large majority of the meeting were opposed to the proposition ; if so, why did they not bring forward some counter resolution ? For himself, he considered parliamentary reform wholly unconnected with the public debt, and, to any such reduction as was recommended in the petition, he would never consent, except in a case of overwhelming necessity —a necessity which at present was far from existing.[1] Londonderry, however, instead of welcoming this opinion, fixed on the expression, " overwhelming necessity," and protested against it as giving only too much countenance to the spoliation of property. Russell protested that he had only meant such necessity as might arise if a foreign enemy were at our gates, and the safety to the country rose paramount to every other consideration. Londonderry retorted that, even in such circumstances, the nation would be justified only in postponing, not in repudiating its engagements. Brougham insinuated that the Government was trying to stop the mouth of county meetings, and spoke as if attention had been drawn to the obnoxious paragraph in order to draw away attention from the rest of the petition, ending by saying roundly that the rider was not more objectionable than the conduct of Londonderry respecting the restriction and subsequent resumption of cash payments. Peel brought some dignity into the wrangle by saying that Russell's " manly and becoming confession " had done ten times more towards setting his party right with the people of England, than the defence The Kent petition.

[1] *Hansard,* vii. 1078.

which had been made for them by Brougham; and blamed the Whig leaders for not explaining to the meeting the impossibility of the course they were following.

Western was astonished at Peel's consummate assurance in denouncing the men of Kent for an expression wrung from them in a moment of irritation. "It was too much for gentlemen to suppose that public justice was due to no one but to the public creditor; why was it not equally to be measured to the public debtor?" Hume poured oil on the flames by saying that the words of the petition might in fairness be construed to mean no more than, say, a conversion from 5 per cent. to 4 per cent. or from 4 per cent. to 3 per cent. Burdett, too, said: "the men of Kent did not say that the public creditor should not have 20/- to his £1, but it was the opinion of many most able men that, in consequence of the measures of the right honourable gentleman opposite, the public creditor was likely to get 30/- in the £1. And, after all, was there anything so very objectionable in the proposal?" Encouraged by this, another member went on to say that the contracting of £800,000,000 of debt was a species of dishonesty, seeing that ministers never could have hoped to discharge it: he thought it their duty to do what the French had done with their assignats, treating all debts contracted in that species of money as in a depreciated currency, and legalising their liquidation in the present currency with reference to that depreciation. Bennett backed this up: the public had no right to pay more than they had borrowed; if they borrowed 20/-, they ought not to be called upon to pay 30/-. Ricardo quietly observed that it was clear that, if the public creditor had at one time received 30/- in place of 20/-, he had, at other times, received 20/- in place of 30/-; he had great doubts whether, in the whole of these transactions, the public creditor had been benefited. Hume was sorry that such opinions with respect to the payment of the public creditor should be held by his honourable friends; but, though he differed from them, he could not shut his eyes to the fact that they were opinions held by the best informed persons in the country. And, certainly, in this year the expression that, sooner or later, repudiation might be thought of, is heard in less and less guarded terms, and, unfortunately for the Opposition, it was from their benches alone that such opinions were expressed.

The farmers' attitude to the Corn Law.   After the publication of the Report and the passing of the new Corn Law, the farmers would seem to have settled down to the conviction that, as nothing was to be expected from Government, they must work out their own salvation and get their rents reduced. They were rather ungrateful, indeed, about what had been done for them. " The alteration in the Corn Law adds to the evil." " It is evident that the curtailment of public expenditure has added much to the distress." The millions of taxes taken off had not perceptibly benefited the occupier of land—the Farm-horse tax amounted to only threepence or fourpence per pound of the farmer's rent; the shilling taken off malt did no good in Scotland or to the consumers of ale anywhere; the reduction in the Leather Tax had not lowered the price of shoes or harness by the smallest fraction—the reduction of taxes, indeed, turned out to be a mere humbug.[1] They never ceased to grumble, prophesy ruin, and revile their leaders for not doing something. " There is scarcely half a dozen of the country gentlemen in the House of Commons who seem to be of the same opinion—it is idle, therefore, to hope for anything from the influence of the landed interest, which is every day sinking both out of Parliament and within it." The economists, too, came in for more than their share of abuse. Whenever an argument could be fortified by a quotation from them, it was done, but generally they were credited with doing great harm to the public judgment. And, from the *Farmer's Magazine,* one might draw up a very pretty tale of schemes for remedying the distress which could only have been conceived, one thinks, by men driven by desperation out of their ordinary senses. There was some little reason for saying that they had asked for bread and gotten a stone. Londonderry, quite wisely, said that the present was a suitable time to arrange the matter of the foreign import, inasmuch as it was at the moment so purely a speculative question—" so adequate is the present principle of protection that, in my opinion, nothing can open the ports short of that species of dearth which must open them even if the protecting price were 100/- instead of 80/-." But this was no remedy for the present distress, and nothing was done to carry out the hope of the Committee as to " affording some temporary relief." [2]

---

[1] *Farmer's Magazine,* 495.

[2] Western was not ashamed to suggest that what had been done was to " reduce the import price from 80/- to 70/-," and that this was a violation of the solemn pledge given by Parliament—a breach of public faith. It had spread dismay in all quarters. Better the former law, defective as it was, than the proposed improvement (*Hansard,* vii. 552).

The King's Speech in February said that a considerable improvement had taken place in the course of the past year in the commerce and manufactures of the kingdom, and that important branches were now in a very flourishing condition. But thereafter there is little reference in Parliament to the course of industry except the frequent statement that the depression had passed away, and that everything was, for the moment, on the upgrade. The fullest information is contained in a speech of Peel [1] on 12th June, in which he quoted returns he had obtained from the chief manufacturing towns as to the condition of industry. At Bolton, an immense quantity of goods had lately been manufactured; the working population was well provided for; and the profits of the master manufacturers were low. At Rochdale, the spinners were said to have plenty of employment and the working weavers never doing better. At Manchester, the profits of the master manufacturers appeared to be smaller upon the average than they had been in former years; but, from the contraction of credit and the improved quality of the currency, the risk of loss was also less; speculation and adventure were less common; consequently profit, though smaller than heretofore, was more secure; at present there was abundant employ for the working classes. At Leeds, more cloth was making than had been known for many years, but profits were comparatively low; the working classes were generally employed; their nominal earnings were less, but their comforts greater than they had been formerly. From Glasgow, the account was equally favourable. At Huddersfield, the profits were low but the whole population was employed; good workmen earning constantly from 16/- to 22/- per week. At Nottingham, all was doing well but the silk stocking trade. [2]

In the *Edinburgh Annual Register*, I find it stated that the cotton spinning trade was never more brisk; the quantity of woollen cloth manufactured exceeded that of any previous year; of raw silk the average consumption for the past three years had been

---

[1] In the beginning of the year, Sidmouth had retired from the Home Office. and Peel, who had given up his post as Chief Secretary for Ireland in 1818, took his place. It is curious to note that the political predilections, sympathies, principles, and prejudices of the two men were generally considered very much the same. But, indeed, very divergent opinions were held about Peel in those days. Croker considered him unambitious and retiring, while Greville believed that, under his placid exterior, he concealed a boundless ambition.

[2] *Hansard*, vii. 1015. In the debate on the Salt Tax, however, Curwen asserted that it was " well known that the average wage of the manufacturer did not amount to more than 8/- a week."

2,100,000 lbs. ; the export of linen from Ireland in 1822 was over £3 millions, being nearly £1 million more than in 1820 ; the Stafford iron trade was "in the fullest state of activity"; in hardware and cutlery, we "were beyond the danger of rivalry"; while the import of tea, "the great luxury of the manufacturing population," was increasing in almost every quarter, being over 23,000,000 lbs. for the year. All the same, I find during the year mention of rioting in Norwich, Monmouth, and Staffordshire against reduction of wages, and a violent strike of the Newcastle keelmen which lasted for months.

The return of good times is so far confirmed by the returns of foreign trade. The Imports were £30,531,141—practically the same as in the previous year. The Re-exports were £9,227,567—a decrease of about one and a half millions. But the Exports were £44,242,532, exceeding those of the most flourishing year which the country had known during the continuance of the war, and showing an increase of £3½ millions over the previous year. The Real Exports were £36,966,023. The export of cotton, said Wallace in the next year, increased 10 per cent., of linens, 12 per cent., of woollens, 13 per cent., of hardware, 17 per cent.[1]

The number of ships built in the United Kingdom was 564, representing 50,928 tons.

[1] It is of interest, for comparison with the figures of 1819 (*Economic Annals, 1801-20*, p. 690), and with those of 1824 (*infra*, p. 276), to give the principal details for the year ending 5th January, 1823.

EXPORTS OF BRITISH PRODUCE AND MANUFACTURES.

Cotton Manufactures	£24,556,000	Fish	-	£208,000
Woollen „	5,940,000	Hats	-	194,000
Linen „	2,594,000	Tin and pewter wares	-	194,000
Linen yarn -	2,353,000	Plate and jewellery -	-	176,000
Iron and steel	1,140,000	Lead and shot -	-	148,000
Refined sugar	949,000	Stationery	-	143,000
Brass and copper manu-		Si ..s	-	141,000
factures	611,000	Glass	-	136,000
Hardware	534,000	Unwrought tin	-	129,000
Coals	241,000	Soap and candles	-	116,000
Salt	236,000	Leather -	-	114,000

RE-EXPORTS.

Coffee -	£2,217,000	Pepper -	-	£240,000
Cotton wool	1,279,000	Tobacco -	-	156,000
Piece goods of India	1,088,000	Brandy -	-	143,000
Raw sugar	612,000	Rice	-	139,000
Rum -	547,000	Wines	-	134,000
Indigo	456,000	Saltpetre	-	127,000
Corn -	315,000			

Steam
carriages.

There does not seem to have been any notable advance in industrial invention during this year. But, here and there, we find great expectations of a new application of steam. The *Edinburgh Magazine* for April contains an intimation that " the long-considered problem of propelling, by steam, carriages capable of transporting merchandise and also passengers upon common roads, without the aid of horses, has at length been solved." Such steam carriages were at the moment being built at the manufactory of Messrs. Bramah ; the power would be equal to that of six horses, and a carriage of 28 feet in length would run at from three to seven miles at pleasure. The patent had been taken out by Mr. Griffith, of Brompton, and one such carriage was already being operated with success in Vienna. A roseate anticipation of the future of steam coaches occurs in the same magazine in December.

Steamboats.

Among the shipping notices, one marks the appearance of steam packets of 300 tons to run from Liverpool to Bristol and Greenock, and, among the advertisements in July, appears one of the *Swift*, a steam yacht running twice a week from Brighton to Dieppe. An iron steamboat, the *Aaron Manby* is announced in June as arriving at Paris *via* Rouen—" for ever memorable in the history of shipbuilding as being the first attempt to traverse the ocean in a vessel composed of any material but wood." In America, ships were running between Quebec and Baltimore, a distance of 700 miles.[1] Among the petitions to Parliament, appears one from the coach proprietors and innkeepers along the Dover Road, complaining of the injury sustained by the steam vessels sailing direct from London to France, and praying for a tax on steamboats.

IMPORTS.

Cotton wool	£4,735,000	Piece goods of India	£283,000
Tea	2,736,000	Skins and furs	255,000
Flax	1,197,000	Linen yarn	229,000
Coffee	2,672,000	Dyewoods	221,000
Raw silk	943,000	Pearl and pot ashes	198,000
Tallow	828,000	Brandy	197,000
Wool	695,000	Butter	163,000
Wines	675,000	Mahogany	143,000
Timber	609,000	Flax seed and linseed	142,000
Thrown silk	591,000	Bark	139,000
Madder	541,000	Iron in bars	124,000
Hides	513,000	Pepper	119,000
Hemp	509,000	Pitch and tar	116,000
Train oil	426,000	Corn	115,000
Indigo	380,000	Cheese	111,000
Rum	367,000	Currants	108,000
Tobacco	329,000	Cochineal	105,000

[1] *Glasgow Herald, passim.*

CHAPTER XI

1822. ANOTHER UNEVENTFUL YEAR

THE very first subject brought before Parliament was the state In Ireland, of Ireland. For some months previous to the King's visit, from fresh outrages, which so much had been hoped—he was the first English sovereign who had appeared in Ireland on a mission of peace—there had been one of the periodical outbreaks of violence. They began again in the end of the year, and, in the beginning of 1822, many parts of the southern and western counties were aflame with riot and savage outrage, identified with the " Whiteboys " or " Rockites " ; partly, no doubt, the result of those religious differences which have so often made the people of that country forget the fundamental principles of all religions, partly the expression of that contempt for the law as an alien thing characteristic of the very poor Celt. These outrages were, of course, used for party purposes. But both parties were agreed that the majesty of the law must be asserted before remedial measures were taken, and the only opposition to the coercive measures proposed was based on the assertion that outrage could be put down by more vigorous administration and did not call for suspension of public liberties. The Insurrection Act was re-enacted, and the Habeas Corpus Act, for the fifth time since 1800, suspended. Thanks to these measures, comparative tranquillity was restored before the summer.

While some blamed the currency, the want of manufactures, overpopulation, the institutions, the administration of justice, the denial of emancipation, absenteeism, the taxes to support a Protestant establishment, there were not wanting, as might be expected, some who ascribed the lawlessness to the revolt of desperate men against want, low prices, rack-rent, tithes, and distraining. However this element may have entered previously, it was witnessed by the end of July that famine was abroad in the land.[1] Incessant rains

[1] *Hansard*, vii. 146.

failure of the
potato, and
typhus. had totally rotted the potato, on which, speaking generally, the
whole population of the south of Ireland lived during a great portion
of the year. Thousands, it was said, were reduced to a single
meal of oatmeal and water a day. There was, indeed, plenty of
corn in the market,[1] but there was no employment and no money
to buy anything. The newspapers for weeks were full of the horrifying details of starvation and of the typhus which followed. By
July, Cobbett was suggesting a Poor Law for Ireland—at least
saying that "these terrible scenes could never have been enacted
if there had been in Ireland that system of Poor Laws which so
many ignorant and unfeeling men were endeavouring to undermine
and destroy."

In these circumstances, the Lord Lieutenant made appeal to
the Irish gentry, and great sums were spent in immediate relief.
The Government added a quarter of a million for food and seed
potatoes, and, besides, empowered the advancing of money for
the undertaking or completion of any work, public or private, on
the security of the rates thence arising or expected to arise. A
central London committee collected another quarter of a million
by subscription ; "nor was there a town of any note in the island
which did not hold its public meetings for promoting the success
of this labour of love." In the autumn, the new crop brought
relief ; and, after all, the London committee in September found
itself with such a surplus that it devoted £5,000 for clothing, £8,000
for the encouragement of the fisheries, £8,000 for the general purpose
of improving the condition of the Irish poor, and no less than
£40,000 for the encouragement of the linen manufacture in the
southern provinces. As the distress died away, however, the outrages commenced again.[2]

A Superannua-
tion Act, The principal parliamentary events of the year come in sequence
of the agricultural agitation, and have been discussed in that connection. But, indeed, almost everything during this Session turned
on this agitation. Among other things, it forced the Government
to have respect to the universal cry for economy. Acting, it would
seem, on recommendations from a committee which had been sitting
for three months, the Government brought in a Superannuation
Act Amendment Act, designed to carry out the twofold purpose

---

[1] It was found in Clare, said Liverpool, that the oats were being used for
illicit distillation, and that exportation of grain was going on from that
county (*Hansard*, vii. 672).

[2] *Hansard*, vii. *passim*, and *Annual Register*, 33.

of compulsory insurance of Government servants, and of reducing the total charge of the salaries in the Government departments. Before 1810, the provision for persons retiring from public offices was very uncertain, arbitrary, and unsatisfactory. One way was by appointing them to sinecure offices ; another was by obliging the successor to pay the person who retired a portion of the salary of the office. In 1782, a superannuation system had been recommended by a committee of inquiry ; in 1797, a committee of the House made the same recommendation ; and, in 1803, a first step was taken towards carrying out the principle. It was the Superannuation Act of 1810, passed during the inflation of prices, and " imposing on the country a great and unnecessary expense," which was now to be amended.

The general principle adopted was to fix the salaries as nearly *and revision of* as possible on the standard of 1796 or 1797 ; to specify the various *salaries.* officers who might be entitled to receive superannuation allowances ; and to make them contribute to a Superannuation Fund. Salaries of £100 and upwards would be reduced, for this purpose, by 5 per cent. ; those below £100, by 2½ per cent. And, where salaries were marked down for revision on the retiral of the present holders, the actual salaries would be subject to 5 per cent. on the amount of the revised salary, and to 10 per cent. on the excess. As the existing superannuation allowances amounted to about 10 per cent. on the existing salaries, this would be a saving of about 5 per cent. At the same time, the Chancellor of the Exchequer intimated that the King, " of his special command and generous feeling," had set an example by giving directions for a reduction to the extent of 10 per cent. upon all those departments of the royal household " which contributed more immediately to the personal comfort of the sovereign," that of the Privy Purse, the Lord Chamberlain, the Lord Steward, the Masters of the Robes and of the Horse—in all representing a sum of £30,000.[1] His Majesty had also further directed a reduction of 10 per cent., to continue for five years, on the salaries of all offices above £100 held at his pleasure, such as that of the Lord Chancellor, the Cabinet Ministers, and the great officers of the household. These reductions, when they had all come into effect, would represent a saving, he expected, of over

[1] It does not seem to have struck anyone that the King's " generosity " was at the expense of the household officers. We learn from the Budget speech of 1824 that, at the same time, the great officers of state gave up 10 per cent. of their salaries, amounting to £50,000, following the example of His Majesty (*Hansard,* xi. 590).

£370,000 a year—a large sum considering that " the whole reduction turned upon an establishment not exceeding £2 millions."

Almost the only opposition, strangely enough, came from Canning, who denounced it as a " clear breach of faith." Take, he said, the case of a young man of the highest promise, who, at the time when he was obtaining the highest honours of his college, and had every prospect of distinguished preferment in the Church, was induced to accept a public situation under the Crown on the conditions of the statute of 1810. He was now to be told that a large part of his emoluments were to be taken from him. This Bill would be to him a grievous injury. The reply to this extraordinary claim, of course, was that, if the Crown had a right to dismiss a servant altogether, surely it had the right to reduce his salary, and the Bill duly passed into law.[1]

Enthusiasm for retrenchment.   All through the session, the Government was badgered to death by the new enthusiasm for retrenchment. Creevey, on 27th February, took what he called his " benefit," making an attack on the Civil Offices Pension Bill of 1817, by which, he affirmed, members of the Cabinet had secured themselves pensions of from £3,000 a year downwards independent of the Crown. Later, he attacked the " snug, comfortable, family party," the Board of Control for managing the affairs of India, and " rolled the new Board about to their hearts' content and to the universal satisfaction of the House." Lord King, Normanby, and others joined in the attack. Davies complained that no account was rendered to Parliament of how the £4 millions of charge for collecting the public revenue was spent ; asserted that, since 1793, the salaries of collectors had been enormously increased ; and urged that it was notorious that this expenditure was one great source of the patronage enjoyed by the Government and of the power and influence which they possessed over the votes of the House.[2] Brougham formally attacked the daily increasing influence of the Crown—" the increased means of patronage which had accrued

[1] *Hansard*, vi. 1015 ; vii. 1844. The salaries of the civil servants, however, were restored to their old amounts in 1824 (*Hansard*, xi. 726, 1451) in spite of the opposition of Hume, who contended that the salaries had been reduced on account of, and proportionally to, the change which had then taken place in the currency. In 1829, by a Treasury Minute, every person thereafter accepting office under Government was required to submit to an annual reduction according to the amount of his salary, to be formed into a fund out of which the superannuation allowances were paid (*Hansard*, xxiii. 325).

[2] *Ibid.* vi. 753, 1048, 1120; *Creevey Papers*, ii. 34, 35.

from the increase in the revenue and income of the country "—
reprobating " the habit of looking up for the means of subsistence
to a Government which had the disposal of so much revenue within
its patronage "—" the influence was felt by members through their
friends ; it was first felt at elections and then in the votes of the
House ; and it signified very little whether a man was bribed by
holding an office himself or by having another to hold it on trust
for him ; the obligation was the same and the influence was the
same." [1]

But the hero of the retrenchment crusade was undoubtedly Hume, its
Hume. Not an estimate was presented but Hume, fortified by his leading spirit.
" happy spirit of blundering," and his entire want of humour, was
ready to move a reduction, supporting it by endless tables of figures,
and never deterred from making a strong statement by the suspicion
that he had not all the facts in his possession.   He objected to the
Navy estimates for their want of detail, routing Croker on his own
ground.   He moved reductions on the Army estimates, and called
forth the rebuke from Wilmot that, " if the honourable member took
no more care in his other financial assertions, he would feel it right
to reject his propositions in future with disdain." He attacked
the Ordnance estimates ; found fault with the Commissariat and
Barrack Establishments ; threw suspicion on the Post Office ;
criticised the Irish Civil List and the Superannuations, and the
Miscellaneous estimates—how on earth could they spend £40,000
on Secret Service in time of peace ?   One of his friends (Maberly)
recommended him to abandon the useless task of disputing the
estimates, entreating him not to exhaust his own strength and
that of his friends, night after night, since all his exertions were
rendered unavailing by the overwhelming majorities of Ministers.
Hume merely expressed his determination to persevere, and cheerfully went on to say that the pay of the Commander-in-Chief was
too great.   But, although he was nearly always unsuccessful in
carrying his points, the cumulative force of the attack compelled
the Government to economies of their own initiation, and, in the
end, to appear before the public as having stood for the same policy.[2]
And one result very obviously due to Hume's perseverance was
that, in April, the Chancellor of the Exchequer himself moved

---

[1] *Hansard*, vii. 1265.

[2] Hume's manner as a speaker, it is interesting to know, was plain, dry,
steady, destitute of any flow, richness, or ornament (*Edinburgh Annual
Register*, 1824).

for a Select Committee for the Simplifying and Better Arrangement of the Public Accounts—the more significant that he had
already indicated that the Sinking Fund would be made a particular
object of its attention.[1] Amid all these economies, it is pleasing
to note that the House was unanimous in approving of one new
expense, calculated at £2,000 a year, namely, the publication by
Parliament of a complete edition of the *Antient Historians of this
Realm*, under the conduct of Petrie, the Keeper of the Records.[2]

The agricultural agitation, skilfully used as pointing to the
necessity of better representation of the farmers,[3] also served to
keep alive and strengthen the demand for parliamentary reform,
which otherwise played no great part in the debates of the year,
and Russell moved a Resolution for it in a speech of $2\frac{3}{4}$ hours—
" an excellent and appropriate statement," said Hobhouse, " which
it was very difficult to touch." The concluding words of Canning's
reply are perhaps worth quoting. " That the noble lord will
carry his motion this evening, I have no fear, but, with the talents
which he has shown himself to possess and with (I sincerely hope)
a long and brilliant career of parliamentary distinction before him,
he will no doubt renew his efforts hereafter. Although I presume
not to expect that he will give any weight to observations or warnings of mine, yet on this, probably the last opportunity which I
shall have of raising my voice on the question of parliamentary
reform,[4] while I conjure the House to pause before it consents to
adopt his proposition, I cannot help conjuring the noble lord
himself to pause before he again presses it upon the country.
If, however, he shall persevere—and if his perseverance shall be
successful—and if the results of that success shall be such as I
cannot help apprehending—his be the triumph to have precipitated
those results—be mine the consolation that, to the utmost and the
latest of my power, I have opposed them." [5]

In another field, the advance in liberal ideas was manifest. The
modern reader has some difficulty in crediting the callousness of
past generations to the sufferings of the brute creation at the hands,
not only of the mob, but of fine gentlemen and sportsmen like
William Windham. In the first two decades of the century, the

Marginal notes: Canning on parliamentary reform. / Cruelty to animals.

[1] *Hansard*, vi. 864, 1462.   [2] *Ibid.* vii. 1737.

[3] " It would be interesting to know," said Harriet Martineau, " how many
of that order of reformers (the agricultural classes) obtained their convictions
through the distress of these years."

[4] At the moment Canning was preparing for India.   [5] *Hansard*, vii. 51.

only attempts to recognise by legislation the "rights" of the brute creation were the Bull-baiting Bill of 1802 and Erskine's Bill of 1809, both of which were thrown out chiefly by Windham's ridicule.[1] In the records of 1820, we come across an Ill-treatment of Horses Bill passing through the Lower House. It seems to have been a well-intentioned measure for the prevention of cruelty. But it was ridiculed on the old grounds that "it arose out of that spirit of legislation which was too prevalent at the present day," that legislation was not required, that "Parliament might as well protect dogs and cats," etc.—in the same strain of argument and prejudice as threw out Erskine's Bill. Ricardo said bitterly that, when so many barbarities prevailed in fishing, hunting, and other species of amusement, it was idle to legislate for horses alone.[2]

But, in 1822, the first Cruelty to Animals Act was brought in by Richard Martin.[3] It provided that any person accused of wantonly and cruelly beating, abusing, or ill-treating any cattle, might be summoned before a magistrate, and, if convicted, either upon his own confession or by the oath of any witness or witnesses, should be fined in a sum not exceeding £5 and not less than 10/-, or imprisoned up to a limit of three months. The only objections now made—probably with some reason—were that the offences mentioned were "of too vague and indefinite a nature," and that, if the principle of punishing cruelty were adopted, the line was drawn in an arbitrary manner at cattle. The Bill, however, passed (c. 71 : "to prevent the cruel and improper treatment of cattle").[4]

The chief events after the rising of Parliament are three. In August, the King—who was now figuring far less in political life than he did while Regent—paid a state visit to Scotland ; to be received there with a fervour of enthusiasm which can be explained only by the surmise that the Scot had a philosophic power of separating the office from the man which the Englishman—who knew him better—never manifested.[5]

---

[1] Economic Annals, 1801-20, 59, 206.   [2] Hansard, v. 1098.

[3] "Humanity Martin" (1754-1834); Member of the Irish Parliament (1776-1800) ; Member for Galway since 1801 ; chief agent in the formation of the Royal Society for the Prevention of Cruelty to Animals.

[4] Hansard, vii. 758, 873; Annual Register, 87. The Act, it was acknowledged in 1824, had done some good. An overwhelming majority of the cases presented under it were of so atrocious a nature that conviction regularly followed accusation—although Martin admitted that he generally had to pay the fine himself, the parties being too poor to pay it.

[5] The paean in Blackwood—with its text, "a king of whom Scotland might be proud"—must be read to be believed. There was some not unnatural

Castlereagh's
suicide.
In the same month, Londonderry, at the age of fifty-one, his
mind unhinged for the moment by thankless and unpopular work,
evaded the vigilance of his attendants, and took his own life. One
who knows him only through the parliamentary records and his
dispatches when our representative at the various congresses after
the war, finds difficulty in understanding Harriet Martineau's bitter
diatribes and Creevey's ungenerous depreciation, and welcomes the
verdict of later historians that few statesmen of George III.'s reign
have left a purer reputation, or rendered greater services to their
country, than did Castlereagh.[1] One good thing, however, came of

Canning
succeeds.
his death at that moment. Canning, who since his resignation
from the Board of Control had been a private member, had taken
leave of his constituents at Liverpool, and was preparing to sail
for India as Governor-General when the news came. The choice
of a successor lay between him and Peel—the " Merry Andrew "
and the " low miserable Spinning Jenny," as Brougham called
them. The King, who had an active dislike to Canning, gave way
to the strong remonstrances of Wellington and Peel.[2] It was
Canning, then, who gave Wellington his instructions as British
plenipotentiary at Verona, but it is only just to Castlereagh's
memory that the strict neutrality in regard to France and Spain,
which Wellington announced as the British policy, was the instruction drafted by Castlereagh before his death.

The continental events of the year, which mirrored themselves
Congress of
Verona.
in the proceedings of the Congress of Verona in October—originally

annoyance, however, that Sir Walter Scott, who acted as Master of Ceremonies,
had made too much of the bagpipes, and let his countrymen figure as a
nation of Highlanders, and the appearance of the King at a levee in full
uniform of Stuart tartans, with a broadsword, pistols, and philabeg, savoured
somewhat of comic opera.

[1] Croker wrote of him in December of the past year : " Londonderry goes
on as usual, and, like Mont Blanc, continues to gather all the sunshine upon
his icy head. He is *better* than ever ; that is, colder, steadier, more *poco-
curante,* and withal more amiable and respected. It is a splendid summit of
bright and polished frost which, like the travellers in Switzerland, we all
admire ; but no one can hope, and very few would wish to reach." Brougham
writes to Creevey a few days after the event : " Put all their other men together into one scale and poor Castlereagh in the other—single, he plainly
weighed them down. One can't help feeling a little for him, after being pitted
against him for several years pretty regularly. It is like losing a connection
suddenly. Also he was a *gentleman* and the only one amongst them."

[2] " Canning succeeds to the Foreign Office, Lead of the House, etc." wrote
Brougham to Creevey—" in short, to all of Castlereagh except his good
judgment, good manner, and bad English." It is curious to read that, by
January, the King was seen walking about the Pavilion with his arm round
his Secretary for State's neck (*Creevey,* ii. 59).

called to consider the evacuation of Italy by the Austrian armies and the state of affairs in the East of Europe, but occupied almost entirely with the proposal of the Holy Alliance to interfere in Spain—were of intense interest to the country, but do not much concern the economic historian. Enough to say that the French *cordon sanitaire*, drawn in August 1821 against the plague which raged on the other side of the Spanish frontier, had risen to 100,000 armed men, and remained, months after the plague had disappeared, as a *Corps d'Observation*, professing to watch against the invasion of republicanism into French territory; and that England, sympathising with Spain, was anxiously looking on at what might have turned into a European struggle but for the firmness of Wellington and Canning. The object of Canning in these negotiations at Verona—an object so much condemned in the debates of the next Session because so much misunderstood—was admirably put by him subsequently. " Whatever might grow out of a separate contest between Spain and France (though matter for grave consideration) was less to be dreaded than that all the great powers of the Continent should have been arrayed together against Spain ; and, although the first object in point of importance, indeed, was to keep the peace altogether—to prevent any war against Spain —the first in point of time was to prevent a general war—to change the question from a question between the allies on one side and Spain on the other, to a question between nation and nation. This, whatever the result might be, would reduce the quarrel to the size of ordinary events, and bring it within the scope of ordinary diplomacy. The immediate object of England, therefore, was to hinder the impress of a joint character from being affixed to the war—if war there must be—with Spain. . . . And this, I say, was accomplished." [1]

The chief contribution to economic science was Ricardo's *Pro-* Economic *tection to Agriculture*, a *chef d'œuvre* inspired by the current dis-* publications. cussions. Joseph Lowe's *Present State of England* has been justly characterised by Jevons as one of the ablest treatises on the variation of prices, the state of the currency, the poor law, population, finance, and other questions of the time, which he ever met with. It contains *inter alia* an admirable calculated estimate of the gains and losses of the war, showing how much of the apparent internal prosperity was real, how much fictitious, and how much due to a temporary stimulus which had to be paid for at peace, and it

[1] *Hansard*, viii. 1483.

deserves special attention as giving the first sketch of an Index Number, or, as he called it, a Table of Reference for Time Contracts.

Among the book advertisements, I find the following—many of them, I daresay, of as much importance as *The Analytical Investigation of the Scriptural Claims of the Devil*, which appears in the same lists : *Considerations on the Accumulation of Capital and its Effects on Profits and on Exchangeable Value ; Economical Enquiries relative to the Laws regulating Rent, Profit, Wages, and the Value of Money*, by T. Hopkins ; *Observations on Trade*, by R. Heathfield ; *A Letter to Sir Humphry Davy on the Application of Machinery to the purpose of Calculating and Printing Mathematical Tables ; The Principle of the English Poor Laws illustrated and defended*, by Frederick Page ; Wm. Spence's *Tracts on Political Economy* ; Whitmore's acute *Letter on the Present State and Future Prospects of Agriculture* ; Western's *Address to the Landowners of the United Kingdom* ; Sir John Sinclair's *Address to the Owners and Occupiers of Land*.

MISCELLANEA.

The lectures of " Mr. Lawrence, the celebrated anatomist," delivered before the Royal College of Surgeons, were pirated by a bookseller named Smith, and, on an injunction granted, Smith appealed to the Lord Chancellor on the ground that the book was not entitled to the protection of the law, " being irreligious and denying the immortality of the soul " (*Annual Register*, 62).

CHAPTER XII

1823. THE PASSING AWAY OF AGRICULTURAL DISTRESS

WE saw that, in the end of 1822, heaven sent the farmers all they could ever pray for in the way of abundant crops. And yet the distress seemed as bad as ever. Prices, of course, were low—lower than they had been in thirty years—but this, one would think, was to be expected. Gregory King's Law—that, when there Gregory ensues a scarcity in an absolute necessary of life, and the quantity King's law. falls off in an arithmetical ratio, the price is exalted in a geometrical one, with its corollary that, when there is a surplus, the price will fall in the inverse ratio—had never been denied. And no one but a singularly short-sighted person could dream that the mere exclusion of foreign grain would keep up prices if a home harvest yielded so much beyond the average consumption of the nation. All the same, surely something must be wrong when a splendid harvest ruined those who raised it. The true explanation—that a system which encouraged the extension of cultivation to poor and costly soils, by the stimulus of a regulated monopoly, must end in disaster [1]—was often enough given, but the ears of those who had sunk their capital in this extension were stopped against the truth, and all they could suggest was something to " mend matters," while insisting on the retention of the monopoly. Hence the " causes " alleged and the " remedies " called for, and the connection of the remedies with the causes, become more and more difficult to follow and explain.

As has been said, the *mot d'ordre* of the agricultural agitation "Equitable in 1821, was the currency, and, in 1822, the taxation. In 1823, it adjustment of contracts," was the currency again—the difference being that, in 1821, the favourite remedy was to raise the prices by again debasing the standard ; in 1823, to revise contracts made during the period of

[1] See Whitmore, *infra*, 141.

the debased standard. This was called the " equitable adjustment of contracts." [1]

All January and February, the price of wheat remained at the level of 40/-, and the King's Speech in February spoke of the continued depression of the agricultural interest—" the most important of them all." Before Parliament met, then, there remained a considerable amount of agitation throughout the country, engineered for political purposes, and very strong language was used. But the portentous alliance of the country gentlemen and the Radicals got a shock at Norwich, where a great meeting was captured by Cobbett, and a petition drawn up by him was carried with rapturous exclamations, recommending such trifles as appropriation of part of the property of the Church and the sale of the crown lands for the liquidation of the debt, an equitable adjustment with regard to the public debt, and also with regard to all debts and contracts between man and man, suspension for one year of all distraints for rent, all process for tithes, and all processes arising out of mortgage, bond, annuity, or other contract affecting house or land.[2]

The new struggle began in the Commons on 14th February, when Lethbridge complained .that the Speech had given no pledge that anything would be done. Again the old statements were repeated ; the distress was due to the policy of the legislature, which allowed the import of cheap foreign produce, etc. But Canning at once intimated that it was the sincere, deliberate, and honest conviction of the Government that no measure could be devised for the immediate relief of agriculture ; the only thing proposed would be the remission of direct taxes, to be submitted by the Chancellor of the Exchequer.[3]

preached by Stanhope

But the new cry was first sounded in the House of Lords, and by Stanhope. Moving the addition of a clause to the Address, he argued that the agricultural distress proceeded from the return to cash payments—" Could any favourable season or abundant harvest by any possibility have had the effect of lowering the price of corn 50 per cent. in three years ? "—and boldly advocated cutting down the interest on the debt. " If we contemplate,"

---

[1] Wodehouse, the Tory member for Norfolk, used the expression at a Pitt Club dinner in November 1822, and claimed to be the first person to do so—seemingly afraid that Cobbett would take the doubtful honour.

[2] When the petition was presented, Coke did his best to minimise the gravity of Cobbett's success, and only one member professed agreement with it.

[3] *Hansard*, viii. 117.

he said, " the effects which the change of currency has produced
upon taxation, we find that the public annuitants now receive
twice as much in the produce of the earth as they did in 1819,
and nearly twice as much as they then did in other commodities.
Is not this to be considered as a most nefarious fraud practised
on the nation and as an act of public robbery ? " [1]

Throughout the Session, the revision of contracts was repeated
in different ways, and with varying emphasis, and it became clear
that the idea had caught hold.   Western professed himself entirely and Western,
persuaded of it.   As the year went on, indeed, the feet were cut
from the agitation by the sudden return of high prices.   Wheat
was over 50/- in March ; over 60/- in June.   In view of the changed
position, Lethbridge withdrew a motion of which he had given
notice, on the ground that the state of things now afforded a hope
of great alleviation, if not entire extinction, of the distress. [2]   Western
however, persevered, although it is not easy to see what he now
hoped for. [3]   It would seem, indeed, as if the idea of " equitable
adjustment " of the contracts which most affected them had taken
possession of the landed class—the crazy belief that the terms
of mortgages, etc., made years before, could be revised.   At any
rate, on 11th June, Western brought up the evils of the resumption
of cash payments, with, he affirmed, increasing confidence in the
correctness of his views.   The metallic currency, he would contend should have been established in 1819 as near the average
value as possible of the paper currency which had lasted twenty-
two years, and this could have been easily ascertained by " the
paramount and real standard of value, Bread Corn "—every one
knew that corn was more steady in value over a long period of
years than the precious metals.

Ricardo, in reply, made what was for him a long speech—sub- and consequently written out by himself for *Hansard*, and sent to the Ricardo.
editor only a few days before his death.   What he approved in
Peel's Bill, he said, was that it established a fixed currency.   He
had cared little comparatively what the standard established was
—whether it continued at its then value, or went back to the old

---

[1] *Hansard*, viii. 12.   This was Cobbett's teaching.

[2] *Ibid.* ix. 609.   He was bitterly abused for this by Cobbett, who had
now discovered that the rise in prices was due to the season, and must be
injurious to the manufacturers and all the labouring classes !

[3] *Ibid.* ix. 833.   It was noted that, at least when he began his speech,
none of the country gentlemen was present—" though they are the first
victims," he said bitterly, " they are the last to perceive it."

level ; his object had been a fixed standard of some description
or other. What he sought was to guard against the many and
the severe mischiefs of a fluctuating currency ; fluctuating, not
according to the variations in the value of the standard itself,
from which no currency could be exempted, but fluctuating according to the caprice or interest of a company of merchants, who,
before the passing of that Act had the power to increase or diminish
the amount of money, and consequently to alter the value whenever
they thought proper. Owing to the unnecessary and mischievous
operations of the Bank subsequently, he was ready to admit that
the Bill had raised the value of the currency 10 per cent. Western
had affirmed that it was 30 per cent., but his chief proof rested
on the altered price of corn, of which the cause had, of course,
been the abundance of the crops. To prove this, he recalled
Western's own words in 1816 : " It is perfectly well known," he
had said, " that, if there is a small deficiency of supply, the price
will rise in a ratio far beyond any proportion of such deficiency ;
the effect, indeed, is almost incalculable. So likewise, on a surplus
of supply beyond demand, the price will fall in a ratio almost tenfold
the amount of such surplus." He then repeated the argument
he had given on a previous occasion.[1] " As the honourable gentle-

---

[1] On 26th February, when irritated at the perpetual attacks on the fundholder as the person who was profiting at the loss of the country. " If the
interest which the fundholder had been paid in depreciated currency, upon
capital which, when lent, had not been depreciated, were to be set against the
interest which he was receiving in undepreciated currency now upon capital,
which, when lent, had been depreciated, not only would the loss in the one
case compensate all that had been hitherto paid in the other but would actually
be equal to a perpetual annuity of that amount which he was at present
receiving." Mr Mushett of the Mint, in his *Tables* exhibiting the gain and
loss to the fundholders from the fluctuations in the value of the currency
from 1800 to 1821, had demonstrated this. Of the £800,000,000 of debt,
£400,000,000 were borrowed before the Bank Restriction Bill had operated
any depreciation whatever, and another £100,000,000 had been lent to the
Government before any considerable depreciation had taken place. Hence
there had been £500,000,000 lent to the public in capital which was not
depreciated. Interest in the depreciated currency had been paid on this for
twenty years, and the loss, at simple interest, was about £27,000,000, or, at
compound interest—and that was the fair allowance—about £12,000,000 or
£13,000,000 more. It would appear that the whole loss which the stockholder
had sustained, in consequence of having been paid in a depreciated currency
the interest on the sums borrowed previous to and immediately following 1797,
was about £40,000,000. Take next Mr. Mushett's calculation of the advantages since the depreciation had ceased, by the alteration of the currency.
This he calculated at £2,000,000 per annum. Converting the previous loss
of £40,000,000 into a perpetual annuity, we should also have the sum of
£2,000,000 a year. Thus the profit and loss would be found to balance each
other (*Hansard*, viii. 255).

man stated the question, it would appear as if all the advances
to Government had been in a depreciated currency, and all the
payments from Government to the stockholder in currency of the
mint value." [1]

The Marquis of Titchfield (fourth son of the Duke of Portland) Titchfield's
next took up the advocacy of Western's views, in a long and super- rash speech.
ficial speech—the kind of thing which might be expected from a
young man who started by saying that his own acquaintance with
the subject was very recent, but went on to express his " most
entire confidence that, to understand it sufficiently to decide upon
it, was open to almost any person's comprehension upon a very
little attention to a mere statement of the question." He demanded
justice—simple justice—for the aristocracy of the country, who
would inevitably be ruined, torn from their paternal estates, and
reduced to spend a miserable existence in a foreign land—and all
because, when money was abundant and prices high, they " borrowed
fearlessly," without a suspicion that wheat could ever be 39/- a
quarter—" while they were receiving 140/- they took it for granted
that they might safely calculate upon bad times not bringing it
lower than perhaps 70/- or 80/-." [2] Warming to his subject, he
said that, if the currency had been fixed at a juster standard in
1818, the interference of France in the affairs of Spain would not
have taken place, and committed himself to the monstrous state-

---

[1] Ricardo usually consumed his own smoke, but, on this occasion, he was
tempted to retort with some indignation. Western, in a recent pamphlet,
had said that it required the utmost extent of charity to believe that, in the
advice he (Ricardo) had given, he was not influenced by interested motives.
" He did not pretend to be more exempted from the weaknesses and errors
of human nature than other men, but he could assure the House, and the
member for Essex, that it would puzzle a good accountant to make out on
which side his interest predominated. He would find it difficult himself from
the different kinds of property which he possessed (no part funded property)
to determine the question. But by whom was this effort of charity found so
difficult ? By the honourable gentleman, whose interest in this question could
not, for one moment, be doubted—whose whole property consisted of land—
and who would greatly benefit by any measure which should lessen the value
of money. He imputed no bad motives to the honourable gentleman. He
believed he would perform his duty as well as most men, even when it was
opposed to his interest. But he asked the honourable gentleman to state on
what ground he inferred that he (Ricardo) would, under similar circumstances,
be wanting in his ? "

[2] He felt much relieved, said Huskisson, with unwonted irony, to hear it
stated—though as a great misfortune—by the Marquis that the rents of land
had fallen within a few years from 25 per cent. to 30 per cent. ; he recollected
that the greater part, if not the whole, of the lands which had so fallen had
previously risen to double. This freed his mind from the dread of seeing the
whole of the present race of landlords swept away.

ment that the Government had not stepped forward in defence
of "a cause that it would have been both honourable and wise
to defend" because of our peculiar circumstances with regard to
the debt—"he could not believe that any English Minister, whether
Tory or Whig, would have consented to remain a passive spectator
of these occurrences, or that he would have confined himself to
dispatches politely written, if the public debt had amounted to no
more than such a comparative trifle as four hundred instead of
eight hundred millions." In the same self-satisfied way, he airily
suggested a few of the remedies which might be afforded ; such
as the "equitable adjustment of contracts," altering the standard
to something between £3 17s. 10½d. and £5 4/-, a "sort of Government paper, depreciated in different degrees, in which contracts
of certain debts should be payable." If these remedies were thought
too extensive, "there was one of a smaller description about which
there ought not to be a moment's hesitation—he meant, to alter
the standard from gold to silver. This measure would at once
diminish the burdens of the country 5 or 6 per cent., and it would
be absurd, indeed criminal, to make light even of so small an advantage as that."

Baring

Baring—who may be supposed to have had the last speaker in
his mind when he said that, "in proportion to the difficulties of
this question, individuals were peremptory and obstinate in their
opinions"—while ready to admit the grievous injury which tampering with the currency had inflicted on the aristocracy, and,
indeed, on every private family, could not think that revising the
standard four years after it had been restored was advisable, but

again
advocates the
double
standard.

took the occasion to say a word or two for the double standard.
It would be a great security against any future deviation from a
metallic currency. "Under the present system of a gold circulation,
he did not think that, if the country were again involved in a war,
two campaigns would elapse before all the commercial classes at
least would call out for a return to the happy days of a paper money.
But if the circulation was placed on the broader basis of two metals
to the currency, there would be less danger of resorting again to
the paper system. ... If the Bank had two currencies to work
with, it would greatly facilitate its operations in case of a demand
for the precious metals, as there was no country of Europe in which
silver might not be had in the event of a run on the Bank."[1]

[1] Sir John Sinclair lent his doubtful support to the double standard in a
communication sent to the provincial press during the year.

Peel, in a very sound speech, managed to defend his Act without repeating the old arguments. Agricultural distress was not a new thing since 1819 ; in 1816, Western himself had spoken of the agricultural classes as in a state of hopelessness—of land paying no rent, and not covering its expenses of cultivation. Surely that distress had not been caused by the Bill of 1819 ! As to " equitable adjustments," so confidently spoken of, how was it to be discovered who were the debtors, and who were the creditors, when the individuals were constantly changing, and those who were now the public creditors were not those who originally advanced the money ? " I borrowed money when the pound note was worth only 13/-," said the noble marquis, " and I am called on to pay it back when it is worth 20/-." But he seemed to forget that there were periods when the pound note was worth 15/-, 17/-, 19/-, and sometimes even more than 20/-. How, then, was the particular sum to be fixed at which the adjustment was to be made ? And if improvident speculations were to be made the subject of equitable adjustment, why should the noble lord limit that adjustment to speculators in land ? " It really was a pretty summer amusement which the honourable member had cut out for them when he proposed, on the 11th of June, 1823, to revise all contracts that had taken place since 1793." Huskisson followed and further tore the argument to rags, and, after two evenings' debate, Western got only twenty-seven to vote with him.[1]

Peel's defence of his Act.

For the moment, " equitable adjustment " got its quietus. But, as might be expected, the new Corn Law, although inoperative, pleased nobody, and was not left without criticism. In February, Whitmore raised a discussion on the subject,[2] premising that the reason why he chose that particular time was that it was only at a moment when any alteration in the law was in the future that a sober and rational discussion was possible. The evil which mainly affected the agricultural interests, he said, was the fluctuations of price. Under a law which prohibited the importation of corn till a very high price was reached, there was, inevitably, a rush of capital into agriculture, poor soil brought into cultivation, and old pastures broken up. If the territory was sufficiently extensive, this involved that, in average years, we had a produce sufficient for the consumption of the country ; but it also involved that, in good harvests, we had a superabundance ; and the surplus fell back on the market, and forced prices very low. Then came distress

Whitmore's illuminating statement.

[1] *Hansard*, ix. 834, 902.   [2] *Ibid*. viii. 264.

—deterioration of soil from economising in manure—poor land thrown out of cultivation—and the result, in two or three years, was a positive deficiency of produce. And then the same circle would repeat itself. Applying this to the present position, he was forced to the opinion that we were approaching the final stage thus antici-pated. Owing to the low prices, the consumption of wheat had greatly increased—by 22 per cent., it had been calculated, between 1821 and 1822. The advanced wages of the manufacturing classes had put brown bread almost out of use—they were now using the best wheat.[1] The stocks in the hands of the farmers were running low. On the other hand, a great deterioration in the poor lands had taken place, because the poorer farmers were unable to buy manure, and were using one-half or two-thirds less. He himself had a limework ; the average sale for ten years had been over 42,000 bushels ; in 1821, it was a little over 30,000 ; in 1822, it was a little over 20,000. The " protecting price," in fact, was ruining the farmers. Politically speaking, such a system set class against class ; it embittered the other classes of the community against the aristocracy, who used to be thought their friends and protectors ; it hurt the manufactures on which depended so greatly our strength and prosperity ; and it encouraged the emigration of capital. Considering how encumbered the agriculturists were with the payment of poor rates, he certainly could not be an advocate of free trade in corn. But it was his intention to propose the lowering of the importing price by 2/- a year, till it came down to 60/-—that being the price below which foreign corn could not be imported in any considerable quantity. All that was wanted by the country was to avoid the injurious fluctuations of late years, and to secure a fair level price. And he moved for leave to bring in a bill to amend the Corn Laws on these lines.

Curwen on retention of poor lands.   Curwen, opposing, gave voice again to his old sentiment, that " every acre of land that could be made available should be under cultivation," and admitted that he " was most undoubtedly one of those who would wish that a single quarter of foreign corn might never be imported into this country." But the existing law was, he believed, the best that we could have under existing circumstance. He urged the remission of the taxes on the lowest classes of the labouring community—on malt, which interfered with the con-sumption of " a beverage not more essential to the labourer's comfort and strength than to his happiness and well-being "—on

[1] This is the first statement, I think, of that important historical stage.

candles which cost the poor man 10/- a year—and on the windows
of every cottage under £5 rental.[1] Such a reduction would soon
call into cultivation millions of now unprofitable acres.

Attwood, of course, was faithful to his currency creed. He Attwood.
denied that the great fluctuations in the price of grain were primarily
occasioned by the Corn Laws—the opinion was " erroneous and had
been frequently refuted "—they were due to the metallic currency.
The high prices of 1818, when wheat was 84/-, were " the prices
of the cheap money of the Restriction Act, which operated alike
on all prices ; which increased wages as well as the price of food ;
and which, whilst it gave high prices to the farmer, gave at the
same time to the labourer the means of supporting them," and
made all classes prosperous. Ricardo agreed with Whitmore as
to the effects and dangers of the existing law, and said that the
greatest good would be done by bringing the question before the
House at the present time. But Whitmore did not go far enough :
he left " the mischief of a fixed price " ; and this he considered
a great error. A duty should be imposed on corn equal to the
peculiar burdens borne by the grower of corn, with a corresponding
drawback on exportation. " Then, and then only, would corn
be kept at a price nearly equal to what it was in other countries."
But he would not oppose any measure which was an approach to
a free trade in corn. The motion, however, was lost by 25 to 78.[2]

As has been noted, while politicians were crying haro and alas Prices
over low prices, prices suddenly rose of their own accord, and, at suddenly
the prorogation, the King's Speech spoke of his satisfaction in rise.
contemplating " the gradual abatement of those difficulties from
which the agricultural interest had so long and so severely suffered."
One comes across statements like the following : " Something like
a new era has begun in agriculture ; rents have been reduced and
leases renewed ; things, in short, are getting into something like
their old train—the effects of the revulsion from war to peace are
beginning to disappear." After Parliament had risen, however,
it became evident that the statement had been somewhat premature
—had, in fact, rested on the precarious ground of a rise of prices
in anticipation of a poor harvest. After a winter of the old-fashioned

[1] Curwen's reputation for reliability must have suffered when Huskisson
asked how the penny per lb. duty on candles, say at 40 lbs. a year, could
possibly come to 10/- ; and reminded him that the labourer actually paid
no window tax at all unless his cottage had more than six windows and, even
then, unless he were rated above £5.

[2] *Hansard*, viii. 264.

sort—severe frost and deep snow blocking the roads in the north—
the weather all over the country was wet and bleak, the summer,
one of the coldest on record, and, when the late harvest was gathered,
the deficiency in all kinds of grain was from one-fifth to one-fourth.
Oats was the only crop which, in Scotland at least, came near an
average. Nor were beans, peas, and turnips any better, while
potatoes were particularly poor. The quartern loaf in Scotland
varied between 9d., 10d., and 11d.

The course of wheat prices is rather staggering. Sustained,
perhaps, by the expectation of war—in which, the farmers thought
cheerfully, " Great Britain, as a matter of course, will have to
take a part "—the price kept about 60/- till well on in August,
and fears were expressed that the ports might be opened before
the farmers got their grain to market. But, when the harvest
results were declared, it fell below 47/-, and, in the middle of December, was still under 51/- : the condition of the farmer, said his
own organ hopelessly, is no better than it was. How, then, is the
general conviction to be accounted for, that the agricultural depression was passing away ? Short crops and low prices, one would
think, are surely worse than abundant crops and low prices !

Conviction
that distress
was passing.
The explanation—if there be an explanation—seems to be that
rents and wages were becoming adjusted to the new conditions.
Farmers are apt to make outcry enough when rents are too high ;
perhaps they are not so ready to publish the fact that rents have
been reduced. And the little that is said of wages speaks of reduction, seldom of increase. Meanwhile one notes the growing tendency
to lay some part of the depression at the door of Ireland. Was
it quite fair that Irish corn should be allowed to come in in any
quantity when the cultivators paid less tithe and no poor rate ?
" Assist Ireland with bounties," wrote one in the *Farmer's Magazine*,
" to export her produce to other nations, instead of glutting the
British markets with it."

CHAPTER XIII

1823. INDUSTRY: A QUIETLY PROSPEROUS YEAR

AGAIN and again in the annals of the century one is reminded of the likeness between the individual and the economic organism—that the healthy body is unconscious of its well-being. In this year, it seems peculiarly emphasised : if one did not know how to interpret the silence, it would not be easy to pronounce on the condition of trade and manufacture. The King's Speech, indeed, spoke of " the increasing activity which pervaded the manufacturing districts and of the flourishing condition of commerce in most of its principal branches." And the inference that industry was quietly and steadily pursuing the up-grade is confirmed by an enquiry which Peel made in the beginning of the year. In order Peel's second to compare the current state of things with the statement made inquiry. by Brougham in March, 1817,[1] he addressed letters to various local and municipal authorities in the manufacturing districts. The account from Huddersfield was that the working classes were never better employed ; spinners were receiving 25/- a week, and weavers from 18/- to 21/- ; there was a great increase in building ; the poor rates, which had been 10/- in 1815, had been reduced to 6/8. In Sheffield, he found the poor rates reduced from £36,000 in 1820 to £19,000, with an estimated fall for the current year to £13,000 ; scarcely a single house was unoccupied. In Halifax, the labouring classes were employed and generally well off ; the poor rates greatly diminished ; and there was a large increase in houses let from £7 to £8 per year. In Birmingham, which had suffered terribly after the war, the whole body of the working classes was well employed ; a great number of new houses had been built ; the poor rates had fallen from £52,000 in 1820 to £20,000. In Manchester, the cotton trade was larger than ever before known ; the number of buildings

[1] *Hansard*, xxxv. 1004. *Economic Annals, 1801-1820,* 594.

146   Industry : a quietly Prosperous Year   1823

in course of erection greater than at any former time ; fine cotton
spinners earned 30/- per week, coarse spinners from 20/- to 28/-,
cotton weavers, 10/-, silk weavers, 16/- ; poor rates had fallen
from £27,000 in 1820 to £15,000.   In Bolton, there was more
employment than ever was known ; population was rapidly increasing, and many new buildings were being erected.[1]

Flourishing
commerce and
manufactures. The Speech at the prorogation in July, again, spoke of the flourishing condition of all branches of our commerce and manufactures,
and, that the latter part of the year witnessed similar progress, is
confirmed by local newspapers.   In Blackburn at midsummer,
owing to great demand for cotton twist on the Continent, the
manufacture was very busy ; seventy new cotton mills had been
built or were in course of erection—two of them 200 yards in length
by 20 in height, with two steam engines of 70 and 100 horse-power.
In Glasgow, for the past eighteen months the cotton trade had
been more prosperous than usual, employment regular, and wages
adequate : a great many additions had been made to the old cotton
mills and new ones built—one costing £40,000 : the coarse linen
trade also was in a very thriving state : it was, besides, an almost
unprecedented year of building, and all building operatives were
in demand : the consumption of stones and bricks had been so
great that a number of quarries and brickfields were exhausted—
bricks which had sold at 25/- in the early part of the year were
at 40/- in the end.[2]

All over the manufacturing districts of England one finds the
statement that goods were bought up as soon as made.   The total
consumption of raw cotton exceeded that of 1822 by one-fifth ;
the output of woollen and silk goods increased ; the demand for
iron, hardware, and cutlery fully revived after the long stagnation
in these trades—even the gun trade was fully active ; shipping
participated in the recovery and shipbuilding with it.   The only
complaint made was that profits were low—a welcome and healthy
change from the bold speculation of the last twenty or thirty years
which had reared so many princely fortunes.   In December the

[1] *Hansard*, ix. 925.

[2] It was in this year that the deepening of the Clyde at Glasgow began to be
seriously entertained, under the stimulus of decreasing entries from foreign
ports.   In the end of the eighteenth century the river was fordable at the
Broomielaw, in the heart of the city.   Previous to 1818, no vessels engaged
in foreign trade came up the river further than Greenock or Port-Glasgow.
The new steam dredger was introduced in 1824, and in 1825 the work was
actually begun—to the great disgust of Greenock, which pronounced the
scheme chimerical, hopeless, and impracticable.

3 per cents. were at 87—"investors not knowing what to do with their money."

Now and then, however, one is reminded of the other side to all this. In May, for instance, a petition, numerously signed, was presented from the manual weavers of Stockport, representing their great distress from the extremely low rate of wages, the remedy proposed being that the House should fix a minimum rate of wages ; complaining also that certain improvements in machinery had had the effect of reducing the quantity of employment of those who wove by hand. The debate was notable for the reiteration on the part of Ricardo that the extensive use of machinery, by throwing a large portion of labour upon the market, while, on the other hand, there might not be a corresponding increase of demand for it, must, in some degree, operate prejudicially to the working classes. But still he would not tolerate any law to prevent the use of machinery.[1] In the same month, again, a petition was presented to the House from the cotton weavers of Manchester, attributing their present distress to the employment of machinery. Huskisson, on presenting, expressed his dissent from it. Peel said that, from the enquiry he had made, he could say that the wages of labour were such, considering the price of provisions, that the weavers could afford to live in comparative comfort.[2]

Only once do I find any record of industrial disturbances. It was in Glasgow, in September, when the proprietors of the power-

The handloom weavers.

Disturbances in Glasgow.

[1] *Hansard*, ix. 598. *Vide* his *Principles*, chap. xxxi. The two points on which he dwelt now were that, if we did without machinery, other nations, to whom we sold, would not, and that the supply of low-class labour, when men were "made such machines of by the poor laws," might easily be redundant. The reminder has a wider scope, and, as such, is perhaps of more importance now than it was then when machinery was comparatively in its infancy, and was not so definitely a rival of labour. The best friends of the human worker are those who point out to him that, so far as he is fit only to do work that machinery can do better, the value of his labour will fall—that is, the progress of the production of wealth will mean lower wages—and that his safety is to train himself for that work where machinery either needs him as complement or cannot compete with him—that is, where he uses his brains. The lesson gets a curious emphasis in the intimation, in this same year, that James Cross of Paisley had invented a harness-weaving loom which dispensed with the previous auxiliary labour of the " draw boy."

[2] *Ibid.* viii. 1292. In 1819 (*Economic Annals, 1801-20,* 711) we found an " abstract idea " ventilated, that machinery should be taxed, in order to equalise its product with that of human labour which paid all manner of taxes on the necessaries of life. In 1822, Maxwell of Pollok, it seems, attracted some attention in Scotland by openly recommending the imposition of taxation " on that description of machinery which came most directly in competition with human labour." On the present occasion, however, he expressed doubts as to the propriety of his former advocacy.

loom factories appear to have taken on new tenters and dressers after some dispute. At the breakfast hour a crowd of several thousands assembled, and began to throw stones and roughly handle the intruders. The police was overpowered, and a strong force of the Enniskillen Dragoons was brought up from the barracks. At seven o'clock, when again some of the new hands were preparing to go home under military protection, the rioters began to break the factory windows. In one mill, " while the work of destruction was going forward, the new hands sallied out in a body, and, being mostly provided with pistols for their own protection, fired several of them among the mob. Not expecting such a reception, the terrified delinquents fled in all directions, and the streets soon afterward became as quiet as usual. The next morning, no opposition was offered at any of the mills." [1]

Steam navigation.   The progress of steam navigation is marked by an advertisement of a packet, engined by Boulton and Watt, running from London to Rotterdam and back within a week, and by the notice of a steamship of 500 tons register, built at Calcutta and launched in July. One notes that, in May, 215 miles of streets in London were lit by gas.

Foreign trade.   This growing activity, however, was not strikingly reflected in the figures of foreign trade—perhaps for the reason that the exports, as we saw, had already risen in the previous year by £3½ millions. There was, indeed, a slight diminution both in exports and re-exports ; but the imports showed an increase of about £5 millions. The figures are as follows : Imports, £35,798,000 ; Re-exports, £8,603,000 ; Exports, £43,826,000. The value of the Real Exports was £35,357,000.

The number of ships built and registered in the United Kingdom was 594, representing a tonnage of 63,151.

[1] *Edinburgh Magazine*, October, 502.

CHAPTER XIV

1823. ROBINSON'S FIRST BUDGET

AMONG the changes made in the Cabinet before Parliament met was the appointment of a new Chancellor of the Exchequer. Vansittart, whom Huskisson once called " the real blot and sin of the Government," [1] retired from the office which he had held but scarcely adorned since the beginning of Lord Liverpool's administration in 1812, and became Chancellor of the Duchy of Lancaster as Lord Bexley. With that strange perversity which, so often in English history, has put the care of the national purse into the hands of an inferior man, Huskisson, who had been Chief Commissioner for Woods and Forests since 1814, was passed over, and Robinson, President of the Board of Trade since 1818, [2] took Vansittart's place. *A new Chancellor of the Exchequer.*

The King's Speech had promised that the estimates would be found materially below the expenditure of the past year : the diminution of charge, combined with the progressive improvement of the revenue, had produced a surplus exceeding expectation ; and it seemed that, without affecting public credit, a further considerable reduction might be made in the burdens of the people. The new Chancellor of the Exchequer lost no time in following this up. On 21st February, he anticipated the Budget by what he called an Exposition of the Financial Situation of the Country. [3] *His Financial Exposition.*

---

[1] This, however, was not the popular opinion. "There never existed a statesman who had fewer infirmities and more virtues than Mr. Vansittart," said the *Glasgow Herald* on his retiral. Why Creevey called him " Mouldy," I do not know.

[2] Frederick John Robinson, afterwards Viscount Goderich, and, later, first Earl of Ripon. Robinson was universally liked as a courteous and liberal-minded gentleman, whose manners disarmed opposition. His speaking was sensible, agreeable, and "with a great tone of candour and perhaps rather much attempt at humour."

[3] *Hansard*, viii. 194.

The actual revenue of the past year had been £54½ millions, and the expenditure £49½ millions, realising, as Vansittart had expected, a surplus of £5 millions. His estimate for the coming year was, roughly, a revenue of £57 millions and an expenditure of £50 millions ; showing a surplus of over £7 millions, of which he proposed to devote £5 millions to the reduction of debt, and the balance to remission of taxation. In detail, his calculation was :

REVENUE.

Customs - - - - - - - -	£10,500,000
Excise - - - - - - - - -	26,000,000
Stamps - - - - - - - -	6,600,000
Post Office - - - - - - - -	1,400,000
Assessed Taxes - - - - - -	5,900,000
Land Tax - - - - - - -	1,200,000
Miscellaneous - - - - - -	600,000
Half-Pay Annuities - - - - -	4,800,000
	£57,000,000

EXPENDITURE.

Total Charge of Unredeemed Debt - - -	£28,124,000
Other Charges on Consolidated Fund - - -	2,050,000
Half-Pay Annuities - - - - -	2,800,000
Army - - - - - - - - -	7,362,000
Navy - - - - - - - - -	5,442,000
Ordnance - - - - - - -	1,380,000
Miscellaneous - - - - - -	1,494,000
Interest of Exchequer Bills - - - -	1,200,000
	£49,852,000

His reasons for estimating the revenue somewhat sanguinely were : the increasing consumption of excisable articles—beer, bricks, candles, hides, glass, malt, paper, pepper, printed goods, salt, soap, British spirits, starch, tea, tobacco—as compared with the average of the three preceding years ; the improved condition of the people in the manufacturing districts ; and the savings banks' returns, both as regards contributors and amount of deposits. The taxation which he proposed to remit was confined to the Assessed Taxes— those among them which were particularly vexatious, and difficult to collect, and which weighed most heavily on persons connected with agriculture. Dividing the various taxes under this category into those on (1) windows ; (2) houses ; (3) horses, carriages, and servants ; (4) dogs, armorial bearings, game certificates, etc. ; he would leave (2) and (4) untouched. In (1), there would be a

Assessed
Taxes
reduced,

diminution of 50 per cent. on all windows, and a total remission of the tax on all those on the ground floor of shops whether attached to a house or not. In (3) he would remove entirely the tax on persons employed in trade and husbandry who might be employed occasionally in some other menial capacity, such as the care of a horse or as occasional gardener ; [1] that on the lower classes of taxed carts, the 3/- duty on ponies and mules, and the 3/- duty on horses employed by small farmers who were also engaged in trade. And, on the remaining taxes on horses, carriages, and servants, he proposed a reduction of 50 per cent. This would amount in all to £2,200,000. But, as regarded Ireland, the whole of the Assessed Taxes which remained after the repeal of the Hearth and Window Tax in 1822 —representing about £100,000—would be removed, and some alterations would also be proposed involving a large reduction of the duty on spirits.[2]

and, in Ireland, removed.

Robinson was warmly complimented from all sides ; even the leading members of the Opposition vied with each other to eulogise his clear and satisfactory statement. Baring pronounced it what the honour of the British nation required in a minister of his rank. Hume had never heard a speech from the ministerial side which gave him more pleasure ; no Chancellor of the Exchequer for many years had given so luminous a statement. Ricardo said that the science of Political Economy, which he had so often to defend, had never before had so able an expositor. There was one point, however, on which he differed from him. In his surplus of £7 millions was contained an amount of £2 millions, got by putting on one side of the account £2,800,000 to be paid for half-pay and pensions, and, on the other, £4,800,000 to be obtained from the trustees who were to pay the pensions. But who were these trustees paying the £4,800,000, but the same persons to whom the £2 millions were to be repaid ? Undoubtedly, from the assumed surplus of £7 millions, must be deducted those £2 millions which the Sinking

---

[1] In 1821, Curwen had said that a poor woman in the neighbourhood of Berwick, who had paid sixpence to a man to prune a favourite fruit tree, was surcharged with an " occasional gardener," and that her goods were actually sold to pay the tax (*Hansard*, v. 1185).

[2] This latter alteration eventually took the shape of a reduction to 10/6 per gallon in England, and to 2/- in Ireland and Scotland. It was intended as an effectual blow at illicit distillation, and, as a fact, was so successful that, within the next two years, there was an actual gain to the revenue. In 1840, we find Robinson (now Lord Ripon) claiming that his surplus had enabled him to make the successful experiment (*Hansard*, liv. 476).

Fund itself was to supply, and the clear Sinking Fund, accordingly, was £3 millions, not £5 millions.[1]

The Dead Weight Scheme.

Vansittart's unfortunate Dead Weight Scheme now took on another shape. As we saw, no purchaser had come forward when it was carried through. But now the Bank of England offered to take part of the contract to run for five and a quarter years. The acceptance was keenly opposed by Grenfell, Baring, and Ricardo as an extremely improvident bargain for the public, and a violation of the statute which forbade the Bank being a dealer in public securities. Sir Joseph Yorke put what seems a pertinent question. He could understand the policy if, at the end of forty-five years, every man on half-pay was to be as dead as Julius Caesar. But what was to be done with those persons who were daily coming on the half-pay list ?—for there was a constant supply of them.[2]

A new Sinking Fund.

The allocation of £5 millions to the reduction of debt was not passed without much discussion. The state of the old Sinking Fund was honestly faced by Robinson ; " under the existing law, the total amount annually paid over (out of the Consolidated Fund) to the Commissioners for the Reduction of the National Debt was about £15 or £16 millions, but he conceived that, as a great portion of this amount was at present either lent to the Government or diverted to other uses, it was unnecessary to continue such a complicated machinery," and he proposed to repeal " those parts of the Sinking Fund Acts which directed the payment of the particular sums that were now payable out of the Consolidated Fund to the Commissioners." They were now, he said, to start a new Sinking Fund on the lines of the old. The £5 millions would be paid over, in quarterly instalments, to the Commissioners, who would use them to buy up a corresponding amount of debt. But the debt thus purchased would not be cancelled, but go on bearing interest, and this interest would be intercepted by the Commissioners, who would lay it aside to constitute " that sort of principal or capital which Mr. Pitt originally contemplated," till such time as the interest regularly accumulating would reach

[1] At the same time, Ricardo avowed himself so concerned as to the indispensable necessity of getting rid of the tremendous debt, as to repeat his suggestion of 1819, that there ought to be a general contribution from the capital of the country for that purpose. He himself would contribute any proportion of his own property if others would do the same. On Ricardo's scheme, see Cannan, *The Economic Outlook*, p. 133.

[2] *Hansard*, viii. 682, 822, 1123.

an amount equal to 1 per cent. on the total of the debt, funded
and unfunded.[1]

Calcraft at once brought up a recommendation that the whole Ricardo
surplus should be appropriated to the relief of taxation. Ricardo disapproves.
backed him up—not that he did not approve of a real Sinking Fund,
but that he did not think the national purse safe in the hands
of the present Ministers ; it was too great a temptation to entrust
them with. There was every reason to believe that this Sinking
Fund would become fictitious ; every Sinking Fund had, in its
origin, been real, but every one had been turned from its purpose.[2]
Had it not been said in so many words that the Sinking Fund
would furnish ministers with the means of going to war in cases
of extremity ? If that was the real reason, why call it a Sinking
Fund ? Tierney, adverting to the "clear surplus of revenue,"
pertinently asked what was to be done in the case of any deficiency
—the only resource would be to impose new taxes to make good
the deficiency, as no resort could be had to borrowing. Liverpool,
however, rested on the fact that, since 1816, £22 millions per annum
of taxes had been remitted—fully one-third of the taxation of the
country during the later years of the war ; it was time, he said,
to look the financial system of the country in the face, and it was
impossible to place that system upon a solid basis without an
efficient Sinking Fund. Robinson's proposition, accordingly, was
carried.[3]

---

[1] It will be seen that this is just No. 7 in the financial proposals put forward
by Londonderry in 1822. The Act (4 Geo. IV., c. 19) bears that the payment
of all sums then charged upon and issuable out of the Consolidated Fund to
the Commissioners should cease on 5th April, 1823, and that the Capital Stock
held by the Commissioners should be cancelled on that date, "and interest
to cease." Presumably, the £5 millions surplus of 1822 was devoted to the
reduction of debt in the old way—by being added to the old Sinking Fund.
The history of the Fund is given in the Report of the proceedings of the
Commissioners for the Reduction of the National Debt from 1786 to 1890
(C. 6539, 1891).

[2] The Sinking Fund instituted by Walpole in 1716, which was directed
"to and for none other use, intent, or purpose whatsoever," and had for
some years made effectual progress in reducing the debt, was abandoned by
himself in 1733, when he took half a million from it for the purpose of keeping the Land Tax at 1/- in the pound : "The honourable gentleman," said
Pulteney, "has been called, and once had the vanity to call himself, the father
of the Sinking Fund ; but, if Solomon's judgment was right, he who is thus
for splitting and dividing the child can never be deemed the true father."
Thereafter, so far from possessing any efficacy as a Sinking Fund, it soon
came to be looked upon as the principal fund upon which ordinary items of
expenditure could conveniently be charged.

[3] Hansard, viii. 340, 501, 534, 543, 579, 635. I daresay many of those who
supported the Sinking Fund did so because the doctrine that the Debt was

Hume again.   When the various votes passed through the House, no great
discussion was raised and no change was made. Hume, however,
continued his ungrateful task of calling attention to all expenses
which might, in his opinion, be economised; moving reductions
on the army, navy, ordnance, and miscellaneous estimates; protesting regarding the crown lands, the Irish yeomanry, the expense
of colonial governments; and, finally, proposing to dispense with
the Lord Lieutenant of Ireland and all offices in connection with
him.[1]

Tallow
candles.
Only one attempt was made to extend the Government's relief
of taxation. This was in the shape of a motion to repeal the tax
on tallow candles. The annual amount yielded to the exchequer
was £313,000 in England, and £16,500 in Scotland—where the duty
was about one-twentieth part of the English duty. It was a tax
on the poor man's farthing dip, a necessity of his labour in winter
time, costing him, perhaps, 3d. a day out of his wage. The manufacturer, too, suffered excessively from the restrictions of the excise
laws—one maker was quoted as having taken no fewer than thirty-
three oaths since last July! Robinson's reply was the old one—
that the revenue could not spare £150,000 more; that other branches
had more need of consideration and other taxes were more loudly
complained of, such as those on coal, beer, and tobacco. It was
the intention of the Government, moreover, in the next Session, to
abolish the lottery—he would propose the lottery resolutions this

not sacred had spread from Cobbett to the landed classes. On the other hand,
one should not condemn too hastily the many who conscientiously advocated
taking the Sinking Fund for taxation. They had no thought of repudiation.
No stipulation had been made about repayment—the debt was an interminable
annuity—and, so long as the national credit was upheld, no creditor was
likely to want repayment. And it ˙was argued that the growth of wealth
was being checked by the many taxes which weighed directly and indirectly
on industry, and that the resumption of a Sinking Fund after a few years of
" breathing time " would find the national thews and sinews both rested and
strengthened. " There should be no hesitation," said Parnell in 1830, " about
suspending the Sinking Fund, till funds could be got for it without doing so
much injury to industry " (*Financial Reform*, 221).

[1] " The invariable principle on which he acted," said one, " was that wrong
could be found in everything." In some of these efforts he was seconded by
Creevey, who, among other things, rooted up a curious precedent of economy
in the conduct of Queen Elizabeth when, on one occasion, there was a deficit
of one-half, and her Chancellor of the Exchequer announced that her Majesty
had supplied the rest out of her own revenues, " sparing from herself to serve
the necessity of the realm, and shunning thereby loans upon interest as a most
pestilential canker that is able to devour even the state of princes." Nor
did he hesitate to draw the moral that giving up part of the Civil List would
have " most beneficial consequences."

year for the last time. The latter announcement was received
with cheers, and the tallow candles motion was negatived without
a division.[1]

When the Budget was opened formally on 2nd July, little change
was made. The Supply, which had been put at £16,600,000 in
February, was now close on £17,000,000. But there was a more
than corresponding increase in the Ways and Means, which were
now taken at £17,385,000; and the surplus had risen to eight
millions instead of seven. The extra—which amounted to about
half a million net—was unappropriated, and no further reduction
was made in taxation.[2]

In the list of Acts passed during this Session appears one under Intermediate
the curious title, " An Act to Encourage the Consumption of Beer " Beer.
(c. 51). Its history is as follows. There were at this time two
duties payable, one of 10/- per barrel on strong beer, the other of,
2/- on table beer. The want of an intermediate strength was said
to be a hardship. To provide for this, it was proposed that brewers
should be allowed to brew a beer of not less than five or more than
five and a half barrels of 36 gallons each for every quarter of malt,
at a duty of 5/- per barrel, and that licences could be taken out by
any one for the sale of such a beer—not to be consumed on the
premises. The seller would have considerable advantages over the
publican, as he would not require to pay the usual licence, and would
not be under the control of the magistrates. Such beer could be
sold for 2½d. per pot. It would be a sound drink, and the increased
consumption would, incidentally, benefit the agricultural classes.
But, to secure the revenue against fraud—and the consumer against
prejudice—from the temptation on the brewer to mix this with
the strong beer which had paid the 10/- duty, it was provided that
this " intermediate beer " should be brewed only in a separate
building at least 200 yards away from the ordinary brew-house.
This last clause excited vehement hostility, as either crippling the
manufacturer of the new beer, or compelling the sinking of fresh
capital in what was avowedly an " experiment." Ricardo and

---

[1] *Hansard*, ix. 390.

[2] *Ibid.* ix. 1412. While the preliminary statement of February was a
simple and clear presentation of the entire revenue and expenditure, the Budget
remained in its old form. The income of the Consolidated Fund (£46,000,000)
and its charge (£38,000,000) showed a " surplus on the Consolidated Fund "
of £8,760,000. The lottery was £200,000, and there was a new sum of £90,000
representing eighteen months' charge, payable by the East India Company on
account of half pay and pensions of troops employed exclusively in their
interest.

others pointed out that the " gloomy control of the excise " could
be avoided, and the unfair advantage of those who were rich
enough to brew their own beer removed, by taking the tax off
beer altogether and putting it on to malt. " The whole quantity
of malt consumed in England," said Maberly, " was about 26
million bushels, and, of this, nearly 7½ millions were consumed by
the rich in private brewing and thus paid no beer duty." The Bill,
however, got through.[1]

[1] *Hansard*, viii. 646, 661 ; ix. 214, 592, 975, 992, 1432.

CHAPTER XV

1823. TOWARDS FREE TRADE

As we have seen, the first steps in the new commercial policy had been taken by Wallace, who had held office as Vice-President of the Board of Trade since 1818. As Chairman of the Committee on Free Trade which reported in 1820, he had revised the Timber Duties in 1821, and recast the Navigation Acts in 1822. When moving the reappointment of the Committee in February, he could say that none of the evils confidently predicted from these measures had happened : both the Norway trade and the North American trade had actually increased ; foreign vessels in danger of ship-wreck, no longer deterred by heavy duties, had found refuge in our ports ; several nations had placed English ships on the same footing as their own ; the old prejudice of British manufacturers, that every advantage gained for a foreigner was a positive injury to them, was disappearing.[1] For reasons which have never been made clear,[2] when Robinson, then President of the Board of Trade, became Chancellor of the Exchequer, Wallace was not shifted up, but became Master of the Mint. The occasion was taken, however, to render a very sincere tribute to him. There was but one opinion among the merchants of London, said Baring, and it was that, since the first establishment of the Board, all the exertions of all its former presidents were not, when united, equal to those which had been made by the right honourable gentleman alone during the time he had filled the office. Ricardo paid his tribute of respect to his merits : much as his plans had benefited the commerce of

The praise of Wallace.

---

[1] David Hume was far in advance of his times when he ended his essay, " On the Jealousy of Trade," with the words : " Not only as a man, but as a British subject, I pray for the flourishing commerce of Germany, Spain, Italy, and even France itself."

[2] It was said that " feelings of delicacy " had induced him to relinquish his office (*Hansard*, viii. 105).

the country, they would have benefited it still more had all of them been fully carried into effect ; and Hume and Canning swelled the chorus of praise. Happily, however, the succession followed a legitimate line : Huskisson became President of the Board of Trade, and the most notable economic events of the year mark the beginning of his regime. But it is only fair to Wallace's memory to recall that the first measures were merely the carrying out of the plans laid down in his Report.

Warehousing Bill. One of these was the Warehousing Bill, the object of which was to allow foreigners to deposit their goods in British warehouses, and to take them out for exportation without payment of duty.[1] The Bill was cordially approved by Ricardo, and there was no opposition to its principle. But several changes were made in detail as it passed through the House ; the chief being, that goods warehoused for re-exportation could be taken out for home consumption on paying the difference ; that stores not consumed on one voyage might be transferred to another ship going on another destination ; and, in deference to Irish feeling, that foreign linens were exempted from the warehousing privilege. On this occasion, Sir John Newport, a former Chancellor of the Irish Exchequer, took the opportunity of saying that, having on former occasions opposed the principle of a free trade, he now considered the opinions which he formerly entertained upon that subject to be quite erroneous, and had arrived at the conviction that the trade of Ireland would be greatly improved by throwing it quite open ; an opinion in favour of a free trade was fast gaining ground in that country.[2]

Reciprocity of Duties. The other, the Reciprocity of Duties Bill, was no less than an entire departure from the principle which had, up till then, governed our foreign commerce. The policy embodied in the Navigation

---

[1] The " natural situation of this realm " suggested to statesmen, as early as the time of Charles II., that England might become an entrepôt for the world. Before there were any warehouses under the King's Lock, a merchant was allowed to store his importations in his own warehouses upon payment of a small portion of the duty, giving bond for the payment of the remainder within nine or twelve months. By the 12 Chas. II., in the case of most articles, a drawback of half the amount first paid was allowed if the goods were exported within the time mentioned. The system grew, and the facilities were extended by the Warehousing Act of 1803, but were confined to the Port of London. Wallace, in 1821, echoing the First Report of his Committee, avowed the principle in the words, " I wish to give to the commerce of foreign nations the freest possible access for the purpose of exportation from England. I am desirous of making this country the general depot, the great emporium of the commerce of the world " (*Hansard*, v. 1292; *Customs Tariffs Blue Book*, 41).

[2] *Hansard*, viii. 642, 666, 1121

Act, of imposing higher duties on cargoes brought in foreign vessels and giving smaller drawbacks, said Huskisson in June, was all very well so long as the nations with which we traded acquiesced. But first the United States retaliated by imposing duties upon all articles imported into that country in British ships, and, as consequence, two sets of ships, British and American, were employed, each leaving its own ports in ballast. To get rid of this inconvenience, we were obliged, in 1815, to place American vessels, with respect to the duties, on the same footing as British. Then Portugal retaliated, and we placed her on the same footing. The Netherlands, in 1821, passed a law allowing a premium of 10 per cent. upon all articles imported in Dutch vessels—a differential duty of 10 per cent. upon all others. And now Prussia had raised the duties on our ships, intimating that she would go further if we continued our present policy. In such circumstances, it was obvious that we must either commence a commercial war, or admit other powers to a perfect equality and reciprocity of shipping duties. The latter, he was persuaded, would lead to an increase of the commercial advantages of this country, as being that which had the largest trade, and, at the same time, promote a better political feeling among the maritime powers. What he meant to propose, then, was that our duties and drawbacks should be imposed and allowed upon all goods equally, whether carried in British or in foreign vessels ; giving the King in council a power to declare that such regulations should extend to all countries inclined to act upon a system of reciprocity, but reserving to the same authority the power of continuing the present restrictions with respect to those powers who should decline to do so.

One or two members, as might be expected, said that this would ruin the shipping trade, but generally the proposals were welcomed, and the relative Resolutions were agreed to. Parliament, said Ricardo, " had at length begun to find out that restrictions on commerce were restrictions, not on other countries, but on our-selves. It certainly was a question of policy whether England should take off the duties without receiving reciprocal advantage from foreign powers ; but, if foreign powers recognised the same liberal principles, there could be no doubt that the advantage to England would be double the advantage which any other country could derive from the regulation." It had been said that personal advantage ought to be sacrificed for the good of the navy, but for that he had no fears : " The state of that navy, the facility for

Ricardo on international trade.

building ships, the superiority of this country in that branch of art, the great capital and enterprise of the people, were so many securities that the navy would not fall into decay. He hoped soon to see Canada deprived of the preference which she enjoyed in the timber trade, and placed, in that respect, upon the same footing as Norway and Sweden." [1]

Retaliation.   The statute, as has been said, which empowered the King in council to place the shipping of a foreign state on the same footing as the shipping of Great Britain, empowered him also to impose countervailing duties in case any foreign state imposed duties upon any goods or shipping of this country arriving in the ports of that foreign state. It is interesting to note that this latter power was first exercised against America. Notwithstanding that the Act of 1822 had settled the permanent intercourse between our West Indian Islands and the United States, allowing the latter to trade with our colonies in their own vessels, the United States continued the alien duty on the tonnage of British ships as well as on the cargo. Countervailing duties accordingly were imposed—though with great regret and reluctance—equal to 94 cents per ton upon the ships and 60 cents per ton upon the cargo. [2]

West Indian sugar preference.   Another Free Trade debate arose over the question of East Indian sugar. As things stood, a duty of 10/- in one instance and of 15/- in another, was imposed on sugar brought from the East Indies extra to that charged on sugar from the West Indies. [3] This was admittedly a duty imposed for the protection of the slave colonies; defended partly on the ground that the colonial sale for sugar was restricted by the " colonial compact " as it was

---

[1] The Reciprocity Treaties concluded on this basis are enumerated in Levi (*History of British Commerce*, 166). The model on which they were drawn up was that adopted by the Convention of Commerce with the United States in 1818, the principle being that " all articles of produce, trade, or manufactures, should be received in either country, on the payment of duties as low as were paid on the same articles by any other country, and that there should be no discriminating duty with respect to the ships in which they were imported " (Huskisson, in *Hansard*, xix. 1769 (1828)).

[2] *Hansard*, x. 154. The American claim—a pretension, said Huskisson, unheard of in the commercial relations of independent states—was that United States products should be admitted into our colonies upon the same terms and duties as the like products of Great Britain. Till this was granted, they would impose alien duties (*Hansard*, xii. 1106). The dispute was not settled and retaliation was indulged in by both sides till 1830.

[3] It seems interesting to find Adam Smith classing sugar along with rum and tobacco as " nowhere necessaries of life," although, he admits, they had become " objects of almost universal consumption."

called, partly on the curious contention that slave labour was
more costly than free labour. For some time, attention had been
drawn to this differential duty, both by the Free Traders and by
the East Indian interests. In 1821, the Manchester Chamber of
Commerce had protested against it.[1] On that occasion, we find
Ricardo objecting to the principle of giving a preference to the
produce of one country as compared with another, and Bennet
adding, particularly when the preference was given to " people
who had vested their capital in dealing in human flesh"; while,
on the other side, it was said that it was impossible for the trade
of the West Indies to go on unless by the aid of such a protecting
duty, and that those colonies were entitled to some relief, as they
were bearing burdens twenty times greater than had been imposed
on any other body.

In the present year, Whitmore and others, asking for a Select
Committee to consider the subject, urged that the colonial compact
had now been revised and relaxed by the recent Acts which allowed
the West Indies commercial intercourse with the United States,
with independent Spanish America, and with the Continent; that
the handicap on the import of East Indian sugar prevented the
soil of that great dominion being turned to the best advantage,
and, by restricting their exports, restricted our exports to a market
of a hundred million heads in favour of a market of some three-
quarters of a million; that such a handicap was particularly unfair
to the East Indies seeing that our cotton manufactures had destroyed and taken the place of the Indian home manufactures;
that the use of sugar as a dead weight to ships returning from
India was essential to our shipping; and that the great interest
was that of the British consumer, who had a right to get his sugar
in the cheapest market. But Huskisson would not grant the
enquiry. He was satisfied that, in the existing circumstances, it
would not be confined to the mere commercial question, but would
be conducted solely with a reference to " the fearful and delicate
subject " of slavery. He intimated, however, that he was willing
that the 15/- duty should be reduced to 10/-.[2]

But the protectionists were not yet convinced that the current Tallow again.
was setting against them. Undeterred by the failure of the previous
year's attempt, we find the butchers of Leadenhall market, in May,
presenting a petition complaining of the glut of Russian tallow,
and praying for a further duty on that import. Lethbridge, who

[1] *Hansard,* v. 508.   [2] *Ibid.* viii. 337 ; ix. 444.

introduced it, argued that the additional duty would not fall on the consumer. Lord Milton retorted ;—how, then, could it be of any use to the Leadenhall butchers ? and Ricardo, observing that the principle advocated might be applied to any foreign commodity whatever, recommended that, as Lethbridge had discovered so easy a way of reducing the National Debt by throwing the burthen of taxation entirely on foreigners, he ought to be made Chancellor of the Exchequer—no other Chancellor had ever yet been found who could impose taxes without inflicting serious burdens on the people.[1]

Protection of the kelp burners. A step essentially protective, however, was taken in the interests of the kelp makers. Mineral alkali, a principal constituent of soap and glass, was got from common salt, from barilla, the ash of certain plants grown in the salt marshes of Spain, and from kelp, the ash of a seaweed growing on rocks. Kelp burning became general in the Hebrides and Orkney after 1745, and was said to be the only industry of many parts of Ireland. It seems that, a month after the reduction of the Salt Duties, the duty on barilla had been reduced from £11 to £5 5/- per ton. The kelp makers of Scotland, thereupon, sent a memorandum to the Treasury praying that the duty might be raised again—at the same time as the importers of barilla sent a petition to the House praying that it should not. In June, accordingly, we find a Bill going into committee to raise the existing duty for five years to £8 8/-, and the Chancellor of the Exchequer defending it—as a merely temporary measure—solely on account of the eighty or a hundred thousand kelp burners. Lord Binning claimed the increase of duty on the ground of humanity—he did not care one straw for political economy in a case of this kind. Ricardo contended that the only ground on which the measure could be supported was that of humanity ; but the same reasons that now induced this augmentation would exist at the end of five years to warrant its continuance, and he objected to temporary expedients of this kind and to the principle on which they were established. Bennet feared that there was a good deal of self-interest mixed up with the appeal to humanity, and Hume pointed out that, since the duty on barilla had been taken off, the price of kelp had risen. The Bill appears among the list of Acts as cc. 44 and 57.[2]

Wool Duties threatened. Evidently it was being suspected that the duty on foreign wool would be the next object of attack. In 1821, a petition from a

[1] *Hansard*, ix. 213.   [2] *Ibid.* ix. 738, 973.

number of dealers in wool had been presented, affirming that the high duty was checking importation, and hurting the woollen manufacture. Baring strongly supported it, while Huskisson denounced " the fallacy of the assertion." In May, of the current year, Sir John Sinclair thought fit to send to Parliament a special petition from himself against the repeal of the duties. Sir J. Sebright, who presented it, took a novel method of pointing the moral. To convince the House how needless the importation of foreign wool was, he arrayed himself in a coat of the finest cloth made from English wool, and waited " a reasonable time " in the lobby, to give members an opportunity of satisfying themselves. The Government, however, was not yet prepared to take the step, but hinted at a " deal." On presentation of two petitions from the woollen manufacturers of Leeds and Huddersfield against the duties, Liverpool again pointed out that they were now more productive than ever—they had risen from £250,000 to £400,000; and suggested that they could be doing no injury to the manufacturers, as the exportation of woollen goods had increased. But, as to the justice of the tax, he would only say that he was willing to give up all the advantage of the £400,000 to the revenue, provided that the manufacturers would agree to the free exportation of wool ; so long as they objected to the one, he would not, in the interests of agriculture, feel justified in giving up the other.[1]

While the trend of legislation was thus very markedly in the direction of removing the duties and restrictions which gave protection to British manufacturers as against foreign competition, a parallel movement had, as markedly, for some time been freeing British industries from the vexatious interference and regulation of Government.[2]

The linen trade had been more favoured than most by Government regulation. After the famous Linen Compact of Will. III., when His Majesty pledged himself to " discourage the woollen manufacture in Ireland," the Irish linen trade had been made the

Linen restrictions removed.

---

[1] *Hansard*, v. 89 ; ix. 239, 648.

[2] The two sets of restrictions were really branches of one and the same regulating policy. In the past, some industries were protected against foreigners, others against rivals at home—both on the ground that the interests of production demanded protection against " undue competition." The " infant industry " argument—that a new trade is a tender plant which must be guarded against winter and hard weather—seemed to apply in either case. Protection had not then hardened into the modern form—that the utmost competition within a country should be welcomed, while competition with other countries should be banned.

special object of encouragement, particularly by bounties. The Scottish trade, which came under a Board of Trustees in 1727, was encouraged in the same way. But the regulations which were thought necessary for its well-being had long ago been found burdensome and restrictive. This year, accordingly, we find Huskisson moving for leave to bring in a Bill for the repeal of several statutes which imposed regulations injurious to the Scotch linen manufacture. They had been " passed at a time when the House was in the habit of interfering with the business of individuals." The 13th of Geo. I., for instance, professed to regulate not only the shape of the cloth but the number of threads in every hank of yarn. The stamping, too, had been found an instrument of fraud instead of security. The Bill, it was said, would be received with satisfaction and gratitude by the people of Scotland, and Parnell thought it ought to be extended to Ireland. In *Hansard* we hear no more of it, but it appears among the Acts as c. 40.[1]

Agitation against the Spitalfields Acts.
The length to which regulation had been carried in the silk trade was brought strikingly to the notice of the House of Commons, in May, by a petition from the master manufacturers of London and Westminster against the statute of 13 Geo. III., usually called the Spitalfields Act. The petition gave a gratifying account of the flourishing state of the British trade generally. Formerly France, on account of her proximity to the raw material in Italy and her superior machinery, had such predominant advantages as entirely confined the sale of English manufactured silks to the British dominions. But the supply of raw silk from Bengal had improved so greatly in quality, and so prodigiously in quantity, that we were no longer dependent on Italy for the raw material. As a fact, the whole import of silk, raw and thrown, for the year 1820 was $2\frac{1}{2}$ million lbs.—a twofold increase in twenty years and " greatly exceeding the consumption of the French manufacturers." The petitioners expressed their conviction that, by judicious arrangements, silk might be rendered, like cotton, one of the staple commodities of the country. But the trade was carried on under very injudicious and vexatious restrictions, and the following list of grievances was given. (1) The raw material was burdened with heavy duties. (2) Wages both of journeymen and journeywomen were fixed and regulated by the local magistrates. (3) Masters could not employ weavers in other districts without incurring ruinous penalties. (4) The same provisions extended to the manufacture of silk mixed

[1] *Hansard,* ix. 150.

with other materials. (5) The magistrates' regulations prescribed the minutest details of the manufacture—number of threads to the inch, width of work, quantity of labour which might not be exceeded without extra wages. (6) Breach of these regulations through ignorance might involve enormous penalties. (7) From being thus arbitrarily fixed, wages had been carried extraordinarily high, so much so as to drive the manufacture to other parts of the country beyond the jurisdiction of the magistrates. (8) Masters were compelled to pay an equal price for all work, well done or ill done, so retarding improvements and repressing emulation. (9) Machine work was fixed at the same wage as hand, and machinery was so discouraged that, while improved machinery was in full operation among foreign rivals, the London silk loom remained in the same state as when introduced by the French refugees. (10) Manufacturers while resident in London were not allowed to employ any portion of their capital in other parts of the kingdom. (11) In consequence, any stagnation in the demand was met by the masters stopping their looms, and the weavers were frequently thrown on charity. (12) Many large works had been transferred to Norwich, Manchester, Macclesfield, Taunton, Reading, and other towns, where the cost was half or two-thirds that of London.[1]

The petition represented that the Select Committee on Foreign Trade of 1821 had reported that, unless some modification of the law took place, it must be, in the end, ruinous to the silk manufacture of Spitalfields, and as injurious to the workmen as it would be to the employers. Ricardo, Wallace, Huskisson, and others expressed their full recognition of the evil ; not a voice was raised for the existing Act ; and Huskisson intimated that it was his intention at once to ask leave to introduce a Bill for its repeal.[2] But, immediately thereafter, a most numerous and respectably signed petition was presented by the Lord Mayor from the silk weavers of Sudbury against this—the result, it said, would be to reduce their means of subsistence and increase the poor rates. The silk trade was flourishing and the men satisfied. Ricardo

---

[1] To the list of restrictions, Lauderdale added some others in a speech in the following year. A weaver could not take more than two apprentices ; the wages varied, not with the activity and prosperity of the trade, but with the price of the loaf ; in fancy work, where machinery had superseded hand labour, the master was required to employ two labourers where he needed only one (*Hansard*, xi. 750).

[2] *Hansard*, ix. 143. For Ricardo's part in the discussion, see Cannan, *The Economic Outlook*, p. 114.

pointed out that such a petition, coming from a district which was free, and praying that a restriction might be continued upon another district, was a most powerful argument in favour of the very measure which it opposed.[1] Another petition, signed by 11,000 weavers was also strongly hostile. A good many voices were now raised for delay and for reference to a Committee—not that anyone defended the existing laws, but that the weavers might be convinced that the laws were injurious to the workers themselves, and Huskisson, in spite of his conviction that the case had already been long enough before the country, gave in to the appointment of a Committee.

A Bill to repeal them.

The next notice is when the report of a Bill on the subject was brought up and counsel was heard against it. Fowell Buxton felt unequal to go into the merits of the Bill " upon the principles of political economy," but pointed to the high wages in Spitalfields, and the low ones in Coventry, and said that the moral effect of the measure would be to pauperise the working population of Spitalfields. And " a more moral and industrious manufacturing population did not exist among the working classes." Huskisson replied that, if there existed a competition in any part of the country by which work could be done for half the price paid in London, the effect would be to deprive the London masters of all business, and, of course, the workmen of employment. Brougham, with some reason, said that the regulation of wages by the magistrates in London was half a century old, and, seeing that this regulation was the work of the House itself, it was but fair to hear the evidence of the workers themselves before a Committee. The Committee, however, was refused, and the Bill passed.[2]

When it came to the House of Lords, Liverpool, approving of the Bill, thought that the petitions against should have a full and patient hearing before a Select Committee. Ellenborough, speaking in high terms of the silk weavers as a body of men, said that the trade had greatly advanced. The raw material imported twenty-one years before was 830,000 lbs., and now it was 2,500,000, while the duty collected had risen in the same time from £200,000 to £600,000 : " there was no proof that the trade stood in need of the proposed alteration. . . . The Acts in question had reference to a distance of ten miles round the metropolis—a mere speck. He verily believed they were interfered with merely to gratify the theoretical views of political economists." But he had always

[1] *Hansard*, ix. 377.   [2] *Ibid.* ix. 810, 831.

looked upon the Spitalfields Acts " more as a measure of police than of trade ; they were most efficient in preserving peace and a good understanding between masters and journeymen. Nothing, in principle, could appear more absurd than that the Lord Mayor and Aldermen should regulate the scale of wages between masters and journeymen, but, looking at the practical effect of that regulation, it did not appear so absurd. . . . The list of prices was made out by a committee of the journeymen and the masters, and, in many instances, an umpire was called in to decide between them. They then went before a magistrate, and the agreement was ratified." The Bill and the petitions were then referred to a Select Committee.[1] This Committee also, it seems, was in favour of repeal. On coming up for the third reading, Harrowby condemned the Bill on the ground that " the residence of a large manufacturing body in the metropolis was *prima facie* a great evil, which could be counteracted only by regulations that might nevertheless not be in themselves conformable to general principles." If the effect of the existing law was gradually to diminish the trade in London, it would be an advantage. In the use of machinery, there was much to admire : still, as in all human affairs, there was a drawback. The best description of manufacture was that which was domestic. This repeal would introduce the factory system, " where they would be exposed to every evil, and where their excellent moral habits would be destroyed, while half a dozen large manufacturers would amass large fortunes."

In deference to the majority, the Bill was now amended in the Lords : the power of the magistrates to regulate the wages of journeymen within the districts in question was left untouched, but the masters were to be allowed to employ any part of their capital out of these districts, and the period within which information should be allowed for offences against the existing law was limited to three months. In this form, the Bill passed.[2] But, with these amendments, the Commons would have none of it ; Huskisson said the mutilations would render it worse than useless ; and for this year the measure dropped.[3]

The old vexed question of apprenticeship came up in a special form during the passing of the Merchant Vessels Apprenticeship

Apprenticeship.

---

[1] *Hansard*, ix. 985.   [2] *Ibid.* ix. 1529.

[3] *Ibid.* ix. 1540. The weavers celebrated the Lords' action by three days of public rejoicing ; " at each trade-house was exhibited the bill, ' Peace and goodwill between master and man for ever.' "

Bill, which regulated the number of apprentices to be taken by merchant vessels in proportion to tonnage. Ricardo and Hume opposed it, as, on the one hand, putting injurious restrictions on a particular trade without any peculiar circumstances being shown to justify it—" it would not be more unjust," said Ricardo, " to enact a law that every surgeon should take a certain number of apprentices to encourage the progress of surgical science "—and as, on the other, tending to reduce seamen's wages by manning ships largely with apprentices. The argument on which all the weight was put was that good seamen could be obtained only by educating them in this way, and Huskisson affirmed that the measure had given universal satisfaction to the shipowners, and, he believed, to every member of the House except Ricardo. On the third reading, Ricardo withdrew his opposition, and the Bill passed.[1]

[1] *Hansard*, viii. 551, 663, 1125.

CHAPTER XVI

1823. IRELAND

CONCURRENTLY with the Spanish negotiations, the affairs of Ireland divided the attention of the House for some time after the opening of Parliament. The state of things in that part of the kingdom was again causing uneasiness. As the King's Speech said, the provisions made in the previous Session had been productive of the happiest effects. But now the disturbances in the southern counties, which had come to an end during the potato famine, broke out again, with the usual savage accompaniments of arson, cattle-maiming, and murder, while the Orangemen were continually rioting in the north; and, in May, the Insurrection Act was continued—not without the old remonstrance that such measures did no good and that "something else" should be done. The outrages became more pronounced during the summer. By the end of the year, however, the country enjoyed more tranquillity than it had for some time.

It was to meet one of the acknowledged grievances—the main cause of the outrages, said some—that the subject of tithes was now taken up in earnest. In March, Goulburn [1] introduced a Bill to establish a composition for tithes in Ireland. The difficulty, as explained by Vesey Fitzgerald, was that, in Ireland, the tithes were paid, not as in England by the middle and higher classes, but almost entirely by the very lowest of the peasantry. This necessarily brought the clergyman into hostile contact with his people; it placed him in the painful situation, either of abandoning the greater part of his income, or of getting into a course of litigation with the greater number of his parishioners. The chief subject of dispute was the value of the crop. The law required the peasants

Goulburn's composition for tithes.

---

[1] Henry Goulburn (1784-1856), one of Pitt's most intimate friends; in 1810, Under-Secretary for Home Affairs, and, later, Under-Secretary for War and the Colonies; Chief Secretary to the Lord-Lieutenant, 1821-27.

to set out the tithe before the crop was removed. They could not comply with this law ; their necessities frequently compelled them to make a premature use of the crop for immediate sustenance, and, having done so, it became impossible to ascertain the value. The principle of the Bill, then, was to encourage a voluntary agreement between the party who paid and the party who received tithes.[1] It proposed to do so by directing the assembly of a special vestry to discuss with the incumbent the propriety of compounding for twenty-one years for the tithes of the whole parish. An attempt was made to compel the incumbent to a composition even against his will, but this was violently opposed, and the Bill passed. In the succeeding February, Liverpool could say that " the success of the measure had far exceeded his most sanguine expectations." [2]

Account of the 40/- freeholders.

But, perhaps, more light was thrown upon the disturbances by the amazing account of the Forty Shilling Freeholders under joint tenancy, given by Dominick Brown, the member for Mayo. The system of joint tenancy, he said, was very ancient, dating from times when it was desirable to protect clans of husbandmen from wild beasts or other hostile clans. As it now existed, from ten to five hundred acres were let from two to a hundred tenants jointly, every one of whom was responsible for the rent of all the rest as well as his own. They held the land in common, making a new division of the arable every year or two, but leaving the pasture undivided. They generally paid a rack rent, and, after they had built their huts without mortar, chimney, or window, they all swore to 40/- profit on registering their freeholds, arising from a joint lease for one or more lives. The uniform results of this system were the naked, squalid beggary of the whole, and extreme indolence, the necessary consequence of the industrious paying for the idle and profligate—each tenant trying merely to preserve his existence and that of his family. Any effort at improvement was out of the question. Their life was reduced to that of brutes ; among themselves, there was constant disunion and petty litigation ; against all the others, there was continual union for every bad purpose. They resisted the ordinary process of law altogether ; they distilled illegally ; they fought together against other clans at fairs and markets. Sedition and disease spread like wildfire among them. They were at once in a state of savage licentiousness and of abject slavery to the landlord. Being all bound for each

[1] *Hansard*, viii. 494, 1132 ; ix. 366, 602, 802, 989, 1434, 1452, 1490.
[2] *Ibid.* x. 29.

other, the landlord could at any moment ruin any one, though worth far more than his own proportion of rent, by distraining him for the rent of all the joint tenants. In short, the landlord had every power over them save that of life and death. He could strip any one of his whole property, including his miserable food. Even where joint tenants were in the best circumstances, much of their time was lost in watching the proper application of their common funds. They all attended whenever money was to be received or paid for the general account. This system contributed more than anything else to the multiplying of a beggarly population. As people never valued a common right like an individual one, joint-tenants readily admitted into their partnership all their sons and frequently their sons-in-law. Under such circumstances, was it extraordinary that the greater part of them could hardly get a sufficiency of potatoes to keep them from starving?

So far from these ghastly facts being questioned or denied, they were confirmed by other speakers. Newport said that nothing had brought greater misery upon Ireland than this subdivision of the land. Another member mentioned one instance where a farm of the value of £15 was subdivided among forty tenants, all of whom voted as freeholders. When Brown introduced a Bill to deal with the matter, the only opposition made was that " it would deprive the Catholics, who were the mass of the freeholders and joint-tenants, of the influence which they at present enjoyed," [1] A Bill to that it " embraced a principle calculated to create great discontent discourage joint-tenancy. in Ireland," and should not be proceeded with in a House where not more than a dozen Irish members were present.

The Bill provided, says the *Annual Register*, that it should not be lawful for any person to register, or to vote at an election, in respect of any freehold under the yearly value of £20, held under a lease executed to any persons jointly, in common, or in partnership, after the 1st of July, 1823. The Act appears as c. 36 : " To Discourage the Granting of Leases in Joint-tenancy in Ireland." [2]

In March, Hume made the first of his attacks on the Irish Church.[3] Hume attacks the Irish Church.

[1] The Bill, however, as the mover explained, had no retrospective effects, though it would " certainly prevent freeholders being created by new joint leases."

[2] *Hansard*, ix. 560. *Annual Register*, 64.

[3] *Hansard*, viii. 367. A writer in the *Edinburgh Review* of 1822 calculated that the real rental of the Irish ecclesiastical property could not fall short of a million—Hume made out that " the annual revenue in the hands of the Irish Protestant Church " was over three millions—while the entire expense of

Premising that an established church was "altogether a civil institution, a creation of law," and that its property was assigned to it for the performance of specific duties, for a limited time, and revocable under a variety of circumstances, he claimed the reduction of the church establishment—with, however, the most scrupulous attention to vested interests—the prohibition of non-residence, and the reduction of benefices on the model of the Church of Scotland. The debate seems unreal, most people believing that it was merely a prelude to an attack on the Church of England, and the Resolutions were lost.

Report on the Labouring Poor. During this Session, a Select Committee was appointed to enquire into the condition of the Labouring Poor in Ireland, with a view to facilitate the application of the funds of individuals and associations for their employment in useful and productive labour, and, shortly before the rising of Parliament, the Report was submitted. In May, 1822, it said, about half the superficial contents of all Ireland might be called "distressed," and, in these districts, considerably more than half the population depended upon charitable assistance for their support. The distress had this peculiar feature, that, while the potato crop had failed, there was plenty of corn and a considerable amount of export ; that is to say, the distress was due less to want of food in general than to absence of purchasing power and want of employment.[1] Perhaps the most immediate cause of this want of employment was the rapid increase of population—from 4,200,000 in 1791 to nearly 7,000,000 in 1821. During the war, the high price of corn and the demand for export

the Scottish Established Church, the efficiency of which had never yet been questioned, did not exceed £250,000, or, at most, £300,000 a year.

[1] "This peculiarity in the character of the late distress appears to have arisen from the entire dependence of the peasantry upon the food raised by themselves." The argument is not fully drawn out in the Report, but it comes to this. The Irish peasant, as a rule, did not make a living, as the modern crofter does, by raising cattle for sale, using his small area of arable simply for feeding and bedding the beasts that graze on the outrun, and buying everything for his own living from outside, but by raising potatoes which he himself with his family consumed. The potato crop was very variable and uncertain, and the surplus of one harvest could not be reserved to supply a deficiency in another. "They are unaccustomed to have recourse to markets " ; even if they had been, the weight and bulk of potatoes threw great difficulties in the way of transport. So far as this was true, the misery of such peasants—with no outside crop to sell and therefore no purchasing power whatever—was easily explained quite consistently with the comparative well-being of those who raised grain for the market. But this export of grain gave great play to Cobbett. He would have prevented it by police power—presumably compelling its sale to those who " had no purchasing power whatever," instead of sending it wherever the best price was obtainable.

gave a stimulus to the extension of arable husbandry, and—partly from political motives—an extraordinary subdivision of farms took place ; many of the evils of Ireland, in fact, both moral and political, might be traced to the mischievous and frequently fraudulent multiplication of the elective franchise. With the depression of prices, it became desirable to consolidate these again into larger farms, and lay down much of the arable into pasture, and the first effect was to deprive many of the peasants of their former homes. At the same time, the fall of prices injuriously affected the gentry, already burdened by fixed payments, and their reduced incomes necessarily affected the employment of the people. The want of capital in Ireland was generally referred to as a principal cause of this want of employment, and the want of security, it was often said, had frightened capital away. This want of capital had led to payment of wages, not in money but, in allowances, and sometimes labour on the roads was set off against the rent of the holdings. The Committee went on to recommend instruction of the peasantry in agriculture, and to examine Robert Owen's plan, which they dismissed as impracticable ; earnestly to recommend the extension of the linen manufacture in the south and west ; to approve of the emigration experiment about to be tried ; and ended by saying that, while they admitted the danger of all artificial encouragements to industry, they feared that capital would not be attracted until peace and tranquillity were fully restored, and that tranquillity could not be secured without encouraging industry among the people " with the aid of the public, relying afterwards on the operation of natural causes." [1]

[1] The Report is printed in the *Edinburgh Annual Register*, Chron. 77, and in Cobbett's *Register*, 7th August, 1824. How Cobbett gathered from it that half our National Debt had been contracted " to get the means of compelling the Catholic National Church of Ireland to submit to the Protestant Church," and that, " to effect this purpose, the English people had been reduced to beggary," is beyond my comprehension.

CHAPTER XVII

1823. THE YEAR

BEFORE Parliament met on 4th February, several important changes, as we have seen, were made in the Cabinet. Peel was now recognised as " manager " of the House of Commons. Canning, Foreign Secretary and most brilliant of parliamentary speakers, dominated the Ministry—which was, indeed, now looked upon as Canning's Ministry.

The sympathy with Spain. Everywhere there was intense sympathy with Spain—at a meeting in the London Tavern, " to consider of the best means of affording assistance to the Spaniards," the chief names are Lords W. Bentinck, Erskine, and Lynedoch, Mackintosh, Baring, Hume, Lambton, Hobhouse, Waithman, and Francis Place—and, for some time, it looked as if the peaceful development of the country would again be interrupted by a great war. It was the danger of being dragged into the quarrel which bulked most largely in people's minds in the beginning of the year ; and, till Government had thrown down the pledge of strict neutrality, and war actually broke out, a great part of the attention of Parliament was taken up with the conduct of Ministers in the affairs of France and Spain. To most reasonable persons, the experience of the late war was too fresh to allow them to entertain the idea of a new one. " No war—no eloquence," wrote Sydney Smith, " but apathy, selfishness, common sense, arithmetic ! Are we to be eternally raising fleets and armies to make all men good and happy ? " But, inside Parliament, the feeling against France was very strong. Brougham, among thunders of applause from both sides of the House, spoke the plainest truths that ever were told to friendly powers regarding the " three gentlemen of Verona." Althorp proposed the repeal of the Foreign Enlistment Act, to enable us, while professedly neutral, to give assistance to Spain. Hobhouse spoke " for war—at least for preparing for war." Ellenborough, Holland, Lansdowne, King, Grey, Mackintosh, all threw their influence against neutrality. The debates—which, by the way, are excellently and fully condensed in the *Annual Register* of the year—while they furnish the keynote to the policy of Non-intervention, clearly declared by Canning and thenceforth adopted by the country, show also how strong was the feeling for oppressed nationalities, and how ready a great many —the Opposition as a whole, and, certainly the most advanced Radicals—were to go to the very verge of war for a very ill-defined principle. Moreover, the fear of what might happen if France succeeded in realising her old aspiration contained in the words " il n'y a plus de Pyrenées," is seen in the note sent to our Minister at Paris : " With respect to the provinces in America which have thrown off their allegiance to the crown of Spain, time and the course of events appear to have substantially decided their separation from the mother country. . . . Spain has long been apprised of His Majesty's opinions upon this subject. Disclaiming in the most solemn manner any intention of appropriating to himself the smallest portion of the late Spanish possessions in America, His Majesty is satisfied that no attempt will be made by France to bring under her dominion any of those possessions, either by conquest or by cession from Spain." In the end Canning carried his policy—not without many a jibe that, if the country had not been so deep in debt, it would have adopted firmer measures.[1]

Canning's policy towards the Spanish colonies.

The rest of the story is soon told. On 28th January, came the extraordinary speech of the King of France : " I have ordered the recall of my minister ; a hundred thousand Frenchmen, commanded by a prince of my family, are ready to march, invoking the God of Saint Louis to preserve the throne of Spain to a descendant of Henri Quatre, to save that fair kingdom from its ruin and to reconcile it with Europe. . . . Let Ferdinand VII. be free to give to his people institutions which they cannot hold but from him. Hostilities shall cease from that moment." On 7th April, the French crossed the frontier; on 23rd May, they entered Madrid, meeting with no more resistance, as the Duke had prophesied, than he did in going to the Ordnance Office ; on 1st October, the Spanish Constitutionalists set Ferdinand free to join the French ; on 1st November, the war ended by the surrender of Barcelona to the royalists. All the

[1] " We are bound over in a sum of eight hundred millions to keep the peace," said Brougham. " The best security for the peace of mankind at present," said the *Glasgow Herald* very sensibly, " is the poverty of governments."

Acts of the Constitutional Government were declared null and void, and the contemptible Ferdinand, who had promised a general amnesty, constitutional rule, etc., began a course of conduct to his people which the French Government were powerless to moderate, and of which they must have been heartily ashamed.[1]

The Monroe Doctrine.

Canning's declaration as to the now independent Spanish colonies was followed by a pronouncement on the part of the United States which has ever since determined the relations between the old world and the new. In the Message to Congress of 2nd December, President Monroe used the words : " We owe it to candour, and to the amicable relations existing between the United States and those (the allied) powers, to declare that we should consider any attempt on their part to extend their system to any portion of this hemisphere as dangerous to our peace and safety. With the existing colonies or dependencies of any European power, we have not interfered, and shall not interfere. But, with the governments which have declared their independence, and maintained it, and whose independence we have, on great consideration, and on just principles, acknowledged,[2] we could not view any interposition for the purpose of oppressing them, or controlling in any other manner their destiny, by any European power, in any other light than as the manifestation of an unfriendly disposition towards the United States. . . . Our policy in regard to Europe, which was adopted at an early stage of the wars which have so long agitated that quarter of the globe, nevertheless remains the same ; which is, not to interfere in the internal concerns of any of its powers ; to consider the government *de facto* as the legitimate government for us ; to cultivate friendly relations with it, and to preserve those relations by a frank, firm, and manly policy ; meeting in all instances the just claims of every power—submitting to injuries from none. But, in regard to those continents, circumstances are eminently and conspicuously different. It is impossible that the allied powers should extend their political system to any portion

[1] It is some makeweight of a very doubtful policy that, once in Spain, the conduct of the Duc d'Angoulême was unexceptionable. "History," said Canning, "never furnished a similar example of the discipline of a foreign army engaged in the invasion of another state—or, rather, called in by invitation to assist a predominating party in putting down a rival faction " (*Hansard*, x. 992).

[2] The revolted colonies of Spain had been recognised as independent and sovereign states by the United States in 1822 ; in the same year England recognised their commercial flags, and, in 1823, appointed consuls. By the end of 1823, Portugal no longer possessed a single station in South America.

of either continent without endangering our peace and happiness ;
nor can anyone believe that our southern brethren, if left to themselves, would adopt it of their own accord. It is equally impossible,
therefore, that we should behold such interposition, in any form,
with indifference." In the same Message, we find it laid down
as a principle that " the American continents, by the free and
independent condition which they have assumed, are henceforth
not to be considered as subjects for future colonisation by any
European powers."

The enunciation of the Monroe Doctrine was hailed by Brougham,
in the debate on the King's Speech in the following year, as an
event which had dispersed joy, exultation, and gratitude over all
the freemen in Europe.[1]

Meanwhile Parliamentary Reform advanced another step. Fortified by the presentation of many petitions—among them, one, 380
feet in length, from some two-thirds of the freeholders of Yorkshire, containing over 17,000 *bona-fide* signatures—Russell moved
for " a plain arithmetical statement of the number of voters who
returned members to the several cities and boroughs, and the right
of voting as it was usually exercised in those cities and boroughs,"
and got 169 votes out of a House of 449. On this occasion Ricardo,
for the first—and, as it proved, the last time—took a prominent
part in the discussion. " The simple question," he said, " for
them to determine was, whether they would not purify the House,
when it was notorious that it could not be considered, in the fair
sense of the words, to represent the people." Although the suffrage,
he was convinced, ought to be extended, and much beyond its
present limits, the more important question was the mode of election
and the duration of Parliaments. As things were, no House could
be a true representative of the people, and there was but one mode
of obviating this, vote by ballot. Unless this were adopted, the
House would continue to be what it was now—the representative
of the aristocracy and of the aristocracy only. And he would
insist on the necessity of more frequent elections. He differed
from Russell as to the vested rights of individuals in boroughs ;
there were no such rights, and no compensation was called for.
He would agree with Canning that the people never had been better
represented. But were we never to have a good House of Commons
because we never had had a good one ? " The demands of the
people might be easily satisfied. They asked only for that which

Ricardo on parliamentary reform.

[1] *Hansard,* x. 68.

was perfectly reasonable—that they might have a voice in the public councils, and the power of restraining the expenditure of their own money," and that they had a right to have.[1]

The parallel question of Burgh Election Reform in Scotland had been raised by Reports obtained by Parliament in 1819, 1820, and 1821, and, since then, the subject had been ably kept before the House by Lord Archibald Hamilton. Its necessity was now illuminated by the "dreadful example" of Inverness, and backed by a petition from 7,000 householders of Edinburgh, setting forth that the sole representative in Parliament of their 100,000 population was elected by thirty-three individuals whose property did not exceed £2,800.[2]

Slavery : a new chapter. In the gloomy history of slavery a new chapter was opened. Fowell Buxton—confessing that the only reason why he did not move for the immediate emancipation of all the slaves was that the adult slave, debased by slavery, enfeebled in powers, changed in character, was not ripe for liberty—moved a Resolution that "the state of slavery is repugnant to the principles of the British Constitution and of the Christian religion ; and that it ought to be gradually abolished throughout the British colonies, with as much expedition as may be found consistent with a due regard to the well-being of the parties concerned." The means of carrying this out, in his view, was to proclaim that all negro children born after a certain date should be free : thus "slavery would burn itself down in its socket and go out." "We do not say, 'retrace your steps,' but 'stop' : we do not say, 'make reparation for the wrong you have done,' but 'do no more wrong ; go no further.'" Canning, objecting to the opening statement of the motion, submitted three moderate Resolutions, and, after a long and able debate, they were **Bathurst's Circular.** carried *nem. con.* Thereupon Lord Bathurst, the Colonial Secretary, issued a Circular to the different islands communicating the Resolutions, and recommending a schedule of reforms to the local authorities—among them, the absolute prohibition of the whip.[3] This "interference with colonial affairs" was much resented in the **Smith, the missionary.** islands. In Demerara, an insurrection of the slaves was put down by armed force, not without bloodshed. The memorable sequel was that a zealous missionary named Smith was charged with being concerned in the conspiracy, tried by court-martial under a

[1] *Hansard*, viii. 125, 172, 1149, 1260.
[2] *Ibid.* viii. 735 ; ix. 30, 611 ; cf. Walpole, ii. 287.
[3] *Ibid.* v. 1285, 1325 ; vii. 1399 ; ix. 255 ; x. 1047

mockery of justice, and condemned to death. When the King's message arrived rescinding the sentence, Smith was already dead of an illness due to the severity of his treatment in prison.[1]

A foreigner of distinction once asked a British Member of Parliament what had passed in the Session of 1823—"Five months and fourteen days," was the reply. Similarly, in the events of 1823 there is little to catch the attention of the general reader. It may be located as the year when Edward Irving, Locating the engaged for five years at the Caledonian Church at a salary of £150 year. a year, "in addition to the seat rents," was attracting all London, including Liverpool, Canning, Brougham, Peel ; when Birkbeck, copying the parent type in Glasgow, founded the first Mechanics' Institute in London ; [2] when Prince Hohenlohe was performing his marvellous cures ; when Vauxhall was the new place of fashionable resort; when Lockhart's *Spanish Ballads*, Galt's *Entail*, *Peveril of the Peak* (published the same day in French at Paris), *Quentin Durward*, *St. Ronan's Well*, Moore's *Loves of the Angels* appeared, and Grimm's *German Popular Tales*, illustrated by Cruikshank, entered into the heritage of English children ; when £150,000 was granted by Parliament for the building of London Bridge, and the first plate of the Menai Bridge was laid ; when the newest advertisements which catch the eye are Rolands' Macassar Oil, Atkinson's Bear's Grease, Pears' Genuine Transparent Soap, Cockle's Antibilious Pills, Gowland's Lotion, and Warren's Blacking.

The obituary of 1823 is very heavy. Among others, it included Obituary. Jenner ; Mrs. Radcliffe, the novelist ; John Philip Kemble, the actor ; Sir Henry Raeburn, the great painter ; the venerable Lord Erskine ; and the good Pope Pius VII., the grateful and attached friend of England, "revered by the whole Christian world."

---

[1] The colonial proceedings are given in a petition from the London Missionary Society (*Hansard*, xi. 400). " There is more outcry about the death (a natural one) of this mischievous CANTER than there was about all the cuttings and killings of 1817 and 1819. This fellow was labouring to plunge a whole colony into bloodshed. He was tried and condemned, and then he was *pardoned*. He has since *died*. What, was the fellow to be immortal ? " This was Cobbett's comment—*ex uno disce omnes*.

[2] It is interesting to note what the *Quarterly*, in October 1825, said of these Mechanics' Institutes which were now taking root everywhere—apropos of the 19th edition of Brougham's *Practical Observations upon the Education of the People* : " Much undoubtedly of the alarm which they have occasioned, and of the opposition which they have experienced, is to be attributed to the patronage and advocacy of Lord Brougham. ... It is his singular infelicity to prejudice every cause which he undertakes to advance."

But the greatest loss to England was that of the man who " educated the House of Commons," David Ricardo. The son of a Dutch
Jew, who settled in England and became a member of the Stock
Exchange, Ricardo followed his father's profession.   " His complete
knowledge of all its intricacies ; his surprising quickness at figures
and calculations ; his capability of getting through, without any
apparent exertion, the immense transactions in which he was concerned ; his coolness and judgment, combined certainly with (for
him) a fortunate tissue of public events, enabled him to leave all
his contemporaries at the Stock Exchange far behind ; and to
raise himself infinitely higher, not only in fortune, but in general
character and estimation, than any man had ever done before in
that House."   From his earliest youth, he showed a bent for abstract
reasoning, and he found his *métier* when, in 1799, he came across
the *Wealth of Nations* in a circulating library at Bath.   His first
appearance as an author was in 1809, in the tract *The High Price
of Bullion a Proof of the Depreciation of Bank Notes*.   His friendship
with Malthus, formed about this time, and with James Mill, the
historian of British India, ended only with his death.   In later
life, he became an extensive landed proprietor, and retired wholly
from business with a fortune of half a million.   In 1819, he entered
Parliament as member for the Irish borough of Portarlington.
" You will have seen," he wrote to a friend, " that I have taken
my seat in the House of Commons.   I fear that I shall be of little
use there.   I have twice attempted to speak, but I proceeded in
the most embarrassed manner ; and I have no hope of conquering
the alarm with which I am assailed the moment I hear the sound
of my own voice."   His first prominent appearance was on 24th
May, 1819, in the debate of Peel's resolutions respecting the resumption of cash payments, when he was " loudly called upon from
all parts of the House."   Thereafter Ricardo was an acknowledged
power.   His voice, indeed, is described as " harsh and screamy " ;
he used no arts of eloquence, said what he had to say in the fewest
words and plainest way, and never abused his opponents.   But
his calm, serious exposition of principles, his severely independent
tone, his habit of bringing everything to the test of economic theory,
distinguished him from every man in the House.   Behind it all
was the respect commanded by a noble character and an unblemished
record.   In private life, he was a most lovable man, and his great
wealth he used generously, subscribing to almost every charity in
the metropolis, and supporting at his own expense an almshouse

and two schools in the neighbourhood of his estate. As one said, he was at once the firmest and the gentlest of human beings. " He seemed free from every bad passion," said Hobhouse, " and those who came within the sphere of his gentle and resistless influence felt that he was born for the consolation of those around him and for the happiness of mankind." His death, at the age of fifty-one, was entirely unexpected. After Parliament rose, he appeared in excellent health and spirits, and completed his tract on the establishment of a National Bank. But, in the beginning of September, he was seized with a violent pain in the head, which developed as disease of the middle ear, and, " after a period of indescribable agony," he died on 11th September. One is reminded of Mackintosh's words : " I have known Adam Smith slightly, Ricardo well, and Malthus intimately. Is it not something to say for a science that its three greatest masters were about the three best men I ever knew ? " [1]

Among the economic publications of the year, I find the following : Ricardo's *Plan for the Establishment of a National Bank* ; Malthus' *The Measure of Value stated and illustrated* ; Tooke's *Thoughts and Details of the High and Low Prices of the last Thirty Years ; New Ideas on Population*, by A. E. Everett ; *A Letter to Malthus answering his Criticism of Godwin*, by David Booth ; *Essay on Political Economy* (Supplement of the *Encyclopaedia Britannica*, vol. vi.) ; *A Compendium of Finance*, by Bernard Cohen ; *Outlines of a System of Political Economy*, by T. Joplin (advocating the establishment of Banks on the Scottish system) ; *An Inquiry into the Principles of the Distribution of Wealth most conducive to Human Happiness, applied to the newly proposed system of Voluntary Equality of Wealth*, by Wm. Thompson ; *Elementary Propositions illustrative of the Principles of Currency ; An Essay on the Employment of the Poor*, by Robert A. Slaney (awarded a silver medal by the Board of Agriculture) ; *Defence of the Usury Laws*, by Robert Hannay ; *The Poor and their Relief*, by George Ensor ; *The Domestic Policy of the British Empire viewed in connection with its Foreign Interests ; A Letter to the Proprietors and Occupiers of Land*

Economic publications.

---

[1] The very large space which I have given to Ricardo's speeches is due to my conviction that they supply a most valuable commentary to his books. As Professor Marshall has noticed, Ricardo has suffered more than most economists from his excessive condensation, and his habit of taking principles as to which he had no doubt for granted. The necessity of making himself understood in the House throws much the same light on his economic theory as the letters of a great man often throw on his public actions.

on the *Declension of Agricultural Prosperity*, by Lord Erskine;
Remarks on the Erroneous Principles which led to the New Corn Law,
by John Wright; *Two Letters on the reputed Excess and Depreciation
of Bank Notes*, by Daniel B. Payne; *Relative Taxation, or Observations on the Impolicy of Taxing Malt, Hops, Beer, Soap, Candles
and Leather*, by T. Vaux ("one of those few publications relative
to Political Economy from which we can derive either pleasure or
instruction," said the *European Magazine*).

CHAPTER XVIII

1824. GREAT PROSPERITY EVERYWHERE

WE saw that, since the early summer of 1823, there had been a definite conviction that the long depression in agriculture was passing away, and that already the remedies suggested by Western and others seemed unreal. Difficult as it is to understand this, in view of the very poor harvest of that year and the fall of price which followed it, the conviction was confirmed in the course of 1824.

For once, almost nothing was heard in Parliament of agricultural distress. In February, we read the grudging admission that, " in so far as it depended upon price, agricultural distress might be considered in some degree removed." Farmers—to Cobbett's deep disgust—with their usual optimism, retook their farms, and the new generation, like soldiers in an engagement, closed up the depleted ranks. In Fife—where, however, as was said, rents based on fiars' prices had been somewhat extensively adopted—many estates were sold at thirty years' purchase of their estimated annual value. In Cumberland, it was noticed that agricultural improvement, particularly drainage and making of roads, had never made such rapid strides. Everything seemed to bear out the somewhat banal words of the King's Speech in February, that " agriculture was recovering from its long depression, and, by the steady operation of natural causes, was gradually reassuming the character to which its importance entitled it among the great interests of the nation." [1]

Disappearance of agricultural distress.

[1] Cobbett becomes even more hysterical this year. There is no recovery in agriculture at all, he says. The state of the farmers generally is worse than it was last year. Landed estates are passing into the hands of " Jews and Jobbers." The rise in price is a thing to be sorry for ; it is nothing but the result of the partial repeal of Peel's Act by the permission to issue " bales of paper," by which money is depreciated by one-seventh. So, for want of something else to attack, he turns on the Bible Societies—" the printers and

The farmer's year. The new contentment was strengthened by a good harvest, unaccompanied, this time, by any serious fall in price. "Winter had not made its appearance," by March, and the spring was open and favourable to all farming operations. A dry summer followed, some parts, indeed, suffering from drought—the farmers in the Clyde valley, for the first time in thirty years, had to carry water for their cattle. Labour was fully employed and at fair wages. In Scotland, at any rate, the harvest was generally above the average : wheat and oats plumper and fuller than in ordinary years ; barley excellent ; beans, as a rule, good ; potatoes most abundant and in the finest condition ; turnips remarkably good. At the same time, lean and fat cattle and sheep were in demand.[1]

The price of wheat was above 67/- in February and April, and fears were entertained that the ports might be opened by a rise to the 70/- level which would admit the grain bonded before 13th

publishers of the Bible have done a great deal of mischief in the world "—and sets to to write a History of " the most unfortunate event the country ever saw, the Reformation," and promises to " do the job effectually "—in a few weeks. In the end of the year, for no very obvious reason that I can discover except that manufacturing was " prosperous " while agriculture, according to his superior knowledge, was not, he made an attack on the factory system as " the great cause of pauperism and of the degradation of the people," connecting it with the Funding System. " Before this infernal system, which has corrupted everything, was known in this country, there were none of those places called Manufactories. . . . The man who invented the funding system should have been burned alive the moment he opened his lips upon the subject." The logic is as obscure as his tracing of the Irish potato famine to small notes, but it seems to be : (1) that it was " the natural tendency of a system of loans and funds to draw money into great masses," which then became " the means of commanding the common people to stoop in abject submission to the few ; (2) that it depopulated the farms of the " profitable labours of women, girls, and little boys." I feel inclined to apologise for giving so much space to Cobbett, but it is good that the present generation should know the quality of what was called " the most powerful voice in England."

[1] Tooke, however, says, that " according to all reports, the produce was again deficient." I have only the reports for Cumberland, Liverpool, and Yorkshire beside me, but they do not bear this out. In Cumberland, wheat, barley, and oats were a full average ; rye, beans, and peas, considerably above the average ; potatoes and turnips, very superior. In Liverpool, the crops generally were reported scarcely to reach an average. In Yorkshire, wheat had not for many years been more generally good in quality, though not a very heavy crop ; oats were light, but barley fair as to quantity ; while peas, beans, and turnips were all a good crop. As regards Lincolnshire, too, a member said, in 1825, that he had been assured by his tenants that " the late harvest was superabundant—considerably more than an average crop —and would exceed the supply of former years " (*Hansard*, xiii. 344). One reason for diverging accounts of any harvest was that the counties far away from London did not thresh their wheat till the crop of the nearer counties was exhausted ; hence the results were not known till well on in the next year.

May, 1822, on payment of the duties. But oats and barley alone rose to the requisite height, and the imports of both were absorbed without materially affecting the price. As the harvest was gathered, wheat fell below 55/- in September, but it shortly recovered and closed about 66/- in the end of the year. " Two years have scarcely elapsed," said the *New Monthly* in December, " since landed property was a complete drug in the market, and thousands who then refused to take leases at an abatement of a third or perhaps nearly half the amount of former rents have already discovered abundant reason to regret their folly." The average price of wheat for the year was 63/11.

Some figures of agricultural wages are given in the Report on the Condition of the Labouring Classes. In the northern counties, Agricultural wages. which were nearly if not totally exempt from the evil of paying wages out of the poor rates, wages were from 12/- to 15/- a week. In Northumberland, they were 12/- ; in Cumberland, 12/- to 15/-. In Lincolnshire, they were generally 12/-, " and the labourers live in comfort and independence." In Oldham, they were 12/- to 18/- —the average, presumably, includes manufacturing wages— while, in Wigan of the same county, where relief was given to a man with three children, they were 7/- to 8/-. In Staffordshire, they were about 10/-, " and labourers having families only receive occasional relief from the poor rate." In Yorkshire generally, they were 12/-, but, in some parts, the practice of giving married labourers assistance appeared to be very prevalent. In the southern counties, however, where the practice had been carried to the greatest extent, wages varied from 8/- or 9/- down to 3/- for a single man and 4/6 for a man and his wife.[1]

The Corn Laws were scarcely mentioned this Session. But, on 13th May, an interesting " conversation "—not mentioned in *Hansard*—took place, when Curteis, the member for Suffolk, voiced a grievance very often mentioned outside, that the averages which regulated the foreign importation were never properly taken, and asked for the names of persons who had made returns of

---

[1] The bulk of the Report is given in the *Annual Register*. I find 1/5 to 1/8 per day of ten hours quoted for Perthshire in the *Edinburgh Magazine* for April. It should be noted, however, that the question of agricultural labour in Scotland is scarcely comparable with that in England. In 1831, it was found that more than two-thirds of the occupiers of the soil in Scotland " did not employ labourers " ; they worked the land with the aid of their families (the figures are, of 79,853 male occupiers above twenty years of age, 53,966 worked in this way), the average to each holder in the remaining category being only 3¾ labourers (*Porter*, 160).

market sales—" in order to check the frauds practised in striking the averages." Huskisson acknowledged the evil complained of— very often "the fractional shilling made all the difference." On this occasion, he spoke again of the desirability of " free importation guarded by a sufficient protecting duty " in preference to the existing system.[1]

Warehoused
Wheat Bill. One relaxation, however, was made. On 17th May, we find a Bill brought in by Huskisson entitled the Warehoused Wheat Bill. Something between a million and a half and two millions of English capital was locked up in the foreign wheat put in bond. This might be exported as wheat but not as flour, and the colonies were dependent on us for their supply of flour. To allow this to get into circulation again, he proposed that a certain quantity of it might be ground and exported to the colonies, reminding the House that wheat was perishable, and that, as the law stood, whatever the state of the wheat, it could not be ground, nor even taken for cattle feeding or changed into manure. It was urged that a measure like this was encouraging foreign countries again to deluge the British market with foreign grain, but Huskisson easily disposed of the objections, and the Bill passed.[2]

Flourishing
industry. As to the general industry of the country during the whole year, there was scarcely an expression of doubt, either in Parliament or outside : it was flourishing beyond any example. The King's Speech in February said that trade and commerce were extending themselves both at home and abroad ; an increasing activity pervaded almost every branch of manufacture ; the growth of the revenue, among other things, evinced a diffusion of comfort among the great body of the people : and Liverpool added that, without one word of exaggeration, it could be said that, at no former period had the country enjoyed a more general state of internal happiness and prosperity. In the end of June, in closing the Session, the King repeated his congratulations in much the same terms.[3] It seems desirable, then, to examine, with some care, the economic

---

[1] *Edinburgh Magazine*, xv. 371.   [2] *Hansard*, xi. 760.

[3] It is very suggestive that, among all this abounding prosperity, one class remained outside. In a memorial, the handloom cotton weavers of Bolton said that, while the importation and consumption of raw cotton was " swollen to a sum total never known before," the rates for weaving were " never in such a state of depression." This was the result of the powerloom system, and, they added inconsequently, " these powerlooms produce neither soldiers nor sailors to fight the battles of the country, but, as the absorbers of profitable manual labour, are eminently injurious to the agricultural interest by diminishing the consumption of agricultural products " (Cobbett's *Register*, 13th March).

phenomena of this year, in order to find, if we can, how it was that the upward movement, begun in 1821, met with a sudden check in 1825 which plunged industry once more into depression.

Tooke has noticed that, from 1821 to 1824, the trade and manufactures of the country had never before been in a more regular, sound, and satisfactory state. During the latter part of 1823 and the greater part of 1824, in most of the great branches of trade there prevailed a general character of prudence and sobriety, without any apparent resort to an undue extension of credit : there still prevailed the caution which had been taught and enforced among the commercial classes by the reverses and losses sustained by the great fall of prices since 1818.[1]

But, in 1824, the rapidly increasing capital of the country, no longer heavily taxed and absorbed by Government expenditure, began to take new and speculative channels of investment. The first in point of time was foreign loans and foreign mining shares. Between 1817 and 1823, various loans to continental states had been negotiated in this country, and, as the return was high and the dividends were regularly paid, these became a somewhat favourite form of investment for those who were discontented with the low rates now obtainable from Consols and Exchequer Bills. But, in 1822 and 1824, several loans were asked in London for the new South American states, and easily found subscribers. In all, the foreign loans contracted between 1821 and 1825 amounted to £48 millions, of which £22 millions were South American—Portuguese and Mexican, Greek and Brazilian, Peruvian and Buenos Ayres loans were in equal favour.[2] This was accompanied by the flotation in England of numerous companies to work the silver mines temporarily abandoned during the civil wars—in Mexico, Chili, Peru, Brazil, and the Plate. A similar, and even more speculative field, was found nearer home : by February, British capital was flowing towards Ireland, to work " the numerous rich mines with which Ireland abounds," [3] and Parliament was kept busy discussing the propriety of relaxing its rules in favour of these, presumably, beneficent undertakings.

Beginning of the speculation.

[1] *History of Prices*, ii. 142.   [2] Levi, 178.

[3] By the end of March, three influential companies had appeared to exploit —as was said with unconscious truth—" the immense mineral wealth in Ireland which was almost unknown." It is curious to notice the confident statement that there was, after all, something to be said for even rash enterprises in Mining, where " every pound of coal or metal extracted is something added to the stock of national wealth," while in Assurance there " can be neither profit to the shareholders nor benefit to the public."

From this the fever spread. Within a few weeks, in the early
part of the year, the following, among others, were subscribed:[1] The
Alliance Fire and Life Insurance Company, with a capital of five
millions (brought out by Rothschild, and rising to a premium of
22½ per cent. on the issue of the prospectus) ; The Palladium Fire
and Life Insurance Company, with two millions ; The British
Annuity Company, with three millions ; The Metropolitan Investment Company, with one million. Then there was a company
for obtaining from Government a grant of a million of acres of
land in New South Wales and for improving the growth of wool ;
an association for cutting a canal across the Isthmus of Darien ;
a company for navigating the Thames and Isis by steam ; a company, formed by certain noblemen and others in Ireland, for the
purpose of draining and reclaiming three millions of acres of bogs
in that country, etc., etc.—the very titles suggestive of the South
Sea Bubble.[2] Many of these companies asked no special help
from the legislature, but, by the month of April, there were something like 250 private Bills before the House of Commons, to give
legal existence to loan, road, market, dock, bridge, canal, Irish
mining, and, particularly, gas companies.

Gambling in
stocks

Before long, the inevitable gambling in small called-up capitals
and in first instalments began.[3] " This possibility of enormous
profit by risking an (apparently) small sum, was a bait too tempting
to be resisted ; all the gambling propensities of human nature
were constantly solicited into action ; and crowds of individuals
of every description—the credulous and the suspicious—the crafty
and the bold—the raw and the experienced—the intelligent and the
ignorant—princes, nobles, politicians, placemen, patriots, lawyers,
physicians, divines, philosophers, poets, intermingled with women
of all ranks and degrees—spinsters, wives, and widows—hastened
to venture some portion of their property in schemes of which
scarcely anything was known except the name." [4]

[1] Annual Register, 2.

[2] Juglar says that a company, which actually found subscribers, was formed
to drain the Red Sea with a view of recovering the treasures of the Egyptians !
(Les crises économiques, 334).   Francis remembers having seen the prospectus
(History of the Bank of England, ii. 3).

[3] The ignorance which underlay some at least of the speculations, is shown
by no less a person than the Speaker thinking it worth while to warn shareholders that they were liable for the full amount of their subscriptions, although
the " deposit " was only one pound for every hundred (Hansard, xiii. 1032).

[4] Annual Register, 3.

All this was in the early part of 1824, and nobody seems to have
had any apprehension of coming evil.   Indeed, the first note of
alarm I find in contemporary literature is in the *European Magazine*
of April, where, under the heading of Domestic Affairs, it is said :
" The most prominent feature in them at present is the rage for
new projects and new loans, which pervades the whole country
and seems to have turned people's heads quite giddy.   Never since
the South Sea Bubble has the mania been so endemic.   There is
not a capitalist nor moneylender all over the empire that is not
infected with it, and, where it will end, no man can foresee."

But the rush of capital to stocks and shares, and the gambling
in these, was only one part of the phenomena of speculation in
the early part of 1824.   More serious perhaps—because it dealt
with raw materials and the legitimate objects of merchant industry
—was that which led to enormous inflation in the prices of goods.
During the preceding year, with the exception of a temporary rise,
during the early months, in colonial produce and other commodities
likely to be affected if war broke out over Spain, and a speculative
rise in cotton later, the prices of goods generally were either
stationary, or dull, or drooping, and continued so during the first
six months of 1824, and, in some cases, till its close.   But, towards
the end of the year, the increasing rate of consumption gave markets
a decided upward tendency.   Attention was drawn, in circular
letters from merchants and brokers, to the reduced stocks of various
articles in comparison with the stocks of twelve months before,
and confident statements were made of the failure of certain crops,
such as cotton and silk, and of other causes which were likely to
diminish the forthcoming supply.   At a time when money was so
cheap and easily obtainable, these two causes are amply sufficient
to account for the beginning of a great speculative movement in
prices.

and in produce.

All this was not quite unnatural and without basis.   The wealth
of the country had, for the moment, outgrown its investments.
Consols, which had been below 74 in April, 1823, were 92 in January
and above 96 in November, and the premium on Exchequer Bills
rose from 10/- and 12/- to 60/- between the same dates.   I find
it stated in November that the Scots Banks were " loaded with
money " ;   their interest on deposits was reduced to 2 per cent.,
and yet they had £5 millions for which they could not find any
advantageous investment.   There was, indeed, some reason to think
that the country was only at the beginning of a vast extension of

Reasonable basis of the speculation.

its industry and trade. The great expectations of the peace, be
it remembered, had never yet been realised. The Continent had
been too exhausted by the twenty years of war to react at once.
But things had now settled down. Nations that turn their spears
into pruning hooks get a new purchasing power ; and an era of
active international exchange of commodities seemed in sight.
Besides, the most exaggerated expectations were entertained of
the markets of the new world, now released from Spanish and Portuguese control. As of old, it was the precious metals of these countries that attracted attention and hope. Some economists lamented
the probable depreciation of money, and became apprehensive that
the National Debt might be paid off. The capital raised for mining
companies was taken out in engines and equipment manufactured
at home ; this set many industries in activity and swelled the
exports. At the same time, the loans made to these states were
largely transmitted in British manufactures, and people did not
stop to consider that this was a temporary export of capital and
not part of the normal annual cross-current by which exports are
balanced by imports. All the while, the increase of the revenue
and the visible prosperity of the country, loudly proclaimed in the
King's Speech, added to the prevailing optimism.

So far, it seems to me, the movement was natural and legitimate
enough, and did not necessarily lead to evil consequences. It was, in
fact, only the overflowing of capital which was, in after years, to
make England a great creditor country. But now the outsider
"took a hand." As prices rose and profits were realised by the sale
of goods bought a short time before, the example became infectious,
and, in each great branch of goods, the public were tempted to
join in the money-making game. Cotton was the first and prominent article into which the speculation rushed : [1] then came silk,
wool, flax, and other goods, where some advance was justified by
the shortness of supply. But soon the mania spread to articles
where there was no such justification. The stock of coffee, for
instance, was greater than in former years ; yet it rose 70 per cent.
to 80 per cent. Spices rose, in some instances, 100 per cent. to
200 per cent. without any reason whatever. "In short, there was
hardly any article of merchandise which did not participate in the
rise." [2]

The outsider takes a hand.

---

[1] It is interesting to note that hitherto only coarse cotton had come from
Egypt. But, in 1822, cotton was grown in Egypt from Brazil seed, and, in
1824, 50,000 bags of it were available for export to England.

[2] Tooke, *History of Prices*, ii. 140.

As might be expected in such a year, there was a great increase Foreign trade. in all the branches of foreign trade. Imports and re-exports rose each by over £1½ millions; exports, by nearly £5 millions; real exports, by £3 millions. The figures are as follow: Imports, £37,468,000; Re-exports, £10,204,000; Exports, £48,730,000; Real Exports, £38,422,000.

The number of ships built and registered in the United Kingdom was 799, representing a tonnage of 91,083.

CHAPTER XIX

1824. THE FIRST FREE TRADE BUDGET

APART from the phenomena of the culminating year of an industrial cycle—the splendour of the sky when the stormclouds are gathering at the edge—the chief interest of 1824 to the economist is that it was the year when Huskisson, definitely and with a clearly announced programme, took off the prohibitions and began to reduce the protective duties.[1] This involved financial changes the consideration of which is inseparable from the financial statement of the year, and it seems to me most advisable to deal with the two questions, the reform in taxation and the commercial policy, in the chapter which deals with an otherwise interesting Budget.

Financial *exposé.* On 22nd February, Robinson, following the course he had adopted in the previous year, gave an *exposé* of the financial situation of the country.[2] In most of the departments, the revenue had exceeded the estimates, and, in the Miscellaneous revenue, there was a considerable excess owing to the payment on account of the Austrian Loan.[3] In all, the revenue of the past year had amounted to £57,672,000, and the expenditure to £50,962,000, leaving a surplus of £6,710,000.[4] Deducting the £5,000,000 which, by the Act of last Session, was laid aside for the reduction of the

[1] The programme was completed in 1825, and the Budgets of the two years should be studied together.

[2] *Hansard,* x. 304.

[3] By a convention with the Emperor, £2,500,000 were accepted in satisfaction of all our claims upon him, namely the £6 millions of principal lent in 1795 and 1797, and the guaranteed dividends which had been paid by England all along —a total of, at compound interest, about £22,000,000. Reids, Barings, and the Rothschilds enabled him to find the money, and their charges brought down the sum repaid to about £2,200,000 (*Economic Annals, 1801-20,* 145 ; and *Hansard,* iv. 19, 1219 ; v. 1280).

[4] Robinson, as we saw, had expected a surplus of £8 millions.

Debt, the surplus available for any immediate public purpose was £1,710,000.

His estimates for the current year were as follows :

REVENUE.

Customs	£11,550,000
Excise	25,625,000
Stamps	6,800,000
Taxes (including Land and Assessed Taxes)	5,100,000
Post Office	1,460,000
Miscellaneous	730,000
Remaining payments of Austrian Loan	1,500,000
Half-pay and Pensions Annuity	4,620,000
	£57,385,000

EXPENDITURE.

Interest and management of Public Debt (not dependent on annual votes of the House)	£27,973,000
Interest on Deficiency (Exchequer) Bills	100,000
Civil List—Parliamentary Pensions, etc. (charged on Consolidated Fund)	2,050,000
Half-pay Annuities	2,800,000
Sinking Fund	5,135,000
Interest on Exchequer Bills	1,050,000
Army	7,441,000
Navy	5,763,000
Ordnance	1,410,000
Miscellaneous	2,611,000
	£56,333,000

This would show a surplus at the end of the year of £1,052,000, or £2,762,000 for the two years.[1]

So much of the surplus as arose out of the repayment of the Austrian Loan, he would propose to devote to certain objects of great national importance. It was to be looked on as a God-send ; few people expected ever to see a penny of it, and it was greatly to the credit of the Emperor—and he was as good and honourable a man as ever lived—that he had managed to persuade his finance minister to part with so much in the circumstances of the country. This " unexpected treasure that had found its way into the Exchequer," he would appropriate in three ways : (1) £500,000 for

[margin note: The Austrian Loan.]

---

[1] It will be noticed that, instead of estimating for a surplus of six millions, and " proposing to devote five millions for the redemption of debt," he boldly puts the five millions among the Expenditure as Sinking Fund, and leaves only a million as surplus.

building more churches [1]—" the manner in which this proposition seems to be received by an honourable member opposite (Hume) does not impress me, remembering, as I do, the light in which he has always viewed church establishments "; (2) £150,000 for repairing and adding to Windsor Castle (and other £150,000 within the next two years); (3) £60,000 for laying the foundation of a National Gallery.[2]

Another conversion— to 3½ %. Before entering on the disposal of the remainder of the surplus, he announced another conversion scheme, made possible by the fall in the rate of interest. The 4 per cent. stock, amounting to £75,000,000, with a charge of three millions, he proposed to convert to 3½ per cents., giving the six months notice required. Those who accepted the conversion would receive £100 of 3½ per cent. stock for every £100 of 4 per cent. stock. The inducement would be a guarantee of not being paid off for five years thereafter. Of those who did not accept, one-third would be paid off in October *pro rata*, and the remaining two-thirds in successive years. The saving, he calculated, would be £375,000 a year.

He now begged the House to accompany him a little beyond the present year, and consider how they were likely to stand at the end of 1827. The revenue in general might be assumed to be at least the same as at present. But there were certain items of charge which intercepted a part of the revenue in its progress to *Reduction of bounties.* the Exchequer, and on these he meant to propose a reduction. (1) The whale fishery bounty, amounting to £50,000, which Huskisson and he were convinced was entirely unnecessary, expired in the present year and would not be renewed.[3] (2) The bounty on the curing of herring and other fish, amounting to £70,000—a

[1] " When it is thought that religion is declining," commented Carlyle, " we have only to vote half a million's worth of bricks and mortar " (*Signs of the Times*).

[2] In view of this, the Government had already bought the Angerstein Collection of thirty-eight pictures—originally selected by Sir Thomas Lawrence, with " not one moderate picture among them "—for £57,000. The purchase met with unanimous approval ; even Hume was glad that the " disgrace " of not having a national gallery was now to be removed (*Hansard*, xi. 101).

[3] This bounty dated from 1732, when 20/- a ton were granted to every whaler of more than 200 tons burden, in order to encourage the British whale fishery against the Dutch. At various dates, it was 40/- and 30/- ; since 1795, it had been again 20/-. M'Culloch calculated that, since 1750, £2½ millions had been spent in this bounty, and suggested caustically that Franklin's remark, that he who draws a fish out of the sea draws a piece of silver, did not apply when, in fishing up one piece of silver, we were obliged to throw in another of greater value.

bounty which might have been necessary years ago, when British
fisheries were less advanced than those of other countries, but
was not now, when we were able to meet our ancient competitors,
the Dutch, in all the markets of Europe, would likewise die a natural
death.[1] (3) As to the linen bounties, on which £100,000 a year
might be saved, he was convinced, not only of their inutility but
of their mischievousness, but the reduction would not be immediate
and sweeping ; the bounty on inferior linens, indeed, would cease
immediately, but that on higher descriptions would fall by 10 per
cent. gradually until the whole was abolished.

The total result, then, would be a surplus, for 1825, of £372,000 ;
for 1826, of £477,000 ; for 1827, of £522,000. Adding these to the
surpluses of last year and this, the total surplus, at the end of
1827, would be £4,135,000.

The next question was, What should we do with it ? The most
immediate and obvious mode would, of course, be to use it for
reduction of the Debt, but, on many accounts, the remission of
taxation seemed to have the first claim. He would propose, then,
to use this surplus " as a means of commencing a system of alteration in the fiscal and commercial regulations of the country."

First, he would reduce the duty on Rum by 1/1½ per gallon, in Rum.
order to bring it to a level with the duty on British spirits. Whether
this would do good to the West Indies or not, might be a question,
but the reduction was sound in principle. This would cost the
revenue £150,000.[2]

---

[1] The deep-sea herring bounty was instituted in 1750, when, in addition to
remission of the duty on salt used, 50/- of tonnage bounty was given—as
Adam Smith said, vessels were fitted out for the sole purpose of catching, not
the fish, but the bounty. In 1808, it was made 60/- per ton burthen on vessels
from 60 to 100 tons, besides a sum of 2/- per barrel of herring. In 1815,
as the fishing was making no progress, this was raised to 4/- per barrel. This
was at a time when the price per barrel was about 16/-. On asking the opinion
of the Commissioners for the Herring Fishery, the Board of Trade had been
advised that the 4/- bounty might now be diminished without detriment,
but that the reduction should be gradual—a shilling a barrel to begin with.
The tonnage bounty, however, was an expenditure of money which might
very well be saved, and it was a fruitful source of fraud and perjury ; they
recommended, accordingly, that it should be wholly withdrawn. Although
not noticed in *Hansard*, Robinson's good intentions evidently were not carried
out. In 1827, £92,000 was still paid in bounties for Scotch and Irish fisheries ;
" the putting an end to them has, of late years," wrote Parnell, " been so often
enacted by law and so often postponed, that it may be set down as certain that
every effort will be made to continue them " (*Financial Reform*, 127).

[2] In this case the event proved that the revenue was fully recouped by the
increase in imports.

Coals.   Second, he would reduce the long-standing duty on Coals, which pressed very unequally on various parts of the country and with peculiar and unnecessarily aggravated severity on London. The duty on sea-borne coal was 6/- per chaldron on the country at large, and 9/4 in the port of London.[1] This latter burden—the 3/4 extra on London—would be swept away at once. The gain of the metropolis would be increased by another measure, namely, the removal of the practically prohibitive restrictions on the importation of inland coals into London—the 10/- local duty, when they came by Thames, the 7/6 duty when brought by canal. This would end the monopoly in coal. But it would increase the consumption, and the immediate loss to the revenue of £200,000 would probably in the end be no more than £100,000.

But the most important of the changes now proposed were so, not from the point of view of revenue, but from that of " a more free and liberal system of policy in matters connected with trade."

Wool.   First came Wool.[2] Of late, the Government had made public the " deal " they proposed with the manufacturers—" if you will consent to the removal of the impolitic restriction (as we consider it) on the exportation of British wool, we will propose to Parliament the repeal of the duty on the importation of foreign wool." [3] Many

---

[1] The general tax on sea-borne coal was imposed by William III. The 3/4 extra payable in London was really an octroi, levied in 1667 for the rebuilding of the city after the Great Fire, and since continued for city improvements.

[2] At various times, in past centuries, the exportation of raw wool had been prohibited, sometimes to annoy other countries, sometimes to allow our sovereigns to increase their private revenue. In Elizabeth's time, when the manufacture was very prosperous, the export was entirely free. The policy of absolute prohibition, which aimed at the protection of the home manufacturer by securing him, not only the monopoly of what was considered a superior raw material, but an abundant and cheap supply of that material, was formally adopted by the 12th of Chas. II., and had continued ever since. This, of course, was a grievance of the farmers, and, to give them their " just " share of protection, the importation of foreign wool—mostly from Spain—which had hitherto been entirely free, was checked, first, by a duty of 5/3 per cwt. in 1802, then of 6/8 in 1813, and, finally, of 56/-, or 6d. per lb. in 1819. The injury this was doing to the woollen manufacture was obvious, and was dwelt on by the Lords' Committee of 1828 ; for (1) English wool, thanks to the improvements which had increased the weight of the carcass and the quantity of the fleece, had by no means maintained its high quality, and (2) foreign wool was necessary for many descriptions of cloth—particularly the cloths exported. See M'Culloch, *ad verb.* ; also a strong article in the *Edinburgh Review*, October 1823, on the decline in the wool trade since 1819.

[3] Robinson affirmed that the rise in the import duty from 1d. to 6d. in 1819 was not for protection, but for revenue. But it was certainly put forward at the time frankly as a duty of protection (*Annals, 1801-20*, 685). The arguments for the repeal of this duty were given in February, in a petition from

meetings had been held over the country where the subject was fully discussed, and a decided majority were willing to accept the compromise. He proposed, then, to reduce the 6d. per lb. duty on foreign wool, imposed in 1819, to the old figure of 1d., and to allow the free exportation of British wool (and of manufactures so put together as to be capable of reduction to and use again as wool) on the payment of 1d. also. He could not anticipate evil to the agriculturists in this ; the consequence would be a great extension of our foreign trade, and it was beyond his comprehension how this could be otherwise than beneficial to the growers of wool in this country who supplied the raw material.[1] The diminution of revenue would be about £350,000.

Next came Silk.[2] The position was a curious one. There were Silk. revenue duties on raw silk, heavy protective duties on thrown

London wool merchants and factors and in the debate thereon. (1) The tax could be justified only by the most pressing necessity, whereas, now that English woollens were in competition in foreign markets with foreigners subject to no such tax, the duty, which was all but prohibitive, made it impossible for British manufacturers to compete. (Incidentally, the interesting calculation was given that if, in any year, the wool crop at home was one-tenth over the average, the price would fall by 30 per cent. ; if one-fifth, by 60 per cent.) (2) Since 1822, the exports of woollens had decreased by upwards of one-fourth. Our coarse cloths were accordingly shut out of Italy, " where nothing but coarse wool was now grown," and Germany had secured the monopoly of supplying Egypt and Turkey. (3) France had taken off her duty on importation. (4) The manufacturers would be forced to employ agents on the Continent to wash the wool, in order to effect a reduction of the duties. (5) The duty was imposed in 1819, for the protection of agriculture, as a counterpoise to the new duty of 18d. per bushel on malt, and a half of this malt duty had been removed (*Hansard*, x. 267). To this might be added (6) that the existing and heavy duty imposed in 1819 was not that under which the wool growers had gained wealth and importance (*Hansard*, xlvi. 35, 1839).

[1] The Act also repealed the prohibition of exporting and carrying coastwise live sheep.

[2] Introduced into England in the fifteenth century, the manufacture made great progress in the age of Elizabeth, and was firmly rooted by 1666, when it employed some 40,000 persons. And all that time—in fact, till 1697—the importation of foreign silks was, generally speaking, quite free. It is worth noting that from £600,000 to £700,000 worth of foreign silks were annually imported during the very period when the British silk manufacture made the most rapid advances, from 1685 to 1692. It was only at the solicitation of the French refugees that Parliament passed an Act, in 1697, prohibiting the importation of all European silk goods, and, in 1701, extended the prohibition to the silks of India and China. As might be expected, in the early days of the manufacture, the importation of the raw material was taxed only with a view to revenue. But, in 1719, in consequence of the patent granted to Lombe's machine for throwing silk, and the high hopes entertained that England would become independent of foreign supply, a large amount of capital was invested in throwing mills, and the interests of this infant industry were the reasons given for the enormous duties on organzine—that is, two or more single fibres twisted together reversely or " thrown " (M'Culloch, *Dictionary, ad verb.* Silk).

silk, and a positive prohibition of the use of foreign silk goods. As to the latter, our antiquated system was seriously standing in the way of commerce with foreign countries. Whenever a foreign state imposed a new duty on any of our manufactures, the Government was immediately assailed by letters from all quarters asking them to make representations and remonstrances. How could they do so, when the answer was inevitably a *tu quoque* ? Now there never was a more favourable opportunity for emancipating ourselves from ancient prejudices, for cutting the cords which tied commerce to the earth, for making a new start in the race for national wealth and prosperity, than the present, when our manufactures were in a state of universal activity, and capital was eagerly searching for employment.

Smuggling.   But there was another reason for it.   " I remember, and I daresay there are many honourable gentlemen who have not forgotten, that, when the honourable member for Aberdeen (Hume) last year produced his bandana handkerchief even in this place, and, having triumphantly unfurled the standard of smuggling, blew his nose with it,[1] I reminded the honourable gentleman of that of which he did not seem to be aware at the time ; namely, that there was not an honourable gentleman near him who had not an absolute right to take possession of that handkerchief. . . .   Every one who has been on the coast and has watched the arrival of vessels from the neighbouring Continent, must have frequently observed females step out of them apparently in a state of the most uncomfortable corpulence ; who, in time however, and without any surgical aid, were safely delivered of their burdens, and restored to the natural slimness and grace of their own figures."   But it was not ingenuity only, but fraud, perjury, and every bad moral consequence, that flowed from it.   A young man might bring over a piece of silk, perhaps " as a present to a female friend."   This act, in itself not only innocent but laudable, our law had converted into a crime. *Nemo repente fuit turpissimus.*   This young man might go on to turn the practice to a profit—get familiarised with false oaths, perjury, etc.   Then followed a navy to keep the contraband trade

---

[1] The incident occurred on 30th June, 1823—it is not reported in *Hansard*—when Hume, flourishing his own yellow bandana, said that he would bet that every silk handkerchief in the House was smuggled. " Aye, there it is," he cried, when many handkerchiefs were produced, " is it not monstrous that law makers should be law breakers—I mean should be compelled to be so ? " The House was convulsed when Hume went on gravely that a man who began with smuggling would go on to the commission of the greatest crimes !

in check. Battles, bloodshed, and murder ensued[1]—all for the interests of a few silk manufacturers who, he sincerely believed, could already drive their foreign rivals out of the field, wherever the market was open.

In the first place, then, said Robinson, he would reduce the duty on raw silk from the East Indies—and this led him to say, in passing, that, as our cotton manufactures had completely superseded their domestic cottons, the original staple manufacture of the East Indies, we owed them some reparation, and, as they could not buy without selling, he proposed to admit their manufactured silks at a fair duty. The duty on raw silk from the East Indies would be reduced from 4/- to 3d. per lb. ; on raw silk from China and Italy, from 5/- to 6d. ; the duty on organzine, from 14/10 to 7/6. As regards foreign manufactured silks, all prohibitions would be removed—he trusted, for ever—and the following substituted : on plain silk goods in the piece, 15/- a lb. ; on figured silk goods (which were much more valuable), 20/- a lb. ; and, on all other silk goods, 30 per cent. *ad valorem.* He would likewise propose that " shoes, gloves, and other articles of that sort which everybody knew were not now kept out at all, but which, being prohibited by law, were introduced into the country by fraud, should be admitted on paying a duty of 30 per cent. *ad valorem.* He was not prepared to say, with regard to the last-mentioned articles, that there ought to be no variation in the scale of duty, or that the duty ought always to continue as high as he had stated it ; but, at all events, it was fair, in the commencement, to let the advantage, if any, be in favour of the British manufacturer. The loss to the revenue would be £462,000.[2]

The whole annual decrease in the revenue would thus be £1,062,000. " If we multiply this sum by three, in order to ascertain the loss of the years 1825, 1826, and 1827, and add half that sum as the loss which will accrue in this present year, 1824, we shall find that the total loss down to the end of the year 1827 will be £3,717,000." Deducting that from the total surplus of £4,135,000, there would remain, at the end of 1827, a balance in favour of the Exchequer of £418,000. He then adverted to the remaining part of the Salt Salt. Duty, amounting to 2/- a bushel, which the Government was pledged to remove in January next. He had an open mind about this. But if there appeared to be—as he thought there was—a general feeling that no evil would accrue from the continuation

[1] For confirmation see *Hansard* of 1821, v. 215.
[2] The same Act repealed the bounties on the exportation of silk manufactures.

of that small portion of the duty, he would prefer to continue it. He finished by expressing his gratification that a Government, which had taken off £8 millions of taxation in the last three years, should still find it in their power to take off another million, and sat down " amidst loud cheers " from all sides of the House.

Criticism:

The proposals were received on the whole with appreciation, and the criticism does not strike one as doing anything more than

Baring,

the presumed duty of an Opposition to oppose. Baring had never of late years heard so gratifying a statement ; he doubted, however, if this plan of finance, extending over years, was not based on more certainty of results than was justified ; he thought the conversion to $3\frac{1}{2}$ per cent. was a greater reduction than the means of the country warranted ; and, while professing to have no objection to the principle of introducing foreign manufactures, he asked if any communications had been opened with other countries for reciprocal

Ellice,

concessions. Ellice justly pointed out that an immediate reduction of the silk duties would cause great inconvenience and distress ; the present duty on silk amounted to a heavy percentage on the value of the article, and of late there had been very large pur- chases ; persons with large stocks of manufactured goods for spring consumption would be heavily hit. Agreeing on the expediency of ultimately reducing the duties, he protested against it being

Brougham,

done suddenly. Brougham, in a captious speech, expressed his disappointment. The only results would be cheaper coal—a benefit to the poor, indeed, but only to those less poor than others, the poor of London ; cheaper silk—a benefit to the rich ; cheaper rum—and " he was one of those who would rather support that which would make it dearer, for the sake of public morals." He would have liked to see some part of the Sinking Fund taken for the relief of taxation. For the Austrian repayment, he had nothing but ridicule. Was it a " God-send " that the Emperor had had the common honesty to pay us half a crown in the pound upon the money he had borrowed of us so long ago ? He hoped that the panegyric pronounced that night would bring out—not another half-crown, for that would be too much to hope for—but another sixpence. As for building churches, this was half a million taken from the whole people to be spent on a section—" the whole respect- able and liberal body of dissenters in the country were to be excluded from any participation " : with such a sum, no fewer than 2,500 schools might have been erected, and every parish provided with a school of some sort.

Hume went much further. The whole of the Sinking Fund Hume. should have been taken to reduce the burdens. The duty on rum should be reduced to 5/- —" he allowed that the immediate effect of making spirits cheap might be morally injurious, but it would not continue so ; for it was always the case with any dear article that, when accidental circumstances enabled the poorer classes to obtain it, they gratified themselves to excess ; but, as soon as it became easily accessible, it was comparatively neglected " : [1] the French, for instance, were a soberer people than the English. All the assessed taxes should be taken off—it was owing to them that the mansions of our gentry were deserted ; so should these most iniquitous taxes on law proceedings. It was monstrous to let the Emperor off with half a crown in the pound. As to churches— " really, if ever any public proposition deserved to meet with universal reprobation, it was this."

Robinson, in replying, said that his idea was that the reduction on the Silk Duties should take effect from 5th July ; that the duty on inland coals should be 1/- a ton ; [2] that the sum needed to pay off the 4 per cents. converted should be got by loan or by Exchequer Bills ; and the resolutions were then agreed to.

The preliminary items in the Budget were disposed of without much difficulty, though strong language continued to be used about the Austrian " God-send " which made them possible.[3] The grant

[1] In 1796, Pitt had laid it down as a principle that " the consumption is so pernicious that no man could wish that there should be any limits to the duty, so far as is consistent with the means of safely collecting it." Hume evidently was not aware that his experiment had been tried in 1689 when distilling had been thrown open, with the result that, by 1724, the passion for gin drinking spread among the masses with the rapidity and the violence of an epidemic, and the fatal passion for drink was at once, and irrevocably planted in the nation. " Small as is the place which this fact occupies in English history," says Lecky, " it was probably, if we consider all the consequences that have flowed from it, the most momentous in that of the eighteenth century—incomparably more so than any event in the purely political or military annals of the country " (History, ii. 479).

[2] Apparently Scotland was exempted altogether from the 1/- duty: see infra.

[3] One member hoped that, in justice to other bankrupts, the name of the Emperor would appear in the Gazette. Hume raised a vigorous opposition to the amount being taken as a discharge in full. Lord Holland calculated that the sum due without compound interest was £17½ millions, and, with compound interest, £24 millions ; suggested that part of the loan had actually been handed over to the enemy of this country; and made great fun of the " payment—great talent must have been displayed by the persons who managed this affair in persuading His Imperial Majesty that his large debt was paid." It was for this speech, presumably, that Lord Holland appears among the list of persons prohibited from entering Austrian territory, as a person entertaining

Grant for churches.

for Churches was defended mainly on the ground of the existing want of accommodation. The last million granted by Parliament in 1818 had built ninety-eight churches and given accommodation to 53,000 persons, and all the new churches were full to overflowing : besides, it had stimulated auxiliary subscriptions of £200,000. But there were still 179 places, containing 3,548,000 inhabitants, which had church accommodation only for 500,000 souls, or about one in seven. " If we were to have any established church, that church must take contributions from the dissenters as well as from its own members." Hume protested that the churches might be built without the aid of Parliament—the only object of the vote was to increase the church patronage ; that the money might be applied to better purposes, etc.; and obtained some support in his opposition, but the measure was passed by overwhelming majorities.[1]

Grant for Windsor Castle.

The grant for Windsor Castle needed no other justification than the many inconveniences of the existing building, and the reminder that the splendour of the royal dwelling should correspond with the dignity of the sovereign and of the country over which he reigned. But there was considerable criticism of the work being begun without detailed plans and estimates, and Hume was not alone in thinking that, without some such limits, more would be needed when the grant was spent. If any one doubted that, said Grey Bennet, he need only repeat two words—" Caledonian Canal ! "[2]

"notoriously very bad sentiments "—" an enthusiastic adherent of radicalism "—distinguished by his " insolent abuse against the allied monarchs." Canning defended the transaction as really the settlement of a claim which had lapsed. Liverpool pointed out that, at the time the loan was granted, the whole question was whether it should be a subsidy or a loan—" there was no individual who voted for the loan who would not have voted for giving the money as a subsidy."

[1] *Hansard*, xi. 171, 328, 384, 1080, 1093, 1430. It is painful to read, in parliamentary debates, but, usually more frankly, in contemporary literature, the language used about dissent in these years. Sir Isaac Coffin, supporting the Government, said that there had been a lamentable increase of those devil-killers called Methodists—such an increase as, he was sure, must eventually undermine the Church of England. These Methodists were such rooting fellows, that, let them once get into your house, they would soon get into the kitchen, from the kitchen, they would go into the cellar—and the inevitable consequences among servants were prostitution and dishonesty ; and this disgraceful speech was greeted with a laugh and cries of "hear " (*ibid.* 384).

[2] The Caledonian Canal had been opened from sea to sea in 1822, at a total expenditure of £900,000. In 1823, there was an extra grant of £25,000, and now another " last grant " had just been asked for—to make it of a uniform depth of 20 feet throughout, " without which the canal would be utterly useless " (*Hansard*, x. 630).

Hume obtained 54 votes for his amendment, asking for postponement generally, but the resolution was passed by 123.[1]

The objections to the alteration in the Coal Duties were, many Sea-borne and
of them, rather captious; such as that other taxes were more inland coal.
grievous and should be repealed first, and that the change would
give an undue preference, in the relief of taxation, to one part of
the community which had least need of it, the city of London.
But the strongest opposition came, of course, from the coal masters
on Wear and Tyne, who asked, with some show of reason, why the
duty of 6/- should be continued on their coal sent to London while
all duties (except 1/-) were taken off the coal of their competitors
in Staffordshire. The ready answer was that the carriage charges
on inland coal were so heavy as to be entirely prohibitive—instead
of sending 50,000 tons, as was now allowed, the actual sending
had dwindled to a tenth part of that—and it was further said that,
even when these duties were repealed, inland coal would still be
unable to compete. Stuart Wortley, however, acutely raised
another point: Was the abolition of duties on inland coal, while
the duty was continued on the competing coal from Newcastle,
not a highly artificial protection? was it not going against Free
Trade principles altogether, and handicapping the sea-borne coal
because, owing to natural circumstances, it could be brought cheap
to London?—" upon exactly the same principle, a tax might be
laid upon Kent or Essex wheat to balance the additional cost which
attended wheat coming from Yorkshire." The opposition to the
measure then took the form of a demand that the sea-borne duty
also should be removed, and the trade made entirely free, letting
the market go to those who could naturally supply it most cheaply.
To this Robinson's answer was that, while he admitted that the
tax on sea-borne coal was very unequal on different parts of
the country, and pressed with peculiar severity and inequality on the
metropolis, it was a duty for which the present Government was
not responsible, and that he was not prepared to sacrifice the £900,000
of revenue.[2]

It was not to be expected that the Budget alterations in the The " stun of
prohibitory duties would be allowed to pass without a vigorous surprise."
struggle. Within the House, indeed, there was a kind of enthusiasm
for Free Trade which blinded the members, perhaps, to the greatness
of the change. But, outside, the *Times* probably was right when
it said, " we perceive that stun of surprise in the nation, which

[1] *Hansard*, xi. 147.   [2] *Ibid*. x. 270, 301, 1448; xi. 49.

imposes silence at first but will shortly break forth in indignation and execration." The whole thing, it continued, was not a finance measure at all—not one which could with any propriety be introduced into the Budget. And, it may be granted that it was a new thing to find a Chancellor of the Exchequer rejoicing in the giving up of large revenues, not, as was said, to lift the burden of taxation from the people, but " to indulge a set of theorists in their mania for politico-economical experiments." Nothing was to be heard in the interested circles but complaints of the financial arrangements—from clothiers, silk-weavers, linen-weavers, distillers.[1]

The wool manufacturers petitioned, stating energetically that there never was such a serious blow struck at their industry as by the removal of the ancient prohibition of export. The long wool used in the manufacture of worsteds was the exclusive growth of this country, and, indeed, of certain districts in this country ; in the manufacture three or four times its value was added by British labour ; to allow it to go abroad and be manufactured by foreign countries, was to throw away the natural advantage which this country had. Presumably there were representations also that it would not be fair to those manufacturers and merchants who had stocks of woollen goods on which the high import duty had been paid ; and, later on, Robinson announced that he had made

Change in the wool proposals. a change in his proposals. First, the import duty on foreign wool would be reduced by degrees—by 3d. in September, and by the remaining 2d. in December : in view of this, he did not think it necessary to give rebates on duties already paid.[2] And, second, the existing prohibition of the export of raw wool would be replaced by an export duty of 2d. instead of the 1d. he had proposed. This latter compromise, however, was not well received by the agriculturists. Western said that 2d. was practically prohibitive—it

---

[1] One newspaper put forward a new reading of *Laisser-faire*: " It certainly is most unaccountable that, although our new political economists in the Cabinet profess to go on the old French story of *laissez-nous faire* in mercantile affairs, yet they will not let people alone who were perfectly contented, but thrust the new principles down their throat to nearly absolute choking."

[2] The subsequent history of the import duty is that, soon after the reduction, there was a great fall in price. In 1828, accordingly, innumerable petitions were presented, predicting ruin, and asking for reimposition of the high duty. In the Lords, a Committee was appointed, and witness after witness declared that the low price was entirely occasioned by the glut of foreign importation. Parliament, however, refused to listen ; and, by 1839, Lord Howick said that, while the import had increased from 30 to 60 million lbs. the price of English wool was much higher than it had been during the highly protective period (*Hansard*, 1839, xlvi. 553).

amounted to 20 per cent. on low priced wool—and, in the end,
the Chancellor of the Exchequer promised that, if it should turn
out to be prohibitive after a trial, the subject could be reconsidered.[1]
In committee, again, there was some opposition : the measure
would be " ruinous to agriculture " ; it was " the first-fruits of
that new school of philosophy which had lately sprung up respecting
Free Trade " ; it was pressed by " gentlemen who were led away
by their love of spinning-jennies " ; it was not fair that a million
of drawbacks should be given to the silk industry and nothing to the
woollen, etc. The Bill, however, passed without further alteration.[2]

The battleground between old and new, however, was the pro- Baring's
posed alteration in the Silk Duties. This seemed accepted pretty arguments
generally as an *experimentum crucis* ; if silk could stand Free Trade, silk proposals.
anything could, the raw material being purely an exotic and already
manufactured in the countries of its origin. The arguments against
it were marshalled by no less a person than the former protagonist
of Free Trade, Baring. In presenting a petition signed by " nearly
all the most respectable individuals in London and neighbourhood
concerned in the manufacture and trade of silk," he felt bound to
say that the petitioners were in the right.

(1) Everybody connected with the trade was dead against the
alteration.

(2) The manufacture was extremely flourishing, and employed
an immense number of persons.

(3) 30 per cent. was an insufficient duty ; it ought to be 50 per
cent. to put English silks on anything like a footing in point of
price with those of France.

---

[1] *Hansard*, x. 370, 650, 751, 1423, 1442. So far as I can find, the original
proposal of 1d. per lb. export duty became law. In December, 50 bags were
exported to the United States—the first export for about 200 years.

[2] *Ibid.* ix. 804. The result of this great change was given by Huskisson
in 1826—and Huskisson himself, in 1823, it will be remembered, had denied
that the heavy import duty was doing much harm. It made him more and
more distrustful, he said, of the predictions of the " practical " authorities.
Instead of the manufacture being ruined, we had, since the abolition of the
restrictions on export, sent abroad the " amazing quantity " of 100,000 lbs.
of British wool, while, of foreign wool, we had imported no less than 40,000,000
lbs. ; that is to say, we had exported, comparatively, none of native growth
—because we had a better market for it at home (*Hansard*, xiv. 779). We
learn from Porter that the immediate result of allowing the export of wool
was that the French soon produced new stuffs from English wool superior to
anything ever produced in England. But the stimulus thus applied was so
effective, that, in a very few years, our manufacturers were turning out
merinos and other stuffs in every respect equal to their rivals (*Progress of the
Nation*, ii. 11).

(4) —in answer to the argument that high duties were evaded by smuggling—The real protection was not the Custom House, but the power existing at home to seize foreign silk articles whenever they made their appearance.

(5) This was a trade of fashion, and the prevalent opinion in favour of French goods was so strong—and the French had such an advantage in point of dyeing and of patterns—that French silks would be bought in preference to English.

(6) There was no reciprocity at all in the case of France.

(7) The conditions in the two countries were not equal; food here was double the price, and labour was dear, while, abroad, the price of labour was low, and the raw material was obtained on much better terms; to compete with Lyons, all the statutes establishing regulations between workmen and masters must first be done away with. In short, " if we introduced so much of the principles of Free Trade as to allow foreign manufactures to be brought into this country, we must go the whole length of the free system, and get rid of all those laws which prevented the equalisation of the terms on which labour could be procured in this and in foreign countries." [1]

(8) The silk interests would rather give up the reduction in the duties on raw silk than consent to the entrance of manufactured silks. [2]

Towards the end of the debate, however, Baring said that he had never gone further than a free trade in the raw material and a free transit of all goods, so that England might enjoy the carrying trade of the world ; and that the reason why he had dwelt on the handicap of dear labour in England was that, while cotton, from the first operation to the last, went through machinery, silk was thrown off by hand, and, from the nature of it, could not throughout be so much worked by machinery as was cotton. Subsequently he reiterated that it was " a dangerous experiment for the country." He himself had a strong inclination towards the principle of Free Trade, but Huskisson appeared to him to have selected the most dangerous instance for the trial of his experiment. It was beginning at the wrong end.

---

[1] " While the subsistence of the people was at twice the price here that it was in other countries, they might live on the purest system of political economy, but they might die with the book in their hand " (*Hansard*, x. 1230).

[2] The silk manufacturers of Staffordshire, however, disowned such a compromise (*Hansard*, x. 1328).

That such perverse ingenuity in arguing against the practical application of Free Trade principles should come, of all men, from Baring—even although he was member for a silk manufacturing constituency—who had presented the petition of the London merchants in 1820, and had so often and so ably advocated these principles, was as unexpected as it was unwelcome,[1] and Canning rather bitterly commented on it—if one were unwilling Canning. to make any change till the whole system could be altered, he might preach to all eternity on the excellence of his general principles with a perfect certainty that they never would be carried into execution. Huskisson was surprised to hear Baring say that Huskisson. the "real protection" against smuggling was one which had so frequently been denounced as unconstitutional; to find him base his principal argument on the proposition that English labour was dear in the silk trade, as if it were not dear in every other—*e.g.* in cotton and wool, which yet competed successfully with the foreigner; to have the fact ignored that, even with all the restrictions and heavy duties, the British export of silk manufactures " exceeded the whole export of France "; and he protested against the assumption that either the House or the trade had been taken by surprise, as the silk trade had been the first to suggest the removal of restrictions. Ellice and others, professing Free Trade in principle, urged that the beginning should be made with some other trade than that branch of industry which was exposed to the greatest chance of successful competition—" how was it possible to rival the principal and favourite manufacture of France while the price of bread in England was twice as high as in any other market of the civilised world ? " To this Peel, making his first appearance as Peel. a Free Trader,[2] made a very pithy reply : Let them point out any

[1] Baring's attitude is all the more puzzling that we find him, in the very next year, making a strong Free Trade speech, expressing his satisfaction at Huskisson's reforms, deprecating the argument that some private and particular interests were prejudiced, questioning if any considerable quantity of manufactures would come into the country in consequence of the new policy, speaking strongly against the Corn Laws as pressing most heavily on the country's manufactures, commerce, and foreign relations, and saying that he could not help expressing the opinion, however it might differ from that of the economists, that the low price of labour was not a conclusive criterion of the capability of a country for manufacture—he need only refer to Ireland (*Hansard*, xii. 1224).

[2] Peel, immersed in the business of the Home Office, had supported the commercial policy of Huskisson, as he had the foreign policy of Canning, but hitherto had taken no part in the debates. He was already showing " all that manliness and tact for which," said Moore in 1827, "Peel is so distinguished." It is rather notable that Cobbett, who seldom had a good word

other branch of manufacture in which any such prohibition existed :
there was none ; they assumed the general policy to be prohibition,
whereas silk was the one exception. On steel, cotton, wool, and all the
other great articles of manufacture, there was no prohibition, and yet
in these it had been found that we were able to defy all competition.
Again, in the silk manufacture, it was said, Great Britain was
inferior to France in point of taste and machinery. Now did not
this fact lead to the suspicion that it was on account of the prohibition that the same improvements had not been made in this
manufacture that had been made in all others ? Was silk not
quite as much a native manufacture of this country as cotton or
linen ? had it not flourished in this soil for forty or fifty years ?
Far from this plan having no sponsors, as Baring had affirmed,
those general principles, which Baring himself had invariably
advocated, were the sponsors—and a higher authority than any
Hume. parties interested in the silk manufacture. Hume reminded the
House of what the evidence before the House of Lords'. Committee
had proved, that, if we could get the raw material of silk as cheap
as we obtained it of cotton, there was no reason why our silk trade
should not be as flourishing as our cotton trade.[1] Many speakers
seemed to see in the proposals nothing but a political move, and
warmly recommended the Government to take up the Malt, and
Hops, and Leather Duties, or the Window Tax, or the Taxes on Justice
or the Corn Laws—anything but silk. Philips, however, with some
justice, praised Ministers that they had not put forward these liberal
measures to catch popular support—for certainly they were not
popular. Almost alone, Lethbridge heartily denounced the Free Trade
principle. The House was running wild with its theories ; such
principles could never be carried into operation. Neither corn,
wool, cotton, nor silk would bear Free Trade. The activity of the
country had grown up under a different system. The " insinuating
eloquence " of Ricardo—whose memory, all the same, would long
be cherished, and most sincerely by those who knew him best—
had done much mischief by leading the House from practical views ;
his writings showed contradiction on contradiction ; and, however
charming his theories were to political economists, they were dia-
for anybody, said that he had a great opinion of Peel's judgment (*Register*,
1824).

[1] He might have quoted Adam Smith : " If raw silk could be imported
from China or Hindostan duty free, the silk manufactures in England could
greatly undersell all those of both France and Italy, and there would be no
occasion to prohibit the importation of foreign silks and velvets."

metrically opposed to practical results.   But he confessed that he
would be very willing to see the Corn Laws revised ; he thought
the prices now likely to rise too high.[1]

A few days later,[2] Huskisson—in place of the Chancellor of the **Huskisson**
Exchequer, who, perhaps happily, was indisposed—announced **compares Cotton and**
how far the Government would go in concession to the opinions **Silk.**
expressed.   After some amusing banter, fancying what Baring,
forty years ago, would have said if free trade in cotton (then
subject to the same heavy duties as silk now) had been proposed—
" how can you expect that England, which possesses so little
machinery, can compete in the cotton trade with India, where labour
is so cheap " ?—made a very fine defence of the new policy.   There
was nothing in the history of commerce that could compare with
the growth of the cotton trade.   In 1780, the whole export of cotton
manufactures was not more than £350,000.   In 1785, it did not
exceed £864,000, while the woollen exports amounted to nearly
£5,000,000.   By 1822, the cotton exports had risen to over £33,000,000
while the woollen exports were not more than £6,000,000.   These
were the official figures of the exports.   But the real value of the
cotton goods consumed at home, during the past year, amounted
to no less than £32,000,000.   " When I state that, of these
£32,000,000, not more than about £6,000,000 are invested in the
raw material, and that the remaining £26,000,000 go to the profits
of the capitalist and to the persons employed in the manufacture,
will any man who takes a statesmanlike view of the subject doubt
the proposition with which I set out ; that, when you remove the
restrictions and burdens from any one branch of industry, you
not only afford relief to the amount of the tax remitted, but you
lay the foundation for commercial enterprise, of the beneficial
effects of which it is impossible to foresee the event. . . .   I would
ask whether the 1,200,000 persons employed in this manufacture,
whose wants are supplied in return for their labour, do not afford
more real encouragement to agriculture than any regulations to
force up artificial prices could do ?   It is to the growth of wealth
and the progress of industry that this country must look, not only
for relief from her present burdens, but for the power of making
fresh exertions whenever her situation may demand them. . . .
The most remarkable feature in the history of the cotton manufacture is the impetus which it has given to invention, the numerous
important and valuable discoveries which it has brought forth,

[1] *Hansard*, x. 731.   [2] *Ibid.* x. 800.

the ingenuity which it has called into action, the tendency and effect
of all which have been to produce the article at the lowest possible
rate ; and we find that, in the end, a greater number of persons
have been employed to direct the machinery in proportion as the
manufacturer had the prospect of fresh resources." As compared
with this, monopoly in the silk trade had produced what monopoly
was always sure to produce, an indifference with regard to improvements—a chilling and benumbing effect,—till, to the shame of
England be it spoken, in this branch alone, in the whole range of
manufactures, we were completely left behind by our neighbours.

The evils of
smuggling.

But this was not all.   Were there any evils in our penal code which
could be at all compared with those wrought by the system of prohibition which many gentlemen were so desirous to uphold ?   " By the
present laws, any individual, no matter who, the commonest ruffian
in the street, might snatch from a gentleman any article which he
suspected to be of foreign manufacture.   Could anything be less con-
genial to the spirit of English law than that a man might enter the
dwelling house of his neighbour, and make a diligent search, because
he suspected that there was some prohibited article to be found in
his domicile ? "   Had they not heard of Excise officers stopping a
gentleman's carriage and subjecting it to a diligent search, upon
bare suspicion of its containing contraband goods ?   To what an
extent of perjury and fraud did not such regulations give encouragement ?   The higher classes of society would have the prohibited
articles.   " In fact, these prohibitory regulations are like the game
laws—if you continue them, you must expect to have poachers."
He referred to evidence before the Lords' Committee : a Spitalfields
manufacturer, Mr. Hale, had stated that, when he was in Paris,
French merchants offered him, for an insurance of 10 per cent., to
send any quantity of manufactured silks he chose to select to any
part of London he pleased, notwithstanding their liability to be
seized as French wherever they were found.   It was very significant
that Mr. Hale did not consider this an evil ; for, such was the disposition to wear anything that came from France, that the few
silks thus introduced were immediately copied and sold by the
thousand—indeed these English goods were very often sold by the
fishermen and smugglers at Brighton, as French, at higher prices
than was given for them in London !   Surely, with a protecting
duty of 30 per cent., the French patterns might be fairly copied,
" without ministering to the vitiated taste of those who can derive
no satisfaction from a garment unless it be worn in opposition to

the laws of the land and affords encouragement to smugglers ! "
As a fact, not the least part of the secret confederacy against the
proposed arrangement was the influence exerted by ladies' maids
and their mistresses, who benefited by the smuggling.

Granting, however, that postponement of the change was likely
to produce stagnation meantime, he proposed that the remission
of the duty on raw silk should take place on the 25th March—it
was now the 8th—and that persons having raw silk on hand should,
on returning it into the warehouse, get drawback of the duty paid
thereon, and be allowed to take back the silk on 25th March at the
new rate. This arrangement, however, would not extend to any
stock worked and distributed. Further, silk manufactures intended
for exportation might be warehoused for that purpose, and, immediately on exportation, would be admitted to the full benefit of the
drawback. As to the prohibition of manufactured silks, he confessed that, in machinery, in working, and in colouring, British
makers were as yet inferior to our continental neighbours ; and, so
long as this was so, some consideration must be shown to them.
The repeal of the prohibition, then, would not take effect till July,
1826. The concession was received with loud cheers, not only from
the members, but from numerous individuals concerned in the trade
who had found their way into the gallery.[1]

The debate is extremely interesting as showing how the most
intelligent debating society in the kingdom might be quite unanimous on a principle so long as it was not reduced to practice, and
further, how every member thought that, while Free Trade might
very well be applied to other industries, the industry in which he
was interested, either personally or as representative, ought to be
made an exception. And it awakes the suspicion—which was to
come to plentiful expression later—that those who were most
enthusiastic about Free Trade expected that it would be applied,
first at least, to the industry in which they were not interested,
namely, agriculture.

But this was very far from ending the matter. The struggle Drawbacks.
was now concentrated on the drawbacks. It was all very well, it

---

[1] Petitions had been presented in March from 23,000 journeymen silk
weavers of the Metropolis and from 7000 weavers and householders of Bethnal
Green, apprehending " entire ruin " from the importation of foreign silks.
The crowd in the gallery was largely composed of these workers. A very full
report of Huskisson's speech was given subsequently in the newspapers—
presumably the Government thought it the best defence of the new " liberal
principle in commercial affairs."

was said, to give an allowance on goods warehoused and exported. But what about the manufacturers, some of whom had worked up immense stocks merely to keep their people in employment ? What about the merchants who sold for home consumption ? Huskisson promised to take this into consideration ; and, next day, moved that one-half of the drawback, which otherwise would be given on export, should be allowed on such manufactures as, having been warehoused, should be taken out for home consumption within thirty days after 5th April, 1824 ; and this satisfied many of the manufacturers.

Meantime, Baring was exerting all his energies still further to postpone the repeal of the prohibition, and intimated that the silk manufacturers of London were willing to forego the whole amount of the drawbacks if they were allowed a further extension of time. This, he explained, was no trifling inducement, as the petitioners were convinced that the drawbacks would exceed a million sterling —some, indeed, said a million and a half. The Chancellor of the Exchequer answered that such a calculation was absurd ; as the drawback was to be given only on goods uncut, the expense could not be more than £250,000. But, on the same evening, a petition was presented from the retail silk mercers of London, asking that the drawback should be extended to cut pieces. Ninety-nine hundredths of their stock, they asserted, consisted of cut pieces, and, if no allowance were given, the loss to them would not be less than £800,000. Hume and others strongly supported the prayer ; it was very serious if those who had large stocks should get no drawback if even a pattern was cut off ; some rule should be adopted to give the drawback to all cut pieces of not less than a certain number of yards, say 30 or 40—as had already been laid down in regard to ribbons, where all pieces exceeding 18 yards were to receive it. In that case, said Baring, " all the old and unsaleable rubbish, lying in the corners of shops and warehouses, would be poured in to receive the drawback." Other cases were presented as showing hardship : why, for instance, should mixed goods, like silk twist, where twelve parts of the composition were silk and one mohair, not get allowance on the twelve parts ? when a piece had been taken off to send out with travellers as patterns, was this to be counted " cut " and not get the drawback ? Finally, counsel was heard on the matter, and Robinson announced his decision. The drawback would be given on any quantity, not less than 300 lbs. in weight, " and in entire pieces or such as had been only cut for exhibiting patterns thereof." Even then, Hume moved that pieces, being cut, of not less than 30 yards in length should get the drawback, and Baring made a last motion—" rather with a view of recording his opinion than with any hope of inducing the House to adopt his proposition" —that the repeal of the prohibition should be postponed till 5th July, 1829, instead of 1826 ; but both motions were negatived, and the Bill passed the Commons.[1]

In October, one notes that several French manufacturers were in Manchester with a view of starting work there—" this is one of the effects of the repeal of the silk duty," said the *Glasgow Herald* bitterly—and, in 1826, Huskisson told of the persecution endured by one of them who had brought his looms and his patterns from Lyons and set up establishments in Manchester and Spitalfields.[2]

By an irony of politics, it was Hume who made the first complaint against the removal of the Bounties ; the burghs he represented, it seems, made a great deal of the coarse linens—a million sterling was invested in Forfarshire alone in the making of coarse linen,— and he protested against the bounty on coarse being withdrawn suddenly while that on fine was gradually taken off. An English member immediately joined him in the protest ; there was a considerable production of coarse linen in the north of England. But the chief outcry came from Ireland. Belfast was the great centre of the trade. But the linen manufacture had just been introduced into the west and south ; it was giving much employment and promised success. Whatever it did in the north, where the industry was established, this measure would kill the industry in the west and south. As a general principle, said one, bounties were objectionable —every speaker was agreed on that—but " the situation of Ireland was not one that would justify the application of general principles." Petitions were poured in in great number, some protesting altogether against the repeal and saying that it would be totally destructive of the linen manufacture of Ireland, others asking for delay from one year to ten years, and the " infant industry " argument was plentifully used.[3] A sidelight appears in the statement that the measure

Linen bounties.

---

[1] *Hansard*, x. 371, 719, 731, 780, 800, 849, 869, 1221, 1285, 1290, 1312, 1446. The total amount of repayments in consequence of the alterations was £500,000 (*ibid.* xi. 590).

[2] *Ibid.* xiv. 801.

[3] In 1820, Ricardo had asked if twenty years of Protection was not enough to prepare an infant industry to do without it (*Economic Annals, 1801-20*, 759). But a Select Committee in 1822 recommended the continuance of the bounties as regards Ireland, " for wherever the linen trade has obtained a footing, industry, moral habits, content and tranquillity have followed."

was due to the fraud of certain London merchants who had exported
a large quantity of bales of cotton, in the shape of Irish linen, with
the name of a Coleraine manufacturer forged upon them—
presumably, to gain the bounty. And for this Ireland was to be
punished! In the end, the Chancellor of the Exchequer gave
way as regards the immediate reduction, and announced that the
bounties on coarse linens also would be reduced gradually, but by
one-fifth every year, beginning in January 1825.[1]

Repeal of
the "tax on
justice."

There were other two fiscal changes made in 1824, not unimportant, although they are only noticed in *Hansard* in passing.
One was a Stamp Duty. In the debate on the financial situation,
John Smith, the useful member for Midhurst, appealed to the
Chancellor of the Exchequer to look into the evils of the stamps
on law proceedings—the tax on justice, as it might be called.
No one sufficiently appreciated the extent of these taxes, their
exorbitant amount, and their hardships, especially to the poorer
classes. "For instance, in order to recover a debt of from £3 to £4,
you must expend £3 or £4 more in stamps.". Actions were brought
because it was known that the parties could not defend on account
of the expense. "Among the labouring classes, no man was ever
unlucky enough to get into litigation without its being predicted
by all his friends and neighbours that he was pretty sure to go to
gaol before it was terminated. . . . He would venture to say that
there was not a man in that House, who had attained the age of
thirty, without having submitted to some injury to his property
rather than incur the still greater injury which he must sustain
by entering into a law suit."[2] A few days afterward, Robinson
acknowledged most handsomely the weight of these arguments;
he was now "so strongly impressed with the infinite evils (that
word was not, he thought, too strong) arising from these duties,"
that he had applied himself, and had found a way of reducing them
without in the slightest degree infringing on the calculations he had
already laid before Parliament. He was surprised and gratified
to find, on examination, that the amount of these duties in England
did not exceed £180,000, and £20,000 might be a fair estimate as
regards Ireland. He saw his way to get that money from two
sources; first, by the increasing productiveness of the Crown
Lands, which, by 1827, would show a surplus of £100,000; and,

---

[1] *Hansard*, x. 452, 641, 706, 943, 1216, 1309; xi. 426.

[2] *Ibid.* x. 347. "The taxes on law proceedings seemed to him," said
Ricardo in 1820, "the most abominable taxes that existed in the country."

second, by the saving on the collection of the public revenue,which
Mr. Wallace told him, could be counted on to yield another £100,000.[1]
There was no debate on this, but the Act appears as c. 41 : " To
repeal certain duties on law proceedings in the courts of Great
Britain and Ireland respectively."

The other was the abolition of the " Union Duties," which were Repeal of the
Union Duties.
now recognised as having obstructed the reciprocal intercourse of
produce and manufactures between Great Britain and Ireland.
It will be remembered that, in 1800, by the terms of the Act of
Union, certain scheduled articles were excepted from the general
rule of perfect freedom of trade between the two countries. By a
Resolution of 1820, these protecting duties were to continue till 1825,
and then be gradually diminished. Unnoticed in the parliamentary
debates, several of these, thanks to Parnell, had been repealed in
1823 (4 Geo. IV. c. 26). In the present year, the total repeal was
effected at the wish of the Irish themselves (c. 22). The loss to the
revenue was estimated at £300,000.[2]

When the Budget was formally brought in on 7th May, incorporat-
ing the changes made since the preliminary *exposé* in February,
Robinson was able to announce that the assents to the conversion
scheme represented £68 millions out of the £75 millions, and that
the £7 millions of dissents would be paid off by 10th October—the
money to be obtained by Exchequer Bills charged, principal and
interest, on the Sinking Fund.[3] And, in the next issue of such bills,
the interest would be reduced from 2d. per day to 1½d., which would
be a saving of £230,000 on £30 millions of Exchequer Bills. Parnell Parnell on the
Budget.
approved of the financial arrangements generally, and congratulated
the Chancellor. But he warned him that the measures in regard
to silk and wool and bounties were but half measures. He did
not think that Robinson could have done more, as to the silk
trade, than he had done, but it would be the duty of Parliament to
persevere until this trade was placed on a footing of perfect freedom.
The timber trade, too, called for revision of recent arrangements ;
we were paying £300,000 or £400,000 more for timber than we
ought to do. But the most unsatisfactory branch of our finances
was the Debt. It was absurd to suppose that a Sinking Fund of

---

[1] *Hansard*, x. 681.

[2] *Economic Annals, 1801-20*, 38, 759; Dowell, ii. 265; *Hansard*, iv. 720;
v. 5, 459.

[3] Hume protested against thus again complicating the Sinking Fund, when
everybody acknowledged that, if persevered in, it ought to be simplified.

£5 millions could ever be effectual in reducing a debt of £800 millions. For himself, he thought it incorrect to call the surplus a Sinking Fund; its proper name was a surplus or reserve fund, and it was only as such that he approved of it—he never believed that, in event of a war, any Government would leave it untouched. He wished to suggest again [1] to the consideration of the House Ricardo's plan of reducing the debt by means of annuities. It might, indeed, be difficult to convert perpetual into long annuities, but he wished to see the beginning of an attempt—doubtless many persons, for the sake of a larger income, would prefer determinable annuities. Thus the memorable Budget passed.[2]

The Sugar Duties. Great as was the reduction of taxation thus made, it did not satisfy those who thought that other taxes needed immediate attention, and that the Sinking Fund should be utilised for that purpose. On 8th March, Hume moved for the consideration of the Sugar Duties. Imposed during the war " under the pretext of convoy charges," they amounted to 27/- to 30/- per cwt. according to the prices of the article. It seemed to him that the consumption of sugar, like that of tobacco and wine, was checked by the imposition of high duties; practically, it had not increased since the termination of the war. The West India planters, too, were entitled to some relief—the reduction of rum was " paltry and insignificant "—and he proposed, by way of experiment, a reduction of 7/- per cwt. Baring, who seems to have been suffering from a reaction to Protection, called attention to the fact that barley had risen so much of late as to threaten the opening of the ports—" a prospect which could not be considered without considerable alarm in the interests of English growers "—and asked the Government rather to favour sugar by allowing its use in the distilleries instead of barley.[3]

Consumption of sugar. Huskisson answered that Hume was entirely wrong as to the consumption of sugar; no other article had experienced such an increase of consumption since 1814. For the past year, it was 3,330,000 cwt., equal to an increase of 40 per cent. on that of the previous nine years; it had more than kept pace with the increased supply from the colonies, and the price was rising on that account;

[1] Parnell had advocated this in 1823 (*Hansard*, viii. 536, 548).

[2] *Hansard*, xi. 589.

[3] Frankland Lewis, however, contended that, at any time when the ports were opened, only a very small quantity of barley was imported, and protested at the West Indies being relieved at the cost of the barley growers alone.

as the expert opinion was that it was impossible for the British
West Indies to produce a greater supply than in the last year (namely
3,785,000 cwt., of which 655,000 only were exported), it was
" not most urgent, in the present state of the country, that the
impost should be reduced." It was suggestive and interesting that,
in 1791, the whole consumption of sugar in Great Britain and Ireland
was only 1,400,000 cwt. and that the tax was then 12/4 ; while, in
1823, the consumption had considerably more than doubled, although
the tax was 27/-. But, said Huskisson, as a fact no country in
Europe, of three times the population of Great Britain, consumed
as much sugar as was annually employed here. Personally, he
would be glad, in principle, that the distillers should be free to use
sugar instead of barley if they pleased. But arrangements could
not be made for this before the distilling season was over, and,
besides, it seemed hard to exclude from the distilleries the barley
grown in our own country. Finally, it should be remembered
that every shilling of a reduction on the sugar duty was a loss of
£150,000 to the revenue.

Several speakers warmly approved of Baring's proposal, considering the distressed state of the West Indies, but Huskisson
would give no pledge. During the debate, the interesting fact
was brought out that, in 1807, rum was the favourite—almost the
exclusive—drink of Scotland. It had ceased to be so because, owing
to the scale of duties, whisky had become so much cheaper. Thanks
to the reduction of the duties on spirits distilled in Scotland, even
the reduction in the duty on rum, it was said, would not bring it
into consumption again. Hume, protesting that the consumption
of sugar had by no means kept pace with what they had a right to
expect—had not increased proportionally with the growth of
population—withdrew his motion.[1]

An interesting subject, from its resemblance to the Continental Sugar
Sugar Bounties question in the end of the century, was brought Bounties.
up, in May, when Whitmore asked for a Select Committee to consider the drawbacks or bounties paid on the exportation of sugar.
The sugar imported from the West Indies paid a duty of 27/- when
the price was under 47/-, and of 30/- when the price was above 47/-.
His first point was that, with this small difference between the two,
when sugar was re-exported to the continent, it received a drawback of 3/- more than the duty paid on import. This fact, he said,
" could not be denied." But this sugar received a second bounty

[1] *Hansard*, x. 782.

when refined in this country and exported. When used for home consumption, the calculation was that every 112 lbs. of unrefined yielded 56 of refined. But, when intended for export, it was not thus completely refined : 112 lbs. of raw sugar yielded from 60 to 65 lbs. refined ; that is to say, several lbs. of molasses were left in, to be extracted by another refining abroad. The price of molasses in the market was 25/- to 30/-, and so " there was an enormous profit on the exported sugar." [1] Unfortunately, Whitmore diverged to the general question of slave labour—the encouragement this gave to it—and rested his motion much more on this than on the bounty ; and, on grounds of policy—for the facts were not in dispute, said Huskisson subsequently—the motion was negatived.[2]

Smuggling of Brandy.

In March, Col. Davies moved for a reduction in the duty on foreign Brandies, when some curious particulars were given both as to the spread of smuggling and as to the effect of reduction of duties on the revenue. " The extravagantly high duties," he said, " induced many persons to embark large capitals in the contraband trade. By the very high profits they made when they succeeded in securing a cargo, they were enabled to give high wages to all those who assisted them in landing it. The consequence was that, whenever a ship so laden appeared off the coast, the whole of the peasantry were ready to assist in landing and secreting her cargo, confident that they would be well paid for the risks they ran. The demoralising effects of such a trade upon the manners and habits of a people were too well-known and admitted to render it necessary for him to describe them. It had been truly said (by Baring) that one consequence of our high duties on foreign spirits and other articles was to place nearly the whole of the southern coast in a state of civil war. The effect of a discovery on some of the individuals themselves was most ruinous. If a man were detected carrying a keg of contraband spirits, he was taken before a magistrate, fined £100, and, in default of payment, was impressed on board one of His Majesty's tenders. . . . Such exorbitant rewards were given for the discovery of smuggled spirits, that persons engaged in the contraband trade were even known to cause information to be given against themselves, in order to come in

[1] That is to say, each 56 lbs. of refined sugar exported got a drawback as if duty had been paid on 112 lbs., whereas only 60 or 65 lbs. of refined should have got such an amount.

[2] *Hansard*, xi. 730.

for a share of the reward, which was sufficiently large to cover the expenses they had gone to and leave a handsome profit on the adventure. . . . In 1806, when the duty was 12/6 a gallon on foreign spirits, the produce of the duty was £1,463,000. In 1810, it was increased to 15/1½d., and the quantity imported was greatly reduced, but the produce increased to about £1,500,000. This increase, though small, encouraged the Chancellor of the Exchequer in thinking that a still further increase would be a ready way of increasing the revenue. In 1811, the duty was raised to 19/1½d., and the produce fell off. In 1815, it was reduced to 17/9 and the produce increased; but it was only £815,000, being, even yet, not much more than half the produce in 1810 when the duty was lower. The same result of an increase of duties was seen in wines. In 1806, the produce was £1,267,000 ; the rate of duty had since been increased £30 a pipe on French and £20 on other wines, and the produce had decreased to £1,020,000—a loss of nearly £200,000 to the revenue and a reduction of a third of the quantity consumed." Again, the expense of collection greatly increased with the high duties. "In 1806, the rate of the expense of the collection of the Customs duties was £5 4s. 7d. per cent. In 1822, it was £8 7s. 8d. per cent. The expense of collection in the Excise, in 1806, was £3 0s. 7d. per cent., in 1822, £3 15s. 5d. per cent. In Ireland, the expense per cent. in 1806 on the collection of both duties was £10 ; in 1822, it had risen to £17." [1]

The Chancellor of the Exchequer agreed with the principles expressed, but demurred to the subject being brought up in this way. He admitted that the duty on foreign spirits was very high, but he thought that the present was not the proper time for making any reduction in it, seeing that such reduction must operate to the prejudice of the manufacturers of British spirits. It might, perhaps, be said that it would be well to make a reduction in the duties on British spirits also. Perhaps it might be so, but that, it would not be denied, was a great question, and it would not be wise to go into it now until we had seen the effect of the reductions made in the duty on spirits in Ireland and Scotland. No man, he thought, would deny that it was desirable to have the duties on ardent spirits as high as could be safely collected. Hume repeated his

Effect of high duties in checking revenue.

[1] This was a favourite text of Parnell. In his *Financial Reform* (p. 117), he pointed out that the gross receipt of revenue in 1806 was over £58 millions, and the charge for collection £2¾ millions, and that, in 1826, the revenue had fallen to under £55 millions, while the charge had risen to over £4 millions— a total charge of about 7½ per cent.

contention that it was "the difficulty of coming at the spirits, by the high duties which were placed upon them, which caused the temporary excesses of many persons when they got it within their reach." And he did not see why every poor man should not have whisky within his reach, as the rich man was allowed to have wine when he could pay for it. The fact was that there was no branch of our internal industry which was so mismanaged as the distillation of spirits : it was a complete monopoly, and the profits arising from it were never greater than at the present moment. He understood that the reduction of the price in Scotland had so increased the demand that the distillers in that country were unable to supply it ; one half of the spirits distilled in Scotland came into England. The system of smuggling had taken a new direction; it was now as active from Scotland to England as it had ever been before from Holland. "He had taken occasion last Session to deprecate the absurdity of preventing the importation of whisky into England. He had stated at that time that he had whisky in his house ; he avowed that he had smuggled whisky in his house then ; and he avowed it still ; for, if such foolish laws were made, they ought to be broken. He would continue to break such a law, and let them find him out if they could."

Again, on presenting a petition against the high duties on foreign Wines, the member for London pointed out that, in 1801, when the duty was 8/9 per gallon, the sum paid into the revenue was £2,307,000, while the average from 1821 to 1823 was under £2,000,000 "though the duty was nearly doubled." Hume really hoped the Chancellor of the Exchequer would take the matter up. He was convinced that, by taking half the duty off French wines, the quantity consumed would be more than doubled, the revenue benefited, and smuggling—which cost a million a year in the preventive service—would be checked. But Robinson would not be drawn ; as the discussion, he said, placed him in the difficult position of having his silence or his declarations alike misconstrued, he considered himself justified in withholding any expression of opinion on the subject.[1]

The effect of high duties in revenue was again called attention to in a petition from the Bristol manufacturers of tobacco and snuff.

---

[1] *Hansard*, x. 226, 945, 1310. Hume subsequently obtained returns for ten years of the produce of all excisable and customs-paying goods, in order that the effect of certain legal measures in increasing or diminishing their consumption might be distinctly ascertained (*ibid.* 451).

The Tobacco duties amounted to 1,000 per cent. upon the original value of the article, and the evil emphasised was the inevitable smuggling. Its vast amount might be seen from the fact that, when the duties amounted to 1/5d., the quantity paying duty in Ireland was eleven million lbs., and, now that they were 4/-, the quantity was no more than two and a half millions. Thus the tax, while impolitic in a financial point of view, was perhaps a more fertile source of crime than any other branch of the revenue.[1]

In March, Hobhouse, in a wandering speech bringing in the Corn Laws, the Austrian repayment, the Church Grant, Windsor Castle, and a few more things, moved for the repeal of the Window Tax, as unjust, irregular in operation, and oppressive to the least opulent portion of the community—to be effected at the expense of the Sinking Fund—and Maberly, Althorp, and Hume, in the same discursive way, supported him. The tax deprived the labouring classes of light and air, compelled many families to reside abroad who might live at home, produced many of the worst diseases and a good deal of bad morality, checked the increase of buildings, and, consequently, checked the employment of artizans and the additional consumption of our produce and manufactures. Baring opposed, expressing his surprise that anyone could doubt the policy of maintaining the Sinking Fund as a necessary support to the public credit, and the Chancellor of the Exchequer reasserted that he had gone as far with the remission of taxation as he was justified at the present moment.[2] *The Window Tax.*

Maberly went further, and moved for the repeal of all the Assessed Taxes, amounting to about £3½ millions, and got 78 members to vote with him—possibly on the ground, frankly expressed by Lord Milton, that the only chance of driving Ministers to a general repeal of taxes was by voting for the repeal of every particular tax that it might be proposed so to deal with.[3] *Assessed Taxes.*

In May, Calcraft moved to repeal the remaining duty on Leather. In its reduced form, it yielded little more than £300,000, and it took three times that amount from the people ; besides, the restrictions *Leather Tax.*

[1] *Hansard*, x. 369.

[2] *Ibid.* x. 652. Lethbridge subsequently suggested to the Chancellor of the Exchequer that he should allow all windows which had been stopped up in consequence of the tax to be reopened : this would create a large demand for glass, and give employment to a number of useful and industrious individuals who were now out of employment without in any way interfering with the financial arrangements already made ! (*ibid.* x. 1397).

[3] *Ibid.* xi. 617.

involved prevented the combining of two trades that ought to be united, tanners and curriers—for the tanner could not touch the skin—thus causing great waste. Robinson in reply did not defend the tax. But he had already remitted £4½ millions of taxes since he took office, and, if he had £350,000 at his disposal, he would much prefer to reduce other taxes than that on leather. There was coal for instance ; there was the tobacco duty of 4/- on an article whose cost price wás about 3d.—a duty which gave rise to a moral evil in smuggling ten thousand times greater than the inconvenience of a leather tax. This gave occasion to Sir Joseph Yorke's indignant astonishment that the Chancellor of the Exchequer should have declared that he would sooner repeal the tax on tobacco, the use of which was so unnatural, and which was so offensive to the stomach, lungs, and nasal organs, than the tax on so necessary an article as leather, without which nobody could move. Canning, with ready wit, retorted that it was rather hard on the Chancellor that he should be called upon to show, not only that every tax which he thought it expedient to maintain was not oppressive, but that there was something in it peculiarly amiable and lovely. The motion was, of course, lost.[1]

Legacy Duties.   In February, Hume moved for returns " with the view of bringing the Legacy Duties under the consideration of the House at a future period." From 1797 to 1806, no less than £22 millions had been levied in these duties ; in 1822, the amount was over £1,000,000. Such taxes he denounced as " pernicious and impolitic : they had been admitted by all who had written on the subject to be taxes on the capital of the country, and they ought, therefore, to be repealed." They were, moreover, harassing and vexatious, as claims were made even after fourteen and fifteen years. Robinson demurred at discussing the general principle, but admitted the latter grievance, and said that it had already been remedied. The motion was agreed to ; but, later on, Hume asked for further returns in order to call attention to the hardship and impolicy of imposing legacy duties on sums under £100. The whole duties on probates, administrations, and inventories in Great Britain amounted to £1,800,000 and the portion arising from duties on sums under £100 was by no means great compared with the vexation and trouble they caused. In one instance, the expense of obtaining probate on a property of £106 amounted to £14 ; in another, to £4 14s. 6d. on a sum of £55. The inconvenience was even greater

[1] *Hansard*, xi. 776.

in Scotland, where the collection was very strict: the officers
there, he was told by a magistrate, would insist on a man's old
nightcap and slippers being included in the inventory of the goods
which he left for his widow and children. Robinson had no objection to the motion—it was no less his wish than his duty to give
the community every relief in his power upon those minor matters
which, without diminishing the revenue, were likely to render the
raising of it less severely felt by the public—and the return was
agreed to.[1]

Amid all these reductions and attempts at further reduction, The remaining Salt Duty.
it is almost refreshing to come across a proposal to arrest the flowing tide. Wodehouse, in May, moved for the continuance of the
2/- still levied on Salt. He was aware that the faith of Parliament
stood pledged for the entire abolition of the salt duties. But he
did not consider that such a pledge was indissoluble. The repeal
would be of very slight advantage to the country. And then he
unfolded the reason for his advocacy—it was "that His Majesty's
Government might thereby be enabled to give a more effectual
relief to the country in the ensuing Session of Parliament by the
remission of the duty payable on Windows!" The Chancellor,
reminding the House of the wording of his pledge, could not say
that any strong feeling had been expressed in favour of the continuance of the Salt Tax, and he advised Wodehouse to withdraw
his motion—which Wodehouse did.[2]

In the debates on the various estimates, Hume, now more sure Hume's crusade against Colonial expenses.
of himself and of what was expected of him, and, therefore, more
truculent, put in an objection to almost every category of the
expenditure.[3] But perhaps the most notable of his appearances
was the crusade which he now began against the expenses of the
Colonies. When £600 was moved to defray the civil establishment
of the island of Dominica, he protested—to be answered by the
Chancellor of the Exchequer that Dominica was, and always had been,
one of the most distressed spots in the West Indies. When £22,549
was asked for Sierra Leone, he wanted to know what benefit this
country derived from Sierra Leone ; the loss of lives in it, he knew,
was very considerable, and the expenditure, as the House saw, was
very great. This time he got the answer that the House was called
on to vote this sum as the consequence of a certain Colonial System—

[1] *Hansard*, x. 134 ; xi. 48.
[2] *Ibid.* xi. 741. The duty was entirely taken off from January 1825.
[3] *Ibid.* x. 167, 271, 296, 366.

among other things, as an expenditure to promote the civilisation of Africa—and this was not the time to discuss that system. The same answer was given on the resolution to grant £44,000 for the Settlement on the Gold Coast.

He made similar objections to the grant of £2,440 to defray the expenses of certain Colonial Services. On a vote of £15,500 to defray the charges of the Society for the Propagation of the Gospel in the Canadas, Nova Scotia, New Brunswick, Newfoundland, Prince Edward Island, and the Cape, he asked if, in addition to the civil and military establishments of these colonies, we were to support their ecclesiastical establishments as well. Why not pay every medical gentleman who proceeded there ? Ascertaining that the money was applied to the support of the Protestant religion only, this, he said, was worse and worse : why were the Catholics of Ireland and the Dissenters to be taxed for the benefit of another sect.[1]

But, when £8,229 was moved " to defray the charge of the Civil Establishment of Upper Canada," Hume was more outspoken. It was extremely unfair that the people of England should be called upon to pay the expenses of the civil as well as the military establishments of her colonies. Among other things, he asked what became of the money received from the sale of lands—a source which yielded so many millions to the United States revenue ? In reply, it was pointed out, that, up till 1816, all the expenses of that colony were borne by England, whereas now the colony raised £20,000 out of £30,000, and the vote was £4,000 less than in the preceding year : as to the land sales, surely the honourable gentleman knew that the lands produced no pecuniary value, but were granted to those who would undertake their cultivation : if, however, Hume would give notice of a motion having for its object the abandonment of these colonies, he would soon see the kind of feeling it would produce throughout the country. Hume, however, had the courage of his convictions : " he was of opinion that the best policy which this country could pursue with regard to the Canadas would be to render them independent at the end of ten years, by which we should be relieved from a large annual expense, and avoid the probability of being drawn into a war with the United States on their account, which might cost us millions." [2]

Promotion by purchase.

To Hume, too, belongs the credit of being the first to bring up the methods of promotion in the two services. In the previous year, he had prayed for enquiry into the manner in which promotion

---

[1] *Hansard*, x. 953, 962, 963, 964, 968.   [2] *Ibid.* x. 955.

took place in the navy—the scandalous way in which a few fortunate
youths were advanced over the heads of three or four thousand
others.[1] He now took up the parallel question in the army. A
certain sum only, he said, was allowed to be given for commissions.
Anyone purchasing promotion had to declare in writing, " on the
word and honour of an officer and a gentleman," that he had " made
no clandestine bargain," and did not give more than this amount.
Yet, contrary to the regulations of the Commander-in-Chief, there
was scarcely one case in ten in which officers received their commissions at the regulation price. This was notorious, and he hoped
that a respect for the honour of the army would induce the House
to approve the clause he proposed, that officers be not required to
make any such certificate. The army authorities acknowledged
that the declaration was " very objectionable." Palmerston alone
opposed Hume's clause, on the ground that the question was
" full of difficulty " and was already under consideration of
" those to whom the consideration of such questions properly
belonged " ; and Hume, " after the reprobation which the system
had met with from both sides of the House," withdrew his clause.[2]

On the vote for defraying the charge of the Ordnance, there
was a debate supplying information that may be new to most
people, viz. that the barrack system came in only at the beginning
of the century, and was still strongly reprobated. Although the
Petition of Right protested against the quartering of soldiers on
the people—at a time, indeed, when there was no standing army—
the custom had continued in one form or other. But, in 1803,
when troops were sent to the coast to guard against invasion, it
was impossible to provide them with quarters at the public
houses, and various petitions against private billeting were forwarded
to Parliament. Accordingly it was determined, in order to relieve
the people from the inconvenience, that several barracks should be
built within those districts. Hobhouse now protested against the
disposal of part of the vote to the building of a permanent barrack
on the site of the King's Mews at Charing Cross. The system
separated the character of the soldier and the citizen. He quoted
Blackstone in support : " Nothing ought to be more guarded against
in a free state than making the military power a body too distinct
from the people. It ought only to be enlisted for a short and limited
period ; the soldiers also should live intermixed with the people ;
no separate camp—no barracks—no inland fortresses should be

The barrack system.

---

[1] *Hansard*, ix. 1079.   [2] *Ibid*. x. 1039.

allowed ; and perhaps it might be still better if, by dismissing a stated number and enlisting others, at every renewal of their term, a circulation could be kept up between the army and the people, and the citizen and the soldier be more intimately connected together." Sir Henry Hardinge said that, before the revolutionary war, all the soldiery were dispersed in billets about the town, and that their discipline was so greatly destroyed, and their morals corrupted, that, in 1791, 1792, and 1793, among the public executions, out of every fourteen there was one guardsman. Since the establishment of barracks, the case was so far altered that it was a rare thing to hear of a guardsman being arraigned. Obviously the soldiers were not only much more exposed to acquire profligate habits under the billeting system, and to commit outrages when removed from the control of their officers, but were also more likely to relax in their discipline. Hume, however, contended that a man did not cease to be a citizen when he became a soldier, and should not be regarded as a mere automaton to be moved only by the will of his commanding officer. The sum asked for barracks was monstrous, and the object of it, he considered, was to maintain a military despotism.[1]

[1] *Hansard*, x. 861.

CHAPTER XX

1824. THE REPEAL OF THE COMBINATION LAWS

In 1819, Hume had voiced the growing conviction that the Combination Laws of 1799, which declared all combinations to obtain an advance of wages to be unlawful, and, on the oaths of one or two credible witnesses before a Justice of the Peace, punishable by three months' imprisonment in the common gaol, required looking into.[1]   The first definite action towards revising them was taken by Peter Moore, the member for Coventry, in 1823, when he printed and circulated a Bill for the purpose.   Huskisson complained that one Bill, as consolidating 44 Acts of Parliament, contained regulations so minute, inapplicable, and impossible that it was enough to control, embarrass, and perplex the regulations of any trade, and he asked Moore to postpone it till the coming session.[2]

But, in the end of the same year, Hume gave notice that he would take action on the subject, and, on 12th February, indicating that he had acted by the advice—he had hoped for the assistance—of Ricardo, he asked for a Select Committee to enquire as to the Emigration of Artizans, the Exportation of Tools and Machinery, and the Combination Laws.[3]   He was warmly seconded by Huskisson, and the Committee appointed contained about 50 members, including Chas. Grant, Sturges Bourne, Bennett, Frankland Lewis, Parnell, Philips, Stuart Wortley, Acland, Hobhouse, and Huskisson, Hume being Chairman.   On 21st May, instead of making a report to the House stating the grounds on which the Committee had come to their determination, a string of Resolutions was presented.[4]

Hume's Committee.

---

[1] *Economic Annals, 1801-20*, 712.

[2] *Hansard*, viii. 366, 751 ; ix. 546.   [3] *Ibid*. x. 141.

[4] *Ibid*. xi. 811.   In the succeeding year, Huskisson, stating this, apologised that his official duties had prevented him paying much attention to the business of the Committee, and called attention to some very extraordinary provisions which had been allowed to pass (*Ibid*. xii. 1289).

As regards the Combination Laws, the resolutions were as follow :

(1) " That it appears, by the evidence before the Committee, that combinations of workmen have taken place in England, Scotland, and Ireland, often to a great extent, to raise and keep up their wages, to regulate their hours of working, and to impose regulations on the masters respecting apprentices or others whom they might think proper to employ ; and that, at the time the evidence was taken, combinations were in existence, attended with strikes or suspension of work : and that the laws have not hitherto been effectual to prevent such combinations.

(2) " That serious breaches of the peace and acts of violence, with strikes of the workmen, often for very long periods, have taken place in consequence of, and arising out of, the combinations of workmen, and been attended with loss to both the masters and workmen, and with considerable inconvenience and injury to the community.[1]

(3) " That the masters have often united and combined to lower the rates of their workmen's wages, as well as to resist a demand for an increase, and to regulate their hours of working ; and sometimes to discharge their workmen who would not consent to the conditions offered to them ; which have been followed with suspension of work, riotous proceedings, and acts of violence.

(4) " That prosecutions have frequently been carried on, under the Statute and the Common Law, against the workmen, and many of them have suffered different periods of imprisonment for combining and conspiring to raise their wages, or to resist their reduction, and to regulate their hours of working.

(5) " That several instances have been stated to the Committee, of prosecutions against masters for combining to lower wages, and to regulate the hours of working ; but no instance has been adduced of any master having been punished for that offence.

(6) " That the laws have not only not been efficient to prevent combinations, either of masters or workmen, but, on the contrary, have, in the opinion of many of both parties, had a tendency to produce mutual irritation and distrust, and to give a violent

[1] In the *Glasgow Herald* of 9th April, 1821, for instance, I find it positively asserted that, for some time, there had been a combination among the cotton spinners, extending over the cotton districts of the three kingdoms, with membership enforced by threats, spoiling the work of recalcitrants, throwing vitriol, shooting into the houses of " knobs " (what we now call " blacklegs "), etc.

character to the combinations, and to render them highly dangerous to the peace of the community.

(7) " That it is the opinion of this Committee that masters and workmen should be freed from such restrictions, as regards the rate of wages and the hours of working, and be left at perfect liberty to make such agreements as they may mutually think proper.

(8) " That therefore the Statute laws that interfere in these particulars between masters and workmen should be repealed, and also that the common law, under which a peaceable meeting of masters and workmen may be prosecuted as a conspiracy, should be altered.

(9) " That the Committee regret to find from the evidence that societies, legally enrolled as benefit societies, have been frequently made the cloak under which funds have been raised for the support of combinations and strikes, attended with acts of violence and intimidation; and, without recommending any specific course, they wish to call the attention of the House to the frequent perversion of those institutions from their avowed and legitimate objects.

(10) " That the practice of settling disputes by arbitration between masters and workmen has been attended with good effects ; and it is desirable that the laws which direct and regulate arbitration should be consolidated, amended, and made applicable to all trades.

(11) " That it is absolutely necessary, when repealing the Combination Laws, to enact such a law as may efficiently, and by summary process, punish either workmen or masters who, by threats, intimidation, or acts of violence, should interfere with that perfect freedom which ought to be allowed to each party, of employing his labour or capital in the manner he may deem most advantageous."

As regards the Emigration of Artizans, the resolutions were : and on the

(1) " That it appears, by the evidence before this Committee, Emigration Artizans.

that, notwithstanding the laws enacted to prevent the seduction of artizans to go abroad,[1] many able and intelligent artizans have

---

[1] The 23rd of Geo. III. cap. 13 enacted that any person who should " contract with, entice, persuade, or endeavour to persuade, solicit, or seduce, any manufacturer, workman, or artificer in wool, mohair, cotton, or silk, or in iron, steel, brass, or other metal ; or any clockmaker, watchmaker, or any other manufacturer, workman, or artificer in any other of the manufactures of Great Britain or Ireland, of what kind or nature soever, to go out of the

gone abroad to reside, and to exercise their respective arts, in foreign countries, and that it is extremely difficult, if not impossible, in this country, by any mode of executing the present laws, or by any new law, to prevent artizans who may be so determined from going out of the country.

(2) "That, although the penalties which the laws inflict on artizans who disobey them, are not distinctly understood by the workmen, yet an unfavourable opinion is generally entertained by them of the partial and oppressive operation of these laws, as preventing them from taking their labour and art to the best market, whilst all other classes of the community are permitted to go abroad, and to take their capital with them, whenever they think proper.

(3) "That it appears also by evidence that many British artizans residing abroad have been prevented from returning home, from an erroneous opinion that they have, by going abroad, violated the laws of their country, and consequently incurred penalties under them.[1]

(4) "That, in the opinion of this Committee, it is both unjust and impolitic to continue these laws; they, therefore, recommend their entire repeal, and that artizans may be at liberty to go abroad, and to return home, whenever they may be disposed, in the

---

kingdom into any foreign country not within the dominions of the Crown, was liable to be indicted, and to forfeit £500, to suffer imprisonment for twelve months, and until the forfeiture was paid, every subsequent offence being further punishable with £1000 penalty and two years' imprisonment." Before an emigrant can pass the customhouse, said the *Edinburgh Review* in January, he must be furnished with a certificate, signed by the churchwardens and overseers of the parish, declaring that "the bearer is not, nor hath ever been, a manufacturer or artizan in wool, iron, steel, brass or any other metal; nor is he, nor hath he ever been, a watchmaker or clockmaker or any other artificer whatsoever."

[1] Very divergent statements were made before the Committee as to the numbers of emigrant artizans. One witness put them as high as 16,000 during 1822 and 1823. A more cautious estimate made out that there were no more than 1300 or 1400 English artizans in France altogether. At the iron works of Charenton, 250 Englishmen were employed in 1823, and new works for rolling iron were being built by some of our countrymen on the banks of the Seine near Paris. In several large cotton factories, it was said, the majority of the workmen were obtained from Scotland or England. The law was by no means a dead letter. In February 1822, I find two stocking weavers, who had emigrated to the Netherlands some time before and had returned to take their families, arrested and charged with "quitting the kingdom contrary to 5th Geo. I. c. 27." It seems strange to read in the Lyons newspapers of the time loud indignation being expressed at weavers being "seduced away to their eternal rivals, the English!"

same manner as other classes of the community now go and return." [1]

But, as regards the Exportation of Machinery,[2] the Committee asked for time to make a more complete investigation.

This is all we learn as to the Combination Laws and the Emigration of Artizans from *Hansard*. But, among the Acts passed during the session, we find c. 95 : " An Act to repeal the laws relative to the combination of workmen, and for other purposes therein mentioned " ; and, further, c. 97 : " An Act to repeal the laws relative to artificers going into foreign parts." The Journals of the House of Commons, vol. 79, show that Hume obtained leave to bring in these Bills on 24th and 25th May, and that they passed through both Houses without a division.[3]

It is usually the case that the last year of a "boom" is marked by labour unrest and strikes,[4] and it is not difficult to see why. The "boom" provokes the strike, and the strike, if extensive enough, is sufficient to end the "boom." The working classes, witnessing

The last year of a "boom."

---

[1] Adam Smith had spoken very strongly against these regulations for giving masters " the monopoly of the ingenuity of all their countrymen." They were contrary, he said, to the liberty of the subject of which we affected to be so very jealous, and which, all the same, we so plainly sacrificed to the futile interests of our merchants and manufacturers.

[2] See *Economic Annals, 1801-20*, 738. The exportation of " instruments of trade " under forfeiture and heavy fine was prohibited since at least the time of William III. (*Wealth of Nations*, IV. viii.). In May of the current year, a special meeting of the Manchester Chamber of Commerce passed strong resolutions against permitting artizans and machinery to be exported.

[3] One of the influences in bringing about the repeal was the famous article written by M'Culloch in the *Edinburgh Review* of January. The most striking passage, perhaps, to the people of the time was on the " miserable error " of supposing that low wages could ever be advantageous : " the essential interests of society require that the rate of wages should be elevated as high as possible —that a taste for comforts, luxuries, and enjoyment should be widely diffused, and, if possible, interwoven with the national habits and prejudices." But the efficient agents were Francis Place and Hume. After long and patient wire-pulling, those two " contrived privately to talk over and to silence the few members who were alive to the situation : and the measure passed, as Place remarks, ' almost without the notice of members within or newspapers without.' " So quietly was the Bill smuggled through Parliament, that the magistrates at a Lancashire town unwittingly sentenced certain cotton weavers to imprisonment for combination some weeks after the laws against that crime had been repealed (*The History of Trade Unionism*, by S. and B. Webb, 10th edition, 92).

[4] Geo. Philips noted the fact that combinations did not, for the most part, take place when wages were low but when they were high ; the most ferocious combinations had taken place in Glasgow and Manchester when the rate was 30/- to 50/- a week (*Hansard*, xi. 410).

the loosened expenditure and extravagance of the masters, get
impatient of the contrast between their respective conditions, and
strike for a larger share of the prosperity—and it must be acknowledged that masters are not in the habit of raising wages till they
have to do so by scarcity of workers or are forced by a strike.   The
stoppage of supply affects the demand : sometimes it may only
postpone it, more often it sends it to other countries or checks it
altogether.   The suspension of wages and profits, of purchases of
raw and auxiliary materials, of transit, involves loss of purchasing
power generally and at once affects all other supplies.   The dislocation involved is, of itself, enough to account for the depression
which then begins and spreads by natural contagion.[1]

Strikes,   We should then, in any case, expect to find 1824 marked by labour
disturbances.   But the repeal of the Combination Laws, for the
moment at least, aggravated the tendency.   Trade societies sprang
into existence on all sides ; for the next six months the newspapers
are full of strikes and rumours of strikes.   In the month of September
alone, there were serious stoppages among the dyers, the cloth-lappers,
the journeymen shoemakers, and the colliers in and around Glasgow,
accompanied by rioting, picketing, and intimidation.   But the most
prominent was in the cotton trade, where from the end of August
till the following January, cotton spinners and powerloom weavers
struck work almost in a body.   They formed themselves into associations, held public meetings—the Weavers' Association sent weekly
reports of their proceedings to the newspapers—sent delegates to
Ireland to promote combination on the same principles, established
a regular system of organisation, fixed the terms on which they were
willing to negotiate with their employers, dictated the rules by which
the conduct of the workmen was to be regulated—and all in a
peaceable and orderly way.   The masters, on the other hand, took
joint action in their own defence.

The same phenomena·happened up and down the country.   So
serious was the reaction towards Combination that Hume, on 14th
September, wrote to the operative weavers of Glasgow : " I still
do expect that great benefit will be derived from the Repeal if the
imprudent conduct of the operatives does not urge the masters to
obtain a renewal of the power they formerly had to oppress," and,
more distinctly in December, to the Manchester Cotton Spinners :
" I should be very uncandid if I did not inform you that, unless
the operatives act in a manner more moderate and prudent than

[1] See author's note on Industrial Cycles (*Economic Annals, 1801-20*, 606).

they have done in some parts of the country, I fear that many members of the House of Commons may be disposed to re-enact the laws that have been repealed—I allude particularly to the secret unions in Stockport and Dublin, the association and declaration of the colliers of Lanark, Dumbarton and Renfrewshire, which are estranging their best friends, and gradually raising the community against them."

CHAPTER XXI

1824. SOCIAL AND ECONOMIC

IN general history, the year 1824 occupies a small place. There was no movement in politics, and apparently little interest in them —neither intrigue nor agitation—the people too busy making money and attending to their own affairs. But one who reads a little deeper than facts and phenomena would probably discern the emergence of something like a new spirit—something which brings the reader into the atmosphere of modern times. In the beginning of the decade, it was still counted the privilege of the many to be thought for and ruled by the few. The idea of democracy as a norm of government had not entered the mind of any but a few scholars. It was not even an ideal, to be dreaded only because the people were not ready for it. It was, as Ward called it, a " whirl-pool " towards which, if reform were once entertained, we should be drawn by an irresistible force. But, by 1824, all seems to be different. " Liberality," wrote Lord Redesdale, who by no means approved of it, " is the word of the day." " The people," said the first article in the new *Westminster Review,* " no longer sit quietly by as spectators, while Whig and Tory, that is, a few great families with their connections and dependents, and a few pensioned or expectant creatures, play out the political game in their own way and for their own benefit. . . . There is an obvious deference for the people, and an implied appeal to them in the transactions of every department, whether political, religious, or literary. . . . In short, the prodigiously increased importance of the people is recog-nised in the speeches of the statesman, the sermons of the divine, the lucubrations of the author, and the criticisms of the reviewer. All seem impressed with the rise of a new power, and, blessing or cursing, they pay to it a certain degree of homage." The enthusiasm for free institutions comes out strongly in the hatred

A new spirit.

of the Holy Alliance, which, acting as a kind of royal, imperial, military police all over the Continent, as Brougham put it, kept interfering with the liberties of the minor German states and Switzerland, muzzling the press, suppressing societies, and generally governing them " for their good." It is strongly marked in the discussions on France and Spain, and on the related question of the new American states. Increasingly difficult as it was to regard Spain as a deeply wronged people held down by force—was not the Duc d'Angoulême hailed in Madrid as " The Deliverer " ?—many, as we saw, were willing to go to war for the " oppressed nationality " at the cost of estranging every court on the Continent. It appears in the angry debates on the continuance of the Aliens Act ; in the annual discussions which were bringing Catholic Emancipation nearer its goal ; in the reformation of the criminal code and the recasting of punishments with a view to respecting the rights of the criminal ; and, above all, in the growing determination to set our own house in order, and remove the anomaly of a nation ready to fight for the freedom of other countries while a million of the King's own subjects were in actual slavery. As we might expect, then, an examination of the parliamentary records discovers many interesting sidelights on economic and social progress.

First in importance was the repeal of the Spitalfields Acts. After the strong opposition led in the previous year, one would hardly have expected to find this coming about in the most unobtrusive way. On 4th May, Lauderdale, in the Upper House, intimated that he would introduce a Bill for the repeal of certain laws relative to the Silk Trade—the same in substance as that which had passed the House of Commons in the previous Session, but been thrown out by their lordships.[1] The time, he thought, was most opportune, as those persons who were, last year, the principal supporters of restrictions on manufactures and trades had materially changed their opinion, and, in his opinion, the journeymen weavers had done the same. The Bill passed with little debate in the Lords, and with none in the Commons, and appears as c. 66 : " To repeal certain Acts of his late Majesty relating to the wages of persons employed in the manufacture of silk, and of silk mixed with other materials." Thus quietly passed away the elaborate and artificial system of restrictions which had long kept the silk industry in fetters.[2] In October, I find it stated that Spitalfields was never more prosperous than since the repeal, wages being 15 per cent. better ; and, in

Repeal of the Spitalfields Acts.

[1] *Supra,* 167.   [2] *Hansard,* xi. 433, 750, 792.

February of the next year, the mover of the Address in the Lords could say that, so far from the trade having decayed as had been anticipated, it had advanced more rapidly than before, " and had since extended almost as much as the cotton trade had done." We no longer dreaded the rivalry of the foreigner in our market, and were able to contend with him in the markets of the continent.[1]

Duties of the Bank of England.

In 1822, as we saw, there was some pretty plain speaking about the Bank of England, and, as the expiry of the charter came within sight, its critics were resolved that the charter should not be renewed on the same terms as before. In 1824, the old question began to be asked in a more distinct form—the rights of the Bank as a private company as against their duties to the Government. It came up first on an enquiry as to the current note circulation. Manning (evidently a director) said that the Government had no claim on such returns, any more than it had to call for copies of the books of any private merchant, though the directors might give these returns as a matter of courtesy or for private information to a member. Grenfell said sharply that he differed in all points as to this. It was, in fact, the imperious duty of the House to call for such returns—" absolutely necessary to know how the Bank conducted its business," and " whether it was or was not in a state of solvency."[2]

Grenfell.

Grenfell then, asking for a number of returns, resumed his favourite task of criticising the Bank. The points he emphasised were : (1) that it was being paid far too much in the £4 millions to which the public balances had been reduced—it was not less than £120,000, or at the rate of 3 per cent., and any private banker would willingly take it for £20,000 ; (2) that the £260,000 for managing the public debt and paying the dividend was also too much—by £100,000. The Chancellor of the Exchequer pleaded that the House would not be justified in revising a contract while the charter lasted. Hume went further than Grenfell. The bargain made in 1800 had already been revised, in 1808, when the allowance for management was raised ; why should it not be revised again when circumstances called for its reduction : and urged the Government to " shake itself free of the trammels in which they had long been held by the Bank"— as the interest of money was now nearly on the same level as when

[1] *Glasgow Herald*, 15th October ; *Hansard*, xii. 8.

[2] *Hansard*, x. 123. In contrast with the secrecy maintained here, it had been noted in 1821 that the Bank of France was inspiring confidence by the clear description it gave of the state of its affairs—its discounts, accounts, current receipts and payments in specie and paper, and current expenses (*Annual Register*, 1821, 135).

the Bank lent a large sum to the Government, let the Government pay off every shilling that had been borrowed—it could be done in five minutes. The Bank was now acting as a pawnbroker on a large scale, lending money on estates ; [1] if the £15 millions were repaid, the Bank could give more effectual relief still to the country gentlemen—" they would not know what to do with their money and must lend it at a very reduced interest." Parnell, following the same line, declared that it was time to look into the renewal of the Charter, which would expire in nine years ; he was very anxious to prevent any new arrangement without a full examination of the policy of again conferring on it any exclusive privilege. Ellice cordially agreed as to the impropriety of ever again granting an exclusive charter, and he also criticised the large loans made by the Bank on landed estates, as tying up money in a security not easily realisable—the policy which had brought down the country banks in 1815 : suppose money were suddenly wanted, he asked, how could the Bank raise it ? Grenfell's motion meantime was agreed to. [2]

The subject of Marine Insurance occupied much of the attention of Parliament, and an important measure was passed. As the law stood, there were only two corporate bodies with which marine insurance could be effected—the Royal Exchange and the London Assurance Company, incorporated in 1720 by the 6th Geo. I. c. 18, the reasons then given for granting them exclusive privileges being the special danger of loss, the great sums involved, and the number of bankruptcies among individual insurers. A Select Committee, which reported in 1810, said that these two companies between them did not insure much more than five millions of property, or under 4 per cent. of the insurances of Great Britain ; so that, for the remaining 96 parts, the merchants continued exposed to all the consequences from which the Act of Parliament had thought to relieve them. They seldom insured risks in hazardous and remote voyages. The commerce of the country, in fact, had very much outgrown the capital, as well as the system, upon which these two companies were originally formed. The great bulk of the business, then, was done on individual security—individuals assembling together to underwrite separately, and prevented by

Marine Insurance.

---

[1] In the end of 1823, we read that the Bank had come to the resolution of employing a large capital in loans at 4 per cent. to landowners who could offer adequate security (*Farmer's Magazine*, November, 479).

[2] *Hansard,* x. 226.

law from associating to make insurances jointly. " Hence the
establishment of Lloyd's coffee house, where every person meaning
to underwrite must attend during the time necessary for that
purpose. But the first merchants in the city of London did not,
and could not attend Lloyd's coffee house. This exclusive privilege,
therefore, operated as a monopoly, not merely to the company,
but to Lloyd's." The inconveniences, however, were so great—
particularly for merchants outside London—that, notwithstanding
the prohibition and the penalties, there were upwards of twenty
known associations in different parts of England for the purposes
of marine insurance. The Report said further that the superiority of
companies for the purpose, as regarded facility, security, and cheapness, appeared from the concurring testimony of all the merchants
who had been examined, and might be inferred from the fact that,
where there was no restriction (that is, anywhere but in Great
Britain), insurances were invariably done by companies. In view
of all this, the Committee recommended that the exclusive privilege
for Marine Insurance of the two chartered companies should be
repealed, saving their charters, powers, and privileges in all other
respects.[1]

In May, Fowell Buxton brought in a Bill for the repeal thus
recommended, contending that the two companies had been
chartered in the old days of exclusive privileges, and that no good
reason could now be adduced in support of the monopoly—particularly as no such monopoly existed in other forms of insurance.
The objections made were trifling ; such as that it was an interference with vested rights, inasmuch as the companies had paid for their
privileges on the understanding that the exclusive charters were to
be in perpetual succession, and could not be withdrawn unless on
grounds of public inconvenience—and there was none such, as it was
perfectly easy to fall back upon Lloyds ; and that, among other
things, it would destroy Lloyds. Huskisson, Robinson, and Hume
supported the Bill, asserting that the public had a right to get their
business done in the best and cheapest manner ; that the counsel
heard for the companies had shown no case ; and that the
insufficiency of the payments originally made for the charter, and

---

[1] The Report is given in full in the *Edinburgh Annual Register* for 1824.
Down till the end of 1824, each partner in a Chartered Company was liable
only to the extent of his share or interest in the stock of the Society (*vide* an
instructive article on Joint-Stock Companies in the *Parliamentary Review*
for 1825, p. 709).

the long continuance of the privileges, took away all right to compensation ; and, in the end, the Bill passed both Houses.[1]

The reckless plunge of capital into Joint Stock Companies, which *Joint Stock Companies.* was such a marked feature of the year, induced Lauderdale to try to lessen " the mischief which was going on," by providing that such companies should not be incorporated by Act of Parliament without the assurance of their being possessed of the requisite capital.   He secured two additions to the standing orders of the House of Lords, to the effect that companies for making turnpike roads, canals, bridges, for lighting, paving, and cleansing cities, and the like, which should acquire the right of suing or being sued, must prove that three-fourths of their capital were already paid up and deposited or invested in securities.   On this occasion, it was moved that Irish mining companies should be exempt, on the ground that such a provision would effectually prevent their formation, but the motion was lost. It is a little surprising, then, to find, shortly after, a Joint Stock Company, " to encourage the working of mines in Ireland by means of English capital," passed without the provision, and to notice Lauderdale merely calling attention to, but not opposing it.   The Earl of Harrowby defended the exemption by saying that " as, in considering the state of Ireland, their Lordships had thought it right, for the purpose of securing the tranquillity of that country, to overlook those great principles of legislation by which they were usually guided, so it surely might be proper, for the sake of finding employment to a miserable population, to overlook some of those principles of political economy, the general advantage of adhering to which they acknowledged." [2]

But impediments were sometimes thrown in the way of Joint Stock Companies just because they were associations of capital. We find, for instance, an Equitable Loan Society Bill petitioned against by numbers of individual pawnbrokers in London and Leicester, and the petitions supported by well known Radicals. Burdett looked with suspicion on such companies, particularly as they were directed against a class of persons who were, in some degree, obnoxious to the public : pawnbrokers were, he knew not why, considered as unfair traders, and it was said that they made exorbitant profits: the fact was that they were placed under greater restrictions than any other class of traders, and it was absurd to

[1] *Hansard,* xi. 766, 1086, 1202, 1357, 1430, 1470.
[2] *Ibid.* xi. 856, 1076, 1100.

talk of exorbitant profits when their business was open to the competition of all, as all trades should be. Whitbread looked with great jealousy at the combination of gentlemen to destroy the trade of individuals. Hobhouse joined with him, for, if "this Bill were carried, there was no reason why joint stock companies of butchers or bakers should not be established : the real object of the Bill was private profit, and by that profit the public would be losers." Another member contended that the Bill, though Christian in profession, was Jewish in principle, as the object of the speculators was to monopolise the profits which the Jews at present enjoyed.[1]

Two studies in competition. Two more studies in the conflict between old and new ideas regarding competition are presented in the discussions over a new dock and a new bridge. The second reading of the St. Catherine's Dock Bill was moved by Grenfell, the ground taken being that the new dock would secure a very great public advantage, namely additional dock and warehouse accommodation for the growing navigation of the Port of London. No exclusive privileges were asked.

The objections raised were these :

(1) That there was already more than enough accommodation ; the London Dock Co. had foundations laid for warehouses capable of containing 200,000 or 300,000 tons of goods, which "had not been proceeded with for want of sufficient encouragement."

(2) That, of the six existing dock companies, two paid no interest ; one paid $3\frac{1}{2}$ per cent. ; the London Docks paid $4\frac{1}{2}$ per cent. ; and only the two others paid more than 5 per cent., and that on account of a transient monopoly—"what sort of prospect does this hold out ? "

(3) That the 25 acres of ground required now contained 1,100 houses, and 10,000 souls entitled to six or eight months' warning ; every Bill of this sort was an invasion of private property for an alleged public purpose ; moreover, the ground had been refused to the London Dock Co. twenty years before.

The answers given to these objections were :

(1) That, if a new company could do business better or cheaper, there was no reason for refusing the Bill.

(2) That the entire inhabitants of St. Catherine's parish did not amount to 5,000 ; of the 1,100 or 1,200 householders, 300 had given their assent to the Bill ; and that the ground had never been refused

[1] *Hansard*, xi. 857, 960.

—in fact, the London Dock Co. had been authorised to purchase it, but had then preferred a spot lower down.

(3) That the opposition came mainly from the rival docks, the East India, West India, and London ; if they succeeded in throwing out the Bill, they would have a complete monopoly.[1]

In the debate on the Hammersmith Bridge Bill again—a bridge not calling for any public grant, but to be erected by private capital —the arguments used against it were :

(1) That the bridge would lead to a part where there were scarcely any inhabitants.

(2) That Kew bridge and Fulham bridge were within a mile and a half.

(3) That it would be most damaging to the rights of the proprietors of the above mentioned bridges.

(4) That it would entail compensation to the proprietors of those bridges.

(5) That it would be of no use unless new roads and approaches were made, and this could not be done without sacrificing property to a great extent. " It might be very well," said Sir Joseph Yorke plaintively, " to have good level roads to walk upon, but it was really a heart-rending thing when roads were cut in every direction round gentlemen's estates which previously were quiet and retired." [2] The Bill, one is glad to see, was read a second time without division.[3]

Since 1819, the necessity of standardising the Weights and Weights and Measures of the kingdom had been the subject of several parlia- Measures. mentary reports. In all Acts subsequent to Magna Charta, the Winchester bushel was declared to be the only legal one, and yet its dimensions were never specified till the 3rd William III., and the bushel which was in use at the Port of London, at Mark Lane, and at the Guildhall, did not agree with the standard bushel at the

---

[1] *Hansard*, xi. 95 ; xii. 612.

[2] Yorke, however, had his revenge. A few days later, he is found denouncing the objection urged against the Tees and Weardale Railway, that it would come near a nobleman's park. This, he explained, was a vast public work by which coals would be furnished to the Metropolis and the existing monopoly weakened ; and, if the question of private property was not allowed to interfere with the erection of Hammersmith Bridge, it should not be allowed here (*Hansard*, xi. 419).

[3] *Hansard*, xi. 397. It is not without interest to recall the fact that, in 1671, a proposal to build a wooden bridge at Putney was lost, after a very serious debate in which it was said that, if the bridge were built, the watermen would be ruined, the navigation of the Thames ruined, and London itself ruined (*European Magazine*, September).

Exchequer either in shape or contents. In 1822, wheat was sold in London by the quarter, in Scotland by the boll, in Ireland by the barrel; in one place by weight, in another by measure.[1] In the present year, a Weights and Measures Bill, based on the report of the last commission, and only delayed from the past session for want of time, was brought in by Sir George Clerk, and passed without objection, under the title, " For ascertaining and establishing uniformity of weights and measures." The old denominations were retained, but were now determined by reference to natural standards.[2] The "imperial standard yard" became the only standard measure of extension, every other measure in the kingdom, lineal, superficial, or solid, being computed and ascertained from it, and this yard was determined by a pendulum vibrating in a vacuum at sea-level in the latitude of London. The "imperial standard troy pound" was to contain 5760 grains, and all other weights were to be derived, computed, and ascertained from it. The "imperial standard gallon," containing 10 lbs. avoirdupois weight of distilled water at 62° Fahr., was made the standard of capacity. The new Act was to come into force on 1st May, 1825, and, after that date, all contracts for sale were to be holden to relate to these standards, unless the contrary was specified : if any agreement made reference to local weights and measures, it should be null and void unless it specified the rate or proportion which they bore to the standards. No new weights and measures could be made ; but the ones existing in any person's possession might be used, provided that their rate or proportion to the standards were painted or marked on them.[3]

Decimal System.   In connection with the more scientific standards thus adopted, it is perhaps worth noticing that—not for the first time [4]—the Decimal System was advocated in Parliament, though only as regards coins. The proposal put forward was to adapt the existing coins by making three denominations, pounds, double shillings, and farthings—the latter raised by 4 per cent. Wallace, now the Master

[1] *Quarterly Review*, January 1822.

[2] It is curious from the point of view of " natural standards " to know that Henry I. ordered the length of his arm to be the criterion of the yard measure.

[3] *Hansard*, x. 450 ; *Edinburgh Annual Register*, 365 ; *Annual Register*, 65. In 1825, however, the Act was amended, and the date of its coming into force was postponed till 1826.

[4] A Select Committee had recommended, in 1821, that " the sub-division of weights and measures employed in this country be retained, as being far better adapted to common practical purposes than the decimal system."

of the Mint, admitted the theoretical advantages, but was doubtful
if the practical disadvantages did not more than counterbalance.
He pointed out suggestively that the decimal system had been
adopted in France after the revolution, that is, when there had been
an overthrow of every previous system, and when no existing
interests or prepossessions had to be contended with. The motion
was not pressed to a division, the proposer contenting himself with
anticipating that the young members of the House would live
to see the principle of his measure carried into effect.[1]

In April, an interesting petition was presented from several Sale of
fishmongers and poulterers in London, asking for the repeal of a mackerel on
Sundays.
clause in an Act of William III. which permitted the sale of mackerel
on a Sunday, the ground taken being that the permission was
abused to sell other fish on that day. Hume asked why they needed
an Act "not to compel them to do a certain thing which they needed
not do, unless they chose " ; why did these conscientious Sunday
observers not agree among themselves not to do it ? The answer,
of course, was that others would not follow—particularly " Jews
and low Irish "—they would lose their customers and their connection. Nothing came of it, but the petition is worth recalling
from the statement therein that, " from the excellent state of the
roads, and the great improvement of wheel carriages, machines
laden with mackerel and other fish could arrive overland from the
coast of Sussex, and other places of similar distance, at the London
market, in the short space of seven or eight hours, not to mention
the facility with which Billingsgate was supplied by steam boats
and other vessels." [2]

The Game Laws were now become the subject of annual dis- Game Laws.
cussion. The poacher, among his own class, was looked on very
much as the smuggler among all classes—not a criminal but a
" free trader." " I like a smuggler," said Lamb. " He is the only
honest thief. He robs nothing but the revenue,—an abstraction
I never greatly cared about "—and one wonders how many even
to-day do not share the same feeling ! Earl Grosvenor affirmed
that nearly one-half of the persons confined in gaol were there for
violation of the Game Laws. The evils connected with them were
so far-reaching that everyone, it may be said with perfect truth, was
agreed that the laws should be amended. The kind of amendment
wanted, however, varied as widely as the interests of landowners,
farmers, sportsmen, philanthropists, and consumers of game. The

[1] *Hansard*, x. 445. [2] *Ibid*. xi. 414.

only unanimity of opinion was that "any change would be for the better." A Committee appointed amid warm approval reported, in 1823, that the law was everywhere evaded, that its breach was not counted any moral offence, that the market was constantly supplied by poachers; and came to the conclusion that the evil would be diminished if persons qualified to kill game in virtue of real property were permitted to sell it to persons who should be duly licensed to retail it. But the Bill brought in on these lines did not pass. In the present year, two Bills were brought in but came to nothing.[1]

Cruelty to Animals.

The friends of animals had another innings this Session. In 1823, Martin, encouraged, not so much by the success of his Cruelty to Animals Bill, as by the sympathy shown in cultivated circles with its object, had moved for leave to bring in a Bill to prohibit bull-baiting—it had been decided in court that bulls were not cattle, and therefore not included under the Act of 1823—and dog fights. The old difference of opinion at once showed itself, some contending that it was wrong to interfere with the "amusements" of the lower classes, others, like Brougham, that it was wrong not to extend legislation to similarly cruel sports among the upper; and the motion got no further. In the current year, Martin brought in another Bill to prevent bear-baiting and other cruel practices. Peel opposed very much on Brougham's ground—let them abolish fox-hunting and partridge shooting, and then they might abolish bear-baiting. Dropping this Bill by advice, Martin brought forward two others, a Cattle Ill-treatment Bill—which was met with mere levity —and a Horse Slaughtering Bill, directed against the cruelty inflicted by knackers on animals which were not worth treating decently— which was thrown out. Lord Calthorpe then brought in a Cruelty to Animals Bill; it was objected to on the ground that it aimed at "teaching people humanity by law," and it also dropped.[2]

---

[1] *Hansard*, v. 38; viii. 541; ix. 79, 644; x. 187, 224, 266, 444, 902, 1415; xi. 389, 956, 1097, 1199. The Report is given, with hostile comments, in Cobbett's *Register*, May 17, 1823. From this time, Cobbett gave the agitation his vehement support.

[2] *Ibid.* ix. 433; x. 130, 131, 368, 865, 1186; xi. 1089, 1431, 1095. Martin—who was well known for bringing actions for cruelty against poor people and then paying the fines himself—confessed that, on a recent occasion, he had taken the law into his own hand. He had brought in a few trusses of hay for the unhappy animals, and found that the horses never got it. So he sent some 200 letters by the twopenny post to the knacker informing him that horses, mules, asses, cows, etc., could be had at particular places if sent for at once—"if he did not make haste the dead animal would be removed "— and caused the ruffian an expense of £15 in postages and expenses !

During the year, there was much and passionate discussion of the state of affairs in the slave colonies. In June, Brougham moved an Address to the Throne on the fate of John Smith. In one of the most splendid examples, both of forensic ability and of passionate love of justice—the speech extends over 40 pages of *Hansard*—he went over the trial in Demerara step by step, denouncing the proceedings, the sentence, and the subsequent remission as all illegal. The motion was defeated, but only by 193 to 146.[1] Canning, expressing his " unequivocal abhorrence of slavery in the abstract," urged the repeated sanctions of the legislature and the settled rights of inheritance, the dread of mooting " the awful question of the transcendental power of Parliament over every dependency of the British Crown," and the disastrous effects which would follow sudden emancipation, as reasons for moving cautiously, and ended by carrying through a Bill which declared the Slave Trade piracy—a curious *non sequitur*, as it seems to me.[2]

From this time onward, both in petitions and in outside discussions, three things began to be dwelt on : that, unless slavery itself were abolished, there would never be an end to the slave trade ; that the emancipation must be gradual ; and that those who might thereby suffer loss should be compensated.[3] Meanwhile, however, the colonies went on as if they were " fey." Demerara passed a resolution that all missionaries of every kind should be excluded from the colony. The House of Assembly of Dominica declared the inability of the colonies to contribute any pecuniary aid towards the instruction of the slaves. In Jamaica, determination was shown not to introduce any of the proposed amendments into the slave code ; and very strong language was used against the British Cabinet, particularly Canning. In Barbadoes, the year passed away and the slaves remained as they were. In Trinidad, the regulations were put in force under strong protest. Only in St. Kitts was the Order received without murmurs and some attempts made to carry it out loyally. Wilberforce could assert that there was a growing rather than a diminishing disposition to oppose the reforms which England had suggested, and, indeed, the colonies got not a little encouragement from the attitude of many at home. Baring stood forth as the champion of the planters in the House,

---

[1] *Hansard*, xi. 961, 1206.   [2] *Ibid*. x. 1064, 1091.

[3] Hume took a strong position on this last ; property in slaves was abominable, but it had been acquired under the sanction of English law, and recompense was only just (*Ibid*. x. 1331).

and *Blackwood* outside denounced the " saints " as canting hypocrites covering "intrigue, worldliness, heartlessness, and the spirit of money getting" under the guise of philosophy and religion.

In general literature, one notes the appearance of road books and guide books, and of specialist magazines of all kinds. The greater reviews attract attention by their violent attacks on each other. There are vast numbers of tracts on the West Indian question. Among book notices appear the following:

Economic literature.

M'Culloch's *Discourse on the rise, progress, peculiar objects, and importance of Political Economy*; De Quincey's *Dialogue of Three Templars on Political Economy, chiefly in relation to the principles respecting Value of Mr. Ricardo*—" unequalled, perhaps, for brevity, pungency and force," says M'Culloch; *The Principles of Political Economy*, by M. Juicson; *An Inquiry into the principles of National Wealth*, by John Rooke; Richmond's *Narrative of the Condition of the Manufacturing Population; Effect of the Employment of Machinery, etc., upon the Happiness of the Working Classes*; W. Thompson's *Enquiry into the Principles of the Distribution of Wealth*; *An Inquiry as to the Poor Laws*, by J. E. Bicheno (hostile to a compulsory provision); *A further Enquiry into the present state of our National Debt and into the means and prospect of its redemption*, by Francis Corbaux; *Thoughts on the Funding System and its Effects*, by Piercy Ravenstone; *A Treatise on the Principles of the Usury Laws*, by Robert Maughan; *Outline of the system of Education at New Lanark*, by Robert Owen; Slaney's *Essay on the beneficial direction of Rural Expenditure*.

In the obituary of the year, appear the names of Louis XVIII., Byron, George Webb Hall, and Joseph Marryat, the champion of the shipping interest.

MISCELLANEA.

" It is reported that the Senatus Academicus of Edinburgh University have passed a resolution in favour of examining medical candidates for graduation through the medium of the English language in all time coming, and it is expected to receive the municipal sanction " (*Glasgow Herald*, 6th August, 1824).

CHAPTER XXII

1824. THE PROGRESS OF THE POOR LAWS

For some time now, the discussion of the Poor Law had formed part of the annual parliamentary business, though little came of it.[1] In 1821, as no member of the late Committee took up the matter, Scarlett (created Lord Abinger in 1855) brought in a measure consisting of three parts : (1) to declare the poor rate assessments of the current year ending 25th March a maximum never to be exceeded ; (2) to deny parish relief " where the parties merely grounded their claim upon being unable to obtain work," limiting it to cases of actual infirmity of body, old age, or debility by sickness or accident ; (3) to deprive justices of the power to order the removal of paupers. The Bill was received with much praise and read a second time. But, after some rather unreal debate—for evidently no one expected so crude a Bill to get beyond academic discussion— it was withdrawn.[2]

(margin: Scarlett's Bill, 1821.)

In the same year, Chetwynd, member for Stafford, asked for a Select Committee to take into consideration the existing laws relating to vagrants. The country was overrun with them, he said —people who sallied forth from lodging houses to seek for opportunities of theft, and, in the last resort, committed an act of vagrancy in order to be passed on to such places as they described as their settlements ; then swore to another place to which they were passed on in like manner, and thus were always travelling about the kingdom. The Committee was appointed, and, in May, Chetwynd got leave to bring in a Bill based on its report. From a debate in June at the report stage, we learn that the chief objects of the Bill were to prevent the removal of vagrants, which was costing the country no less than £100,000 a year, " while the practice too often

(margin: Chetwynd's Vagrancy Act.)

---

[1] See *Economic Annals, 1801-20, passim.*

[2] *Hansard,* v. 572, 987, 1228, 1479. Scarlett's Bill is discussed in a friendly way in the *Edinburgh Review* of October 1821.

presented scenes shocking to humanity and decency"; to substitute imprisonment and labour; and to abolish the system of rewards for the apprehension of vagrants.[1]

Scarlett's Bill, 1822.

In 1822, Scarlett renewed his attempt. The vice of the whole Poor Law administration, he thought, might be traced to three causes : (1) the restraint on the circulation of labour ; (2) the unlimited provision for the poor ; (3) the indiscriminate application of that provision, leading to profligacy, idleness and vice. The Bill he now introduced was intended to be one of a series carrying out these principles, and dealt with the first only. Its leading feature was to do away with the compulsory removal of paupers—the law, as it was at present, obliged persons, as soon as they became chargeable to the parish, to remove to another parish where they had a settlement—and so to reduce at once the amount of litigation and the enormous expenses and hardships of removal. Numerous petitions, however, were presented against the Bill, and, after much opposition, it was thrown out on the second reading.[2]

Movements in 1823.

In 1823, we hear less, in petitions and parliamentary debates, about the pressure of the evil. Possibly because of the revival of trade, the Poor Rate for 1822 had fallen to £6,358,000—a lower figure than in any year of the preceding six. Nolan obtained leave to bring in a Bill to amend the laws relating to the maintenance and employment of the poor, similar to one he had submitted in the previous Session. T. P. Courtenay brought in a Bill with the same title. Wood proposed a set of resolutions relative to settlement, but withdrew them with an intimation that he would bring in a Bill to amend the Settlement Laws. But of these measures we hear nothing more.[3]

Russell's Committee.

In the current year, more progress was made. On 25th March, Lord John Russell asked for a Select Committee, " To enquire into the condition of the labouring classes, particularly with a view to the practice of paying part of the wages of labour out of the Poor Rates." Peel pointed out that this would be, practically, an enquiry into the condition of the labouring poor generally, and the remit was limited to : " To enquire into the practice which prevails in some parts of the country of paying the wages of labour out of the Poor Rates, and to consider whether any and what measures can be

---

[1] Hansard, iv. 1216 ; v. 983, 1192. In 1822, the Act—thenceforth known as Chetwynd's Vagrancy Act—amended this, and consolidated into one about fifty Acts relative to Vagrancy in England (Ibid. x. 86).

[2] Hansard, vii. 761.   [3] Ibid. viii. 367, 750 ; ix. 693.

carried into execution for the purpose of altering that practice." [1] Among the members were Peel, Sturges Bourne, Bennett, Western, Althorp, Acland, Scarlett, Brougham, Spring Rice, and Geo. Philips, Russell being chairman.[2]   The Report was presented on 4th June, but the matter was not discussed before the end of the Session.

The Report—which is very short—reads like a condensed state- Its Report. ment of the more famous one of 1832.   It begins : " From the evidence and other information collected it appears that, in some districts of the country, able-bodied labourers are sent round to the farmers, and receive a part, and, in some instances, the whole of their subsistence from the parish, while working upon the land of individuals.   This practice was, doubtless, introduced at first as a means of employing the surplus labourers of a parish ; but, by an abuse which is almost inevitable, it has been converted into a means of obliging the parish to pay for labour which ought to have been hired and paid for by private persons.   This abuse frequently follows immediately the practice of sending the unemployed labourers upon the farms in the parish.   The farmer, finding himself charged for a greater quantity of labour than he requires, naturally endeavours to economise, by discharging those labourers of whom he has the least need, and relying upon the supply furnished by the parish for work, hitherto performed entirely at his own cost. An instance has been quoted of a farmer's team standing still, because the farmer had not received the number of roundsmen he expected.   Thus the evil of this practice augments itself ; and the steady, hard-working labourer, employed by agreement with his master, is converted into the degraded and inefficient pensioner of the parish.

" This practice is the natural result of another, which is far more common, namely, that of paying an allowance to labourers for the maintenance of their children.   In some counties, as in Bedford- shire, this payment usually begins when the labourer has a single child, wages being kept so low that it is utterly impossible for him to support a wife and child without parish assistance."

These evil consequences were these :

(1) " The employer does not obtain efficient labour from the labourer whom he hires."   Men who are sure of a subsistence for themselves and their families will, naturally, be idle and careless— four or five labourers frequently do only the work of one.

---

[1] *Hansard*, x. 1413.
[2] *Journals of the House of Commons*, vol. 79.

(2) " Persons who have no need of farm labour are obliged to contribute to the payment of work done for others."

(3) " A surplus population is encouraged ; men who receive but a small pittance know that they have only to marry and that pittance will be augmented in proportion to the number of their children "—they are heard to say, " We will marry and you must maintain us."

(4) " By far the worst consequence of the system is the degrada- tion of the character of the labouring class." Subsistence being assured to all, however, lazy or profligate, all inducement to obtain a good character is taken away. The effects correspond with the cause—" the parts of the country where the system prevails are, in spite of our gaols and our laws, filled with poachers and thieves." And to punish those who refuse or neglect to work would be re- pugnant to the national character—or would tend still further to degrade the labouring classes of the kingdom.

" The effects of this system very clearly show the mistake of imagining that indiscriminate relief is the best method of providing for the happiness of the labouring classes. Employers, burdened with the support of a surplus population, endeavour to reduce the wages of labour to the lowest possible price. Hence, where the system to which we allude has gained ground, the labourers are found to live chiefly on bread, or even potatoes, scarcely ever tasting meat or beer, or being able even to buy milk ; while, in other parts of the country where high wages are still prevalent, the food and whole manner of living of the labourer are on a greatly better scale. This difference is, doubtless, to be attributed to the excess of popula- tion in particular parts of the country ; but that excess is, in great part, to be attributed to the maladministration of the Poor Laws during the latter years of the great war.

"Without assigning any precise period when the system of paying part of the wages of labour out of the Poor-rate commenced, we are of opinion that, although perhaps it began earlier in some districts, it has generally been introduced during the great fluctuations of the price of provisions which have occurred in the last thirty years. In the year 1795, especially, a year of scarcity, parishes, finding that employers could not afford to pay their labourers a sufficient sum to support their families, even on the most stinted scale, added a contribution out of the Poor-rate to healthy labourers in full employment."

The evil, however, they were glad to say, was partial ; many counties in England were nearly, if not totally, exempt from it. It was scarcely found in Cumberland and Lincolnshire. It prevailed in parts of Lancashire and Yorkshire. " In Suffolk, Sussex, Bedfordshire, Buckinghamshire, Dorsetshire, and Wiltshire, the plan of paying wages out of the Poor-rate has been carried to the greatest extent. Norfolk, Huntingdonshire, and Devonshire are likewise affected by it. In some of these counties, wages are 8/- or 9/- ; in others, 5/- ;—and, in some parts, they have been, and are, so low as 3/- a week for a single man, and 4/6 for a man and his wife."

" With respect to the remedy for the evils pointed out, it is obvious to remark that a great, if not the greater part, arises from the maladministration of the laws. Yet, when this remark is made, it does not appear how, under the present system, the laws which regard the poor should be otherwise than ill administered. Where no select vestry or assistant overseer has been appointed, the poor are assigned to the care of a person named only for one year, and in general anxious chiefly to get rid of his office with as little trouble to himself as possible ; or, if he endeavours, in spite of clamour and vexation, to improve the practice, his designs are liable to be overset by the order of magistrates who, with excellent intentions, are often not conversant with the details of the management of the parish in whose concerns they interfere.

" The great object to be aimed at is, if possible, to separate the maintenance of the unemployed from the wages of the employed labourer ; to divide two classes which have been confounded ; to leave the employed labourer in possession of wages sufficient to maintain his family, and to oblige the rest to work for the parish in the way most likely to prevent idleness.

" By the 43rd of Elizabeth, it is ordered that ' the churchwardens and overseers shall take order from time to time, with the consent of two or more justices, for setting to work the children of all such who shall not be thought able to keep and maintain their children.' This provision, while it clearly shows that the framers of that Act never had it in contemplation to raise a fund for the support of all the children of all labourers, affords the means of remedying, in some degree, the existing evil of adding to the wages of labour from the Poor-rate. Wherever, from disinclination to work, parents earn less than they might do, in order to draw from the parish fund, it might be found highly useful that the parish officers, with the consent of the magistrates, should, instead of giving money to the parents, set to work their children, who would, at the same time, be removed from the example of idle or dissolute parents. But this remedy must be used with caution, and might be inexpedient, if applied in cases where the best labourers, with their utmost exertions cannot earn sufficient to bring up their children without parish assistance.

" According to the system at present pursued in many counties, a scale of allowance is drawn up by the magistrates, fixing, in money, the sums which a labourer is to receive, in proportion to the size of his family and the current price of flour or meal. On this allowance, whether idle or industrious, the labourer relies as a right; and, when he receives less, he makes an angry appeal to the magistrate, not as a petitioner for charity but as a claimant for justice. Without questioning the fitness of the scale upon which these tables have been framed, we cannot but regret that the magistrates should promulgate general regulations, the obvious tendency of which is to reduce the rate of wages, and create dissatisfaction between the labourer and his employers.

" With respect to the second object,—the mode of finding employment for those who profess themselves unable to obtain it—it appears to your committee that the parish should, if it be possible, provide them with labour less acceptable in its nature than ordinary labour, and at lower wages than the average rate of the neighbourhood. Your committee can add that this method has been found practically beneficial in all places wherein it has been carried into effect.

" It must never be forgotten, in considering this subject, that the evils produced by the Poor Laws are different in different places ; that all the good effects hitherto produced have been accomplished by improved management ; and that, if those effects have not been more general it is because the management of the poor has in the greater part of the country improved very little."

The Committee then went on to recommend the appointment of Select Vestries, and of Assistant Overseers receiving a salary ; and ended by saying that, even as the law at present stood, much might be done by the vigilant and enlightened attention of the magistrates—particularly by pointing out to the farmers the mischievous consequences of placing their labourers upon the public fund, by discountenancing abuses, and by supporting those who endeavoured to reform the existing system. " There never was a more favourable moment for reforming an abuse which, in very few places, is as yet of thirty years' growth." [1]

In view of the sitting of this Select Committee, it is not surprising that little else was heard of the Poor Laws during the Session. Leave was given to Nolan, however, to bring in and print an amending Bill, and to Althorp, for one to abolish that source of enormous and expensive litigation, Settlement by Hire and Service.[2] What was thought an ill-considered Bill brought in by Kennedy—" without the slighest encouragement from any public body in Scotland " —to prevent assessments from spreading further than they had done in Scotland, and finally to abolish that " vicious system," was universally opposed and was withdrawn.[3]

Chetwynd's Vagrant Act came in both for defence and criticism. Littleton said that it had saved the counties of England and Wales £100,000 annually, which had heretofore been expended in passing vagrants from one part of the country to another, and that the clamour which had arisen against it was due, not so much to the law, as to the indiscretion of some of the magistrates who had administered it. Hume, however, submitted that the discretionary powers vested in the magistrates to convict under the oath of one witness had been in some cases subject to very serious abuse. When the Act, which would, in course, have expired in September, was renewed, some members objected to that part of it which empowered the magistrates to cause " incorrigible rogues " to be whipped— whipping was never reformatory but always made the person worse. Peel granted this, but contended that the punishment was not for the purpose of effecting reform, but as an example to others, and that in this regard it was found to be often effectual. The Act apparently was renewed very much as before.[4]

Vagrancy Act renewed.

---

[1] The Report is given in full in the *Edinburgh Annual Register* of the year, chron. 66, and, in great part, in the *Annual Register*, *49.

[2] *Hansard*, x. 450 ; xi. 32.   [3] *Ibid.* xi. 900.

[4] *Ibid.* x. 86, 106 ; xi. 1081.

CHAPTER XXIII

1824. THE ETERNAL PROBLEM

" What's
wrong with
Ireland?"

" EVERYTHING seems prosperous but Ireland," wrote Croker. The Speech at the beginning of the Session said that there were "many indications of amendment." In the south and west, however, the old outrages were heard of from time to time, although the new constabulary were effective in repressing daring violations of the law. But, whether the disturbances were the cause of the distress, or the distress was the cause of the disturbance, was a much debated subject. " What's wrong with Ireland ? " was the question asked in many forms and answered in many ways. Most, perhaps, in their hearts, thought that the chief cause was that the people " were Irish," but they generally spoke of the "moral state of the people" as due to want of education and of a " free circulation of the Scriptures "—meaning that the religion of the majority was to blame. Others thought that the root of the matter was the want of employment—a huge and increasing [1] population depending on the land, and with no manufactures to speak of. The old explanation, of course, was always in evidence—absenteeism—the annual drain of some £2 millions spent out of the country.[2] And it was generally agreed that the land system was about as bad as possible.

Maberly
proposes an
advance of
capital.

Early in May, Captain Maberly, the member for Northampton, asked the House to take into consideration the propriety of an Advance of Capital to be employed in the provinces of Munster

---

[1] In this year, M'Culloch committed himself to the statement that the population of Ireland had doubled in the previous 33 years, that of England in about 80. At the Census, be it remembered, it showed 365 persons to the square mile against Scotland's 86, and was the densest rural population in Europe.

[2] *Les absens ont toujours tort*, said one in reply. "Absentees ' are certain Irish proprietors who stand in danger of being knocked on the head if they stay at home, and are sure of getting no rents if they go abroad. Irish proprietors will inhabit their country when the country becomes inhabitable.

and Connaught. His argument was that one of the most prominent evils in that country was the excess of population relative to the means of employing it, taken in relation with the fact that the population lived on the cheapest form of food, the potato—a crop always precarious. This ratio of population to employment, in which redundancy emerged, might be remedied in two ways ; by checking the increase of population, or by increasing the employment. In Ireland there were two special stimulants to population, the small holdings and the fact that the Catholic clergy depended for their subsistence largely on the fees accruing from the celebration of marriage. These stimulants might be lessened, but he wished to direct attention to the other term, and suggest the swelling of the fund which furnished the means of employment. But employment depended upon capital, and capital could not be tempted without security, and in Ireland generally there was no security. On the other hand, it was well known that, where there was sufficient employment, there was tranquillity and order, and capital had security ; these were reciprocally cause and effect—there was want of employment because there was insecurity, and there was insecurity because there was want of employment. If, then, no private individual would embark his capital while the country was in so disturbed a state, was it too much to ask that the Government should interpose its relief ? He did not think of more public works— which, by the way, he called unreproductive expenditure of capital ; they only suspended distress, and, the moment the works were completed, the employment was totally withdrawn. But two branches of industry in Ireland were susceptible of artificial encouragement, the Fisheries and the cultivation of Flax, in both of which capital could be "reproductively" expended. What he proposed was the advance of a sum not exceeding a million sterling, to be distributed and lent out, at the discretion of commissioners, at a low rate of interest or none at all, to "individuals who would engage to employ it, the parties giving proper security for its repayment." He was aware of the danger here ; "the landed gentlemen of Ireland, embarrassed, as they were, might be tempted to receive the capital given by the Government at a low rate of interest, and to discharge the incumbrances under which they at present laboured." Thus checks would be necessary to show what amount of capital they had expended and how it was employed. The scheme, however, was exceedingly nebulous, Maberly probably expecting that it would never come to be worked out.

Many speakers set forth the obvious objections. Robinson said he was very much afraid that, instead of inducing Irish gentlemen to trust to their own resources and exertions, and to the energies of their country, they would be led to lean for support upon Government, and rely upon temporary loans for the purpose of keeping their heads above water; such a system of advances must come to an end some time or other, and then they would be less capable of exerting themselves. As to fisheries, it was already in the power of the Lord Lieutenant to afford them assistance by the appropriation of five or six thousand a year for the purpose of building small piers and making small harbours for the protection of fishing boats. Goulburn pointed out that, if any difficulty occurred in repayment, and Government had to resort to means of severity to recover the loans, it would have the preference over all other creditors; this would cause the other creditors to withdraw the money due to them by every possible means; and the consequence would be that Government must either forgo the debt, or, by proceeding, produce a greater inconvenience. Besides, a great part of the money granted by Parliament was still in the hands of the Irish Government. Canning reminded the House of the *Spectator's* aphorism—that "nothing was so amiable as a lender, while nothing was so odious as a creditor; we went cap in hand to a lender, admiring his liberality and generosity, while, in a year or two, when he assumed the aspect of a creditor, we dreaded to see his face; yet these were the same individuals in different stages of their progress."

Althorp, however, cordially supported the proposal on two grounds: first, that Ireland had no other resource on which it could depend but the Government; and second, and more questionably, that "in a country where labour was so cheap, living might, with a very little sacrifice on the part of England, be made cheaper than in any other part of the British dominions"; if this were effected, people who now resorted to other countries for cheap living would spend their money in a country where the necessaries and many of the luxuries of life might be procured at so cheap a rate. Spring Rice quoted cases where benevolent individuals had invested capital in setting people to work, and had been repaid; to which Canning, however—who spoke with authority as one who had advocated similar views before he became a "convert"— replied that this amounted to arguing that, because a landlord had been able, beneficially, to advance money to his tenants, *ergo* a loan should be made to the landed gentlemen throughout Ireland.

Newport supported the proposal on the ground of reparation—
that the great impediment to the circulation of capital in Ireland
was to be found in the bad administration of the laws of that country.
John Maberly complained that his relative had been misunderstood.
His plan was, not to lend money on landed security, but to advance
money for specific purposes. Abercromby retorted that the result
was the same : Government could not afford to lend on mere
personal security, and what beyond personal security could they
look to except to the land ? whether, therefore, it was lent on land
directly, or whether the land was only pledged as a collateral security
for its repayment, the evil was the same, and the remedy by the
Government also would ultimately be the same. Moreover, this
would destroy the sale of land for a considerable time ; for who,
under any circumstances, would think of purchasing land pledged
for a debt to the Government, whose process would follow it into
the hand of every successive purchaser ? The motion was lost
by 33 to 85.[1]

In the same month, Althorp moved for a Select Committee to
enquire into the state of Ireland, proposing that it should take
up such extensive questions as : the connection between landlord
and tenant, the employment of capital and of the people, the
possibility of establishing large manufactures, the system of grand
jury presentments, the church establishment, the tithe system, the
Orange and Riband lodges, the exclusion of the Catholic laity
from offices. Parnell supported him in a speech which was very
pretentious but came to very little. It was essential, he said,
before entering on such a discussion, to establish some distinct
notion of the nature of the evil. This, in his opinion, was the state
of the peasantry—their extreme poverty—not poverty arising
from high rents, exorbitant tithes, county cess, or the want of resident
landlords, but from a deficiency of wealth to admit of proper wages
being paid to the labouring class.[2] If so, the object aimed at
must be the establishing of wealth in Ireland, and this to such an
extent that labour should be so rewarded that new habits of living
might be universally introduced. The remedy, then, was the direction of effort to augment capital, and in such a way that employment

Althorp's Committee.

---

[1] *Hansard*, xi. 450.

[2] In the subsequent year, he said it had been shown by several intelligent
witnesses before the Committee that, if the whole sum paid in the course
of one year (as wages) was divided among all the labouring class, it would
not make a higher average per man per day, throughout the year, than 4d.
(*Hansard*, xii. 622).

would be so general, and so constant, and bear such a proportion to the numbers of the labouring class, as would secure good wages to them—to make the labourer, in short, independent of making his living out of a piece of land for which the competition of his own class fixed a high rent.   The capital already existing in Ireland, indeed, was greater than was generally supposed—he was no friend to the transfer of capital from England by legislative interference —but it might be very much increased.   The entire repeal of the Union Duties, "which shut out no less than sixteen branches of Irish manufacture from the British market," would tend to this —" the experience of only a few months afforded reason for expecting that the cotton manufacture would become one of great importance" ; so would the proposed removal of the restrictions on Irish banking, the establishing of new banks on the Scottish system, and the repeal of the Usury Laws.   Something, however, must be done to establish a due administration of the law, and, more important still, to put an end to disturbance and insurrection.   But no success could be hoped for unless the present rapid increase of population was checked.   Seventy years ago, Ireland was one of the thinnest peopled countries in Europe : now she was one of the most densely peopled.   This could not be done by direct legislative provisions, but it could be helped by enabling the people to earn higher wages and live upon a better food than the potato, by preventing the excessive subdivision of the land under the middle-man system—that of joint-tenancy—and by encouraging the tendency already manifest towards the consolidation of holdings. Finally, he warned the House that, if the increase of population were not checked, there must be an emigration, not to foreign countries but to England, which would introduce the potato diet, bring down the standard of wages, and swell the poor rates.

The Government opposed the enquiry on the ground that it was far too large and complicated for a Committee ; and, after a very long discussion, Goulburn's amendment was carried, that the enquiry should be limited to the nature and extent of the disturbances that had prevailed in those districts of Ireland which were then subject to the operation of the Insurrection Acts.[1]   A similar Committee was appointed by the Lords in the same month.[2]

Insurrection Act renewed.   The first result of the enquiry was an almost unanimous recommendation to renew the Insurrection Act, and this was done, not without the usual protest that force was no remedy, and only

[1] *Hansard*, xi. 654.   [2] *Ibid.* 753.

" tended to perpetuate the disturbances which it pretended to allay." [1]

One of the most fruitful sources of outcry, the evils connected Tithe. with the payment of Tithe, had, as we saw, been tackled in Goulburn's Tithes Composition Bill passed in the previous session. The Act had been put in operation very extensively and with good results. Over a thousand applications—about one half of them from the clergy—had been made for special vestries : of 966 parishes in which endeavours had been made to carry it into effect, it had been completely successful in 216. Goulburn now introduced an amendment bill to " give increased efficiency " to his measure, and the Bill was carried with general approval.[2] Hume bluntly insisted that no good would be done to Ireland by this sort of legislation ; the real remedy for the evil was to break up the church establishment in Ireland—nothing else would be effectual. He accordingly renewed his attack of the past year, but again without success.[3] One result, however, was the introduction of a Bill by Goulburn (c. 91), in most respects similar to the existing law in England, to compel, so far as possible, the residence of the Irish clergy upon their benefices.[4]

The first indication of a desire for a Poor Law in Ireland is given A Poor Law in a petition from the parish of Kilmore (Co. Armagh), signed by mooted. Catholics, Dissenters, and Churchmen, and presented by the Bishop of Raphoe, praying for a law " to enable the inhabitants of any parish in Ireland to maintain their own poor." He admitted that the introduction into Ireland of the English Poor Law was neither practicable nor desirable. All the petitioners asked was " that the power of attending to the distress of the poor might be made, not a compulsion, but a legitimate part of vestry business." The Earl of Limerick said that such a request and from such a quarter, was " truly astonishing "—" calculated to spread horror and alarm from apprehension of the consequences which must attend the adoption of any such plan." [5]

---

[1] *Hansard*, xi. 1102, 1322.

[2] *Ibid.* x. 851, 1385 ; xi. 68, 501, 1104.

[3] *Ibid.* xi. 532. Hume had a, possibly, unwelcome ally in Cobbett, who said that the only thing to restore peace and contentment to Ireland was to " unestablish the church."

[4] *Ibid.* x. 183.

[5] *Ibid.* xi. 1098. In August, at a Catholic Association meeting, O'Connell avowed himself a convert to Cobbett's view on the propriety of a Poor Law for Ireland.

CHAPTER XXIV

1824. THE PROGRESS OF PROTECTION IN OTHER COUNTRIES

WE find surprise expressed in many quarters that other countries should be adopting and confirming the commercial restrictions which we were getting rid of as fast as consideration for vested interests would allow. The reason, however, is not far to seek. The progress of Britain, both in internal industry and external trade, was the envy of the world, but it was, perhaps, a little difficult to account for on grounds of natural resources : indeed, it was rather an example of how natural drawbacks may be counteracted. Thus attention was attracted to the legislative system under which the progress had been made—the fostering care of the Government, the prohibitions and tariffs—and the historical conditions were confused with the cause. The fact that Britain was now dispensing with her system was answered by the consideration that, after a building is put up, the scaffolding may be removed.

Netherlands. The methods adopted by the Netherlands are the more interesting because of the resemblance between the economic conditions of the two countries and their ancient rivalry. In August, 1823, as result of the special enquiry into the interests of the farmers relative to those of the consumers,[1] the King's Speech to the States General declared that the interference of the law was not required. The harvest had again been very productive, and prices of provisions were low. This favoured all the undertakings of the national industry. But it also made it necessary to find an outlet in foreign markets,[2] and the failure of commercial negotiations with France obliged him, with regret, to deviate from the former liberal principles, and " adopt reciprocal measures to hinder or limit the import

[1] *Supra*, 111.

[2] The King's Speech in 1821 had adverted principally to the rising state of manufactures in the Netherlands (*Annual Register*, 1821, 148).

of foreign products." Certain articles of import—" so far as they were of French origin or imported from France "—were now subjected to special duties, such as porcelain, china, earthenware, stockings, caps, mittens, and other knit or woven articles of wearing apparel of cotton, wool, or thread, and slates. Others were entirely prohibited, such as glassware of all kinds (except lookingglasses), cloths and kerseymeres, muriatic, nitric, and vitriolic acids, and brandy distilled from grain ; while distilled liquors, vinegars, and wine from France, could not be imported except by sea. The Speech also announced that, in the province of Groningen, a society of farmers was forming, " with a view to found a system of credit on the land and its produce." Another interesting experiment was the exemption from land tax for fifteen years of certain buildings erected by the Benevolent Societies of the Hague and Brussels, which aimed at the cultivation of waste and barren lands, and finding useful employment for a large number of destitute poor.

In the present year, the King's Speech in October said that, while the harvest had again been abundant, the continued fall in the price of grain had rendered it necessary to institute a further examination into the interests of the farmers. Regulations for limiting the entrance of foreign grain were, accordingly, agreed on, and, pending their issue—as " the state of agriculture required immediate relief "—importers were compelled, besides paying the existing duties, to give security for paying the higher duties which might be imposed. But relations with our country had become very friendly by the conclusion of the treaty on 17th March, for exchange of territories in the Indian Archipelago—giving them Bencoolen and Sumatra, and getting in exchange Malacca and all the Dutch ports on the Indian continent—and for reciprocal privileges to Dutch and British ships trading in the respective ports, and negotiations went on for a general treaty of commerce on a liberal basis. A provisional agreement was issued in August, declaring that all goods imported from the United Kingdom by ships under English colours should be considered and treated, in respect of duties, as if the importation had been made by a Netherlands ship—exception being made where importation under the Netherlands flag was specially favoured by the general law or by the tariff. An ordinance of April commanded that no Netherlands fisherman should carry on the pickle-herring fishery at a less distance from the coast of Scotland than two leagues.

In 1823, Sweden, influenced by loud complaints of poverty, retraced the absurd steps she had taken in absolutely prohibiting the import of any foreign commodities which could be made at home, and replaced the more burdensome direct taxes by import duties. The sumptuary laws, which imposed large sums for the liberty of wearing silk, drinking wine, and consuming other luxuries, were also repealed, in spite of the remonstrances of the peasants. In 1824, she also adopted reciprocity in shipping. After April, British commerce was to enjoy the same advantages in Sweden as were enjoyed by the Swedes in Great Britain. Ships of either nationality were to be on the same footing with respect to dues and commodities carried—this, however, not to extend to goods imported in British vessels carrying direct from the British colonies, " as Swedish merchant vessels do not enjoy the liberty of visiting the ports of the colonies and foreign possessions of England."

Portugal.   Portugal, possibly propitiated by the firm attitude of Britain in her favour, reduced her tariff on British woollens, which had been increased in 1821, to the old figure of 15 per cent., pending the conclusion of a final treaty.[1]

Prussia.   As regards Germany, Prussia, in April, signed a convention of commerce with this country establishing reciprocal equality as regards shipping. Among the several German States, where there was much depression of manufactures, and loud complaint of the prohibitive laws of their neighbours, the conflict of interest between these States, as we saw, was leading, on the one hand, to steps being taken towards commercial treaties between particular States, and, on the other, to the emergence of the aspiration for binding them all together in a commercial league " to protect native against foreign industry."

United States.   But it was in the United States that the most striking change was made. In 1816, the first avowedly protective tariff had been imposed : 25 per cent. being laid on cottons and woollens and " on articles of which a supply was being made at home," while the duties on other articles—principally for fiscal reasons—were on average about 20 per cent. The protective duties, however, were temporary—intended to remedy a serious situation—and were to

---

[1] The value of the British market to Portugal is strikingly shown in the official statement of wine exported from Oporto during 1822 : to England and her dependencies, 27,535 pipes ; to Hamburg, 111 ; to Holland, 37 ; to France, 1, etc. (*Annual Register*).

fall to 20 per cent. in 1819.[1] In 1818, some modifications were made in the direction of further protection; the textiles tariff was prolonged till 1826; the duty on all forms of unmanufactured iron was considerably increased; and the average of the tariff rose to 35 per cent. *ad valorem*. But, although the New England States grew clamorous for protection, and Monroe associated himself with the policy from the date of his first Message, it did not get a hearing from Congress.

But now, in 1824, a new tariff came into operation which had not even the pretence of aiming at revenue, and was specially directed at English staples—" for the purpose of affording additional protection," said the President's Message, " to those articles which we are prepared to manufacture or which are more immediately connected with the defence and independence of the country." Its principal object was the encouragement of wool, iron, hemp, lead and glass. The duties on cottons—already high enough—were raised very little, but the duty on raw wool was advanced from 15 per cent. to 30 per cent. ; on iron in bar and bolt, from 75 cents per cwt. to 90 cents ; on leghorn hats, from 30 per cent. to 50 per cent. On all articles not specified, the 7½ per cent. duty was raised to 10 per cent., and the average rose from 35 per cent. to about 40½ per cent.[2] Considerable apprehension was expressed in the Southern States that we might retaliate as regards cotton, and that, in any case, the friendly relations now existing between the two countries might be endangered. But England had learned her lesson.

---

[1] *Economic Annals, 1801-20,* 495.

[2] " Had no restrictions on the importation of foreign grain existed in Europe generally, and especially in Great Britain," wrote our minister at Washington, " I have little doubt that the tariff would never have passed through either House of Congress, since the great agricultural states, and Pennsylvania especially, the main mover of the question, would have been indifferent, if not opposed, to its enactment."

CHAPTER XXV

1825. THE SECOND FREE TRADE BUDGET

"Prosperity
Robinson's"
Financial
Exposition. PARLIAMENT resumed on 3rd February, and, on the 28th,
the Chancellor of the Exchequer made his usual Exposition of the
Financial Situation of the Country.   At the moment, everything
was *couleur de rose* ; everybody was carried away by the activity
in every branch of industry, not excepting agriculture ; nobody
dreamed of coming disaster ; and the congratulatory terms in which
the Budget was introduced earned for its author the name of " Prosperity Robinson."   After estimating in the past year for a surplus of
£1,052,000, the House, he said, had made some further reductions in
taxation, which, in ordinary course, would have reduced the surplus
to £420,000.   As it was, the actual surplus was no less than £1,437,000.
The excess came from all branches of revenue, and witnessed, not
only to prosperity, but to successful policy.   In Customs, the
proximate cause was the increased capacity to consume the produce
of other countries, aided by the reciprocal facility which that
increased consumption gave to the extended use of the products
of our industry by other nations.   In the Excise—which showed
an excess of £1,143,000 over what he had ventured to anticipate—
the increased consumption in nearly every category testified to
the increasing ease, comfort, and happiness of the people.   Last
year's reduction of £200,000 in law stamps was followed by a greatly
increased revenue, showing that we had obtained the benefit of
" cheap justice " without making the sacrifice which we were prepared to encounter.   The Post Office increase of £60,000 was the
natural consequence of increasing activity in the general business
of the country.

Estimates.   Passing to the estimates for the current year, he calculated the
produce, including everything, at £56,455,000 ; the expenditure,.

including about £5½ millions for the Sinking Fund, at £56,000,000.
In detail :

REVENUE.

Customs	£11,350,000
Excise	26,400,000
Stamps	7,100,000
Taxes	4,875,000
Post Office	1,500,000
Miscellaneous	750,000
Trustees on Half Pay	4,470,370
	£56,445,370

EXPENDITURE.

Consolidated Fund—	
Interest of Debt	£27,233,670
„ Exchequer Bills	40,000
Civil List, etc.	2,050,000
Half Pay Annuity	2,800,000
Sinking Fund	5,486,654
Supply—	
Interest of Exchequer Bills	820,000
Army	7,911,751
Navy	5,983,126
Ordnance	1,376,641
Miscellaneous	2,300,000
	£56,001,842

Carrying out the plan of last year, and casting his eye forward
to 1826 and 1827, he estimated that he had now to dispose of the
following :

Surplus of 1824	£1,437,744
„ 1825	443,528
„ 1826	864,676
„ 1827	1,254,676 [1]
	£4,000,624

Last year, he had used his surplus " as a means of commencing The new
a system of alteration in the fiscal and commercial regulations of principle.

[1] The excess expected in 1827 over 1826 was due to a diminution he proposed
to effect in the bounty upon the exportation of West India refined sugar,
by changing the existing graduated duty—which inevitably led to the calculation of drawback on muscovado as if it had paid duty at a higher rate than it
actually had—to a fixed duty of 27/- per cwt. on raw sugar ; this should save
3/- per cwt. of bounty on the drawback, or £300,000. This seems indicative
of the changing feelings towards the West Indies, when it is remembered that
Whitmore's proposal to enquire into the bounties had been rejected in the
past year on the ground of the distress in the islands, and because the question
was " fraught with such fearful consequences." At anyrate, it was regarded
as a blow at the West Indies (*Scots Magazine*, July).

the country ; " putting rum on a level of competition with home spirits, taking off certain bounties, reducing the tax on coal brought into London, reducing the import and export duty on wool, reducing the import duties on raw and thrown silk, and changing the prohibition of foreign silk manufacturers into a 30 per cent. duty. In disposing of the present surplus, he had three objects in view : (1) increased consumption at home, combined with increased extension of commerce abroad ; (2) the restriction of smuggling ; (3) some alleviation of the burden of direct taxation—the first two being, in his opinion, ten thousand times more advantageous than the third. The country was by this time convinced of the good sense of getting rid both of positive prohibitions and of prohibitory duties ; and he intimated that the President of the Board of Trade would take an early opportunity of submitting a plan for reducing within moderate and reasonable bounds all the remaining prohibitory duties—" thus to strike, as it were, from our recollection all those errors and prejudices which have so long shackled the energies of our commerce and restricted the productive industry of the world."

Reduced duties on Iron,   The most important reduction would be that of the duty on foreign Iron in bars and unwrought, from £6 10s. per ton—which was in a great measure a prohibition—to 30/-. The demand for iron had risen of late in such a wonderful degree that the produce of our mines was unequal to meet it at any reasonable price. Instead, then, of the narrow and short-sighted policy which would say, " Let us use none but our own," he would say, " Use all you can get." [1] But this change would not apply immediately to all countries. They meant to set an example to other governments, and act reciprocally—" we are not bound to abstain from making distinctions in favour of those nations whose views and principles are conformable to our own."

The next reductions would be on duties which were neither avowedly nor really prohibitory, but were so high as to impede

[1] The late progress of the iron industry had almost rivalled that of cotton. Long confined to Kent and Sussex by the necessity of smelting with wood, it was a matter of discussion, down till the middle of the eighteenth century, whether we should give up the iron manufacture or face the depletion of our timber. But, after the resuscitation at Colebrookdale, in 1740, of Lord Dudley's almost forgotten invention of 1619—smelting with pit coal—the industry steadily grew. By 1799, we were exporting a million and a half sterling of cast iron. During the war, when the demand was very great and when foreign supplies were checked, the increase was phenomenal—aided by the fact that iron, almost alone, escaped taxation.

consumption. The first of these was on Hemp, an article seriously Hemp,
affecting our mercantile marine ; it would be reduced by one half,
at a loss to the revenue of about £100,000. Coffee was now taxed Coffee and
differentially at 1/- per lb. on West Indian, 1/6 on East Indian, Cocoa,
and 2/6 of foreign, and, particularly since the increase of the duty
in 1819, the consumption had not kept pace with population and
wealth : the reduction of duty, which would be extended to cocoa,
would cost the revenue £150,000.[1] In foreign Wines again, not Wines,
only had the consumption not increased in twenty years, but it
had actually fallen off—not per head but absolutely. This might
be due to change of fashion, but he thought it due mainly to the
high price, and he would propose a reduction on the existing duty
of nearly one-half, being at the rate of 1/3 per bottle on French,
and 1/- on all other foreign wines—a loss to the revenue of probably
£230,000. He hoped that this would bring back the consumption,
in England and Scotland at least, to the amount drunk in 1801-3.
" I trust that, in the latter country, they will now drink their
claret with as much zest as they were formerly wont to do." [2]

The next change needed was of peculiar importance : it was a British Spirits,
reduction of the present duty on all British Spirits—not, indeed,
to the level already established for Scotland and Ireland of 2/- —
but from 10/6 per gallon to 5/-, on all spirits distilled from malt,
and to 6/- on those distilled from a mixture of malt and raw grain ;
and a reduction of the duty on Rum from 10/6 per gallon to 8/- — Rum,
the differential duty of 2/- being only just, as the colonial manufacturer was " not liable to that increased charge upon his raw
material which affects barley and malt from the restrictive operations of our corn laws." At the same time, it would be permitted
to the colonies to make whisky from grain, and send it here either
to be rectified or sold as whisky. He did not defend this reduction
on the ground of increasing the consumption and benefiting the

---

[1] The new rate on foreign coffee was 1/3, with a differential rate of 6d. to any
British possession in America, and 9d. to any within the charter of the East
India Company. Pepper, which was taxed about 500 per cent. on its value,
was subsequently reduced from 2/6 to 1/- —in the interest of the East Indies
as well as of the consumer (*Hansard*, xiii. 1222).

[2] By 1828, it was found that this reduction had materially increased the
exportation of wines from Bordeaux, and France reciprocated by reducing
the duty on English iron. Subsequently, the duty on Cape wines, which had
entered at one-third the duty on Portuguese, was made 2/- per gallon till
January 1830, then to revert to 2/6 (*Hansard*, xii. 1140). In the next Budget,
it was intimated that the drawback paid on account of the reduction on wines
to the holders of stock was no less than a million sterling (*Hansard*, xiv. 1322).

revenue—he knew some would hear with horror and think that it would spread universal drunkenness over the land—but as a means of coping with smuggling : it was really a choice of difficulties ; smuggling was an evil of immense magnitude, the cause of excessive and varied immorality, and the parent of innumerable crimes ; it was questionable if this measure would make spirits cheaper than they were already, considering the immense quantities smuggled across the border and across the channel.   They had tried the most rigorous measures to prevent this smuggling ; they had surrounded the coast with ships and guards, imposed penalty upon penalty, but all in vain.   Why ?   Because the cause of the evil was the law, and the alteration of the law had not yet been tried.   Let them try it now, and apply to England that change which had had such trium-

Distilling,   phant success in Ireland and Scotland.   He proposed, moreover, to equalise the system under which distilling might be carried on throughout the United Kingdom ; numberless restrictions would be removed from the trade, and the intercourse between different parts of the country rendered indiscriminately open.[1]   As the law stood, the distiller must begin by making a raw spirit which he could not sell for consumption, but must consign to the rectifier, in whose hands it underwent a fresh distillation, and, being mixed with various compounds, was then distributed to the consumers under the denomination of gin ; whisky, which was the pure extract from grain, unrectified and uncompounded, could not be sold for consumption.   He proposed now to legalise the sale of whisky : it was but reasonable that the people of this country should be at liberty to drink whisky instead of gin if they chose, and Mr. Hume would be able to indulge in his favourite beverage without qualms of conscience or unpleasant liability to penalties.   The annual loss

Cider.   to the revenue might be stated at £750,000.   For the same reason —the excessive smuggling—he would reduce the duty on cider from 30/- to 10/-, which would make a deficit of £20,000.[2]

Assessed Taxes.   As to direct taxation, he proposed to remove a number of small vexatious items on the Assessed Taxes—on four-wheeled carriages drawn by one pony, on occasional waiters, on coachmaker's licenses, on carriages sold on commission, on mules employed in carrying

[1] " The duty on the distillery in England was lowered from 11/8½ per gallon to 7/-, and the method of charge in use in Scotland was applied to England. . . . In two years the revenue was recouped in consequence of the enormous increase in the consumption of duty-paid spirits " (Dowell).

[2] At the same time, the taxes on wine, foreign spirits, coffee, cocoa, nuts, pepper, and tobacco were transferred to the head of Customs.

ore, on husbandry servants occasionally employed as grooms, on husbandry horses on hire, and on taxed carts. Houses vacated after the beginning of the year, he would charge—not for the whole year as now, but—during the time of occupation only. Untenanted houses, occupied only by a caretaker, he would relieve from duty altogether. In dairy farms, he would exempt two windows instead of one. On houses under £10 rental, now charged 1/6 per pound, he would remit the whole of the Inhabited House Duty, and, on houses having not more than seven windows, the whole of the Window Duty ; these two items, giving a substantial boon to many thousands of the poorer householders, would cost the revenue £276,000.

The total reduction would be £1,526,000, of which about £650,000 would fall upon the present year. Thus, he concluded, " I propose to give additional facilities to foreign commerce and internal consumption ; thus I strike a blow at that giant, the smuggler ; thus I exempt from the weight of direct taxation those who are the least able to bear it."

Some dissatisfaction was expressed ; for instance, that the West Indies were handicapped by the smaller reduction on rum than on spirits[1] and by the removal of the sugar bounty; that the East Indies were still handicapped by the preferential duty under which their sugar paid 37/-, as against the 27/- on West Indian ; that tobacco —" that great article of notoriously contraband consumption "— now taxed 1,200 per cent. on its cost, had not been touched— nor had tea ; that the wine duties were not equalised, and that the absurd monopoly of Portuguese port was continued. The reduction of the Spirit Duties called out a strong remonstrance from W. Smith, the member for Norwich. The immorality of it, he said, was beyond all question ; there was no necessity to enable a man to get drunk for a shilling—he could do that easily enough already. It appeared, from the most incontestible evidence, that almost every crime of the most atrocious character, such as murder, robbery, and burglary, was committed under the influence of ardent spirits. Why, then, reduce the price to one half ? It was said that the Scots were a sober people notwithstanding the low price of spirits in Scotland. The fact was that the poverty of the lower classes there was a check upon their intemperance. He might remind the

Reception of the Budget.

---

[1] There was some reason for this complaint, as, in last Budget, the reduction on the rum duty was based on the principle of putting it on an equal footing with British spirits.

House of the reply of Dr. Johnson to a person who observed that
a person might buy a solan goose in Scotland for twopence :—
" Granted, but where will he find the twopence in Scotland ? "
Hume, on the other hand, strongly recommended the Chancellor
of the Exchequer to equalise the duties between England, Scotland
and Ireland to a greater extent, giving the example of France and
America, and repeated his old argument—" it was the disposition of
man, when he could obtain an indulgence only occasionally, to get
as much of it as he could ; but, if circumstances enabled him to
obtain the gratification regularly, the temptation to excess was
removed. Good wages and low prices were the best security for
good conduct." But, on the whole, the Budget was received with
cordial appreciation.[1]

Attempts at further reductions.

Subsequently a few attempts were made to amend Robinson's
proposals. Maberly, supported by the large towns, moved for the
repeal of the whole of the Assessed Taxes, particularly the House
and Window Taxes. Criticising the Budget in detail, he contended that more relief would be given by getting rid of direct
taxation than by the Budget alterations, and that the general
opinion of the country was with him. At any rate, the Sinking Fund
should be applied to the reduction of taxation—instead of effecting
its purpose, the Debt was actually greater by £12 millions than in
1816. Huskisson argued that it had always been held by the
gentlemen opposite that direct taxes operated less mischievously
than indirect ; and that the Income Tax was as free from objection
as any other but for the inquisitorial power which accompanied it.
Now the Window Tax was not liable to this objection, and he
therefore thought it was not one of the taxes which should be
selected for repeal. Maberly, in reply, admitted that " direct
taxation was just in principle, and, on this account, he preferred a
property tax ; but, from its odious inquisitorial character, he hoped
never again to see it adopted." Althorp committed himself to the
proposition that he, for one, would not be at all afraid of leaving
the Debt even at £800,000,000, so long as the interest and all the
annuities charged upon it could be punctually and honestly discharged—although he might be of a very different opinion if the
Debt were of such an amount that there was any possibility of buying it up. The motion was, of course, lost.[2] A similar fate befel
Hobhouse's proposal to repeal the Window Tax, Maberly's proposal

[1] *Hansard*, xii. 719, 1081.   [2] *Ibid.* xii. 901.

to repeal the Beer Duties,[1] and Sykes' motion to reduce the Soap and Tallow Candles Duties. Hume entreated the Chancellor of the Exchequer to try for one year the effect of reducing the Newspaper Stamp Duty to 2d. : so anxious was he on the matter that " he would almost become personally responsible if any loss should accrue," to which Robinson answered unkindly that he would wish to have a security of another description.[2]

The general answer of the Chancellor to all these proposals was that he had gone as far in the reduction of taxation as he felt at present justified—" you must not ride a willing horse to death "—and the various changes passed into law without material alteration.[3]

An Emigration Grant raised some discussion in Parliament. In Emigration. 1823, a grant of £15,000 had been voted for facilitating the emigration of some 5,000 persons from the South of Ireland to the Cape. The experiment at first had not been very fortunate ; the crops had failed and the settlers were reduced to great distress. But of late "most flattering accounts of success" had come home, and now an " experimental grant " of £30,000 was asked for conveying the same class to the Canadas. The error of past emigration, said Wilmot Horton, was that people were sent out, and, when they arrived, had not the means of procuring subsistence. The present system aimed at placing the settlers in such a situation as to enable them to support themselves by their own industry. Hume, however, looked upon the grant as a most wanton piece of extravagance, and said he would oppose it in every way till he had further evidence from Canada : he was credibly informed that eighteen out of every twenty emigrants to Upper Canada passed on to the United States. The grant was made.[4]

As the Chancellor of the Exchequer had indicated, many of the Huskisson's changes already intimated as immediately affecting the revenue larger scheme. were part of a larger scheme adopted by the Government for increasing the industry and wealth of the country. Three weeks later, Huskisson unfolded the scheme, dividing it into three : the commercial policy with respect to the colonies, the revision of the

---

[1] The chief argument was that there was a tax of 35/- on beer and one of only 20/- on malt, and that this taxed the poor man, who bought his beer, 200 per cent. or 300 per cent. more than the rich who often brewed it. Why not put all the duty on malt ?

[2] Thanks to the paper duty and the stamp, the ordinary newspaper of the day consisted of four large pages, issued twice a week, at a price of 7d.

[3] *Hansard*, xiii. 374, 771, 1064, 1275.   [4] *Ibid.* xii. 1358.

protective duties, and the further encouragement to the interests of shipping and navigation.

From time to time within the last two or three years, as we have seen, mutterings of discontent had been heard in Parliament regarding the burden imposed on the mother country by the colonial establishments, and, within the past few days, very outspoken sentiments had been expressed with regard to the future of the colonies themselves. Baring pressed upon the Government the expediency of considering in good time what must, of necessity, be the future condition of Canada. It was impossible that it could very long continue to be a colony of Great Britain, for all experience proved that no colony, the productions of which were similar to those of the parent country, could, for any great extent of time, continue in that relation to the parent country. It would therefore be wise to consider the propriety of doing that, freely and in time, which might otherwise be accomplished after great bloodshed and expense. He would recommend to the Government to call on the legislature of Canada to enquire whether they felt themselves strong enough to separate from the mother country, and if they desired to be set on their own legs. This would ensure good feeling and advantageous commercial intercourse, and it would also be an act of generosity consistent with the dignity of a great nation.[1] Three days later, Captain Maberly, in a debate on the Sugar Duties, said that the trade to the West Indies was, to all intents and purposes, a losing trade to this country ; the sooner England got rid of those colonies and of the heavy expenses incurred, the better would it be for her interests.[2]

The new Colonial policy.   It was with these revolutionary sentiments in his ears that Huskisson, on 21st March, called the attention of the House to the system of our commercial policy in respect to the colonies, previous to proposing a set of resolutions on the subject.[3] The long established policy of all the European powers, possessing colonies in the New World, he began, was that of an entire and rigid exclusion of those colonies from all commercial intercourse except with the mother country : to uphold this exclusion and forbid all such intercourse, seemed of the very essence of colonisation.[4] But, within the past

---

[1] *Hansard*, xii. 1033.   [2] *Ibid*. xii. 1085.

[3] *Ibid*. 1097. The speech, which is of historic interest and deserves a fuller summary than space allows me to give, is reported very adequately in the *Annual Register*, p. 99.

[4] It is well known that Lord Chatham once said from his place in Parliament that the British colonists of North America had no right to manufacture even a nail for a horseshoe.

fifteen years, vast inroads had been made in this system. The Portuguese Brazils, St. Domingo, Cuba, and other Spanish colonies, had been thrown open, to say nothing of the new South American States. Could the British colonies, under our system of monopoly, now stand up in competition with the freedom of trade of these countries, and ought we to risk the good will and attachment of our great possessions oversea by continuing to make their interests subservient to ours ? The consequences of such a policy were seen, for our guidance, in the case of Ireland, which " was held in the most rigid subserviency to the supposed interests of Great Britain" down till 1780, and, for our warning, in the case of the United States. The conclusion clearly was that, so far as the colonists themselves were concerned, their prosperity was cramped and impeded by the old system of exclusion and monopoly, and the next inference was as clear, that whatever tended to increase the prosperity of the colonies could not fail, in the long run, to advance in an equal degree the general interests of the parent state.

Certain relaxations had already been made,[1] particularly as regards allowing the United States to trade with our colonies in their own ships—a privilege not granted to any state in Europe. The privilege indeed had as yet met with rather a sorry return, but in any case he would ask why the same indulgence should not be extended to the ships of European states ? Were we more jealous of the navigation of Denmark, Sweden, Holland, Russia, or the Hanse towns, than that of the United States ? His proposals were, then, briefly, " to open the commerce of our colonies to all friendly states upon the same principle (though, of course, with some differ- ence in the detail of its modifications) upon which they are at liberty to trade with Jersey or with Ireland." With the exception of some articles which it would be necessary to prohibit, such as fire-arms and ammunition of war generally, and sugar, rum, etc., in the sugar colonies, " I propose," he said, " to admit a free inter- course between all our colonies and other countries, either in British ships or in the ships of those countries, allowing the latter to import (into the colonies) all articles the growth, produce, or manufacture of the country to which the ship belongs, and to export from such colonies all articles whatever of their growth, produce, or manu- facture, either to the country from which such ship came or to any other port of the world, the United Kingdom and all its depend- encies excepted. All intercourse between the mother country and

[1] Cf. *supra*, 106.

the colonies, whether direct or circuitous, and all intercourse of the colonies with each other, will be considered as a coasting trade to be reserved entirely and absolutely to ourselves." The importation of foreign goods into the colonies would be made subject to moderate duties, " but such as may be found sufficient for the fair protection of our own productions of the like nature " : [1] these duties would, of course, form part of the colonial revenues. The existing prohibitions would be replaced by *ad valorem* duties ranging from 7½ per cent. to 30 per cent. Three other changes would be made : the warehousing system, familiar in England, would be extended to certain colonial ports ; the large fees levied at almost all the ports would be abolished, the customs officers being paid by a salary ; and Mauritius sugar, which now paid 10/- per cwt. more, would be admitted at the same duty as that from the West Indies.

Canadian wheat.

The last change was more startling ; it was that Canadian wheat would be allowed free entry at all times on payment of a fixed duty of 5/- per quarter. This he defended as a matter of common justice —corn was the staple of the colony, with which it paid for its supplies from Great Britain : was it fitting that, when the Canadians made their remittance in that staple, they should not be able to know whether it could be received here or not ? And the British grower could scarcely complain, as the freight from Quebec to England was not less than from 12/- to 15/-, and the greatest quantity which Canada could supply was no more than 50,000 quarters.[2]

Some criticism.

In the short debate which followed, Baring, expressing his gratification at the " broad and liberal views of commerce," pointed out

[1] In 1830, Parnell said that these clauses had made the principle of free trade entirely inoperative ; the duties were so high that England still practically enjoyed all the advantages of the old monopoly in supplying the colonies with her productions ; the attempt to establish a free colonial trade, and, at the same time, to give protection to British manufactures, had failed, because the two things were quite incompatible. He went on to argue that the only conditions on which it could be wise or politic for us to continue to keep colonial possessions, were that the number of them should be greatly reduced, and that those retained should contribute to the whole expense incurred in their defence. And, with respect to Canada, no case could be made out to show that we should not have every supposed commercial advantage if it were made an independent State (*Financial Reform*, 226, 236).

[2] No objection was made to this at the time, but subsequently it was affirmed that the average price of wheat in Canada was 38/- ; with freight, 12/- and a 5/- duty, this would admit it at 55/- ; was this a fair protection to our own agriculture ? Robinson's answer was that Canada was a colony belonging to this country ; that the Canadians were our fellow-subjects and entitled to our peculiar favour and protection. If the argument were good

that, to the North American colonies, this was really a measure of emancipation, for whatever remained peculiar in their situation would be privileges and not restrictions, but suggested that it would be necessary to provide against the possibility of any larger masses of corn coming from other parts of the American continent through Canada. Huskisson explained further that there would be some articles on which prohibitory duties would still be kept up, among them sugar, rum, molasses, cocoa, and coffee, the production of any foreign country—say Havannah—which might be carried into our colonies and thence exported here, on the favoured colonial terms. A question was asked as to the preference given to West over East Indies : the main intention of the measure seemed to be to ensure a valuable monopoly to the West Indies, and, upon paying a duty of 27/- per cwt., to admit sugars from all colonies—including now Mauritius—having a slave population ; upon what principle was it contended that the same advantage was not also to be enjoyed by the free labour of the East Indies ? But the proposals as a whole met with great acceptance, and the resolutions were passed without dissent, the only alteration being that the new regulation of admitting Canadian corn at a duty of 5/- was limited to two years.[1]

The second and more important part of the scheme—that which dealt with the Protective Duties—was taken up by Huskisson on 25th March, when, it is as well to remember, there was still no cloud in the industrial sky except the gambling mania which had seized all classes.[2] It was, no doubt, advisable, he said, to proceed with caution ; but, in every instance, so far as they had hitherto gone in the new commercial policy, the fears and forebodings of those opposed to the change had proved visionary and unfounded, and the expectation of its most sanguine supporters had been more than realised. There might be some doubt if the substitution of 30 per cent. *ad valorem* duty on foreign silks, instead of absolute prohibition, would prevent smuggling, but " if alarm now exists anywhere, it is transferred to the other side of the channel, and is to

The Protective Duties.

against Canada, it would have been good against Ireland in 1806 (*Hansard*, xiii. 350).

[1] In the course of the year, it was noticed that there had been large quantities of foreign wheat imported into Canada, and the explanation was suggested that it was not for re-export to England, but for home consumption, so as to allow Canada to export the whole of its growth. Possibly this was the reason of the limitation to two years.

[2] *Hansard*, xii. 1196.

be found only among the manufacturers of France—in consequence of the great progress and improvement since made in this country in every branch of the silk trade."

The new canon of Protection.   " Having thus ruled that 30 per cent. was the highest duty which could be maintained for the protection of a manufacture in every part of which we were most behind other countries [1]—that extensive manufacture which, on the score of general inferiority, stood in need of general protection "—surely it was time to turn our attention

Cottons.   to our other great protected industries.   In Cotton, it could not be denied that we were superior to all other countries ; we could undersell all competitors in markets open alike to them and to us—even the East Indies.   The official value of cotton goods exported in 1824 was over £30 millions,[2] and yet—would the House believe it ?—there were on our book of rates import duties on certain descriptions of cotton goods of 75 per cent., 67½ per cent., and 50 per cent., all the time that our goods were admitted into the East Indies almost duty free.   He proposed, then, to admit all foreign articles manufactured wholly of cotton at one uniform *ad valorem* duty of 10 per cent.   This would " countervail " the duty on raw cotton, and the duty upon any other articles used in the manufacture.[3]

Woollens.   As to Woollens—the manufacture most nursed and dandled by the legislature—that favourite child which had suffered by the spoiling [4]—the present duties varied from 50 per cent. to 67½ per

---

[1] The words challenge attention. No such " rule " had been laid down in the reported speeches : probably it was the reflection of some understanding in the Cabinet.

[2] The principal official exports of British produce for the year ending 10th October, 1824, were : Cotton manufactures, £26,880,000 ; Cotton twist and yarn, £3,138,000 ; Woollen goods, £6,880,000 ; Linen manufactures, £3,174,000 ; Iron and Steel, wrought and unwrought, £1,490,000 ; British refined sugar, £1,121,000 ; Hardwares and Cutlery, £680,000 ; Brass and Copper manufactures, £582,000 ; Glass and Earthenware of all sorts, £284,000 ; Silk manufactures, £189,000.   Among the exports of foreign and colonial produce, Coffee and Cocoa came first with £2,413,000 ; then Raw Sugar, £1,042,000, and Piece Goods of India, £1,033,000. This may be compared with the exports of 1822 (*supra*, p. 123).

[3] In 1823-4 the duty on cotton wool was 6 per cent. if imported in a British ship, 12 per cent. if in a foreign. From 1825 to 1830 it came in from foreign countries at 6 per cent.. and, from any British possession, free.

[4] The following interesting comparison was made : In 1764, the raw cotton imported was about 3,360,000 lbs., and the value of cotton goods exported, £200,000 ; in 1824, the figures were, respectively, 147,000,000 lbs. and £30,795,000.   In 1764, the raw wool imported was 1,926,000 lbs., and the value of woollen goods exported, £5,159,000 ; in 1824, 23,858,000 lbs., and £6,926,000. In 1764, the raw silk imported was 418,000 lbs. and, in 1824, 3,000,000 lbs.

cent.   He was satisfied that 15 per cent. would answer every purpose
of reasonable and fair protection.

Linens—another object of more nursing and interference than Linens.
was good for the manufacture—were now protected by very complicated duties ranging from 40 per cent. to 180 per cent. : he
would reduce them all to 25 per cent.

The altogether prohibitive duties on Paper he would reduce, Paper and
" so that they should not exceed double the amount of the excise Books.
payable on home made goods."   This would extend to printed books:
the existing duty of £6 10s. per cent. on bound, and £5 on unbound
books, would be reduced to £3 10s. and £3 respectively—due regard
being had to copyrights, which might require specific provisions.[1]

Foreign Glass, which also was subject to heavy excise duties, Glass.
would be reduced from 80 per cent. to 20 per cent. ; and, instead
of the heavy duty on common glass bottles, amounting to 16/2 per
dozen—which, now that wine was reduced in price, amounted to
more than half its value—he would recommend a duty of 3/- only.

Upon all description of foreign Earthenware, an article supplied Earthenware.
by us to so many countries, the present duty was 75 per cent.,
the effect of which was that ornamented porcelain was abundantly
smuggled from the continent.   He proposed to reduce the duty on
earthenware and plain porcelain goods to 15 per cent., and on
porcelain, gilt or ornamented, to 30 per cent., which was quite as
much as could be demanded without throwing this branch of import
into the hands of the smuggler.

To foreign Gloves, another manufacture altogether prohibited Gloves.
but " to be bought in every shop," the same observation applied
and the same duty, of 30 per cent., would be imposed.[2]

The reduction of the Iron duty from 130/- to 30/- per ton, already Iron.
intimated, he thought it necessary to defend further.   Many
deputations from iron masters had waited on the Board of Trade,
all their representations partaking of the same character—all great
advocates of free trade, but all assigning a quite conclusive reason
why their particular calling should be made an exception !   But

[1] The beginning of the manufacture of paper in England is generally credited
to Sir John Spielman, who was knighted by Elizabeth for his paper mill
erected at Dartford in 1588, and given a licence for ten years for " the sole
gathering of all rags and other articles necessary for making paper."   The
excise on paper ran from 30 per cent. to 150 per cent. according to the kind.

[2] Hume, however, pointed out that this would not prevent smuggling,
as gloves, like other such articles, could now be brought into the country at an
insurance against seizure of 20 per cent.

was it fit that we should be suffering from scarcity of an article of universal use like iron, which raised the price to almost double, simply for the protection of the ironmasters ? Could our hardware manufactures at Birmingham and Sheffield go on if this price continued ? would the orders not be transferred elsewhere, and the share of this country in their execution be confined to models and drawings for the guidance of foreign artificers ? Then, again, Swedish iron was superior to our own, and its admixture with British iron would improve the quality of our manufactures, particularly in the making of iron cables. Besides other advantages, more free admission, he was confident, would check the late extreme fluctuations in price.

Copper.   The duty on Copper, now entering largely, as Baring pointed out, into the manufacture of steam engines, was at present £54 a ton, as against £10 in 1790. He was aware that, under the encouragement of this monopoly, much capital had been invested in copper mining,[1] and he knew the difficulty of doing what the public interest demanded without injury to those particular interests—it was always the most arduous part of the task which a sense of public duty imposed on him. He thought it safe, however, to reduce this duty to £27 per ton. Another metallic substance went with this,
Zinc.   Zinc or spelter—which entered into the composition of brass in the proportion of one-third, and paid a duty of £28 per ton. With a duty on copper of £54 per ton, and, on spelter, of £28, what chance had a British exporter of brass goods ?—as a fact the briskest demand in this trade was in the preparation of moulds and patterns for foreign manufacturers. This duty also he would reduce by one half. On
Tin.   Tin, the existing duty of £5 9s. 3d. per cwt. was excessive, and he would reduce it more than one half, viz. to £2 10s. per cwt.[2] The
Lead.   duty on Lead (the price of which had risen within a few months from £19 10s. to about £30 per ton) was now 20 per cent. *ad valorem* ; a reduction to 15 per cent. would, he hoped, be sufficient to admit of a foreign import and to check the existence of exorbitant prices.[3]

[1] The capital invested in copper mines was said to be about £2½ millions, employing 70,000 to 100,000 persons.

[2] This 50/- duty proved quite inoperative for protection, as our production of tin remained uniformly greater than our consumption, and no foreign produce could enter into competition (Porter, ii. vi.).

[3] Subsequently, this was still further reduced on the ground that it was so essential in many branches of domestic improvement (*Hansard*, xiii. 1217).

There were others among the enumerated articles which he would
deal with on the same principle, according to a schedule annexed
to the resolutions.   But, although everything which could by any
accident be considered as an object of jealousy to any of our manufacturers was enumerated by name in the Book of Rates,[1] there
were several articles which could not be so—objects which derived An omnibus
their value solely from their connection with art, science, and litera- clause.
ture.   These cost the importer 50 per cent. on their estimated
value, under a sweeping clause which provided that, upon all goods
in part or wholly manufactured and not enumerated, a duty of 50
per cent. was payable, and 20 per cent. when not, either in part
or wholly, manufactured.   These duties were of little value to the
Exchequer—some of them ludicrous—some not very creditable
to the good taste and character of the country.   For instance a
mummy was imported from Egypt.   The importer, anxious that it
should not be seized, declared its value at £400.   It could not
be called a raw material, and was therefore taxed at 50 per cent.
as a manufactured article !   He proposed, then, to reduce the
duty on manufactured articles not enumerated from 50 per cent.
to 20 per cent., and, on unmanufactured, from 20 per cent. to 10
per cent.[2]

The result of the alterations would be that the purely protective Defence of
duties would, in no instance, exceed 30 per cent.   " If the article the 30 per cent.
maximum.
be not manufactured much cheaper or much better abroad than
at home, such a duty is ample for protection.   If it be manufactured
so much cheaper, or so much better abroad, as to render £30 per
cent. insufficient, my answer is, firstly, that a greater protection is
only a premium to the smuggler ;   and, secondly, that there is no
wisdom in attempting to bolster up a competition which this
degree of protection will not sustain.   Let the State have the tax,
which is now the reward of the smuggler, and let the consumer
have the better and cheaper article, without the painful conscious-
ness that he is consulting his own convenience at the expense of
daily violating the laws of his country.   When my right honourable
friend, the Chancellor of the Exchequer, is labouring to put an end,
as fast as he can, to the evils of smuggling, by lowering the duties,
increased during the pressure of the war, and for the purposes of

[1] Before Huskisson began his reforms, it has been said, " the tariff list of the
United Kingdom formed a tolerably complete dictionary of all the products
of human industry."

[2] Subsequently he calculated the immediate loss to the Exchequer by all
these reductions at £400,000 or £500,000 per annum (*Hansard*, xiii. 1221).

revenue, upon articles of consumption, the last thing which we ought
to countenance is the continuance of high duties, not for the benefit
of the Exchequer, but for the supposed protection of certain branches
of manufacture. Is the illicit importation of foreign spirits to be
checked, merely to give fresh life to the smuggling of cambrics
and lace from Flanders, or of gloves and porcelain from France ?
I cannot think that gentlemen are aware to what an extent all the
moral evils of smuggling are encouraged by the prohibition of these
comparatively petty articles. Let any one go down to Brighton,
and wander on the coast from thence to Hastings ; I will undertake
to say, that he shall most easily find, at every place he comes to,
persons who will engage to deliver to him, within ten days or a
fortnight, any prohibited article of manufacture which he can
name, and almost in any quantity, upon an advance of £30 per cent.
beyond the prime cost at Paris. What is the consequence of such a
system ? A number of families, that would otherwise be valuable
and industrious members of society, exist, and train up their children,
in a state of perpetual warfare with the law, till they insensibly
acquire the habits and feelings of outlaws, standing rather in the
relation of pirates, than of fellow-subjects, to the rest of the community. And is this abominable system to be tolerated, not from
any over-ruling necessity of upholding the revenue, nay, possibly,
to the injury of the Exchequer ; but merely because, in a few
secondary branches of manufacture, we do not possess the same
natural advantages, or the same degree of skill, as our neighbours ?
If cambrics are made better at Valenciennes, is that a sufficient
reason for imposing a prohibitory duty on all linens ; a duty from
which the revenue gets next to nothing, whilst the country is full
of the proscribed article ? If certain descriptions of paper for
engraving are made more perfectly in France, are we always to be
condemned to the use of an inferior and dearer article of home
manufacture ? The time has been when it was found quite a
sufficient reason for imposing a prohibitory duty upon a foreign
article, that it was better than we could make at home ; but, I
trust, when such calls are made upon this House hereafter, our
first answer at least will be, let us see what can be done by competition ; first try to imitate, and by and by, perhaps, you will
surpass your foreign rival. This is the feeling, this is the hope and
the emulation which we have now created in the silk trade ; and, I
believe, with a very reasonable prospect of the most complete
success. But this feeling never would have been called forth

under the old and helpless system of prohibitory Protection. Prohibitions, in fact, are a premium to mediocrity. They destroy the best incentive to excellence, the best stimulus to invention and improvement. They condemn the community to suffer, both in price and quality, all the evils of monopoly, except in as far as a remedy can be found in the baneful arts of the smuggler. They have also another of the great evils of monopoly, that of exposing the consumer, as well as the dealer, to rapid and inconvenient fluctuations in price.

" With the knowledge of this fact, that we furnish, in a proportion far exceeding the supply from any other country, the general markets of the world with all the leading articles of manufacture, upon which I have now proposed greatly to lower the duties, I own that I am not afraid of this country being overwhelmed with foreign goods. Some, I know, will come in, which are now excluded ; I shall be glad of it. In various ways, their admission will be beneficial to the general interests of the country. That it cannot be extensively injurious to any of those interests, may be inferred, not only from the arguments with which I have already troubled the Committee, but from actual experience. In the year 1786, we entered into a commercial treaty with France. Under the stipulations of that treaty, the cottons and woollens of France were admitted into this country upon a duty of £12 per cent.—I now propose for the latter £15 ; hardware, cutlery, turnery, etc. upon a duty of £10—I now propose £20 per cent. ; pottery and glass, etc. under a duty of £12—I now propose £15 upon the former and £20 upon the latter. What was the result of this treaty ? We sent goods of various descriptions to the French market, and England was supplied with other goods of French production ; but no injury accrued—no check was given to any particular branch of our staple manufactures in consequence of this interchange. One advantage arising from it was, to create a spirit of emulation, an instance of which occurred in the woollen trade. Soon after the opening of the intercourse between the two countries, French cloths of a fine quality were imported in considerable quantity. They were preferred to our own. No fashionable man was to be seen without a coat of French cloth. What followed ? In less than two years, the cloth of our own manufactures became equal to that imported from France ; the one could not be distinguished from the other ; and coats of French cloth were still the fashion, whilst the cloth of which they were made was manufactured in this

No fear of swamping.

country. In like manner, we shall now, in all probability, import some printed cottons from Alsace and Switzerland, of richer and brighter colours than our own ; some fancy muslins from India ; some silk stuffs, some porcelain from France, objects for which curiosity of fashion may create a demand in this metropolis ; but they will not interfere with those articles of more wide and universal consumption, which our own manufactures supply cheaper and better ; whilst they will excite the ingenuity of our artists and workmen to attempt improvement, which may enable them to enter the lists with the foreigner, in those very articles in which he has now an acknowledged superiority."

The heavy taxation objection.

He was aware of the objections that might be urged. One was that, since the war, we had to support heavy taxation. But other countries were not exempt from this, and, moreover, in many of them concrete capital had been impaired and diminished by the war, while our trading capital on the contrary, was not only intact, but, even during the war, had been continually increasing. And, in respect of the comparative cheapness of foreign labour, since the great inventions the part played by manual labour was insignificant in comparison with that played by the creative powers of mind. It was the union of those powers, of the great capitals which called them into action, and of the enterprise, perseverance, and steadiness of action that distinguished British industry, and had placed it in the commanding position it now held in the world, and on these he relied to retain that position.

The reciprocity objection.

Another objection was that we ought to defer any improvement in our own commercial system until we could persuade foreign states to view it as a concession to them which we were ready to make in return for similar concessions. He could not see much wisdom in such a line of policy—at the best, it referred only to the foreign market, and he did not see that, if any measure was really beneficial to us, it should be withheld because other States were not yet advanced enough in the knowledge of their own interests.[1] Let foreign countries see our Chancellor year after year largely remitting public burdens, and at the same time exhibiting a prosperous Exchequer, still flowing to the same perennial level, and he had no doubt that, when they had contemplated for a few years longer the happy consequences, their eyes would be opened, and they would imitate our present rather than adopt our cast-off system

[1] Huskisson quoted here in support a letter from Kirkman Finlay, the late Member for Glasgow.

of restrictions and prohibitions.[1] At the same time, as a stimulus
to them, he would reserve a power of making an addition of one-
fifth to the proposed duties upon the productions of those countries
which might refuse to place our commerce and navigation upon the
footing of the most favoured nation.[2] And no part of the arrangements would interfere with the power of the Crown to enter into
specific treaties of commerce with particular states still further
varying or modifying the duties.

He then went on to consider what advantage might be given to the British manufacturer in his competition for foreign markets by reducing some of the duties levied upon the raw materials he was obliged to use. The duties on articles used in dyeing—imposed or increased during the war—he would largely reduce ; as well as some others, such as that on olive oil—much used in the manufac-ture of wool—from £15 13s. per ton to £7, and that on rapeseed, which would now be merely nominal. The duty on coarse foreign wool, not exceeding the value of 1/- per lb., which now pressed heavily on the manufacture of coarse woollens, he would reduce from 1d. per lb. to $\frac{1}{2}$d.[3] *(margin: Auxiliary materials.)*

In the same speech, he took up the third part of the scheme, that which related to the Shipping and Navigation of the empire. There was, he said, already a Bill on the table repealing all the quarantine duties, which pressed very heavily—and so unequally—on the particular ships and goods compelled to go into quarantine. The expense of this would henceforth be borne by the country at large.[4] As already intimated, the fees upon shipping and trade *(margin: Shipping and Navigation of the Empire.)*

---

[1] By July it was stated that Portugal, following our example, had repealed
the whole body of prohibitory laws, and substituted duties of 30 per cent.
But Huskisson, who went on a mission to France in the autumn to effect
a commercial treaty, entirely failed, owing, some said, to resentment of the
allies at the recognition of the South American States, but really, said the
Etoile, to the impossibility of arranging with a country which prohibited
the import of that which France wanted to export. In a Waterford paper of
April, it was said that the Netherlands had signified their readiness to remove
all restriction on the import of British manufactures into their territories and
colonies on condition that our duty on Dutch butter and cheese was withdrawn.

[2] By a general clause added subsequently, the addition was actually made
of 5 per cent.—" on imports from all countries which did not allow trade to
be carried on with them on equal terms " (*Hansard*, xiii. 1462).

[3] Another clause was that wool from any British possession was allowed in
free.

[4] When the new quarantine regulations were formally brought in by bill,
however, the entire discussion was directed to quite another matter. It
seems that the opinion was gaining ground that the epidemics against which
quarantine was directed were not propagated by contagion, and many seriously

in our colonies would be abolished. The (quite exceptional) stamp
duty now payable upon the transfer of a whole ship, or of any share
in a ship, from one person to another, would be repealed, and the
stamp duty on debentures for the payment of drawbacks, and on
bonds given by merchants for the due delivery of the goods declared
for exportation, would be reduced to a fixed duty of only 5/- upon
each instrument. The fees at present payable to consuls, either
upon ships or goods in foreign ports would, as already proposed, be
abolished, with the exception of certain small fees for personal acts,
such as notarial instruments, and the consuls would henceforth be
paid by salaries. Certain other small taxes upon shipping, such
as those for the maintenance of a place of worship, the payment
of a chaplain, etc., would disappear. The Levant Company which,
for two hundred years, had levied considerable duties on all British
ships resorting to the Levant, for the maintenance and establishments of consuls, had made a voluntary surrender of their charter,
and those consuls also would now be paid by the Crown.

If these measures—which were open to alterations and amendment—were approved, he thought that this session would not close
without our having proved to this, as well as to other countries,
that we had not lost sight of the recommendation from the Throne
—to remove as much, and as fast as possible, all unnecessary
restrictions upon trade.

General
approval.
Huskisson sat down amidst loud cheers, and the debate shows
that the House of Commons had fully made up its mind that the
principles acted on were beyond question. The interests directly
affected, of course, had something to say. Copper, for instance, could
not be raised from the Cornish mines under £100 a ton—another
member said £150—while it might be imported at £50 ; the glass
bottle makers had enough to do to meet competition with old bottles
without this further blow ; Staffordshire ornamental china could
never compete with the superior clay and the cheap painting of
France, etc., etc. Others took the opposite view—that the proposals did not go nearly far enough. Parnell, in a strong free trade
speech, said that many of the duties retained were inconsistent
with Huskisson's own theory, and would prove prohibitory; urged
that, after all, the consumers were the great body of the people ;

advocated the revision of the regulations on that assumption. But, fortunately,
the common sense opinion prevailed, that, till medical opinion was more agreed
than it was, it would not be wise even to appoint a Committee to examine the
matter. The interesting debates on the subject are worth reading (*Hansard*,
xii. 1315 ; xiii. 601, 788, 1036).

blamed the opponents of the measure for not seeing that capital, displaced from a trade which needed protection, was not lost but transferred to others where it would be more profitably employed as regards the community : for himself, he would take the duties proposed as the duties from which a gradual reduction should be made, and reduce the whole of them from year to year, so that, in a few years, the whole trade of the country would be free from everything like a protecting duty—Protection was bound to keep up prices, lead to the making of inferior goods, and uphold smuggling. Baring, Hume, and others pointed out that the measures now proposed were totally at variance with the principles which the Government had pursued respecting the Corn Laws—the time must come, and that shortly, when this subject of the protection of agriculture would force itself upon the attention of the House. Charles Grant,[1] again, considered that the great value of the proposals would be their effect upon foreign nations ; we had grown to be the first commercial country in the world even under our restrictive system, and to that system did foreign nations impute our wealth and our aggrandisement.

When the changes proposed came up in the Customs Consolidation Bill,[2] and some slight alterations and further reductions on the schedules were made, Huskisson concluded by the significant intimation that the Committee was not to be considered as coming to any final adjudication on all the reductions that it was proposed to effect in the existing system of duties. Parnell took this for text of a very notable speech, on the lines of his former one, criticising the want of principle in the various duties retained. He was content to adopt the changes, but it would not be just to allow the public to invest capital and embark on new engagements on the idea that this was the final settlement of the protective policy. The measures now taken would not establish a universal freedom of trade ; indeed, nothing could possibly be more at variance with those principles than almost every duty in the very voluminous schedule. The President of the Board of Trade had most ably and accurately enumerated the evils which belonged to protecting duties : (1) that, by preventing competition, these duties destroyed the best incentive to excellence and the best stimulus to improvement ; they were in fact a premium upon mediocrity ; (2) that

Parnell's fine speech on Huskisson's Free Trade.

---

[1] Grant (Lord Glenelg from 1835), Chief Secretary for Ireland from 1819 to 1823, was Member for Inverness.

[2] *Hansard*, xiii. 1215.

they condemned the community to suffer, both in price and quality, all the evils of a monopoly ; (3) that they exposed the consumer, as well as the dealer, to rapid and inconvenient fluctuations in price ; (4) that they were a premium to the smuggler, encouraging all the moral evils of smuggling ; (5) that they excited suspicion and odium in foreign countries.   These were the five distinct and substantive evils which must always be borne in mind, and, " when any member should thereafter stand up in his place for the purpose of resisting the repeal of a protecting duty, he would have to show that the right honourable gentleman was in error in his opinion as to the effects of such a duty, or that the repealing of the duty would be attended by some greater evil to the community than the five evils which were stated by him to be the natural consequences of it." The commonplace argument used was that this or that branch of manufacture would be ruined if foreign goods were allowed to come into competition with it, and then a ready inference was drawn that a protecting duty was absolutely necessary for the purpose of upholding the profits of our capitalists, and securing a demand for the employment of our people.   But the object of that argument was to shut out from our use foreign cheap goods, and to keep up the price of our own, or, in other words, to secure to the British manufacturer what was technically called a remunerative price. But this remunerative price, being a higher price than the goods would bring if there were no protecting duty, obliged every member of the community to pay a higher price for the commodities he wanted than he ought to do, in order to benefit that small portion of the people who were engaged in making those particular goods. Under the plea, therefore, of upholding the public interests by imposing a protecting duty on a manufacture, the interests of the whole community were sacrificed to those of the infinitely lesser number of persons who carried on the manufacture, and every case of a remunerative price secured by a protecting duty, when the fallacy on which it was claimed was removed, would appear to be nothing less than a tax levied on the public at large for the benefit of some small portion of it.   In this way it was that the general system of protecting duties formed a mass of very severe taxation ; but having this peculiar character, that, while it took immense sums out of the pockets of the people, it contributed nothing to the Exchequer. The erroneous opinions as to the effect of importing foreign goods arose from neglecting this elementary principle, that, if we buy, we must also sell ; just, therefore, in proportion as we imported more foreign goods, should we create by the importation a new demand for domestic manufactures to pay for them ; and, though it might be possible that some particular manufactures were hurt, others would be greatly increased.

But, as to Huskisson's schedule, on what principle were the various duties arrived at ? Taking it that the 10 per cent. on cottons was justified, not as a protective but as a revenue tax on an article which could very well bear it, what was the explanation, as a protective duty, of 15 per cent. on woollens when we had perfect machinery and either a decided superiority or equal advantages in raw materials ; of 25 per cent. on linens—simply a premium on the non-introduction of machinery and on the neglect of flax growing and dressing in Ireland ; of 20 per cent. on hardware and steel, where we had machinery, materials, and coal in a much greater degree than any foreign country ; of 15 per cent. on earthenware—a manufacture in which, of all others, we had least need to fear foreign competition ? What object could a duty of 50 per cent. on beads, pomatum, skates, toothpowder, etc., have but to vex and torment the public ?—for there were no corresponding industries to protect, and the revenue would be insignificant. As to the duties on foreign luxuries—the 100 per cent. on currants and oranges, the penny per piece on eggs, the 50 per cent. on grapes, etc.—they were particularly objectionable as falling upon those whom the legislature ought to take under its special protection, the industrious middle classes. And, for the duties on food, bacon, butter, cheese, potatoes, rice, cattle, and grain —well, it really was time to reconsider the policy of sacrificing everyone who was not a landlord to the interests of landlords. He did not blame Huskisson—who had probably gone as far as he was allowed—but he asserted that the schedules were wholly at variance with the principles of " open competition " laid down.[1]

Eventually the changes proposed passed into law with a few alterations made by Huskisson himself ; principally that the new duties on linen, glass, and paper were made specific, to decrease

A few modifications.

[1] The speech was a very fine one and deserves much fuller quotation than I can give it. It is a good reminder of how very far Huskisson's " freer trade " was from " free trade," and of how little it was based on any settled principle, either as regards protection, revenue, or the interests of the consumer. Parnell could say in 1830 that " little or no change was really made by the alteration of the protecting duties and prohibitions in 1825—if free trade is the right policy, the work of introducing it still remains to be done " (*Financial Reform*, 68).

annually till the *ad valorem* figure mentioned was reached,[1] and that the duty on all imported books was made £1 per cwt. on those published before 1801, and £5 on those published subsequently. Liverpool, like other speakers, thought it probable that the changes would make other countries adopt a similar course of policy.

Opinion outside. It was not to be expected that this notable reaction against Protection should meet everywhere with the favour which was shown in Parliament. Strangely enough, none of the great quarterlies gave any special attention to it. But *Blackwood* grew almost pathetic in confessing inability to understand it, and laid all the blame on those visionaries, the political economists.[2] Four of the arguments given in an article entitled " Free Trade " are perhaps worth quoting, as showing how far the new science was understood outside. (1) Adam Smith's two objects were the destruction of monopolies and cheapness of prices. But Free Trade, thoroughly carried out among nations, would leave us a gigantic monopoly of

---

[1] Huskisson's argument for allowing eight years of gradually diminishing duties to linens was, that while, in Ireland, the labour had hitherto been entirely manual, machinery was rapidly introducing itself, and that time should be given to make the change. Parnell objected that, on the principles laid down, there seemed, indeed, some justification for continuing the high duties for some short period, as little machinery was yet in use and flax was cheaper abroad, but that there could be none for continuing permanently a protecting duty. Machinery was being introduced, and great improvements could be made as regarded the old bad habits in the preparing and dressing of flax in Ireland, and nothing could more conduce to this than the knowledge that, in a few years, all protecting duties would be repealed (*Hansard*, xiii. 1234). It was maintained (by Maberly) before a Committee that the Scottish linen manufacturers got their flax from Holland and France, not because the quality was any better, but because the Irish flax was so badly cleaned.

[2] In a venomous article, ridiculing his " Practical Observations upon the Education of the People, addressed to the Working Classes and their Employers," in which Brougham had advocated that the artizans should form themselves into Book Clubs or Reading Societies, and advised them to study, among other things, Political Economy, *Blackwood* says :

"We believe to a certain extent in political economy, for it comprehends a number of old stale truths which were familiar to all men before the name was ever heard of ; but we say that it combines with these truths many false-hoods, that it joins to some sound theory a great deal that is erroneous, and that, as a whole, it will ruin this empire if reduced to practice by the Government. . . . Its doctrines bring into question a very large portion of our political system ; they strike at some of the main pillars of British society ; they seek the destruction of many sentiments and regulations which, in our judgment, are essential for binding man to man and class to class—for cementing together and governing the community. They are in their nature democratic and republican, hostile to aristocracy and monarchy ; and they are generally taught by people who virtually confess themselves to be republicans. This is sufficient to convince us that a large part of political economy is yet anything but knowledge, and that it is therefore unfit to be taught to the working classes " (*Blackwood*, May, 542).

manufacturing, and other countries as gigantic a monopoly of growing corn, and these two monopolies would secure that the prices of manufactures and the price of corn would always be at a maximum. The true beneficial method, according to the writer, was that each nation should give a monopoly to its own producers, because, in that way, the competition of a number of individuals was secured and prices kept down. (2) If our duties were reduced, say, from 80 per cent. to 35 per cent., this " would keep the foreigner constantly in our market as the efficient competitor of the Englishman " : this extreme competition would reduce prices, wages, and profits to the lowest figures—would be a prolific source of fraud and bankruptcy—would dissipate capital and throw labour out of employment. " The extreme of general cheapness must ever produce the extreme of general poverty when it flows from the extreme of competition." (3) The foreigner would take advantage of our policy to the fullest extent, but he would shut his ports against our goods—would take away in exchange, not our goods but our money. (4) " The economists declare that the richer our neighbours get—that the more we enrich them—the more trade they carry on with us, and the more we increase our trade." This is " the most perfect fable that ever was flung in the teeth of history."

NOTE ON HUSKISSON AS A FREE TRADER.

It may be no more than an academic exercise, but, in view of the modern aspiration for a " scientific tariff," it might be worth while to ask what was Huskisson's principle of Protection. A " free trader," in the modern sense, as regards manufactures at least, he certainly was not. He was, of course, as he said, " the decided enemy of anything which established temporary or permanent prohibition." As regards corn, while he advocated a fixed duty, we have it on Warburton's authority in 1840 that, a few days before his death, he declared that a moderate fixed duty would lead, at no very distant period, to total repeal, and so it might be concluded that Huskisson was, in this respect, a Free Trader. But, as regards other industries, he would have " free importation guarded by a sufficient protecting duty."

Perhaps we may get at the answer by analysing his treatment of two extreme cases. Silk was, of all others, the manufacture " in every part of which we were most behind other countries.' All the same, it was worth fighting to keep : (1) because so many and such extensive interests of labour and capital were vested in it, (2) because there was some hope that the disadvantage might grow less or disappear. To this industry he would give the highest possible protection, 30 per cent. ; " highest possible," because (1) more than 30 per cent. would be too great a temptation to the smuggler, and (2) because 30 per cent. was as much as the consumer should be asked to sacrifice—if 30 per cent. was not enough for any manufacture, it was " bolstering up a competition." Cotton, on the other hand, was the manufacture in which we had a clear superiority to all other countries, and to this he would give 10 per cent. At the same time, he explained that the 10 per cent. was to " countervail " the 6 per cent. duty on the raw material coming from foreign countries, which 6 per cent., as Parnell pointed out, should be continued, as it was " a revenue tax on an article which could very well bear it."

Accepting this explanation of the 10 per cent. duty on cotton goods, it seems to follow, logically, that Huskisson would have admitted free any foreign competing manufacture in which our makers had no claim for such a countervailing duty, and in which we had a clear natural *advantage*—in such a case Protection was absurd because quite unnecessary.

But, apparently, he would not admit free any manufacture on which we were merely on a footing of *equality*, or even where we had some considerable measure of superiority. Woollens, *e.g.* were to pay 15 per cent., although we had the advantage of perfect machinery and abundant raw material. Plain earthenware also was to be charged 15 per cent., although it was a manufacture in which we had least need to fear foreign competition. Hardware, where we had a clear advantage in materials, machinery, and coal, was to be taxed 20 per cent. So was glass. So were all unenumerated manufactures. And linens were to pay 25 per cent.

In short, in spite of occasional utterances as to "fair competition," "equal footing," etc., Huskisson must, I think, be credited with the view that all British producers had a right to a certain amount of protection because they were British. If the foreigner got in at all, someone—either the foreign producer or the home consumer—must make up his mind to a sacrifice.

To put it concretely : Say that the Protection which a British trade might justifiably demand, because it was British, was 10 per cent.; then, in the case of silk, the extra 20 per cent. might stand (1) against the disadvantages of the home producer, such as heavy taxation weighing on the industry, dear food, high wages ; (2) against the advantages on the side of the foreign producer, such as fashion, colouring, skill, machinery, cheap food, low wages.

It is obvious how far this is from the " scientific " principle of Protection adopted, it would seem, by the American Tariff Board of 1909, that the object of Protection was simply to establish *equality of competition* between the protecting nation and its foreign rivals—a principle which, while it refuses to the consumer the benefit of foreign natural advantages that would enable the foreigner to undersell, refuses to the home producer any advantage based simply on the ground that he is a home producer.

But how far Huskisson would have gone if he had had a free hand, will never be known. Huskisson was eminently a practical politician : he "opened his hand," as Harriet Martineau said, " by one finger at a time, because the people or their rulers could not receive a whole handful of the truth about Free Trade." And, again, he had little anticipation that, for many years at least, there would be Free Trade in corn ; and, as he said, he could not see why one produce of the skill and industry of the country should not be protected as well as another.

CHAPTER XXVI

1825. THE SPECULATIVE MANIA.

FOR the past few years, the chief interest to the economic student has been the emergence of the country from the long distress which succeeded the war. 1815 and 1816 were very bad years. The first half of 1817 was also bad, but the tide turned in the second half. In 1818, there was a quick return of prosperity, and, in the early part of 1819, the " trade, commerce, and manufactures of the country were in a most flourishing condition." But this was a mere flash in the pan—the distress began again before the year was out, and continued till the latter part of 1820, when there were signs of revival. The improvement was steady all through 1821 and 1822. In 1823, the adjective most often used was " flourishing." 1824 was what we now call a " boom year." Even agriculture, which had not shared in the revival hitherto, forgot to complain. And now, in 1825, we are to see a reaction as sharp as it was unexpected.

In the beginning of the year, the prosperity of the country was undoubted. The $3\frac{1}{2}$ per cents. were over 100. The King's Speech in February was optimistic in the highest degree—" there never was a period in the history of this country when all the great interests of the nation were at the same time in so thriving a condition, or when a feeling of content and satisfaction was more widely diffused through all classes of the British people." The mover of the Address said that, in speaking of the general prosperity of the country, he knew of no local or geographical exception, whether in England, Wales, Scotland, or, he was happy to add, Ireland. In Glasgow, for instance, it was noted that the demand for machinery was such that almost as many mills had been set up for making it during two years as in the preceding thirty.[1] Agricultural distress, said the *Annual Register*, had disappeared.

The turn of the cycle.

[1] In an official report, dated 1st March, made by Cleland, the Superintendent of Public Works in Glasgow, the following table of building wages is given :

How much of this activity was, industrially and commercially, sound, and how much longer it might have continued, is only the question which meets us at every recurrent turn in the trade cycle. The economist, resting on his theory that, under normal conditions, every new supply is a new demand, is persuaded that, if supply would wisely take its guidance from demand, both might go on expanding till such unlikely time as demand cried " hold, enough ! " But, again and again, he has to record that the condition required is more than can be expected of human nature. Some dislocating cause intervenes. Where there is no catastrophic circumstance which gives a violent wrench to the equilibrium between supply and demand, the dislocation usually comes from this—that the suppliers have misjudged the elasticity of particular demands—gone on producing larger and larger amounts of the same goods without thought of how far that particular demand can or will expand— and so deeply sunk their capital in stone and lime that they can do nothing but turn out goods for which the demand meantime is satisfied. In this case, the supply, being unsaleable, is *not* demand, and the contagion of reduced employment—emptier pockets— spreads from industry to industry. Much the same thing occurs when goods are exported as means of remitting loans, as was the case with South American loans in 1824. The demand is sudden, and as suddenly stops. But too many have acted as if it were likely to continue.[1]

This is, probably, the explanation of the turn of the industrial cycle during the last few decades of modern times, when wars have ceased [2] and banks have learned their lesson. But, in early periods, the turning point was generally a " crash " or a " crisis " or a " panic " of some kind, which, for the moment, almost brought industry to a stop, like the breaking of a wheel at the heart of a

---

Masons, 3/7 per day ; Carpenters and Joiners, 3/4 ; Sawyers, 4/6 ; Slaters, 3/2 ; Plasterers, 3/6 ; Plumbers, 4/- ; Smiths, 3/- ; Marble Cutters, 3/3 ; Painters, 2/9 ; Labourers, 1/8. At this date, the price of the quartern wheaten loaf was 11d. ; of bacon, 7d. per lb. ; of coals, 8d. per cwt.

[1] Cf. *Economic Annals, 1801-20*; Note on Industrial Cycles, 606. Parnell, in his *Paper Money, Banking, and Over-trading*, gives a suggestive hint as to the primary impulse which starts the movement of the cycle in the opposite direction : " When trade is in a depressed state, the making and importing of goods are lessened, and capital is withdrawn from being employed in these transactions ; the supply of commodities is thus reduced ; in a short time, it ceases to exceed the demand, and prices rise."

[2] I retain the statement—which I let pass when I revised my first proof in July, 1914—as an interesting footnote to history. The war of the nations began in August.

complicated piece of mechanism. In the present case, the prominent feature which preceded the crash was—excessive speculation. The steady growth of industry is possible only if capital, and, in a lesser degree. labour, are kept so comparatively mobile that they can be adjusted to meet a demand which is always more or less changing, and—even more important—if the agency through which capital is provided works smoothly. The speculation, then, of 1825 took two shapes in which this was made difficult or impossible—partly, of the over-investment of capital for distant and doubtful returns ; partly, of blind reliance on continued and expanding banking accommodation and facilities on the part of outsiders who had no business to be " taking a hand " at all.[1]   *Excessive speculation.*

Up till the end of April, although one can see from the newspapers that there was some uneasiness about the enormous activity everywhere, and some questioning as to its soundness, there was no external appearance nor even, it would seem, any anticipation of disaster—except, indeed, by M'Culloch, who distinctly pointed out the convulsion about to happen in a *Scotsman* article in spring. In a debate on 16th March, much regret was expressed at " the rage and folly of the day "—the " gambling mania," said Baring, " which had seized all classes and was spreading in all parts of the country."[2] But, so late as the Speech on 6th July, His Majesty spoke of " that general and increasing prosperity on which he had had the happiness of congratulating the House at the beginning of the Session, and which continued to pervade every part of the kingdom." Those, however, who were better informed, saw danger ahead. They knew, for instance, that, after the highest point of prices was reached in January and February, there had been a pause, and a slight decline, and, in May and June, a rapid decline. This was not difficult to account for. There comes a point, in any general rise of prices, when, for the moment, the question is asked at what point the rise is going to be arrested. In agriculture, that point is often very well marked ; it is when the coming harvest is estimated as over   *A fall in prices,*

---

[1] Thus, at any rate, I should translate the main phenomena which brought it about ; but every crisis, whether predominantly commercial or industrial, is so complicated, and the contagion of panic and depression so widespread, that one can only suggest the main clues of explanation.

[2] It is from 1825 that the regular Money Article of the newspapers dates. The number of new loans and of companies dealt in on the Stock Exchange practically doubled ; mining shares were introduced for the first time ; it was this that drew the attention of the Press, and gave birth to a special column for the speculator.

the average. So, in manufactures, the point is when there is a confident expectation that the crop of their raw material will be abundant. In cotton alone—the chief crop in which British manufacture was then interested—the amount imported from Egypt, which, previous to 1824, had been perfectly insignificant, rose to no less than 20 million lbs. And, as Tooke shrewdly notes, the effect on public opinion was all the greater that it seemed to open up a great and indefinite source of supply. As it turned out, the imports of the year were so enormous that prices must have fallen in natural course. As compared with the average of 1822-4, the imports of wool rose from 20 to over 38 million lbs.—this was the time when, as Huskisson said subsequently, British merchants went " wool-gathering " in every part of Europe ; of cotton, from 161 millions to 222 million lbs. ; of indigo, from 5 to $7\frac{1}{2}$ million lbs. ; of square timber, from 550,000 to 664,000 loads ; of deals, from 41,000 to 58,000 cwts. ; of thrown silk, from 404,000 to 800,000 lbs. ; of raw silk, from 2,600,000 to 3,430,000 lbs. ; wine, tallow, and some others had risen nearly in a similar proportion, and, in fact, every branch of trade had been extended to a degree unparalleled in this country.[1] Generally speaking, therefore, the most marked feature of price, during the first six months of the year, was a great fluctuation of prices at the high level ; and, after that, the fall.

in foreign loans, While this was the state of those who had speculated in commodities, and found themselves landed with stocks of goods which they had never intended to use and were not able to hold, those who had invested in foreign loans were no better off.[2] Once the first glamour of lending to the new South American states—where, it was said, silver was so plentiful that the meanest utensils were made of it [3]—had faded a little, the absence of security and the rise of the home rate of interest had the same depressing effect on them. During a revolution industry stands still ; the troops however, have to be paid ; if they are not paid in paper— that is, by a concealed forced loan—they are paid with borrowed money, and the interest on that can be paid only by further loans—if they can be raised. So the South American loans

---

[1] *Hansard*, xiv. 452. The figures are from an official return laid on the table.

[2] According to an estimate printed in the *Annual Register*, the payments made on foreign loans during the year 1825 were over £11 millions (p. 48 *).

[3] Fowell Buxton, regarding Peru.

returned almost no interest, and the stocks were thrown on a depressed market.

But those who had taken a hand in the gamble in joint stock companies were much worse off, and their distress would seem to have been the proximate cause of the crisis. The number of such companies was stated at 276, and the amount of capital for which their shareholders had made themselves liable by subscription in 1824 and the beginning of 1825 was variously estimated in Parliament from £160 millions to £200 millions.[1] The amount of the national capital thus involved, and the rashness with which the majority of the companies were promoted, gave great anxiety to Parliament. A strong desire was expressed by many members to protect the community from the gamble into which it was plunging— generally taking the rather futile form of asserting that this or that company could not possibly succeed. The Prime Minister warned those persons who were now engaging so rashly in joint stock companies that they entered on them at their own peril ; if distress came of it, both he and his colleagues were determined that they would never allow the introduction of any Bill for the relief of the sufferers or listen to any claims they might make.[2] So much, in fact, was said against " the fury for joint stock companies which had taken possession of the people,"—as if the joint stock principle were itself an evil—that Attwood had to remind the House, that, when any enterprise was beyond the capital of an individual, there was no means of carrying it out but by such a company ; that innumerable great works had already been carried out in this way, such as docks, canals, insurance companies, and that what was done in other countries by Governments under the name of public works was done here by combinations of private capital.

The modern student would not be inclined to say that the majority of the companies promoted merited the name of " bubble companies " [3] or " companies to work mines upon the Stock

in company shares.

Not all bubbles,

---

[1] A French journal gave the amount at £174 millions, principally in insurance and banking companies, mines, railroads, canals, docks, and gas companies. According to the *Annual Register's* estimate, the capital instalments called up during 1825 amounted to £17½ millions.

[2] *Hansard*, xii. 1195. It is not a little significant that, in 1826, the member for London should group railway companies, water companies, and gas associations as " bubbles." *Ibid.* xiv. 700.

[3] There was, indeed, some doubt whether the Joint Stock Companies came under the Bubble Act of 6th Geo. I. or not. Practically, the Act had been a dead letter on account of the severity of the penalties imposed, but, on the

Exchange," although the language used about them afterwards would lead to that conclusion. " It seemed as if all Bedlam had broken loose on the Royal Exchange," said Baring. " Capital was so abundant," said a member in the debate on the Address, " that the merest adventurer might go into the money market and, let his scheme be the wildest that human fancy could suggest, he would find people to support him with it." But, among the list of companies actually formed, it would be hard to find more than one or two of which such language was true. Perhaps the nearest resemblance to it, curiously enough, was a company of which Huskisson, Brougham, Horton, and Grenfell were directors, and Lansdowne and Liverpool, respectively, President and Vice-president, to vest a million of money for the cultivation of mulberry trees and propagation of the silkworm in Great Britain and Ireland ! The charge made against most of them was one that sounds strange to us, namely, that they were combinations of capital competing with individuals, for such competition could have only one end, monopoly—and monopoly was as much dreaded as unlimited competition. The Metropolitan Fish Company, for instance, was a Bill to incorporate a joint stock company to supply the poor of London with fish. It was vigorously denounced as aiming at monopoly. It would take the bread out of the mouths of industrious individuals, and hurt a fine race of seamen. The public " already procured fish at as cheap a rate as the nature of the commerce would allow." If Lord George Seymour, Mr. Mocatta, and other respectable persons chose to become fishmongers, there could be no possible objection, but there was a strong objection to them uniting for the purpose of ruining the poor but honest fishermen. " The idea of conducting retail business by a joint stock association," said the *European Magazine*—" of selling *e.g.* a pound of fish or measuring out a pint of milk, on account of a Company with a court of proprietors, a board of directors, a secretary, and auditors, in competition with the private fishmonger or dairy keeper—is an absurdity which could not have gained admission into the head of the most unreflecting, had not the rage for speculation overpowered the dictates of common sense." " It was extremely iniquitous," said one, " to interfere with the hard earnings of a class of persons whose calling was honourable and of great antiquity, as it was followed by the apostles." It was

representation that it was not right that companies possessing £250 millions or so of capital should not know whether they were acting rightly or not, the Act was repealed (*Hansard*, xii. 1279 ; xiii. 1018).

pointed out that the new company proposed to be purchasers of fish—not fishers ; but this merely diverted the attack—the effect would be a monopoly in the sale and not in the catching of fish ; and it was evident that, when so much capital was brought into the market, fish would rise instead of becoming cheaper.[1] The Equitable Loan Company, again, as we have seen, was promoted to carry on the business of pawnbroking on a large scale ; according to its prospectus, it would be able to lend on pledges sums under £10 at a lower rate than that charged by the ordinary pawnbrokers. The Bill to incorporate it was thrown out in the Lords on the argument of the Lord Chancellor that, as the number of persons composing the company might amount to about 7,000, it was not fair that a body so constituted should compete with individuals ![2]

The immediate evil, however, was that most of the companies had called up small amounts only—about one-fifth on the whole —and the premiums ran up to absurd figures. The £10 instalment called up of the United Mexican £40 share, for instance, was sold for £35 in December and for £155 in January : the £70 instalment of the Real del Monte £400 share, at £550 in December, and at £1,350 in January. As the breezy admiral, Sir Joseph Yorke, said, there were companies to bring salt water from Brighton and airs from Bognor—companies to " bring airs from Heaven and blasts from Hell ! " Earl Grosvenor thought it proper to deny in Parliament that he had cleared between £300,000 and £400,000 by mining speculations.[3] *but with much uncalled capital.*

But returning common sense was reminding the holders that the *The check.* returns from such investments, even when the enterprises were sound, could not be expected till years after the capital was sunk, and that many of them were notoriously unsound. When the continuous rise in the price of shares was checked, the shareholders could not sell at a profit and clear out before another call was made, and the calls still further depreciated the price. Those who had not sufficiency of capital to wait, had to throw their shares on the market or borrow at a higher rate of interest, often pledging their stocks. As the result showed, the Mexican and South American mining companies, with one or two exceptions, simply absorbed the capital, and, instead of sending precious metal up the shaft, swallowed the

[1] *Hansard*, xii. 965, 1020.
[2] *Ibid.* xii. 1350 ; xiii. 899, 1061, 1349.
[3] *Ibid.* xii. 613, 751.

money subscribed, and then closed down.[1] Of the other schemes, most were abandoned.

Any one familiar with the facts of such a movement can see how these three branches of speculation hung together, and how this made straight for a crisis in the trade which is the very heart of organised industry. They could scarcely have been undertaken without the support of banking credit, partly by affording accommodation in discounts, partly by taking securities on pledge. A speculation of this amount would have strained the resources of the soundest banking system. But the dangers of banking were not then understood as they are now. The country bankers had encouraged the speculation, and the issues of many of them had been greatly extended without any corresponding provision of available reserves to meet sudden demand.[2] Several of them had really for some time been insolvent, and were kept afloat merely by the confidence of their customers and the facility of the money market, which had accompanied the increase of the Bank of England issues ; and many more who were solvent—if time had been given—had not, as a rule, counted on the necessity of having their reserves in an available form. Others, again, had never had sufficient available resources for the business they were doing, and the disaster began with one of these, the house of Sir Peter Pole & Co. which, after struggling for a week, stopped payment in the beginning of December.[3] This brought down others connected with it. Panic set in. There was a run on several London Banks and three or four suspended payment. Altogether,

Fall of Pole & Co.

Panic.

---

[1] Not to be wondered at, if there was any truth in the graphic *Rough Notes* of Captain Head, a mining engineer who traversed some 1200 miles in the Pampas inspecting gold and silver mines—not published, unfortunately, till the next year. Never was a country so ill furnished with everything required in mining except the ores.

[2] If two debates in Parliament of June are to be believed, some of the country banks at least were under the impression that there was not any legal obligation on them—such as there certainly was on the Bank of England—to pay their small notes in gold on demand (*Hansard*, xiii. 1271, 1381). The same appears from a petition presented in 1826 (*ibid.* xv. 778).

[3] Up till December there was, apparently, little apprehension of any general convulsion. In a financial article of November it was stated that there had been extraordinary fluctuations and depressions in the money market, and failures on the Stock Exchange, but, " all through this bustle and anxiety public confidence has never been even for one moment in the slightest degree shaken. The nation is, in its general state, flourishing almost beyond parallel." But, in the end of the year, there were many failures connected with the cotton trade in the United States, and the commercial discredit of Liverpool preceded that of London.

nearly seventy banks in town and country—six of them in London
—closed their doors by the middle of the month. This, of course,
besides disorganising all trade, caused a suspicion of all notes and a
rush of the banks to get gold from the one source available, and the
pressure was transferred to the Bank of England. But the Bank ^{The Bank}
reserves had already been brought down by a drain of gold for ^{itself in} _{danger;}
export, and for some time it looked as if a second suspension would
be necessary. On the 17th, the Bank intimated to the Government
that they were " likely to be run dry," and suggested restriction
—which, however, was absolutely declined. The run on gold in
the middle of December might have proved fatal had it not been
for the patriotic action of the London merchants and traders, who ^{but, supported}
met in the Mansion House on the 14th and resolved to support the ^{by the} _{merchants,}
public credit of the country ; declaring that the embarrassments and
difficulties were due to a general panic for which there was no cause,
and that they had the fullest confidence in the banking establishments of the capital and the country ; and deciding to act generally
upon that confidence. As it was, on 24th December, the coin in
the Bank was reduced to £426,000 and the bullion to £601,000—
in all, £1,027,000—and, in Huskisson's words, " we were within a
few hours of a state of barter." Apparently, however, the suspicion
had not extended to the Bank of England notes. The famous
issue of between 600,000 and 700,000 one pound notes which
were discovered in a box lying in the cellars, overlooked when
the Bank called in their small notes in 1824-5, and the perceptible
relief which these gave, proves this.[1] But notes cannot be issued
just because they are printed. At this point, the directors, who had
issued a notice on 6th December that they would continue to discount ^{takes the bold}
mercantile bills at 4 per cent., adopted the bold course of enlarging ^{course, and} _{discounts}
their issues by discounting freely at 5 per cent. (to which the rate ^{freely.}
was raised on the 13th) all mercantile paper that had any pretensions
to security. The issues, which had been £35 millions in the first
two weeks of the month, were over £51 millions in the latter two.[2]
By the 26th, the panic was stopped. The $3\frac{1}{2}$ per cents. which had
gone down to 83 recovered to $91\frac{1}{2}$. " Never was there a less ^{A bad New}
merry New Year in London than the present," wrote Crabb ^{Year.}
Robinson.

[1] In Norwich, the Gurneys are said to have stopped a run merely by placing
a thick pile of these notes on the counter.

[2] At the same time, they asked and obtained assistance from the Bank of
France to the amount of two millions in three months' bills.

In Baring's words subsequently : " Every one desirous to obtain what was due to him ran to his banker or to any other on whom he had a claim ; and even those who really had no immediate use for their money took it back, and let it lie unemployed in their pockets, thinking it unsafe in other hands. The effect of this alarm was that houses which were weak went immediately. Then went second-rate houses, and, lastly, houses which were solvent went because their securities were unavailable at the moment. The daily calls to which each individual was subject put it out of his power to assist his friend, and this added to the general difficulty. All confidence was lost, and, in this country, commercial confidence was carried to an extent never exceeded in any nation. Scarcely one man could be found to trust his neighbour, every one endeavouring to husband his resources for himself. Such a state of panic had scarcely ever before existed amongst us." [1]

Foreign trade.   The direction which the circumstances of the year gave to foreign trade is reflected in the increase of the imports by about £7 millions, while the exports fell by £1½ millions and the re-exports by a million. The Official values are :

Imports - - - - - - - -	£44,208,000
Exports of British produce and manufacture -	47,150,000
Exports of Foreign and Colonial produce - -	9,169,000
The Real value of the British exports was -	38,870,000

The number of ships built and registered in the several ports of the United Kingdom was 975, representing 122,479 tons.

[1] *Hansard*, xiv. 199.

CHAPTER XXVII

1825. AGRICULTURE : A THREATENED CHANGE IN THE
CORN LAW

As we have seen, the position of agriculture had begun to improve
in 1823, and the improvement continued in 1824. So at least one
gathers from the King's Speeches, from the debates in Parliament,
and from the fact that the farmer's organ had given over its loud
complaints. Although I have not come across any evidence that
agricultural conditions had materially changed, the farmers benefited,
no doubt, from the extra demand for produce induced by the general
prosperity. In 1825, says the *Annual Register*, agricultural distress had disappeared.[1]

Disappearance
of distress.

The weather up till February, indeed, had been wet and
tempestuous. But the seed-time was favourable, and, to a hot and
dry summer—hotter than had been known for thirty years—succeeded a very early harvest, got in under the best conditions. In
the home counties, the wheat harvest was general by the end of
July, and the only complaint was that, owing to the activity in
manufacturing, extra field labour was scarcely to be had, and that
wages ran very high—as high, it was said, as in the last years of
the war. The wheat crop was excellent ; barley less uniformly
good, but still an average ; oats defective but not to any great
extent ; potatoes and turnips, however, short by about a fourth.
The prices of all live stock were high. As had been anticipated
in Parliament, the stocks of grain were nearly all exhausted by
harvest time. The price of wheat, accordingly, prevented from
rising by the admission of half a million quarters from bond in
April, kept very steady all over the year, reached 69/- only in May,

---

[1] All the same, we find in a letter from Lord Sefton to Creevey in October :
" Nothing can exceed the distress here among the farmers ; forty per cent.
reduction of rent is the lowest they talk of, and, even then, I don't believe they
will be able to pay the remainder."

ruled about 65/- after harvest, and scarcely fell at all till December. The prices of other crops rose.[1] The official average price of wheat over the year—which, however, it will be noted, does not correspond with the *Annual Register* figures—was 68/6.

Some change in the Corn Laws expected.

Somehow or other—possibly from Huskisson's success in overturning the prohibitory duties, and from the general enthusiasm for a free trade—the impression had got abroad, and it is reflected in current literature, that the Government was going to do something with imported corn—no one knew what. The landed classes, who, hitherto, had looked with complacency upon the reduction of duties on manufactures, and had lost no opportunity of complaining of the new Corn Law—as they had complained of every Corn Law—suddenly discovered that they were well off. "Our reports," said the *Farmer's Magazine* in May, "bear witness to the satisfaction and contentment which prevails, almost without exception, among farmers in every part of the country, and, at the same time, to the full employment of the labourers who depend upon them, at an improved rate of wages. . . . It is in these circumstances that it has been thought expedient again to agitate the public mind with that perpetual bone of contention, the Corn Laws." And great indignation and alarm were expressed. Petitions for and against began to pour in in such numbers that one member called attention to the enormous expense which the country was being put to in printing them. The two great interests in the State began to be sharply defined by hostility to each other. As a rule, the landed classes begged that no change should be made, while the manufacturers cried for anything that would bring down the price of food. The Government were forced to give some indication of their policy.

On 2nd April, Lord Liverpool, in answer to a question, said that, in his opinion, some—he did not say what—alteration must be made in the Corn Laws, with a view to the permanency which was so desirable. In giving the same intimation to the Lower House, Huskisson, defending the delay on the ground that the important changes in regard to other duties could not have been carried through if any attempt had been made to deal with the

[1] The ports were opened to barley and oats again in November, and it was agreed on all hands that the measure was peremptorily called for in the circumstances. Although three million quarters of oats were imported, yet such was the pressure of demand that prices continued above the limit of the Act of 1815, and it was pointed out that they would, if that Act had been in force, have come in without paying any duty at all.

Corn Laws in the same Session, let fall the suggestion that, as
several foreign countries were in some distress owing to our exclusion
of their corn, and had, in revenge, shut out our manufactures, it
might be worth while to consider whether this did not give us the
key for solving the difficulty—whether we had not a right to say :
" We will not admit you to the benefit of a free trade in corn unless
you will at the same time admit the free introduction of our manufactures." [1]

There was very strong criticism as to the uncertainty this intimation would .cause everywhere, and the unsettling effect it would
have, if not the slightest intimation was given as to what line the
Government would take in next Session, and this found more ample
expression on 28th April when Whitmore, whose " Letter on the
Present State and Future Prospects of Agriculture," was already
widely known and quoted, brought forward his promised motion,
proposing to admit foreign corn at a duty of 10/- when the home
price was 55/-, and to add 5/- to the duty for every 5/- of fall in the
home averages. The motion was evidently not taken seriously,
and need not be discussed ; even the 47 who voted for it seemed
to do so merely as a protest against the inaction of the Government.[2]
But it allowed Huskisson to give some intimation that his own
idea of the change he thought necessary, and in which he would
concur, was a fixed duty to be gradually reduced. In the meantime,
a purely temporary measure was passed. The corn in bond—amount- A temporary
ing to 394,000 quarters of wheat, and a very small quantity of other measure.

[1] *Hansard*, xiii. 142, 273. As a fact, according to Villiers in 1840, the
Government was approached in 1826 by Prussia with a proposal to conclude
a treaty of reciprocity, engaging to make no change in the existing system for
a certain number of years, and, specifically, not to increase the duties on
British merchandise, on condition that England allowed the importation of
Prussian corn subject to such duties as should not exclude the possibility of
carrying on that trade with a reasonable profit, and that it would grant
greater facilities to the importation of timber coming from the port of Prussia ;
and Canning had been compelled to answer: " It becomes His Majesty's
Government, when a proposal for altering our Corn Laws is made to us by a
foreign government, as a condition of something to be done or omitted by that
Government, at once to declare that we can never entertain such a proposal ''
(*Free Trade Speeches*, i. 213).

[2] It proceeded on the idea, pretty generally expressed, that 60/- was about
the minimum price which would afford a fair profit to the farmer. Taking
foreign wheat as costing 45/-, the average price at Danzig for the last forty
years, and adding 10/- for duty and 10/- for freight and charges, foreign wheat
could not compete till the home price was a good deal above 60/-, and the home
farmer would still have the advantage of 5/-. Even, then, if it were always
true that foreign wheat cost 15/- less than home wheat, this would prevent it
coming in. If, again, the home price went down to 50/- the duty would be 10/-.

grain—was to be admitted at a duty of 10/- (instead of 17/- as it would otherwise be) if the home price of wheat reached 70/-, the grain to be taken out in three monthly instalments before 15th August. The reason which weighed with Huskisson was, not any consideration for the owners—they had speculated and must abide by the consequences—but the possibility of having the ports thrown open in August to the immense quantity of foreign grain which had been accumulating in other countries all the time our ports were shut : this, besides, would dispose of much of the accumulated corn in this country, before " the period when the Corn Laws must come under the revision of Parliament." [1] The price was rising very rapidly ; the temptation would be for the bonders to hold back on the speculation of its rising to 80/- and of foreign grain being admitted free ; it was desirable that there should be more supply before the next harvest was available ; and he proposed the counter-inducement of admitting it with a moderate duty when the price rose to 70/-. At the same time he proposed that Canadian wheat—of which the quantity in bond probably did not exceed 20,000 quarters—should be admitted at " a prospective duty of 5/- per quarter in lieu of all other prohibitory duties." Both Resolutions were passed without division. [2]

Considerable apprehension was expressed that American corn would be brought in through Canada. Huskisson thought it quite unwarranted, but introduced a clause requiring the same certificate of origin as in the case of sugar, and promised that, if during five years, the average importation of what was called Canadian corn should exceed 100,000 quarters, he would take that as evidence that there had been a fraudulent importation of American corn, and would adopt some measures to guard against it. [3]

The Bill founded on the two resolutions, however, was strongly condemned in the Lords as the " ominous forerunner of a change in the Corn Laws." As Lord Redesdale said, to talk of a free

[1] *Hansard*, xiii. 252.

[2] *Ibid.* xiii. 337. Huskisson stated in the next year that half a million quarters were taken out between June and August, and that this, as he had anticipated, was successful in preventing the ports from being thrown open in August.

[3] *Ibid.* xiii. 590. As a fact, in the first year afterwards the importation from Canada was only between 70,000 and 80,000 quarters, and in the next it fell to 30,000 (*ibid.* xvi. 1056).

trade in corn was at once absurd and dangerous ; it could never exist consistently with the safety and prosperity of the kingdom ; the constitution of the country was founded upon the landed interest, etc. The Bill, however, passed, though by narrow majorities.[1]

[1] *Hansard*, xiii. 952. In November, we find Sir John Sinclair, at a banquet given him by the Inverness-shire Farming Society, as headstrong as ever. Speaking of the interests of the owners and occupiers of land as paramount —they were " the most valuable part of the community "—he harped on at the " wretchedness of depending on a foreign country for food," called for an " augmentation of the cultivation of the worse lands as a means of giving employment," and pronounced for the total exclusion of foreign produce.

CHAPTER XXVIII

1825. LABOUR LEGISLATION: COMBINATION AND FACTORY ACTS

Effects of the repeal. WE saw that the Act of 1824 repealing the Combination Laws—passed without discussion and, as was confessed later, without examination—was almost immediately followed by what some people called a " Saturnalia "—a time when the workmen, like Roman slaves of old, thought themselves entitled to celebrate their freedom by showing that they were not fit for it. Trade Societies sprang into existence on all sides ; for the next six months, the newspapers are full of strikes and rumours of strikes, and of hearty denunciation of the " excesses." By February 21st, we find Huskisson using the words that, " since the repeal of the Combination Laws, the workmen in the dockyards and other trades had committed such excesses as, if they were continued, would compel the House to resort again to the former laws." Hume himself agreed that the conduct of the workmen in all parts of the country had been highly blameable—they had attempted to impose upon their masters regulations far more arbitrary and degrading than those they had so much complained of, and conduct like this would drive their best friends to wish for the reimposition of the old laws.[1]

Huskisson on its evils. On 29th March, Huskisson took blame to himself, as well as to the House, for not having given due consideration to the Bill of the previous Session,[2] and, particularly to not having noticed that, in repealing thirty or forty statutes relative to combinations and conspiracies, they were taking away the possibility of proceeding against them at common law, and precluding the possibility of any legal remedy to what had become a great public evil. In his

---

[1] *Hansard*, xii. 597.

[2] Later in the year, Liverpool confessed that he had not been aware of its extent, and did not, until it came into operation, know its provisions.

official capacity he had received very painful accounts of the conduct
adopted by workmen in many parts of the kingdom, acting under
a misconception of the object of the law, and combining in a way
destructive to property and business—mischiefs which indeed had
grown to such an alarming pitch as promised soon to call for the
interposition of the civil power.   He was a friend of the freedom
of labour, but he, as strongly, contended for the freedom of
employers : property, machinery, and capital ought to be as sacred
and unfettered as the labour which was the admitted property of the
workman.   He held in his hands two sets of Articles of Regulation
typical of many others ; one of the Operative Colliers of Lanark
and Dumbarton, the other of the Ayrshire Association, both
having a constitution and a complete body of functionaries.   One
of the articles provided that the delegates from all the different
works should assemble at one and the same place on certain stated
occasions.   This, the House would note, was not a combination of
all the workmen of one employer against him, or even of one whole
trade against the masters, but something more formidable and
extensive ; namely, a systematic union of the workmen of many
different trades, and a delegation from each of them to one central
meeting—a kind of federal republic, all the trades being represented
by delegates who formed a kind of congress.   Another regulation
was to the effect that the president, the secretary, and the treasurer
were to be paid out of the general funds, and that every member
having employment was to contribute a portion of his wages for the
purposes of these associations.   " So that here was a tax levied
upon each workman for the maintenance of general funds applicable
to purposes of this mischievous character."   Another article clearly
demonstrated the real nature and intentions of the societies.   " It
is the duty of these delegates, first, to point out the masters they
dislike : secondly, to warn such masters of the danger in which
they are placed in consequence of this combination : and, thirdly,
to try everything which prudence might dictate to put them out
of the trade."   All laws passed at the meeting of the delegates
were to be binding on all whom these delegates represented.   Now
one of those laws was " that there should never be allowed to be any
stock of coals in the hands of any of the masters," because, if such
stocks were allowed, they would be less dependent on the workmen,
and might possess some means of rescuing themselves from the
tyranny of the unions.   Other associations, however, were governed
by regulations, if possible, more extraordinary.   One was that no

man, coming into any district or county within the control assumed
by the associating parties, should be allowed to work without being
previously amerced in £5, to be applied to the funds of the association. Another was that any child, permitted to work or to assist,
should, at ten years old, be reckoned as a quarter of a man, and pay
a proportional amercement accordingly. In like manner, it was
provided that any man, being called in by any collier to his assistance, should not be at liberty to work under him unless previously
adopted, like the collier, by the society, and unless, like him, he
should previously have paid his £5. When any measure was adopted
after a full discussion, the decision of the majority was to bind
the rest. What all this led to might be seen from another of the
articles, which ran that no operative, being a member of the association, should be at liberty to engage himself for any given time
or price without the consent of the committee of management.
Who would for an instant endure a control of this oppressive, of
this destructive nature ? The Seamen's Union, among others,
had come to the determination of not submitting to the authority
of any persons whom they had not, among themselves, appointed
or approved. How was it possible to carry on business in mining
if the workmen themselves should have appointed all the overseers
under whose superintendence they were employed ? This same
Union prescribed that they who were employed as seamen in the
coasting trade should not put to sea unless all the rest of the crew
were members of their union. Again, it was positively one of the
articles agreed on that men, thus employed, should do nothing
which they had never before been called upon to do as seamen.
Thus, very recently, a vessel laden with coal got on a sandbank,
and the seamen refused to shift the ballast because " it was
unworthy a seaman to assist in shifting ballast ! " If any man,
after that, could be found to affirm that such principles and
conduct were not matters for the interference of Parliament, he
would only say that Parliament had better at once resign every
idea of giving any protection at all to any species of property.

He was not surprised, however, he continued, when he looked
at the wording of the Act, to see how an artful misconstruction
might easily be put upon it by those who wanted to mislead
and deceive the men. The Act lent itself to misconstruction,
and it was inadequate to meet the evil of workmen being permitted to plot and openly avow their intention to carry such permission (as they presumed it to be) into effect in a manner the

most destructive, perhaps, to the property of their employers which it was in their power to devise. But if such courses were allowed to continue, the inevitable consequence would be that no individual would embark his capital under risks so great, or submit its application to a system of tyranny and control such as no man possessing capital would for a moment choose to endure. As he summed up on a subsequent occasion : the workmen combined to dictate to their masters the mode in which they should conduct their business ; to dictate whether the master should take an apprentice or not ; to prevent certain individuals from working ; to enforce the principle that wages should be paid alike to every man, whether he were a good workman or a bad one ; and they levied heavy fines on those who refused to agree to their conditions. They not only prevented the employers from carrying on their business with their assistance, but they prevented individuals who wished to work from getting employment at all. Finally, without giving any indication of what course he thought should ultimately be followed, he moved meantime for the appointment of a Select Committee to enquire into the effect of the late Act, and to report their opinion how far it might be necessary to repeal or amend it.

Hume admitted that many classes had gone further than could possibly be permitted, although he considered that the increase of employment, and the great demand for workmen, had tended to the mischiefs complained of more than the repeal of the Combination Laws. Still, the men had often acted with extreme impropriety. In Dublin, the Unions had been productive of the greatest evils ; there many persons had actually been murdered. But, he argued, the masters had acted in the same spirit and principle—as for instance when they refused to employ union men, or sent round lists to each other so that no man who differed with one employer could get work from another. If the principle were admitted that the fault did not rest alone with the men, no person would more heartily concur with the right honourable gentleman than he did, in the propriety of punishing any measures connected with threats and intimidations, whether they were adopted by masters or men. *Even Hume speaks plainly.*

Peel said that he was not convinced that the precipitate repeal of thirty-five statutes, without substituting something for that which had been taken away, was the best course which could have been pursued. But he believed that the system of delegation as it existed was an excessive and infamous tyranny. On the Thames *So does Peel.*

lately, four or five individuals presented themselves at a yard and commenced working. They were told that they were not wanted —that there was no room for them. Their answer was that they had been sent thither by the committee of delegates, and that employment must be found for them. On this being refused, all the men left the yard ! He urged that combinations produced counter-combinations, and destroyed all good feeling and good faith between classes. And he thought there was one party well deserving the attention of the House—the man who, in the midst of these com-binations, should resolutely adhere to his master. Such a person would be the object of universal hatred among the men, and he did think that there were more than twenty towns in this country where such a man could not appear with safety after nightfall.[1] Could there be a stronger case for the intervention of the legislature than this ? Many further instances were given by various speakers of the evils complained of—such as the resolutions of the opera-tive coal miners that no person should be allowed to work as a coal miner who had not been engaged in the trade from the age of sixteen. No one defended the late Act as it stood, and the motion was agreed to.[2]

Report of
Wallace's
Committee.

When the Committee reported, a Bill was brought in founded on its recommendations. Wallace, who was Chairman of the Com-mittee and introduced the Bill, stated its principle, and gave a short account of what had come out on evidence before the Com-mittee. Combinations, he said, were greater in extent than formerly, but they were more open in their proceedings : thirteen cases of absolute combinations were proved, of which seven had grown up since the repeal ; the parties met regularly and constantly, with presidents, secretaries, and committees ; their objects were, briefly, to settle when they would work, whom the masters should employ, how many, if any, apprentices should be allowed ; in short, to take all power out of the hands of the masters. Beyond this, they had, in some cases, pointed out individuals to be assassinated. In Scotland, a still more organised system prevailed, and he quoted the oath taken—one may hope not generally—" by the persons engaged in Scotland in those combinations," pledging themselves,

[1] It is some testimony to the truth of such a statement that, when the Shooting and Stabbing (Scotland) Act was passed, the Lord Advocate explained that a clause in it making vitriol-throwing a capital offence was rendered neces-sary by " the scenes which had occurred in the West of Scotland for a consider-able time " (*Hansard*, xiii. 1245).

[2] *Hansard*, xii. 1288.

in the name of God, to execute with zeal and alacrity every task
or injunction put upon them by the majority as to the chastisement
of nobs, the assassination of oppressive and tyrannical masters,
and the demolition of shops that should be deemed " incorrigible."
To gain their ends, every inducement was put in practice. First
of all, persuasion was tried; then money was offered; then warnings;
then threats and intimidation ; and, if these were insufficient, then
murder, or an attempt to murder, was resorted to.

The principle of the Bill was to make all associations Legal
illegal except for the purpose of settling what amount of wages combination
defined.
would be a fair renumeration to the workmen and the hours
or time for which they should work. He thought it safer to point
out the description of association which was legal than to specify all
those that were illegal, in doing which there was great danger either
of putting in too much or of leaving out something which might
be necessary. The Bill gave a summary jurisdiction to the magistrate ; did away with the necessity of a previous information ;
and permitted a conviction upon the evidence of one witness only.
To put it briefly ; every workman or other person, or any number
of persons, were liable to be punished by summary process for
forcing, endeavouring to force, threatening, molesting, obstructing,
or compelling by any means whatever, any person or persons either
to leave his or their work or to join any combination or union of
workmen.

Hume, supported by a great number of petitions from the side Hume fights
of the operatives, protested against the Bill; none of the alleged the Bill.
abuses, he said, has been at all proved ; no proof of violent conduct
to any material extent given. And, after all, what had occasioned
these combinations ? What but the Corn Laws—the combination
of the landowners which had raised every necessary of life
within the last three years from 30 to 60 per cent. in price? It was
a little hard to allow the corn grower to bring his commodity as he
chose into the market, and to shut out all competition in order that
he might obtain his own price for it ; and then to punish the workman, who was compelled to buy this artificially raised commodity
of the landholders, for making what efforts he could to get the
best possible price for his own. For if the masters were to be
protected by the present Bill, the men had a right to protection too.
And had they protection ? If the masters combined to give their
men only half a sufficient rate of wages, and had strength enough
to starve them into taking it, there was nothing in the Bill to prevent

them doing so.   And how could this danger be met by the workmen
except by counter-combination ?   for which, short of carrying it
to the extent of violence, he still thought they ought to have the
fullest permission.   The masters might at all times prevent combinations against working by contracting with the journeymen
for a certain period ; the masters, then, had the remedy in their
own hands, and had no right to call upon Parliament to support
them with the strong hand of power.   Besides this, he objected
to the discretion which the Bill proposed to lodge in magistrates.
From stage to stage, Hume, almost single-handed, opposed the
Bill—somewhat handicapped, one is inclined to suspect, by his
honest declaration that no individual, high or low, should be coerced
or controlled by combinations, and by the weight of evidence
that so many had been coerced.   Peel, indeed, said that he had
never heard, in the Committee or in the House, expressions regarding the combinations of the operative classes so strong as some of
those used by Hume himself.   But, with the exception of two
clauses, one directing that justices should transmit to the sessions
a copy of the commitment, the other allowing appeal to quarter
sessions, the Bill passed very much as introduced.   When it came
to the Lords, the only objection raised was by Lansdowne, who
regretted that so important a Bill should be passed within two
days of the prorogation ; he thought that counsel should have
been heard against it, and intimated that he might yet move
for this in next Session.[1]

Aftermath.   But, for some time after, the year's unfettered freedom to combine
left its marks.   In September, we hear of the combined cotton
spinners of Glasgow trying to carry out their threat of " rooting
out all the new workers," of assaults and outrages, of workmen
taken to their homes under police protection.   Hume, offered a
presentation of " a magnificent and massive piece of plate " from
the Union, declined it, with some home truths as to the folly of

----

[1] *Hansard*, xii. 1351 ; xiii. 149, 298, 353, 362, 1347, 1400, 1458, 1462, 1478.
Thus, say Mr. and Mrs. Webb, " the right of Collective Bargaining, involving
the power to withhold labour from the market by concerted action, was for
the first time expressly established " (*History of Trade Unionism*, 97).   I
have thought it advisable to give some considerable space to these debates,
partly to show that there are few features in the labour disputes of to-day
with which our ancestors were not familiar, but, principally, to show in
what light they were then regarded.   It is interesting to note *Blackwood*
protesting angrily against the new word " operatives "—as if they were so
many doses of Glauber salts—the old word " servant " was surely good enough :
in Brougham's pamphlet on education, it noticed, the terms masters and
servants were never used—always " the working classes and their employers."

their actions. The linen weavers of Barnsley laid down a plan to compel the workers, factory by factory, to strike, and selected the order by lot. Following the same plan, the Clyde colliers and Dunlop's ironworkers at Glasgow were ordered to stop work, although Dunlop's men were much attached to him and voted against the strike. In August, the Association of Seamen of Sunderland, which had been for some time at war with the shipowners, seeing a ship going out of port manned with seamen not belonging to the port, attacked it, and were only dispersed with bloodshed by the military. In September and October, combination seemed to be increasing rather than diminishing, and it was said that the Cabinet had resolved to take further action next Session. Combination, in fact, in its threatening form, was not checked till, in various trades, the masters plucked up courage and fought it with free labour. But, by December, combination, it was broadly asserted, was knocked on the head. Bradford weavers and combers went back to work at the old wages after five months of a strike. So did the Renfrewshire colliers, of whom it was said that, six times in the year, they had demanded an advance of wages, each advance being accompanied by a corresponding diminution of the hours of labour and of the output.[1]

In Hobhouse's *Diary*, March 21, appears the entry : " Spoke to Peel privately respecting the abridgement of the hours of labour for children in the cotton factories. He referred me to Huskisson ; Huskisson referred me to Philips of Manchester ; and Philips, to the Chamber of Commerce at Manchester. The poor operative deputies from Manchester have been often with me, trying to induce me to bring in a Bill for them. I want someone to do it more likely to succeed than myself." But, on 6th May, we find him getting leave to bring in a Bill to regulate the working hours for children employed in cotton mills. He was at once asked to extend it to other mills. His only answer was that he had found so much difficulty in making regulations for the one class of mills that this single object appeared to him enough for one person ; he would not, however, object to a general measure if the House desired it. Peel, while professing no objection, urged the House to pause

Hobhouse's Factory Bill.

[1] It is characteristic that Place should think that combinations would soon cease to exist—" men have been kept together for long periods only by the oppressions of the laws ; these being repealed, combinations will lose the matter which cements them into masses, and they will fall to pieces." For some years, indeed, little was heard of them, but this, no doubt, was because of the great distress (*History of Trade Unionism*, chap. ii.).

before it entered too extensively into this field of legislation. The present Bill was like one which he had before supported, but the House must take care not to carry this sort of legislation too far ; if they made the regulations too severe, the masters might refuse to employ any children.

The regulation proposed was to limit the hours of children (persons under sixteen) employed in cotton mills to eleven per day. This, indeed, was already the legal work day for children according to Sir Robert Peel's Act of 1819, the third clause of which ran : " no child under sixteen years of age shall be compelled to work more than eleven hours a day." But the Bill had proved, and was con- fessed to be, entirely inoperative ; only two convictions had been obtained under it, and no one denied that not less than twelve hours was the usual number.[1]   " In the best regulated mills, the children were compelled to work 12½ hours a day," said Hobhouse, " and, for three or four days in the week, were not allowed to go out of the mills to get their meals. In other mills, they were forced to work fifteen or sixteen hours a day." Why, cried Burdett, had any man a horse that he would think of putting to work for twelve hours a day ? Suppose it were true, as had been asserted, that we should lose two and a half millions by the shortening of hours, asked Hobhouse, anticipating Carlyle, " would it not be better to give up the cotton trade altogether than to draw such a sum out of the blood, and bones, and sinews of those unfortunate children ? "

That the cotton spinners, however, were for the most part un- regenerate on the subject, may be seen from Philips' speech on the second reading. The whole course of his experience, he said, induced him to believe that the Bill would in no degree improve the condition of the labourers. Those persons who were acquainted with the management of cotton factories were much better able to judge of what regulations were fit to be adopted than those who knew nothing about the practical effect of the existing laws. He was satisfied that the condition of the people working in the factories was much better than that of persons who worked out of them : the weavers out of doors did not receive more than one-third of the wages of those in factories ; and the latter were, besides, provided with more convenient and wholesome places to work in. It would be well to limit the hours of children's working if it were possible, but it was not possible without limiting the

[1] See a pamphlet quoted in Hutchins and Harrison's *History of Factory Legislation*, 30.

labour of adults. The only effect of the measures now attempted
would be to deprive the children of work altogether. He was
satisfied that no such number of hours as had been asserted were
ever used for the employment of children. The evasions of the
Act had happened in the least respectable mills, where the owners
were wholly regardless of public opinion. The effect of this and
similar Acts of legislation would be to keep up a spirit of hostility
between the masters and the men—they had already produced
this effect. He concluded by saying that he thought this interference extremely unadvisable. The sale and purchase of labour
by the workmen and their employers ought to be left wholly unrestricted. The best thing that could be done would be to repeal
all that had been enacted on the subject.

When the Bill went into Committee, Hobhouse said that he had A twelve hours'
been " induced to alter a little his original purpose," and propose day.
that the children should work twelve hours for five days in the week
—exclusive of half an hour for breakfast and an hour for dinner—
and nine on Saturdays.[1] He could assure the House that some
masters, employing among them 15,000 operatives, were as anxious
for these restrictions on children's labour as he was. But it grieved
him to hear all this opposition to the eleven hours. Criminals on
hard labour were not compelled to work so many hours—nor, added
a member, were West Indian slaves. From enquiries made, he
found that machine-makers, moulders, house carpenters, cabinet-
makers, stone masons, bricklayers, blacksmiths, millwrights, etc.,
worked no more than ten and a half hours per day ; and, some of
them, in winter, only eight and a half. And one circumstance
which distinguished the cotton manufacture from all others was
the high temperature, and the extreme variations of heat and cold.
Two members spoke of Owen's factory—which " paid sufficiently "
—where the hours of employment had been reduced from eleven
and a half to ten and a half—and as much work was done in the
shorter time. Philips still was unimpressed : the effect would be
to throw children out of employment altogether; the present
complaints were got up by a most formidable combination which
called itself " The Grand Union of Operative Spinners " ; if members
knew these unions as well as he did, they would oppose them. He
did not object to the limitation of hours in the day, if he could be

[1] In case of a mill standing for want of water, or for repairs, the hours
might be extended by one hour each day in the week in which suspension
took place.

convinced that it was called for by circumstances, but those circumstances had not been made out.

Huskisson, it is to be noted, supported the Bill, but in a very tepid way ; " as Parliament had thought it right to interfere with respect to the cotton mills, certainly the more fully the provisions of the former Bill were carried into operation the better." But he by no means believed that the children generally in cotton mills worked fourteen hours a day. He had no doubt that, if they investigated every species of labour, they would find much that they could wish to alter ; but what would become of those children if they were not so employed, and what would they do for the food, clothes, and comforts they were at present receiving ? Any alteration that should induce the masters to withdraw those comforts would be only an aggravation instead of a relief to the children. Peel, who had recommended Hobhouse to confine his Bill to making the Act of 1819 operative, did not oppose the clause limiting the hours, but said that he would have been better pleased to have had no alteration made at all as to the labour, without having a commission first to investigate the facts.

As there is no record in *Hansard* of how the Bill was received by the House of Lords, presumably it passed unchanged, and it appears as c. 63 in the Acts of the session.[1]

---

[1] *Hansard*, xiii. 421, 643, 1008.

CHAPTER XXIX

1825. OTHER HAPPENINGS OF THE YEAR

THIS year again passes almost unobserved in general history—or would have done so, but for its disastrous ending. Greville makes no entry in his diary ; Creevey can talk of nothing but the country houses he visited ; Croker fills up his note-book with reminiscences of the King when he went to " dine and sleep at the Royal Lodge " ; Hobhouse has only a few brief entries of his own parliamentary doings. Outside of the memorable changes in the direction of Free Trade made by Huskisson—which, perhaps, might have been indefinitely postponed if he had not seized the occasion when men were optimistic about the future and prosperity warranted experiment—and of the commercial crisis which was to bring back bad trade, the political, social, and economic happenings of the year may be grouped together in one rather miscellaneous chapter.

The Catholic question again took up an inordinate amount of time. Ireland, said the King's Speech, was participating in the general prosperity, and the outrages had so far ceased as to warrant the suspension of the extraordinary powers given in the previous session. But the growing power of the Catholic Association, which was much discussed, was aimed at in a Bill to put down unlawful societies in Ireland, and its passing had two results : that Cobbett, who had not hitherto taken much interest, now enlisted himself actively on the side of Catholic emancipation, and that O'Connell, hitherto little considered, became a recognised power. But, by the end of the year, the Act was confessed to be a dead letter, and no attempt was made to enforce it. A Catholic Disqualifications Removal Bill, supported by Canning, passed the Commons, and was thrown out by the Lords. Hume made a third unsuccessful attack on the Irish Church by way of Resolutions. Grattan got leave to bring in a Bill for the Relief of the Poor in Ireland, asserting

Ireland.

that it was purely experimental, limited as to time, and having no
resemblance to the Poor Law of England—the only curse, said
Mackintosh, piously, which had not been inflicted on Ireland.

Slavery.

Of Slavery very little was heard directly in Parliament, but the
ignoring of the Order of 1824 by all the islands, and the insane
actions of some of them, were rapidly filling up the cup.

The railway
movement.

This year, 1825, dates the beginning of the " railway movement,"
as it was called—the opening of the first railway, and the first
great fight in Parliament over the new " loco-motion." " Nothing
now is heard of," said an article in the *Quarterly* of March, " but
rail-roads, the daily papers teem with notices of new lines of them
in every direction ; and pamphlets and paragraphs are thrown
before the public eye recommending nothing short of making them
general throughout the kingdom . . . a visionary scheme unworthy
of notice. . . . It is certainly some consolation to those who are
to be whirled at the rate of eighteen or twenty miles an hour, by
means of a high pressure engine, to be told that they are in no
danger of being seasick while on shore ; that they are not to be
scalded to death nor drowned by the bursting of the boiler ; and
that they need not mind being shot by the scattered fragments,
or dashed in pieces by the flying off or the breaking of a wheel.
But, with all these assurances, we should as soon expect the people
of Woolwich to suffer themselves to be fired off upon one of Con-
greve's ricochet rockets, as trust themselves to the mercy of such
a machine, going at such a rate." And the reviewer trusted that
Parliament would at least limit the speed on all the railroads to
eight or nine miles an hour—a speed " as great as could be ventured
upon with safety."

Stage coaches.

Naturally there was great opposition. By this time, stage communication between the great cities had become very perfect. It
was calculated that a person had 1,500 opportunities of leaving
London in the course of twenty-four hours by stage coach, and
that three hundred coaches passed through Hyde Park Corner
daily. While in 1770, a stage coach ran between Manchester and
London, and between Manchester and Liverpool, twice a week,
there were now twenty coaches running daily. " The mail coach
establishment, by far the most perfect public arrangement ever
attempted and carried into practice, is now extended from the
extremity of Cornwall to the extremity of Caithness, a distance
of 1,082 miles." Indeed, " a Mr. Wightman " had published a
pamphlet asserting that a velocity could not be attained on these

railroads equal to one-half that with which " our best stages now travel." [1]

But now the days of the stage-coach were numbered. The Stockton and Darlington Railway, a single line twenty-five miles in length, built by Stephenson, was formally opened in October.[2] The new conveyance is described, with much interest, as making its way majestically through rows of spectators lining the road, accompanied by equestrians, carriages, and coaches trying their powers against the new rival. The first train carried 450 passengers and drew 80 tons of goods, accomplishing the distance in three hours and seven minutes—" in some places the speed was fully twelve miles, and, in one, fifteen." The price of coal in Darlington, it was said, fell from 18/- to 8/6 per ton. Although this line, like all before the Manchester and Liverpool, was designed exclusively for goods traffic, a daily coach, suggestively named the " Experiment," was run to carry six in and fifteen to twenty outside, making the return journey in two hours.

The first public line.

Among the Local Acts of 1825 appear no less than six for railways or " tram-roads." But, during the session, the more serious project of a railway between Liverpool and Manchester was brought before Parliament, and this called out most serious opposition. On the one side, it was alleged that the Bill was supported by the united wealth and influence of the two cities ; that it was projected out of public spirit—the promoters having agreed that no person should hold more than ten shares, and intimated that they would be content with 10 per cent. dividend or even 5 per cent. ; that the goods exported from Liverpool had risen from a value of £11½ millions in 1821 to £19 millions in 1824, and that the canal communication was not sufficient to cope with the traffic —cotton was sometimes detained at Liverpool for a fortnight, while the Manchester manufacturers had to suspend work ; [3] that

Liverpool and Manchester line projected.

---

[1] In 1830, I find that the coaches between Manchester and Liverpool did the distance (inclusive of three changes of horses) in less than three hours, the rate being more than twelve miles per hour.

[2] Before the beginning of the nineteenth century, the railway lines—constructed altogether of timber—were all private undertakings connected with collieries. The first public line with iron rails, constructed under Act of Parliament, and available to the public on payment of tolls, was the Wandsworth and Croydon, opened in 1803, and some seventeen such lines were now in operation (*Economic Annals, 1801-20*, 51).

[3] In the debate of 1826, it was said that the trade of Liverpool had doubled every twenty years since 1760 (*Hansard*, xv. 89). Its population had grown in little more than a century from less than 5000 to 130,000.

there was " as much reason in the complaints of those who were
connected with canals, and therefore wished to stifle this measure,
as there was in the petition of the inn-keepers on the Kent-road
who objected to the steam-packet navigation because it interfered
with their profits." On the other side, it was urged that there
were already three canals between the two cities, all rival companies, competing with each other, and keeping down the rates,
and that the railway would interfere very seriously with private
property.

Philips'
opposition.

But perhaps the most interesting feature is that the project was
heartily opposed by Geo. Philips, the member for Manchester, a
great cotton spinner who, as we saw, made himself conspicuous by
opposing the Factory Act. It had been asserted, he said, that the
canal line was fifty miles long while the railway would be only
twenty-three ; that carriage by canal took thirty-six hours and by
rail would take only six ; that goods could be carried by rail at ten
or twelve miles an hour, by the canal at only four ; that the rail-
road possessed as much advantage over the canal as the canal
did over the turnpike ; that the cost of carriage would be cut down
to one-third. All this he denied. The Manchester and Irwell Canal
was only forty-two miles long, and was being shortened to thirty-
nine. The time occupied in carriage was twelve hours, and could
be reduced to nine or ten. A late formal experiment, with the
best locomotive engine they could find, showed an average rate
of under three and three-quarter miles per hour on the plane, and
four and a half on an incline. A superintendent of a canal and of
a railway had assured him that " a more extraordinary delusion
never was known than that of supposing that a railroad was superior
to a canal ; he wondered that such an assertion could be made "
—and, besides, the expenses of repair of rail and canal were as
six to four. An eminent surveyor he had met by chance was of
opinion that a railway " could not enter into successful competition
with a canal : even with the best loco-motion engine, the average
rate would be but three and a half miles per hour, which was slower
than the canal conveyance." If the canals had an ample supply
of water, they would be perfectly competent to convey, with sufficient speed, all the merchandise that passed between Manchester
and Liverpool.

Finally, a member summed up that the assertions advanced on
one side were as much to be relied on as those on the other, and
that he would vote for the second reading in order that the truth

of these assertions should be investigated before a committee of the House, and the Bill was read.[1] In committee, however, the opponents had a clear majority, and the Bill was withdrawn— "this devil of a railway is strangled at last," writes Creevey.[2] One notes with strange feelings that the strongest speech in favour of the new railway was delivered by the great man who was to lose his life at its opening, William Huskisson.

The corresponding advance in navigation is seen in the sailing of the "Enterprise," a steam vessel of 500 tons, carrying 300 tons of coal, but making use of sails as well—the first steamship to make the passage to India. Great interest was taken in the new departure. She expected to make the passage in eleven weeks, or at the rate of nearly 200 miles a day, instead of the usual seventeen or eighteen weeks, and, if successful, it was said, was to receive a premium of £10,000 from the Government. By the end of the year, however, word came home that she had taken eight weeks to reach the Cape—the usual time of a quick-sailing ship.[3] One notes that, before starting, the crew struck, refusing to do "unusual or extra duty," and were promptly replaced by a new set of men. In June, there appears intimation of a Joint Stock Company being established "for a constant and regular communication of steam vessels between Europe and America," Lord Lansdowne being president. *[margin: The "Enterprise."]*

In May, Wallace, the Master of the Mint, succeeded in removing what he called one of the most important distinctions remaining between Great Britain and Ireland, by moving a set of Resolutions for assimilating the currency of the two countries. The Irish pound and the Irish shilling, which were merely imaginary monies, were abolished, and, in every subsisting contract, £100 British was to be received as equal to £108 6s. 8d., all new contracts to have reference to British currency only. The inconvenience of the existing *[margin: Irish currency assimilated.]*

---

[1] *Hansard*, xii. 845.

[2] Creevey, who was a member of the committee, and acted openly in the interests of Lords Derby and Sefton, speaks of "this infernal nuisance—the loco-motive monster, carrying 80 tons of goods and navigated by a tail of smoke and sulphur, coming through every man's grounds between Manchester and Liverpool," and could see nothing on the other side but interested shareholders, lying promoters, and perfidious Whigs affecting conscientious scruples.

[3] *European Magazine*, 366. This result, however, was not considered a failure. She had to economise her coal, and actually steamed for thirty-five days only. Commenting on the attempt, the *Annual Register* said: "Were the Isthmus of Suez cut, the distance from England to Calcutta would be reduced to 8,600 miles, and the voyage might undoubtedly be shortened by 36 to 40 days" (*Chron.* 171).

system was fully recognised ; there was no opposition ; and the Act appears as c. 79 of the year. It is interesting to find that, in the succeeding year, the workers in the different trades of Dublin struck, demanding " payment of their wages in English money " —that is to say, practically, a rise of 1/8 on every 20/- wage.[1]

Early closing.
What is probably the first emergence of the Early Closing Movement appears in an intimation that, in August, a meeting of shopkeepers, called at the London Coffee House, agreed to shut at 7 p.m. from November to February, at 8 p.m. in March, April, September, and October, at 9 p.m. from May to August inclusive, and half an hour later on Saturdays, with the object of " allowing shopmen, etc., more ease and relaxation." But, at a meeting of linen-drapers in September, the general feeling of the trade was against the proposal, and it was agreed to shut at 8 p.m. from 1st September onwards, and at 9 in summer.[2]

Foreign affairs.
Except for the ratification of commercial treaties with Denmark and Hanover, Columbia and Mexico, there is little of interest to us in the foreign affairs of the year beyond the full recognition of the new states in the other hemisphere. " His Majesty has taken measures," said the King's Speech in February, " for confirming by treaties the commercial relations already subsisting between this kingdom and those countries of America which appear to have established their separation from Spain." " We find them independent," said the mover of the Address : " indeed, the independence of Old Spain is much more questionable than that of her colonies. . . . In Mexico, the domestic government is sustained by a domestic force ; no man dare hold up a finger against it ; if he does, he mounts the scaffold the next day. But Spain is garrisoned by 20,000 Frenchmen." In this year, also, the independence of Hayti was recognised by France, and that of Brazil by Portugal. All the same, there was much excitement over the general recognition, and opinion was by no means unanimous regarding its wisdom.

London Bridge and London University.
Among the events of the year, may be noted the laying of the first stone of London Bridge on 15th June, and the foundation of London University, suggested by Campbell the poet, and championed all through by Brougham and Hume.

Economic literature.
The following appear among economic publications of the year : The Principles of Political Economy, by J. R. M'Culloch ; A

---

[1] Hansard, xiii. 573 ; Dublin Evening Post, July 25, 1826.
[2] European Magazine, August and October.

Critical Dissertation on the Natural Measure and Causes of Value, by Samuel Bailey—" he does not appear to have properly appreciated the Ricardian theory of value, or to have succeeded in any degree in shaking its foundations," says M'Culloch ; *Principles of Political Economy and Population, including an examination of Malthus' Essay,* by John M'Inison.

MISCELLANEA.

In March, Hume submitted a Resolution that no Member should vote for or against any question in which he had a direct pecuniary interest. He was aware that it had been provided that no Member should vote in favour of a measure in the passing of which he had this interest, but there had never been an order that Members similarly interested in opposing a Bill should also be disqualified. It was admitted that the principle was clear enough, but it was urged by speaker after speaker that the difficulties of carrying it out were insuperable, and the motion was negatived without a division (*Hansard,* xii. 973).

Much was heard in Parliament of a project of a Thames Embankment— " a Quay and Terrace Carriage Road on the northern shore, from Craven Street in the Strand at Westminster to Blackfriars Bridge." The justification of it was the choking up of the main artery by traffic. Nothing which he had ever heard of the confusion after the Battle of Leipsic, said Lord Palmerston, where men, horses, and carriages were mingled together, could have equalled the confusion daily to be witnessed in the city. Crabb Robinson describes a panorama of the Embankment exhibited at Covent Garden—" a pleasing anticipation of a splendid dream, which not even in this projecting age could become a reality."

CHAPTER XXX

1826. THE AFTERMATH

Frightful rumours.

THE financial panic was over early in January. After a slight pause, came an unprecedented number of bankruptcies. In February, the distress seemed to return with double force, and, for some weeks, the failures of mercantile houses were many and alarming. The fall of the eminent firm of Goldschmidt particularly—the senior partner died of a " broken heart "—affected public opinion heavily. " There is now no panic," writes Greville, on 12th February, " but the greatest alarm, and every prospect of great distress and long continuation of it. The state of the city, and the terror of all the bankers and merchants, as well as of all owners of property, is not to be conceived but by those who witnessed it." Towards the end of February, " frightful rumours were in circulation " about houses of the highest respectability, and the funds fell over six points. Within five or six weeks, from sixty to seventy banking establishments stopped payment.

What will Government do?

When Parliament met on 2nd February, public opinion was greatly agitated as to what the Government would do, some large measure of relief being generally expected. For this reason the subject of the distress occupies both the first and the final place in the King's Speech. " His Majesty has seen with regret the embarrassment which has occurred in the pecuniary transactions of the country since the close of the last session of Parliament. . . . Some of the causes to which this evil must be attributed lie without the reach of direct parliamentary interposition ; nor can security against the recurrence of them be found unless in the experience of the sufferings which they have occasioned. But, to a certain portion of this evil, correctives at least, if not effectual remedies, may be applied ; and His Majesty relies upon your wisdom to devise such measures as may tend to protect both private and public interests against the like sudden and violent fluctuations, by placing on a more firm foundation the Currency and circulating Credit of the country. . . . His Majesty deeply laments the injurious effects which the late pecuniary crisis must have entailed upon many branches of the commerce and manufactures of the United Kingdom. But His Majesty confidently believes that the temporary check which commerce and manufactures may at this moment experience, will, under the blessing of Divine Providence, neither impair the great sources of our wealth nor impede the growth of national prosperity."

Naturally enough, when it was found that the only measure to be taken was to regulate the country bank paper, there was much dissatisfaction. Sound banking, however prudent as a means of prevention, could not be conceived as any remedy for existing distress. Many views were expressed [1] as to the causes of the crisis, " the most disastrous and most horrible perhaps in our commercial annals," as Canning called it—" one of the most tremendous and searching convulsions ever experienced in any country," added Lansdowne, with this peculiarity that it had happened in a time of profound peace.[2] All were agreed as to the leading feature of the disaster : it was the " general spirit of mad speculation " which had taken possession of the country. There was almost as much agreement as to what had caused the emergence of this spirit : peace and prosperity had caused a " redundancy of capital "— one notes the common use of " redundancy," " surplus," " glut," without any thought as to what they meant or whether they meant anything but abundance—this redundancy depressed the rate of interest, and capitalists, discontented with the small return, threw themselves into projects that promised more.[3] Lansdowne

---

[1] *Hansard*, xiv. 3, 22, 91.

[2] Comparison was naturally suggested with the crisis of 1793, when manufactures were rapidly advancing and interest was very low ; when also there was over-trading, over-issue by the country banks, and stoppage of nearly a hundred banks. But then there was the well-grounded apprehension that we should be involved in a great war : as Robinson said, " the revulsion was occasioned by extraneous causes, and not by the extravagant speculations of individuals " (*ibid.* xiv. 944).

[3] It might be noted, however, that " over-speculation " and " over-trading " were generally spoken of as if they were synonymous. Tierney rather aptly asked what " over-trading " meant. When a man did not succeed, he was nicknamed an over-trader—it reminded him of the old distich about treason :

> " Treason does never prosper—what's the reason ?
> Why, when it prospers, 'tis no longer treason."

So, when success followed the speculator, he became the sagacious and adventurous British merchant ! (*ibid.* 551).

succinctly summed it up thus : " the accumulation of capital caused a reduction of the rate of interest ; by a reduction in the rate of interest, facilities were afforded for speculation ; speculation produced an effect upon prices ; the alteration in prices checked the progress of mercantile exports, and that caused the precious metals to be sent out of the country. Then ensued that lamentable distress which arose from an accumulation of stock purchased at high prices being obliged to be sold at greatly reduced prices under the influence of alarm." But, from all the debates, the only remedy for the existing and urgent distress which suggested itself was a recourse to the old remedy for " scarcity of money "—an issue of Exchequer Bills.

Exchequer Bills proposal.

On the presentation of a petition from the Merchants of London praying for relief in this manner, it became evident that there was a very strong body of feeling both in the city and in Parliament in favour of such a course. The arguments used were :

(1) and chief, that, in 1793, the success of such a measure was immediate and complete. The Government then was ready to issue up to £5 millions, but a little over £2 millions was found sufficient. Nearly £3¾ millions were applied for, but, " the moment it was known that the Government had authorised an issue of Exchequer Bills, assistance was easily procured in various quarters " ;

(2) that this remedy could be applied at once, while the want of confidence and the contagion of distress were spreading every hour ;

(3) that the Government had been greatly instrumental in causing the distress, as their conversion scheme and the reduction of the interest on Exchequer Bills had driven investors to seek for a better return in foreign countries, while their free trade policy had diverted exports to India and South America, where returns were not to be had for twelve, eighteen, or twenty-four months ;

(4) that it was beside the mark to speak of " creating a precedent " for government assistance in all times of distress, seeing that this calamity was unexampled and universal ;

(5) that the relief would not be given to the speculators who had caused it—they no longer existed—but to men of respectability, honour, and integrity, who had unfortunately become the sufferers from the operations of others.

The proposal had the strong support of Baring, chiefly on the ground that, " if all the cases of distress that had ever, in any former time, occurred in this country, were to be summed together, they would fall far short of equalling the mass of distress and suffering which at present oppressed the nation," and that, all the same, the only thing wanted was to restore confidence. And, indeed, if Ministers had not previously asserted their intention of non-interference so strongly as almost to pledge themselves, it is more than likely that they would have given way before the feeling expressed. As it was, although deserted by some of their firmest adherents, they stood firm, and Liverpool threatened resignation rather than yield. The case of 1793, they said, was not parallel : then, everything was thrown out of gear by the entirely unexpected outbreak of war, " when those engaged in commerce could have had no foresight of the events which were to plunge them in distress," whereas, now, the cause was rash and excessive speculation against which the Government should not insure the speculators.

But, said Canning, in our opinion there is but one proper remedy for the distress ; I say plainly and openly but one ; and that is the exercise of the power vested by charter in the Bank to make advances upon the security of property or merchandise to those who may require it.[1] This met with very strong opposition. It was a new system, said Lansdowne, and by far the most objectionable method of relief possible. It would lock up the Bank's funds in an unavailable form, but, worse, it would destroy the mechanism by which the issues should be regulated, the foreign exchanges : thus, for a temporary purpose, the permanent system by which the Bank got back its resources every two months, would be thrown out of gear. Consider what would happen if, after a deficiency of circulation, followed by a great and sudden increase due to advances on goods, the state of the foreign exchanges made it necessary to contract the issues—the burden would fall entirely on persons in trade who relied on the discount of their bills. In 1793, Pitt and Lord Melville had opposed it on these very grounds. Personally, he very much preferred an issue of Exchequer Bills, as they would serve to restore the confidence which was wanted, and would make no addition to the currency.

Liverpool replied that he entirely agreed with Lansdowne, and then went on to show that he did not. The Eank, he said, had already the legal power of right to advance money upon goods, and, in the exceptional circumstances, when relief seemed called for, it was advisable that the Bank, and not the Government, should give it. All the objections which could be made to advances

The Bank to advance on goods.

[1] *Hansard*, xiv. 698.

against goods applied with tenfold force to any attempt to give relief by an issue of Exchequer Bills. Unless the Bank cashed them, there could be no relief ; if it did, it was landed with a security much less available than goods, seeing that the advances would be made for a period of two or three months only. Lansdowne retorted that this was all founded on the assumption that goods unsaleable now would be saleable in two or three months. Liverpool's reply was : (1) that the money advanced would be but a portion of the value of the goods pledged ; and (2) that it was a general opinion that a short period of delay would be of the greatest advantage, as, while there was no want of money in the country, the money was locked up in consequence of the panic.

It is a little difficult to come to a conclusion whether the Government were really convinced that they were right, or whether they considered, primarily, that they were bound by Lord Liverpool's pledge, and, subsequently, thought that vacillation was worse than anything else. The argument consistently advanced by them was that of precedent—sometimes that there was no real precedent, sometimes that any precedent there was was bad, sometimes, again, that this would make a precedent into an expectation. At any rate, if they had wanted a good excuse to give in at the last moment, they certainly had it in the strong expression of opinion on all sides.[1]

Confidence restored. Reluctantly, and only after some pressure, the Bank agreed to make advances to private individuals on the deposit of goods, merchandise, and other securities, up to a limit of £3 millions. From that moment, confidence did begin to return. As a fact, the sums applied for fell far short of the limit.[2] We have it on the authority of Tooke that, by the end of the year, trade and manufacture had resumed their normal course, and that hardly any trace remained of their having been disturbed in their progress.[3]

[1] Croker wrote a very full account of what he thought " the most ridiculous political intrigue he ever saw," to Wellington, who was on the Continent (*Correspondence*, i. 314).

[2] The method adopted was to apportion the total, and appoint Commissioners in the chief provincial towns—generally mercantile persons belonging to the place. Thus I find that the sum allocated to Glasgow was £400,000, to be lent upon goods or unexceptionable personal security. It was announced later that the total amount advanced to the whole kingdom was less than £400,000, Manchester taking £115,000, and Glasgow only £81,000.

[3] *History of Prices*, ii. 170. Tooke, however, was of opinion that the measure adopted had not been called for ; the kind of confidence most required, namely, confidence on the part of the buyers that prices were no longer upheld by

All the same, the suffering to individuals was very great. The South American loans entailed a loss of nearly the whole of the sums subscribed ; there were no dividends except some small sums paid as such out of the capital subscribed. The Mexican and South American mining subscriptions, with one or two exceptions, resulted in a total loss of the capital paid. Of the other schemes, a large proportion was abandoned at the sacrifice of the greater part, if not the whole, of the deposits and first payments.[1]

Loss on loans and mines.

In the manufacturing world, the distress was marked not so much by failures as by stagnation. It was impossible, of course, that a commercial and banking crisis should not get through almost immediately to the industrial organisations and the working classes. The merchant depends very greatly on the banker, and the manufacturer, in most cases, depends upon the merchant. If the merchant is in distress, his first thought is to risk nothing further, and he will not enter into new buying contracts till his financial future is again reasonably safe. But by this time the manufacturer, in many cases, had become independent of the buying merchant. Up till 1819 or so, most goods for export were sold to mercantile houses at home. I do not know how it was in England, but, from the traditions of my own firm, I know that the practice by manufacturers of " consigning " goods abroad, on their own account and risk, had been largely adopted in the West of Scotland by the year 1825. The attraction of " getting rid of the middleman " blinded them to the danger they ran in the locking up of their capital. I have no difficulty, then, in accepting the statement in the *Glasgow Herald* of 3rd February that fully three-fourths of the cotton manufactures of that city had been exported by the manufacturers.[2] The procedure was that the Scots banks made advances

Manufacturing stagnation.

" Consigning."

---

undue credit, had been already restored, and credit was improving and distress abating before the plan was adopted.

[1] Tooke, *History of Prices*, ii. 159. It was not only mining companies that had been projected. Captain Head tells how he found, at Buenos Ayres, a number of Scotch milkmaids, sent out by a churning company. When they had overcome the preliminary difficulty of getting to work on " a set of lawless wild creatures, who looked so fierce that no young woman who ever sat upon a three-legged stool would dare to approach, much less to milk them," and " the shops in Buenos Ayres were literally full of butter," it was discovered that the guachos and natives preferred oil ! (*Rough Notes*).

[2] I find in the same paper, in 1823, a remark that the " recent practice of our manufacturers exporting goods to foreign markets on their own account, and obtaining advances on the goods from the commission merchants to whom they consign them, seems likely to lead to over-production " and greater vicissitudes in trade. In Moore's *Journal* of 14th December, 1825, appears the following :

of one-half to two-thirds of the value, sometimes on short-dated bills accepted by the home representatives of the foreign firms, more often on acceptances at long dates. The temptation to the banks to give such accommodation was the immense sums now deposited with them, for which they had difficulty in finding employment. When the panic set in, and the banks declined to discount bills having more than four months to run, such advances were checked.

In these cases, the universal experience was that, in the optimism of good times, the manufacturers had at least fully supplied their markets. The amount of goods shipped to South American states, when the condition of these states was still anything but settled, is amazing. As early as 1823, for instance, one reads of 300,000 yards of printed calico being shipped to Lima in one week of May, before Great Britain had either acknowledged the new Government or entered into any commercial treaty ; of a merchant in June making a claim for the seizure of a cargo worth £40,000 sent to the same port. If such manufacturers had strained their resources, and discounted on expectations of sale, all they could do was to wait on the sales from abroad before they could get the means of going on ; they could no longer count on discounting in the same easy way as when there was no shadow on the commercial horizon. Hence they curtailed their production as much as possible, and the distress immediately got through to the working classes. This, I imagine, is the explanation of the expression " over-trading " so commonly used.[1] In times of great confidence, manufacturers risk their own capital on far-away journeys, and, besides, they are likely to use as much capital of other people as they can get hold of through banking credit—not themselves realising, probably, how deeply they are trading beyond their depth till the banking facilities are withdrawn. And it is to be suspected that they often speak of a

" Took in a gentleman as far as Oswestry, who proved to be a merchant of some kind at Liverpool ; some interesting conversation on commercial matters ; mentioned the great change that had taken place of late years from the manufacturers exporting for themselves without the intervention of merchants as formerly ; the latter class, accordingly, quite extinct, and the business managed entirely between the manufacturers and their commercial agents abroad. All this done from greediness of profit, and their present sufferings (from bad remittances and the fall of cotton) little, he thought, to be pitied."

[1] " Over-trading," as applied to bankers, is clear enough ; it means overissues of paper, rash discounting, advancing on securities inadequate or not easily realisable, etc. But the expression, when applied to ordinary commerce and manufacture, needs analysis.

" scarcity of circulation " when they only mean that they cannot get the usual credit on which they have been counting to pay their current wages.

As regards the working classes, much credit was given to them in Parliament for their exemplary patience and fortitude. But it is open to doubt if their distress merited the epithet "unparalleled." The seconder of the Address in the Lords congratulated his peers that the agricultural interest had met with no material check by the recent difficulties, and, even as regards manufactures, it was often asserted that the distress was by no means universal. It is easy, in any time of bad trade, to collect enough accounts of unemployment and trade disturbances to make an imposing total and a readable chapter. Those who wished to prove that the " people were starving " have never wanted for evidence in bulk. But when one collects from the periodical press all the instances thought worth recording, it does not seem to prove that the working classes were suffering from the effect of the late crisis so much as might have been expected. The working classes.

In January and February, there were riots at Norwich among the weavers, on suspicion of work being sent outside of the town, when the military were called in—" nearly every kind of business is at a standstill." In Paisley, there were meetings " to take measures for supplying the unemployed classes with the means of subsistence." In April, such unemployed weavers in Glasgow as had been resident there for twelve months, were being set to relief works of breaking stones, quarrying, and digging. In May, we read of 40,000 persons in Manchester receiving pecuniary assistance ; of riots and attacks on the factories at Bradford put down by the military ; of great distress in Dublin. On a suspicion of " forestalling and monopolising potatoes " at Trowbridge, all the gardeners of the neighbourhood were attacked and plundered, and here also the soldiers were called in. In this month, a great meeting was convened at the London Tavern by the Lord Mayor, where a subscription was opened which soon ran up to £100,000 ; the amount was raised " mainly in the agricultural districts," and the King himself contributed £2,000 in addition to £5,000 given previously ; a letter by His Majesty was read in all the churches asking a collection for the distressed manufacturers. In July, there were strikes and riots among the colliers at Dudley. No trade, we are told, was suffering more than that of printing—in Edinburgh, only one-third of the work doing—in London, " absolutely at a standstill." [1]   In Oldham, in October, there were riots and disturbances for some weeks over reduction of wages.

Loom breaking.

But in the above list, I have omitted the events which drew everybody's attention in the month of April. In Blackburn, Accrington, Preston, Clitheroe, Rochdale, Manchester, and other places—as consequence, said some, of the rejection of Whitmore's motion on the Corn Laws—the weavers broke into tumultuous rioting, destroying all the power-looms within reach, but, it was noted, refrained from touching the spinning frames or injuring any other property. The extent of the destruction appears from the fact that, in August, twenty-three actions were raised against various hundreds in Lancashire, claiming compensation for the destruction of over a thousand power-looms, and that more than £16,000 was actually recovered.

The hand-loom weavers.

This, and the frequent mention of the weavers as the chief sufferers in Glasgow, Paisley, and elsewhere, make one suspect that much of the distress of the year was not due to the late crisis at all, but was the coming to expression of the inevitable struggle between machinery and hand-weaving. According to Baines, in 1823 a very good hand-weaver, twenty-five or thirty years of age, would weave two pieces of nine-eighths shirting per week, while a power-loom weaver, about fifteen, tending two looms, would weave seven similar pieces. But, by 1826, the power-loom weaver was tending four looms, and turning out twelve to fifteen similar pieces. It was a common calculation that the steam-loom did as much as three hand-looms. When it is considered that the selling price of calicoes had fallen from 15/8¾ in 1821 to 10/6 in 1827, the distress of the hand weaver needs no further elucidation. The weaving of fine cloths and fancy goods was left to the hand-looms, but the market for the sale of such was a limited and fluctuating one. The great increase in power-looms in England took place between 1824 and 1825, and it was complained that they had not been introduced extensively enough to meet all the demand. And yet, says Porter, " the hand-looms employed in the cotton manufacture are believed not to have diminished between 1820 and 1834, but rather to have increased." The hardship was not so much noticed in the years of the great speculation. But

[1] On 21st January, Constable became bankrupt, and Scott, at the age of 55, set himself to redeeming debts exceeding £100,000. " Even the last Waverley novel was hawked about for a purchaser, when, two years ago, a general skirmish would have ensued among the booksellers to obtain the copyright."

when demand was checked, and the first thought was how to reduce costs of production, it was inevitable that the contrast between the hand-loom and " those engines of stupendous power called power-looms " should be emphasised.

It was natural enough, too, that the nature of this distress should not be fully appreciated at the time as it is now. Bennett, for instance, spoke of the destruction of the power-looms as a case of the workers destroying their own means of living—" a course about as rational as that of the Irish rebels who had burned the bank notes wherever they found them in order to injure the bankers by whom they had been issued." But the bitterness of the situation was that the skill acquired in using the hand-loom was not skill that could be transferred to the steam-loom—and, moreover, was it not the case that the power-loom could be worked by women ?

The probability of this explanation is shown in the mention which, otherwise, seems contradictory, that, as early as March, at Leeds, Halifax, Manchester itself, things were looking brighter ; that, at Liverpool, the demand for colonial produce " continued steady " ; that, at Glasgow, " commercial improvement " began to be spoken of instead of " commercial depression." In June, round about Manchester, there was " a lively demand in the cotton market," and distress seemed be passing away. Finally, in October, it was confidently said that, in the woollen trade of Yorkshire, the tide had fairly turned ; that, in the Macclesfield silk mills, a thousand more hands were at work than three months before ; and that the cotton mills were working full time, under a great demand for calicoes, " especially those produced by the steam loom." " Competition must be crushed," said the *Glasgow Herald*, " for no manufacturer could compete with the British on the terms at which he is now offering the labours of his countrymen, coupled with the unprecedented prices of cotton." [1]

---

[1] *European Magazine*, 647 ; *Gentleman's Magazine*, 66, 362, 547 ; *Hansard*, xvi. 56. It was noted, in July, that serious disturbances, " closely resembling the nature of the late broils in our manufacturing districts," had taken place in several cities in the south of France, from Bordeaux to Marseilles. The French Chamber of Commerce drew a deplorable picture of the state of trade and manufactures, ascribing the evil to want of confidence among capitalists. In December, it was no better—" in Lyons and other manufacturing towns, the artizans are in quite as bad a condition as those of Lancashire." It either indicates the difference in point of view, or the absence of information about a country so close at hand, that Hume, in November, could say : " Look at France ; she is prosperous and happy ; every man there has enough, while,

Emigration.   I find a final confirmation of this view in the new appeal for emigration. Before this time, emigration had been urged, and opposed, as a remedy for *agricultural* distress, particularly from Ireland, and a Committee was at the moment considering the subject. But, so far as I know, Government had never until now been asked for aid to send the hand-loom weavers to the colonies. In December, there came petitions from the weavers of Glasgow and Lanarkshire, saying that many of them were without any employment at all, and that most of them had worked for fourteen or sixteen hours a day, and were earning only six shillings, five shillings, some of them as little as four and sixpence a week. Lord Archibald Hamilton, who presented the petition, said that he knew this to be the fact. The petitions did not ask for charity. It spoke volumes for their sufferings that all they asked was—exile, the means of emigrating. In presenting another, Sir James Graham gave an account of the distress in the place for which he sat. In Carlisle, hand-loom weavers were making no more than 5/- a week for fourteen hours of labour, most of them a year in arrear of rent and liable to be evicted. Perhaps, he said, the chief cause of their distress was beyond the reach of parliamentary interposition ; it was the improvements which had recently been made in the power-looms ; the hand-weavers could not be converted into power-loom weavers, and were thus compelled to continue a hopeless struggle with the power-loom at a rate of wages which was regularly decreasing.[1]

Foreign trade.   The statistics of foreign trade seem to prove that commerce was comparatively little affected. True, both imports and exports were over £6 millions less than in 1825. But the imports were greater than in 1824, and, if the British exports fell much under those of the years since 1822, they exceeded the figures of 1821. And the re-exports were actually a million above those of 1825. The Official values were :

Imports - - - - - - - -	£37,813,890
Exports of British produce and merchandise -	40,965,736
Exports of Foreign and Colonial merchandise -	10,076,287
The Real value of the British exports was -	31,536,723

in England, scarcely any of the labouring classes has more than the bare means of subsistence." It is significant that the *Gentleman's*, in December, notes that, in Philadelphia, power-loom weavers could not be procured in sufficient numbers.

[1] *Hansard*, xvi. 227, 298.

The number of vessels built and registered in the several ports of the United Kingdom was 1,115, representing 118,363 tons. Of these, 72 were steam vessels, representing 8,638 tons (as against 24 and 3,000 respectively in 1825).

CHAPTER XXXI

1826. THE END OF THE ONE-POUND NOTES

As we have seen, the absence from the King's Speech of any pro-posal for meeting the existing distress was severely commented on. We shall find a good deal to explain the subsequent proceedings, if we notice that, before Parliament met, the Government had formed and formulated its view of the distress, of its main causes, and of the few remedies which might be applied. On 13th January, *Government's communication to the Bank.* Liverpool and Robinson signed a communication—usually credited to Huskisson—sent to the Bank of England. It begins thus :

"The panic in the money market having subsided, and the pecuniary transactions of the country having reverted to their accustomed course, it becomes important to lose no time in considering whether any measures can be adopted to prevent the recurrence in future of such evils as we have recently experienced.

"However much the recent distress may have been aggravated, in the judgment of some, by incidental circumstances and particular measures, there can be no doubt that the principal source of it is to be found in the rash spirit of speculation which has pervaded the country for some time, supported, fostered, and encouraged by the country banks.

"The remedy, therefore, for this evil in future must be found in an improvement in the circulation of country paper ; and the first measure which has suggested itself, to most of those who have considered the subject, is a recurrence to gold circulation throughout the country, as well as in the metropolis and its neighbourhood, by a repeal of the Act which permits country banks to issue one and two pound notes until the year 1833 ; and by the immediate enact-ment of a prohibition of any such issues at the expiration of two or three years from the present time.

" It appears to us to be quite clear that such a measure would be productive of much good ; that it would operate as some check upon the spirit of speculation and upon the issues of country banks ; and whilst, on the one hand, it would diminish the pressure upon the Bank and the metropolis, incident to an unfavourable state of the exchanges, by spreading it over a wider surface ; on the other hand, it would cause such pressure to be earlier felt, and thereby ensure an earlier and more general adoption of precautionary measures necessary for counterbalancing the inconveniences incidental to an export of the precious metals. But, though a recurrence to a gold circulation in the country, for the reasons already stated, might be productive of some good, it would by no means go to the root of the evil."

The communication then goes on to say, basing the argument on the convulsion of 1793 when there were no small notes, and on the fact that Scotland had for thirty-five years escaped all the convulsions which had occurred in the money market of England, although all that time it had nothing but one-pound notes, that the issue of small notes, though it were an aggravation, could not be the sole or even the main cause ; there must be something unsound in the banking system, and this led to the question of establishing a sound system of · banking throughout the country adequate to the progress of the nation during the past thirty or forty years. From all this, it might be suspected that, when the experience and debating power of Parliament were brought to bear on the subject, the Government had already taken up a position from which it was, perhaps, more than could be expected of human nature that it would resile, namely, that the principal source of the late disaster was the rash speculation, and that this had been " supported, fostered, and encouraged by the country banks," in the issue of small notes.[1] *The Government position.*

The Government plan was sketched out, after the reading of the Speech : the one and two pound notes were to be gradually withdrawn from circulation and their place taken by gold, and the exclusive privileges of the Bank of England were to be revised. *Withdrawal of the notes.*

In the debates on the Speech, as we have seen, there was agreement that mad speculation, made possible by " redundancy of capital," was to blame for the crisis. And there was still agree- *Effect of the notes on speculation.*

[1] The small notes, it might be noted, were introduced by the Bank of England under the Restriction Act in 1797. The £5 notes had been introduced only in 1794 ; before that date, nothing under £10 was issued.

ment thus far—that the banks had a great deal to do with making the speculation possible. But, beyond this point, opinions were very divergent. Some blamed the over-issue of notes generally ; others, the over-issue' of the country banks alone. Liverpool considered the latter cause so prominent, and so great in magnitude, as to account for all that had happened ; the number of notes stamped had risen from an average of four millions in 1821, 1822, and 1823, to six millions in 1824, and to over eight millions in 1825.[1] Against this, it was pointed out that the Bank of England also had increased its issues, from £17½ millions in April, 1823, to £19 millions in 1824, and to over £20 millions in the spring of 1825. Lauderdale and Hume, almost alone, denied that the crisis was due to the currency. In the course of the past year, said Lauderdale, there had been " a demand on the capital and labour of this country to the extent of £17 millions." The country was not capable of answering that demand. They had better analyse the numbers and qualities of the steam, and mining, and other joint-stock companies recently formed, and the quantity of capital sunk in them. It was a farce, insisted Hume, to say that the misery we had been experiencing was attributable to the country banks ; the true causes were the pressure of taxation and the wasteful expenditure of the public money. .

Very few, it may be noted, except Lauderdale, enquired what was meant by an excess of paper—as if paper might not expand at one time and contract at another, with the change in the level of prices and the amount of transactions for which it was required, or asked, like Hume, how there could be over-issue when notes were convertible and had always been converted into gold. But Lauderdale generally spoiled any case by coupling it with the advocacy of something else in which, rightly or wrongly, he was thought a crank, and, on this occasion, he said roundly that the cause of disaster was the Sinking Fund, and went on to preach a silver standard.[2] And Hume, of course, came from that strange country

---

[1] Tooke, however, calculated the increase between 1822 and 1825 at 50 per cent. only (*On the State of the Currency*, p. 39). But considering that, in 1824-5, the Bank of England had called in their small notes, amounting to about £7 millions, there was surely room for a considerable extension of the country bank issue among people who had got into the habit of using small notes.

[2] *Hansard*, xiv. 466. Robertson, member for Grampound, an unwearied opponent of the reciprocity treaties and of free trade in all forms, had a theory of his own regarding the distress : it is interesting as showing the views still held of the Balance of Trade. He considered the existing embarrass-

where there was no gold, where one-pound notes were the small
change, and where banks never failed.

The conviction that small notes were bad things which should What had the notes to do with the disaster?
never have been allowed, and that country bankers could not have
encouraged over-speculation in any other way, appears so strong
that one is afraid to hesitate a doubt ; but, so far as my judgment
goes, it was by no means clearly made out in the debates what
the one and two pound notes had to do with the disaster. They
did not circulate in London ; they did not circulate for miles round
Manchester ; and it was in these centres that the speculation raged
and there that the first failures occurred. What did encourage
and feed the speculative mania was the facility of getting discounts ;
if this was the evil, what did it matter in what form the discounts
were given ?—or did anyone ever contend that any speculator of
importance took his credit in small notes ? It is one thing to say
that the country banks had encouraged speculation, and that their
favourite issue was small notes ; it is quite another to say that
there is something peculiarly helpful to speculation in the small
notes. Even to-day, in Scotland, we seldom see anything but the
one-pound note, but, on the few occasions when Scots bankers
have " encouraged speculation," we never blamed it upon the
denomination of the note. " There has been over-speculation and
there have been small notes—hackney coaches are the cause of
rain, for there can be no doubt that rain often falls in places infested
with hackney coaches," said the *Globe*. So far as a connection
seems established, it was that, to the extent that small notes were
used, they had driven gold out of circulation, and, presumably,

ments as the unavoidable consequence of the now fashionable policy. The
excess of exports over imports since the peace amounted to £189 millions,
" from which no return had been made to this country to compensate the loss
thus induced." In the first year of the peace, the excess was £13 millions ;
last year it was £24 millions. " Could any country live and thrive under
this draining away and transfer of its resources ? " The House might ask
how the surplus wealth, thus indicated, was to be kept in the country. The
question was not difficult to answer. " Give such capital protection, and
then it would stay at home and create a real prosperity by bettering the
wages of labour and increasing the productive powers of the national industry."
Absolutely free trade would let in foreign commodities, press down home
manufactures by the competition, and draw capital in greater and greater
quantities abroad, to bring in the supplies of foreign industry. This doctrine
of free trade was the most vicious principle that had ever been adopted by
thinking men. As Robinson said, his argument was that the distress was due
to excessive exports, and yet his greatest dread was excessive imports ! On
a later occasion, Robertson asserted that, since the peace, capital to the amount
of £256 millions had gone out of the country, leaving, therefore, little more
than £70 millions to carry on its industry (*ibid.* 388).

made the country carry on its transactions with a smaller stock
of gold than would otherwise have been available—to which
the answer might be that such notes were a comparatively small
part of the circulation, and that the country was not suffering
from a shortness of gold, but from a sudden check to credit.[1]
But, once the Government had taken up the strong position it did,
there was a good deal to back it up in the misery evidently
entailed, by the failure of an issuing bank, on the poorer classes,
who, not only were practically compelled to accept small notes
in payment or go without, but had got into the habit of counting
them " as good as gold." He would ask, said Lansdowne, any of
their lordships, who had happened to be in a country town when
one of those failures had taken place, whether he could bring to
mind the scene of complicated misery and distress which he must
have witnessed, without feeling that it was incumbent on him to
do all in his power to prevent a recurrence of the most dreadful
calamity to which a community could be exposed.

From the discussions in Parliament, however, one would think
that the business of the country was still conducted by bank-notes.[2]
—seeing that they were only small change? Before banking was carried on by transfers and acquitment of
obligation made simply in bank books by the agency of the cheque,
there must, of course, have been a possibility of evil in notes which
does not now exist. But we know that, by this time, notes were
no more than small change. "Let anyone consider," said a correspondent of the *Glasgow Herald* on 17th March, " how many transactions take place between a banker and his customers which require
scarcely the use of a single note, either large or small. Bills are
discounted, the proceeds of which are paid by an order on London
to retire acceptances falling due there ; or London bills are handed

---

[1] Another explanation of the connection between small notes and speculation may be hazarded, although it was not put forward : namely, that the
country bankers were to blame by their eagerness to lend, and that their
having the monopoly of small notes gave them an advantage which made it
easier for them to lend. Large notes are bound to be constantly brought back
to the issuer in order to get small change, but small notes, wherever there is
confidence in them, may be out for long periods, and make the banker careless about having his securities in available forms.

[2] It is curious to hear that other countries had not yet got the length even
of the bank-note. Lowe, in 1822, noted that its use was hardly known on the
Continent. The Bank of France had branches in only a few of the provincial
towns, and " there was not a private bank of circulation in the whole country."
Holland had never yet adopted the note system, while, in Austria, Russia, and
Sweden, the paper was forced currency, not convertible (*On the Present State
of England*, p. 269).

over in exchange for the bill discounted. Loans to a large extent
are frequently transacted by a mere transfer from one name to
another, or a memorandum addressed to a neighbouring banker
may serve the purpose as well as if notes were used. Anyone
acquainted with the mode of doing business in Lancashire will
understand this at once."

The prevailing view was put most logically by Baring, whose Baring's view.
experience and recognised common-sense gave his opinion great
weight. He had no hesitation in attributing the disaster to the
extent to which the circulating paper money had been pushed
about eighteen months before. The Bank of England had been
the authors of the dangerous redundancy of money which started
the wild speculation ; the country banks had added to it, but much
more mischievously. For, while the Bank exercised a wise discretion in the quantity it put out, " the very business of a country
bank was to put out all the paper it could, and this, as every gentleman acquainted with country banks well knew, was their constant
practice. On market days, they employed persons to go out, and,
not only to put out as much paper of their own as they could, but
to withdraw from circulation all the paper of the Bank of England
and substitute for it their own. By these means, the country was
saturated with paper money, and that redundancy produced which
had been the parent of the existing distress." [1] Then came the
frantic speculation, which spread from London over the country
like an epidemic. " He did not mean to say that this was not far
beyond any such cause as the redundancy of money he had alluded
to ; but it was nevertheless true that this fictitious surplus was
the fuel by which the fire was fed. The greatest exertions were
made by everybody to get rid of their capital. The bankers in
London, their agents in the country, and the customers of both,
were actuated by the same universal desire to put out their money
in whatever way they could. Then, all on a sudden, the very
reverse of this system came into practice. A panic seized the

---

[1] Sir M. W. Ridley questioned this ; that the country bankers had been the
means of producing the commercial distress, he entirely denied. They had
no power of over-issue ; they were unable to raise a fictitious credit ; they
could not keep in circulation a single note longer than it was absolutely
necessary—being always obliged to pay in gold or Bank of England notes.
Lansdowne, on another occasion, showed one way in which the theoretical
convertibility was evaded : a bank made an arrangement with the paymaster of a regiment to pay in its notes, giving him a percentage according to
the distance from the place where the notes could be cashed ! (*Hansard,*
xv. 212).

public. Men would not part with their money on any terms, nor
for any security, and the consequence was general distress. . . .
Persons of undoubted wealth and real capital were seen walking
about the streets of London, not knowing whether they would be
able to meet their engagements for the next day. It was impossible
that anything could be more liberal or sensible than the conduct
of the Bank of England as this juncture ; but the causes lay too
deep to be removed by anything that the Bank of England could
do. Their assistance might, and, in a great measure, did relieve
the distress, but they could not cure it. The over-issue by the
country banks was the main cause by which the distress had been
so widely spread, and, as everybody in the country was deeply
concerned in this subject, the more this cause was investigated and
explained, the more it would be likely to be remedied." " I do
not charge the country banks," said Canning, " with having originated the spirit of speculation ; but I think it impossible to deny
that the country banks were the source whence this inordinate
speculation derived its aliment." " The small notes," said
Brougham on the same lines, " did not originate the over-trading
or originate the mischief ; but, when the mischief had arisen, it
was very materially aggravated by the small notes in circulation."

The motion.   The great discussion was entered on in earnest on 10th February,
when Robinson moved " that all Promissory Notes payable to
bearer on demand, issued by licensed bankers in England or by
the Bank of England, for any sum less than £5, bearing a date
previous to the 5th of February, 1826, or which may have been
stamped previously to that day, shall and may continue to be
issued, re-issued, and circulated, until the 5th day of April, 1829,
and no longer." [1] In all great commercial countries, he said,
where activity, enterprise, and speculation formed, as it were, the
very elements of existence, there must be great and sudden changes
—periods of long-continued prosperity and seasons of temporary
and trying adversity : all history proved this. And he went on
to argue, not very convincingly, that such fluctuations were more
likely to occur in a country where the circulation was partly metallic
and partly composed of paper convertible into metallic money—
" in this case there was a facility given, both to the borrower and

---

[1] Meantime; Government had taken the unusual step of prohibiting the
stamping of any more small notes, and this was loudly denounced, on its discovery, as unconstitutional. The defence offered was that, not only had intimation been given of the intention to bring in a Bill, but a day been fixed for
its introduction.

to the lender, the inevitable tendency of which was a quicker rise of prices, and, upon any reverse, a more precipitate downfall." But while such fluctuations were inevitable, they need not be aggravated, and one such aggravation was the small note. This note circulated principally among the poorer classes, and the consequence was that when, from over-speculation, or over-issues, or any other cause, an alarm or panic arose, the first person to press forward and secure his property was the poor man. " He hears of distress—he hears of failures—and is it not natural that he who has invested his little all—to him of an importance of which it would not be easy to form a conception—should be the first to press forward for the payment of his demands—the first to guard against consequences which would to him be absolute ruin." Example is contagious. Then came the holder of five or ten pound notes. He says to himself, " what is the meaning of this ? there must be something wrong here," and he followed the torrent, till the man who did not entertain the least doubt of the solidity of his banker became influenced by the contagion, and became unable to resist the temptation of grasping at that which further forbearance might endanger. This was the history of a great portion of the late disastrous events.[1] The power of issuing these notes, therefore, was one great source of the insecurity of country bankers, and, in their interest as well as the interests of all, it should be taken from them. The proposal to withdraw such notes was no novelty ; the evil of them had been long admitted ; and it was never intended that they should form part of the system after the resumption. The only apprehension worth thinking about was that the with-

---

[1] It may be that a Scotsman, accustomed to nothing else than one-pound notes, is not an impartial judge, but it is, I think, a little amusing to see English prejudice trying to justify itself at almost every debate by a new argument. This point—that the small note started the panic—is undoubtedly ingenious. Canning, however, always ready to take up a new idea, elaborated it finely in the words : " The larger notes, indeed, like the smaller, are so many promises to pay the equivalent in metal ; but it is in the one-pound notes that the promises are daily put to the test. When the labourer or mechanic presents a one-pound note, and finds that, instead of gold, nothing is to be had in exchange for it but another piece of paper like itself—what is the consequence ? A want of confidence grows up amongst the lower orders—through whom, and, from them, to their superiors that want of confidence spreads with increased rapidity—involving in it the destruction of commercial credit and depriving thereby the working classes of the present means of subsistence." And he ended his speech by a paraphrase of Henri Quatre's aspiration—that every man, at the end of his week's toil, should carry home, as the earnings of his week's toil, not a piece of, perhaps, worthless paper, but a portion of the precious metals in his pocket.

drawal might leave a gap in the circulation. But the small notes, which had been, say, £6 millions in 1825, were not likely to be more than £4 millions now, and that such a gap could be easily filled, within the three years allowed, was proved by the ease with which gold had been obtained for the resumption : there were probably £19 millions more gold in the country than in 1820, and now that the exchanges had become favourable, it was, in point of fact, profitable to import gold.

Baring's opposition.

Baring led the opposition. He did not agree with the Government that speculation was the root of the matter. He considered the distress as a banking crisis, brought on primarily by the Bank of England first using its great accumulation of gold improvidently then suddenly contracting its issues and curtailing its discounts— " a few days before no one knew what to do with his money : now no one knew where to get it." And then, its available resources choked up by advances to and agreements with Government, it could not come to the assistance of the people in the rising distress. He agreed that, as part of the permanent system, small notes should be called in, although he admitted that in many cases they were of great, almost indispensable, use in the country. " They had objected to the small notes of the Bank of England on account of the numbers which the forgery of them led to the gallows.[1] They ought now to object to the small notes of the provincial banks on account of the numbers whom they consigned to the poorhouse and to all the miseries of a living death." But he opposed the proposal on the ground that it was entirely inadequate at the moment. The distress was not at an end—the house was on fire, and they must get the people out. Confidence must be restored, and, for that, time must be given to encourage bankers not to press for their dues. The measure proposed would only add to the stringency.

Huskisson's support.

Huskisson, who was the real author of the finance measures, in replying, commented with some warmth on being taunted with insensibility to the sufferings of the people, and with saying that the distress had subsided—with applying milk and water as a remedy. What he had said was that " the panic in the money market had subsided." Was it now the case, as had been the case in the middle

---

[1] The forgery of Bank of England notes was so notorious, and the dread of them on that account so great, that, " if there was a country bank in the neighbourhood, of known stability, there was not a labourer who would not prefer taking its notes." Indeed, this was given as one proof that there was no likelihood of the Bank of England over-issuing small notes.

of December, that the best securities could not be converted into
money—that Exchequer Bills, Bank stock, East India stock, even
Consols were unsaleable ? " If the difficulties which existed in
the money market a short time since had continued for only eight
and forty hours longer, the effect would have been to put a stop
to all dealings between man and man except by means of barter."
That such a money-market panic must derange the ordinary transactions of commerce for a long time to come, he was as sensible as
any man.   The question—and the urgent question—was how to
guard against the recurrence of such a state of affairs.   He would
put it in a simple proposition.   " If there were in any country a
paper currency of the same denomination as coin, the paper and
the coin could not circulate together ; the paper would drive out
the gold.   Let crown notes be made and we should never see crown
pieces ; allow one-pound notes to circulate and we should never see
a sovereign." [1]   So it had happened practically ; the bankers over
the country had to face a sudden demand for gold when they had
none, and the seven or eight hundred country banks applied to the
Bank of England as their only reservoir.   Seven or eight hundred
drains were at once opened through her—gold was to flow from
her into the country.   Not only so, but the banks of Scotland and
of Ireland looked to her as their security.   Was it fair or just that
the Bank of England should be the means of protecting and securing
all these banks ? why should she insure all the other banks in the
country ?   The only question was, whether this was the proper
time for carrying the proposal into execution.   He maintained
that it was—as the proper time to deal with an intoxicated person
was when he was suffering from the effects of his intemperance.
The small notes, thanks to the panic, were already greatly curtailed,
and the country banks had a large stock of gold drawn from the
Bank of England.[2]   If they waited, the notes would be issued
again, and the same danger would be threatened.

In the long debate which followed, a great deal of time was taken The country
up by the vehement defence of the country banks :—they were the banks.

---

[1] Canning strikingly quoted from a letter written him by Burke on his death-
bed—the only letter he had ever received from that great man—" Tell Mr.
Pitt that, if he consents to the issue of one-pound notes, he will never see a
guinea again " (*Hansard*, xiv. 331).

[2] Besides, as Peel pointed out, some £17 millions, of the £25 millions
coined since 1819, remained in the country ; the probability was that a
good deal of these were in the coffers of country bankers, partly from a prudent
motive of precaution, partly because they chose rather to see their own notes
in circulation wherever they could accomplish it (*Hansard*, xiv. 297).

only persons who had not speculated—in fact, they had done all in their power to discourage their clients from speculating ; the disaster began with the failure of banks in London, and it was this that brought down the country banks, etc., etc. Almost the only new point brought forward germane to the subject was Peel and Canning's contention that, in one district (Lancashire, Manchester, and Liverpool) containing two million inhabitants,[1] and in another (London) containing other two millions—that is, in two busy districts which contained two-thirds of the entire wealth of the nation—there were no small notes : how, then, could it be said that the small note was necessary to the trade of the country ? But, from Huskisson's speech onward, it would be impossible to follow the debate briefly and logically. When the country banks, the Bank of England, the Government itself, were in turn attacked, it was natural that their friends should rally to their defence rather than speak to the motion, and inevitable that the debates should become an angry wrangle. Many members, for instance, were personally interested in the country banks ; conceiving that these banks were attacked, they had first to extract the acknowledgment that the bankers themselves were honourable men and that only the system was blamed ; then they had to establish, to their own satisfaction, the proposition that the small notes were not at any rate the main cause of the panic ; in doing so, they suggested that something or somebody else—say the Bank of England, or the Free Trade policy, or this or that—was more to blame ; and this, in turn, roused the indignation of other interests to defend themselves against the charge. And so the debate went on hour after hour, dragging in all sorts of subjects, none of them perhaps quite irrelevant, but hopelessly obscuring the main issue. Where one set of speakers thought the small notes indefensible, and another thought them right in theory but liable to too great abuse in practice, a third, wrong in theory but right in practice, and a fourth, considering them wrong either one way or the other, argued that " this was not the time " to abolish them, while bimetallists, paper money

---

[1] In Lancashire, there were no banks which issued paper, and, in all the manufacturing districts of the north of England, there were few. Almost the entire circulation consisted of bills of exchange passing from hand to hand like notes, covered with endorsements. A witness before the Lords' Committee said that he had seen bills to the value of £10, not with fifty or sixty names attached, but with double that number—" I have seen slips of paper attached to a bill as long as a sheet of paper could go ; and, when that failed, another attached to it."

advocates, free traders, protectionists, all saw a chance of ventilating their views, it might be expected that anything like a short abstract would be impossible. Enough to say that the immense amount of talent in the House of Commons was never better shown than in these debates. One is amazed to find how many people spoke with confidence and decision on such a difficult subject as the currency, and more amazed, perhaps, to find how well they spoke on it. As to the public outside, Greville wrote ; " so great and absorbing is the interest which the present discussions excite, that all men are become political economists and financiers, and every-body is obliged to have an opinion." " I have tried to understand this great question," wrote Hobhouse modestly, " and think the Ministers right. I shall support them."

On the division on Baring's amendment—which, he asked, should be regarded as decisive of the principle, " as a state of suspense was the very worst in which the country could be left "—the votes for the Government proposals were 222 and for the amendment 39, a majority of 183.

Thus ended the first stage.[1] But acceptance of the principle by no means ended the matter. In many places, the country bankers, from motives of precaution—some said, in order to defeat the measure—had precipitately begun to withdraw their small notes. Gurney told of a banker in Yorkshire who had £13,000 in circulation in one-pound notes. He issued them, and re-issued them ; and, in the course of less than a week, had paid the whole amount three times over ; on which he took them all up and threw them into the fire. There being nothing, as yet, to take their place, difficulty was found in paying wages and in carrying on the ordinary business of life. Impressed apparently by this danger, Robinson, four days after, moved that the Bank of England be an exception to the time limit of the other banks, and be allowed to issue small notes dated previously to the 10th October proximo.[2] On this the struggle

The Bank's small notes excepted.

[1] *Hansard*, xiv. 165, 245.

[2] Greville puts the argument very well. " The great evil now is want of a circulating medium, and, as the immediate result of the measure would be another run upon the Bank, and that probably all the gold drawn from it would disappear—for men now are anxious to hoard gold—this evil would be increased tenfold. The whole country is in distress from the absence of cir-culating medium for the common purposes of life ; no country banker will issue notes, for they are instantly returned upon his hands, and exchanged for gold. The circulation of country notes being generally confined within a very limited extent, the holders of them can easily present them for payment. The circulation of a quantity of Bank of England paper will relieve the im-

was renewed, and raged over many debates, with a violence quite
disproportionate to its importance.[1] When the motion was carried
by 187 to 24, Hume took up the running, principally to ventilate
his own favourite scheme, that the banks should be compelled to
deposit with the Exchequer securities equal to the amount of their
issues—a securing of the notes, as was amply pointed out, which
would so much diminish the security of deposits as to put an end
to deposit banking. For this he got only eight supporters. Whitmore said that, if they went to the root of the evil, they would do
away with the issue of the £5 notes, and Lord King, wishful to see
20 or 30 millions of sovereigns in circulation, would agree to put
down the £5 and even the £10 notes. A more important suggestion
that, after 5th April, 1829, all notes under £20 should be payable
in gold at the place where they were issued and at such other places
as the banker might please to insert—instead of in London or some
far-away locality—was adopted ; and, on 7th March, the Bill
passed.

Bill in the   When it came up to the Lords, the Earl of Carnarvon moved its
Lords.   rejection, on the comprehensive grounds of the time, the circumstances, and the error of the abstract idea that a paper currency
founded on a metallic one was the best and safest : there was no

mediate distress arising from this necessity, and the difficulty of exchanging
them for gold will ensure the continuance of their circulation. When men
find that they must take notes, and that gold is not to be had without so much
pain and trouble, they will be contented to take the notes to which they have
been accustomed, and will think the paper of their own bankers as good as
that of the Bank of England, besides the advantages of being less exposed
to the losses arising from forgery." Greville's story is that Gurney, who seems
to have been a fanatical believer in the necessity of the small note, threatened
the Chancellor that, if the Bill were persisted in, he would send up half a
million Bank of England notes and change them for sovereigns, and that all
country bankers would follow his example—so causing another drain for gold
on the Bank. But the reiterated statement of the Government that the only
object of the motion was to retain a power of remedy in case of a small currency
famine, their contention that the Bank disliked small notes and had no interest
in circulating them, and their willingness to accept a clause safeguarding
against over-issue by the Bank, seem sufficient to account for the apparent
inconsistency. Certain it is that they won support from many who had
before opposed the main measure as likely to produce an immediate contraction of the currency (*Greville Memoirs*, vol. i. chap. iii.).

[1] The forgery argument was strongly pressed. The Government was
entreated not to reopen this old sore. It seems certain that the Bank of
England small notes were constantly counterfeited, while those of the country
banks and of the Bank of Ireland almost never were ; and it was, rather rashly,
assumed that it was easier to imitate them. Probably the explanation is that
the small notes of the Bank, circulating everywhere, were more easily and
uncritically passed than the large ones, and than the small notes of the other
banks which circulated only within a limited area.

connection between the existing crisis and the currency ; but, if any change were to be made, it should be by putting the English currency on the same footing as that of Scotland.   Here Lauderdale, saying that his objections applied more to the time of the alteration than to the change itself, parted company with Carnarvon.   There was a very good reason, he said, why the Scots system could not be introduced in England ; it was that that system was founded on the best foundation for any great establishment, namely, the practice of ages.   It had the confidence of the people ; and, when the same could be said in an equal degree of the English system, then no change would be necessary.   It was idle to talk of translating systems from one country to another.   This being all the opposition, the amendment was negatived and the Bill became law.[1]

On the whole subject, what one, looking at the matter from the modern point of view, would be inclined to emphasise is, that the great disaster was a fine example of the dislocation which is the danger of all organised machinery, and that the particular form it took was the sudden shock given to public confidence.   Every person admits that " credit " is the very life-blood of the modern system, but not everyone appreciates that the " credit " in question is, not the time given for payment, but simply " trust "—the trust that every to-morrow shall be as to-day—that everyone will find ready to his hand to-morrow the facilities which he has to-day.   All industry is carried on by contracts and arrangements which run far into the future ; every trade depends on trades that come before and trades that come after ; every consumer gets his spending power—his demand—from the supply of some industry or other ; and any check, either in demand or in supply, sends a shiver through a whole web of related interests.   But when anything throws serious doubt on the solidity of a banking system, where all the members are knit together in the closest way and all depend ultimately on finding gold at the one spot where the gold is accumulated, a blow is struck at the very heart, and panic spreads like a rapid contagion, not only from bank to bank, but from the banks to the class who depend on the banks—that is, the entire world of producers.[2]

---

[1] *Hansard*, xiv. 450, 537, 556, 570, 572, 859, 878, 963, 1184, 1347.

[2] " Will you explain in what way the state of the small note circulation operated so as to interfere in the management of the Bank ? "—" It rendered the Bank liable to a very great sudden demand ; for instance, in the end of the

The six
partners'
restriction.

The other remedial measure announced by the Government at the beginning of the Session was the revision of the exclusive privileges of the Bank of England. Great praise, indeed, was given to the Bank for the prompt and liberal assistance it had rendered at the late crisis. But the effect of the exclusive privileges, as Robinson said, had been to permit elsewhere in the country every species of banking plan to be in full operation save what was of the most solid and beneficial character. It was too much, said Brougham, to trust the whole property of the country to the absolute control and direction of four and twenty men ; other companies should have an opportunity of rising in competition. The particular object intended was the removal of the restriction which limited the number of partners in a bank to six. The original object of this curious provision, which formed a part of the Bank Charter, was to give to the Bank of England a position which no other bank could approach. But the numerous failures of the country banks, said Liverpool, who brought in the Bill, seemed to point to the absurdity of allowing " any small tradesman, a cheesemonger, a butcher, or a shoemaker, to open a country bank, while persons with a fortune sufficient to carry on the concern were not permitted to do so "— forbidding the trade, in fact, to take the shape of large associations of capital as in Scotland, and, since 1824, in Ireland.[1] The great extension of the country banks was comparatively recent, dating from the seven years preceding 1793—years of the greatest prosperity, when a bank became set up in every market town. In the commercial convulsion of that year about a hundred of them stopped payment. But, as Chalmers said,[2] " the whole number of country banks in England was unknown ; their capitals and character were unknown ; their imprudence only was known."

Lauderdale ridiculed the idea. Would men be ready to embark in those schemes in greater numbers than hitherto allowed by law ?

year 1825, the demand upon the Bank was nearly two millions and a half sterling, almost entirely for the support of the small note country circulation. . . . The holders of small notes are the lower orders of the people, whose fears are more extensively acted upon in times of distrust ; and, there having been no exchange for the £1 note but the sovereign, the demand upon the Bank became inevitable " (J. Horsley Palmer's evidence before the Committee on the Bank Charter, 1832, p. 22).

[1] The monopoly of the Bank of Ireland was abolished by an agreement between the Bank and the Treasury in 1821. The establishment of joint-stock banks was recognised by an Act of 1824, amended in 1825. The many joint-stock banks since established in Ireland were now, said Lord Bexley, in full operation, to the great convenience of the public (*Hansard*, xiv. 493).

[2] In his *Estimate of the Comparative Strength of Great Britain*, 296.

Would the noble earl find six men or more who were ready to embark their whole property, with the chance of dividing it to the last shilling in case of failure ?   And did he suppose that an increased number of partners would add one iota to the general security of banks ?   Security there was none, either in the number of partners or their wealth, if there were not skill in transacting business.[1] Even Baring was doubtful as to the establishment of larger banks, and dwelt on the ridiculousness of encouraging country gentlemen to become sleeping partners in such concerns.   " If it was desirable to form banks in the great commercial towns, it should be done either by means of branch banks from the Bank of England, or by allowing a number of gentlemen to embark certain portions of their capital, say, £10,000, in a joint banking company : that sum, from ten men, would be £100,000—an amount, in his opinion, quite adequate to support the respectability of the ordinary run of such concerns."   And, moreover, while he was not prepared to say that " a rule, exempting the property of the individuals composing a company from all liability beyond their subscribed capital, would be proper for the ordinary purposes of trade, for banks, it was his fixed opinion, that, under all the circumstances, it would be found both to confer adequate respectability and ensure sufficient confidence." [2]   Ellice, however, said that it was more by good fortune than by good management that the panic had not travelled northward :   the banks in Scotland had not been behindhand in giving encouragement to over-trading and speculation.[3]

But, as the changes proposed interfered with the provisions of its charter, the consent of the Bank had first to be obtained ;   it was some time before the Bank would give in ;   and in the end it consented only on the condition that it should be placed upon the same footing as the Bank of Ireland, by having its exclusive privileges éxtended—not, as in Ireland, to fifty but—to a distance of sixty-five miles round the metropolis.   Thereupon, in order that the two measures should go through Parliament simultaneously, the Bill for the purpose was brought in in the House of Lords.

[1] *Hansard*, xiv. 475.

[2] *Ibid.* xiv. 81.   This system was familiar in France, said Lockhart, where private individuals might invest small sums in banks without rendering themselves liable beyond the amount of those small sums.

[3] The Scotch system, said Hudson Gurney, was one which went, much more than that of England, towards facilitating speculations of every kind, but it was the customer there who broke, and the banker who swept his securities (*ibid.* 148).

Although amply denounced as unworkable, full of contradictions—a mass of absurdity, said Hume—and confessed by Liverpool to be far from perfect and only as good as they could get so long as the chartered privileges of the Bank stood in the way, the Bill duly passed into law.[1]

The Government had announced at the very first that it was their intention to extend the prohibition of small notes to Scotland and Ireland. But while the measures were passing through Parliament, Scotland had risen as one man.[2] Never was feeling more strongly entertained or more decidedly expressed. Both Houses were deluged with petitions from public meetings and from all the great commercial bodies in the north. And, besides, had not Scott written his famous *Letters of Malachi Malagrowther*—of which, indeed, Earl Grosvenor said that the whole agitation had originated in the fears excited in the minds of ministers by that celebrated personage, "the mightiest magician of the age," as Robinson called him. Impressed by the outcry, the Government, while protesting strongly that they could see no reason for it, took refuge in a Select Committee. In the debate over the appointment of this Committee—which was strongly opposed on both sides as quite unnecessary—the arguments advanced for the extension to Scotland are far from convincing. They were, briefly, that it was impossible for one part of the kingdom to support one system, and another, another—but why, asked the *Globe*, not give them bishops and a Court of Chancery, rasp down their cheekbones and make them speak English ? ; that, in commercial cases, Scotland could not do without England—when distress occurred, the Scots banks must lean on the Bank of England ; that, if the measure were not extended, it must be wholly ineffectual for England.

The case of Ireland, which was remitted to the same Committee,

---

[1] *Hansard*, xiv. 450, 556, 866, 1258 ; xv. 236. The Bill contained the provision that, in case the Bank of England should think proper to establish branches, they should be bound to pay their notes in gold in the same part of the country in which the notes had been issued. This was to provide against the great inconvenience which has been experienced in Ireland where the Bank had refused to pay gold except at Dublin.

[2] Abercromby, the member for Calne, with his usual genius for misrepresenting Scotland, stated that the whole of the press of Scotland argued in favour of the intended alteration (*Hansard*, xiv. 1358). I have not come across anything to justify such a statement except the petition signed by "120 respectable inhabitants" of the town of Duns, hoping that the measure would be extended to Scotland (*ibid.* xv. 155). One landowner, the Earl of Mansfield, excited great indignation by giving notice that he would not accept payment of his Scots rents in notes.

was confessedly different. In 1819 and 1820, nine of the Irish country banks broke, and one in Dublin, and it was not advisable that such banks should spring up again. Of the old banks, only nine remained, and few of them issued their own notes. The paper in circulation, then, was that of the Bank of Ireland, and it at least was sound and unobjectionable. And while, in Scotland, there was a veritable " rebellion of paper against gold," in Ireland there was no marked hostility to the proposed measure—perhaps because, as an ancient historian said of the Irish, " they never rebelled at the right time." Still the Earl of Limerick could say that the measure would be " infinitely more mischievous in Ireland than in Scotland."

Select Committees, then, were appointed by both Houses—that of the House of Commons containing, among others, Robinson, Peel, Tierney, the Lord Advocate, Newport, Bourne, Archibald Campbell (the member for Glasgow), Huskisson, Lord Archibald Hamilton, Parnell, Althorp, Abercromby, Ridley, Grenfell, Brougham, Palmerston and the Reports were presented before the end of the Session. The Commons' Report was much the more detailed, giving an account both of the history and practice of banking in Scotland, and it is easy to gather that the information which the English members now got of Scottish banking was somewhat of a revelation, and that they were much impressed by it.

The Commons' Report.

The Bank of Scotland, it began, was founded in 1695 ; the Royal Bank in 1727. In 1765, the old practice of making notes payable, either on demand, or at the end of six months with interest, at the option of the issuer, was abolished ; all notes were made payable on demand ; and notes under 20/- were prohibited. There were in existence at the present time thirty-two banks, most of them with hundreds of partners. Excepting in the case of the Bank of Scotland, the Royal, and the British Linen, these partners were bound jointly and severally, to the whole extent of their fortunes, for the whole debts of the Bank ; and the law of Scotland, by the establishment of records of purchases and mortgages of estates, gave the creditors great facility for ascertaining the pecuniary position of the individual partners. The various banks had amongst them 133 branches covering the whole country.

The business of a Scotch bank consisted chiefly in taking deposits, on which a varying interest was allowed—at the moment it was 4 per cent. ; in issuing notes upon the discount of bills ; and in advances on " cash credits," on both which the rate at the moment was 5 per cent. The aggregate amount of deposits might be £20 or £21 millions—more than half of this in sums from £10 to £200, contributed by the labouring class in towns, and by servants and fishermen in the country. These deposits were usually added to gradually, till they reached a considerable sum, when they were taken out for the purchase of a house or to start a business—" a great part of the most thriving farmers and manufacturers had arisen from such beginnings." Thus the banks had long given the country many of the benefits derivable from Savings Banks.

The existing amount of paper currency, being in fact (with the exception of silver) the whole currency of the country, was computed to be £3,309,000, of which £2,079,000 were in notes below £5. The question before the Committee being, in substance, whether the existing system could coexist with a metallic currency in England, the presumption, on general principles, was in favour of uniformity over the whole kingdom. But the main object of the witnesses from Scotland was to prove the claim of that country to be an exception ; they were all " decidedly averse to any change." The grounds urged were : that the system had prevailed since the first institution of banking in Scotland ; that, coincident with it, there had been a great and progressive increase in industry and wealth ; that, in 1715 and 1745, confidence was not shaken nor any extraordinary call made for gold—nor yet in 1793, 1797, nor 1825 ; that, for twenty years previous to the Bank Restriction, England had a currency consisting of the precious metals and of promissory notes not below £5, and no proof could be adduced that the paper circulation of Scotland displaced or interfered with, in any material degree, the metallic currency of England ; that bank failures had been extremely rare,[1] and only in two cases did the creditors not ultimately receive the whole amount of their principal and interest ; that the new system proposed would destroy the inducement to continue branch banks, and that " the whole system of deposits and cash credits would be most materially affected if the banks were compelled to forego the profit now derived from the issue of notes below five pounds"; finally, that the directors of the Bank of England who were examined urged no objection to the continuance of the present system, provided that the paper

---

[1] Only six between 1772 and 1822, I believe. One witness said that, in the 130 years during which paper had been in use, the whole loss which the public sustained by the failure of banks amounted to no more than £36,344.

circulation of Scotland could be effectually restrained within the limits of that country.

" Upon a review of the evidence tendered to your Committee, and forming their judgment upon that evidence, your Committee cannot advise that a law should now be passed prohibiting, from a period to be therein determined, the future issue in Scotland of notes below five pounds. . . . They are unwilling, without stronger proof of necessity, to incur the risk of deranging, from any cause whatever, a system admirably calculated, in their opinion, to economise the use of capital ; to excite and cherish a spirit of useful enterprise ; and even to promote the moral habits of the people by the direct inducement which it holds out to the maintenance of a character for industry, integrity, and prudence."

One provision, however, they felt bound to make—that the circulation of Scotch notes should be restricted within the limits of Scotland.[1] And they concluded by expressing some apprehension that the crime of forgery was on the increase in that country.

The Committee of the Lords reported much in the same strain. The Lords' Report. The only noticeable additions were : that the Scotch banks had, for more than a century, exhibited a stability which they believed was unexampled in the history of banking—that they supported themselves from 1797 to 1812 without any protection from the restriction by which the Bank of England and that of Ireland were relieved from cash payments—and that there was little demand for gold during the late embarrassments ; that this solidity appeared to derive a great support from the constant exchange of notes between the different banks, by which they became checks upon each other, and by which any over-issue was subject to immediate observation and correction ; that one part of the system had the best effects upon the people of Scotland, and particularly on the middling and poorer classes, in producing and encouraging habits of frugality and industry—the cash credits, the total amount of which was stated to be five millions, and the average amount advanced by the banks about one-third ; that while, if they were reduced to make an option between the establishment of such a metallic circulation in Scotland and the abandonment of it in England, they would recommend the prohibition of small notes in Scotland, they entertained a reasonable expectation that legislative measures might be devised to prevent the introduction of Scotch

[1] " The notes, being Scotch," said the Lord Chancellor, " it would be in their very nature to travel south ! "

paper into England. In fine, they were not disposed to recommend that the existing system of banking and currency in Scotland should be disturbed.

Irish notes.   In regard to Ireland the recommendations were very indefinite : the whole treatment of the subject, indeed, was very unsatisfactory. As their enquiries had been less extensive, the Commons' Committee hesitated, in the present imperfect state of their information, to pronounce a decisive opinion upon the general measures which it might be fitting to adopt. The prevailing practice of using notes for the payment of sums between one and two pounds, for three guineas, and other fractional sums should be discontinued, as it tended to dispense with the necessity of silver coin, and practically to exclude it from circulation. But, although they were inclined to think that it would not be advisable to take any immediate step for the purpose of preventing the issue of small notes in Ireland, their impression undoubtedly was that a metallic currency ought ultimately to be the basis of circulation in that country. The Report of the Lords' Committee was no less vague. The system of banking in Ireland, they said, instead of remaining unshaken for a long period, like that of Scotland, had experienced so many shocks, that its banking establishments were now almost confined to the chartered Bank of Ireland and its local agencies, the branches of the provincial bank which was established in London, one joint-stock company in Dublin and one in Belfast, the latter of which had local agencies, and a few private banks in Dublin and Belfast. The issue of small notes had been at different periods permitted and prohibited, so that there was no prescription to plead for their continuance ; there were no cash credits ; and there was not the same check upon over-issues by the exchanges of notes. The failures had been many. They abstained from recommending the adoption of any measures for assimilating, by slow gradations, the circulating medium of Ireland to that which would become at an earlier period the circulating medium of England, only under the expectation that further information and more experience as to the effects and operation of the changes which had lately taken place in the banking system of Ireland, might lead to the formation of a more decided opinion.[1]

Tierney.   The presentation of the Report on the very last day of the Session made a great commotion. Tierney scathingly exposed the inconsistency of banishing the small notes from England in order to

[1] The Reports are given in the *Annual Register*, Appendix 64 *

compel gold into circulation, while allowing Scotland to continue
a system which could not but banish gold from circulation. He,
personally, had consented to the Government proposal as a national
policy, while conscious that it was a very severe remedy, and would
inflict hardship in many quarters. But now the Scots were to be
made an exception because of the hardships ! It was the more
grievous that all the Scots members except one (Hume) had supported the new system ; but, when it was dared to think of applying
it logically, the fiery cross was sent round. If a metallic currency
was the best, as he agreed, it was at the same time the hardest to
get at ; why should Scotland not bear her share of the burden ?
He warned the House that, when the evidence was circulated, it
would form ample material for a manifesto in favour of a paper
currency from one end of the kingdom to the other. And he roundly
accused the Government of vacillation and weakness, and of going
back on the pledges by which they had secured adherence to their
scheme for England.

Peel, who had signed the Report, denied that the Government Peel.
had ever given any pledge to extend the system to Scotland. His
own feeling was that it should be so extended, but, after hearing
the evidence in Committee, he owned that he was afraid, without
further evidence to prove that the two systems were incompatible,
to resolve on doing away with that of Scotland.[1] After all, there
was nothing in this inconsistent with the object aimed at, the
return to metallic payments. It was a return to the state of things
before the Bank Restriction, when small notes were prohibited in
England, and when no one mooted the prohibition of them in
Scotland. Evidently the feeling was strong that the English
members had been duped into their hasty acceptance of the abolition
of the small notes by the anticipation that it would be general.
And there is some room for suspicion that many thought that, if
they had seen the evidence from Scotland before the measure was
passed, they would have hesitated before assigning so definite a
place in the distress to the issue of small notes.

[1] *Hansard*, xv. 1411.

CHAPTER XXXII

1826. THE BUDGET

"Still more prosperity." ON 13th March, the Chancellor of the Exchequer, an excellent minister in times of prosperity but obviously unequal to a crisis like this, carrying out the plan adopted by him in 1823, made his Exposition of the Financial Situation.[1] Defending himself against the charge of having misled the country by exaggerated statements of its prosperity, he showed that, taking the past three years together, the actual receipts had exceeded the estimated revenue by £1,398,000, notwithstanding the concomitant repeal of no less than £8 millions of taxes. Going back to 1816, the clear remission of taxation could be shown to be £27,522,000 ; " it is impossible for any man in his senses to argue that this large remission of duties has not mainly contributed to that increased consumption which has itself augmented the revenue." And he gave an interesting list of the quantities of various goods which paid duty in 1816 and in 1825, showing such increases as : tobacco, 13 per cent. ; sugar, 19 per cent. ; tea, 20 per cent. ;[2] leather, 29 per cent. ; candles, 36 per cent. ;[3] coffee and cocoa, 43 per cent. ; paper, 51 per cent. ; hemp, 74 per cent. ; wine, 88 per cent. ; crown glass, 95 per cent. ; flint glass, 104 per cent. ; plate glass, 108 per cent. ; hard soap, 113 per cent. ; raw cotton, 119 per cent. ; soft soap, 121 per cent. ; thrown silk, 180 per cent. ; deals, 182 per cent. ; bricks, 188 per cent. ; timber, 196 per cent. ; tallow, 201 per cent. ;

[1] *Hansard*, xiv. 1305.

[2] It is interesting to find tea spoken of, by Malmesbury, as " perhaps almost a necessary of life among the lower orders " (*Hansard*, xv. 1058).

[3] It is a fine—almost a perfect—instance of how differently statistics may be interpreted, that Hume, subsequently, should bring forward the increase in the consumption of candles as proving, not the better condition of the people, but the greater difficulty which the poor had to earn their bread. " Formerly the artizan, weaver, and shoemaker were able to retire at the close of day, but now their labour, bestowed through the better part of the night, scarcely sufficed to procure them subsistence " : it was a perversion of terms, he said, to apply the figure otherwise (*Hansard*, xv. 860).

raw silk, 274 per cent. ; butter, 317 per cent. ; sheep's wool, 443 per cent. In the past three years, too—from 5th January, 1823, to 5th January, 1826, that is, since the new arrangement of the Sinking Fund—the Funded Debt was reduced from £796,530,000 to £778,128,000—at the rate of nearly £6,134,000 per annum ; the Unfunded, from £36,281,000 to £31,703,000. In the same period, the annual charge of the Funded Debt (including management) fell from £28,123,000 to £27,117,000 ; of the Exchequer Bills, from £1,100,000 to £820,000 : that is to say, the total annual charge on the two descriptions of debt fell from £29,286,000 to £27,946,000, a reduction of £1,340,000 of the annual charge on the entire debt in the course of three years. He added that the expense of collecting the revenue was now half a million less than in 1818.[1]

Omitting to say how far his estimates for the past year had been realised—it would appear from Porter that there was a deficit of over £4,000,000—he budgeted for the coming year as follows :

EXPENDITURE.

Consolidated Fund—

Interest and Management of the Public Debt -	£27,117,186
Interest of Exchequer (deficiency) Bills -	50,000
Civil List and Pensions of a permanent nature	2,065,000
Half-Pay Annuity	2,800,000
Sinking Fund	5,585,235
Annual Votes—	
Army	7,747,000
Navy	6,135,000
Ordnance	1,754,000
Miscellaneous	2,225,000
Interest of Exchequer Bills	850,000
	£56,328,421

REVENUE.

Customs and Excise -	£37,446,000
Stamps	7,400,000
Taxes (including Assessed Taxes)	4,800,000
Post Office	1,550,000
Miscellaneous	1,360,000
Payment from Trustees of Half Pay -	4,320,000
Surplus of 1825 on Sinking Fund	167,000
	£57,043,000

[1] " What, *still* more prosperity !—mercy upon us,
This boy'll be the death of me '—oft, as already,
Such smooth Budgeteers have genteely undone us,
For *Ruin made easy* there's no one like Freddy."—*Moore*

This left a surplus of £714,579 for Parliament to deal with as it might think fit.

Tobacco. By a curious blunder in the drawing up of the late consolidation of Customs and Excise, the 4/- duty on tobacco had been changed to 3/- for one-half of the past year. This " strange mischance," which cost the revenue £450,000, had, however, so much of good in it that, as the reduction had had no inconsiderable effect in checking the smuggling of tobacco, particularly in Ireland where that practice was carried on to an extent " beyond all imagination or belief," it had suggested to the Chancellor of the Exchequer the alteration which he now proposed to make, namely, to continue the reduction ; this would diminish the surplus by £600,000.[1]

Exchequer Bills. The last matter dealt with was the relation of the Government to the Bank. In January, the Bank held about £6 millions of Exchequer Bills upon advances which it had made. In addition to this, at the instance of the Government, it had consented to purchase £2 millions of outstanding Exchequer Bills—" partly to relieve the money market from the pressure which seemed at that time to operate with peculiar force upon this species of security, and partly in the hope that various classes of the community who were suffering from the forced contraction of the currency might obtain a certain degree of relief from this mode of extending the general circulation " ; and the Government had then promised that ˙the amount would be repaid in the current year. To save the Bank from possible embarrassments, he submitted that it should be repaid £6 millions of the Exchequer Bills in its possession, and he proposed to do so by funding £8 or £9 millions in the course of the current Session.[2]

The Chancellor's exposition was received with great approval. Baring had never heard a speech which had given him more satisfaction. Huskisson called it " one of the most luminous state-

---

[1] The smuggling of tobacco was, of course, one of the strong arguments for reducing the duty. Hume pointed out that, from 1810 to 1812, when tobacco paid 2/- per lb., duty was paid on 41 million lbs., while, from 1820 to 1822, when the duty was 4/-, only 33 million lbs. paid duty. Few things, he reiterated, could be more beneficial to the fair trader, more destructive to smuggling, or more advantageous to the revenue, than a reduction of these duties (*Hansard*, xiv. 695).

[2] The Exchequer Bills—which, as Maberly thought proper to explain, were bills on Government payable at sight, issued for a debt previously contracted, and usually denominated the Unfunded Debt—were funded by creating a new 4 per cent. stock, not redeemable under seven years, giving £107 of stock for each subscription of £100 in Exchequer Bills, or £100 10/- cash (*ibid.* xv. 281).

ments that had ever been delivered within the walls of the House." Hume, however, attacked it almost viciously. The increase of Hume consumption of which the Chancellor of the Exchequer had made so much, he was ready to prove, was not in proportion to the increase of population. But the point he laid most stress on was that, " although so much had been talked about the reduction of taxes, more money had been taken from the pockets of the people within the past three years than had been within the preceding years." The average revenue raised in 1817-1819 was £51,700,000 ; the average raised in 1823-1825 was £52,430,000. " Had the people not a right to expect that these immense sums should not be taken from their pockets in the eleventh year of the peace ? " Little attention was paid to Hume's argument—it " was obviously and utterly erroneous," said the *Annual Register*. But there is little doubt that his contention was not as foolish as it seemed.[1]

Before the Budget was brought in, Hume had, as usual, fought criticises all the service estimates. Instead of the permanent establishment everything. being kept at £17,350,000, as had been promised, it had been £20 millions since 1821. In his view, our army, navy, ordnance, and civil estimates might be reduced one-half. No such military establishment was ever thought of at any former time of peace— should it be increased " at the awful moment when tens of thousands were in a state of destitution " ? No naval establishment in the world amounted to one-half of our own ; the American navy con- sisted of 7 line-of-battle ships, while our ships of war were 509. The most effectual strength of the country was, of course, the navy, but it was injudicious to add to its numbers without diminishing the army—the army was not our arm. On the other hand, the naval estimates were defended by Sir George Cockburn as a kind

[1] What Hume does not seem to have realised was that, under a system of indirect taxation, increased consumption is the " visible test " of increased income, and that a reduction of the rate of taxation is compensated if there is a corresponding increase of the national income taxed. He was quite right in saying that the sum taken from the pockets of the people was not dimin- ished ; wrong, in suggesting that the *burden* was not diminished as the ability to pay the taxes increased. The evil of indirect taxation, as everyone now sees, is that it strikes with little reference to ability to bear the burden ; remission of taxation on particular articles may, indeed, take the weight off shoulders which should bear it. But it seems to have been the belief of early financial reformers that something was wrong if the revenue raised by the Government increased unless in times of war. Hume, for instance, seemed to look on all increase of Government expenditure as wholly " unproductive," and certainly would not have acknowledged that the payment for army and navy is—like the payment for police—a premium on insurance, rising with the value of the property insured and with the increased difficulty of guarding it.

of reproductive expenditure—a mercantile police for our universal
carrying commerce—necessary, particularly at the present moment,
in the Mediterranean, the West Indies, and the coast of Africa,
and the explanation given of the increase of the estimates was the
enormously extended range of our trade, owing particularly to the
opening up of South America.[1]

On 5th May, under the comprehensive title of " The State of
the Nation," Hume made an attack on the Government's finance
—or, rather, on everything done and left undone by the Government—in the shape of 47 Resolutions, covering twenty-six printed
pages. Starting with the compliment of saying that he gave
Ministers every credit for the liberal course of policy which had
lately distinguished the administration, and assuring them that
he had no desire to procure their removal from office, he went on
to contend that they had confused the principles of currency with
the principles of banking; that the debt had not been reduced, as
the Chancellor of the Exchequer said, nor had its charge, nor had
taxation ; that the establishments now cost treble of what they
had in 1792 ; that sinecures and pensions had increased ; that the
navy was filled with young noblemen and fine gentlemen instead
of sailors ; that poverty and crime stalked abroad in the land.
The present truly appalling distress was " not a partial distress
against which no foresight could guard. It was a great and general
deprivation, and it could not be accounted for except by a great
and general cause. That great, that general, that pervading cause,
was the keeping up of large, useless, and most extravagant establishments in this country." Then, as Robinson complained, after
speaking for two hours on the subject of the Sinking Fund, he
very coolly turned round and said, " I don't mean to call the attention of the House to this question now, but I shall take some other
opportunity to bring it forward." [2] The Chancellor of the Exchequer excused himself, as he well might, from replying in detail,
on the ground that the Resolutions had been put into his hand
only at eleven o'clock in the forenoon, but replied with some warmth
to some of Hume's rasher and more personal statements—they
were an attempt to lower him in the opinion of the country. The

---

[1] *Hansard*, xiv. 520, 678, 1082.

[2] The only hint he gave as to what he would put in its place was the statement that " all the surplus revenues of the country ought to be applied in
the purchase of long annuities," and that no balance should be allowed to
remain in the hands of Ministers.

motion was not supported except by Brougham and Maberly in very general terms, and was lost by 51 to 152.[1]

[1] *Hansard*, xv. 841.   One does not like to pass judgment on a man who was, in many respects, so much ahead of his times—especially so long as he confined himself to destructive criticism—but I attach much importance to a man's standpoint as revealed in side statements by himself.   The following seems suggestive. He had, he said, expressed an opinion in 1825 which he now wished to support. It was that no nation could, in the nature of things, derive any pecuniary advantage by its inhabitants trading solely among themselves. If two persons of this country exchanged their commodities, it appeared obvious to him that benefit from such a transaction could arise only to one of the parties.   One individual must lose what the other gained : both could not gain, and, therefore, the country could not derive any benefit from the transaction ; it was merely a transfer of advantage from A to B, and no creating of any benefit.   In the same speech, he said that the productive classes were, "only the man who guided the plough, the man who delved at the spade, him who wielded the hammer, him who threw the shuttle "— emphatically not the " country gentleman " ; he was not worth one farthing in the scale of production.

CHAPTER XXXIII

1826. FREE TRADE ON ITS TRIAL

In many directions the new policy of freeing industry from prohibitions and restrictions was already justifying itself by success. Huskisson, for example, could say that, instead of all the British wool being exported, as was anticipated by some on the removal of the restriction on its export, to the utter ruin of all our manufacture, the export since had been only 100,000 lbs., while the importation of foreign wool had risen to no less than 40 million lbs. But, as the existing distress had been very much contemporaneous with the Free Trade measures, it might be expected that Free Trade would be
The late silk blamed for it. It will be remembered that "the last iniquity of
measures. the economists," the removal of the prohibition of foreign silks, and its replacement by a protecting duty of 30 per cent., had been postponed till July of the current year; and, as that date approached, many of those who were interested in the trade, and found a more ready explanation of their depression than the existing crisis, thought that they might be successful in getting their monopoly continued for some time longer. Many petitions, accordingly, were presented, praying for a repeal,[1] or, at least, a further modification of the provisions of 1824. Hundreds of thousands of people, said Baring, now reverting to his 1824 attitude, were anticipating ruin and starvation from the import. The master silk-weavers were unanimous that, if French silk goods were let in, there was no chance of selling a single yard of English silk. The whole trade was unhinged. He wished to know now if the House were going to support Ministers in their "desperate resolution." The impression of the petitioners was that the principle of Free Trade must be greatly injurious to the general interests—unless, indeed, it were extended

[1] On January 23rd, the Board of Trade had an interesting talk "with a deputation from the Spitalfields weavers in which Huskisson defined his position" (*Edinburgh Annual Register*, Chron. 108).

to corn. Lethbridge suspected that this was the sinister intention
in the whole policy; it was an outwork to a similar alteration in
the Corn Laws, and he for one must oppose anything like a free
trade in corn : so long as the National Debt remained, no such
thing could be listened to.[1]

On 23rd February accordingly, Ellice, one of the members for Motion for
Coventry, made a motion on the subject. His line of argument delay.
presents perhaps as good an example as could be given of how
the somewhat drastic measures passed in 1824 and 1825 were
looked upon by many who yet maintained their Free Trade principles,
and, for that reason, it may be useful to give it with some fullness.
He defended himself against change of front. When the monopoly
given by the war had ceased to exist, there was nothing for it but the
removal of the prohibitions and restrictions. But, evidently, in consideration of the complicated interests involved, the greatest caution
was necessary in applying this. The first step was to reform the laws
regarding navigation and foreign trade generally, and here he had
given his unqualified support to the Government. The next step
should have been the reform of the currency and the Corn Laws.
Third, ought to have come the revision of taxation by removing
all duties and taxes bearing particularly upon the productive
industry of the country, and substituting in their place taxes upon
the wealthier and unproductive parts of society. By these means,
the country would have been put in a position to compete with
our manufacturing rivals abroad. But, first, the country ought to
be placed on such an equality. His objection, then, was that the
Government had begun where they ought to have ended. The Act
for finally removing the probibition against foreign silks was passed
without sufficient enquiry as to the consequences that must ensue
from so sudden an alteration. No trade had engaged so much of
the Government's attention in the past. It was, indeed, an exotic
plant, and it was the only extensive branch of manufacturing
industry in which our great political and commercial rivals had
attained an admitted superiority. But, under the encouragement
of a strict monopoly, it had risen to the important place it held
among our staples on the return of peace.[2] When the particular

[1] *Hansard*, xiv. 152.

[2] Certainly, to whatever it was due, the silk trade had made marvellous
strides in the past few years. In 1820, Liverpool had said that he wished
England had never had a silk manufactory, although, considering the capital
and the workers involved, he could not agree that it was possible to relinquish
it. But the Committee on Foreign Trade of 1821 spoke of the rapid increase

measure was passed in 1824, opposition was silenced by the bribe of the two years allowed for preparation, and by the expectation held out that other measures would be adopted, before the expiration of that period, to place the industry, in respect to taxes and the price of provisions, on an equality with its French and Swiss rivals. He did not deny that much good had resulted from the spur of threatened competition, and that our manufacture had improved beyond precedent in the past two years. But, all the same, he agreed with the prayer of the petition " for a little time for further enquiry," before it was determined to expose the trade to dangers which might be either diminished or entirely removed by the delay of one or two more years.

Ellice then went on to bring forward some details which, he hoped, would induce the House at least to refer the whole subject again to a Select Committee. The throwster, the dyer, and the broad-silk weaver declared themselves unable to compete, principally, if not entirely, owing to the difference in the price of labour, the heavy taxes, and the high price of provisions, but they did not complain of their inferiority in skill and machinery. Very different was it with the narrow-silk weavers, particularly the makers of fancy goods and gauze ribbons. There the superiority of the French and Swiss looms was beyond all doubt. One workman, with the engine loom, could now produce six times as much as the workman with the common single hand-loom, and the melancholy fact was that fully three-fourths of the looms still in use in Coventry, to which place this manufacture was entirely confined, were of an inefficient description, and that by far the greater part of them were the property—he sadly feared, the only property—of the operatives themselves. Their buildings and houses were adapted to this machinery, and must be altered for the reception of the engine looms, which required more room and greater height ; and, in the present depressed state of the trade, and the apprehension of the immediate introduction of foreign goods, the weavers were unable, and the manufacturers unwilling, without some assurance

---

in the silk manufacture. In 1822, it was said—not quite truly as it happened— that silk was the only flourishing industry in the country. In 1823, the petitions against the Spitalfields restrictions gave the flourishing state of the trade as an argument for the removal of these restrictions. After the Spital- fields Acts were repealed, in 1824, silk was said to have extended almost as much as cotton. In 1825, new throwing mills were erected, and, even with that, the importation of thrown silk was almost trebled. It was in face of this that a number of merchants met at the London Tavern, and put forth a declaration that France could undersell them by 60 per cent.

of adequate protection, to invest money in alterations which might
only increase their difficulties. And then he went on to the old
appeal—what was to become of those workers, two-thirds of them
now entirely unemployed and the other third at half wages ?

Huskisson, who had already told the deputation to the Board
of Trade that " the distress was but a temporary one which must
be met with patience," answered that the real drift of the argument
was to impugn those principles of commercial policy which, under
the sanction of Parliament, had now prevailed for the past two or
three years, and the point at issue was, not whether a Committee
should be granted, but whether the prohibitory system should be
re-established. " If we re-establish it in one instance, we shall
very soon be called on to do so in many others." To answer the
charge that the new policy was the work of visionaries and theorists,
he began by reading a few sentences of the great petition of the
London Merchants in 1820, and was compelled, by the loud demand
of the House, to read it all. The men who signed that report, he
said, were not only practical men, but men holding the highest
rank in the commercial world. More than that, the petition was
presented by perhaps the greatest practical authority in the country,
the member for Taunton himself (Baring), in a long and elaborate
speech, which he would have liked to quote entire as a most luminous
commentary in support of the doctrines urged in the petition. At
that time—and it also was a time of the greatest distress—Baring
proposed certain measures of relief. They were : (1) an alteration
in the duty on foreign wool ; (2) the simplification of the revenue ;
(3) the abolition of prohibitory duties ; (4) the repeal of the navigation laws ; (5) the removal of the linen transit duties ; (6) the
alteration of the commercial regulations with respect to France,
in order to show that we considered the restrictive system not the
cause of but a bar to our industrial progress ; (7) an extension of
the trade with British India. All these suggestions had been taken
up and acted upon, and all that Baring did at the time was to taunt
the Government with its delay in carrying out a mandate so universally and unanimously expressed. That debate convinced the
Government that the time had come when they might go forward
with measures to which they had long before avowed a friendly
disposition. But when, in 1824, after long taking thought, they
dealt with the silk trade on the principles laid down, from that
moment they lost the support of the member for Taunton, and
his voice was only heard in opposition to measures which he had

Huskisson's
fine defence of
Free Trade.

so long been recommending for adoption. Indeed, he declared at that time that, by the end of the two years allowed before the prohibition should finally cease, the silk trade would be destroyed. Personally, Huskisson considered that the two years' delay was the greatest error then committed.[1] During 1824, the silk trade went on flourishing and increasing in the face of this threatened annihilation. In the spring of 1825, the demand extended to a greater degree than had ever been witnessed before in almost any branch of trade—old factories enlarged, new factories erected, new looms occupied—several of the new mills not roofed in even yet—importation of thrown silk almost trebled. In February, there appeared an advertisement in a Macclesfield paper : " To overseers, guardians of the poor, and families desirous of settling in Macclesfield. Wanted immediately from 4,000 to 5,000 persons, from seven to twenty years of age, to be employed in the throwing and manufacturing of silk. The great increase of the trade having caused a great scarcity of workmen, it is suggested that this is a most favourable opportunity for persons with large families, and overseers who wish to put out children as apprentices, to ensure them a comfortable livelihood." " Humanity," continued Huskisson, " is not the least remarkable part of this precious document, and the House will not fail to observe how admirably the cruelty of confining children of seven years of age to labour in a silk mill for twelve to fifteen hours out of the twenty-four, is tempered by the inducement to parents to provide for their families for life. What sort of provision that has been, the present wretched state of those helpless infants will best evince. And here I cannot help observing that, at the very time such an invitation was sent forth to overseers and parents by the owners of silk mills, this House was very properly occupied in passing a Bill to prevent the employment of children under nine years of age in cotton factories." [2] Some of those children, he had been told, did not receive more than eighteenpence a week ; if so, what became of the difference in the expense of labour between this country and France—would it be said that a French child could not earn eighteenpence a week ? The conclusion, of course,

---

[1] It was said in the *Westminster* later that the opinion was very generally expressed by the manufacturers that they would have suffered less from the immediate operation of the measure than they did from the stagnation which was the consequence of postponement. But this, of course, is not Huskisson's argument.

[2] It is only fair to add that the above advertisement, according to Baring, was made by some master throwsters at the time of a strike.

was obvious. "Can any man wonder, after such an enormous extent of speculation—after such inhuman effort to induce so many destitute children to flock into the manufacture—after such an influx of population—at all branches of this trade being now in a stagnant state, and most of these newcomers being out of work at Macclesfield ? "

But the real crux of the matter, he went on, had not been in the slightest degree touched upon in Ellice's speech. He, personally, had never conversed with a single merchant or manufacturer who did not admit that, if a higher protecting duty were imposed than 30 per cent., the supply of foreign silk goods would be thrown into the hands of the smuggler. The only argument for prohibition in preference to a protecting duty was the right of search which accompanied it—that, after the forbidden goods had been landed in this country, and were in the possession of individuals, even for their own use or consumption, they might be followed into private dwellings, nay, into the very pockets of the wearers, and seized, in the King's name, at the bare suggestion of any common informer. And what did this repulsive provision amount to ? The whole of the seizures of smuggled silk in this country for the past ten years did not exceed £5,000 per year. Now the values of such goods as were regularly entered at the custom-houses of France for exportation to this country were from £100,000 to £150,000 a year, and this was exclusive of the far greater supply poured in through all the channels of smuggling, without being subjected to any entry. In fact, there was scarcely a haberdasher's shop, in the smallest village of the kingdom, in which prohibited silks were not sold, and that in the face of day. As for Bandana handkerchiefs, which figured at the East India Company sales to the amount of between 800,000 and a million handkerchiefs each year, at 4/- a piece, and were shipped off for Hamburg, Antwerp, Rotterdam, Ostend, or Guernsey—were they retained in the Continent ? Was it not notorious and undenied that they nearly all illicitly found their way back to this country, to be sold at 8/- a piece !

"Upon the motion of this evening, then, we have to make our choice between a moderate protecting duty which can be collected, and the going back to the system of prohibition productive of such mischievous consequences." [1]

[1] This speech—which occupied two hours and ten minutes in delivery— was one of Huskisson's finest efforts—" the most masterly I ever heard him or anyone else ever make," said Hobhouse ; indeed, it seems to me one of

Baring's reply. The debate was adjourned to a second evening, when Baring made the best of a very poor case. There was nothing in his speech of 1820, he maintained, that he would not stand up and contend for now as decidedly as he did then. But adherence to the general principles of Free Trade did not exclude the adaptation of these principles, or special temporary exceptions, in particular circumstances, although he was aware that the burden of proof lay with those who called for the exceptions. Huskisson was too much disposed to act ruthlessly upon abstract principles, while it was impossible to sit five minutes in the House without being convinced that no particular rule could be applied to the circumstances of this country. Nobody rejoiced more than he did that a professorship had been founded in the University of Oxford for the teaching of Political Economy.[1] But political economy was a very difficult science, and, as yet, nothing like agreement was to be met with among its professors. His late friend, Ricardo, for instance, had some of the most fanciful theories that could be imagined—take his notion of a compensation between the property of the country and the public debt—take his absurd idea of the extent of capital he thought requisite for a national bank. In the same way, Malthus had written a pamphlet to prove that the Corn Laws had nothing to do with the question of rents. This was to be paralleled only by M'Culloch's doctrine respecting absenteeism in Ireland—if ever an absurdity had been sent forth by a learned and intelligent man, it was the doctrine that absenteeism was no injury whatever to that country.[2] What was to become of a nation if

the finest " fighting speeches " on record. But, like all fighting speeches, it was a little unfair, and was more of a reply to the seconder of the motion, who had called in question the principle of Free Trade, than to Ellice.

[1] This was Nassau William Senior (1790-1864); educated at Eton and Magdalen ; at the Bar, 1819 ; made his first appearance as an economist in a *Quarterly* article on the Corn Law Committee Report ; first holder (for five years) of the new chair founded in Oxford in 1825 by Henry Drummond.

[2] J. R. M'Culloch—always venomously pursued by *Blackwood* as " The Stot," the " stupid savage," the " dour dull fellow," and by Cobbett as " Peter "—examined before a Committee, in 1825, had said : " The income of a landlord when he is an absentee is really as much expended in Ireland as if he were living in it." The statement caused a great sensation, and was usually quoted as another extravagance of the " economists." So far as I can make out from further elaboration by M'Culloch, he confused the ordinary export of produce for sale abroad with the export in remittance of rent ; the difference being that the former is, one way or other, balanced by a corresponding import, while the latter comes to a terminus in the foreign country. " Ireland gets no return except receipts for rents." But, apart from this, the wider question—usually discussed as if it were the same—whether a resident

its legislation was guided by theorists of this description ? But, if Huskisson was bent upon applying these Free Trade principles to the silk trade, he must give them entire and universal operation ; he must take that other step, the freeing of the corn trade from all restrictions.[1] The Corn Laws were to be found in the beginning, in the middle, and at the end of every question in which the price of labour was concerned. But his friend refused to give any certain sound on this great matter. Everybody knew that the price of labour must depend on the price of subsistence. In Basle, he was told that the common wages to good workmen were 4/- a week. The foreign labourer could live upon much less than was required by the English artisan, and he lived at a very different standard of housing. But Huskisson had never touched upon the question of what was to happen if the English weaver could not compete, even with the protecting duty—for he did not believe that his friend was so great an advocate for political economy as to set up the rigid doctrine that, if a trade could not support itself, it ought to be destroyed. And did such a question not arise as to other manufactures ?

By this time, the House was ready for Charles Grant's summing   Grant sums up. up. " It was said that these measures had produced the present stagnation and depression of the silk trade. He denied the assertion, because he found that that stagnation had extended itself to every other branch of industry ; was not confined to the silk trade, but operated upon those trades where no legislative interference had yet taken place, as in the instance of cottons, timber, tallow, Irish provisions, and so on. It was, therefore, neither natural nor just to assign that, as a certain and peculiar consequence, to one trade which was common to every branch of our industry and commerce." When the House divided, the motion was lost by 40 against 222—a majority of 182.[2]

---

landlord is an advantage to his country or not, surely depends on the way in which he spends his rents. The easy inference is that such a landlord " employs labour " in Ireland. But suppose he does, and that this labour is withdrawn from " productive employment " at home, say, in keeping a stable for Punchestown, he might perhaps do just as much good—or harm—by keeping a stable for Auteuil.

[1] So said Hume ; he knew the sentiments of manufacturers generally, including those of silk, and they were not afraid of Free Trade provided that its principles were extended to corn as well as to all others (*Hansard*, xiv. 98).

[2] *Hansard*, xiv. 733, 809. That the silk interests had no real belief that their trade was in danger, may be surmised from the fact that, in April, we read of white mulberry trees being imported into Ireland from the south of

One cannot but admire the steadfastness of Huskisson at this crisis.[1] He was no Ricardo.   But, in consistency with an economic theory which he accepted, he had laid sacrilegious hands on an industry which, up till this year, had been steadily and rapidly increasing—twice as fast, indeed, as cotton. ⌐Of a sudden, that industry collapsed. We hear of 8,000 women and children at Macclesfield out of employ ; of 7,000 Spitalfields weavers living on potatoes ; of great subscriptions headed by £2,000 from the King, at the same time as Lyons, Tours, and Avignon had " three times the demand they could supply." All the while, the country at large was without conviction of the wisdom of his policy, and was particularly sceptical about its application to silk, while, in the Cabinet, it is easy to see that there was only intellectual acceptance of his plans. The two things which gave him courage, I imagine, were, first, the knowledge that silk was not suffering more than other industries, wool being as badly affected and cotton even worse, and that, when the purse-strings of all classes were drawn tight, a luxury like silk was one of the first things on which the richer economised ; and, second, that his measure, while perhaps increasing the legitimate supply of foreign silks, would, as certainly, diminish the illegitimate. And, before long, he was justified by the news that the French silk workers, after a brief speculation to deluge the English market, had fallen into " a frightful state of stagnation," and that three-fourths of the Lyons weavers had no occupation.

It should be noticed that all this happened some months before July, when the new reduced duties came into force. It gave Huskisson occasion for a brilliant rejoinder in May of the next year : " All that was thought necessary, on the part of the advocates of prohibition, was to assume, as incontrovertible, that the silk manufactures of this country would necessarily be altogether ruined, root and branch, by the then pending change in the law. Here was the theory of ' practical men.' That theory once admitted, the inferences were not difficult to draw and state as so many undeniable facts—the total annihilation of a capital amounting to many millions sterling—five hundred thousand industrious people, women and children, deprived of all means of subsistence

France and Italy, to encourage the growth of silkworms, and, in May, that several thousands of mulberry trees were being planted in Devonshire.

[1] " With the exception of Turgot," said the *Westminster*, " the history of the world does not perhaps afford another example of a minister steadfastly adhering to general principles, in defiance of the clamours of the timid and the interested of all parties."

—and I know not how many other horrible consequences; all so much taken for granted that I was pointed out as a ' cold-hearted metaphysician,' who, worse than the devil, could contemplate unmoved the certainty of so much wretchedness and distress." And then he went on triumphantly : " In spite of this frightful denunciation, the House resolved to abide the result of the alteration which was then about to take effect in respect to the silk trade. The new law came into operation in July, at a period of peculiar pressure and difficulty in every branch of our manufactures. Yet, nevertheless, I have now the satisfaction of stating that there is no one extensive manufacture which has suffered so little from the distress of the times, as that of which the total ruin and annihilation had been so confidently foretold. Nay, more; I am enabled to add that the result of a free competition has been this— that more real improvement has been made in the silk manufacture of this country within the last twelve months than had been made for half a century before. I assert this on the authority of the manufacturers themselves ; and I say that, at this moment, those manufacturers are not only fearless of the rivalry of France in foreign markets, but, in some articles, are able to undersell the French manufacturer even in his own market ; and so little do they dread the competition of Bandana handkerchiefs, against which no rate of duty however high, we were assured, could afford protection, that silk handkerchiefs are now actually weaving in England for the purpose of being sent out to the Indian market." [1]

While the new policy was thus being attacked from the side of the manufacturers, it had, at the same time, to meet the forces of reaction among the powerful shipping interests, now suffering like the others from the after-effects of the crisis, and ready, like them, to blame their distress on the withdrawal of protection. We saw that the five Bills which repealed the Navigation Laws passed in 1822 without much discussion or opposition. It was publicly stated, so rapid had been the progress of more liberal opinions, that even the shipowners approved of the Bills, and, certainly, when Wallace retired from the Board of Trade he was presented with an address, subscribed by nearly all the principal shipowners of London, thanking him for the many and great services he had rendered to commerce and navigation, and particularly for the changes he had effected in the Navigation Laws. But, in 1825, we find a petition from the London shipowners setting forth that,

Shipping reaction.

[1] *Hansard*, xvii. 626.

to the great advantage of foreign shipping, the new policy sub-
verted a principle acted on for two hundred years ; that the cost
of building and equipping British ships was higher owing to the
duties ; that the wages paid to British seamen were necessarily
higher ; that, in the past three years, the tonnage of Holland,
France, Norway, Prussia, and Sweden had increased in a greater
proportion than the British ; that, since the peace, the value of
British shipping had fallen one-half while the number of ships was
diminishing and shipbuilding declining; and, finally, that the
principle of affording protection to domestic industry from foreign
competition had been recognised and acted on from the earliest
period of our history.[1]

The agitation came to stronger expression in the current year,
in spite of the emphatic imprimatur in the speech from the throne,
when announcing the conventions with France [2] and the Hanseatic
cities, that His Majesty lost no opportunity of giving effect to the
principles of trade and navigation which had received the sanction
of Parliament, and of establishing them, as far as possible, by
engagements with foreign powers. From the beginning of the
Session, numerous petitions were presented to Parliament all asserting the impossibility of competition, the inequalities of the reciprocity treaties, the vast increase of foreign and the rapid decline
of British shipping, and demanding the reimposition of protecting
duties on British bottoms. When Huskisson proposed that La
Plata and Colombia, having no ships of their own, should be allowed
to trade to England in foreign vessels upon the same favourable
terms as were allowed to the national ships of other states, even
Hume asserted that our mercantile marine was declining, and said
that he had consented to the Reciprocity Bill only on the assurance
that the heavy duties would be taken off timber, hemp, and other
articles necessary for ships.[3] The agitation grew so insistent that
Huskisson, towards the end of the Session, thought it necessary to
take some formal notice of it.

Huskisson on the Navigation Acts.   He admitted in the fullest way that the regulations of the Navigation Laws were founded on the first and paramount law of every
state—the highest ground of political necessity—the necessity of
providing for our own safety and defence ; the necessity for being

---

[1] *Edinburgh Annual Register*, chap. 63.

[2] The text of the Convention, which is dated 26th January, is given in the
Annual Register, 82 *.

[3] *Hansard*, xiv. 359.

prepared to afford security to our numerous colonial possessions scattered throughout all the seas of the world ; the necessity of protecting the different branches of our widely spread commerce against all the risks attendant on a state of war ; and, lastly, the necessity of preserving our ascendancy on the ocean, and thereby sustaining the high station in the rank of nations which that ascendancy, more than any other circumstance, had given to this country. Entertaining these opinions, he was as ready as any man could possibly be to say that it was our duty, on all occasions, to look to the peculiar nature of this state necessity, and that, whenever the interests of commerce and navigation could not be reconciled, the interests of commerce ought to give way and those of navigation to have the preference. What we had to consider, then, was whether the alterations already made in the Navigation Laws had or had not exposed the other great public interests, for the support of which the system was established, to hazard or jeopardy ; whether these alterations had placed any particular branches of the shipping interests in a situation of difficulty such as entitled them to specific consideration ; and whether, in these alterations, the Government had merely been actuated by the gratuitous desire to make experiments.

After an admirably clear exposition of the intention of the Navigation Acts—to create and maintain a great mercantile marine in this country, and to prevent any other nation from engrossing too large a portion of the navigation of the rest of the world—and of their modification down till the reciprocity treaty with the United States in 1815, he went on to explain how it was that our shipping seemed to be declining. The peace of 1815, sending back the commerce of the world to its ancient channels, and making every country anxious that its own trade should be carried on in its own ships, had, of course, given a check to the rapid expansion of our carrying trade—as it had done to that of the United States. But there were other causes : (1) the stoppage of the Slave Trade —" when the necessity of kidnapping cargoes of slaves on the coast of Africa was as coolly defended, on the score of encouragement to our marine, as the taking of codfish on the banks of Newfoundland could be at the present day " ; (2) the establishment of security to the ships of all nations in the Mediterranean as well as our own, by the putting down of the Barbary corsairs ; (3) the stoppage of the war demand for hired transports and the selling of the smaller warships—these together set 1,559 vessels and 363,000 tons free to compete with the commercial marine ; (4) the fact that, under the uninterrupted communications of peace, two-thirds of the number of vessels could do the same amount of carrying as under the war conditions ; (5) the interruption to the foreign grain trade under the Corn Law of 1815.

Still, with it all, between the very prosperous year of 1792 and the end of 1825, the registered ships of the British Empire had increased from 16,079 to 24,174, and the tonnage from 1,540,145 to 2,542,216. The number of ships annually built had been increasing for the past thirty-seven years, and, in the past year, was greater than in any previous. The number of British ships entering inwards in 1825 was 21,786 or 2,786,844 tons, as against 6,561 foreign ships or 892,601 tons—" the increased employment of British shipping alone in 1825 exceeds the aggregate increase of employment in the shipping of all other nations of the world." Taking the trade particularly referred to in the petitions—that with the northern parts of Europe—the increase of British shipping between 1824 and 1825 was much greater than the increase of Prussian shipping, and the number of British ships which passed the Sound in 1825 was " not only positively greater than it was in any of the twenty years, but its proportion, with respect to the number of vessels from all other nations, was equally favourable to this country."

He then went on most convincingly to justify the wisdom of entering into reciprocity treaties with the various states, asking the House to weigh this policy against the alternative of establishing discriminating duties, which would certainly be followed by retaliation on the part of the other nations—" a warfare of counteracting duties." He ended by saying that it would be a matter of surprise if, amidst the almost universal stagnation of demand, the shipping interest, which had fully participated in the extraordinary activity of the preceding period, should not partake of the languor by which it was now succeeded. The criticism which followed was trifling—most of it to the effect that the cheaper cost of building, lower wages, poorer victualling must ultimately give the superiority to the shipping of other nations.[1]

Exportation of machinery. In 1824, the Committee which reported in favour of the repeal of the Combination Laws and of the laws restricting artisans from going abroad, had asked that time should be given to make a more complete investigation into the other matter remitted to

[1] *Hansard*, xv. 1144.

them, the exportation of tools and machinery.[1] In 1825, Hume
obtained the reappointment of the Committee for this purpose,
and Huskisson concurred, making the curious confession that he
had taken upon himself a discretion which, although perhaps not
strictly legal, the House, he hoped, would not consider criminal,
and allowed the export of some articles of machinery, such as the
hydraulic presses and others, " against the prohibition of which
all mankind agreed "—adding that at the moment, so great was
the demand for machinery, the orders, with all the hands that
could be procured, could not be executed for eighteen months
to come.[2] As might be expected, a petition was presented shortly
afterwards (from the inhabitants of Nottingham) stating the great
alarm with which they heard of the proposal ; " if, in compliance
with the present fascinating doctrines of Free Trade, permission
were given to export machinery, they must become citizens of the
world and accompany it : as a continued residence in their own
country, exposed to the evils of extensive competition with foreign
manufacturers, whom such a measure must enable to meet them
triumphantly in the market, would be impossible." Huskisson
observed that he could not conceive how we could allow
the free exportation of labour and check the exportation of
machinery. Hume added that the fact was that, by means
of smuggling, machinery of all kinds was already very largely
exported.[3]

There is no notice in *Hansard* of the Report of this Committee,
but, in May of the current year, we find Hume bringing up the
continuance of the prohibition, and bitterly regretting that he had
allowed himself to be dissuaded by Huskisson from introducing a
Bill for its repeal. First he presented two petitions from manufacturers who had received large orders, and were likely to receive
larger, and were unable to execute them. England might supply the
whole world, he said, with machinery ; as it was, an additional
trade was being lost to this country while men were going about
unemployed. And the prohibition was futile, as, if the machinery
was not exported, the artisans to make it were. Grenfell instanced
what had happened at the end of the American War, when the
Government thought proper to prevent copper sheathing being
sent to France, with the result that the French immediately
established factories of their own, and that Rouen was now one
of our most formidable rivals.

[1] *Supra*, 231.　　　　[2] *Hansard*, xii. 651.　　　　[3] *Ibid*. xiii. 1135.

Hume moves
for a Bill.

Encouraged by the reception he met, he moved, a few days later, to bring in a Bill to repeal the prohibition. Huskisson was apprehensive that, if leave were given to export every species of machine without discrimination, considerable mischief must ensue. Steam engines and other articles intimately connected with machinery were already permitted to be sent abroad, and, in some cases, the exportation of other machinery had been allowed, namely, where the manufacturers did not conceive that their interests could be prejudiced. He would not oppose the motion ; but it would be necessary that the fact of such a motion being introduced should be known throughout the country in order that they might be put in possession of the feelings of those most interested. One member said that the introduction of any such measure at the present time would produce most unpleasant feelings in the community : another, that the Committee which reported in favour of the repeal had taken no evidence from such interested centres as Lancashire, Glasgow, and Birmingham, nor had the House heard the opinion of Boulton and Watt and other scientific men, who, he believed, were not favourable to an unlimited exportation of machinery. Philips, on the other hand, said that the export would not only have the effect of giving employment, but would also enable many persons in the trade who now had machines unemployed to dispose of them to advantage to other countries ; but he thought it better, in the circumstances of the time, to refer the whole matter to a Committee next Session. In the end, Hume deferred to these opinions and withdrew his motion.[1]

Another discussion arose on the same subject in the new Parliament in December, when Hume presented a petition from makers of machinery in Manchester begging for repeal (the Chamber of Commerce had petitioned against it), and went over his arguments again—to the great annoyance of Baring, who asked if nothing could be done to stop long speeches on presentation of petitions : he had heard Hume repeat these opinions more than twenty times

Torrens as
protectionist.

before. On this occasion Colonel Torrens, the member for Ipswich,[2] who, a few nights before, had spoken strongly against Protection and protested against " the assumption that British manufacturers required any protection against foreign competition," if only the

[1] *Hansard*, xv. 908, 1118.

[2] Robert Torrens (1780-1864); served in navy ; colonel in a Spanish legion in the Peninsula ; in 1808, wrote *Economists Refuted* ; in 1815, *Essay on the Influence of the External Corn Trade*—which Ricardo called " unanswered and unanswerable " ; in 1821, *An Essay on the Production of Wealth*.

Corn Laws were removed, now said that, although he was, generally speaking, a friend of Free Trade, yet he thought the principle
must be limited by another, namely, the policy of each country
reserving to itself the sole benefit of those exclusive advantages
which, either from nature or by acquisition, it might enjoy. Why,
e.g. give the advantage of our cheap coal to other countries ? an
export duty of 50 per cent. would benefit the revenue and prevent
the foreign manufacturer from competing. Similarly, if we made
better machinery than our rivals, why give away this exclusive
advantage ? The fact was, we ought to keep with a firm hand all
our exclusive advantages. This seems to have struck many as a
new light on the subject. Baring said that it had so long been
the habit to look upon any man as a Goth who dissented from the
modern doctrine of political economy that he congratulated the
House upon the accession of the member for Ipswich, and hoped frequently to find him coming forward upon his side of the question.
It was true, he continued, that the heavier articles of our machinery,
such as cylinders, wheels, etc., were exported without injury to
our trade ; they were composed of a large quantity of the raw
material. But it was different when the material of machinery
was trifling, and when it derived its main value from the ingenuity
and skill exercised in its construction. If we were driven to the
question of an unqualified exportation or a total restriction of
machinery, he, for one, would prefer the latter. And even Peel
fully agreed in the expression of satisfaction as to Torrens' " conclusive and able statement respecting the true principle on which
our commercial policy should rest." From all which, one may
gather that the hold which Free Trade possessed on the House of
Commons was not very strong.[1] It may be said with some confidence that, if Huskisson had not got his Free Trade measures
passed at a time of great prosperity and of high hopes in the
resources of Great Britain, they would never have been passed
during his lifetime.

The end of the matter was that, although the prohibition of the
export of machinery in general remained on the statute book, a
discretionary power was given after this date to the Board of
Trade of relaxing the law, and that, practically, permission might be
had for the export of all the more common articles of machinery.[2] Parnell's
profession of
On 30th November, Parnell asked for returns of the quantities Free Trade.
of foreign goods imported into the United Kingdom in the years

[1] *Hansard*, xvi. 291.　　　　　　　　[2] *Porter*, 265.

1824 and 1826, with the aim of showing that, under the so-called Free Trade, very little addition had been made to the imports. The fact was, he said, that the Act of 1825 did little more than change a system of positive prohibitions into a system of prohibitory duties, and that this new system was, in point of fact, as exclusive of foreign competition as ever. " The more the nature of these protecting duties was examined, the more evident it was that, in place of being of any service to the manufacturing interest, they actually injured it. For, as agricultural produce was too high to be exported in order to pay for foreign goods, the more that were imported, the more British manufactures must be exported to pay for them ; and, therefore, what was most for the benefit of British manufacturers was, the greatest possible importation of foreign productions of all kinds. The right course to adopt was to abolish every duty that partook of the character of what was called a protecting duty ; and to impose duties on foreign goods solely for the purpose of obtaining revenue, and in no degree by way of giving protection to any branch of national industry. If this were done, there existed no sound reason for supposing that a single branch of manufacture would be incapable of carrying on a successful competition with a similar foreign manufacture ; while it was, at the same time, certain that, if any branch should be injured, some other would be benefited in consequence of the larger exportation that would become necessary to provide the means of paying for the imported foreign manufacture." And then he went on to say that, if the duties on articles of luxury, taste, and food were lowered to about 5 per cent., the revenue would greatly rise.

So far as I know, this is the first profession of faith in what we now call Free Trade, by an authoritative person in the House. One would have liked to know what Huskisson thought of it, but he asked to be excused ; it seemed to him that it would be a fitter time to enter on the " solemn consideration " required when the returns had been obtained.[1]

---

[1] *Hansard,* xvi. 200.

CHAPTER XXXIV

1826. THE CORN LAWS: JACOB'S REPORT

IN the previous year, almost the only thing which threatened the content of the agricultural classes was the dread of a change in the Corn Laws in the direction of reducing protection. In 1826, there was much more reason for the fear. The opposition of interests between "corn and cotton" became more acute, and, from the opening of Parliament onward, petition after petition was sent up by the manufacturing classes, praying for relief from the Corn Laws; among them, one from "the working community of Manchester," signed by 40,000 names, and another from the Corporation of London. Lord King made himself conspicuous in presenting these, denouncing, in unmeasured terms, this "job of jobs"— "the most gigantic job in the whole history of misrule," as he called the Corn Laws, to the intense annoyance of the landed classes; managing, at every fresh petition, to get in one of these "little harangues"—sometimes witty, always outspoken—which, he roundly told the House, were better than long speeches.[1] The petitioners used very violent language, complained a member: there could not be a greater grievance inflicted on the country than cheap bread: who were to purchase manufactured goods if corn became cheap?[2]

The opposition between Corn and Cotton.

---

[1] "Little squibs," Lauderdale called them. Every man has his own method of warfare, retorted King; the noble lord has his paradoxes and crotchets; I prefer my own.
> "How can you, my Lord, thus delight to torment all
>   The Peers of the realm about cheapening their corn?
> When you know, if one hasn't a very high rental,
>   'Tis hardly worth while being very high born.
> "So cease, my dear Baron of Ockham, your prose,
>   As I shall my poetry—neither convinces;
> And all we have spoken and written but shows,
>   When you tread on a nobleman's corn how he winces."—*Moore.*

[2] *Hansard*, xiv. 1000.

On 20th April, was presented a Report which served as text for many a discourse. In the previous June, William Jacob, F.R.S., had been sent by the Government through Northern Europe, to make an examination into the state of those countries whose productions found an outlet by the Vistula into the Baltic, beginning at Dantzic. The remit was very wide in its scope, and he was asked besides to look into " all facts that bear on the subject of the changes that might be produced if such an alteration were made in our laws as would leave our markets at all times accessible to the corn grown in Poland." The Report is long and interesting, giving an account of the land tenure, the methods of agriculture and carriage, and the condition of the people in those countries, and its conclusions were perhaps the more credible that Jacob, in a book published in 1814 and again on examination before the Committee of 1821, had expressed himself hostile to anything like free trade in corn.[1]

The Report had been seen by several members although it was not yet formally presented, and, on 18th April, Whitmore, moving that the House resolve itself into a Committee to consider of the present state of the Corn Laws, availed himself of it to point some of his contentions. His chief arguments may be summarised as follows :

(1) How could Parliament in consistency pledge itself, as it had done, to the principles of Free Trade, and yet refuse to carry them out with respect to corn ? Personally—and he was only a type— he could not be an advocate for Free Trade if its principles were to be partial in their operation. And how could the exclusion of

[1] The Report is printed in full in *Hansard*, xv. 400. Among other things, Jacob noted that, in maritime Prussia, wheat was grown entirely for export ; that the inhabitants ate rye bread from necessity, and those who could afford wheaten bread ate rye from choice—" I have met many Englishmen who, after a long residence in these countries, have given the preference to bread of rye " : that, in Poland, when the peasants brought to market their trifling quantities of produce, part of the money was used first to purchase salt, and the rest was spent upon whiskey : that the whole of the internal commerce of Poland was in the hands of the Jews, who might not become landed proprietors, and were bitterly hated and despised : that the Polish gentry were too proud to follow anything but the military career, though the pay was scarcely enough to pay for their expensive uniforms, while the Church had " too few prizes, among many thousand blanks, to induce any but the lower classes to enter on that profession " : that much of the traffic in Poland was carried on by barter without the intervention of money, and that no paper or any other substitute for metallic money was in circulation. Those interested in the history of our Manorial System would be surprised to find how much of the main features of our fourteenth century survived in Poland in the nineteenth.

corn on our part tend to the reciprocity arrangements from which so much was hoped ?

(2) The country had been under virtual Free Trade in corn up till 1815—for, when corn was imported after 1773, it was for the most•part at the high price and the nominal duty—and, so far from agriculture being injured, those were the years when waste and poor lands were brought under cultivation.

(3) The present system gave a blow to the internal corn trade of the country. It was throwing England on her own resources ; the whole consumption was dependent on one precarious source of supply, which might, at a bad harvest, be totally insufficient. Such a method of supply was tolerable only if merchants, speculating, carried over the surplus of good years and made it available for the deficiency of bad. As it was, the apprehension of coming change in the Corn Laws inevitably discouraged this speculation, and the internal corn trade was on the decline.

(4) In such a position as this, the only hope, in event of a scarcity, was that foreign supply should be readily accessible. But the long exclusion of foreign corn had inflicted upon foreign states more evil than the Milan decrees ; the countries from which we must derive our chief supply were in the deepest distress, were giving over the growing of wheat, and were turning their lands to rye, to pasture for wool, and to other crops.

The alteration which he proposed was the one he had moved in and proposal. 1825 ; a protecting duty of 10/- per qr., along with a temporary provision—to prevent alarm among the agricultural classes—that this duty should be increased if the price at home fell suddenly and considerably. Say that, at the home price of 55/-, the duty was 10/-, this would be temporarily increased to 15/- if English wheat fell to 50/-, to 20/- if it fell to 45/-, and to 25/- if it fell to 40/-. He was convinced that, in no case, was there any fear of " a deluge of foreign corn." Taking the twenty-one years from 1800 till 1820—embracing periods of scarcity and of prices so high that we had corn sent to us from every quarter of the globe—the annual average amount of corn imported was 600,000 qrs., and the price 84/6. And it must be remembered that it was the very high price which had induced the richer countries to afford us any abundant supply ; " it was the poor country, and the poor alone, which furnished that supply of grain which the wants of this country required." Indeed, he had no hesitation in saying that, if the average price in this country were from 55/- to 60/-, they could never expect a larger amount of grain to find its way to this market than the 400,000 qrs., which were the overplus of the maritime countries and those districts near the navigable rivers. And he appealed to Jacob's statement that, if a duty of 10 per cent. or 12 per cent. was imposed upon the importation of corn from Poland, it would, in his opinion, put an effectual stop to the importation of grain from Poland except in extraordinary seasons.

Philips, as a representative manufacturer, seconded, and put forward two new points. One was that while, according to the member for Cumberland (Curwen), the labour employed in agriculture constituted 20 per cent. or 25 per cent. of the value of its products, in the cotton trade, the proportion of labour cost was fully 60 per cent. ; thus a high price of corn led either to a great increase in wages—which would put us out of competition in the foreign market—or to the starvation of the labouring classes. The other was that the land did not, as was so frequently asserted, pay all the poor rates. According to returns furnished at his instance, it appeared that, out of the £6 millions of poor rates, more than £2 millions were assessed on other property than land. But these returns did not tell the whole truth, because it was the custom, in some of the agricultural counties, to pay wages out of the poor rates, while, in the manufacturing counties, this was never done ; this was the reason why the poor rates in Lancashire were only at the rate of 4/- while those of Sussex were at 21/- in the pound.

Lord Milton, the member for Yorkshire, supported the motion by telling his brother landowners some very plain truths about themselves. A revision of the Corn Laws, he said, would not be injurious to the landed interest. It would, indeed, occasion a considerable fall of rents, although this would be so far compensated by a corresponding fall in the price of all articles of consumption. But the " agricultural interests " were not the same thing as the " landed interests." " The same number of acres must still be cultivated whether the rent paid was 20/- or 10/-." The landlords pretended to speak for the farmers and their labourers, but the latter had no interest in the high price of corn. Who asked for the prohibitory laws ? It was the landed gentlemen of England, and their object was to obtain high rents and large profits. He blushed for the order to which he belonged. It was said that the interest of the National Debt could not be paid unless the landed gentlemen were supported by high prices—as if the interest of the debt were not paid by the arm of the labourer, and the capital of the nation, as well as by rents.[1]

The only reply of Huskisson and the Government was to stand firm on the decision come to and announced on the first day of the session, that, considering the very great questions which were to occupy the House—particularly the currency—there would be no time to give that cautious and long deliberation to the Corn Laws which they ought to get ; and they refused to say a word on the specific proposals now suggested. Huskisson took occasion, however, to disavow the extreme Free Trade belief with which he was sometimes credited. To occasional or permanent prohibitions he was a decided enemy. But by Free Trade he did not mean the removal of all duties—and, of course, not the duties imposed for revenue only. But he " did not know why one produce of the skill and industry of this country should not be protected as well as another." His object was " to place our commerce and manufactures in a state in which they could fairly compete with the commerce and manufactures of other countries." It was countervailing protection. " If, in the peculiar situation of this country, there are circumstances which render it necessary to impose upon our manufacturers and agriculturists burdens from which those classes are exempt in other countries, it is but fair that a countervailing duty, to the extent of the advantages enjoyed by other countries, should be imposed as a protection to those classes in this country." " What I have already proposed in this Parliament respecting a free trade in silk was, not that all the ports should be opened without duty, but that such a degree of protection, as appeared to me commensurate with the disadvantages under which our manufacturers of that article are placed, compared with the foreign manufacture, should be afforded in the shape of a duty upon the foreign manufacture, and, by thus

Government refuses to discuss the Corn Laws,

---

[1] Curwen's reply to this is perhaps worth quoting for its naivete. In advocating the interests of the landlords, they were advocating those of the people at large ; manufacturing could not go on with cheap corn, because cheap corn must bring low wages and low wages produced misery ! In the debates, Adam Smith was often appealed to, as saying that wages did not fluctuate with the price of provisions—that, in many places the price of labour remained uniformly the same sometimes for half a century together—that the high price of provisions during the ten years previous to his time had not, in many parts of the kingdom, been accompanied by any sensible rise in the money price of labour. But it may be granted that, so long as one party said, with conviction, that cheap corn involved low wages and dear corn high wages, and another said, with equal conviction that, while wages did not fall with cheap corn, they could not rise with dear corn, and a third contended that wages had nothing to do with the price of corn, there was not much chance of agreement on the reform of the Corn Laws.

putting our manufacturer upon an equal footing with the foreigner, to excite his emulation and industry."[1] Finally, answering the charge that the Government had begun where they should have ended, he asked the House to remember the different circumstances under which the two branches of commerce were then placed. Webb Hall, and others had shown that one branch of manufactures had a protection of 80 per cent., another of 60 per cent., and so great was the impression created that the answer of the agriculturist, to every proposal for any alteration in the Corn Laws, was "take off the protection given to the manufacturer, and we shall then be able to enter into competition with the growers of foreign corn." This objection being now removed, they could go on to say to the agriculturist that the manufacturer was suffering from the duty imposed in the shape of corn. Whitmore's motion was, of course, defeated, by 250 to 81.[2]

Meanwhile, there was utter stagnation of manufacture, and the distress among the operatives was very great. In April, as we saw, it broke into dreadful rioting and reckless destruction of the power-looms in Lancashire. On 1st May, accordingly, the matter came up, and Lansdowne earnestly pleaded with the Government "not to allow the session to terminate without making some provision to relieve distress that was so excessive as almost to induce despair." True, the distress was a consequence of "that unexampled spirit of speculation which existed last year"—a cause over which the people had no control, though they were unhappily the victims. But when he considered that the late currency measure, though inevitable and necessary, had given a check to commercial enterprise, he thought a case could be made out for the interference of Parliament. As Burke said, "When a man is starving, his case is taken out of the ordinary principles of justice and necessitates in others a departure from the principles of punishment, and brings the case within the jurisdiction of mercy." Voluntary subscriptions, indeed, such as were being made in many places, were an obvious and desirable method of assistance in case of local distress, but

---

[1] It will be noticed how far this was from what Ricardo meant by "countervailing protection." And, even in this, he gave two accounts of what he meant to "countervail"; one was the burthens imposed by this country—presumably taxes—the other, the "natural" advantages enjoyed by foreign manufacturers. Apparently, too, Huskisson had forgotten that, in the duties imposed by himself on woollens, earthenware, glass, hardware, he had put foreign manufacturers on anything but an "equal footing."

[2] *Hansard*, xv. 318.

this distress was too great and extensive to be met in that way.

Without much introduction, Liverpool at once announced the Government proposals : first, to release the corn now in bond— amounting to some 250,000 or 300,000 quarters—and throw it on the country at a duty of 12/- per quarter ;[1] and, second, in view of the coming dissolution of Parliament, to invest the King in Council with the power of admitting a further supply after giving the usual six weeks' notice of such intention.[2] but proposes a measure of relief.

So far as the mind of Ministers may be read from their speeches— and, however it may have appeared to political opponents at the time, there seems no reason to doubt their absolute sincerity —the reason of the proposal was this. The great distress was due to the sudden cessation of demand, chiefly for cotton goods, two-thirds of the production of which were for export. But wheat had been rising for some weeks, and was now over 60/-. How far the Corn Laws were to blame for this high price was beside the question, for the subject could not be considered now. But, if the rise of wheat to 80/- was, at any time, a sufficient reason for opening the ports, it was reasonable, in this time of exceptional distress, to count something less than 80/- a famine price, and to admit a limited quantity.[3] Now a great deal of corn lay in the warehouses in bond, much of it in the very centre where the distress was greatest. To allow this to come out at a duty of 12/-, if not much of a direct boon, would at least prevent prices going higher. But Parliament was to be prorogued, for a general election, in a month, and after that, while Parliament was not sitting, worse might happen. The distress might continue—might increase ; there might be a bad harvest ; wheat might rise to what was now generally called " famine price " of 80/- [4]—might, indeed, rise to 100/- or more. But till the average of six weeks before 15th August showed a figure of 80/-, no wheat could be imported. In such an event, it seemed very desirable that the King in Council should be empowered to open the ports, if necessary, at a fixed duty. These temporary Reasons for

---

[1] In its final form, the Bill enacted that the bonded grain should be admitted at intervals ; one-half on July 15 and the other half within a certain period thereafter.

[2] *Hansard*, xv. 742.

[3] Indeed, said Liverpool, considering that £27 millions of taxes—many of them bearing directly on agriculture—had been remitted since 1815, would it not be admitted that 60/- now was equal to 80/- then ?

[4] Lord King spoke of " the pauperism price " as 60/- and " the famine price " as 70/- (*ibid.* xv. 207).

measures did not prejudge the general question of the Corn Laws—
were no condemnation of them—did not even reflect on them.[1]
They were only measures of relief for an exceptional state of matters,
not caused, though aggravated, by the Corn Laws.

and against
the measure.   On the other hand, although most agreed that something of the
sort must be done, and that the present measure would not, in
itself, have much effect one way or another, it was set forth that
the Government, intentionally or unintentionally, was letting the
people believe that the cause of the distress was the high price of
food, and that this was a practical condemnation of the Corn
Laws : as Lord Ellenborough put it, on the ground that the
present was not a fit time for altering the Corn Laws, the Government, at the beginning of the session, refused to enter into consideration of them ; now they were taking advantage of the
feelings awakened by the distress of the country to alter the
Corn Laws, but without consideration.   The Marquis of Salisbury
conjured Liverpool to pause before he plunged the country deeper
into the mire of Free Trade.   " The country gentlemen are furious,"
writes Hobhouse, " and the Tory ministerialists in the other House
call for vengeance on the head of Huskisson."   But only one or
two members said, in so many words, that this was a direct blow
at the agricultural interests, that it would induce depression among
them which " would take away the only means that remained of
giving employment to the labouring poor " and would throw two
millions of the most laborious class of the population out of employment.[2]

Opposition of
the landed
interest.   While, however, the first of these measures did not meet with
much opposition—the same had been done in the previous year,

---

[1] I should not think that this was exactly true.   The measures—particularly
the second of them—were a reflection of the belief, almost universally held and
stated, that there must be, sooner or later, a revision of the Corn Laws, and
that the first point of revision would be that 80/- would never again be the
figure for prohibition of import.

[2] It strikes me as rather strange that nobody argued that the measure was
a " dodge " for saving the Corn Laws.   The price of bread is at all times a
serious consideration to the working man, but the situation is intolerable if
bread goes to famine price at the same time as he is suffering from want of
work and wages.   Was the measure adopted, then, it might have been argued,
not one way of withdrawing attention from the permanent evil of the Corn
Laws ?   The working man was not, indeed, likely to say, as the Lords seemed
to suppose, that the Corn Laws were the cause of his distress, but he was very
sure to find them a grievous aggravation of it.   A man suffering from cancer
and suffering from a cold in the head at the same time, has, I imagine, pretty
definite ideas as to the relative place of these ailments as " causes " of his
misery.

and the price of corn had not been affected—the second was stubbornly, and at every stage, contested by the landed interest, and also, to some extent, by those who considered that the measure was altogether futile, as lowering the price of bread by a halfpenny would neither give relief to starving people, nor give employment, nor "restore confidence," and by those who saw no reason why Parliament should be prorogued in a month, or why it should not be called together again in case of necessity emerging. To meet the storm, the Government agreed to limit the quantity which might thus be admitted to 500,000 qrs. But this only focussed the opposition on the futility of the measure, and the objection of vesting a dangerous power outside of Parliament. The House divided again and again, but the divisions showed either that the strong feeling was confined to a few, or that the landed interest had not the courage to face unpopularity.[1]

The occasion to use the powers given by the second measure was not long in coming. The summer was marked by almost

Alarm as to the harvest.

[1] *Hansard*, xv. 784, 917, 971, 1053, 1122, 1135, 1139, 1203, 1366. Creevey's comments are very outspoken and suggestive. On 3rd May, when the first Resolution was passed, he wrote : " I was one of the majority last night in support of his Majesty's Ministers for cheaper corn than the landed grandees will now favour us with. . . . It certainly is the boldest thing that ever was attempted by a Government—after deprecating any discussion on the Corn Laws during the present session, to try at the end of it to carry a Corn Law of their own by a *coup de main*, and to hold out the landed grandees as the enemies of the manufacturing population if they oppose it. . . . And, unhappily for Toryism, that prig Peel seems as deeply bitten by ' liberality,' in every way but on the Catholic question, as any of his fellows." On the 5th, when the second Resolution was passed, he wrote : " Well—the villains jibbed after all. . . . In *language*, the Ministers are everything we could wish, but in *measures* they dare not go their lengths for fear of being beat, as undoubtedly they would. Indeed, it is very doubtful if even this temporising scheme of letting in 500,000 quarters of corn, *in the event of scarcity*, will go down in the Lords. . . . I never saw anything like the fury of both Whig and Tory landholders at Canning's speech ; but the Tories much the most violent of the two. . . . It is considered, in short, as a breaking down of the Corn Laws." On the passing of the Report on the second Resolution, he wrote : " The *land* has rallied in the most boisterous manner. The new scheme is considered as a regular humbug, and a perfect insult to the *agricultural intellect*. In short, Canning and Huskisson are rising (or falling) hourly in the execration of all lovers of high prices, Whig and Tory, but particularly the latter. . . . We beat the *land* black and blue ; but the Lords, it is said, are not to be so easily beaten as the booby squires. There is to be a grand fight." And, when the Bill passed the second reading : " Well, you see the landholders, high and low, are the same mean devils, and alike incapable of fighting when once faced by a Government without any land at all. Was there ever such a rope of sand as the House of Lords last night ? to be beat by 3 to 1 after all their blustering. . . . The charm of the power of the Landed Interest is gone, and in a new Parliament Canning and Huskisson may effect whatever revolution they like in the Corn Laws " (*Creevey Papers*, ii. 100).

unprecedented heat, sunshine, and drought over the whole country, the thermometer often ranging from 80° to 90°.[1] In Aberdeenshire, at the foot of the Grampians, fire broke out in the peat moss and heath, burning to a depth of five to seven feet, and raged for a fortnight over an area nearly seven miles in breadth by five in length : it was making for the great forests of Glentanna at the rate of three miles an hour, when the whole population turned out and saved them. Great tracts of sheep walks in Yorkshire were entirely destroyed, the fire going to a great depth, and even running below the surface and bursting out at other spots. In St. John's Wood, " every greenhouse, hothouse, and all the glass used in the extensive gardens and nurseries," were smashed to pieces by the hail. There was one fortnight in autumn, said Liverpool subsequently—the last week in August and the first in September—" as alarming with respect to the produce of the earth as any period that had ever been remembered." Reports from all quarters entirely concurred that wheat was deficient in quantity and quality ; barley, two-thirds of an average ; oats, generally deficient ; peas and beans much more so. All July, prices of everything except wheat were rapidly rising. The prospect as regards oats—in many districts the most important crop for food—was most alarming. By the end of August, the price was well above the importing point, but still the average of the quarter would not have allowed the opening of the ports, and no relief could have been obtained before the 15th of November. It was known that, in several foreign countries from which oats usually were imported, the crop was a failure. And, besides, there was every prospect that the potatoes crop would be ruined, while the hay crop, in the richest parts of England, was calling forth fears of the utmost scarcity—the fact, indeed, being that it was absolutely necessary to feed cattle with dry fodder just as in the depth of winter.

Ports thrown open.   It was in these circumstances that, on 1st September, by an Order in Council, the ports were thrown open for oats, oatmeal, rye, beans, and peas—though not for wheat—the importers coming under a bond to pay the duty hereafter specified by Parliament.[2]

---

[1] The drought seems to have extended over Europe. In Stockholm, it lasted for seven weeks ; every green thing was burned up, and all hope of a crop vanished.

[2] The text of the Order in Council—which contained the reasons for it— is given in *Annual Register*, 80.*

When the agricultural results were declared later, these measures were fully justified. The harvest was very early—it was got in by about the 15th of August, thanks to the aid of an influx of un-employed manufacturers. Oats, peas, beans, and rye were very short. Wheat, on the other hand, it was found, had suffered but little from the drought, except in regard to straw, and was average in quantity and of fair quality. Potatoes, thanks to the genial showers of September, were abundant, particularly in Ireland. The price of wheat fell after May, went down to 54/- and rose again to 58/- in December. The average for the year was 58/8.[1]

---

[1] One misses, in this year, the homely, naïve, honest gossip of the *Farmer's Magazine*. Like the *Edinburgh Magazine* (whose copyright was purchased by Blackwood for £25), it had gone down in the crash with Constable. Its place was taken by the *British Farmer's Magazine*, published by Ridgway, the bias of which was stubbornly Protectionist. "I am well aware," said Simon Gray (author of a quasi-economic treatise called the *Happiness of States*, which he constantly quoted as a kind of sacred text), to whom was given the leading article in the first number, "that our cultivators, both landowners and farmers, are, in general, disposed to treat what is called, in the cant of the day, *political economy*, with a mixture of hatred and contempt. They perceive that their solid prosperity and comforts are to be sacrificed to the wild, fantastical fancies of a false science so called. In this, I entirely coincide with them. They cannot treat the system with more sovereign contempt than I do. It is founded on absurd principles, and the super-structure, like the foundation, is sheer nonsense." The new magazine con-tained a special section of Sporting Intelligence—mostly the Turf.

CHAPTER XXXV

1826. ·POLITICAL, SOCIAL, AND ECONOMIC

THE session of 1826, says the *Edinburgh Review*, was remarkable for nothing so much as its want of interest ; there were not within the memory of man so few points of difference between the contending parties in both Houses.[1]

Parliamentary Reform. The great measure was Russell's motion for Parliamentary Reform, his general plan being to take a certain number—say 100— of the small and decayed boroughs, and allow them to return only one member instead of two, filling up the vacancies by adding to the number of representatives of counties, and also by giving the right of representation to the large towns which had recently grown up. The debate was languid ; none of the chief men spoke on either side, and the motion was lost by 123 to 247. The same fate befel Abercromby's motion involving Burgh Reform in Scotland. But Russell carried resolutions dealing with bribery at elections, though only by the casting vote of the Speaker.

Ireland. Irish affairs did not occupy any very important place in the proceedings of Parliament. Although Ireland shared in the distress with the rest of the kingdom,[2] there were no industrial disturbances such as marked its course in England, and the only outrages were those to be expected of religious differences at election time. Several recommendations of the Committee of 1825 on the state of Ireland [3]

[1] October 1827, 421.

[2] In August, the distress was aggravated by an outbreak of typhus in Dublin, where camps were erected by the Government in the open fields as places of refuge.

[3] The notable points in the Report were : Acknowledgment of " excessive population " ; the eager competition for land, let by private auction—" the competition for land, or rather potato gardens," said a witness, " has attained an appearance something like the competition for provisions in a besieged town " ; the practice of leasing of large tracts to a set of landjobbers, known as middlemen, who made it their business to sub-let small patches at a high

were acted on, others—such as the abolition of the " fictitious forty shillings freeholder "—had not yet got beyond discussion. O'Connell now declared that he had changed his opinion, and would not now accept of emancipation accompanied by any infringement whatsoever of the elective franchise of the 40/- freeholders. An amendment Act was passed for the establishment of asylums for the lunatic poor. But a mere mention of the propriety of some sort of Poor Laws was enough to call out the unmeasured invective of the Earl of Limerick—a more mischievous, a more impoverishing, a more demoralising system never existed, and this system it was wished to extend to Ireland. In the course of voting the estimates, a great deal of strong language was used regarding the misuse of state funds in assisting schools [1] and institutions, particularly in reference to their alleged proselytising tendencies. An Act " to amend the law respecting the assignment and sub-letting of lands and tenements " was passed with a view to check that fruitful source of poverty in Ireland, the subdivision of tenancies ; and another, " to consolidate and amend the laws which regulate the levy and application of church rates and parish cesses." But the Roman Catholic Disabilities were brought forward only on presentation of petitions, and Burdett and Brougham, while convinced as ever of the policy, expediency, justice, and necessity of conceding the claims, considered that it was most judicious not to bring on any formal discussion.

One other matter may be mentioned, as giving an interesting picture Market tolls. of " local taxation." In February, Spring Rice raised a debate on Tolls and Customs in Ireland. The great evils alluded to were amply admitted. There were many markets and towns invested by royal prerogative with the right of levying certain tolls and duties—there were no less than 2,000 patents granting tolls—the annual amount

rent ; the phenomenon of, wherever possible, " dispeopling estates " ; above all, that " the Irish farmers cultivated their land as a means of procuring, not a return to capital, but subsistence merely."

[1] A statement by Fitzgerald, the member for Kerryshire, seems worth quoting : " So far from being in the state of ignorance attributed to them, he was convinced that the peasantry of any district in Ireland would be found better educated than the inhabitants of any corresponding portion of the Empire—perhaps he should except Scotland. . . . With the exception of the learned professions, and perhaps some coteries of blue-stocking ladies, the poor peasantry of the County Kerry were more learned than the majority of those who composed even the higher circles about London. It was not an unusual thing to see a poor bare-legged boy running about with a Homer, a Cicero, or a Horace under his arm." As Peel said, he did not think this was the kind of education that would best fit them for the usual purposes of life (*Hansard*, xv. 18).

of them something between half a million and a million sterling. Not only were they a grievous tax on the poor, but they were levied with much oppression—in open and insolent violation of the law, said one. It was the practice, said Newport, for the collector to stand at the entrance to the market-place with a huge bludgeon in one hand and a prayer-book in the other. He imposed the oath upon the vendor in a summary way, and, if he met with resistance, took the law into his own hands with the bludgeon. No poor man could afford to try the legality of the charges. The difficulties presented by the situation were as obvious. To buy them up at the lowest calculation would involve £10 millions. The same system prevailed throughout England—say, for instance, in Covent Garden : was this country to be taxed for removing that evil from Ireland which was to be continued upon herself ? If a Commission were to enquire into the matter, it would have to investigate some 40,000 cases ; that is, it would be an endless one ; a very snug thing for the commissioners, said one ; he hoped he had put in his claim in time for a seat upon it ! In the end, an understanding was given that a Select Committee, with limited powers, would be appointed to ascertain whether any, and what, remedy could be applied to the existing evils without trenching upon private rights.[1]

Alien Act.   This year, the Alien Act was recast. Originally passed with the intention of keeping a hold over the propagation of revolutionary opinions, its main provision was that the Crown was empowered, on occasion shown, to direct aliens to leave the country. It was fiercely resented by many, such as Althorp, Hume, and Mackintosh, on the ground that it was a breach in national tradition and therefore unconstitutional, liable to abuse—although abuse was never proved—and a concession to the absolute ideas of continental monarchs. Since 1822, it had been renewed for two year periods, and was defended by Peel and Canning as a measure of precaution and a check on foreigners making this a hatching-ground for plots against their own Governments. The Act having now expired, Peel brought it up again in the form of a Bill for the Registration of Aliens. The power of compelling aliens to leave the country, he said, had been used by his predecessors five or six times, and, by himself, only once ; no one, then, could say that it had been abused. But he was happy to say that they did not consider it necessary to renew this power. The Bill now introduced—which was intended not as a temporary but as a permanent measure—would

[1] *Hansard,* xiv. 439 ; xv. 30.

merely enact the registration of such aliens as thought proper to take up their residence in the country. The Government was warmly congratulated on their decision. Hobhouse, overflowing with gratitude, said that the old Aliens Act, whether in actual or threatened operation, had always been reckoned by enlightened foreigners as one of those measures by which England had suffered herself to become connected with the arbitrary system of the Continent, and this would be a principal step towards a return to the policy which so long made Britain the protectress of the oppressed.[1]

The growing impatience with slavery showed itself in many Slavery. forms. The table was covered with petitions. Canning intimated that he was about to direct our own officers in the colonies to introduce into each of the colonial legislatures a Bill embracing all the instructions of the Order in Council of 1824, which would test the sincerity of their professions. A Resolution was adopted relative to the execution of eight slaves in Jamaica, after a trial on which, said Denman, no conviction could possibly have followed in England, stating that in this the House saw " further proof of the evils inseparably attendant upon a state of slavery, and expressing its increased conviction of the propriety of the Resolutions passed in 1823." The planters, on the other hand, began a counter agitation embodied in petitions which did not want for support at home.

Many of the controversies still connected with the regulation of Public-houses. public-houses began to take shape in this year, and drew forth some interesting expressions of opinion. In presenting a private petition, recommending the abolition of the application to magistrates as leading to jobbery in the granting of licences, Hume roundly declared that he did not see why any licence should be required for a public-house more than for a house in which tea and coffee were retailed ; if any abuses were discovered, the law was sufficiently powerful to put them down—" they all knew that, when a licence was granted, it raised the value of a house from £500 to £1000." Again, in presenting a petition from the Licensed Victuallers of St. James', complaining that magistrates had the power of punishing publicans for keeping their houses open at " unseasonable hours " while they were left with the definition of that expression, Hobhouse said that it was too bad that tradesmen in general, unable to leave their business before ten or eleven at night, should be deprived of that

[1] *Hansard*, vii. 805, 1092, 1453, 1717, 1851 ; x. 1332 ; xi. 113 ; xv. 498.

fair recreation which they were in the habit of indulging in the parlours of public-houses. The publicans had no objection to clearing their tap-room—the place most likely to be visited by idle and disorderly persons—at the prescribed hour ; but it was a hardship to close their doors and empty their parlours at that time— particularly as oyster shops, coffee shops, saloons, and other disorderly places, were allowed to remain open all night.[1]

Usury Laws.   Apart from the great measures mentioned in special chapters, the purely economic matters dealt with by Parliament were not very many. It was in 1816 that Onslow began his long campaign against the Usury Laws. In 1818, a Select Committee recommended their repeal, and a Bill was postponed in 1819. By 1821, it was thought that their revision at least was in sight. As Ricardo said : " Money ought to be placed on the same footing as any other commodity ; the lender and borrower ought to be allowed to bargain together as freely as the buyer and seller did when goods were to be disposed of " ;[2] as in the case of the laws against exporting coin, the only effect was to place the traffic in the hands of characters who had no scruples against taking a false oath—they were encouraged to evade the law and made a great profit by doing so. But Onslow's Bill was lost. In 1824, he was supported practically by the Government and by a consensus of opinion, but again the Bill was lost, though only by 63 to 67. The same fate befell it in 1825, when Onslow intimated that the subject had been so well threshed out in previous sessions that he would not fatigue the House with further arguments. And now, in 1826, though Peel said that it was a serious question if the Usury Laws had not contributed in a most important degree to increase the late distress, the Government asked Onslow to withdraw his Bill, to which—congratulating himself that the measure had made many converts, and that many who had at first opposed were now its warmest supporters—Onslow agreed.[3]

Liverpool and Manchester Railway Bill.   In 1825, as we saw, the Liverpool and Manchester Railway Bill was withdrawn, and Creevey congratulated himself that " this devil of a railway was strangled at last." In April of the present

---

[1] *Hansard*, xv. 157, 534.

[2] A witty writer in the *New Monthly Magazine* defined the Usury Laws as punishing a man for making as much as he could of his money, although he was freely allowed to make as much money as he could.

[3] *Economic Annals, 1801-20*, 470, 575, 641 ; *Hansard*, v. 175 ; viii. 1144 ; ix. 1014, 1319 ; x. 157, 551 ; xi. 36, 283 ; xii. 150, 531 ; xiv. 409, 1373 ; xv. 280.

year, however, we find the same Bill at its third reading, though
the canal proprietors and landowners concerned had gathered to
its attack. All the arguments which could be mustered were the
following : The measure had been rejected last year ; the original
claim of speed was twelve miles per hour—now three miles only
were claimed, which gave the railroad no substantial advantage over
the canal ; originally, the whole work was to be done by steam—
now it appeared that nearly the whole work was horse-labour ; the
experiment of the Darlington Railway had shown that one fourth
or one fifth of the whole time on the road was consumed in stoppages ;
goods could not be carried more cheaply than by canal ; many had
already suffered from this " mad and extravagant speculation "
—shares which at the first projection had gone to 40 per cent.
premium were now at 1 per cent. discount ; to purchase the land
and carry out the scheme would take £435,000 ; and to pay 1/-
interest, 313,000 tons per year, or 857 per day, would require to
be carried—" it was impossible such a quantity would ever be
conveyed by the rail-road." Sir Isaac Coffin said that the Bill had
been taken up again to meet the views of some noble personages ;
he would not consent to see widows' premises invaded to promote
the views and interests of certain high persons—" he would ask
how any person would like to have a rail-road formed under his
parlour window." [1] Philips reiterated his belief that the rail-roads
would be of no general advantage commensurate with the injury
they would inflict upon private property.

Huskisson brushed all this aside ; private interests must give
way to public services, and measures like this must always invade
private property ; if the railway could not do better for the public
than the canal, all that would happen would be that the public
would not use it ; his own reason for assisting the Bill was to break
down the overgrown monopoly now enjoyed by the canals. It
was a special condition that the profits upon the undertaking should
always be limited to 10 per cent. ; would the canals limit their
profit to this extent—" taking, as they were now doing, more than
100 per cent. " ? With this, the Bill passed by 88 to 41,[2] and
Stephenson was appointed engineer to this line.

---

[1] In 1828, it seems that the scheme of a railway between Newcastle and
Carlisle was blocked by a landowner asking £8000 as compensation for the
line passing near his house.

[2] *Hansard*, xv. 89. The promoters had offered to abandon the use of steam,
or to submit to any restriction on its use (*Walpole*, iii. 20).

The limits of competition.

I have noticed more than once the curious ideas still prevailing as to the proper limits of competition—coming out, it may be remembered, most strikingly in the contention that Newcastle coals should be handicapped by a tax of 6/- in order to give inland collieries a chance. The records of the present year afford at least one more illustration. In opposing a Bill to enable the Welch Iron and Coal Company to sue and be sued in the name of their secretary, Littleton, the member for Staffordshire, asserting that this was to give a kind of parliamentary sanction and authority to the purposes for which the company had been formed, said that he drew a very great distinction between companies formed to do what none but great companies could do—such as working the mines containing precious minerals in other countries, and various other undertakings which required the hazard of immense capital without the fear of great individual loss—and companies like the present, which were created for undertakings of a mere ordinary description, and which were likely to prove ruinously injurious by competition with meritorious individuals. Another member said that everybody knew that this company was not at all necessary ; instead of there not being enough iron, there was too much there, and the great evil of this Bill would be that it would increase the competition to a mischievous extent. Calcraft said that he had always stood up for individuals embarked in trade against those overwhelming efforts of capital, and he would do so now.[1]

On the other hand, the extreme " hands off " policy—based on what were considered Free Trade principles—is shown in a debate when the Lord Advocate brought in a Bill to regulate vessels navigated by steam in Scotland, containing such now recognised rules as that the person appointed to navigate such vessels should be properly qualified ; that the vessels should undergo examination and be obliged to carry lights ; and that the same rules should be observed at sea as those observed by carriages in the streets. Hume said he would not directly oppose the Bill, but he had great doubt as to its utility. It was brought in in consequence of some recent accidents—which everyone must lament—but he did not approve of the system of legislating upon particular events. The public might be left, he thought, to take care of itself. People then would

[1] *Hansard*, xv. 76. Baring noted, as a characteristic of the time, that last year, the House passed all Bills relating to companies of the most trumpery description, and now they seemed indisposed to pass any Bill which was at all connected with a company.

choose their steam packets as they chose other conveniences, and take those which had the best reputation for safety. Parnell agreed with him. Sykes objected to any such intricate regulations : it would be better to leave the conduct of the captain at least free, and not to interfere with him. Newport said that, if the people of Scotland were not to be trusted with the management of their own steamboats in their own way, it would be much better to introduce a Bill to prevent them from using steamboats altogether. Finally Hobhouse said that the people of Scotland would not thank the Lord Advocate for this interference : he might just as well bring in a Bill to prohibit then from navigating by steam.[1]

As regards foreign affairs, 1826, says the *Annual Register*, was a busy year in almost every part of the world—in Burma, Ashantee, Russia, Greece, Turkey, and the Peninsula ; but the only matter which calls for notice here is the agitation and discussion in France over Protection. A Committee of the Chamber, under pressure of agricultural distress, recommended a Corn Law, by which importation from abroad would be prohibited when the home price of wheat was 26 francs per hectolitre, with a fixed duty, when the price was above that, of 25 centimes per quintal if brought in a French ship, and 2 francs if in a foreign. It is worth noting, perhaps, that the Minister of Finance went the length of saying that French linens required no protection, as, even in foreign markets, they were preferred to those of any other nation. More important is the proclamation that, from 5th April, France adopted the principle of our old Navigation Act : the new regulations prevented the introduction into France of the products of our colonies in British ships, or even in French ships clearing out of ports of the British dominions in Europe. The products of other countries of Europe could not be imported into France in British vessels except from the ports of the United Kingdom.[2] This, of course, like the retaliation on America, was one of the trump cards in the play of those who clamoured that the British reciprocity system had entirely failed. Canning made a visit to France in the autumn : he was well received, but nothing came of it in the way of a commercial treaty.

Besides many pamphlets on Currency and the Corn Laws, the following publications may be noted :

An attempt to define some of the first principles of Political Economy, by Thomas Smith ; Tooke's *Considerations on the State of the*

In France, a
Corn Law,

and
Navigation
Act.

Economic
literature.

---

[1] *Hansard*, xiv. 1244.   [2] *European Magazine*, 443.

Currency; Sir James Graham's *Coin and Currency, an Address to the Landholders; Three Letters to the Editor of the Edinburgh Weekly Journal from Malachi Malagrowther, Esq.; Two Letters on Scottish Affairs from Edward Bradwardine Waverley, Esq., to Malachi Malagrowther; Free Trade, an inquiry; Corn Laws, Foreign and Colonial Trade, Navigation System*, etc., by Alex. M'Donnell; M'Culloch's *Essay on the circumstances which determine the rate of wages and the condition of the labouring classes*; Chalmers' *Christian and Civic Economy of Large Towns* (the concluding volume was published this year); West's *Prices of Commodities*; Drummond's *Cheap Corn.* In foreign economics, appeared Ganilh's *Dictionnaire d'Economie Politique*, Van Thünen's *Isolirte Staat*, St. Simon's *Nouveau Christianisme*, Rau's *Lehrbuch der Politischen Oekonomie*, vol. i.

CHAPTER XXXVI

1826. THE NEW PARLIAMENT

The existing House of Commons had sat since January, 1819, and, The general election. accordingly, died a natural death in June of the current year. The general election in July was chiefly remarkable for the absence of party voting ; " on no previous occasion had Ministerial influence been less openly and less actively exerted." [1] The two fighting issues, indeed—the Corn Laws and, above all, Catholic Emancipation —did not lend themselves to determination by party. In England, the result was an accession of strength to the opponents of Emancipation. In Ireland, on the other hand, the Catholic Association made it the test, and, wherever they held sway, no candidate who declared against the Catholic claims had a chance. One can only hope that the stories told in England, of the clergy bringing all the terrors of their religion to bear on the contest, were exaggerated, but it seems certain that the church took an open and violent part in the struggle. One priest is quoted as declaring that the whole body of the peasantry had risen in tumultuous revolt against their land-lords, and boasting that this extraordinary political phenomenon was, to a great extent, the result of the interposition of the clergy, whose influence had been brought into full and unrestrained activity.[2] Possibly nothing else could have explained the fact that, in Water-ford, the 40/- freeholders swept the landed interest from the field. But, on the whole, no impression was made on the Ministerial majority.

Among those who failed to get seats were Lord John Russell, Lord Howick, and Brougham. The only contest in Scotland was for Kirkcudbrightshire. Cobbett—who, as early as 1809, had been of

---

[1] Sometimes, as in the case of Palmerston's candidature, it was divided against itself.

[2] *Annual Register*, 172.

opinion that it would be " very beneficial to the country " if he were in Parliament—supported by a voluntary subscription stood for Preston, which, it was said, " enjoyed almost universal suffrage," and, amid " a scene of unmixed blackguardism " and tumultuous uproar, polled nearly a thousand votes. The quality of the man is shown in his triumphant boast that he had " bled " his opponents to the extent of many thousands of pounds. As a whole, the elections were conducted with much violence. At Carlisle, where the whole police force consisted of two constables, the military were called in to keep the peace. " The Government continued its course, neither very much loved nor very much feared."

The new Parliament met on 14th November, and was opened in person by the King, who was received among great demonstrations —" all former mistakes either forgotten or forgiven." He had the satisfaction of saying in the Speech, that, though the revenue was affected, " there had been no such diminution in the internal consumption of the country as to excite any. apprehensions that the great sources of wealth and prosperity had been impaired : at the same time, the depression under which the trade and manufactures of the country had been labouring had abated more slowly than he had thought himself warranted in anticipating. But, it was emphasised, Parliament had been called together for the one purpose of communicating the opening of the ports, and asking an indemnity for the Government. The measures taken were universally approved, and the duty for oats was fixed at 2/-, and 2/2 per boll on oatmeal, while 3/6 was imposed on the quarter of rye, beans, and peas, these duties to continue till 15th February, when the next averages would be struck. But, ignoring this one special purpose, many members took occasion to attack the Government for an Address, as Brougham called it, " composed from end to end of blanks," and much criticism was expressed that no mention was made of the Corn Laws. Could a heavier censure fall upon these laws, asked Whitmore, than the simple fact that this was the third instance of their infraction within three years ? To all this, Liverpool's answer was that, at the earliest convenient day after the recess, he would call the attention of the House to the subject of the Corn Laws.

An indemnity asked for opening the ports.

Non-intervention defined

But, as it happened, one important thing was done during the brief sitting, and it seems necessary to quote it as defining the limits of our national policy of non-intervention. Some time before, bands of deserters had crossed from Portugal into Spain, where they were cordially received, and established themselves threateningly on the frontier. The Spanish Government, when requested to disarm the deserters and send the arms back to Portugal, in terms of a convention recently made between the two nations, winked at the matter, sent eloquent statements that had nothing to do with it, gave repeated assurance to England that his Catholic Majesty would neither consent to nor allow any aggression against Portugal, and did nothing. Finally, an army of several thousand men, drilled and equipped, it was said, by Spain, crossed the frontier at several points, carrying terror and devastation, and proclaiming sometimes a brother of the reigning sovereign, sometimes a Spanish princess, sometimes even Ferdinand himself, as the rightful occupant of the Portuguese throne. On 3rd December, the Princess Regent, in virtue of the ancient obligation of alliance and amity, renewed as late as 1815, claimed His Majesty's "aid against a hostile aggression from Spain." The Government waited till the news was confirmed. "On Friday night," said Canning, in one of his most brilliant speeches, "this precise information arrived. On Saturday, His Majesty's confidential servants came to a decision. On Sunday, that decision received the sanction of His Majesty. On Monday, it was communicated to both Houses of Parliament— and this day, Sir (Tuesday)—at the hour in which I have the honour of addressing you—the troops are on their march for embarkation."

The action of the Government was enthusiastically applauded by all parties. Indeed, the case seems quite clear : we were bound, not only by ancient ties, but by a treaty renewed as late as 1815, to defend Portugal against aggression. One voice almost alone broke the harmony; it was that of Hume. He could not deny, he said, that such a treaty was in existence. But such treaties were to be deprecated, and it would not be amiss to discuss the question whether or not, in sound political expediency and discretion, we were to be bound by them. Were we to give Portugal our aid and protection, although it was morally certain that we could never expect to receive any assistance from her ? The question was whether we were called upon, in sound policy, to plunge rashly into hostilities of which no man could see the end. Canning had wholly overlooked the most important point of all, namely, whether this country was in a condition to go to war, or able to bear the new burdens which such a state of things would impose upon it. It was all very fine to talk of keeping faith with foreigners, but the right honourable gentleman was about to place this country in a state that it must

in the case
of Portugal.

Hume's
protest.

either break the national faith with its own creditors at home or with its allies abroad. He did not think, besides, that a *casus foederis* had been made out—the aggression had not been made by Spaniards. Canning was mistaken in supposing that he would carry with him the feelings of the people of England with regard to the proposed war at a time when the workmen, in the most important branches of industry, were unable to obtain the means of subsistence. The war could not be carried on without the imposition of fresh taxes, and therefore nothing but the necessity of defending themselves ought to induce the House to consent to the commencement of hostilities.[1] He was seconded by Wood, the member for Preston, who said that self-preservation was the first law of nature ; " to our own people we were bound by the ties of nature—foreign ties were merely conventional."

Baring on treaty obligations.
    To this, Baring made a very strong reply. Was an exhibition of pusillanimity the way to secure respect and peace ? It was not to the point to say that the treaty with Portugal was imprudent— on the whole, he thought it was : the only question for the House to consider was, Is the faith of England engaged to afford protection to Portugal ? Could any man with a spark of honour say that this was the moment to discuss the prudence of such treaties ? Was it to be contended, said Brougham, in a magnificent burst of indigna- tion, that this country could go on for twelve years without ever objecting to the treaty ; taking all the benefit of it, admitting the obligation of it, calling upon foreign powers to fulfil their share of it ; and that we could now, with security or honour, because it happened to suit our purpose to stand by the treaty no longer, turn round and say that we renounced it, because it was impolitic to have entered into it and we regretted that we had done so ! Would any nation ever make a treaty with England again ? As to the contention that this was not acting " in defence of Portugal," but " interfering in the internal concerns of other countries," he would put it thus : Suppose a body of discontented subjects of this Empire were to take up a position on the other side of the channel, and suppose them to be permitted to recruit on the French coast, and make all the arrangements for a hostile expedition—imagine them marshalled, and armed, and accoutred, and furnished with

---

[1] I have given this speech as far as possible in the *ipsissima verba*. Hume, to me, is such an interesting personality, and, apparently, so typical of a school of thought, that I try to do him justice even when his action seems most outrageous.

every necessary resource at the expense of the French Government
at Paris, or by the agency of the local authorities at Calais, Dieppe,
or Boulogne ; suppose them seen hovering in French vessels upon
our coasts, or landing to carry the brand of invasion into the country :
then suppose our Minister representing at the foot of the throne in
Paris—" This is an act of aggression on the part of the French
Government " ; how would he like to be told in reply that it was no
such thing—" it so happens that every man of your assailants is an
Englishman or an Irishman, and not a Frenchman." Hume's
amendment was negatived, only three members supporting him.[1]
It was on this occasion that Canning made his memorable declaration of how, without going to war, he had restored the balance
of power, overset by the entry of the French into Spain. " I looked
another way—I sought materials of compensation in another
hemisphere. Contemplating Spain such as our ancestors had
known her, I resolved that, if France had Spain, it would not be
Spain ' with the Indies.' I called the New World into existence
to redress the balance of the Old." [2]

The rest is soon told. By Christmas day, British troops entered
the Tagus, and the rebels were driven out of Portugal. France
informed Spain that she must expect no assistance. Spain made
haste to implement its promises, and the crisis passed.

---

[1] The Press, however, terrified at the danger of a war with France, was by
no means so unanimous. One newspaper gave the names of the four members
" with much respect." And yet this same newspaper, no later than August,
had said that a war might be of some service at present, as " it would put
money in circulation no matter from whence it came," and would interrupt
the whole system of liberal policy, and enable us to go back to the commercial
regulations under which we had hitherto flourished (*Glasgow Herald*, 14th
August).

[2] *Hansard*, xvi. 334, 336, 350.

CHAPTER XXXVII

1827. THE INTERREGNUM TILL EASTER

On 5th January, died the Duke of York, heir presumptive to the throne;[1] and the Duke of Wellington succeeded him as Commander-in-Chief. On 8th February, Parliament resumed, and Liverpool at once announced that, on Monday se'nnight, he would bring under its consideration " one of the most important measures, both politically and economically, ever agitated "—the Corn Laws—adding the ominous words, " if nothing in the interim should happen to make it necessary to put off the motion to a further day." On the 16th, " never better or more cheerful," he gave notice of the proposed grant to the Duke of Clarence. On the 17th, the something " in the interim " had happened ; he was struck down suddenly with apoplexy, and the long Ministry of fifteen years came to an end.[2]

The passing of Lord Liverpool.

[1] Many statesmen—among them Huskisson and Canning—owed their subsequent ill-health to the bad arrangements of the funeral. Lord Eldon escaped a chill only " by standing on his hat " on the cold flags :

> " At sea, there's but a plank, they say,
> 'Twixt sailors and annihilation.
> A hat that awful moment lay
> 'Twixt Ireland and Emancipation."—*Moore.*

[2] It may be that Liverpool was not a great statesman, although one who knows him intimately, if exclusively, by the records of *Hansard*, would gravely dispute Disraeli's epithet, the " Arch Mediocrity." But it was no small thing that, during these fifteen troublous years, the reins of government were held —if not controlled—by one of whose honour and perfect uprightness no one ever had the smallest doubt. His weakness and his strength are best, perhaps, summed up in Brodrick's words : " He looked at party divisions almost with the eyes of a permanent official who can work loyally with chiefs of either party." Full justice, it seems to me, has never been rendered to Liverpool's sound good sense and freedom from party bitterness. The ability he showed of working harmoniously with colleagues of different views was, to my mind, due to the recognition which all sensible men—except politicians—avow, that all good men think pretty much alike in the really important questions of life.

For some weeks, partly out of respect to the stricken Minister, partly owing to the vacillations of the King—" he is a poor devil," said Creevey—the country was nominally without a head.   But the Corn Laws could not wait ; petitions on both sides were being poured into both Houses ; [1] and, on 1st March, in the absence of Huskisson, who was still suffering from severe indisposition and was perhaps aware that he would require to explain away his very different attitude in 1813-1815, Canning, evidently quite as ill as his friend, expounded the principles on which the Government had resolved to legislate.   He claimed as one qualification for the task that he had taken no part whatever in the Corn Bills of 1815 and 1822.   But really the difference between parties was infinitely less than they were stated to be.   He had never met any person who maintained, absolutely and without qualification, the extreme opinions, either for perpetual, unmitigated prohibition, or for perpetual, unrestricted importation—never met with an advocate of Free Trade in corn, who, when pressed in argument, had not admitted that, to the agricultural interest of this country, some protection must be given.   The law of 1815 appeared to him to be " an experiment to combine these most opposite principles in one and the same act of legislation—absolute prohibition up to 80/-, unlimited importation above that.[2]   The consequence of the law was that each in its turn prevailed with its own peculiar mischief, and that they had, within the seven years from 1815, every result that could deter men of observation and experience from ever again resorting to either extreme principle, and, most undoubtedly, from any attempt again to unite the two together.

Referring to the experience of 1816-1819, he summed up : " Thus by the system of 1815, the ports were shut when the supply at home was deficient and when the introduction of foreign grain was loudly

The new Corn Law proposal.

[1] Lauderdale ill-naturedly ascribed the authorship of many of them to Lord King.   Whoever was the author, retorted King, he was not ; but the petitions must give his noble friend considerable pleasure, as they would convince him that other persons could make as great mistakes in matters of political economy as he had made himself (*Hansard*, xvi. 600).

[2] Robinson, who spoke of the law of 1815 as " founded on the extraordinary principles of an extraordinary man, Mr. Webb Hall," put its chief evil very well :   " When corn came to the importation price, the ports were thrown open, and the speculators poured in all the corn they could from every quarter of the world—not in reference to the demand or to the certainty of the market, but because the time for importation was limited, and, if they did not take advantage of that moment and import all at once, they might not have the same opportunity for ten years again " (*ibid.* xvi. 1052).

called for, and opened when the home market was glutted,[1] and when it was most expedient to shut out foreign supply ; and the one opera-tion and the other were produced by fractions of 5d. and of 2d. respectively." And the fluctuations of price from 1815 to 1822 were from 112/- in 1817 to 38/- in 1822. In the latter year, the House had listened to the prayer of the agricultural interest, and revised the law of 1815. Of that revised law, it might be sufficient to say that it had never come into operation at all. " If then, unlimited prohibition, or unrestricted importation, whether singly or jointly, do not afford the proposed protection to agriculture in an unexceptionable manner, and, if it be admitted that a duty is the better mode of protection, let us consider the question of duty."

A fixed duty rejected.

Could any fixed duty ever be effectual to answer its own purpose ? If wheat were again 112/-, would any fixed duty, say of 12/-, be maintained ; if it were again, 38/-, how would a 12/- duty protect agriculture ? It seemed perfectly clear, therefore, that a duty, to be effectually a protection on the one hand, and not an undue burden on the other, must vary with the price of corn. But what should be the base line—the price corresponding to 80/- in 1815 and to 70/- in 1822 ? If it were considered that, in addition to the diminution of public expenditure and reduction of taxation, there was, in 1819, another material change effected in the state of the country by the restoration of the currency, it would be allowed that, on the very same principles on which, in 1822, the price of 70/- might have been a proper one, 60/- would, for all purposes of justice and equity to all parties, be sufficient at the present moment. 60/- was the medium between the average of the past twelve years and the average of the last six years of that period ; it was, besides, the exact average of the past four years. Was it not fair, therefore, to consider this as the price to which the protection of the agricultural interest should be limited and which Parliament would be justified in fixing ? He agreed with Lord Liverpool that 60/- was the price upon which the landed interest were entitled to protection.

The 60/- pivot price.

Taking this as base, the Government were satisfied that a protect-ing duty of 20/-, when the price of the quarter of wheat was 60/-, was as much as it would be reasonable and fair to impose and not

[1] The harvest of 1818 was most abundant, here and elsewhere, yet, " by some accident or some contrivance," the ports were continued open on the 15th of November, by a fraction of 2s., and, by consequence, for the next three months, from then till the quarterly average of February, 1819, an extraordinary influx of foreign corn continued to inundate a country already inundated by a plenty of its own growth.

more. They proposed to diminish that duty by 2/- for every 1/- of increase of the·average price above 60/-, and to increase that duty by 2/- for every 1/- which the average price should fall below 60/-. The effect would be that, at 65/- the duty would be 10/-, and that at 70/- all duty would cease, and importation be perfectly free, except for the nominal registration at the Custom-house, while at 55/- the duty would amount to 30/- ; in other words, to a prohibitory duty, " as it is intended that, at that price, it should be." This would prevent jerks and impulses arising out of extraordinary emergencies. It would equalise prices and keep the equalisation of prices steady. The fluctuation would probably be found limited in a small circle from about 55/- to about 65/-.[1]

They proposed, at the same time, to get rid of another evil of very great magnitude by taking the averages weekly, and making each week's average govern the duty of the ensuing week. This would prevent any deep speculation and take away all temptation to fraud, and vindicate the respectability of the Corn Trade by giving it a character more analogous to the regular trade of British merchants in other branches of commerce. The Resolution proposed contained in detail the price and duty for the other grains— all, however, calculated on the same average of years, and not by the old rough and ready principle of barley being one-half and oats one-third the price of wheat—and for flour, on the calculation of the amount of wheat which would produce it. Preference was to be given to the Colonies, on the principle of imposing a duty of 5/- per quarter on wheat up to a price of 65/-, and, beyond that, of 6d.

The scheme seemed to take the House by surprise, and, indeed, to please very few. Western said that it would be more injurious to the landed interest and more obnoxious to the country at large than the existing system ; among other things, it would spell bankruptcy to the farmers—even prohibition was better than this. Scotland would be ruined, said Ferguson, the member for Kirk- ·cudbright—he repeated it, ruined. So would Ireland, said Newport. Knatchbull was deliberately in favour of prohibition rather than a

The House taken by surprise.

---

[1] It must be carefully noticed that these calculations are in terms of the (smaller) Winchester qr. But the duties were afterwards put in correspondence with the larger Imperial qr. The effect was that the pivot price became 62/- and the duty 20/8. In the debates of the next year, great confusion was made by some speaking in Canning's (Winchester) terms and others in the actual (Imperial) terms. The scale is drawn out in Imperial qrs. in full, *infra*, p. 439.

duty. Althorp, however, as representing an agricultural county, said that the plan was a great improvement, and would not in any way compromise the interests of his constituents. Brougham tried to console the landlords by reminding them that, buying wheat in the Baltic at 25/-, they would actually have a prohibitory duty when the price was 55/-, and promising that, when the British market was thrown open to the Continent, wheat there would rise to 30/- or 35/-. If the duty proposed had been 10/- when the price was 60/-, began Whitmore—but was coughed down, and wrathfully said that, on a future occasion, he would not be stifled. Burdett almost alone ventured to hint that this was very far from being " Free Trade." [1]

Lauderdale's attack.   The first attack on the proposal was made in the Lords by Lauderdale, who now resumed the attitude of a full-blooded Protectionist,[2] under cover of asking for a Select Committee to enquire into the prices at which corn could be shipped from various foreign ports, distinguishing the qualities of grain, and stating the quantity which might be supposed capable of being supplied for importation into this country. The " mysterious secret," as he said, at last was out, and such a plan had never been heard of in any community endowed with common reason—" a plan to levy a duty upon a commodity to be taxed, to be rated, by the price of another commodity which was not to be taxed." Surely the reasonable course would have been for the legislature to ascertain the fair price at which corn could be grown in England ; the fair price at which it could be exported from abroad ; and to impose such a duty as would have made the one equal to the other. He knew, of course, why the present slovenly method had been preferred ; it was that there were scarcely two ports on the Continent at which the price of corn was the same. Excessive difficulties would have been encountered in making out a graduated scale for different prices and qualities, and our ancestors accordingly—who must have seen the advantage of establishing a fairly graduated scale—did not attempt it. But the present Government was evidently ready for any experiment.

What would be the first consequence ? he went on. Let any man in the House tell him what data any tenant could have under the present scheme to offer rent for a farm, or any landlord to accept it—considering that some lands were let on lease, others held at

[1] *Hansard*, xvi. 758. Wheat rose 5/- or 6/- per qr. on the speech.
[2] In 1826, he had affirmed that the maintenance of the Corn Laws was the only way to get cheap bread (*Hansard*, xv. 209).

will. A party of theorists said that the landed interest enjoyed a monopoly. Monopoly! How could 560,000 persons, of all different interests, combine to affect price? But there would soon be monopoly enough under a system of weekly averages—" the most fatal system for the country that ever had been invented." Was it an extravagant supposition that a party of merchants, purchasing a million quarters of foreign corn and having it ready to throw into the market of this country, might, by a sudden purchase of British corn to the amount of £200,000, raise the average from 60/- to 70/-, thereby getting their foreign corn in at 1/- a qr. duty instead of 20/- and clearing a million? The effect would be no less than allowing corn to come to England duty free from all quarters of the world, and this could only end in the utter ruin of British agriculture, leaving us dependent upon foreigners for our supply. " The deception of the new plan was, that it hung out a sort of semblance of considering 60/- an average remunerating price." As a fact, it gave no security up to that price. The probability was that, one year with another, foreign corn could be brought into this country at 25/- a quarter. Say, then, that the price here was 55/- (and the duty, accordingly, 30/-) ; then foreign corn would come in at 55/-, so that, even at the present low price of corn, the new scale would give no protection to the home farmer.[1] The fact was that these calculations as to the price of foreign corn were made altogether too high. " Corn had been landed at Hull under 25/- within the last two months. And, even if foreign corn were at the absurd and impossible price of 40/-, with a 20/- duty, it only amounted to a protection of the home farmer as high as 60/-." The plan, besides, would put an end to fair importation, for few merchants would care to give a commission upon the faith of a weekly average. The project was strangely called Lord Liverpool's project. He would not believe that, unless Lord Liverpool personally gave him an assurance of it ; the Prime Minister was not the man to throw the country into confusion for the sake of a set of wild theories. The project was Huskisson's, whose boasted Free Trade measures had nothing else for their real object than this attack on the Corn Laws. The best possible law that could be framed was to prohibit the

---

[1] The possibility, it will be noted, of Brougham and Lauderdale coming to such opposite conclusions was that Brougham took the price in the Baltic ports at 25/-, while Lauderdale took 25/- as the price landed in British ports. Whitmore said that the freight might be taken at 12/- to 15/-, and the insurance and importer's profit at 7/- more.

importation of all foreign corn, leaving it to the discretion of the Privy Council or Parliament to open the ports.

Bathurst defends.

Bathurst, reminding the House with some indignation that Lord Liverpool had given notice that he himself would bring forward this measure, excused himself from replying in detail on the ground that he did not intend to oppose the motion ; but pointed out that, under the existing law of 1822, the protection was less than that now proposed. For instance, when the price of home grain rose above 70/- on the averages of the past three months, the ports were thrown open at a duty of 17/- and remained open for three months whatever the market price might be in the interval. If it were true that foreign grain could be landed here at 25/-, it could thus be sold at 42/-. And if, meanwhile, the price of home wheat had gone down to 50/-, was the farmer not absolutely without protection ? Yet this was the law of which the petitioners—the landed interest— were so fond, and in which they wished to have no alteration ! The motion was agreed to, and the Committee appointed.[1]

Stubborn resistance of the landowners.

When, however, the measure was formulated in Resolutions and the Bill began to pass through, the agricultural interest had made up their minds to give it the most stubborn, even unreasoning, opposition. It now appeared, contrary to ordinary belief, that agriculture was in a state of extreme depression—indeed, of poverty ; if rents had been paid, it was at the cost of " starving the land " ; the 60/- price, based on the average of the past six years, was a wrong basis, as, " during the whole of the last six years, the agriculturists, instead of making a profit, had been growing at a loss." Nothing would serve them but prohibition or " protection amounting to prohibition." The evils of the law of 1815, against which they had protested so vehemently in 1822, were forgotten ; they asked nothing else than to go back to it. Far from recognising that the measure proposed to give them " protection," they assumed that it was " Free Trade," and denounced it as the work of " the economists " ; [2] took any statement they could hunt up of the price at which wheat could be sold on the Continent—Western quoted 20/-, and one member went the length of 7/- ; flaunted the $\frac{24}{25}$ of

---

[1] *Hansard*, xvi. 1020.

[2] The landed classes, said George Philips, who, after all, were only one-third of the population, were to receive a protection of 33⅓ per cent., and yet they were dissatisfied ! They asked prohibition that they might demand high rents, and they asked the Usury Laws to be continued that they might borrow money cheaply (*ibid.* xvi. 1112).

the poor rates paid by land ;[1] asserted that imported corn would be paid, not in manufactures, but in gold—was it not known that ships bringing grain went out " in ballast " ? (he wished it were " in economists," said Gooch) ; unblushingly argued for the retention of the poor lands—which, perhaps, " ought never to have been put under cultivation "—as a means of " giving employment to labour " ;[2] their premises often so divergent from their conclusions that Peel could truly say that some of the arguments employed against the measure were the very arguments on which he relied for its support. It would be unprofitable to follow their confused reasoning—weak in every respect but the manner of its expression—but the speech of Western may be given : to me, it reads rather like the spluttering of an angry man than the sober utterance of the representative of a great party.

He thought the common-sense of the people, of the manufacturing portion especially, would have been satisfied with the effect of the law of 1815 ; they would have been, but for the invective of the Ministers. Had not the people been misled, their common-sense would have told them that corn had been sold at as low a price as it possibly could. They would have seen that the distress of the farmer was at least as great as their own. The cause of that distress was the restoration of the gold currency ; in fact, it was the value of money which had fluctuated, not the price of corn—it was a fact which could not be denied. (His proof of this somewhat novel proposition was that, where there was free trade in corn, as in Hamburg, Cracow, Berlin, and Dantzig, the fluctuations had been much greater.) His objection to the new Corn Law was that it extended to corn that principle of Free Trade which had so unfortunately been applied to other articles. If this measure were carried, it would throw open the British market to the speculator ; " the immense mass of British capital would find its way into this employment and be

Western's speech.

---

[1] This was Malmesbury's calculation (*Hansard*, xvi. 1295). But did not one single town in Yorkshire pay £90,000 in poor rates ? asked Lord Milton. Land did not really pay a third of the poor rates, said Hume—and what about wages ? were not agricultural wages in England 20 per cent. below those of Scotland, as counterbalance ? (*ibid.* xvii. 98).

[2] " As these sages record, 'twas an axiom of yore
That he who raised two ears where one grew before
Was the country's best friend and protector :
But the sage Doctor Huskisson scouts the old saw,
And proves in his wisdom, by making it law,
That he ' who rears nane where his forebears grew twa,'
Is the nation's great prime benefactor."

continually absorbed in it "—in this, and in the cultivation of foreign lands. It would increase foreign tonnage to carry the grain. It might be true that the high prices had brought poor lands into cultivation ; had they not also brought an amazing extent of the most productive land previously totally neglected ; introduced a better system of agriculture ; increased the quantity of animal food and woollen clothing used by the poor ?   True, we had a super-abundant population : at this moment, a Committee was sitting to emigrate them to Canada " at the incredible expense of £100 a man."   At the same time, it was proposed to admit foreign corn. Thus " Parliament was, at one and the same time, decreasing domestic agricultural labour and importing foreign agricultural labour to the same amount." [1]

On the other hand, the measure was heartily endorsed by Robinson and Peel, who took full responsibility for it along with Canning and Huskisson.   But the most notable incident was the recanta-tion of Parnell,[2] who, it will be remembered, was the great protagonist of the law of 1815,[3] and had not said a word on the subject since 1820.   He had, he owned, changed his opinion ; this was a subject which perhaps, of all others, justified such a course. " If gentlemen would consider what the knowledge was that we had of it in 1813 when he first took it up, or, rather the acquaintance we had of the science connected with it, it would appear that there were ample reasons on which anyone might, and ought to, change his opinion.   Since 1813, the subject of rent had been fully explained for the first time ; whatever were the differences of political economists on other points, nearly all were unanimous in adopting the new views promulgated about rent.[4]   Since 1813, too, Mr. Ricardo published his new doctrines regarding wages and profits and upon the tendency of low profits to promote the transfer of

Parnell's recantation.

---

[1] *Hansard,* xvii. 185.   [2] *Ibid.* xvi. 1101.

[3] See *Economic Annals, 1801-20* for the almost overshadowing part played by Parnell in the long struggle of 1813-15.

[4] The general understanding and adoption of the Ricardian theory—the common use of Ricardo's very terms—is one of the most notable features in the debates.   Indeed, Ricardo's concession, that the agriculturists had a right to be protected exactly in proportion to the greater share they paid of (onerous) taxation than other classes, was very generally put forward, though without recognition of Ricardo's authorship.   All the same, one has to note again how far the great majority were from dreaming of what we now call " Free Trade."   " Who ever disputed," cried Robinson, " that the agricultural interest should be protected ?   The thing was in itself so rational, so self-evident, that the noble lord had little occasion to press his argument in that particular " (*Hansard*, xvi. 1051).

capital from this country to foreign countries." But, perhaps, the
information we had of late obtained, respecting the means of foreign
countries to grow corn and the price at which it could be sold in
this country, was the most important and most calculated to lead
to changes of opinion. When he was chairman of the 1813 Committee, he was so convinced that corn could be grown to an unlimited
amount in Poland, and brought here at a very low price, that he
believed a protecting duty necessary. Now he felt that the agricultural interest had nothing to fear from a more free system even
than that now proposed. Contrary to what was said of him, he had
never been an advocate of high prices ; his whole object was to
secure, by a high duty, a sufficient supply of corn at moderate
prices. He wanted, at that time, to protect Ireland against Poland,
conceiving that with encouragement an immense quantity of corn
could be grown in Ireland, and bring about a fall in price as well ;
we now received 1,400,000 qrs. on the average of the last eight
years from Ireland, and a fall of price—though, indeed, not such a
fall as he had anticipated—had taken place. But the subject
might now be considered with more extended views of the different
interests concerned. The general prosperity of the country was
not equally promoted with that of the landed interest by protecting agriculture. As the consequence of protection was to raise
the price of corn, those who were the purchasers of the 40 to 50
million qrs. annually consumed in this country were obliged to pay
several millions a year more than they would otherwise do for what
they bought. " The effect of an increased price of corn on wages was
very injurious." If the labourers received a rate of wages which was
higher than the rate just sufficient to keep up the stock of labourers
that was necessary to supply the demand for labour, then the increased
price of corn, by protecting agriculture, was nothing less than a tax
on the labourer. If the wages of labour, on the other hand, were
just at that rate which was absolutely necessary to keep up the stock
of labourers, then the effect of the increased price of corn was to
raise wages ; but this would be an operation of some time, and, while
it was going on, the labouring class would suffer greatly. " Again, if
it was true, as it was generally allowed to be, that every increase
of wages was followed by a corresponding fall in the rate of profit,
then one of the effects of protecting agriculture would be to injure
all the master manufacturers of the kingdom, reduce the returns
on the great number of millions of capital invested in industry,
and, consequently, reduce the annual fund for making new accumu-

lations of capital and the general wealth of the country. Such protection would depress capital in another way, namely, by lending a great amount of it to be employed in a less productive manner in agriculture than it would be employed if no protection existed." It was thus that one of the consequences of protecting agriculture was the diminishing of the means of the country to bear taxation. No doctrine was less founded than that of the country not being able to bear its present amount of taxation if wheat were to be as low as 55/- a qr. It was evident that the power of the country to bear taxation could depend upon nothing else than its general wealth ; but, if the consequences of protecting agriculture were to check the accumulation of capital in the way just described, protection, instead of affording the means of paying taxes, would have a contrary effect. All that the advocates of the Corn Law had to say in defence of it was, that the increased incomes of the landlords contributed, by their expenditure, to benefit certain classes of society. But it would be proved that, just in proportion as the landlords had large incomes to spend, did other classes have smaller.[1]

Amendments proposed.

At various stages, several amendments were proposed, voted on, and rejected. Gooch said that no one would have a right to complain if the proposal gave a protection at 60/- to the agriculturist ; but, when the agriculturist sold wheat at 60/-, he did not put that sum in his pocket—the factorage, commission, and other charges took 4/- off the quarter ; and, on this curious basis, Bankes proposed that the determining price should be raised from 60/- to 64/—a proposal to secure so many shillings more of rent, sneered Lord Milton. Whitmore, on the other hand, proposed 50/- and the 2/- sliding scale, with the provision that, when wheat rose to 55/- and

---

[1] Emphasising this in a later speech, he said : If, by any law, the 50 million qrs. of corn annually consumed were purchased at the rate of 10/- a qr. higher than they need be, the charge to the public would be £25 millions—and imagine what would be said if the Treasury proposed to levy a tax of 10/- upon every qr. of corn consumed ! Suppose the landlords got one-third of this, and grant that this much was simply a transfer from one set of pockets to another —what became of the rest of the £25 millions ? It was directly wasted— thrown away—laid out in producing that from a lower soil which a higher would have produced without its expenditure—wasted in growing corn at a higher price than we could purchase it. It was clear, then, that this lessened the power of accumulating capital, and so curtailed both the power of employing labour and the resources of taxation (*Hansard*, xvii. 102). The *Edinburgh Review*, September, 1826, emphasising that, if corn rose, wages, seed, feeding, and farmer's subsistence all rose correspondingly, calculated that, of the excess price drawn from the consumer, not more than one-fifth went to the landlords ; the rest was " absolutely and totally lost to the country."

did not exceed 65/-, there should be a fixed duty of 10/. To both proposals, Canning urged that the 60/- price had a basis ; it was the medium average price of several years, and was considered favourable to the agricultural classes : to depart from it, was to name a price arbitrarily. Hume, again, moved for a fixed duty of 15/-, from July 1st, to be reduced 1/- a year till 1833, when 10/- would be the permanent and fixed duty, " except for Canada as hereafter provided for." But the only alteration carried was that the averages should be calculated, not, as before, on the Winchester bushel, but on the new Imperial bushel, which, as has been said, made the determining price 62/-, and the duty 20/8 ; and the Bill passed the Commons on 12th April, just before adjourning for Easter.[1]

Besides the Corn Laws, little of economic or social interest came Other matters. before Parliament during the interregnum except Burdett's Resolution for Catholic Emancipation—lost by four votes ;[2] the grant to the new heir presumptive, which experienced a chill reception ; and a debate on the expediency of a Poor Law for Ireland, opposed by almost all the Irish members.[3]

[1] The most acute criticism of the Government's proposal I have come across is in the *Westminster* of January, 1827. It was something, no doubt, said the writer, to substitute for prohibition a system under which corn might be lawfully imported at all times. But coals might lawfully be carried to Newcastle and steam-boats to the moon. Dismissing the fears of those who imagined that the foreigner produced corn as if it were a weed, and would give it gratis, and taking 52/- as the lowest return which would indemnify the merchant for importing into this country, it followed that, till wheat rose to 64/- (when the duty would be 12/-) there could, in ordinary circumstances, be no importation. The sole advantage, then, was that a virtual prohibition up to 64/- replaced a legal prohibition at 70/-. What would have been said about Canning if he had simply reduced the importation price to 64/-, instead of dressing out his proposal with a complicated apparatus of figures which could not be comprehended without some trouble ? But if 60/- had been the average price for so many years, how could any regular importation be expected when it could not, normally, take place unless the price were 64/-? And if regular importation were not encouraged, the foreigner would not lay himself out to supply our market, and, at any scarcity, we should have to bribe him to part with his own supply by high prices. The only good of the Bill would be that its inefficacy would tranquillise the fears of the landlords, and perhaps induce them to listen to reason when another change was proposed. The article, it may be noted, quotes largely from Perronet Thompson's witty and trenchant *Catechism on the Corn Laws*, published shortly before.

[2] As Creevey said, this time it was a fight for power, not for the Catholics. One notices, however, that, since 1826, it was suspected that a reaction had set in against Emancipation.

[3] There was some reason for Cobbett's jibe that it was not till England was flooded with Irish paupers that a Poor Law for Ireland was ever thought of ; and the advocacy came almost entirely from Scots and English members. " He had no disposition to speak ill of his countrymen," said Newport, " but he felt that a majority of the Irish poor had a propensity, beyond the people

On 12th April, a new writ was moved for the borough of Newport in consequence of the Right Hon. George Canning having
accepted the office of First Lord Commissioner of the Treasury,
and the House then adjourned.

of almost any other country, to live without labour ; if it was once held out
to them that they could live, under any circumstances, without labour, he
was convinced that no labour would be done." It would destroy industry in
Ireland, said Enniskillen, and a great deal of mischief might be done by the
very proposal to introduce it (*Hansard*, xvi. 1086 ; xvii. 128).

CHAPTER XXXVIII

1827. CANNING'S BRIEF MINISTRY

THE inner history of the protracted negotiations which followed the withdrawal of Lord Liverpool has been so amply told by Croker, Creevey, and Greville, that only the results need be mentioned here. After some weeks, Canning was sent for. Deferring to the King's wishes, he consented to put aside his Catholic convictions meanwhile, and agreed to form an administration " on the principles of that of which Lord Liverpool had been the head." The negotiations carried on during the recess showed how little he had to expect from his old colleagues ; within forty-eight hours, seven The leading members of the Cabinet out of twelve resigned, followed resignations, by eleven members of the Household, and, when Parliament resumed on 1st May, it was found that the administration was practically a coalition, the leading men of the Whigs, with the exception of Lord Grey, having joined the Government.[1] Robinson was raised to the peerage and took the office of Colonial Secretary as Lord Goderich, and Canning united the post of Chancellor of the Exchequer with that of Prime Minister. Wallace resigned. For the first time, Tierney took office, though only as Master of the Mint ; Copley, as Lord Lyndhurst, succeeded Eldon ; Burdett and Brougham were now found on the Ministerial benches.

The chief interest in Parliament, for the greater part of the next and the reasons two months, was the explanations given by the late Ministers why assigned. they had resigned. Though there was no general consent among the seven, the reason given was that they differed from Canning on the Catholic question. Peel said that hitherto he had preserved an uncompromising but a temperate, a fair, and, as he believed, a constitutional resistance to the making of further concessions to

---

[1] A " disgusting concubinage," Lord Londonderry called it. Lord Mansfield said it reminded him of the quotation in the *Anti-Jacobin* : " A sudden thought strikes me ; let us swear eternal friendship."

the Roman Catholics—"I could not remain in office after events
had rendered it probable that I should be the single Minister of the
Crown who was likely to continue opposed to them." Wellington
resigned because he thought that, under Canning, Liverpool's principles would ultimately be abandoned ; Eldon, because he was
against the Catholics, and had intended to resign at any rate ;
Bathurst, because his colleagues had resigned. Sturges Bourne
accepted the Home Office provisionally—it was understood as stop-
gap for Lord Lansdowne, who—with more courage than discretion,
said Althorp—stepped into the place shortly after.[1]

It had become a matter of common remark that, since Canning
acted for Lord Liverpool, the old lines of party had faded out.[2]
There were, of course, *Blackwood* on the one hand, and the irre-
concilables of the *Westminster* on the other, and any person or any
measure disapproved of was "whig" to the one and "tory" to
the other. But, for some time, a stranger coming into the House
of Commons would have been at a loss to know whether any of
the great speakers at the moment belonged to the one party or the
other. But this came to an end when Canning became Prime
Minister ; immediately violent and bitter party spirit reappeared.
This comes out strongly in almost all the debates.

---

[1] No one put much belief in the reasons given, and it seems a little puzzling
that so many who had no objection to hold office along with Canning utterly
refused to take office under him. The fame of Canning, indeed, was an after-
glow. Everyone acknowledged his varied and brilliant powers—"a genius
—almost a universal one ; an orator, a wit, a poet, a statesman," said Byron
years before—to which one might add "an eminently practical politician."
If he had lived a few years longer, his stubborn clinging to a few obsolete
traditions would have been gracefully abandoned, and his inconsistencies
forgotten. But he was yet far from having attained. He had not been tried
by the highest office in the State. He was still a "young man," and was
thought "self-seeking"—perhaps without much analysis of what "self"
meant to such a man. He was ambitious, and ambition, in popular estimation,
is a crime till it is crowned by success. At any rate, it is clear that his colleagues
had little confidence in him, any more than the Opposition had in Brougham.
Grey was honest enough to make a strong attack on his political life and
character—"during the whole course of the right hon. gentleman's career,
there is not any man who has less approved of his conduct than myself." But
this was mild language compared to that used by the high Tories. Newcastle,
for instance, called him "the most profligate Minister that had ever been
placed in power."

[2] It was, perhaps, in recognition of this that Hobhouse's expression, "His
Majesty's Opposition," was counted such a "fortunate hit." The proceedings
of the Government, said Tierney, using the occasion, "for some time have
proved that, although the gentlemen opposite are in office, we are in power.
The measures are ours, but all the emoluments are theirs" (*Recollections*,
ii. 150 ; iii. 130).

The chief subject dealt with by Parliament was the Corn Bill. Redesdale's resolutions against the Corn Bill. A preliminary discussion was raised on 15th May, by Lord Redesdale, who had printed and circulated a formidable set of Resolutions— " a series of essays in political economy," Goderich called them— which went to assert the reasonableness and expediency of the existing Corn Law. The principal contention was contained in the ninth Resolution ; that a Bill to admit foreign wheat on payment of a duty of 20/- when the average was at 60/- would, indirectly, fix 60/- as the highest price for wheat even in the most unfavourable years. He now moved the Resolutions, " with a view to decide whether their Lordships should reject or agree to " the new Bill. After a reply from Goderich, Redesdale declared himself content at having his opinion recorded on the Journals of the House, where, said Lauderdale, with extravagant emphasis, " containing, as they do, the soundest political doctrines, they will go down to posterity and will be read with admiration by future generations." [1]

When the Corn Bill, which had passed the Commons before Easter, was brought up to the Lords by Goderich, the debates, though vehement enough on the part of its opponents, did not add anything to the arguments already urged. As Somerset said, it was " assailed by arguments that had long ago been answered, by facts that had long ago been explained, by prejudices that had long ago been exploded, and by feelings which should not be found in a British House of Parliament," and it went into Committee with a majority of 57. In Committee, however, an untoward incident happened. Wellington wrecks the Bill. Wellington, impressed by the necessity of preventing the ware- housing system " from being made a pretext and converted into a means of practising fraud " in the taking of the averages, and under the impression that the Ministry was not indisposed to accede,[2] moved an amendment that " foreign corn in bond should not be taken out of bond until the average price of corn should have reached 66/-." Goderich immediately declared that the amend- ment was at direct variance with the principles of the Bill, and would tend at once to encourage that prohibition which the measure was calculated to remove. But Wellington persevered ; the clause

---

[1] *Hansard*, xvii. 789.

[2] The correspondence of Wellington and Huskisson on what Greville subsequently called " perhaps the most enormous of all the Duke's political misdeeds," shows that what Huskisson thought might be agreed to by the Government, if necessary to get the Bill passed, was that the corn *already in bond* at the passing of the Act might be so treated, whereas Wellington's amendment applied to corn in bond at any time.

was carried by four votes ; and Goderich announced that he would
not proceed with the Bill.[1]

This was on the 13th June. The harvest prospects were not
assured ; the price of wheat had been rising steadily all the year,
and was now in the vicinity of 60/-. On the 18th, Canning— " looking dreadfully "—conceiving that, in the circumstances, the Corn
Laws could not be left as they were—that it was urgently necessary
to provide against the alarm and excitement which would prevail
if the report should get abroad that nothing was intended to be done
A temporary by Parliament—introduced a Bill, framed on the uncontroverted
measure as
regards bonded portions of the late measure, in such terms as should not occasion
corn. its loss in the Upper House, and should, at the same time, do no
more than was necessary—" since," said Canning, " after what
has passed here and in the other House of Parliament, everybody
must be satisfied that, in the next session, the whole subject must
be fully reconsidered." There were at the moment about 560,000
qrs. of foreign corn in bond. This amount, and any which might
come into warehouse before 1st July, he proposed to let out " under
such restrictions and regulations, both with respect to price and
duty, as would have been in existence had the Bill which passed
this House assumed the authority of a law." In addition, Canadian
corn, at the moment in bond, or shipped from Canada on faith of
the Bill, and for which bills had been drawn and accepted, should
be admitted under the same restrictions. The Bill was to remain
in force only till 1st May, 1828—" by the experience we shall have
had, I think that we shall then possess the best means of entering
on that reconsideration "[2]—and this would ensure that one of
the first acts of the legislature in the coming year would be
to reconsider the Bill of the present session. This, the Warehoused Corn Bill, Geo. IV. c. 57, passed both Houses without
opposition.[3]

While those who represented the landed interest thus failed to

[1] *Hansard*, xvii. 984, 1066, 1139, 1217, 1258. Lord Holland compared
Wellington to Diomed in the fifth *Iliad* : whether Greek or Trojan—friend
or foe to the Corn Bill—was not easy to make out.

[2] The " experience " thus gained was that, of the 633,000 qrs. of corn in
bond on 1st July, 531,000 were taken out in July and August at a duty of
20/- and 22/-. We shall see how, in the next session, this experience was
interpreted, and what use was made of it.

[3] *Hansard*, xvii. 1302, 1371, 1380. The text of the Warehoused Corn
Bill is given in full in the *British Farmer's Magazine* of August. A protest
against it was entered, signed by Stanhope, Malmesbury, Lauderdale, and
others.

maintain the prohibition of corn, they failed more signally in an attempt to re-establish protection in wool. In the early part of the year, Malmesbury, when asking for some returns of the importation of foreign wool, asserted that the home growers had three years' stock unsold on their hands ; the price had fallen from 16d. to 8d. per lb. ; the cause was, of course, the reduction of the duty in 1824 from 6d. to ½d., thanks to which the annual importation, which had been 21 million lbs. on an average from 1819 to 1824, had risen by 8 or 9 million lbs. The wool trade was completely ruined, and it was a singular fact that, with all this increase of raw wool, there was no corresponding increase in the export of woollen goods. " The foreigner took nothing but money." It was another of the experiments of the Free Trade gentlemen, said the Duke of Richmond, and it had failed.

Attempt to re-establish protection for Wool.

When the question was raised on a petition from the wool-growers of Dorsetshire, Huskisson did not think the matter worthy of any long reply. The root of the evil, he said, was the extraordinary speculation in wool of 1825, when British merchants went " wool-gathering " in every part of Europe ; such was their eagerness to purchase that the continental manufacturers not only did not buy in competition, but actually sold the wool which they had originally intended to manufacture themselves. And it must be remembered that, owing to our Corn Laws, wool was now grown on the Continent instead of corn—four or five times more merino wool was raised in Germany than was ever before known. Since then, owing to the general depression, the British manufacturers of woollen goods had not been able to take off this increased supply. The hope lay in the revival of foreign trade—it would be an Irish way of encouraging woollen exports by raising the price of the raw material, particularly when France and the Netherlands were running this country so hard in woollen manufactures. Baring said that Huskisson's reply was so clear and convincing that it set the question completely at rest. To impose a duty on foreign wool would be quite indefensible. Instead of being a new-fangled doctrine, the free importation of raw materials was an old principle of the policy of this country.[1]

The shipping interest also renewed its bold bid for protection. *and Shipping.* Whether it was that the shipowners had really taken fright, or that they thought it might be possible, by a timely agitation, to regain Protection for themselves while their carrying was increased by

[1] *Hansard*, xvi. 1293 ; xvii. 1035.

general Free Trade, powerful bodies of them in London and Sunderland took occasion, in the early part of the year, to present petitions painting the condition of their trade in very dark colours—as was easy to do in the inevitable reaction after a year of extreme activity and speculation.   Baring, most weak-kneed of Free Traders, was quite won over : he had called for the late alteration, but he had since seen some reason to change his mind, and thought that an enquiry at least was necessary.   But Huskisson, who intimated that he wished to attend to the matter himself, was too ill at the moment, and the subject—happily, as it turned out—was postponed.[1]

On 7th May, Gascoyne, Huskisson's colleague in the representation of Liverpool, put forward what he called the effect of the new " Reciprocity Act falsely so-called."   The distress among the shipping interest was an unquestioned fact.   The £30 millions of capital for which that interest counted had undergone a depreciation of 25 per cent.   Within ten years. the American tonnage engaged in trade with this country had increased while ours had dwindled ; the Americans were now in possession of four-fifths of that carrying trade.   If this was the case in competition with a country where cost of building, fitting, and navigating, was nearly the same as with us, what must it be in competition with the northern powers which could build at £8 a ton against our £18, and whose wages were nearly half ? Owing to this comparative cheapness, they could go up the Mediterranean with half freights while our ships could not unless fully laden. " These were a few of the circumstances which accounted for the fact that the ports of this country were filled with the ships of foreigners, while those of the merchants of Great Britain were rotting in their harbours."   He gave figures to show that far more Prussian than British ships entered Liverpool.   The carrying trade was thus sacrificed for the sake of the exports to Prussia, and the exports were diminishing every hour—the whole of them, he believed, did not amount to more than a million.[2]   So far, the foreigners had succeeded in driving British vessels from the seas, and if the present system were persevered in, the destruction of British shipping must ensue. He expected to be told that the registered tonnage had increased rather than diminished ; but this was of no avail, for shipping must be employed at a profit, and now was employed at a dead loss.

[1] *Hansard*, xvi. 1266, 1312.

[2] As a fact, the exports to Prussia were about seven millions.

Another very alarming fact was that the building trade was rapidly deserting us; nearly one-third of our shipping was now built in Canada : in fact, it appeared that there were only 117 ships building in all the docks of this country. In Hull and other places, sailors in great numbers were obliged to have recourse to parish relief. He concluded by moving for a Select Committee to enquire into the present distressed state of the commercial shipping interest. For some reason or other, Poulett Thomson, a new member, was put forward first to reply to this attack, which he did in a short but telling speech greeted with loud applause.[1] He opposed the Committee, (1) because it might be construed into something like a doubt on the part of the Government of the expediency of the principle adopted; (2) that it would necessarily raise delusive hopes in the minds of the shipowners; and (3) because no case had been made out. Nothing astonished him so much as the extraordinary and unblushing effrontery of those who must have supplied the figures put before the House, and they deserved to be exposed. The cause of the shipping distress was obvious; it was the same as that which affected all industries, the over-trading, with this aggravating circumstance that, in ship-building, capital expended could not be withdrawn and transferred, and with the natural consequence that distress lasted longer than in other trades. With regard to cost of building, the parties left out of consideration altogether the differences in measurement owing to the registry regulations of this country : the foreign ship was built at so much per ton burden; the English vessel at so much per ton register; and the British vessel, so built, carried one-third to one-half more tonnage burden than her registry measurement. There were similar inaccuracies regarding the durability of ships, the time taken by voyages, and the number of men employed per ton. But supposing all these charges were true, what did the shipowners propose ? Re-enactment of the Navigation Laws ? And what would follow ? Of course, retaliation by those powers attacked. And supposing that such barbarous measures were thus commenced,

Poulett Thomson's first appearance.

[1] Huskisson complimented him on " manifesting an extraordinary degree of acuteness and knowledge in respect to the commerce and manufacture of the country." Thomson, a brother of Poulett Scrope, was a young Russian merchant who had imbibed political economy from James Mill and Ricardo, and was apt to be more doctrinaire in his utterances than the House would stomach. In 1830, we find him, according to Dowell, " one of the compact body of Whigs who were then meeting in Althorp's rooms, and combining for the sole purpose of financial reform and the reduction of taxation."

which was likely to be the greater loser in this war of prohibition—
the country which possessed an immense commercial marine and had
such an enormous capital employed in shipping, or that country
whose marine was yet scarcely formed and whose capital employed
was very trifling ?

Huskisson then rose, and, taking point after point in detail,
tore the statements made by the shipowners to pieces. The whole
question, he said, was one of fact. The shipowners assumed that
foreign shipping resorting to our ports had increased in an alarming
degree, and that the shipping of this country had decreased in the
same proportion, and the inference was that our shipping would
soon be superseded. If, as he considered, the true state of things
was the reverse of this assumed fact, the inference might be dismissed.
Taking, then, a return from 1814 to 1826 of entrances and clearances,
he proved that, with the single exception of 1825, and although
the trade of 1826 was necessarily depressed, a greater amount of
British shipping had been employed in 1826 than in any former year
since 1814. From various averages of years before and after the
establishment of the Reciprocity System, the same was shown.
True, there had been an increase in foreign shipping—was a miserable jealousy to grudge this ? But, on looking into the nature of
this increase, would the House believe that one-fourth of it consisted of ships under fifty tons, and that the whole, upon an average, fell short of a hundred tons each ? These small ships were
chiefly employed in carrying on the daily intercourse from the
opposite coast of France, the Netherlands, and other ports adjacent
to this country, supplying us with eggs, butter, vegetables, poultry,
fish, fruit, and other trifling articles which found a market in our
sea-ports. Many came with one tide and returned with the
next. Was this the nursery for foreign seamen which was to dis-
lodge us from our rank among the maritime powers of the world ?—
as well might one compare the stage coaches plying between Paddington and the Bank with the mail between Edinburgh and London.
Again, 40,000 tons of foreign shipping were engaged in bringing
bones for manure from between the Scheldt and the Eider, collected
from all the ports and creeks along that line of coast. Would the
shipowners have a British merchant ship sent to Hamburg to lay
alongside the wharf, waiting to collect a bushel of bones here and a
bushel there till she was able to complete a cargo of manure ? But,
going on to the trade " strictly foreign "—that with all parts of the
world outside of Europe—in the year 1814, the British tonnage

employed in this trade was 465,809 tons. In the year 1826, its amount was 503,024 tons, exceeding the tonnage of any one year since 1814 except 1818; while, with the single exception of the United States, there had been no increase at all in the amount of tonnage of foreign vessels trading between this country and those ports. As to the Colonial trade, he proved that the throwing open of that trade had not in the slightest degree injured our own trade or decreased the amount of British shipping.

On the ground, then, that no case had been made out for a Committee, he opposed the motion. After Peel had spoken on the same side, and Baring—although he did not see how, on a system of perfect reciprocity, we could continue carriers for other nations who paid only half price for every article relating to a ship—had frankly confessed that no case was made out, and expressed his entire concurrence with Huskisson's general principles, Gascoyne, admitting that the feeling of the House was against him, withdrew the motion [1]—to the disgust of the Tories, who had hoped that the palmy days of unreasoning party voting were coming back.

As might be expected in the somewhat distracted state of the administration, Canning's Budget was of the most unambitious character.[2] Taking in the £5,500,000 applicable by law to the Sinking Fund, there was, instead of the surplus of £714,000 which Robinson had calculated on, a clear deficit for the year of £2,100,000.[3] Estimating the expenditure for 1827 at £51,800,000, and adding £5,700,000 as the amount applicable to the Sinking Fund, there would be a deficit in the current year of £2,900,000. This he proposed to meet by taking a credit on the Consolidated Fund and adding to the Exchequer Bills outstanding. It was the most expedient course and the wisest—" the country is at present in a state rather to be left to itself than even to be aided, in its return to prosperity, by measures which, as remedies, would be premature."

Canning's Budget.

[1] *Hansard*, xvii. 592. Huskisson's speech was very long, and every point was driven home with a sure hand. It was declared by all parties to be a masterly defence of the new system. I have mentioned only a few of the chief features.

[2] *Ibid.* xvii. 1098.

[3] He pointed out that the legal Sinking Fund for the years 1822 to 1827 inclusive amounted to £26,927,765, and that the income in the corresponding years had been so far insufficient as to leave a deficiency for that period of £1,804,765. In other words, the sum required to meet the legal exigencies of the Sinking Fund, not being forthcoming from income, was raised by borrowing.

The Supply, then, for the year was :

Army - - - - - - - -	£8,194,466
Navy - - - - - - - -	6,125,850
Ordnance - - - - - - - -	1,649,972
Miscellaneous - - - - - - -	2,275,034
Interest on Exchequer Bills - - - -	650,000
Vote of Credit for Portugal - - - -	500,000
	£19,395,322

The Ways and Means were :

Surplus Ways and Means - - - - -	£88,044
Military and Naval Pension Money - - -	4,155,000
East India Company - - - - -	100,000
Duties on Sugar, Personal Estates, etc. - -	3,000,000
Grant from Consolidated Fund - - -	11,600,000
Exchequer Bills to answer Vote of Credit - -	500,000
	£19,443,044

There was some criticism by Hume of the various items of supply, and of "that delusive humbug which was entitled the Sinking Fund." Parnell spoke again of his plan of 1823 for securing the redemption of a considerable part of the debt by converting perpetual into terminable annuities—approved by Ricardo as the only plan that would place a Sinking Fund out of the power of Ministers. Brougham expressed himself perfectly satisfied with the mode in which the Chancellor of the Exchequer was about to provide for the exigencies of the year, and the resolutions were then agreed to.

Peel's reform of the Criminal Laws.　　　The session saw a notable advance in the reform of the Criminal Laws. Since 1818, the crusade which Romilly—"gentlest, sweetest soul that ever lived"—began in 1808 against the barbarous and unscientific laws,[1] had been continued by his friend, Sir James Mackintosh. Mackintosh had some success in 1820, and, in 1821, he introduced three Bills, which, however, were lost. In 1822, he carried a Resolution—" amid loud cheers from both sides "—pledging the House to take the matter into their most serious attention in the next session. In 1823, he carried four Acts on the subject, the chief substituting transportation or imprisonment for death in the case of cutting down river banks, cutting down hop-binds growing on poles, personation of Greenwich pensioners, destroying textile manufactures and machinery, stealing from the King's stores, burglary, housebreaking, robbery in shops, warehouses, and

[1] See *Economic Annals, 1801-20, passim.*

coach-houses, horse-stealing, robberies upon navigable rivers, etc.[1] Mackintosh then gladly handed over further reform to Peel, who proposed to make it a Government measure, and the current year saw the completion of his work. Five Bills, c. 27 to c. 31, repealed about 137 statutes dating from Henry III., abolished the benefit of clergy in cases of felony, laid down the law of offences against property in its new and simplified form, and, abolishing the death penalty in about a hundred cases, limited it to a few definite offences.[2]

Almost the only point of interest in the Royal Speech, when Parliament rose on 2nd July, was the statement that the consideration of the Corn Laws would be resumed early in the ensuing year. Thus ended a most barren session. As was wittily said at the time, " during one half nothing was done because there was no Ministry, and nothing during the other half because there was." The whole tale of general Acts passed during it was 75, as against an average of 113 in the preceding six years. It could hardly be said, remarked Eldon in next January, that there had been an administration in the country for the last nine months. Next year, it was fondly hoped, the great Minister, who had at last come to his own and gathered the strongest of his old opponents into a Cabinet irrespective of party, would begin a new series of beneficent reforms. But it was not to be. " What is your real opinion as to who is to supply Liverpool's place ? I think somehow it must be Canning after all, and that then *he'll die of it.*" So wrote Creevey to Miss Ord on 19th February. The prophecy was soon fulfilled. Canning had

Death of Canning.

[1] *Hansard*, ix. 397, 550, 1244. The following extract from his *Journal* seems to me characteristic of Mackintosh : " While sitting on a stone under the tree my mind was soothed by reading some passage of —— in the *Quarterly Review*. With no painful humility, I felt that an enemy of mine is a man of genius and virtue and that all who think slightingly of me may be right." " What a man that would be," said Sydney Smith, " had he a particle of gall, or the least knowledge of the value of red tape."

[2] *Hansard*, xvi. 632, 1155 ; xvii. 591, 934, 1261. The *Annual Register*, 185, gives a summary of the main provisions. " Peel is a good man," wrote Hobhouse, relative to this, " and he has gained a great and—if he goes on— a lasting reputation " (*Recollections*, iii. 170). A good deal, however, remained to be done in view of what Ellenborough wrote in 1828 : " I am shocked by the inequality of punishment. At one time a man is hanged for a crime which may be as two, because there are few to be hanged, and it is some time since an example has been made of capital punishment for his particular offence. At another time, a man escapes for the same crime, having a proportion of five to two to the other, because it is a heavy calendar, and there are many to be executed. The actual delinquency of the individual is comparatively little taken into consideration. Extraneous circumstances determine his fate " (*Political Diary*, i. 154, 267).

been in poor health ever since the chill caught at the Duke of York's funeral. The fatigue and anxiety of forming an administration, the defection of his old colleagues, and the personal abuse showered on him, showed heavy traces. Ten days before the "short but violent session" was out, on the King noticing his ill looks, he replied that he did not know what was the matter with him but he was "ill all over." On 8th August, he died, of inflammation of the kidneys, at the early age of 57 : "so goes another man killed by public life," wrote Creevey. In tardy acknowledgment of his greatness, the wish of his relatives for a quiet funeral was disregarded, and men of all opinions crowded to the Abbey to do him honour.

Goderich's still-born administration. The Cabinet agreed to stand by one another. The King at once sent for Goderich, who undertook to form an administration. The post of Chancellor of the Exchequer, after being refused by Tierney, Huskisson, and Sturges Bourne, was given, on the King's urgent wish, to Herries—"a gentleman utterly unknown to the country"—who had been successively private secretary to Vansittart and Perceval and was then Secretary of the Treasury.[1] Wellington resumed command of the army, but without a seat in the Cabinet, and Huskisson became Colonial Secretary to lead in the House. But as the new Ministry broke up in the hands of Goderich [2] before Parliament met—the only Ministry of modern times which never faced a debate—its further constitution, and the atmosphere of intrigue in which it breathed, need not detain us. Enough to say that the old rancour of party was never more manifest or more disgusting than during its brief existence.

[1] As a fact, Herries was credited with being the framer of Goderich's past financial statements.

[2] Goderich—"Goody Goderich," as Creevey called him—scarcely deserves the epithet so plentifully applied of being "a weak man"—unless the expression is expanded as "weak in the management of men." The management of a Cabinet needs, not so much special as specialist abilities, and the management of a coalition Cabinet requires an almost superhuman excess of these qualities, for in this case there have to be reconciled not only the jealousies of very able men, but the jealousies of two parties scheming to get a preponderant influence. Goderich seems to me to have made the mistake of thinking that, in a co-operation of equals, there need be no head—that each member might manage his own department. So, after first resigning and then withdrawing his resignation, and thereafter going about with the resignations of Herries and Huskisson in his pocket, he threw up the task.

CHAPTER XXXIX

1827. "HOPEFUL BUT NOT CONFIRMED CONVALESCENCE"

THE chief economic interest of the year, the revival of industry, is one Revival of industry, that gets little attention in the parliamentary records, and, very much for that reason, gets little attention anywhere else.[1] As we have seen, some had ventured to say, even at the crisis of the distress, that it was an unfortunate but a temporary interruption—that the heart of the nation was sound—that no great amount of national capital was lost—that a little blood-letting was not a bad means of bringing back the body economic to its natural state. Anyhow, the distress, which began, it will be remembered, only by the middle of 1825, was as brief as it was acute, and the grant without demur of £9,000 to the National Gallery in 1826, to buy three pictures during the session, does not argue the necessity of retrenchment.

All through the year, we can gather evidence of Canning's all through the year. description, "hopeful but not confirmed convalescence." In January, the situation in Yorkshire is "not materially, if at all, worse than is usual at this time of the year" : the applications for poor relief are on the decrease. In Paisley, there is "decided improvement." The *Globe* says "the great internal business of the country has now resumed its normal course." In February, all the weavers of Glasgow are employed, though at lamentably low wages. In April, an amendment, though neither great nor rapid, is taking place in Manchester ; the wages in most descriptions of cotton fabrics, even of handloom weavers, are rising. In the manufactur-

---

[1] What one must remember is that, at this time, there was not the vast journalistic connection which now brings all the happenings over the three kingdoms into a focus in the next morning's newspaper. Apart from local news, the parliamentary debates formed the chief item, and, when Parliament was not in session, there seems to have been some difficulty in filling up the statutory number of columns.

ing districts of Scotland, trade has now so far revived that every
weaver can get work, " although the prices of weaving are very
low." In May, there is increasing demand in Manchester, says
Huskisson—better wages and more employment ; and Philips says
that the calico printers are doing more than they ever did : at
Blackburn and other places, wages have risen.   There are excessively
heavy imports of cotton into Liverpool.   In June, the demand for
exportation from Manchester is lively.   Steady prosperous improvement in the amount of exports and imports within the last three.
months give unequivocal proof of renewed commercial improvement
in Glasgow, and the transit of goods to London in that period has
increased more than one-third.   At Leipsic Fair, the products of
Spitalfields almost rival the variegated articles of Lyons : the
dealers in English manufactured cottons are making extraordinary
sales, surprising and attracting buyers by many new and beautiful
patterns—the beautiful dressing and the extraordinary cheapness
in the purchase of the yarns and the raw material have been very
favourable to them.   In July, the King's Speech speaks of " a
gradual revival of employment in the manufacturing districts."
In August, the steady improvement in the provinces is shown in a
continued advance of wages—" not less than cent per cent on the
price paid twelve months ago "—and even then the supply of labour
is said to be insufficient.   In September, the autumn orders are
coming in more freely in the silk trade.   Birmingham is in a satisfactory state.   The manufactures of the West Riding have already
attained " a steady and prosperous condition " ;· the prospects
from abroad are more favourable.   In October, great activity is
reported from Scotland, particularly in the trade with India and
Burma.   On the whole, one must agree with Tooke that, after the
late violent changes, the trade and manufactures of the country
resumed in 1827 their usual and steady course at the reduced prices
to which the increased supplies and diminished cost of production
had inevitably led.[1]

Foreign trade.   The almost complete revival, in the foreign trade at least, is put
beyond doubt by the figures of the year.   The British Exports
were over £52 millions as compared with about £41 millions in 1826,
the Real Exports, £37 millions as compared with £31½ millions.
The Imports were close on £45 millions as compared with a little
under £38 millions.   Thus, in 1827, the Exports and Imports rose
again to a higher figure than they had touched even in 1825.   The

[1] *History of Prices*, ii. 193.

Re-exports, however, were slightly under those of 1826, namely, £9,830,000 as against £10,076,000.

The ships built in the various ports of the United Kingdom Ships. numbered 894, representing 93,144 tons. This was a considerable decrease as compared even with 1826. But now the numbers and tonnage told very little of the carrying power, in view of the fact that an increasing proportion were steamships. In 1826, as we saw, 72 such vessels, with a tonnage of 8,638, were built—a number three times that of any previous year. In 1827, " large and powerful " steamers were sailing three times a week between Bristol and Dublin, making the passage in twenty-four hours. As consequence, we read in the *New Monthly Magazine* for February that a numerous meeting of merchants, shippers, and shipmasters, held at Swansea, agreed to a petition. " praying for the interference of Parliament to devise and adopt some means to protect Sailing Vessels against the further increase of Steam Vessels for the conveyance of goods," and entrusted it to the member for the county.

Very little, indeed, was heard of anything like distress except The handloom in February, when a strongly worded petition was presented by weavers again. Hume from the Starving Weavers of Blackburn, demanding, " with the rectitude of injured men, the relief which their unmerited sufferings required." They had, it said, for many years suffered more than language could express, but, within the past two years, they had not had half food, of the worst kind, for their support ; consequently, hundreds of weavers, their wives and children, had died from absolute want of food ; the petitioners, being able-bodied men, could not earn more than 5/- each, and, with two workers in each family averaging six souls, 10/- weekly was the whole for food, clothing, fuel, and rent, and, with all deference to the House, they would respectfully ask if that sum was sufficient for the moderate wants of a man. Why should they who laboured sixteen hours per day not for that labour obtain food and clothing for comfortable existence ? there was a point when endurance became a crime, and at that point they had arrived. The petition went on to say that, after calm and considerate examination, they were convinced that their calamities were due to the people not being represented in the House, and to the Corn Bill, that monstrous monopoly of the landed interest. Believing, therefore, that a reformed Parliament, chosen by ballot and by the whole of the population, would grant unto the people relief, the petitioners, as the forlorn hope, humbly asked that the House would begin a god-like work by repealing the Corn Bill.[1]

Probably this truthfully enough represented the state of the handloom weavers in their pitiful competition with the steam loom.

Petitions for fixation of wages. And, as might be expected, there was a disposition, in some quarters, to idealise the old state of things when wages were, so far, protected from competition. In June, we find a petition presented from the operative silk-weavers of Spitalfields, asking for a law " making agreements with respect to wages between masters and journeymen duly convened operative on both parties," and the member presenting it got occasion, at least, to ventilate his opinion that this might be a palliative, although " the evil resided in the state of the currency." [2] More interesting was a petition signed by 10,000 operative manufacturers of Norwich, accompanied by another signed by certain of the master manufacturers concurring, praying that the House would devise some means for settling by law the rate of wages in that city—all the more remarkable that, as may be remembered, in the previous year there had been riots in Norwich because of work being sent out of the city to be executed at a cheaper rate. Peel pointed out that, if such a law were confined to Norwich, it would be as " injurious as it would be unjust," and, after an interview with the Board of Trade, the Norwich delegates gave up the idea of a local Act and called for a general measure affecting the whole kingdom.[3]

A good harvest. The farmers had little to complain of in the weather of 1827. A mild winter and a genial spring gave promise of a great crop. The summer, indeed, was " of a medium description," but harvest began in the south by the end of July, and, despite a great storm which beat down the grain, and a week of heavy rain in August, harvest home was celebrated by almost every farmer in the south by the 1st and, in every part, by the 10th of September. Beans and peas were an average crop, oats were over, and wheat and barley considerably over, the average. In Scotland, the wheat crop was not so good, being very inferior in quality, below an average in bulk, and very deficient in straw, but other crops were fair. In Ireland, wheat was a fair crop, barley and other grains realised expectations, and potatoes were abundant.[4]

---

[1] *Hansard*, xvi. 412.　　　　[2] *Ibid.* xvii. 1241.　　　　[3] *Ibid.* 1060.

[4] " The crops of 1827," says Tooke, " were computed to have yielded a full average of all grain in point of quantity ; but the wheat, in condition and

Wheat, which in the beginning of the year was about 55/-, rose Prices. to over 61/- in July. Afterwards, the admission of the stock in bond and the favourable harvest depressed the price to about 52/- for the last three months of the year. Oats experienced the same course, rising from about 28/- in January to 31/- in spring, and falling after September to about 22/-. The average price of wheat for the year was 58/6. As this was practically the same as that of 1826, when " the agricultural interest had met with no material check by the recent difficulties," the landlords' statement, when they wanted to find grounds for opposing the new Corn Law, that agriculture was in a state of " extreme depression," seems scarcely borne out.[1]

As to the position of the agricultural labourer, it was com- The influx of Irish harvesters. plained that the distress measures taken to relieve the manufacturing operatives had deprived the country of much of the employment which would naturally have fallen to it, and the grumbling in Scotland as to the influx of labourers from Ireland in harvest time became very pronounced. Some 12,000 of them came over in six weeks, " ready to take any wage offered," aided by a " rate war " between the Belfast steam packets, which brought them at a shilling a head. These " floating bridges " between the two countries, thought Parnell, would at last bring down the wage of the wheat-fed population to the level of the potato-fed.

The obituary of the year includes, besides Canning and the Duke Obituary. of York, the name of Lord Archibald Hamilton, whose independent and manly conduct in Parliament, often mentioned in the first volume of these *Annals*, was gratefully acknowledged by his country. And one notes with regret the great Beethoven dying in poverty at the age of 57, and honoured, of course, by a magnificent funeral.

Of economic books published during the year, may be mentioned the following :

Senior's *Introductory Lecture on Political Economy, delivered before* Economic literature. *the University of Oxford* ; Malthus' *Definitions in Political Economy* ;

quality, was greatly inferior to the crop of the preceding year " (*History of Prices*, ii. 138).

[1] I find that, according to a calculation made before the Select Committee on Emigration in 1827, the number of statute acres in cultivation in the United Kingdom, including meadow and pasture, at the end of 1826, was 46,139,280—as near as possible two acres to each inhabitant. But Porter laments that, even by his time, there were no agricultural statistics ; no attempt had been made to ascertain what proportion of the cultivated land was applied to the production of any one crop, except that of hops, where the interest of the revenue came in.

Thomas Hopkins' *Popular Political Economy; Practical, Moral, and Political Economy*, by T. R. Edwards—a wild extravaganza; Sismondi's *Nouveaux principes d'economie politique* (2d edit., the first published in 1819); Parnell's *Paper Money, Banking, and Over-trading; Currency and Circulation*, by J. A. Yates; Cedric's *Distribution of the National Wealth, considered specially in its bearings on the Corn Laws and Restriction in general; Remarks on certain modern theories respecting Rents and Prices; The True Theory of Rent in opposition to Mr. Ricardo and others*, by a Member of the University of Cambridge (Perronet Thompson); *Views on Corn and Currency*, by Thomas Joplin—the author, said the *New Monthly Magazine*, "has nothing in common with the modern political economists; as for Adam Smith, it had been better for the science if he had never written"; *A Treatise on Free Trade*, by Macdonnell; *Thoughts on Taxation*—bitterly opposed to the whole existing system of indirect taxes, and suggesting that it be replaced by a general tax on houses; *Catechism on the Corn Laws, with a list of fallacies and the answers*, by T. Perronet Thompson.

MISCELLANEA.

"Not only is the present the first year in which a gentleman of Mr. Gordon's rank has attained the highest place upon the tripos; but, which is much more remarkable, it is the first time that gentlemen of that rank have been subject to examination at all. Hitherto the sons of noblemen and the heirs to titles have received their degree of M.A. at the end of two years, as a matter of course!—a peculiarity which, instead of a privilege, ought rather to be considered, and doubtless began to be considered, a reproach. . . . We hail the alteration as one of the most valuable signs of the times, and as a proof that we have *one* university that keeps up with the march of intellect, and leaves the regulations of monkish times far in the rear" (*New Monthly Magazine*, March).

"The members of the Canterbury Philosophical and Literary Institution were lately gratified with the delivery of a Lecture on Gymnastics. The subject, being a novel one, attracted a crowded and brilliant audience" (*New Monthly Magazine*, October).

"At the Lincolnshire Agricultural Society, a prize of ten guineas was given to James Jackson for having had seventeen children (ten living), and been forty years in the service of Mr. W. Taylor of Gayton-le-Marsh. A second prize, of five guineas, was awarded to Amos Greby, for twenty-five children (ten living), and a service of forty-one years in the family of the Bournes" (*British Farmer's Magazine*, November).

CHAPTER XL

1828. THE DUKE'S ADMINISTRATION : THE NEW CORN LAW

On the 8th January, Goderich—" as firm as a bullrush "—placed in a dilemma between acepting Herries' resignation if Althorp were made chairman of the new Finance Committee and accepting Huskisson's resignation if Althorp were not, solved the difficulty by himself resigning, and the Canning Coalition came to an end after seven months of uneasy existence. Within a fortnight of the opening of Parliament, the country had no head.

The King sent for the Duke of Wellington, who, in spite of his assertion a few months before that he would be " mad and worse than mad " to take the office of Prime Minister, surrendered his inclinations, and promptly entered into negotiations with Peel and other members who had seceded when Canning took in the Whigs. Peel, " though not without great reluctance," accepted the Home Office and the lead in the Commons. The Duke, somewhat unwillingly, gave up the office of Commander-in-Chief. Lansdowne, Tierney, and the Whigs generally went out. Goulburn became Chancellor of the Exchequer, and Herries was consoled with the Mint—Wallace going to the Upper House as Baron Wallace. Lord Melville, who was a Catholic, took the Board of Control, Ellenborough the Privy Seal.[1]

Wellington's Ministry.

---

[1] Ellenborough, whose *Political Diary* begins at this point, says of the first Cabinet meeting : " The courtesy was that of men who have just fought a duel." The incredible vulgarity of party politics at the time may be suggested by the following paean from the genial—or " surly "—Christopher on the occasion : " There is a change in the Ministry. The Whigs have melted like so many blobs—not of dew—but of fetid grease—of kitchen-fee (see Dr. Jamieson) drippings fit to be sold only to afternoon mendicants—and have left behind only—a stench. We saw them—we smelt them melting—as the political articles in our present number, written weeks—months ago—sufficiently testify. Shall we henceforth leave the fishy fumes of the Faction of themselves to be dissolved through the air, or shall we dig a hole for the dead body of

Huskisson
remains in the
Cabinet.
But the Duke recognised that any exclusive Ministry of either party was at the moment impossible—he was not going into the House of Commons " with half a party to fight a party and a half " —and the important thing for the policy lately adopted by the country was that Huskisson, after some hesitation, remained in the Cabinet, taking the Colonial Office. The defence he made—that the commercial and foreign policy of the Government was to continue the same, and that the Roman Catholic question was to remain as it was—is, to my mind, complete—for Huskisson. After all, the assertion that he was deserting his old colleagues and " joining Canning's enemies," was quite beside the mark. He had not come in with the coalition. He never did belong to the Whig party. He was a member of Lord Liverpool's Government, and made no sacrifice of consistency, as he understood it, in adhering to the political successor of an administration pledged to carry out Liverpool's principles. If Huskisson believed that Free Trade was, above everything, necessary to the country, he was right in keeping a position in the Cabinet which guaranteed its continuance—and the Corn Law is his justification.[1] But it must be difficult for politicians to believe that anyone in Parliament can honestly prefer policy to party, and Huskisson was much criticised for his " sticking to place." What made his position possible was that other three of the " Canningites " remained with him, namely Charles Grant, President of the Board of Trade, Lord Dudley and Ward, the Foreign Secretary, and Palmerston, the Secretary at War. Otherwise the Ministry became almost what it was under Lord Liverpool, except that Lord Eldon did not reappear, his place being taken by Lord Lyndhurst.

The Corn Bill,
The anxiety of the country as to whether the new Ministry would keep the promise of the old, was set at rest by the Duke's declaration on the Address, that it was the intention of the Government to submit immediately, not the same, but a Corn Bill " founded upon the principles of the measure which was introduced last session." It was inevitable, however, that the Corn Bill of an administration which contained Wellington and Huskisson should be a compromise —the one was bound to justify his wrecking of the Bill of 1827 ;

Whiggery, and inter it deep down in a corp-safe, beyond the pick and shovel of the resurrectionist ? Wait and see " (*Blackwood*, February, 1828).

[1] " If he has already liberalised Wellington and Peel's administration— which is just probable—I think the Ministry is as good as the last," said Hobhouse with his usual honesty.

the other would not be allowed to forget his speech at Liverpool.
All March, it was the subject of constant and heated discussion,
and more than once it threatened to break up the newly made
Cabinet.[1]

It will conduce to clearness to put down the Sliding Scale as it
finally passed, and, as much of the discussion which followed was
based on comparison with that proposed in 1827, to add the latter
scale in a parallel column.

When the Home Price was	the Duty was	Duty proposed in 1827 Bill.
52/-	34/8	40/8
53/-	33/8	38/8
54/-	32/8	36/8
55/-	31/8	34/8
56/-	30/8	32/8
57/-	29/8	30/8
58/-	28/8	28/8
59/-	27/8	26/8
60/-	26/8	24/8
61/-	25/8	22/8
62/-	24/8	20/8
63/-	23/8	18/8
64/-	22/8	16/8
65/-	21/8	14/8
66/-	20/8	12/8
67/-	18/8	10/8
68/-	16/8	6/8
69/-	13/8	4/8
70/-	10/8	2/8
71/-	6/8	1/-
72/-	2/8	1/-
73/-	1/-	—

The above is by Imperial measure. Where the old Winchester
measure was used, the duty was 30/- when the home price was 54/-,
decreasing in the same manner as in the Imperial scale.

In intimating the terms of the Bill to the House of Lords, the —" to con-
Prime Minister explained why he had dropped the amendment ciliate all
which wrecked the previous Bill : the object of that amendment parties."

[1] According to Ellenborough, Huskisson insisted on it being a Cabinet
measure, saying that he was so pledged to the principle of the 1827 Bill that
he must resign if that principle was not preserved. The Duke's proposal was
that at 55/- (Winchester) the duty should be 30/-, diminishing shilling by
shilling to 65/-, and then more rapidly till it disappeared at 72/-. Peel sided
with Huskisson. From day to day, changes and modifications were suggested
and fought over. On 12th March, the Cabinet separated with every prospect
of breaking up. Grant sulked and absented himself. Ellenborough negotiated
in vain. On the 25th, Grant notified his resignation, which, however, was not
accepted. Even on the 29th, it was thought that Grant would be " indisposed "
and leave the Bill to be brought in by Peel. But, at the last, he gave in, and,
on the 31st, Wellington and he intimated the proposals in the two Houses.

had been " to prevent frauds in the system of the averages from
being carried into execution by means of the warehousing system " ;
it was unnecessary now that these frauds were prevented by including
the Irish and Scotch corn in the market, and extending the number
of places at which the average was struck. As to the principle
of the Bill, all were agreed that some protection should be given to
agriculture, but, on the amount of the protection desirable, opinions
differed very widely. The country could no more bear a price of
70/- as a prohibition than it could 80/-, while too low a duty would
throw the poor lands out of cultivation, and make the country
dependent on foreign supply for subsistence. The Ministers then
had steered a course between the two extremes, and proposed a
measure which would " conciliate all parties."

Grant's speech was tepid, almost apologetic. He did not like
the present Bill better than that of 1827—in his opinion it fell
short of it ; but he liked it better than the law at present in force,
and it had the great merit that it was likely to pass and set this
troubled question at rest.[1] He begged the House to consider the
measure as " an arbitration or compromise between conflicting
interests and opinions "—as Canning had called it, a peace-offering.

Huskisson was even more plain spoken. He " did not think
it the best that might have been brought forward," but it was more
likely to abate those angry squabbles which the absence of final
measures had given rise to than any other likely to be adopted.
As to the law of 1815, which some wished to see continued, he
lamented from the bottom of his soul the mass of evil and misery
and destruction of capital which that law in the course of its twelve
years' operation had produced. Peel, however, was convinced
that the new Bill was fair, equitable, and just, and " at least as
practicable " as that of 1827.[2]

---

[1] " For God's sake," said Goderich, " let the question be now settled."

[2] In view of Peel's great recantation in 1844, his attitude on the Corn Law
in 1828 is particularly interesting. The following passage shows that his
education had begun. " He should be sorry to purchase a depression of the
price of bread at the risk of interfering injuriously with those vested interests
which were so essential to the maintenance of the other classes of the State.
But there was another circumstance which had not been adverted to during
the present discussion. It could not be denied, that, in consequence of the
growing population of this country, there was a necessity for looking to other
countries for a supply. It was impossible not to see that, in proportion to the
increase of population of late years, the quantity of land employed in the
production of corn was diminished ; but it was appropriated to the production
of more profitable articles. The increase of manufactures might diminish
the growth of corn, but it did not follow that agricultural property was thereby

Later on, Huskisson acknowledged that the change in the " pivot A more efficient protection. price " from 60/- to 64/- was an increase in the protection presumably due to agriculture,[1] and he " supported the Bill because it would afford a more efficient protection. When the price of corn was from 60/- to 65/- (Winchester measure), the importation of foreign corn would be checked ; [2] when the price was above 65/-, the corn from our colonies would come in free ; and, when the prices were higher, the duties would operate to prevent the importation of an overwhelming quantity of foreign corn." The " experience " gained from the results of the Warehoused Corn Act of the last year was that a 20/- duty was not sufficient to exclude foreign corn from coming in in large quantities when the price was about 60/- ; 531,000 qrs. had come in from bond " when the price of British corn showed that no further supply was necessary " ; in short, the scale of the 1827 Bill, it was proved, did not afford adequate protection.[3]

depressed. The land was devoted to the production of milk and butter and other articles, yielding an equally profitable return. If it were proved to him that, at any particular time, there was less corn grown in the country, he would not therefore admit that agriculture was less flourishing. He would first enquire whether other articles were not produced in its stead which furnished a suitable price. The land, for instance, in the neighbourhood of London and Manchester was not now applied so generally as heretofore to the production of grain ; a great portion of it was devoted to pasture. It was quite clear that Great Britain did not produce sufficient corn for her own consumption. But let it not be forgotten, when they were legislating with a view to the general interests of all portions of the Empire, that there was, in conjunction with this island, another country which did not flourish so much in manufactures, but which possessed great fertility, great powers of production, and vast capabilities of improvement, to which he looked forward for a material addition to the prosperity of the nation at large. It should be considered that, the more the House unduly encouraged the importation of foreign corn, the more it interfered with the supply from Ireland. He did not see what difference should be made between the agricultural interests in Ireland and here. The more agriculture was extended in Ireland, the more the demand for British manufactures would be widened. He did not mean to argue that agriculture in Ireland should be encouraged to the exclusion of foreign nations, but the House should not forget its importance in the scale and its great powers of production and improvement."

[1] Grant made the questionable statement that, as the temporary measure regarding bonded corn was meant by Canning as an " experiment " to guide him in reintroducing the Corn Bill, the present modifications—the additional protection to agriculture—were " in conformity with what he presumed to have been the intentions of Mr. Canning." But this presumption was emphatically denied by others.

[2] Huskisson, who had to fill the rôle of Protectionist—which he did very cleverly, if not very candidly—said, on another occasion that, at 60/-, the introduction of wheat would be prevented pretty nearly altogether.

[3] This was Huskisson's defence, but Whitmore gave a very different explanation of the corn coming in. The corn bonded in 1825 and subsequently, he

What may be called legitimate objection to the Bill was confined to unfavourable comparisons with the Bill of 1827. It was pronounced very complicated; it was a compromise, indeed, but a compromise of conflicting opinions in the Cabinet and not in the country. It was apparent, said Baring, from the manner of Grant's statement, that, before it was submitted to the Committee, a hard battle had been fought to reconcile the conflicting principles of this and of the former measure; it was less favourable to agriculture, because more protection was required when the home price was from 52/- to 58/- than when it was from 62/- to 68/-, whereas the new scale acted in the converse way—in Baring's words, when the price was low, the protection would be diminished, when high, increased : it was dangerous because it was calculated to keep up very high prices, and it afforded a degree of protection which the greediest advocate of protection could never wish for : it gave the agriculturists no real protection when they wanted it, while it exposed them to great obloquy by giving them the appearance of a protection which they did not call for.

Of a more mixed character were the criticisms of Lauderdale, and some of the other objections raised by Baring. Lauderdale, as before, very much preferred the law of 1815 as it stood. A prohibitory system, he said, with a power to the Privy Council to alter or relax it as circumstances demanded, was the system most likely to be practically beneficial. How was a landlord to calculate his leases, which fixed the rent for a number of years, under a system which made the price of corn so uncertain ? [1] Bad as the law of 1815 was, said Baring, it was a despotic law whose very limitation had the power of forcing up prices until they reached a point at which foreign grain became immediately admissible. He would say that any price above 60/- was an indication of incipient distress, and that, the moment the price got beyond that, the duty ought to decline rapidly. If at 60/- there was a duty of 24/-, and, at 61/-, a duty of 23/-, it was a scale which ought not to continue. If the price were

contended, had been imported because it was believed that no higher duty would be imposed than 12/-. It will be remembered that, by the Act of November, 1826, the Crown had power to admit 500,000 qrs. at 12/-. When the scale of 1827 was declared, " a sort of panic arose," and it was thought better to pay 24/8 than keep it in bond : that is to say, it was taken out at a loss.

[1] Lauderdale, like many others, was strong in his aspiration for " steady prices," but he seemed to overlook that nature does not, from year to year, give steady crops, and that the calling in of other countries' supply was the only way yet suggested to keep the amount of corn in the country anything like constant.

to rise beyond 60/-, there would be a degree of alarm in the country which would be productive of the most serious consequences. But much of the other criticism was beside the mark. A still higher duty would be preferable, said Fergusson. There were no bounties on exportation, complained Lethbridge. The measure was not asked by anybody, said Lauderdale ; it emanated from the philosophical spirit of discontent that was abroad, and had been forced on the Ministers in spite of their wishes. The measure had been prepared by someone who wished to make it a source of revenue, said Stanhope. The Bill would lessen the amount of agricultural produce, said Redesdale ; take seven millions out of the pockets of the agriculturists, and, consequently, diminish in an equal degree the employment of labour. The trade, commerce, and manufactures of the country were, in comparison with agriculture, of little consequence. " The only way to have corn permanently cheap was to produce it ourselves. . . . They should always remember that what was produced in a country cost it nothing ; but that what was brought from other countries must be paid for."

When the Bill was in Committee, an amendment was put forward by Calcraft to substitute the scale of 1827 for that now proposed, and it obtained some support. Hume, as a forlorn hope, moved that, for the coming year, a fixed duty be imposed of 15/-, to be reduced by 1/- a year till 1834, when 10/- would become the permanent duty—Ricardo's suggestion, except that he would have started with the figure of 20/-. Western proposed a set of Resolutions condemning the Bill out and out, on the general thesis that the exclusive encouragement of British agriculture was the more effective and safer policy for the attainment of the most secure, steady, and abundant supply possible. Lord King recorded a Protest against the Bill as imposing high and most unreasonable duties on the importation of foreign corn, as affording no expectation of establishing a final settlement of the Corn Laws, and because a varying scale of duties made the importation of corn irregular. Protests on the other side were entered by Eldon and others and by Redesdale and Kenyon. *Suggested amendments.*

But, in the end, all amendments were rejected, and the Bill passed in its original form. As proposed in 1827, the average home price was struck from weekly returns provided by 152 cities and towns, and the average regulated the rate of duty until receipt of the next weekly average ; and wheat from any British possession outside of Europe was admitted at 5/- per qr. until the average *The Bill passes.*

British price was 67/-; above that, at 6d. The scale (and the
colonial preference) adopted for other produce was the same as
that of 1827, contained in the Warehoused Corn Act.[1] An
attempt was made—plausibly enough—to get "further protection"
to oats and barley as well as to wheat, but this was refused on the
ground that the protection given to these grains had already
been increased relatively to wheat ; that is to say, the pivot price
of oats had been advanced from 21/- to 25/-—and 25/- was a
higher ratio for oats than 60/- was for wheat—and that of barley
from 31/- to 33/-.[2]

Huskisson
resigns.

A few days, however, before the Bill passed in the Commons,
Huskisson was no longer in the Government. From the first, the
Duke found that he had more than he could do to hold the incon-
gruous elements of his Cabinet together: "There," he said to Croker,
pointing to a formidable heap of green bags and red boxes, " there
is the business of the country, which I have not time to look at—
all my time being employed in assuaging what gentlemen call their
feelings." As a soldier, he could not understand the freedom of a
staff to disobey : in a few weeks, he was thoroughly tired of his
mutinous colleagues, and felt that, if he could not bring them to
heel, he would be better without them. The four Canningites, he
complained, " always hang together, and all entertain an enormous
and exaggerated view of their own consequence, and they are always
endeavouring to lord it." Huskisson gave him the opportunity
by sending in his resignation, owing it to his chief, he said, for a vote
he had given contrary to an understanding in the Cabinet. To
his astonishment and chagrin, the Duke, whose blood was up,
accepted it as final.[3] The other Canningites threw up their offices,
and, before May was out, the Duke was at the head of a purely
Tory administration.[4]

[1] The provisions of 1827 and of 1828 are given in *Customs Tariffs of the
United Kingdom from* 1800 *to* 1897 (C. 8706, 1897).

[2] The principal debates on the Corn Bill are in *Hansard*, xviii. 1364, 1379 ;
xix. 16, 142, 208, 1333, 1518.

[3] " Huskisson was an able man," writes Ellenborough in his *Diary*, " but
he would never do as a member of a Cabinet in which he was not chief. The
Government would not have lived if he had continued in."

[4] One notes, in this year, the emergence of a new name among political
parties. After the retiral of Huskisson and his friends from the Cabinet,
Blackwood writes : " We have at last, thank God, got rid of the Liberals, and
once more have the happiness to live under a pure Tory Government."
This is the first time, I think, that the word " Liberal " appears for the party
opposed to the " pure Tory." The expression seems to have " caught on " at

After the Corn Bill, the chief measure of the session was the repeal of the Test and Corporation Acts, passed in the time of Charles II.—that is, when the Protestant succession was in danger—but now both obsolete and vexatious. The Act appears as c. XVII., " for repealing so much of several Acts as imposes the necessity of receiving the Sacrament of the Lord's Supper as a qualification for certain offices and employments." As was to be expected, this repeal of dissenters' disabilities was followed by renewed assertion of the Catholic claims, and, on the rearrangement of the Cabinet, came a startling revelation of the power of the Catholic Association. Vesey Fitzgerald, who succeeded Grant as President of the Board of Trade, had been member for Clare, and a new election was, of course, necessary. O'Connell, though a Catholic, and, as such, disqualified to sit in Parliament, was set up as a candidate, pledging his word as a lawyer that he would take his place in the House of Commons without taking the oaths. The organisation was perfect ; the obedience implicit. The clergy exerted all their powers, giving their chapels for election meetings—" every altar became a tribunal." The 40/- freeholders to a man deserted their landlords, and marched to the poll in perfect order, each led to the hustings by the parish priest, to vote " for God and O'Connell." "No whiskey was allowed to the people." After a few days' polling, Fitzgerald retired from the contest, and O'Connell was returned by an immense majority. This wholly unexpected revolt against a popular landlord and friend of the Catholic claims made a very great sensation in the country. During the rest of the year, the Association continued its activity, gaining in strength and determination. The Act which had been passed to restrain it expired in July, and the Association reassembled in its original form : Orangeism again raised its head in the shape of Brunswick Clubs : Ireland was divided into two hostile camps. Fears were expressed everywhere by the friends of Ireland that Emancipation would be delayed till the Catholics had gone so far as to make it impossible. Everything depended upon Peel, and Peel was embarrassed by his Oxford connections, by his past record, and

Repeal of the Test Act.

Return of O'Connell for Clare.

once, and is used elsewhere during the year as an adjective of political abuse. In the course of its twelve numbers, *Blackwood*, in various articles, shows what might be expected from a " pure Tory " party. It denounces impartially the repeal of the Test Acts, of the Roman Catholic disabilities, and of the Usury Laws, the reform of the Poor Laws, the Emigration proposals, the appointment of the Finance Committee, and calls on the Duke to put down " the absurd and pernicious Free Trade system ! "

by being, in spite of himself, recognised as head of the anti-Catholics. On 11th August, however, he wrote confidentially to the Duke, stating his reluctant conviction that it was indispensably necessary for the Government to change its policy on the Catholic question.[1]

Various happenings. It seems scarcely credible, but the Corn Law and the Repeal of the Test Acts make up almost the entire tale of legislation carried through in this session. A good many things, however, were actively discussed, and measures set in motion or carried a stage further. Seven or eight proposals were before Parliament at one time, all intended to remedy the anomalies and reduce the expenses of elections, by such means as shortening the polls, registration of electors, forbidding the use of corporate funds for election purposes, etc.[2] Brougham secured two Commissions, on the state of the Common Law and of the Law on Real Property.[3] Lansdowne's two Bills for the Consolidation and Improvement of the Criminal Laws passed. There were the usual fruitless debates on the Game Laws.[4] Peel got a Committee of Enquiry into the Police of the Metropolis.[5] The Poor Laws were discussed in many connections—the claims for such a provision in Ireland, the grievances connected with the passing of Irish vagrants, the vexed question of Settlement. Slaney got leave for a Bill as to the payment of wages to able-bodied persons out of the poor rates. Wilmot Horton, Chairman of the Emigration Committee, who had been Under Secretary of State for War and the Colonies from 1821 to the present year, began, in season and out of season, to preach emigration as remedy for "redundancy of population."

Pauper lunatics. And at least a beginning was made in the rational treatment of lunatics, up till now a class treated as outside the pale of common humanity. A Committee of the House of Commons gave horrifying details of how pauper lunatics were dealt with in London, and a

[1] Peel's *Memoirs*, i. 189.

[2] *Hansard*, xviii. 599, 989, 1234, 1348, 1411; xix. 728, 868, 903, 1297, 1643, 1647, 1743.

[3] *Ibid.* xviii. 127, 833.

[4] Some progress, however, was being made. In 1827, the Act c. 18, to "prohibit the setting of spring-guns, man-traps, and other engines calculated to destroy human life or inflict grievous bodily harm," had been passed, and now the Night Poaching Act, c. 19, which still forms part of the Game Laws, " for the more effectual prevention of persons going armed by night for the destruction of game," was placed on the statute book.

[5] *Hansard*, xviii. 784.

conscience-stricken Parliament at once passed two Bills : one, c. 40, to give counties the power of establishing asylums, not only for the reception but for the medical treatment and cure of those unhappy persons; a second, c. 41, to establish a body of fifteen Commissioners with the power of licensing and visiting such asylums, and, generally, to provide for the care and maintenance of pauper and criminal lunatics in England.[1]

Among other features of the year may be mentioned : the appearance of Bulwer Lytton's *Pelham*, claiming, no doubt truly, "to retail the opinions and customs of the class to which he belonged," the dandies ; the projection, at a public meeting in Dublin, of a ship canal across Ireland, to cost £8 millions—to be assisted, of course, by a Government grant ; the starting of medical teaching in the University of London in October, and the institution of a rival church scheme—for the former did not " teach religion " —when the Duke took the chair and £30,000 were subscribed for King's College ; the excitement in Scotland over the Burke and Hare murders, perpetrated to sell the bodies for anatomical purposes. *[marginal note: Features of the Year.]*

The obituary includes Dugald Stewart, the spiritual father of many famous men ; the Earl of Liverpool ; and J. C. Curwen—the " father of the soiling system," whose example and teaching gave a new character to the business of farming. *[marginal note: Obituary.]*

Among economic publications, one notes the following :

An Essay on Political Economy, Parts I. and II., by Captain Pettman—" an extravagant enthusiast for paper money " ; *Elementary Thoughts on the principles of Currency and Wealth, and on the means of diminishing the burdens of the people*, by J. D. Basset ; *Essay on the supposed advantages of a Sinking Fund*, Part I., by Lord Grenville ; Senior's *Three Lectures on the transmission of the Precious Metals from country to country and the Mercantile Theory of Wealth* ; Lewni's *Poor Laws* ; Bayldon *On the Poor's Rate* ; Sadler's *Ireland, its Evils and their Remedies*. *[marginal note: Economic literature.]*

---

[1] *Hansard*, xviii. 575 ; xix. 196.

CHAPTER XLI

1828. FINANCE: AGRICULTURE: INDUSTRY

A new Finance Committee. AT an early period of the session, Peel, after making a clear and frank statement of the existing position,[1] obtained the appointment of a new Finance Committee of 23 members—such as had sat every ten years or so since 1786—to enquire into the State of the Public Income and Expenditure, advise as to securing effectual control of all charges, and report on possible reductions. The Committee embraced, among others, Parnell (chairman), Goulburn, Tierney, Herries, Althorp, Hume, Maberly, Bankes, Baring, Fitzgerald, Horton, Ridley, Stanley, and Huskisson.[2] From time to time, the Committee issued reports presenting ample information as to almost every branch of revenue and expenditure. One of the first fruits of its labours was the resolve not to renew the " dead weight " contract with the Bank which expired in July, but to return to the old system of meeting the pension charge as it rose. That " mischievous act," said Hume, had already cost the country a million, and would, if continued, cost it three more.[3] Another was to discuss and come to conclusions on the Sinking Fund [4] which were embodied in the speech with which Goulburn, the new Chancellor of the Exchequer, opened the Budget on 11th July.

[1] Among other figures, he gave the following: Total capital of the unredeemed funded debt, £777,476,000 ; total annual charge (unredeemed debt, funded and unfunded, including annuities), £29,254,000 ; decrease of the capital of the unredeemed funded debt since 1815, £38,835,000 ; total decrease of charge on account of funded and unfunded debt since 1815, £4,424,000 ; total surplus revenue applicable to the liquidation of the National Debt during the past five years, £12,000,000 ; amount paid by the Commissioners of the Sinking Fund for the past five years, £29,414,000.

[2] *Hansard*, xviii. 447.   [3] *Ibid.* xix. 1645.

[4] Lord Grenville's *Essay on the Supposed Advantages of a Sinking Fund*, published in this year, had done much to educate public opinion.

The total revenue of the past year (including the " dead weight " Goulburn's first Budget. receipt of £4¼ millions from the Bank) was £54,486,000. The total expenditure (including the " dead weight " payment of £2,800,000, but excluding the sinking fund) was £52,690,000.[1] The actual surplus (allowing for the public works account) was £1,132,000.[2]

Coming to the estimates for 1828, he calculated on an increase in the ordinary revenue of £800,000. In 1827, the large importation of grain under a heavy duty had yielded £800,000. This, indeed, could not be counted on in the present year. But, in the Customs from sugar, rum, brandy, and wine, and from the Excise, he expected a large increase; the amount from stamps should be more favourable, as that duty improved according as the value of property was raised; the assessed taxes already showed an increase; the Post Office and other returns, he would take at the same as last year. The revenue, then, for 1828, he estimated at £53,902,000.

The expenditure (including Army, £8,049,000; Navy, £5,995,000; Ordnance, £1,597,000; Miscellaneous, £2,184,000;[3] and £2,134,000 for naval and military pensions—" which payment would not occur again "—but again excluding the Sinking Fund) he estimated at £50,104,000.

The clear surplus, then, would be about £3 millions, as against £1,132,000 of the previous year. It was obvious, however, that, " if we were to provide according to the forms now prescribed for the annual payment of the Sinking Fund, the sum required for that purpose would be, in addition to the surplus, little short of £3,000,000," and the money would have to be raised either by adding to the burdens of the people or by fresh borrowing. The former was impossible in the circumstances of the country; nor did he " apprehend that there was any necessity (arising from the natural desire of maintaining the public credit) [4] imposed either on those

---

[1] He did not mean to conceal that the difference between the sums advanced by the Bank on account of the naval and military pensions and the money paid to the trustees, could not, properly speaking, be considered as income, but rather as a loan made in aid of the expenditure of the year, though long before the commencement of the year's account.

[2] It will be remembered that Canning, in his Estimates for the past year, included a Sinking Fund allocation of £5,700,000, and, with this, calculated on a coming deficiency of £2,900,000. By, rather cavalierly, ignoring this allocation, Goulburn changed the deficit into a surplus !

[3] The reduction on all these heads from the past year amounted to £418,000.

[4] One notes, with some amusement perhaps, the way in which the Chancellor of the Exchequer now treats the venerable argument of " supporting the national credit."

who administered the finances or on Parliament, to adopt that mode of supplying the deficiency of the Sinking Fund." As regarded the latter, " he had long felt, what he was sure must have been a general feeling, that, to borrow money in time of peace to discharge debts which the country had already incurred, was a measure objectionable in principle, not defensible with reference to reason, and calculated to create delusion without affording any substantial advantage." It appeared to him, as it appeared to the Finance Committee, that there was no alternative but to commence, from the present period, to reduce the nominal amount of the Sinking Fund to the real surplus of revenue. This was Pitt's principle, although, ultimately, he had to choose between abandoning the system of a Sinking Fund altogether, or maintaining it by borrowed funds, and did choose what he considered the lesser of two evils. Though this was to reduce nominally the amount of the Sinking Fund, there would still be as much money to apply to that purpose as heretofore. " The only difference would be that, instead of redeeming an apparently larger sum by creating a fresh debt, we should in future redeem a certain sum annually without incurring any new debt. If the House should acquiesce, they would in future apply £3,000,000 to the redemption of debt." [1]

A new
Sinking Fund.

Goulburn concluded by expressing the satisfaction he felt at the general appearance of the country ;—the increase of exports over any of the five antecedent years, the corresponding augmentation of tonnage, the increase of Excise revenue, extending equally to Ireland, on every article which the lower classes consumed, such as 4 per cent. on candles, 22 per cent. on paper, 42 per cent. on printed goods, 9 per cent. on spirits.

There was no division on the Budget, and, indeed, scarcely any criticism—probably owing to the fact that the chief critics had been, wisely, put on the Finance Committee. It was only natural that Maberly and Hume should indulge in some little glorification of what they had done to expose the fallacy of the Sinking Fund, and "thrice re-slay the slain." Parnell, however, called attention to the ambiguous statement of the Chancellor relative to the £3,000,000, as if the whole change were to apply £3,000,000 instead of £5,000,000 as a Sinking Fund. The Committee had positively refused to recommend a fixed Sinking Fund. But an understanding had been come to by the Committee that the Govern-

---

[1] The recommendations of the Committee, in the Report presented in July, are given in the bluebook C. 6539, 1891, entitled *National Debt*.

ment should proceed, in the first instance, as if there was a real surplus of £3,000,000 ; if there were not so large a surplus, it should provide the money wanting by deficiency bills ; and if, at the end of the year, it appeared that the surplus did not amount to £3,000,000, should make good the difference out of the surplus of the succeeding year. The reason for agreeing not to have a Sinking Fund was that those taxes which must be continued to provide the fund would, inasmuch as they fell so heavily upon industry, do a great deal more harm than this Sinking Fund would do good. For his own part, seeing that £6 millions were raised by taxes on raw materials, that there were taxes on many manufactures which were exceedingly injurious, such as the Excise duties on leather, glass, and paper, and that another class of taxes created smuggling, he thought that, when it became a question what had best be done with the surplus of the revenue, it ought to be applied in reducing those taxes which fell on industry. After the taxes were placed on a proper footing and the country had recovered a healthy tone, he would have no objection to taxes of five or six millions, or even more, for the redemption of the debt. Meanwhile he would be content that the debt should in no case be added to.[1]

Thus, then, ended " that glorious piece of nonsense," the Sinking Fund. In 1829, by 10 Geo. IV. c. 27, the whole of the previous legislation affecting the Sinking Fund was swept away except that part which constituted the Commissioners, and what is *now* known as the " Old Sinking Fund "—the actually realised surplus—was introduced.

End of Pitt's Sinking Fund.

One other result of the proceedings of the Finance Committee may be noted. In 1808, Perceval, when Chancellor of the Exchequer, had introduced the system of life annuities as a means of extinguishing the National Debt, and Peel had just stated that, last year, out of a total charge on the funded debt of £28,381,000, £2,602,000 was the amount on account of the annuities.[2] The annuities were calculated on the tables of Dr. Price, which were then thought authoritative. In 1819, it became suspected that the expectation of life—especially of female life—was greater than that laid down in these tables ; within the past forty years, the rate of mortality in Great Britain had fallen from 1 in 40 to 1 in 56 ;

Suspension of Annuities.

---

[1] *Hansard*, xix. 1652. " In case the eventual annual surplus should not amount to £3 millions, the deficiency ought not to be supplied by borrowing," said the Finance Committee Report.

[2] See *Economic Annals, 1801-20*, 168.

thus the annuities had been sold at too low a price ; and the loss to the present revenue was estimated at no less than £8000 a week. The Finance Committee, in its first Report, recommended an immediate alteration, and though nothing could, of course, be done as regards annuities already granted, a Bill was passed to suspend the operation of the Act meantime.[1]

Reduction of Savings Banks' interest.

In February, Hume, who had been one of the earliest and most active in the promotion of Savings Banks, called attention to the enormous expense at which they were being maintained. His aim, he said, had been the security of the poor man's savings, but never that he should get a higher rate of interest than the public creditor. The rate still allowed was £4 11s. 3d. per cent., which showed a loss of nearly £1000 a week. With the countenance of the Chancellor of the Exchequer, a Bill was introduced " to consolidate and amend the Laws relating to Savings Banks," reducing five Acts with some 150 clauses to one with 30 or 40. By this Bill—which appears among the Acts as c. 92—the interest was reduced to £3 8s. 5d. per cent. No individual could deposit more than £30 in any one year, nor more than £150 on the whole ; when, by accumulation of interest, the stock reached £200, interest was to cease.[2]

Scots notes in England.

It will be remembered that the Act of 1826 prohibited all English Banks from issuing small notes dated later than 5th February of that year, and intimated the withdrawal from circulation of such notes after 5th April, 1829. At the same time, the small notes of Scotland were not interfered with, and fear began to be expressed that the Scots notes would cross the border—as, indeed, they already did in the northern counties—and defeat the object of the English Act. Goulburn, accordingly, in June, brought in a Bill " to restrain the Circulation of Scottish Bank Notes in England." He stated —as seemed to be thought necessary [3]—that the present Govern-

---

[1] *Hansard*, xviii. 1135, 1314, 1623. The grant of life annuities was resumed under an improved system in the next year.

[2] *Hansard*, xviii. 258, 1124 ; xix. 1053, 1646. Doubleday's theory of the intention of Savings Banks is, perhaps, worth quoting : " That the whole was a plan for connecting persons of very moderate means with the funding system, I cannot for a moment doubt. . . . It is curious, but, from first to last, hardly a word has been uttered anywhere against the injustice of this cunning scheme, which goes upon the principle of taxing those who cannot save, to take care of the money and pay the interest of those who can " (*Financial History of England*, 253).

[3] When Goulburn, in May, announced unequivocally that, in eleven months' time, all notes under £5 would cease to form any part of the English currency, the statement was received, it seems, with utter astonishment. " We would

ment had no intention of departing from the Act which their predecessors had passed. A great many of the small notes had been
cancelled in the late bank panic ; the bankers had been preparing
for the cessation of issue after 1829 ; there were, he calculated,
not more than £2¼ millions of English small notes in circulation.
Altogether, circumstances could never be more favourable for what
the Government had agreed to in 1826—" the experiment of a
withdrawal of the small notes."   And, after all, those who so much
condemned this withdrawal did not take into account that the total
amount of circulation at present was £20 millions of Bank of England
large notes, £13 millions of country large notes, £2½ millions of small
notes, £22 millions of sovereigns, and £8 millions of silver ; that,
in short, the proportion of small notes to the total circulation was
only 3½ per cent. If, then, they persevered with the Act of 1826
as regards England, he did not think that anyone would dispute the
absolute necessity of preventing the circulation of Scots small notes
in England.

But, as events proved, those who had opposed the withdrawal of
the English small notes conceived that, as the Act did not come into
force for another year, there might still be time to get its execution
stopped, and the tactics adopted were to move the appointment
of a Select Committee " to enquire into the State of the Circulation
of Promissory Notes under the value of £5 in England, and to report
their observations thereupon to the House, with reference to the
expediency of making any alteration in the laws now in force thereto."
In the adjourned debate over this, the whole battle of the small
notes was fought over again at great length, but, as the arguments
for and against have already been considered in Chapter XXXI.,
they need not be repeated here. Enough to say that the amendment
was defeated by 154 to 45—the minority, however, including very
few well-known names except those of Maberly and Hume. But,
even after this defeat, Hume fought on. When it came to Committee, he read the House a little lecture on currency. On Adam
Smith's authority, he would contend that the medium of exchange
ought to be as cheap as possible. Taking a sovereign and a pound
note, the sovereign was not necessary for the internal operations
of the country, but only for the external. If, therefore, they mixed
the two, they ought to have as much paper as possible, and as much

wager our existence," said the *Watchman*, " it is never done."   Even in
December, the *Liverpool Chronicle* said, " We believe few men in the country
expect that Mr. Peel's Bill will be enforced."

gold as might be necessary for transactions abroad. Was it right, then, to reduce the paper currency ? If the object aimed at was to put banking on a secure footing, let security be demanded of bankers—let no person without capital be allowed to coin money. But this Bill left the bankers as they were. " The true foundation for the security of a paper circulation lay, not in the denomination of the notes issued, but in the instant convertibility of these notes, of whatever denomination, into gold."

This was sound enough, but, as the House was not then discussing the continuance of the small notes in England but the possibility of an invasion of England by the Scots notes, the lecture had nothing to do with the subject. Indeed, Hume gave the case away by starting with the assertion that the measure " must lessen the circulating medium of England." Even when the Bill came to the Lords, it was the Act of 1826 that was discussed : very little was said about the Bill itself, which passed in due course as c. 65, "An Act to restrain the negotiation in England, of promissory notes and bills under a limited sum, issued in Scotland or Ireland."[1]

Failure of the English harvest.

Little is said about agriculture in this year. A mild winter and spring promised good results in autumn, and wheat fell to 56/6 in June. But, in that month, the rain began, and, from the second week in July, it was almost continuous till the middle of August, accompanied by storms and great floods. In July, wheat was 60/-; in the beginning of September, over 71/-; in the beginning of November, about 78/-.[2] These prices reflected the failure of the English harvest, generally speaking, in all categories. Wheat was about two-thirds of a medium crop—the first great deficiency in the wheat harvest of England for ten years. That prices did not rise even higher, was due to the circumstances that the Scots and Irish harvests were much more favourable ;[3] that the surplus of the previous year was greater than had been calculated ; and that, of course, foreign supply came in abundantly—including, strangely enough,

[1] *Hansard*, xix. 980, 1054, 1380, 1597.

[2] The prices are from the *Quarterly Journal of Agriculture*. Those given in the *Annual Register* are very much higher, but they do not seem to me reliable. This great rise, coincident with a curtailment of the Bank issues, is given by Tooke as " specimen among many others of the little direct influence of the circulation in counteracting the force of opinion on prices " (*History of Prices*, ii. 195).

[3] The Scots farmer was, this year, in the ideal position of having plentiful crops and famine prices—he had " seldom had a more prosperous season." In December, the quartern loaf was 1/-.

a great quantity from Spain.[1]   In November, the ports were open
at the lowest rate of duty.   Even among the agricultural classes,
there was an expression of thankfulness that the old law had been
repealed—what would the horses have done without the foreign
oats ?—although there was some ungenerous criticism of the
" liberals " that their sliding scale had not produced steady prices.
Fortunately, the price of meat rather fell than rose, and—particularly in Ireland—the potato crop was very abundant.[2]   The
average price of wheat for the year was 60/5, as against 58/6 in the
previous year.

It has been suggested more than once in these *Annals* that, the
less one hears directly in any year about commerce and manufactures,
the more prosperous they are likely to be.   When the cycle is at
its lowest, the complaints of employers to Parliament, and the cries
of the distressed workers against reduced wages and bad conditions
are clamant enough ;   when the cycle is at its highest and just
about to turn downwards, speculation attracts attention and strikes
for higher wages excite sympathy or resentment.   It is only when
the evil days are fresh in memory, and when all classes are thankful
to see the wheels moving again, that there is little temptation to
cry out about distress or ventilate grievances.   In the contemporary
literature of 1828, there is a minimum of positive information.
That in February the cotton trade was very active, thanks to the
great fall in the raw material, particularly in printed goods; that
in November the markets of India were glutted by the enormous
exportation of yarns ;   that the new American tariff was casting a
gloomy shadow over the woollen trade—these scraps of information
would be a small basis for any conclusion as to the state of industry—
and they are, practically, the only ones I can glean.   All the same,
there is every reason to believe that, although prices, wages, and
profits were all low, employment was adequate and the amount
of industry steadily progressive.   The King's Speech, on 26th July,
congratulated the House upon " the general prosperity of the
country and upon the satisfactory state of the public revenue "—
a decisive proof that the condition of the people was one of
progressive improvement.

The foreign trade was, practically, the same as that of the previous

The testimony of silence.

---

[1] Shortly afterwards, the export from Spain was prohibited.

[2] I find potatoes quoted at a penny per stone (14 lbs.) and this given as an
explanation why the influx of Irish to the Scots harvesting was not so great as
usual.

year. The British Exports were £52,788,000, as compared with
£52,221,000; the Re-exports, £9,946,000, as compared with £9,380,000;
the Imports, £45,167,000, as compared with £44,908,000. The Real
value of the British Exports was £36,812,000, as compared with
£37,181,000.

Shipbuilding, however, showed a considerable decline, the number
of ships being 842, against 894 in the previous year, and the tonnage
88,663, against 93,144.

A parliamentary return gives the following figures of our foreign
trade in order of importance :

IMPORTS FROM

British West Indies	£8,908,000
East Indies and China	8,348,000
United States	5,820,000
Russia	3,442,000
France	3,159,000
United Netherlands	1,978,000
Germany	1,669,000
Brazil	1,488,000
Africa	1,175,000
Italy	1,064,000
Prussia	1,027,000

EXPORTS TO

Germany	£9,467,000
United States	6,843,000
East Indies and China	6,388,000
Brazil	6,155,000
Netherlands	4,956,000
Italy	4,642,000
British West Indies	4,049,000
South America	3,287,000
Russia	2,753,000
British North America	2,206,000
Gibraltar	2,078,000
Portugal, Azores, and Madeira	1,764,000
Foreign West Indies	1,450,000
Africa	1,148,000

CHAPTER XLII

1828. PROTECTION AT HOME AND ABROAD

THE two attempts of the previous year to obtain reconsideration Efforts to re-gain protection for Wool, of the Free Trade policy were renewed. In Ellenborough's *Diary* of 8th April, we get a hint that the landed interests were intriguing for a tax on foreign wool : " they would be satisfied," he wrote, " with raising the duty from 1d. to 3d. It was once 6d. If we had no Huskisson in the Cabinet, this would be done." On the 19th, again, he wrote, " we had (after a meeting of committee) some conversation about granting a Committee on Wool in the Lords. Huskisson has pledged himself against it in the Commons. He thinks it would create great alarm amongst the manufacturers, and that, to lay on a duty would ruin our export trade, which, even now, can hardly maintain itself." That the agitation was serious is evidenced by a petition from the London wool merchants on the 28th, " against the imposition of a tax on foreign wool." A duty on wool was " a necessary protection due to the agricultural in-terests," said Lethbridge. Such a tax on a raw material, retorted Milton, would be a reversion to barbarism. Barbarism or not, answered Sir M. W. Ridley, the existing system could have only one issue—the total ruin of the agriculturists : the imports of wool were daily increasing, the exports of woollens decreasing. The agriculturists thought of nothing but themselves, said Philips ; most of the imported wool was worked up and consumed here, and to increase the duty would make the clothing of the people dearer. In May, we find four woollen manufacturers being received at the Board of Trade, representing, among other things, that the raising of the price of wool would lead to the greater use of cotton ; " their information," said Ellenborough, " made me doubt very much whether it would be prudent to lay any duty upon wool." But, in May, on the motion of the Duke of Richmond, a Select

Committee was appointed, " to enquire into the present state of
the Wool Trade "—the Duke of Wellington warning them that
he was satisfied that the Committee would not end in affording the
relief which his noble friend sought.[1]

and for Shipping. General Gascoyne again was the spokesman of the shipowners.
He reiterated the statements of the previous year, that the number
of ships, the tonnage, and the number of seamen all showed a
decrease from 1826 to 1827, and asked the House to pledge itself
to enquire into the causes thereof in next session. Grant controverted the figures; the more the subject was investigated, the
more would the result show that the shipping interest was far from
being in that state which the gallant general had described. Gascoyne seemed to think, finally said Goulburn, that Government
intended to abandon the principles with respect to navigation and
trade which they had acted on previously to the late separation.
How was that possible when so many members of the present
administration were the very individuals under whose auspices
those principles were first promulgated? He could sincerely say
that there never was the slightest disposition to abandon these
principles. Time only was wanting to show how decidedly and
unequivocally they would be followed up. The motion was then
negatived without division.[2]

Thus, if the Free Trade movement did not show any advance
during the year, it obtained official recognition from the new Government—to the dismay of those who thought that the accession of
Wellington and Peel would " put an end to the pest of senseless
meddling innovation."

Parnell counsels bolder Free Trade. Parnell, however, was not pleased with the slow progress which
the policy was making. 1825, he said, was the year when the
Customs duties were altered with the professed design of establishing a free trade. He had obtained the returns of the imports
of foreign manufactures and raw materials in 1824 and in
1826, which he had asked in order to find out what effect the
alteration of the duties had made. The figures showed, as he

[1] *Hansard*, xix. 187, 237, 345.
[2] *Hansard*, xix. 1416. The new heads of the Board of Trade, it is true, did
not give any reassuring statement on the matter. Courteney, the Vice-
President, said that it was the intention of himself and of the President
(Fitzgerald) during the recess to make up their minds on the whole system
of our trade and navigation, " as if their minds were, as respected these, a
sheet of blank paper." Probably this was no more than a reflection of
the political cult of the day—" all decided tints of thought are out of fashion "
—but the words gave rise to considerable misgivings.

expected, that no considerable increase in the import of manufactures had taken place, because the new duties had been fixed
so high as to be prohibitory. The immediate evils of this practical
prohibition were—the raising of the prices of all goods on which
protecting duties were imposed, the reduction of the quality of
home-made goods, and, greatest evil of all, the diminution of foreign
trade which came from preventing several millions worth of foreign
goods from being imported and a corresponding quantity of British
goods exported to pay for them. He asked for similar figurés for
1827 to confirm his contention. But was it not now time to make
some further progress, and to afford to the industry and capital of
the nation new sources of employment ? The complete failure of
all the anticipations of ruin so loudly set forth in 1825 by the silk
manufacturers and glove manufacturers, and other manufacturers,
ought to serve as encouragement to Ministers to take a decided
course. With respect to France, nothing could be more unnatural
than the actual state of our trade. There were no two countries
so well calculated to deal largely together, each had so many productions which were peculiar, respectively, to each other. But the
whole imports from France did not amount to £2 millions, and the
whole of the British exports to France were only about £400,000.
" It was unquestionably a most absurd thing that this country
should be, at this day, levying a rate of duty on French wines which
was established at a period when national wealth was supposed to
consist wholly in gold bullion, and when it was imagined that the
best way of attaining it was by levying a lower duty on Portuguese
wines than on those of France." If we wanted France to be liberal
to us, said Hume, it was not expedient to give such an unfair advantage to the wines of Portugal. The motion, of course, was agreed to.[1]

    That the old idea of regulating wages—that " wages should not   " Regulating
be allowed to find their own level," as it was put—was by no means   Wages."
dead, is again shown in a little debate on a petition introduced by
D. W. Harvey, member for Colchester, who boasted that, springing
from the people, he was of the people, and was proud to be their
champion either in or out of the House. The petition was signed
by nearly 20,000 of the working classes, and asked that, if the House
would not immediately abolish all existing monopolies, admit an
unrestrained importation of grain and all other articles of subsistence and comfort, it would at least give equal protection to
labour with that given to manufacture and agriculture. The

[1] *Hansard*, xviii. 1428.

supporters of the petition, rightly or wrongly, interpreted this as a
reintroduction of the Spitalfields system, by which committees of
masters and journeymen in the various trades might meet at stated
periods, and fix a scale of prices for labour by which the majority
might bind the minority, and the proposal met with but little support.   Later on, the silk weavers of Norwich renewed their attempt
in a petition suggesting the old system for their trade.   Grant said
that the proposition virtually was to establish by law a minimum
of wages, a proposition which had been decided by Committees
of the House to be inadmissible in principle, impracticable in
point of fact, and, if practicable, pregnant with fatal consequences
to the manufacturing interests : and, though some spoke in favour
of it, the matter went no farther.[1]

The foreign affairs of the year, particularly as regarded the war
declared between Russia and Turkey, the chaos in Spain after the
recall of the French troops, and the welter in Portugal, created
unusual interest and excitement both in and out of Parliament,
France. but do not much concern the economic historian.   In France,
where the official figures showed a very rapid advance in the manufacture of cotton, silk, and wool during the past few years,[2] the first
act of St. Cricq, the Minister of the new Department of Commerce—
now suspected of Free Trade leanings—was to appoint a Commission to examine into the state of agriculture, commerce, and
manufactures, especially in regard to such questions as the import
of wool, the effect of the tariff on iron, the preference to French
colonial sugar, the Corn Laws, etc.[3]

[1] *Hansard*, xviii. 1614 ; xix. 260.   As Grant said, in the following year, the
weavers ought to be made aware that the Spitalfields Act, which had been
very properly repealed by the legislature, had driven the capital employed
in the silk trade from Spitalfields into the country, and that the same reason
which had induced the capitalists to remove from Spitalfields, would, in case
that Act were made of general extent, drive them also out of the country
(*Hansard*, xxi. 855).

[2] In May, 1827, Huskisson had stated that France, which, in 1817, imported
only 60,000 bags of cotton, had an import of 216,000 bags in 1826.

[3] It is suggestive that, in this year, we find the vine-growers of the Gironde
petitioning the Chamber, setting forth the injury they suffered from the duties
imposed by foreign countries on French wines as a retaliation for the protecting
duty imposed in France for the benefit of the manufacturers. " What," they
said, " is the basis of the prohibitive system ? A chimera. To sell without
buying. A secret still to be discovered. If we shut our ports to the productions
of other countries, it is good at least to know that theirs must be shut on
our industry ; this kind of reciprocity is inevitable—it is in the nature of
things."   The remedy adopted, as we learn in the following year, was the
abolition of the town octrois, with the view of increasing the consumption.

In Germany, where, in January, the two greatest of the southern Anticipation of a Zollverein. states, Bavaria and Würtemberg, had abolished internal Customs duties on their common frontiers, another approach to a Zollverein was made in February, when Prussia and Hesse-Darmstadt made a convention for entire freedom of trade between the two states with a uniform tariff against foreigners.[1]

Of more vital interest, however, was the passing of a new and The "Tariff of Abominations" in the U.S. stringent tariff by the United States—the " Tariff of Abominations," as it has ever since been called. The tariff of 1824, as we saw, had not only fastened the policy of Protection on that nation, but aimed it specially at the great staples of this country. But it by no means satisfied the protectionists, who had asked for much more. When it failed to protect the new woollen industry—very much because of the removal of our 6d. duty on foreign wool—the cry was, of course, for more protection, and the tariff passed in the present year marks the culminating point of the first period of the American policy. It was based frankly on the intention of making America independent of the outside world, by obstructing and prohibiting the entrance not only of foreign manufactures but of foreign materials— even materials which the country neither grew nor had any intention of growing. The not very creditable story of how this tariff was proposed in order to be rejected, and was passed in despite—" a stray episode in American political history "—is told in detail by Taussig.[2] Enough to say that it greatly increased the duties on almost all materials of manufacture, such as pig-iron, hammered bar-iron, rolled bars, hemp, flax, and wool. It was bitterly opposed by the representatives of all the southern States and by most of those of New England, and was passed only by 105 to 94. Georgia proclaimed a boycott of breadstuffs, horses, cattle, and manufactures against States which had advocated the tariff. For the moment, it appeared to observers like Huskisson as if the conflict of interests might endanger the Union.

The effect on Great Britain was discussed on 18th July, when Huskisson advocates retaliation. Huskisson—who was now out of the Cabinet—made a strong speech. The new tariff was, he considered, aimed at Great Britain ; it imposed duties which were almost prohibitory on our woollens,

---

[1] In 1829, the two groups came to an agreement to suspend all Customs on their mutual interchange of products, to establish duty-free roads, and to enter into no separate treaty with their neighbours. But further progress was interrupted by the Revolution of 1830, and the Zollverein proper dates only from 1833.

[2] *Tariff History of the United States,* chap. ii.

cottons, and hardware, while "the productions of other countries were, in the same proportion, lowered." The United States had, of course, a right to do as they liked, but we had the remedy within our own hands—" a man must be blind to the interests of this country who should consent to deprive Government of the means of promptly meeting the effect of such restrictive measures by corresponding regulations. . . . Whilst we were dependent on America for the raw material, were the Americans to be independent of our manufactured goods, of which they required till now so large a supply ? " It was the most manly course to protect our commerce and protest. The imports from America were of two descriptions ;—articles of consumption, like tobacco, rice, and turpentine, and the material for our great manufacture. We could soon replace their tobacco by giving encouragement to its growth in our own East Indies. The rice of India was already usurping the place of rice from Carolina. Cotton we could cultivate in India if we gave it the same encouragement as we did indigo. There was another consideration : if the United States drove us to other countries for a supply which was now almost all their own, that supply would be brought in English bottoms. " It was become a question of too great importance to be longer overlooked by any Government anxious to protect its commerce from the palpable attempt to exclude the produce of English industry from the market of the United States." He went on to hint that America would not be successful in the attempt to shut out our goods. Smuggling through Canada would be inevitable—although he would deeply regret if things turned into such an illicit channel.[1] But, if America should persevere in this system, the day might yet come when the commerce between her and this country would be as restricted and insignificant as that between us and France. The commerce of America with this country amounted to more than one-half of the whole of her commercial transactions with the rest of the world, while our dealings with America did not amount to one-sixth of our foreign trade. If things came to the worst it was easy to see which would lose most. It was absurd to suppose that we should lose our commerce. All that this fatal policy of the United States could do was to alter its course—to send us into other parts of the

[1] " Free access to Canada will afford our merchants so many facilities for smuggling," said the *Edinburgh Review* in December, " that, unless the Americans place a Custom-house officer in every bush, and station a gunboat in every creek, it will not be in their power to prevent the introduction of our products."

same continent, into Asia, and into the vast islands of the Asiatic seas. He advised the Ministry not to act hastily, but, if they adopted retaliatory measures, to adhere to them with firmness. " Remember that there are limits to forbearance itself : as new interests grow up, the difficulties increase in the way of altering the system." The time should not be too long, nor the difficulties allowed to grow too great, before they legislated in the spirit which might be necessary. Hume advised that the Government should not pay the least attention to the ungenerous policy of America, but leave it to fall by its own weakness. He agreed in thinking that, for every pound which this country would lose by the operation of the tariff, America would lose five. He differed, however, in thinking that, if the resolution to adopt retaliatory measures were once taken, it should be persisted in, reminding the House that the thing which rankled in the breast of the Americans was our exclusion of their staple, corn, from our ports.

Peel thought that America was acting in error, but he did not think that the new tariff was a measure of retaliation on us : " it would be a most extraordinary proceeding, indeed, if America should think fit to adopt measures of retaliation at the very moment when we had relaxed the severity of our Corn Laws." Still he was " not prepared to go the length of admitting that even the perseverance of America should not drive us to the adoption of any retaliatory measures." [1]

President Adams' last Message to Congress of December contains some curious statements about the tariff. " The legislation of one nation is sometimes intentionally made to bear heavily upon the interests of another. . . . Thus the legislation of Great Britain, when, as has recently been avowed, adapted to the depression of a rival nation, will naturally abound with regulations of interdict upon the productions of the soil or industry of the other which come in competition with its own ; and will present encouragement, perhaps even bounty, to the raw material of the other state, which it cannot produce itself, and which is essential for the use of its

President Adams on the tariff.

[1] *Hansard*, xix. 1768. The *Leeds Intelligencer* found some consolation for the passing of a tariff which struck so heavily at British industries by the reflection that it would be the deathblow of Free Trade and Reciprocity with foreigners : " it absolutely knocks on the head—it turns into dust and ashes—it holds up to the scorn of mankind, as a vile delusion and quackery, that accursed cant of the present generation, that pest of nations, corrupter of the human heart and bane of the human understanding—called Political Economy."

manufactures, competitors in the markets of the world with those of its commercial rival. Such is the state of the commercial legislation of Great Britain as it bears upon our interests. It excludes, with interdicting duties, all importation (except in time of approaching famine) of the great staple productions of our middle and western states ; it proscribes, with equal rigour, the bulkier lumber and live stock, of the same portion, and also of the northern and eastern part of our Union. It refuses even the rice of the south, unless aggravated with a charge of duty upon the northern carrier who brings it to them. But the cotton, indispensable for their looms, they will receive almost duty free, to weave it into a fabric for our own wear, to the destruction of our own manufactures, which they are enabled thus to undersell. Is the self-protecting energy of this nation so helpless that there exists, in the political institutions of our country, no power to counteract the bias of this foreign legislation ;—that the growers of grain must submit to this exclusion from the foreign markets of their produce ;—that the shippers must dismantle their ships, the trade of the north stagnate at the wharfs, and the manufacturers starve at their looms, while the whole people shall pay tribute to foreign industry to be clad in a foreign garb ;— that the Congress of the Union are impotent to restore the balance in favour of native industry destroyed by the statutes of another realm ? " The reader will note the suggestion that the new tariff was a retaliation on an avowed intention to " depress " the United States.

Another passage on the " Balance of Trade " is perhaps worth quoting : " In our country, a uniform experience of forty years has shown that, whatever the tariff of duties upon articles imported has been, the amount of importations has always borne an average value nearly approaching to that of the exports, though occasionally differing in the balance, sometimes being more and sometimes less. It is, indeed, a general law of prosperous commerce that the real value of exports should, by a small and only a small balance, exceed that of imports, that balance being a permanent addition to the wealth of the nation. The extent of the prosperous commerce of the nation must be regulated by the amount of its exports ; and an important addition to the value of these will draw after it a corresponding increase of importations. It has happened, in the vicissitudes of the seasons, that the harvests of all Europe have, in the last summer and autumn, fallen short of their usual average. A relaxation of the interdict upon the importation of grain and

flour from abroad has ensued ; a propitious market has been opened
to the granaries of our country ; and a new prospect of reward presented to the labours of the husbandman, which, for several years,
has been denied. This accession to the profits of agriculture, in
the middle and western portions of our Union, is accidental and
temporary. It may continue only for a single year. It may be,
as has often been experienced in the revolutions of time, but the
first of several scanty harvests in succession. We may consider it
certain that, for the approaching year, it has added an item of large
amount to the value of our exports, and that it will produce a
corresponding increase of importations. It may therefore confidently be foreseen that the revenue of 1829 will equal and probably exceed that of 1828, and will afford the means of extinguishing
ten millions more of the principal of the public debt." The logic
which, in one breath, proclaims the practical equivalence of imports
and exports, and states that " the extent of the prosperous commerce of the nation must be regulated by the amount of its exports,"
and, in the next, defends the most violent prohibition of imports,
seems somewhat at fault.[1]

[1] The Message is given in full in the *Annual Register*, 434.

CHAPTER XLIII

1829. SUDDEN RELAPSE INTO DEEP DISTRESS

A break in the usual cyclical movement.

To the people of the day, the industrial condition of the country in 1829 was very puzzling—and, indeed, to the economic historian it remains so still. All through 1828 there had been good reason to believe that the country was passing through the usual well-marked early stages of a " revival of trade." After the sharp and sudden set-back of 1825, prices were low, wages were low, and profits were low ; but trade was slowly recovering, and there was little complaint about want of employment. Suddenly, without any new disturbance or fresh cause, distress came on again, and no one who now painted the condition of industry in the blackest colours was charged with exaggeration. In the middle of April, Charles Grant said, without contradiction, that at the moment no one could deny that the pressure was general—that there was a remarkable stagnation in every department of manufacturing industry—and that the farmer, the agriculturist, and the retail dealer were all feeling the pressure of distress. There was a want of confidence in every class : the power of consumption seemed to be paralysed. And he opposed, as did others, the proposed Committee on the Silk Trade because the pressure was affecting all the great staple trades of the country—the cotton trade, indeed, he believed was still worse off than the silk. With all the elements of prosperity about us, said Western—with abundance of capital—with great energy— with unwearied industry—with foreign commerce pouring in upon us from all quarters—with all the circumstances which are generally quoted as proofs of the prosperity of a country—we are in a state of general calamity and distress.

Many, indeed, kept saying that fluctuations were " natural "— that they belonged to the very constitution of modern industry ; but thoughtful men felt—if they did not express it as clearly as we should—that the usual rhythmical movement of the trade cycle had been broken. Some 180 petitions were presented during the Session, all speaking of great distress. " The Beau's troubles are not over yet," wrote Creevey in April ; " the distress in the country is frightful : millions are starving, and I defy him to do anything to relieve them."

In the debate on the Budget in May, much indignation was expressed at what was considered the indifference of the Government to the acute sufferings of the people. There was, accordingly, some feeling that, before Parliament rose, there ought to be a debate on the State of the Nation, and Sir Richard Vyvyan had given notice that he would, on the 26th May, move for a Select Committee to enquire into the Extent and Causes of the Distress of the Agricultural, Manufacturing, and Commercial Interests. But, on that date, there was no House, and the opportunity was lost. It was just as well, as we learn, from another speech, that the points on which he meant to dwell were :—that there was a cause for our national distress—the withdrawal of the one pound notes had had a great part in producing it, and that " a sufficient remedy " lay in the hands of Parliament—he saw no hope of improvement but " by some ameliorated system of paper currency which, by supplying the public exigencies, would revive trade, and give it the same advantages under which this country had hitherto flourished."

The place of such a discussion, however, was filled by three debates which came close together in the last fortnight of the Session. The first arose on a petition signed by some 8,000 manufacturers of Birmingham, ascribing the distress of the manufacturing districts, and especially of Birmingham, to the Bill which had " tampered with the currency," and " doubled the debt of £800 millions, as well as the £55 millions of taxes." Brougham, in presenting, did it the faint justice of stating its contents and damning its every clause, but there were one or two who warmly supported it. Waithman said that it was impossible to go on like this ; sooner or later, the Government must give protection to the trade of the country so as to enable it to sustain the immense burden of taxation, or else return to a paper currency. Attwood said that the currency question would force itself again and again on the attention of the Government till something were done. Peel naturally complained of such irresponsible language at the fag-end of the Session. He fully admitted that putting the currency back to a sound basis

First debate on the Distress.

had caused distress to many, but, to complain of the evils under which we were suffering without suggesting any remedy, could only unsettle the public mind. Baring contended that it was inherent in the nature of trade that there should be times when it was carried on with profit, and other times when it was impossible to carry it on without a loss : these singular fluctuations were often difficult to trace to any assignable cause : the stagnation had been pretty generally felt throughout Europe, yet no one had had the hardihood to get up and propose a specific remedy. The public were deceived, however, if they thought there was not sufficient accommodation for trade—money was to be had, and in abundance, if credit was good ; and he suggested that one cause of the existing stagnation was the recent rush to supply America before the new tariff came into operation.[1]

Second debate. The second debate was on the same evening—and, indeed, continued the first—when Wilmot Horton brought forward a set of Resolutions as to the Distress of the Labouring Classes. It was a great fallacy, he held, to lay stress on dear corn and consequent high wages as rendering the country unable to compete in the markets of the world. This could hold only if the "labour" compared was manual. But a great deal of our labour was engaged with machinery. Our ability to compete depended on the quantity and excellence of our fixed capital, and we should outstrip other countries in proportion as our fixed capital was greater than theirs. The real problem was with the large amount of able-bodied labourers superseded by machinery. What was to be done with them ? They might, in other times and circumstances, have had recourse to agriculture, but the fact was that the agricultural interest was now "depressed by population." Of three agricultural parishes in Sussex, according to returns laid before the House, in one, there were 220 labourers where the farm work required only 160, and the roads 6, leaving 50 to spare; in another, there were 400 too many; in the third, there were 24. His conclusion was that "both labour and population were redundant"—the supply greater than the demand—and that no improvement could take place in the condition of the labourers till the proportion between the supply and the demand was corrected. If this were true, any other remedy suggested would not reach to the bottom of the case. What influence, for instance, could an alteration in the currency or in the Corn Laws have on the wages of a redundant population ? The

[1] *Hansard*, xxi. 1702.

remedy, of course, to his mind was Emigration.[1] Those who raised the " vacuum " contention—that the place of the paupers removed would be speedily occupied again—ignored the fact that it would take many years to fill the vacuum. He had been charged with cruelty in " promoting the export of individuals from their homes to a distant foreign settlement, where they were exposed to all kind of sufferings, and to the unchecked ravages of disease." He challenged the statement. True, the mortality among the late emigrants to Canada might have reached one in twenty-one, but it was not to be forgotten that most of the emigrants had been reduced to the lowest state of wretchedness before they left the country, so that they were not only more subject to disease but less capable of resisting its attacks.

Sadler, who entered Parliament for Newark in this year,[2] and was constantly speaking, thought that such a confession confirmed the worst that could be said of emigration ; for, in this country, the rate was only one in sixty. As a matter of history he said, truly enough, that there had always been complaints of an alleged redundancy of human beings. He agreed with Bacon that, " while we have waste lands in the country, and whilst we are surrounded by waste seas, the population can never be redundant." And how could anyone say that the agricultural population was redundant when the English harvest could not be taken in without an annual importation of Irish ? So long as mankind were held in slavery, no one was so foolish as to say that slaves were not valuable to those who possessed them : were slaves more valuable than free men ? The fact was that " within our population, now so much complained of, we possessed mines compared with which the gems of India and the metals of America were utterly worthless."

Sadler opposes emigration.

---

[1] The Emigration Committee, which reported in 1826, made great play with " redundancy," and suggested the Poor Rate in England as a fund which might be made applicable for advancing the expenses (*Hansard*, xiv. 1360). The Report was given in full in the *Edinburgh Annual Register* of the year.

[2] Michael Thomas Sadler (1780-1835) ; in business at Leeds from 1800 ; in 1828, wrote *Ireland ; its evils and their remedies*, advocating a Poor Law and a tax on absentees. Malthus' theory, he said, was as unphilosophical and false as it was melancholy, as was proved by the fact that the existing condition of Ireland was much superior to its condition some centuries before when the population did not exceed a million. His theory, elaborated in *The Law of Population* (1830), was that fecundity varied, not according to wretchedness but to happiness and prosperity ; that the power of man to multiply his species diminished in proportion as his numbers increased, and was, *ceteris paribus*, in inverse ratio to the condensation of population.

Huskisson, for once, was tempted to be humorous. Bacon was, no doubt, a high authority, but Bacon himself had said that there was no abstract proposition that was universally true. Speaking of the idleness which existed in England and in Europe, for instance, he said that, if a man had nothing else to do, he should plant a tree. But if Bacon had been brought up in Canada or America, surely his recommendation would have been to cut down a tree ! Sadler has poetically described colonisation as a calamity. But, when we had carried the English language to the utmost ends of the world— when we had raised a population of twelve millions under the United States—when, in Canada, there was now a million of inhabitants against 60,000 in 1763—could it be said that nothing was to be gained by emigration and colonisation ? Would anyone compare the condition of the emigrants to Canada with that of the miserable peasantry of Ireland, with their scanty supply of bad food, and misery the only positive check to the increase of population ? He did not dispute the doctrine that the wealth of a State consisted in its population. If no other circumstances than the extent of Ireland and its fertility were taken into account, it could support a population of ten times its present amount ; but the honourable gentleman, who was the opponent of all " theorists," beggared all theorists when he stated such a position without considering the changes that must take place, in every respect, in that country before such a population could be provided for. In the end, the Resolutions were negatived.[1]

Third debate.   The third debate arose on a petition from Blackburn, complaining of the great distress in which the petitioners, in common with others of the manufacturing classes, were involved, and asserting that the cure was within reach of legislative control. It was presented by Sadler, who claimed roundly that the members of the legislature were " bound to alleviate the distress of the country," but, as Baring reminded him, omitted to say of what description the remedy was to be. Hume agreed with Sadler ; it was the duty of Ministers to find relief for the distresses of the country ; he himself had mentioned three remedies—reduction of taxation, getting rid of the Corn Laws, relaxation of the restrictions on commerce—but nobody had paid any attention.

Peel very sensibly said that the solution of a mathematical problem was a thing entirely different from the administration of practical relief in such circumstances as the present. It was not fair to charge

[1] *Hansard*, xxi. 1719.

the Government with indifference to the distress because they were adverse to the enquiry pressed on them, and did not agree with the remedies which had been suggested. At the same time, he did not take so gloomy a view of the subject as some did. He did not believe that the capital of the country was diminishing or was getting no return—they had heard that kind of statement any time these last ten years. Take the county of Lancashire ; although the improvement in the currency would tend to diminish the nominal amount, the valuation of the rental on land and on the manufacturing establishments had risen, according to a revaluation of 1828, from £3 millions in 1815 to £4 millions. Huskisson, in the same strain, asked how the rapid increase in shipping—testifying to the foreign trade—and the great increase in home consumption, could be reconciled with the statement of universal disaster. The cause of the present distress was not obscure. The mainspring of the mad speculations of 1825 was the fatal facility of obtaining credit upon an insufficient foundation, and it was the reaction from these violent experiments that had caused the present depression.

D. W. Harvey, however, broke in like Thrasymachus in the *Republic*. If no other man was bold enough to tell the plain truth, he would. All the petitions presented, all the orations they had heard upon corn, currency, ships, and free trade were so many schemes of delusion. If honourable members were ignorant, or rather affected to be ignorant, of the cause of our distresses and of the true remedy, the people were not ; every man of common sense and common honesty well understood the national disease and the national cure. The truth must be told ; the country demanded, was entitled to, and must have relief from the grinding oppression of taxation—particularly, he added as an anti-climax, the intolerable pressure of the tithes, an imposition which bore far more heavily and with infinitely less justice upon agriculture than the Poor Laws. The debate ended without result.[1]

As the year went on, things grew worse. The wages quoted are incredible—who, for instance, that has ever made the experiment, as I have, of living on sixpence worth of food a day, can believe that thousands in Huddersfield had no more than $2\frac{1}{2}$d. to live on ?— and, when the low wages were still further reduced, in the endeavour to keep the wheels moving, the starving workers broke into insurrection. In May, there was a considerable amount of rioting round about Manchester ; looms destroyed, webs cut to pieces, factories

Things grow worse,

---

[1] *Hansard*, xxi. 1773.

set on fire, bakers' shops broken into and cleared. In Rochdale, the mob attacked the military who had been called out ; and several were shot down before the streets were cleared. An intimated reduction of wages at Barnsley in August was met with a general stoppage of work ; factories and warehouses were guarded by armed men ; here also the military was called out and some blood shed. It would be tedious to multiply instances ; everything goes to show a very terrible state of privation during the summer and autumn in the chief manufacturing districts. In September, there was no improvement—" neither is there the slightest prospect of any improvement for some time to come "—and, it is added, " the securities of the South American Republics have continued at the lowes quotations, and no prospect whatever yet exists of any dividends forthcoming." In October, we read that, if we " were to judge from the complaints still kept up among the merchants of the City, we ought to come to the conclusion that trade is rapidly departing from these realms." As late as November, some masters and others interested came to the conclusion of taking land near the metropolis " for the purpose of furnishing occupation of a productive nature for such time as may not be filled up with silk weaving "—the Duke had been appealed to " for some Crown Lands " without success. About this time also appeared another phenomenon which must have given gloomy thoughts to those who remembered the early stages of the French Revolution. " Meetings to fix a maximum price upon some of the necessaries of life have been held in many of the manufacturing towns and districts of the north of England. A meeting of this nature was held, not long ago, upon Woodhouse Moor, Leeds, numerously attended, at which it was resolved not to pay more than 1½d. a quart for good new milk, and not more than 8d. a lb. for butter. A similar meeting was held, though upon a larger scale, in Bolton, at which maximum resolutions were also passed."

till, in the end of the year, the cloud lifts. But, in the end of the year, the cloud seemed to lift as suddenly as it had settled. In November, we find a general movement in the principal markets and in some of the manufacturing districts ; there had been indications, for the past four or five weeks, of a much improved trade in cotton and wool. The silk trade was extremely brisk—the silk warehouses in Manchester completely cleared of stock. " In Leeds, every one was employed " ; equally cheering accounts came from Bradford. In other trades, the complaints of distress had altogether ceased, etc. In December, the improvement continued, and the crisis was thought at an end. All the power-looms in Glasgow were at work. Favourable advices were coming from all parts of the world—even the South American Republics seemed to be recovering.

A little unaccountably, the Exports rose from £52¾ millions in Foreign trade. the previous year to £56,218,000, and the Re-exports, from £10 millions roughly to £10,620,000. The Imports, however, fell from £45,167,000 to £44 millions. The real value of the British Exports fell, by nearly a million, to £35,842,000. There was again a reduction in the vessels built and registered in the ports of the United Kingdom. In 1828, the number was 842, representing 88,663 tons : in the present year, it was 718 and 76,635.

As regards agriculture, the weekly imperial average for wheat Agriculture. was over 74/- in January ; fell gradually to 66/6 in beginning of March ; continued in the vicinity of 70/- from then on till the end of June ; kept between 66/- and 68/- till the beginning of September ; then fell to about 60/- in the middle of that month, and remained between 55/- and 57/- till the end of the year. From January to the 6th of March, accordingly, the high prices allowed foreign wheat to come in at the nominal duty of 1/-, from which time the duty rose gradually till it was 16/8 in April, 20/8 all August, 24/8 in October, and 30/8 from the 13th of November onwards. The average for the year was 66/3.[1]

Taking these prices in relation to the agricultural history of the year, it seems clear that, under the new system of the admission of foreign grain, the British prices were far from reflecting the prospects and realisations of the British harvest. The winter and spring, though cold, promised fairly, but the summer was full of changes. In July, came heavy rains saturating the soil. A fair week or two in August raised hopes, which, however, were finally dashed by the recurrence of rain and wind. The harvest accordingly Another was protracted and extremely late, and the grain, got in in bad con- poor harvest. dition and at great expense, deficient both in quantity and quality. Hurried to market ere the end of the year, the importation averages

[1] If one were to judge by the monthly tables given in the *Annual Register*, " from the returns," it would be thought that the year showed a very high range of prices, rising from 72/- in January to about 80/- in early spring ; falling to 75/- in summer, rising to 80/- in August ; falling again to 70/- in October and November, and ending with 73/- in December—an average for the year of about 75/- (p. 285). But whatever the " returns " to which these figures refer, the prices are not the averages which determined the duty on importation.

were much depressed. All the time, fine foreign wheat, as well as a small proportion of British wheat which came to market in a dry condition, was fetching a price about 20/- higher. It is not to be wondered at, then, that the agriculturist found himself bewildered. " In former times," said the *British Farmer's Magazine,* " it was easy to form an estimate of the prices of grain from the state of the weather and that of the crops ; but, since we began to import so much foreign grain, and, of course, came much to the mercy of the grain dealers and importers, we have no rule to look to as to prices except their pleasure. Hence the repeated rises and falls in the grain market every few weeks ; and to such an extent that you can scarcely say what the prices are for a few days together." So much, it concluded, for the sage prognostications of those who assured us that the alteration in the Corn Laws would " ensure steady prices." [1]

[1] 108, 503. The above to some extent accounts for the very divergent tables of prices in different quarters.

CHAPTER XLIV

1829. GOULBURN'S SECOND BUDGET

On 8th May, by which time the relapse of trade into depression had become marked, the Budget was presented.[1] " There were circumstances in the present condition of the country," said Goulburn, " which clouded the general prosperity of the past, and cast a partial gloom over the prospect "—the late bad harvest, the stagnation in commerce, want of demand in manufactures, distress in some branches of industry. But he thought he would be able to satisfy the House that there was nothing in the present state of things which affected the national resources, or interferred with the means of calling them into action—that the country was rather in a state of suspense and uncertainty than of positive ill.

Last year, he had estimated the Revenue at £53,900,000, and the *The past year.* Expenditure at £50,100,000, anticipating a surplus for the reduction of the National Debt of £3,797,000. As a fact, the Revenue had turned out to be £55,187,000, and the Expenditure, £49,336,000. The surplus, accordingly, applicable to the purposes of a Sinking Fund was £5,850,000. The increase was nearly altogether in Customs and Excise—the latter in all categories of consumption, but principally in malt and spirits. The decrease in Expenditure, however, was not all actual saving—some of it being merely postponed payment.

For the current year some reduction of revenue must be expected *The* —" all countries were subject to alternations of prosperity and *Estimates.* depression which no power could ward off." It seemed to be a rule in the affairs of mankind that blessings should not be showered down without a corresponding visitation of depression. His estimates were as follows :

[Revenue

[1] *Hansard,* xxi. 1168.

REVENUE.

Customs and Excise - - - - - -	£37,150,000
Stamps - - - - - - -	7,107,000
Taxes - - - - - - -	4,850,000
Post Office - - - - - -	1,500,000
Smaller branches - - - - -	200,000
Miscellaneous - - - - - -	540,000
	£51,347,000

EXPENDITURE.

Charge of Debt - - -	£27,053,000		
Interest on Exchequer Bills -	850,000		
Naval and Military Pensions -	585,740		
Other charges on Consolidated Fund - - -	2,200,000		
Army - - -	7,769,178—a decrease of	£300,000	
Navy - - - - -	5,878,794	,,	100,000
Ordnance - - - -	1,728,908		
Payments to Spanish subjects (treaty claims) - -	200,000		
Miscellaneous - - -	2,067,973	,,	800,000
	£48,333,593		

leaving a clear surplus of £3,013,407 to the reduction of the National Debt.   He saw no reason to anticipate any change of circumstances which might prevent the carrying out of the recommendation of the Finance Committee, namely, the maintenance of taxation sufficient to give a clear surplus of £3 millions for this purpose.[1]

Criticism.   There was some criticism of the euphemistic " clouded " and " partial gloom "—inadequate expressions for the state of " a country brought to the verge of ruin," with its credit " annihilated " : the Chancellor could not see beyond his full Treasury—and also of the congratulation on the increased consumption of spirits— " as if the amount of gin and whiskey consumed was a proof of the improvement of the condition of the lower orders, although it was not to be denied that thousands had been driven by despair to seek an oblivion of their sorrows in intoxication."   Hume sustained his reputation by a slashing attack on the maintenance of the " reckless expenditure " at a level of £50 millions odd.   " I consider it one of the greatest evils to which the country could be exposed that, during the last seventeen years, the revenue has been so steadily productive.   All history tells me—at least all my experience

[1] This, it may be anticipated, was the only serious attempt made to carry out the recommendation of the Finance Committee ; the policy for many years thereafter was the reduction of taxation in preference to the reduction of debt.

tells me—that, in proportion as you place funds in the hands of Government, they will take good care that they shall all be expended." Was it common prudence even for an individual to live to the utmost verge of his income when he had reason to expect reverses ? He would have used the surplus to remit taxation rather than pay off debt. D. W. Harvey, supporting him, went a step farther. It would be easy, he asserted, to reduce the expenditure by eight or ten millions, but " still greater relief might arise from an alteration of the taxes." He would recommend the substitution of " a well-regulated and equitable graduated property-tax, commencing at one and rising to thirty or forty per cent. Honourable members, of course, laughed at the proposition—he knew very well they would not consent to tax themselves—but it appeared to him that gentlemen possessed of £30,000 or £40,000 a year in the country should pay in proportion for the benefits which they enjoyed ; and, if forty per cent. would be disagreeable, he would be willing to compromise for a tax of twenty per cent. upon their property."

An anomaly in the liquor duties was brought up by Hume. In Scotland the result of reducing the duty on whiskey was that spirits, which used to sell for 8/-, 9/-, 10/-, and 11/- a gallon, were now selling for 6/- and 7/-, and that beer was every day going out of consumption. The amount of beer brewed in Scotland had fallen off from 2,400 barrels in 1822 to 1,500 in 1826, and brewing was perhaps the worst trade in Scotland. In England, on the other hand, the duty on whiskey remained at 7/-, and, in Ireland, there was no duty whatever on beer. It was surprising that Government should suffer the duties on beer and spirits to vary so greatly in the three countries.[1]

Liquor duties anomalies.

---

[1] *Hansard*, xxi. 444.

CHAPTER XLV

1829. THE PROGRESS OF FREE TRADE IDEAS

WHILE all the industries of the country were suffering acutely, silk was the one which most made itself heard—not, perhaps, that it was more depressed than any other, but that, to those in the trade, it seemed that the causes of the distress were not only obvious but removable. As the mill-men and throwsters of Macclesfield put it when protesting against the introduction of foreign thrown silk at a low duty, if laws were found to have failed in attaining their object, and had produced an entirely opposite effect, they ought to be subjected to the revision of Parliament. Petitions witnessing to great distress came from the throwsters of Somerset, Wilts, Dorset, Coventry, and London.[1] 12,000 Spitalfields weavers—" Victims of Free Trade "—marched through the city to present a petition to the Duke. The subject was formally brought up on 13th April by Fyler, one of the members for Coventry, who asked for a Select Committee to enquire into the State of the

The silk trade protest. Silk Trade,[2] promising that he would produce before it such a mass of evidence and incontrovertible facts as would leave no doubt that the principle of Free Trade, as applied to silk, had entirely failed. Free Trade was, he granted, very beautiful in theory, but how could Free Trade in manufactures coexist with a monopoly of corn ? And, if there was one trade more likely to be injured by Free Trade than another, taking into consideration soil and climate, access to raw material, price of provisions, price of labour, it was that of silk. The experiment had now been tried for five years, and the result was—capital lost, one-third of the labour out of employ, and those employed unable to obtain the necessaries of life. The distress of all concerned, in Scotland and Ireland as well as in England, was appalling and unparalleled. In all the

[1] *Hansard*, xx. 567, 608 ; xxi. 444.   [2] *Ibid.* xxi. 744.

silk centres, mills were standing, looms unemployed, wages reduced
to the lowest point. The obvious cause was " the enormous amount
of foreign silk goods which were imported " under the new system
—" a million of money displaced from the work of this country."
One branch of the trade, indeed, and that the most lucrative, seemed
to be entirely leaving us, the manufacture of fancy and figured
articles. He did not know what measures the Government intended
to propose. It was understood that they meant to do their utmost
to prevent smuggling. But that would be of no avail. " It
mattered little whether silk were introduced by legal importation
or by smuggling, so long as it was introduced, and the trade of
the country was overborne. Were vested rights to be obliged
to yield to the influence of political or experimental opinions ?
Half a million of men were at the bar of the House, representing
the distress that had been brought upon them ; let those unhappy
persons be no longer the victims of speculative legislation." The
motion was seconded by Robinson, the member for Worcester,
who honestly confessed, on a subsequent occasion, that, as a
similar distress was being experienced among his own constituents,
the glove-makers, he felt that the best mode of advancing their
interests was to raise the question which professed to relate only
to the silk trade. Every prediction of those who recommended
Free Trade, he claimed, had been falsified. No country had followed
the example of England. America argued that "their manufactures
were in a state of infancy " : France, that the liberal system of
England was admirable, and that she would adopt it—if she were
able to compete. What would be the state of this country when
labour, already abridged by machinery, should be destitute of
employment and driven into prisons and poorhouses by crime
and poverty, instead of being industriously employed ? As to
smuggling, it " increased with the relaxation of the duties, from
the difficulty of distinguishing in the mass the legal from the illegal
article."

Specious as all this was at first sight, it will be seen that there Vesey
was little in the case, as thus presented, beyond the fact that the Fitzgerald's first
trade was in a bad way at the same time that foreign goods were appearance.
being largely imported, the connection of the two, as effect and cause,
being merely stated as " obvious " ; and Vesey Fitzgerald, making
his first considerable appearance as President of the Board of Trade,
easily justified his position as Huskisson's successor. Nothing had
been said, he affirmed, to shake his opinions as to the soundness

and good policy of the existing regulations, but he was not sorry
to be permitted to vindicate the principles on which the Government had acted, and to show that the distress—which he fully
acknowledged and deplored—had flowed, not from the new policy,
but from causes over which neither Government nor Parliament
had any control. He must oppose such a Committee, not only
because it would hang everything up for a couple of months, unsettling all the trade, adding to the stagnation, and encouraging
the opinion, so industriously circulated, that Parliament was likely
to change its policy, but because its object, unavowed but plain,
was nothing else than the return to Prohibition. " Do the petitioners believe," he asked, " that if, by a system of enforced prohibition, they could exclude foreign competition, if they could by
the protection which they seek raise the price and the value of the
domestic manufacture, securing to the merchant those profits
which, they say, he has lost, restoring to the operative those high
wages which he formerly received and which rivalry at home as well
as abroad has tended to reduce—if these gentlemen could guarantee
to the augmented number, both of manufacturers and throwsters,
the same profits and the same monopoly which, under another system,
and with more limited numbers, to the prejudice of the great body
of consumers, they enjoyed—do these gentlemen persuade themselves that that extension of the trade which has been produced
by cheapness and competition will not be affected by the withdrawing of those primary incentives, or that the fashion or the patriotism
of this country is such that its public and its consumers would be
content to pay for our domestic manufacture the same augmented
prices which monopoly would claim ? Does it not occur, Sir, to
the honourable gentlemen that the immediate result of a return to
a prohibitory system, if it produced that increase of price which he
contemplates, must produce also the most fatal effects upon all
those places to which the manufacture has been extended, on
individuals as well as bodies of men who have embarked in it ? "

Smuggling. But it was to the contraband trade that the petitioners had
universally ascribed their present distress. Had smuggling, then,
emerged with Free Trade ? Was it not notorious that, in the old
times of prohibition, French silks were to be seen in every house ?
" If you would encourage the importation of foreign goods, prohibit
them ; if you would confirm the caprice of fashion, and give to the
foreign article a fancied superiority, recur to prohibition." Prohibition was now demanded that foreign goods might be distinguished

from home-made—that the foreign goods might be pursued and their owners made responsible for them wherever they might be found. But could they then be distinguished ? " Under the paralysing effects of undue protection, the goods of this country were once distinguishable at first sight by their inferiority to those of France ; but imitation and improvement, under the stimulus of competition, had been at work, and it had been more than once difficult to maintain a seizure after it had been made. Then allow me to ask the honourable gentlemen by what means, by what authority could that system of prohibition be enforced ? . . . Are you ready to resort to the only means by which it can be enforced—domiciliary visits ? " Were they ready to grant again to the common informer the power of visiting the house of every Englishman of every rank in society, for the purpose of enforcing a fiscal law ? The practical effect of that law was to establish in the minds of the people the idea that the violation of it was no violation of morality ; and this violation of the people's morals made them, by a natural reaction, the more ready agents for the violation of the law ; so that the general result of the system was to render the provisions of the prohibitory laws ineffective for the purpose for which they were intended, and, on this ground alone, namely, the moral and unconstitutional tendency of the laws, he could never consent to see them replaced on the statute book, even though the present system were less effective than it had actually been found to be.

His explanation of the distress was that it did not arise from the measures of 1826, but from prohibition before that year and from over-trading after it—over-extension of the whole trade since 1824 in the confidence that the 30 per cent. duty would afford ample protection. For the moment the manufacture had been extended beyond the demand. It was a circumstance not peculiar to the silk trade—the same was the fact with regard to the cotton trade. The evil, which was the result of excessive manufacturing, was increased by the use of machinery,[1] and its only relief was to be procured by extending the consumption of silk goods—which would indeed be the natural result of the lowness of price. In Coventry, there were nearly a thousand more looms, and three or four hundred manufacturers as against a hundred : in Macclesfield, 60 mills

Over-trading.

---

[1] Grant said that the machinery employed in the silk factories produced at least double what it did before. The spindles, instead of 800 to 1,000 revolutions per minute, were now running at the rate of 2,500 to 3,000, and, in one factory, at 7,000 (*Hansard*, xxi. 853).

instead of 20, and 10,000 looms instead of half the number : " three years ago there was scarcely a silk loom in Leeds—now they are innumerable " : in Glasgow, 7,000 looms now instead of 3,000 ; in Paisley, 20 bales of silk used for one, etc., etc.[1]

The throwsters.   The case of the throwsters required to be specially looked at.[2] Prohibition, as a means to their protection, had never been proposed, nor, indeed, had they ever had it. But, to judge by the petitions, it was now claimed for them that they required high duties more than the manufacturers did, and that to a degree which would, if their wishes were complied with, extinguish the manufacture itself. But the throwsters had been unable to keep out the foreign thrown silk when protected by a duty of 9/2—the importation was then much greater than now. It was plain from this that a certain quantity of foreign thrown silk was indispensable to the manufacturer of the finer order of goods : there was no other way of accounting for the fact that the importation of raw silk had so much increased since the reduction of the duty, while there had been no corresponding increase in the import of thrown silk. It was quite true that the throwster, under the former system, had large profits and was able to pay high wages ; but it was evident that the decrease in his profits had not been occasioned by the reduction of the duty so much as by the extension of his establishments—the natural consequence of the great profits many were making in that business. He had in his hand returns of the trade since 1823. Previous to 1824, there were 780,000 spindles at work in the country ; in 1829, they had increased to 1,180,000, and the mills had increased from

[1] " The fact is," said Parnell subsequently, " that the manufacturers have committed a great error in imagining that all they had to fear was foreign competition, and in failing to take into consideration the home competition among themselves."

[2] Inasmuch as thrown silk was a raw material, the consumption of which was necessarily limited by the use of the finished silk article. To protect it, except in careful consideration of how the protection affected the manufactured silk, was suicidal, seeing that the only way to increase the demand for thrown silk was to increase the demand for silk goods—was, as Hume said, to give one man employment by throwing four men out of work. But where throwing was a separate trade, employing separate capital and separate labour and separate " vested interests," it was anything but easy to administer equal-handed protection to both—and impossible to satisfy both. It is instructive to notice that the same impossible attempt to protect two complementary industries was made in the case of linen. All manufactured linens were charged heavy import duties, but hemp and raw linen yarns also paid duty, and, as has been noted, the Scots linen manufacturers got their flax from Holland rather than from Ireland. Hence the petition of the Perth linen manufacturers in 1825, asking for delay in the reduction of the former, while urging the immediate repeal of the latter.

175 to 266. Was it necessary to add more to prove the over-trading in this branch of the trade ? Indeed, the extension of the throwing trade had added to the difficulties of the manufacturer, inasmuch as the throwster became a competitor in the purchase of the raw material. He could not understand how anyone could say that the interests of the manufacturer and of the throwster were the same. The throwster's interest, in point of fact, and his claim of protection, made the matter more difficult. If he were out of the way, and the English manufacturer could get his raw material on the same terms as obtained by the manufacturer of France, there would be no fear for the future of the trade.[1]

In these circumstances, he was bound to recommend a further reduction on foreign thrown silk. He would reduce the duties on fine thrown silk from 5/- to 3/6 ; on tram, to 2/- ; and on singles, to 1/6. He would be told that many throwing establishments would suffer from this, but the whole question resolved itself into this short point—" under present circumstances, the legislature is bound to protect the home market and the home manufacturer by the highest protecting duty which can properly be levied, but it would be vain to impose any excessive duty, and thus to hold out to the smuggler temptations which he could not resist. It is against the contraband trade that the home manufacturer most requires protection. If, out of the highest duty which can be levied for the protection of the home manufacturer, there should be any which can be extended to the throwster, the House is bound to support him to that extent, but further than that they cannot go. To go further would be to increase the duty of the manufactured article so as to hold out a temptation to the contraband trader, to the destruction of the home manufacturer." *A reduction on thrown silk.*

His second proposal was the giving of a drawback on the export of home-manufactured silks, to an amount equal to the duty on foreign thrown silk employed in its manufacture. Here identity of import and export would not be required ; he would follow the procedure adopted in sugar, where, not the identical article manufactured but, an equal proportion was demanded. " What I propose is to preserve the right of drawback to the person who has paid the duties ; so that the quantity exported may be written off against the duty paid. The drawback will be payable only to the *A drawback on exported silks.*

---

[1] One would have thought that, from all this, the throwsters would have taken warning. As a fact, we shall find that, by 1832, they had invested more and more capital in throwing.

importer when he becomes also the exporter ; or to his nominee when another is the exporter." In other words, the amount of drawback would be equal to the duty paid upon the foreign thrown silk consumed in the manufacture of the article.

Foreign silks   He came, last, to the most important point, the regulation of the competition in the home market between the foreigner and the domestic manufacturer. The legal importation last year was £600,000 ; if it were true, as Fyler asserted, that the total import, legal and illegal, was £2 millions, the contraband trade was much the greater evil of the two. Various suggestions had been made to meet it. There was, for instance, a project for stamping foreign goods. This would give the foreign article a positive advantage. " The sale of silk depends much upon fashion and caprice ; and nothing would be so likely to give a notion of superiority as to affix a stamp proving it to be foreign." In fact, the experiment had been tried. " Some time since, an Act was introduced to protect the lace manufacturers of Buckinghamshire, who required that a stamp should be placed upon foreign lace coming into this country. Who were the first to ask that it should be repealed ? The lace manufacturers themselves ; and on what ground ? ' For God's sake,' said they, ' remove the stamp, for it prevents us selling our lace for French lace ! ' " All such methods would only increase the evil. He confessed that he looked to the regulation of the duty as, not only the best, but as the only means of putting down smuggling.

As to the amount of duty necessary for this purpose he would lay down this principle ; the amount of protection to be extended to anything the subject of home manufacture, to prevent the unfair competition of goods illegally imported, ought to be governed and measured by the difference in the price of labour in the two countries, and by a reasonable reference to such other disadvantages as might affect the manufacturer in this country. He proposed, then, to

to be charged return to the old plan of an *ad valorem duty*, which had never had
25 per cent. *ad* a fair trial. They were told occasionally that smugglers could
valorem, introduce goods at ten, twelve, or fifteen per cent. He did not believe that. The member for Coventry had stated that the average expense of smuggling was from 24 per cent. to 30 per cent. He thought, then, that we might control smuggling in a large class of articles by imposing an import duty *ad valorem* of 25 per cent., giving, however, an alternative to the custom-house officer of making it a rated duty on that basis in such cases as he might

think fit to prevent articles of high value from coming in unfairly, as they had done, at a duty much lower than was intended.[1] At the same time, he would limit the importation of foreign silks to London, Dover, and one or two other principal ports in England, and to one port in Ireland, and would revive an Act lately expired by which silk might not be imported in any vessel of less than seventy tons burden. As to silks from India, there was no principle to justify us in continuing as high duties on the produce of our fellow-subjects, and on the manufactures of our own dominions as on those of foreign countries, at a time when we compelled these people to receive our manufactures duty free, with all the advantages *and Indian* of our capital, skill, and experience against them. He would, *silks 20* then, admit India silks on paying a duty of 20 per cent. *per cent.*

The speech with which Baring followed is extremely interesting, *Baring's* as taking the attitude of philosophic doubt about the applicability *philosophic* of Free Trade to all the industries of the country, and as reflecting, *doubt.* I think, the half-formulated feelings of many intelligent people in these days. It might be necessary, he said, to counteract the smuggler by lowering the duties, but, on the principles laid down by Fitzgerald, it was clear to him that the silk trade stood condemned as a manufacture, and must, sooner or later, perish. Personally he was convinced that, whatever good might result from the application of the Free Trade principle to other branches, it could never justly be applied to silk. Looking at the other leading manufactures of the country, he found that they had a decided preponderating advantage, from one circumstance or another, that would enable them to stand up against the great difficulty arising from the difference in the price of food and clothing abroad. Take iron, the potteries, even the cotton manufacture—which " possessed a great advantage from our being the nearest European country to the New World "—Free Trade had succeeded in these industries ; it was only on the silk manufacturers that the experiment operated so unfortunately, and he could not contemplate the ruin of tens of thousands without shrinking from the responsibility of participating

[1] The existing duty (*supra*, 197) was a rated one, calculated generally on a basis of 30 per cent., but actually amounting to a good deal more—even 42 per cent. or 44 per cent. on some articles. The 25 per cent. *ad valorem* duty now imposed applied to " manufactures of silk or of silk mixed with other material—silk or satin, plain." The 30 per cent. was retained for figured or brocaded, gauze, crape, velvet, ribbons. The ground of the difference was that the former were not injured by compression nor hurt by package, were in general—not seasonal—consumption, and therefore could be easily smuggled.

in the experiment. Silk was the only manufacture in which a foreign country had a decided advantage—in recent inventions of machinery, in labour half the price, in easier access to the raw materials, in "having the start of us in every respect," and in colours. He would add that France had always set the fashions to the rest of the world : "to dress like an English gentleman is the rule, but it is equally the rule to dress like a French lady." [1] Could we bear up against such a complication of advantages ? He thought not ; and all he regretted was that, by the manner in which the subject had been spoken of, persons had been induced to persevere, expecting, by the false lights held out to them, that they would be able to fight the battle against other countries. If the throwster was protected, it was quite clear that the manufacturer could not stand. The chief complaint he made was that protection was afforded to the throwster in the first instance, and that he had been induced by it to lay out his capital in mills and machinery which were not now worth more than the bricks and timber employed in their erection ; expecting to beat all the world out of the field, the poor dupes were doomed to disappointment and ruin.

This led him to repeat what he had said on former occasions, that he could not conceive it possible that, so long as Europe remained in a state of peace, this country would be able, for any great length of time, to continue an exporting country. Looking at the difficulties which the labourers had to endure, their low rate of wages, the difficulties which merchants were experiencing in purchasing so as to be able to meet the competition of foreign markets, he could not think it possible that this country should continue to be a manufacturing country for the rest of the world.[2]

If this were the case, should we be able to carry out the whole of the system of Free Trade ? He did not think, indeed, that similar difficulties would ever arise as regards iron and our potteries. But was it possible for our wool and cotton trades to continue if the present state of things went on ? The cotton manufactories in the

---

[1] "Members must be aware," said Alderman Waithman in the subsequent debate, "that if a shop for the sale of English silks were opened, and a shop for the sale of French silks were to be opened close to it, the latter, though selling twenty per cent. higher, would be surrounded with carriages while the former would remain neglected."

[2] As Baring had just put forward the cheapness of foreign labour as a reason why the foreign manufacturer could export his manufactures to us, it is a little puzzling to find the cheapness of English labour put forward as a reason why we could not export manufactures to him !

United States were pushing forward with amazing vigour, and their success must be certain, so long as cheap food continued to be (as it always would be) the criterion. "Every year evinces greater progress on the part of our rivals." These were questions on which he felt it his duty to speak as they struck him and to court discussion.

As to the admitting of Indian silks at 20 per cent. instead of 50 per cent., Fitzgerald's argument was undoubtedly a very specious one. At the same time, he could not help feeling that we had fellow-subjects rather nearer to us, who might perhaps be harder pressed to make a living than those in India were ; and he could not help coming to the conclusion that, if we allowed this class of goods to come into the country at so low a duty, it would be the means of breaking up the only portion of our trade which we had any chance of keeping.

"A favourite argument in support of Free Trade principles is that we are bound to pursue the right course ; while, as to other nations, if they choose to go wrong, why let them. I must confess that I cannot go the whole length of this proposition, for I think that it will never do for one country to take anything while others take nothing ; the only remedy for which will be that it will, at length, be checked from taking by its absolute poverty and incompetence to do so. . . . I doubt, while one country pursues a policy at variance with all the rest of the world, whether any particular good can be effected by it."

As, however, "his mind was made up on the general principles which had been adopted by the Government," and he entirely concurred with them, he went on that he would not say that he was prepared to recommend going back to the old system of prohibition ; unless he had made up his mind to that, he could not vote for the Committee of enquiry. To go into such a Committee would be to lead the country into supposing that some change was going to be effected in the system. Further than this, it was clear that, if they went into a Committee, the figures were all against the petitioners. He thought it would be difficult, not to say impossible, to make out a case in a parliamentary Committee against the fact of a continuing increase in the import of raw material. "In conclusion, I will only say that I most sincerely lament the position in which the manufacturers are placed; and shall be extremely happy to find that the measure proposed by the right honourable gentleman will have the effect he supposes ;

An unsatisfactory summing up.

though I may say that I do not look at it with such a strong anticipation of success as he appears to do."

The Bill passes. On a division, only 31 voted for a Select Committee, as against 149, and Fitzgerald's resolutions were agreed to. When the Bill founded on them went into Committee, there was another long debate, although "to empty benches," when only 22 opposed. The debate was adjourned and continued at great length. But, while the Bill was passing through, meetings had been held in the silk districts to protest against it, and in Macclesfield and Bethnal Green [1] the operatives had broken into rioting and destruction of the masters' property. On the third reading, in May, Peel said that the interests of the manufacturers, the work-people, and the public tranquillity called for the immediate passing of the Bill : the outrages which had lately taken place were, he knew, perpetrated for the purpose of intimidating the legislature against agreeing to this measure, and he was convinced that every day it was delayed would add to the number of those outrages.[2] Subsequently Fyler and his supporters, expressing their unabated hostility to the measure, declared that they would offer no further opposition, as they saw that it would be fruitless, and the Bill passed (c. 23).[3]

[1] The case of Bethnal Green is a first-rate example of what happens in regard to wages when trades fall into hereditary groups, and the growth of population is not affected by the rate of wages or other economic causes, and of how impossible it is, if labour becomes immobile, for the increasing national wealth to be reflected, as it should, in steadily rising wages. "They are all weavers," wrote Greville in 1829, "forming a sort of separate community; there they are born; there they live and labour; and there they die. They neither migrate nor change their occupation; they can do nothing else. They have increased in a ratio at variance with any principles of population, having nearly tripled in twenty years—from 22,000 to 64,000. They are for the most part out of employment and can get none. 1,100 are crammed into the poorhouse, five or six in a bed; 6,000 receive parochial relief. The parish is in debt; every day adds to the number of paupers and diminishes that of ratepayers—principally shopkeepers who are beggared by the rates. The district is in a state of insolvency and hopeless poverty, yet they multiply; and, while the people look squalid and dejected, as if borne down by wretchedness and destitution, the children thrive and are healthy."

[2] Some colour was given to this by a petition from a master silk manufacturer in London, stating that some of the weavers in his employment could earn on a single loom 35/- per week and many others from 18/- to 25/-, and that he had been obliged to dismiss many hands who were earning upwards of 20/- because he dared not trust his property in Spitalfields.

[3] *Hansard*, xxi. 595, 702, 744, 817, 889, 914, 1160, 1241. In autumn, we hear of an application by the Spitalfields weavers to Government to enable 4,000 of them to emigrate to Australia, and, on the failure of this, an appeal to the benevolent public to send at least a proportion of them (*New Monthly Magazine*, 409).

The economic historian will attach importance to this debate, ow "Free
not so much for its practical result as for the light it throws on derstood.
the evolution of free trade doctrine—the stage which educated
opinion had reached on the subject. As has been hinted, the policy
which was undoubtedly in fashion was not Free Trade but Open
Trade, or merely freer trade, and it had been adopted, not from
economic convictions, but from practical necessity. But, as the
policy developed—whether in success or in apparent failure—and
as statesmen were driven either to attack or defend it, many were
revising the crude ideas with which they started, seeking light from
Adam Smith and the " economists," and either accepting or recoiling
with apprehension from the consequences to which it was logically
leading. The two or three who were already " convinced free
traders " were impatient and contemptuous. " To talk of Free
Trade as applied to this country," said Poulett Thomson, " is
almost ludicrous. Look round at the ' free ' trades. Almost
every article imported into, or made in, Great Britain is loaded with
heavy duties ; and, at this moment, we are discussing, not whether
a duty should or should not be imposed, but whether a duty should
be reduced from 35 per cent. to 25 per cent." " The whole of the
alterations which have been made in our laws concerning trade and
manufactures," said Parnell, " are no more than a very slight
modification of the old system, and merely the first steps towards
a freer system "—as he had said before, they amounted to little more
than substituting prohibitory duties in the stead of absolute prohibitions. Very prevalent must have been the feeling expressed
by Fowell Buxton : " I am not sure that the free principles are
not sound with reference to the silk trade, but I have considerable
doubts upon the subject. It has some peculiarities that perhaps
entitle it to be an exception. If the employment of machinery
here would give us the same advantage it gives in other manufactures, I should say go on with the competition ; but we are to
recollect that the silk trade allows only of a very little use of
machinery ; that the cost of manufactured silk consists almost
entirely of the value of the raw material and of the expense of
the labour bestowed upon it. Can we compete with France in the
raw material when she grows it ? and is it not equally vain to
expect that we should be able to compete with her in the cheapness
of labour ? "

It is to Parnell that we owe the first complete answer—so far as I arnell on
know—to the difficulty which seemed to most people at the time eap labour.

insurmountable, the cheap labour of other countries. " With
respect to the price of labour, it is not true that France has any
advantage over this country ; all experience proves that low-
priced labour is, in the end, dear labour to those who pay for it.
Let the money paid in England to a workman, the number of hours
he works, the constancy of his working, and the skill with which he
works, be compared with the money paid in France to a workman,
and to the hours he works, his constancy at work, and his skill,
and the result will be a clear demonstration that the labour of the
English workman comes, in the end, cheapest to the employer
of it. It is not, however, a correct way of arguing this point.to
look only at the price of labour, in contrasting the cost of it in
England and France ; other circumstances, such as capital and
machinery, ought to be brought into the account ; and, as we have
the advantages in these respects, they serve to counteract the effect
of high wages. The extent of our capital directly leads to that
division of labour which makes it so much more productive than it
is where, for want of capital, this principle is of little avail. . . .
The worthy alderman (Waithman) has discovered that the excise
is the cause of the high price of labour ; but a better acquaintance
with those principles he is so ready to decry would have taught
him that great national wealth is the true and only cause of high
wages ; that high wages lead to such habits of living among the
labouring classes that the smaller luxuries become necessaries,
and that this wealth, which occasions high wages, affords the means
to a country to contend successfully against those countries which
have low-priced labour." [1]

That " cheap labour is dear labour," had already been suggested
by Adam Smith, and emphasised by Arthur Young in his comparison
of the Irish and English labourer. But it must be added as a *caveat*
that " dear labour is cheap labour " only where high wages are spent
in improving the workman—where what the workman thinks of
as " necessaries of life " are " necessaries of efficiency "—not where
wages go in drink and foolish extravagance. And one may admit
that the answer was not entirely reassuring, if it were true, as often

---

[1] *Hansard*, xxi. 940. One notes that it was a favourite contention among
the more economically minded writers of the time—based, no doubt, on
Ricardo's proposition that " whatever increases wages, necessarily reduces
profit "—that high wages were the cause of low profits, and that it was by the
lowness of his profits that the English manufacturer was able to undersell
his foreign competitor in every market of the world (see *e.g. Parliamentary
Review*, 1825, 703).

stated, that France had the superiority in machinery, and that skilled labour in Lyons was half the price of English labour.

What passed for Free Trade with most was nothing more than what we now call Reciprocity ; other nations must give us similar advantages ; there could be no thought of attempting it single-handed. What Waithman considered Free Trade was the export of the surplus of this country in order to obtain the surplus of another country of which we stood in need. But if France or any other country would not agree to act upon the same system, why should England determine to do so ? And many others, of course, saved their reputation by admitting that Free Trade would be the right policy—in other circumstances. "It involved a principle evidently inapplicable," said Bankes, "to the complicated condition of an old commercial community. It might do in a new country, or in a small and isolated state, but never in an old country with engagements and connections wrought into the long-established system of other countries." "Free Trade"
meant
Reciprocity.

Most interesting of all, perhaps, was the assurance with which the equivalence of imports and exports was now stated—not the less interesting that the phenomena and the method of the equivalence were not yet clearly understood. "Did not the honourable gentlemen know," asked Hume, "that, for every pound's worth of foreign produce or manufacture which came into England, an equivalent amount of English produce or manufacture must be exported to pay for it ?[1] And yet it was maintained that every article of foreign produce or manufacture introduced into this country displaced an equal quantity of the industry of this country and *pro tanto* created want of employment, idleness, and distress ! " " These gentlemen misunderstand the nature of trade," said Poulett Thomson. " In order to buy, we must also sell. We may open our ports to the silks and wines of France, to the corn of Germany and of Russia, to the drugs of Asia and of India, but we can get no pound's worth of any commodity without giving in return a pound's worth of our own productions. Our manufacturers will give away nothing ; they will not send their goods to foreign ports without getting an equivalent in return ; and I will venture to say that the producers of foreign commodities, of French silks and German cloths, with Equivalence of
imports and
exports.

---

[1] Fyler's answer to this is too fatuous not to be quoted : " The honourable member never considered the large quantity of silk wasted in the manufacture ; nor did he seem to have taken into his account the large amount of stock that was left in the hands of the merchant at the end of the year ! "

which, according to the statement of these gentlemen, the country has been and will be overwhelmed, are as little likely to make a present to the British consumer of their hard-worked produce without taking in return the staple articles of this country. . . . If, by some magic wand, the nations of the Continent could suddenly surround their dominions with the wall of brass fabled by Bishop Berkeley—if they could effectually exclude every article of British produce, whilst their ports opened to permit the free egress of all their corn—not a vessel of theirs could find its way to our shores ; or, if it did, their cargoes must be made a present of to our people."

The passing of gold.

One notices, however, that the " invisible exports," as we call them, were not yet thought of. Any balance unpaid by goods was credited to the unseen passing of gold.[1] This was accepted by many —and was considered by them enough to condemn any such exchange ; but Hume at least had no such thought. " Good God ! " he exclaimed, " could it be contended, at that time of day, that the export of gold was an evil ? Where did the gold come from ? Did we not send our goods, our hardware and our cottons, to the Rio de la Plata—have the advantage of a freight thither and a freight back—and exchange the gold which they produced, with the additional advantage of a third freight, for the silk or luxuries of the Continent ? What did it matter to us if France would not accept our manufactured silks if she took the gold which we obtained for our goods elsewhere ? " Poulett Thomson alone, so far as I am aware, had a clear conception of the " three-cornered exchange " with which we are familiar. " Italy," he said, " rigidly excludes all our manufactures from her ports ; and yet we take from her annually to the value of two millions sterling. How do we pay for it then ? Her custom-houses are shut to our produce, and the objects of our industry are as strictly prohibited as the works of Voltaire or of Rousseau. I have had the curiosity to endeavour to trace this, and what will the House think of the result ? Upon a

The three-cornered exchange.

---

[1] A paper laid before Parliament giving the imports into and exports from each country for 1828 must have given some puzzlement to those who held this crude idea. France imported £546,000 and exported £2,600,000. Russia imported £2,500,000 and exported over £4 millions. With Portugal, our imports exceeded our exports by about £2 millions. " With Germany and the Netherlands, our intercourse is most beneficial ; we do not import much more than £3 millions from both, and we export to the amount of about £14 millions." (The words are from the *Gentleman's Magazine*.) America sent us £8 millions and took £8,600,000. To the Brazils, we exported £3,800,000 and imported £1,380,000. To the South American Republics, our exports exceeded our imports by about £2,200,000, etc. (*Gentleman's Magazine*, vol. 99, supp. 637).

careful examination of the bills which are drawn from Italy in payment for this silk by several houses in the trade, at least three-fourths of them are remittances from Austria and the German states, which have been made to Manchester and Glasgow for British manufactures." [1]

One is glad, too, to find Huskisson putting clearly the political advantages of Free Trade. " The present wise system of com- mercial policy has inculcated an important doctrine on the pacific relations of one country to another, by showing that one state is not enriched by the impoverishment of another, but that mutual interchange of their respective produce is the only sure basis of mutual prosperity. . . . By the general principles of our present liberal system of commercial policy, we have disarmed other countries of their former usual resource of excluding our manufactures, by convincing them that they must, more than ourselves, suffer by retaliation of their conduct. I will go further, and say that, if we had not altered our prohibitive laws, we should long since have been engaged in a mischievous war with some state equally blind to their own interest." *(marginal: The political advantages of Free Trade.)*

The only utterance on the protectionist side deserving mention was a very powerful speech by Attwood, whose voice had scarcely been heard in the House since the great currency debates, resting his case on the arguments (1) that no other Government had acted on " the new system of political economy " ; (2) that, where Pro- tection had preceded, Free Trade must sacrifice some trades to save others (*e.g.* throwsters and manufacturers) ; (3) that the easy statement that, if one trade goes down, capital and labour will be transferred to others, ignores the impossibility of transferring fixed capital and specialised labour ; (4) that the statement that " no import can long be continued without a corresponding export " ignores the two facts that the import may cease from poverty and pecuniary embarrassment, and that the commerce of the eastern with the western world was carried on at the expense of a constant drain on the precious metals of Europe. " It is a miserable policy which would weigh the interests and security of the people in the balance against a little cheapness or a little dearness of French silk." It is worthy of notice, perhaps, considering the abuse of *(marginal: Attwood's protectionist speech.)*

---

[1] That is to say : Italy sent £x value of goods to England ; England sent £x value of goods to Austria and Germany ; Austria and Germany sent £x value of goods to Italy ; and the actual payment was arranged by a transfer of the bills originating in the transactions.

political economy current among the adherents of the old system, that the only speaker worth quoting on the side of Protection had to defend his case by economic arguments " of such an abstract character " that he apologised for laying them before the House, and that he finally blamed most of the current evils on "the juggling and tampering with our standard of monied value."

Growing recognition of Political Economy.

From such utterances, and from the tone of the debates generally, one finds the growing recognition that economic science was not a web spun by a few scholars from their own brains, but a body of doctrine got, like other scientific theories, from the accumulation and analysis of facts,—often indeed embodied, almost unconsciously, in the statements of practical men. Sadler, who had attempted to decry the change in our commercial system by calling it the work of " the theorists," was reminded that he had shown himself but little acquainted with the facts of the case ; for, if ever there were legislative measures that originated wholly with practical men, they were the measures adopted between 1821 and 1825 : they originated with the petitions of the merchants of London and Glasgow, and with the Reports of Committees of both Houses of Parliament, founded upon the evidence of merchants and manu-facturers, and drawn up, after the most cautious and deliberate consideration. "Some gentlemen got up," said Hume, " and exultingly said ' Thank God ! we are no political economists.' " For his part, he found that political economy was " the science of those laws which regulate the production, distribution, and consumption of those articles or products of exchangeable value that are agreeable, necessary, or useful to man. What an enviable state it was to know nothing of those laws which were of so much importance to the welfare of the country ! "

Wool.

The continued protective agitation in regard to wool was early disposed of. A petition was presented from the landowners of Cumberland, complaining of the great depression in the price of British wool ; attributing the distress to the large quantity of foreign wool imported ; [1] and begging for the re-importation of a higher duty " sufficient to amount to protection." Sir James Graham, in presenting the petition—at the same time stating that he did not agree with it—noticed the anomaly that the grower of

[1] Among the wool imports of 1828—amounting to over 30 million lbs.—we hear of nearly a million lbs. coming from New South Wales, and over 600,000 from Van Diemen's Land (*New Monthly Magazine*, 409). In 1830, it was said that half the wool sales in London were the growth of New South Wales.

wool told them he was selling his wool at a price infinitely too low, while the manufacturer declared that he was working up that wool almost at a loss. Fitzgerald at once gave a reply which showed that the Government was quite decided against any going back, and reminded the House that the duty which, within these few years, had been taken off, was not one under which British wool-growers had gained wealth and importance, but a duty imposed only in 1819 for the purpose of making up a sum of £3 millions for the support of public credit.[1]

While the interests concerned with silk and wool were still agitating for a return to Protection, there were, on the other hand, a few attempts to accelerate the leisurely progress of the Government towards Free Trade. The duty of 93/- on hemp, as a burden on a raw material of the shipping interest, was quite indefensible. As a fact, of the £86,000 raised by the tax, at least £10,000 was paid by the Government itself. The law was constantly evaded by vessels trading with the Baltic taking in their cordage at the ports on that sea, and, to meet this, in 1828, a reduced duty was charged on cordage taken in by British vessels in foreign ports. The understanding then was that this would be followed by a reduction of the duty at home ; otherwise the British rope-maker could not compete, the repairing of ships at home would be damnified, and the trade driven abroad. The motion was now made by Poulett Thomson to reduce the duty from 93/- to 5/-. The Chancellor of the Exchequer admitted the contention, but urged the old argument that the financial arrangements of the year did not permit of the indulgence of his wishes, and the motion was lost by 40 to 60.[2]

Hemp.

In May, petitions were presented from Manchester and Birmingham to the House of Lords, begging them to consider the expediency of opening the trade to the East Indies ; and, on the same day, on presenting another petition, Huskisson raised a debate in the House of Commons in view of the expiry of the Company's charter in 1834. At the last renewal, in 1813, men of the greatest intelligence and discretion, he said, stated that the wants of the people of India were so few and so simple, their habits so long formed, and the whole of their private as well as their social existence so completely controlled by their religious feelings, that any attempt to introduce amongst them those comforts and conveniences which

The East India Company's Charter.

---

[1] *Hansard*, xxi. 1252. *Supra*, p. 196. *Economic Annals, 1801-1820*, 185.
[2] *Hansard*, xxi. 1599.

British commerce might afford would be totally unavailing, that loss and disappointment must be the result to those who should make the attempt, and that the history of India confirmed this view. Fifteen years had passed since the trade was then partly thrown open, and all this was falsified. Our exports eastward of the Cape in 1814 were no more than £1,600,000 : in 1828, they were £5,800,000, and the 28,000 tons of British shipping employed had grown to 109,000 tons. Before 1814, the returns to India were habitually made in the precious metals ; now the difficulty was to find returns from India for the immense amount of goods sent there. Then, again, except for political reasons, China ought not to be excluded from intercourse with this country. But its commerce was exclusively monopolised by the East India Company. And there were grounds far higher than commercial considerations to be weighed in reviewing this subject, to wit, improvement in civilisation, the increase of the comforts, the raising of the moral character of the people of India. They must not forget that they held India by conquest ; and, recollecting that, it was their duty to atone for past and present faults by extending such benefits to the people of India. If India were to be a permanent possession, it must be made permanent by consulting the happiness of the millions of its people ; by consulting that, they would consult also the prosperity and the power of this country. Baring agreed as to China, that there could be no reason why our ships should be excluded from a trade which was open to every other country.

Whitmore asks for a Committee. A couple of days later, Whitmore brought up the matter formally, also recalling the predictions so confidently made in 1813—that only a few glass bottles might be sent, that our costly manufactures could find no vent in a country where wages were threepence a day, etc. There had, indeed, been some ground for such views in the days of monopoly from 1790 to 1813, when there was a gradual falling off of the trade—a time when the Company made a loss of £4,000,000, and boasted of it as a signal instance of patriotism and self-devotion to the interests of India. But it was different when one witnessed the expansion under Free Trade since 1814 ; the trade had nearly trebled in value. He was convinced that there was no assignable limit to our commerce with the east, " provided a profitable investment for a return cargo could be procured in India "—the extent of Indian demand was limited only by their power of payment. What prevented this return cargo was that the products of India were of a very inferior description to similar products of other countries where more capital and skill were employed in their cultivation. The exception was indigo, previously a very inferior product hardly saleable in Europe but now superior to that produced in any other part of the world, and the reason of this was suggestive ; it was that, forty-six years ago, the preparation of indigo was put into the hands of Europeans. There could be little doubt that, if British subjects were permitted to hold lands in India, and their property were rendered secure, the same effect would be produced in all other articles of tropical production, particularly cotton, sugar, and silk. What prevented this again was the extreme jealousy of admitting British subjects to settle in India, and the obstacles put in their way. The other grievance was that the trade with China was a strict monopoly in the hands of the East India Company. By charter, they had the exclusive privilege of trading with that immense empire, containing 150 millions of inhabitants, from which so important an article of our consumption as tea was exclusively drawn. What made it worse was that the Americans found no difficulty in carrying on their free trade with China, supplying not only the United States but all the world except Great Britain with Chinese produce, and importing even British manufactures into Canton.

Goulburn hoped that, in all the circumstances, Whitmore would not press for the appointment of a Committee at present. He admitted the necessity of an enquiry ; he only wanted it to be complete. A great deal of documentary evidence should first be got, and the principles to guide such an enquiry laid down. As the charter did not expire till 1834, it would be ample time to appoint the Committee in 1830. Huskisson saw no reason for this delay—particularly as he thought that an enquiry would satisfy the East India Company that it was for everybody's interest to make some alteration as regarded China, even in the present charter and previous to its legal termination. There was great danger that the United States, and even the South American states, might get too great a hold. Hume strongly supported this view, but Whitmore's motion was negatived without division.[1]

But the most interesting incident in this direction was Hume's attack on the new Corn Law. What he hoped to effect by it— why he should raise the whole question again almost before the Sliding Scale, which was at least a great advance on the old

Hume's attack on the new Corn Law,

[1] *Hansard*, xxi. 1270, 1292, 1335.

prohibition, had had a trial—is somewhat of a mystery. As Peel said with some indignation: " What advantage could accrue to the country if, on every question such as that of the Corn Laws, the legislation were never allowed to be settled even for a single year: having made an experiment respecting it last year, was it desirable for the House to pledge itself to enter into an enquiry on the subject next year : were such questions to be always at the mercy of any man who chose to agitate them and propose that they should be unsettled ? if, whenever distress existed in any particular place—distress attributed to machinery, or to the importation of foreign wool, or to the system of Corn Laws—an enquiry was immediately demanded, there would be an end to all confidence and no one would venture to embark his capital in any commercial enterprise." In presenting a petition, a few weeks before, from the Carpenters and Joiners of Manchester, ascribing their want of employment and starving condition to the restrictions on importation of grain, Hume, indeed, had said that a free trade in corn was " the only measure by which the prevailing distress could be alleviated." But he was too wise a man to think that the Corn Law was the direct cause of the existing distress, and too honest a man to say so. At any rate, on 19th May, he introduced the subject in a speech which took three and three-quarter hours to deliver. He started by avowing that his object was " to have a perfect Free Trade in corn," and he undertook to prove that this would be no injury to the landed interest. Whatever the existing distress might be due to, we could not go back ; we had an immense population depending on manufacturing and a vast capital invested in it ; we supplied the greater part of the world with manufactures, while it sent us the raw materials. We could not throw this large portion of the population for support on the other classes ; our duty, then, was to open up a demand for their products. The Corn Laws prevented this by raising the price of provisions, and making us less able to compete in the foreign markets. Free Trade in corn would not ruin the English agriculturist—would not reduce the price of grain ; what it would do would be to raise the price of corn in other countries and equalise the competition. For a hundred and twenty years, this had been the case ; the price of corn in England and the price on the Continent had never varied by more than the cost of transit, whereas the difference in price was now so great that we should have lost every market in the world had we not, in the better division of our labour and in the superiority of our enterprise, machinery, fuel, and roads, had advantages which counterbalanced the fearful odds in the price of food. Corn was the last article with which the manufacturing labourer could dispense. When the price of it was high, he worked ten, twelve, and even fourteen hours a day in the hope of procuring by his extra hours of work an additional amount of wages to purchase bread for his family ; he did not understand it, yet all he did was to create a glut of articles which might easily be got rid of if he were permitted to take corn in payment.

What Hume proposed was the gradual introduction of Free Trade —not a sudden change : a fixed duty of, say, 15/- on wheat, 10/- on barley, and 8/- on oats, that being about the relative amount of their value. He would propose that there should be an annual reduction of 1/- a quarter on these rates, and he relied, not so much on the advantage of this gradual reduction, as upon the acknowledgment of the principle that the ports were to be open at a fixed rate. This would put an end to fluctuations in price ; the more markets were scattered over the wide world, the less chance would there be of a reduction of demand for manufactures and the less probability of any deficiency of food. This, too, would get rid of the tricks and frauds of the averages. He would also give a bounty on exportation, which would have the effect of levelling the prices pretty fairly throughout Europe, and preventing the farmer being ruined as he sometimes was by a plentiful harvest. It was said, by way of objection, that, if corn reached a very high price, it would be impossible to levy the duty. But there never would be such a necessity, because a scarcity could never occur ; if the harvest failed in one place, we should be supplied from another. It was said that this country could never enter into competition with other states because it was so heavily burdened with taxation. But this was the very reason why we should extend our commerce, for in that way only could we get free from the load which oppressed us. It was said that countries where corn was cheap were very miserable. But the reason of their misery was not cheapness of corn but the want of manufactures—witness Ireland and Poland. It was said that we should not trade with other countries, but on terms of Reciprocity. This was no reason for declining to take from them whatever we could get cheaper than elsewhere. And in the end there was reciprocity. Russia put us under a ban, and yet we took her hemp, tar, and tallow. Was this a dead loss ? " Russia was supplied by France with

urging a fixed duty to be gradually reduced.

brandy, wine, etc., and Portugal sent her wine, olives, etc. Our hardware and cloth found their way into France; our jackets went to Portugal; and thus we paid for Russian hemp and tallow, as if our clothing and hardware went direct to Russia in exchange for them." [1] There was one point more—the statement so often made of "over-production." He denied that there could be general over-production; temporary over-production in one place there might be, but it could not exist in all. "If cloth which was now sold at 20/- a yard could be produced in such quantities as to fetch only 1/- a yard, the only difference would be that nobody would go naked." It was one of the greatest blessings of this country that there was no limit to production. Give us liberty of exchanging the produce of this country for the produce of other countries, and we should hear no more of over-production.

The motion was not taken seriously, but something had to be said. The Session was too far advanced: a time of manufacturing distress was not the time to bring forward this question—not a time, said Huskisson, to let loose all the interests and passions which a meddling with the Corn Laws would call into motion: Hume, most disingenuously, had made it a question between the landed interest and the manufacturers: the sliding scale had not yet had time to be tried, but, in 1828 and 1829, the fluctuations of price had been no more than between 58/8 and 76/7, whereas, in former seasons of similar bad harvests, the price had gone far above the hundreds: a fixed duty could never be maintained in times of scarcity: the Corn Laws were not the cause of the present distress, etc. Hume answered that not one of his arguments had been answered. His only object, however, was to engage the Government to consider the operation of the Corn Laws, and he would press his motion to a division in order to ascertain how few there were of his opinion. On a division, only 11 voted with him. [2]

---

[1] It may be suspected that Hume had already learned something from the last debate as to the "three-cornered exchange."

[2] *Hansard*, xxi. 1464.

CHAPTER XLVI

1829. THE YEAR OF CATHOLIC EMANCIPATION

SINCE Plunkett, in 1821, carried his six resolutions in the Commons, and the onus of maintaining the Disabilities was thrown upon the House of Lords, the question of Catholic Emancipation had been raised in one form or another in 1822, 1823, and 1824, but made no progress in the Upper House.   In the beginning of 1829, however, nothing else was spoken or thought of inside the Houses, and, up till Easter, the parliamentary annals are the annals of Catholic Emancipation.   The whole of volume XX., and 700 pages of volume XXI. are taken up with it.   I had only the choice, said the Duke subsequently, of concession to the Catholics or civil war. "I am one of those who have probably passed a longer period of my life engaged in war than most men, and principally, I may say, in civil wars, and I must say this ; that, if I could avoid by any sacrifice whatever even one month of civil war in the country to which I am attached, I would sacrifice my life in order to do it." [1]

The provisions of " Emancipation " need not be mentioned here, except to say that the Relief Bill opened to Roman Catholics, on the taking of a new oath, both Houses of Parliament, and all military, civil, and corporate offices, excepting those of the Regent, Chancellor, Keeper of the Great Seal, Lord Lieutenant of Ireland, and those connected with the Church Establishment, the Ecclesiastical Courts of Judicature, the Universities, public schools or schools of ecclesiastical foundation ; and that one part of the price was the disfranchisement of the whole of the 40/- freeholders,[2] and the

Provisions of the measure.

---

[1] *Hansard,* xxi. 46.

[2] It may be as well to emphasise again that the great mass of these voters were not freeholders in the English sense of the term, but tenants on leases for lives, holding from " middlemen."   No change was made in the system of holding, but all freeholders, whether in fee simple or derivative, to an annual value under £10, were disfranchised.

raising of the qualification to £10—thus substituting, in Peel's words, an independent constituency for a constituency either under the control of the landlord or the priest.

Dramatic accompaniments.
The dramatic events which accompanied this great constitutional change—how, twenty-four hours before Peel was to introduce the Relief Bill, the King accepted the resignation of Wellington, Peel, and Lyndhurst—how Peel resigned his seat for Oxford, and was defeated at a new election by the protagonist of the high Tories, Sir R. H. Inglis—how the Prime Minister demanded and obtained from Lord Winchelsea "the satisfaction which one gentleman owes to another"—how Wetherell, the Attorney General, revolted from the Government and was dismissed—how the Tories raged and the Whigs made merry over the "treachery"—how both Houses were bombarded with thousands of petitions [1]—how the King, "the weakest man in England," first vacillated and talked of abdication and then regarded the Bill as "his," and the Duke of Cumberland intrigued—all this has had ample justice done to it in the chronicles of political history. It is still an interesting question, however, what would have been the result if Catholic Emancipation had been put to the test of a popular referendum—one may perhaps agree with Walpole that it was not a triumph of democracy, but "the triumph of the thinking few over the unthinking many."

Disappointing results.
Unfortunately, by the end of the year, its opponents were able to say, with some satisfaction, that, whatever else the measure had done, Catholic Emancipation had not brought peace or contentment to Ireland. The state of the country was as bad as ever—religious blackguardism, general lawlessness, murder a thing of no account —and O'Connell was promising the restoration of the 40/- franchise and the repeal of the Union. Still, in February of the next year, Baring could make mention of the happy results which had attended the measure for restoring tranquillity to Ireland, and, indeed, speak of "the complete pacification of Ireland." [2]

The passing of Catholic Emancipation left little time for anything else. As a fact, only 73 General Acts were put on the Statute Book for this year, and most of them are routine incidents of any
Coming of the Peelers.
Session. The only other measure of any importance was that which first instituted a Police Force in London—Peel's Metro-

---

[1] By the end of March, between three and four thousand petitions had been presented to the House of Lords alone.

[2] *Hansard*, xxii. 240.

politan Police Improvement Bill. In 1816, 1817, 1818,[1] and again in 1822, Committees had been enquiring into the system of guarding the metropolis. But the alarming increase of crime both there and in the country generally since 1824—particularly from 1826 to 1827—had emphasised the urgency of the matter, and another Committee was appointed in 1827. On its first report, in February 1828, Peel, asking for a continuation of the Committee, said that, as regards the Metropolis, the increase of crime, in his opinion, was to be attributed, in some measure, to the exposed and insecure state in which property was placed in many parts, and to the facilities afforded of removing it from one part of the country to the other—in a word, to the increased means of committing and concealing the commission of an offence, and to the increased ingenuity of those who lived by preying upon their neighbours. Allowing for argument's sake that we had a tolerably good police during the day, when its services were not so necessary, at night, when we most stood in need of it, it was most defective. But he confessed that he despaired of being able to place the police upon a general footing of uniformity, because of the distinct and discordant jurisdictions of the three divisions. As to the suburbs, which had increased to such an extraordinary extent, the whole reliance of the inhabitants was placed on such gentlemen as resided in the neighbourhood and were inclined to act in the commission of the peace. But, in some places, individuals had to travel seven or eight miles to procure the interference of a magistrate, and many rather put up with the injury and abandoned all attempts at redress. In short, the time was come when, from the increase in its population, the enlargement of its resources, and the multiplied development of its energies, it might fairly be pronounced that the country had outgrown its police institutions, and that the cheapest and safest course would be the introduction of a new mode of protection.[2]

The Committee reported again in the autumn ; and on this Peel's Bill was founded. It is not necessary now to give the arguments by which he justified the taking of the protection of life and property out of the hands of the parochial authorities, and putting it under the control of a Board of Police, replacing the watch taxes by a general police rate. The Bill passed without opposition, and appears among the Acts of the year as c. 44.[3] " It has given me from first

---

[1] See *Economic Annals, 1801-20, passim.*   [2] *Hansard*, xviii. 784.

[3] *Hansard*, xxi. 867, 1487, 1750. The provisional instructions for the different ranks of the police force are given in the *Annual Register*, 377.

to last," he wrote subsequently, " more trouble than anything I ever undertook." Four months after, Wellington wrote him :—" I congratulate you on the entire success of the Police in London ; it is impossible to see anything more respectable than they are." By June of the next year, there were 2,906 " constables "—irreverently known ever since as " Bobbies " or " Peelers "—of good physique, intelligence, and character on the London streets at a wage of 19/-[1] a week. Happily the blue uniform was adopted from the first, instead of red and gold as originally intended.

If to this we add c. 56, " to consolidate and amend the laws relating to Friendly Societies," [2]—in which the principal provision seems to have been that every society should present annually to its members a statement of the funds and, quinquennially, a statement of the sickness and mortality—and Hobhouse's, c. 51 and c. 63, amending his Act of 1825 relating to the employment of children in cotton mills and factories,[3] we have almost exhausted the legislative output of the Session. One or two matters of interest, however, were debated.

Cruelty to Animals.

Since Martin's failure in 1824, nothing had been done to extend the range of legislation against Cruelty to Animals. In 1825, he introduced a Bill to prevent bear-baiting and other cruel practices. Peel took his old ground ; if Martin wished to repress all cruelty to animals, let him include in his Bill hunting, shooting, and fishing. But if he succeeded now, he would come down next year and say " I find there are still some animals unprotected, and, as you have already given your sanction to two Bills and thereby acknowledged the justice of the principle, you are bound to give me your support." This and two other Bills of the same tenor were lost.[4] In the same year, we find the *Parliamentary Review*, commenting on the matter and putting forward this as " principle " ;—that legislation against cruelty to animals was permissible where there was a direct tendency to injure the disposition of the spectators " by making them brutal and vicious " ; otherwise, as brutes had no rights, everything that

---

[1] *Vide* an interesting correspondence between Peel and Croker as to the wage. Croker considered 3/- a day too low—" every artizan has 5/- a day." To which Peel replied that he had already over 2,000 applications ; " no doubt, three shillings a day will not give me all the virtues under heaven, but I do not want them—angels would be far above my work " ; and the real question, to his mind, was that, out of 3/-, a single man could live in comfort and save 10/- a week (*Croker Papers*, ii. 17).

[2] *Hansard*, xxi. 1390.   [3] *Ibid.* 1487.

[4] *Hansard*, xii. 657, 1002, 1160, 1252.

proceeded on the principle of contemplating the good of animals alone was quite beyond the province of legislation and was absurd and vicious.[1]

In 1826, Martin tried again to bring in a Bill against bear-baiting, dog-fighting, and other cruel sports, backed by no less than 52 petitions from populous towns, but got very little support. Peel protested that, personally he abominated all such atrocious cruelty as much as any man. But the question was whether, upon individual cases of abuse, the House was prepared to make an enactment of general application. Where was legislation to stop if one gentleman wished to protect lions, and another to protect dogs. There was scarcely an animal that was capable of being ill-treated in favour of which an Act of Parliament would not at last be sought. Let those honourable gentlemen state some positive principle upon which they would correct such abuses, and which would apply equally to all cases of cruelty. Take pigeon shooting, for instance, —to say that the wanton cruelty perpetrated in it was a perfectly innocent pastime, while dog-fighting and bull-baiting were held infamous and punishable because practised by the lower orders of the people, was a course of legislation which he would never consent to.

Leave being refused, Martin asked to extend the protection of his former Bill to all domesticated animals. The opposition now was that this would be petty and vexatious legislation; where would the House stop if it once began to legislate with regard to the feelings of animals?[2] Still undeterred by failure, he made a third attempt, and asked leave to bring in a Bill " to prevent the cruel and improper treatment of dogs." Why not cats also? asked Hume, adding, angrily, that the House should protect itself from the ridicule which such measures would bring upon it. Only, retorted Martin, because the noble Lord, who led the opposition to one of the Bills, said that he would have supported it if it had included dogs. Surely, all cases of excessive cruelty to dogs and cats and other animals, said another member, could fairly be left to a British jury as the law now stood. Peel was irritated by Martin's persistency—more injury, he said, was done to the cause he wished to support by the manner in which he brought it forward than by anything else : why not let public opinion, and the acts of individuals, remedy the evil ? Martin accordingly withdrew the motion, stating that he would on a future day introduce a

[1] p. 756.   [2] *Hansard*, xiv. 647, 1391.

more comprehensive measure. Peel thanked him, but guarded himself from being expected to say a word in its favour.[1]

Pallmer's Bill.   The only mention of the subject in Parliament since 1826 would not be worth recording were it not to show how little advance was taking place in educated opinion.   It was in the current year when Pallmer, the member for Surrey, asked leave to introduce a Bill to remedy a defect in the Act of 1822 which punished cruelty to cattle—owing to the omission of the word " bull " in that Act, it had been decided in law that bull-baiting was not illegal.   The objections now made were almost precisely what they were in former years : the principle of abstract humanity was not in itself sufficient to justify the House in sanctioning such a Bill ; it was petty legislation unworthy of the House ; the evil had in point of fact no existence, as bull-baiting had become obsolete ; why were the amusements of the poor always selected for legislation ?—if they passed this Bill they would probably be called on to legislate on the subject of cock-fighting, etc.   And again Peel asked, why not bears and badgers as well as bulls ? why not pigeons ?—why not lions ?—for the public, it appeared, had been much offended by a recent lion-baiting.   " In a word, why should not the measure be general, impartial, and consistent—or the means of checking all acts of cruelty be left to the improved habits of the people ? " The motion was lost by 28 to 72.[2]

Early Co-operative Societies.   The following extract from the *Gentleman's* of August recalls the almost forgotten " Union Shop " movement, which collapsed in 1833-4.   " There are several societies in Leeds bearing the

---

[1] *Hansard*, xv. 530.   Perhaps Peel was thinking of his *Blackwood*.   Christopher North strongly objected to legislation because it was " not possible to define cruelty to animals," but went on to boast that his own fist had levelled many a brute in the act of unmercifully beating his horse, his ass, or his wife—" every man ought to take the law into his own hands on such an occasion."

[2] *Hansard*, xxi. 1319.   Objection may be taken to the space I have given in these *Annals* to a subject not directly connected with industry.   My object has been, mainly, to bring out that there has been a very great advance in humanity within the nineteenth century, and to suggest that experience shows that, while " you cannot make people moral by Act of Parliament," the law can " create a conscience " among the unthinking and the brutal by stamping certain practices with its disapproval.   I might suggest also that the callousness of the times, which made England " the hell of dumb animals," was only part of the lower standard of right feeling which permitted the defence of cruelty to children in the factories.   And it may also explain, to some extent, the long patience with the cruelties of slavery.   If a lawyer, in a colonial court of justice, could say that " there was no more harm in killing a negro than in killing a dog " (*Hansard*, xv. 503), it may be suspected that the one callousness reflected the other.

designation of Co-operative Societies, the principal object of which
is to afford their members good provisions at a cheap rate. Each
member of the society contributes sixpence a week towards the
creation of a capital, which is laid out on provisions at the wholesale price, and sold to the members on advantageous terms. Other
persons, not being members, are also allowed to purchase at the
store on as good terms as at other places. All the transactions
are for ready money. The Co-operative Societies also relieve
their members in sickness, and by these combined operations
become at once capitalists and protectors to each other." Another
article in the *New Monthly Magazine* observes that the labourers
are taking into their own hands the management of their own
interests ; every town of any size has already its Co-operative
Society, some only purchasing goods at wholesale prices and "keeping their own shops," others renting land and sharing the returns of
market gardening, others engaged in silk and carpet weaving and
dividing the profits which would otherwise fall to a master. " Only
let these societies go on, and the dominion of great capitalists is
at an end."

In foreign affairs, the only thing of economic importance is the Saint Cricq's
appearance of Saint Cricq's Royal Commercial Commission [1] which Commission.
reads rather like a defence of a bad financial system. The present
Budget showed a sum of 99 million francs received under the head
of Customs, of which about 25 per cent. went in collection and
management—a very expensive impost if the matter were considered
merely in a pecuniary point of view. But the Customs, it pointed
out, were not merely a tax—they were also, and indeed specially,
an instrument of administration, the necessary regulator of the
efforts of industry and national commerce, a means of defence
against the invasion of foreign trade and industry, a charge like
that of the administration of justice. Nowhere was the consideration of the amount of pecuniary produce more secondary. The
industrious population was divided into two productive classes
in many respects opposed in interest, the extractive and the manufacturing. In every country the former had more to lose than to
gain by importation. To keep control of the internal market, it
was necessary to shut out the competition of foreign products—a
competition which they could scarcely sustain upon any point—
grain from Odessa, the sugar of India, the iron of Sweden, the
hardware of England, the wool of Spain, and black cattle from

[1] Given in full in the *Annual Register*, 400.

beyond the Rhine. This class accordingly called for the assistance
of the Customs, and always found the tariffs too low. The latter
class, too, had some interest in excluding certain rival foreign products, but free importation, reducing the price of necessaries, would
generally more than compensate for any injury it might sustain
from foreign competition.

Again, the consumers at large, without understanding the question
generally, perceived in the operation of the Customs nothing but
an obstacle to their procuring provisions, clothing, and household
goods at the lowest price. But beyond these clashing private
interests, were the interests of the public ; the necessity of holding
equally, if not inclining in favour of France, the balance of trade
with foreign nations, so as not to give to the latter the advantage
which a creditor has over a debtor. Such was the end and
such the incontestable utility of the Customs, considered as an
instrument of government, and such were the clashing interests
which the Commission was called upon to consider, and, if possible,
reconcile. The practical conclusion of the Report was that, as
regards iron, the period had not yet arrived for abandoning the
trade to itself, and that, for the present, there should be no
change in the import duty ; that the " altogether new " beetroot
sugar industry should continue to be assisted by the duty for some
years to come ; [1] and that, in general, for the present, there should
be scarcely any change in the tariff.

U.S. Tariff.   In March, General Jackson—" no friend of this country "—was
installed President of the United States. His inaugural speech
declared that the great interests of agriculture, commerce, and
manufactures should be equally favoured, and that the only exception to this rule would consist in the peculiar encouragement of
any products that might be found essential to the national independence. No change was made in the tariff.

In looking over the newspapers of the year, the eye is caught

[1] In 1810, Napoleon founded an imperial establishment at Rambouillet,
where crystallised sugar was produced from beetroot in considerable quantities.
When the French ports were opened again to the colonies in 1814, the manufacture declined, but was revived under the high duties of 1820 and 1822—the
home sugar paying no duty. By 1829, there were 89 factories in active operation, producing about a fifth of the foreign sugar consumed, and attention
was being drawn in this country to the new source of supply as possibly a
substitute which would supersede slave-grown sugar—to the great annoyance
of Glasgow, which characterised the idea as " absurd." In 1820 the first
parcel of beetroot sugar from Poland was received at Odessa, about 70 tons
weight, the quality like good Muscovado and particularly dry (*State of the
Commerce of Great Britain*, 1830, 30).

by three interesting pieces of information : that, in London, the first omnibus—the latest novelty in Paris—started from Paddington to the Bank on 4th July ; that the first Temperance Societies in England were established ; and that Hampstead Heath was threatened with enclosure by an Estates Bill, but saved by the exertions of the copyholders.

1829 was a year of literary Annuals, Keepsakes, Friendship's Literature. Offerings, Forget-me-nots, Souvenirs,[1] with little that remains outstanding, if we except the appearance of Carlyle's glowing *Signs of the Times* in the "buff and blue," with its text, "It is the age of machinery."

Among books on economic subjects may be mentioned the following :

Outlines of a New System of Political Economy ; Read's *Political* Economic *Economy ; Lectures on the Elements of Political Economy*, by literature. Thomas Cooper, M.D., of Columbia College—"the best of the American writers on Political Economy which we have met with," said M'Culloch ; *Economie politique*, par Joseph Droz ; *A Dissertation on the English Poor, with a plan for the gradual abolition of the Poor Laws*, by B. Haworth ; *What is Luxury ? ; The Scottish Banker* (republished from the *Globe*) ; Tooke's *Two Letters on the Currency* ; Wakefield's *Letter from Sydney*—"advocating self-supporting emigration " ; Senior's *Two Lectures on Population* ; *Taxes, or Public Revenue* ; Monteath's *On draining the Bogs of Ireland*.

The obituary includes the names of Sir Humphry Davy and Obituary. of Lord Colchester, better known as Charles Abbot, the Speaker from 1802 to 1817.

---

[1] The part which such ornamental literature played in these days may be surmised from Moore's story that, in 1828, Heath offered him £700 a year if he would edit the *Keepsake*, and afterwards offered Scott £800 (*Journal*, vol. v. 173, 272).

CHAPTER XLVII

1830. INDUSTRY AND AGRICULTURE

IF one were to judge of industrial distress by the time which
Parliament gave to discussing it, 1830 would occupy a very high
place in the annals of calamity.[1] But when we find lurid descriptions of the "dreadful state of the country" made the basis of
revolutionary demands by landowners in an unreformed Parliament,
it is as well perhaps first to weigh the evidence of the distress. I
think we may find another explanation of these demands than
merely intense sympathy with the sufferings of the poor.

After the unexpected plunge into deep distress in the previous
year, it will be remembered that, towards the end, there were
many indications of revival of trade. The official exports had
risen by £3½ millions, and made a record for the century.
In spite of the American tariff, the exports to the United States
exceeded those of any former year. It is doubtful if there
was much complaint among the manufacturers of Scotland and

Misgivings in
early part of
the year. of Ireland. In England, however, in the early part of the year,
there was still enough of depression to justify a good deal of
misgiving. In the silk trade, as might perhaps be expected.
the depression and the reduction of wages were very great. The
iron trade in three counties was said to be "very bad." The
shipping interests made loud complaint that freights showed no
profit.[2] In the few petitions presented, weaving put in the strongest
statements. 7,000 cotton weavers of Preston said that they had
to work twelve or fourteen hours for 10d. a day, blaming their con-

---

[1] 1830 is not one of Jevons' "sun spot years," but I find it noted, in February,
that the spots of late had been "so unusually large as to be visible to the naked
eye." In 1826, also, the *New Monthly Magazine* had spoken of the sun spots
as very numerous and large.

[2] One ventured the remarkable statement that shipping property had
depreciated 100 per cent. (*Hansard,* xxiii. 1220).

dition on the introduction of machinery, and, for some mysterious reason, on the increasing exportation of cotton twist—on which they asked an export duty of 8 per cent.[1] In Glasgow, 4,600 weavers petitioned, saying that the average income of their families amounted only to 3/6 per week, and that after 96 hours of incessant labour, attributing their condition to the rapid growth of population and the still more rapid increase of machinery in that city. Irvine weavers also asserted that they were working sixteen hours per day for 3/6 a week, and asked for the free admission of corn from abroad.[2] The weavers of King's County thought that there might be an escape from their distress by imposing a duty on English goods imported into Ireland.

Such petitions, of course, must be discounted : it was recognised that nothing could be done for those who tried to compete by hand against the power-looms. But other trades, such as the calico printers and the paper makers, took up the same cry, and one sees here and there statements attributing their distress also to the " excessive " or " undue " or " extensive " use of machinery.

But, by the month of March, accounts from Manchester, Leeds, Bradford, Halifax, Blackburn, Bolton, Huddersfield, and Glasgow all agreed in affirming that trade was improving and that wages were rising. In some places, there was a scarcity of weavers. Even in the glove trade, it began to be said that the introduction of foreign gloves had been a blessing in disguise ; formerly French gloves were in every respect infinitely superior to English, but now on equal terms preference was given to the English. In the same month, Sadler admitted, in his turgid way, that for the moment " the country was in a state of comparative ease," though, he said, a deadly blight was hanging over the spring, and the tide of distress would flow again. In April, one report speaks of " a quite remarkable stillness " after the clamour so long kept up by the grumblers. In May, the turn of the tide seemed confirmed. The member for York said that " the average wages of workmen in the manufacturing districts were now as great as at any former period ; Philips

but revival of trade by March.

---

[1] It appears, from an official report, that the fine numbers of cotton twist were so extensively smuggled into France, both by land and sea, as to provoke the suspicion that the Government connived at it.

[2] Leeds was more candid. In March, it seems, a numerous meeting was held, where a petition was agreed on for presentation to Parliament praying that a tax might be imposed on power-looms (*New Monthly Magazine*, 180). The same magazine, in 1828, computed the number of power-looms in the United Kingdom (water and steam) at 58,000.

could say, both from observation and information, that wages in
Lancashire had lately risen, and that few persons were now out
of employment ; while, in London, Alderman Thompson acknowledged that there was a considerable improvement in the manufacturing and commercial interests. In June, Littleton observed
that prices were rising generally throughout the manufacturing
districts ; there was no want of employment ; and gold and silver
were never more abundant nor more easily obtained. During that
month, indeed, there was for the moment a check owing to the
death of the King, but, by July, everything was cheeerful again.

As the year went on, the cloud of depression lifted even from
industries which, a few months before, were said to be *in extremis*.
In a September market report, we read that, in the home silk manufacture, an extraordinary degree of activity had prevailed for some
time, while the manufacture of bandanas was more extensive than
ever ; many cotton weavers were betaking themselves to the silk
looms. In a November report, we find the wool trade in Leeds
and Huddersfield very brisk—" the accumulation of wool in the
farmers' hands, is worked up and the manufacturers are now at
work on the present year's clip "—at the same time as half the wool
sales in London were announced to be of the growth of New South
Wales. In moving the Address on 2nd November, the Marquis
of Bute said that every day brought fresh proof of increasing activity
in the manufacturing districts—particularly in the consumption
and wear of the labouring classes. Wages were rising every day.
He had not heard any difference of opinion upon the point that
there was not a man who did not now find full employment. True,
considerable pressure still prevailed in many of the agricultural
districts, but it could not be denied that there were signs of progressive improvement. By the end of the year, the improvement,
at least in everything outside of agriculture, was beyond
question.[1]

Foreign trade.   There was a rise in the official exports of the year of nearly
£5 millions—from £56,218,000 to £61,152,000, though the re-exports
fell from £10,620,000 to £8,548,000. The imports rose from
£44,000,000 to £46,300,000. The Real Value of the British exports
rose from £35,842,000 to £38,271,000.

[1] I find it quoted subsequently as a proof of the prosperity of 1830, that in
Ashton, 52 mills and 30,000 persons were thrown out of employment for ten
weeks by the turning out of 3,000 coarse spinners who could clear at the time
from 28/- to 31/- a week ; for, says the writer, " trade unions almost invariably
make their appearance when trade is prosperous " (*Annual Register*, 1838, 206).

Shipbuilding, too, began to revive after its three years of decline. The number of ships built rose from 718 to 730, although the tonnage —possibly from the new methods of registration—fell from 76,635 to 75,532. According to Porter, the steam vessels built in the four years from 1827 to 1830 numbered respectively 28, 30, 16, 18.

In one quarter, however, there was no break in the clouds ;— agriculture seemed settling down to despair. All tell the same story, wrote Greville in January, as to the universally prevailing distress—" greater than any since the war " among the farmers. All over England there was failure of rents. In Ireland, by June, it was seen that the potato crop was an entire failure, and many places broke into riot : by July, it was worse—in Queen's County, it was said, the lower orders were perishing from famine. Of Scotland alone was anything cheerful ever said : although the accounts are conflicting, there does not seem to have been any particular distress : rents remained steady, and there was the usual competition for farms when leases fell in. *Distress of agriculture.*

The price of wheat, which, according to the averages regulating the duties, was 56/- at the beginning of the year, rose to 66/- in spring, as the full deficiency of the last year's harvest was realised, and a considerable amount of foreign grain came in. The farmers' complaint of distress seemed justified when it was pointed out that, although price was nominally high, it was for the most part the foreign grain which fetched the high price, the home grain being scanty at the best, and much of it of poor quality. The summer was no more than fair, and prices, which had fallen a little, went up again to 75/- in August, when the low duty of 2/8 for wheat and 3/3 for oats let in immense quantities of both grains—2,000,000 quarters it was said. In some places, the crop was gathered before the 13th of August, when the weather broke ; and, by the end of the month, some three-quarters of the whole were harvested in fair condition. The good prospects, coming at the same time as the large imports, for the moment sent prices down sharply, and, had the prospects been realised, the price might have fallen as low as in 1822. But, at the finish of harvest, when the estimate was " decidedly below average," prices rose again, and, at the end of the year, reached 68/-. In face of these prices, it was decidedly bold to assert that contraction of the currency was the cause of the distress—Tooke, indeed, gives this high range of prices as another proof of the absence of connection—but, all through the year, the ineffable Simon Gray fulminated in the *British Farmer's* *The farmer's year.*

Magazine (which generally allowed him two articles every issue) " that nothing would do us good but a rise in price "—to be effected, he said, by the issue of one pound notes and shutting out silk and gloves from our markets.

Rick burning.   Autumn saw the beginning in England of that portentous phenomenon which had appeared a year before in France, rick burning.[1] It broke out in Kent, in August. In October and November, it spread to Hants, Wilts, Bucks, Sussex, Surrey, Cambridge, Essex, Middlesex. Growing bolder, rioters pillaged by day—levying contributions on gentlemen's houses, asserting their right to higher wages —and burned barns and ricks by night. Accompanying this, went the wanton destruction of threshing machines. " The state of the country is dreadful," wrote Greville on 21st November, " every post brings fresh accounts of conflagrations, destruction of machinery, associations of labourers, and compulsory rise of wages." " The insurgents of Kent," said the *New Monthly Magazine* in the same month, " go about in bands of 150 and coolly demand the keys of the barn to destroy the threshing machines ; all idea of resistance is out of the question. Signals are given by sky rockets, and as many as fourteen stackyards have been in flames at the same time. What adds to the alarm of the farmers is the refusal of the insurance offices to insure them except on the most ruinous terms." So serious was the matter as to call for mention in the King's Speech. The cause of it all seemed to baffle investigation. By many it was ascribed to the general distress. When, in question of this explanation, it was pointed out that the outrages occurred on the estates of popular landlords, where wages were higher than anywhere in the country (2/- a day) and employment was most plentiful, and that destroying food for man and beast at the expense of the farmer was a strange way of expressing distress, the excuse was the same as suffragists give for breaking the windows of innocent tradesmen— that it was by way of calling attention to the badness of the system. It was not the work of the agricultural labourers at all, said others, —it was " contrary to all we have known of the English character," said Lord Grey, therefore it must be the work of scoundrels unconnected with agriculture. It was an " exotic growth'" said Wyndford—the lust of destruction must have come across from France like a bacillus. And the discovery of a remedy seemed as difficult as that of a cause. Peel said in November that four to five hours of every day of his life were spent in endeavouring to discover the

[1] For a similar outbreak in 1816, see *Economic Annals, 1801-20,* 489.

perpetrators : he himself thought that nothing but extraordinary
local vigilance would provide effectual security against it, but
promised that there was no plan promising to be effective which
the House would not cheerfully sanction to terminate a system
so disgraceful.[1]

The mention of this interlude would not be complete without Cobbett.
some notice of the part which Cobbett played—particularly as, in
many quarters, he was blamed for it all, and as some of the
labourers who paid the penalty gave as their last testimony that
their fate was due to listening to " the notorious demagogue."

He indignantly denied that the fires and machine breaking
were the work of foreigners, or " scoundrels unconnected with
agriculture." They were the work of the labourers, and were the
natural result of their miseries. His explanation of the Rural War,
as he called it, was twofold. (1) The labourers, reduced to a worse
condition than they occupied before the war, demanded a wage
enough to keep them alive. The farmers could not pay the wage
demanded because they had so much to pay in rent, taxes, and tithes.
So they made common cause with the labourers, and the labourers
helped in onè way—they went to the parson and compelled him for
the moment to reduce his tithe. (2) The farmers, pressed on by
heavy taxes, resorted to machines which worked cheaper than
men. The labourers, seeing that the threshing machines were
robbing them of wages, destroyed the machines and fired the barns
and ricks of those who owned them. The only remedy was a

---

[1] There had been all along some misgivings about the introduction of
agricultural machinery In 1828, for instance, I find a correspondent of the
Quarterly Journal of Agriculture all but apologising for Patrick Bell's new
reaping machine. It would, to a certain extent, he admitted, displace labour,
but it was justified (1) by all the corn crops coming to maturity nearly at the
same time, (2) by rural depopulation, (3) by increase in the corn grown, (4)
by increasing wages of harvest work, (5) by a consequent saving of a million
sterling a year. And there was undoubtedly some sympathy with the destruction of threshing machines—labour saving appliances not much appreciated
by those whose labour was " saved." But more extraordinary, in the present
year, is the distinct expression of dislike, if not actual hostility, to machinery
in general. Not only did many petitions ascribe the distress to the spread of
machinery, but many members were bold enough to give encouragement to
such petitions. ,There is an excessive glut of manufactures, said Wyndford,
which might be accounted for by the use of machinery : he was no enemy
to machinery, if the employment of it were properly regulated ; but, when it
produced a glut in the market, it injured the manufacturer, and it injured the
poor man, and the poor man had as good a right to have his labour protected
as the manufacturer his goods. Stanhope said that justice and regard for
the rights of the labouring poor ought to impose some restriction on those
who possessed any of the recently invented agricultural machinery—it was
their duty to discontinue its use (*Hansard*, i. 833, 887).

radical reform of Parliament, such as would adopt an "equitable adjustment," and reduce the taxes to £6 millions.[1]

For this "inciting of the labourers to acts of violence," Cobbett was tried for sedition in the next July, but after the jury had been shut up for fifteen hours two of them held out, and the case was discharged.

[1] Cf. with what he said in 1822, *supra*, 116.

CHAPTER XLVIII

1830. DEBATES ON THE DISTRESS AND ITS CAUSES

SUCH being the condition of industry and agriculture so far as may be gathered from outside evidence, we are in a position to form some opinion on the strong statements made about the dreadful state of the nation, and the drastic remedies advocated—always remembering that the improvement in industry did not show itself definitely till March.

The concluding paragraphs of the King's Speech in February, were as follow :

" His Majesty commands us to inform you that the export in the last year of British produce and manufactures has exceeded that of any former year. His Majesty laments that, notwithstanding this indication of active commerce, distress should prevail among the agricultural and manufacturing classes in some parts of the United Kingdom. It would be most gratifying to the paternal feelings of His Majesty to be enabled to propose for your consideration measures calculated to remove the difficulties of any portion of his subjects, and at the same time compatible with the general and permanent interests of his people. It is from a deep solicitude for those interests that His Majesty is impressed with the necessity of acting with extreme caution in reference to this important subject. His Majesty feels assured that you will concur with him in assigning due weight to the effect of unfavourable seasons, and to the operation of other causes which are beyond the reach of legislative control or remedy. Above all, His Majesty is convinced that no pressure of temporary difficulty will induce you to relax the determination which you have uniformly manifested to maintain inviolate the public credit and thus to uphold the high character and the permanent welfare of the country."

A King's Speech, if seldom a literary, is always a very responsible document. It reflects the views taken and opinions arrived at

The King's Speech as text.

by a number of important persons who have first-hand knowledge
of many things not always made public. It is nearly always the
anticipation of a policy. It is usually a compromise. Hence it
challenges investigation of what is " behind it." And what may be
gathered from this particularly cryptic Speech, is that the Ministry
were prepared for a serious attack on their policy, taking occasion
of what would be described as a desperate condition of national
affairs.

Attack by
Tory peers.

The attack was not long of developing, and the seriousness of
it, from the political point of view, was that the principal speakers
did not belong to the Opposition but were leading Tory peers.
Stanhope, without preface, denounced the Speech as the most inept
and most inappropriate ever delivered from the Throne ; it would
be received from one end of the kingdom to the other with contempt
and derision. In the midst of distress unusual, universal, unprecedented, and intolerable, it was said to be prevailing in " some "
parts of the United Kingdom. The Duke of Wellington—who had
everything to lose and nothing to gain from becoming Prime
Minister—" found the vessel of the State surrounded by rocks
and quicksands, and yet he consented to steer the very same course
which had been so ruinously pursued by his predecessors at the
helm; persevered in the same system, adopted the same errors, and
followed all the mistakes which had occasioned the difficulties
and dangers universally felt." The distress, he affirmed and
would prove, was not temporary, but permanent : it arose from mistaken legislative measures which must be repealed. "Unfavourable
seasons ! " He knew that their invariable effect had hitherto
been to injure the producers of grain, but when had it been a usual
effect of unfavourable seasons to lower the price of grain ?[1] Such a

[1] This strikes me as rather a bold argument to use in face of the prices of the
past years. Stanhope can only have meant that the average level over the years
since the war was not the 80/- level which was thought the land's due. But
Stanhope was as irresponsible as his father had been. As a fact, however,
it was very often stated that prices generally were " low " ; Western, e.g.
spoke of " every part of the produce of the farm " being sold at ruinously
low prices, and this was on February 12th when, according to the Annual
Register, wheat was between 73/- and 75/- : barley, 34/- and 36/- ; oats,
28/- and 29/- ; rye, 32/- and 34/- ; beans, 36/- ; and peas between 36/- and
38/-. As I have said, the " returns " which the Annual Register quotes for
two or three years past were usually a good deal higher than those which determined the importing average, but, compared with the annual averages of 1822,
when wheat was 44/7, barley 21/10 and oats 18/1, the average of 1829 (respectively 66/3, 32/6, and 22/9) could scarcely be called " ruinous." It should
be remembered, however, that the poor quality home grain of last harvest
ruled much lower in price than the imported good grain.

statement was an absurdity without a parallel. That the price of corn had been lowered was the consequence of pernicious measures founded upon no just principle, or, rather, upon no principle at all. And, apart from corn, did any one ever hear before of an unfavourable season lowering the price of wool ? In the outset of that system, the wool grower was plundered to benefit the manufacturer, and the result was that, while the grower had been reduced to pauperism, the manufacturer was not benefited, for he lost his best market, the home consumer. The country, in fact, was rapidly approaching a condition which threatened to tear asunder all the bonds that united human society. Stanhope then intimated that he would shortly propose an enquiry by a Select Committee, not to be nominated by the Duke but by the whole House, indicating not obscurely that the *fons et origo* of the distress was the " pressure produced by the alteration of the currency : a measure that had actually raised the current amount of the taxes above the sum paid by the country in the last and most expensive year of the war."

The Earl of Carnarvon went even further. The Speech—" this most extraordinary speech "—was quite unworthy of the sovereign —it was nonsense—the allusions to the distress were most insulting, unfeeling, and cold-blooded. " The great and overwhelming cause, which had brought down this country from the pinnacle of prosperity to its recent depression, was the line of conduct which the ministers, within the last few years, had thought fit to adopt." It would be easy to prove that " every measure, in other times and other countries, which had for its object the contraction of the circulation, produced uniformly public distress. . . . Wiser and happier statesmen had supported successfully the principle that the currency could not be too extensive, provided it represented something substantial ; or, in other words, that it represented property, whether agricultural, commercial, or manufacturing." Another great error was the adoption of the gold standard. No other country had adopted it. Metallic currency, indeed, he could consider in no other light than the small change of a great state : in view, however, of silver being " more easily procurable than gold," and to be had in larger quantities, he would propose a silver standard, and have gold for circulation with a view only to convenience. " The resources of the country would then be emancipated from the artificial fetters in which they were bound, and it would be shown, to the confusion of political economists, that they could be made the means of feeding as well as starving the population of the country." Still another evil was the course of conduct imposed upon bankers : " they could not, consistently with their interests, afford the slightest accommodation to farmers who might suffer by a wet and backward season." As for a parliamentary enquiry, it would answer no good purpose. " If ministers could not propose a remedy for the distress, others should be found who could."

The Prime Minister's reply.

Wellington made a spirited reply, defending the Speech, asking if Stanhope's readiness to adopt as remedy an alteration of the currency, was an example of the cautious way in which they should enter on the discussion of such a subject. Was the question so simple ? " I want to know whether the competition of machinery with labour in all departments of mechanics—the general application of steam—the competition abroad with our manufacturers—and the general imitation of our fabrics—have not produced very great distress among the manufacturers at home. These are the circumstances to which His Majesty refers as important to be considered in connection with the subject of distress, and they are those over which Parliament has no control. Can this House prevent competition by foreign markets with our own ? Can we prevent improvements in machinery ? Can we prevent steam from being applied to foreign manufacture ? " And was the distress really " universal " ? Not to speak of the testimony of the exports, there was not a railroad or canal upon which the traffic had not increased of late years, including last year. The profits were smaller, no doubt, but, if there were none, would the increase of traffic exist ? Were the retail dealers distressed ? Were they unable to pay their rents ? Who was building and renting the new houses that one saw in every direction ? Surely these were indications that the country, notwithstanding the pressure upon it, was still rising and in some points must continue to rise. As to Carnarvon's ascription of the distress to a deficient circulation, why, the largest sum ever known to be in circulation during the Bank Restriction was £64 millions. But, last year, the circulation was over £65 millions. Who, then, could say that money was scarce ? " [1]

[1] Attwood, however, repeated the charge on 11th February. The Duke had estimated that £28 millions of gold coin were in circulation. But, if the landlord did not receive the same rent and the merchant the same profit, if the manufacturer did not employ so many hands, if the money " had much greater power," was it not deducible that there was much less money in the country ? " Having thus shown from argument that this must be the case," look at facts. The Exchequer was receiving £20 millions less ; the landowners

" The truth of the matter," he said, " is that noble lords want, not extended circulation, but unlimited circulation; that is, to give an unlimited power to some individuals—not the Crown, anyone but the Crown—to coin as much money in the shape of paper as they please, that they may be enabled to lend a fictitious capital to all sorts of speculators,—to lend as much money as they please upon land or no land, upon security or no security. . . . I submit to your lordships that the noble Earl has not proved the want of money—there never was a period when money was less wanted. Is there any man, however speculative—any scheme, however visionary, provided only it is a little plausible—which nowadays lacks support ? Is there any power, however bankrupt, even Portugal and Brazil, though the creditors of these countries have been so ill-treated, but can borrow money in this city upon any security or no security ? In fact, capital is more abundant now than it ever was known to be, and the evil is certainly not too limited a circulation."

Lord King, in one of his characteristic speeches, taunted the landowners. Carnarvon, he said, had remarked how well things went when paper formed the circulating medium. Did this not bear with it a strong hankering after the fleshpots of Egypt ? At that time rents were high. But this could not last long ; and now those who had caused the distress did not want to feel any of it. The true reason of the distress was the odious monopolies which met them at every turn—monopolies of beer, of corn, of sugar, of tea ; and the effect of all these fell on the consumer. He paid for all. America, France, and England—the three countries, none of which was oppressed from the absence of a paper currency— were all destroying their own prosperity by setting up monopolies against each other. He believed there were means of raising this country to a higher pitch of prosperity than she had ever yet possessed if she could but be prevailed on to become a customer of those nations which were her rivals, yet he doubted the firmness of

Lord King's Free Trade amendment.

£20 millions less ; the labouring classes half as much as heretofore—indeed, were forced to take truck for wages. The Duke had taken the amount coined since 1824, and assumed that every sovereign of it was still afloat in the country, making no deduction for exportation of gold, for the currency carried away by the 100,000 absentees, for the melting down of gold coin. Goulburn's answer was easy : £44 millions had been coined, and the Duke had allowed for £16 millions going out of circulation ; so long as the exchanges were favourable, there was no danger of gold going abroad as an article of commerce ; no one believed that rent remitted abroad was sent in sovereigns. Attwood, unmoved, however, repeated that he had heard nothing to induce him to change his opinions (*Hansard,* xxii. 381).

those whose duty it was to execute such a task. King then proposed what was practically a Free Trade amendment, containing the words "that we can only expect to derive permanent relief from the abolition of all exclusive privileges and monopolies, from an unrestricted supply of the first necessaries of life and of the materials of manufacture, and from a real free trade." The original Address was carried by 71 to 9.[1]

In the Commons.

In the Commons, the same reckless statements, about the distress being universal and unparalleled, were made and the same cause was suggested—the "surreptitious enhancement of the currency," which doubled the taxes, and doubled the debt. The Chancellor of the Exchequer very sensibly said that the Speech reflected the best information Ministers could get as to the condition of the country. There were parts of the kingdom which, so far from being visited with great distress, were enjoying a state of comparative ease and comfort. If the mover of the amendment proposed—to the effect that the distress was general—had investigated the state of agriculture in Ireland, he would have found there great prosperity and comfort. In fact, there were parts of England in which much of the pressure that existed had arisen from the free introduction of Irish produce. In the northern part of Great Britain, too, there were districts in which the distress complained of had not been felt in any such degree. He was still further precluded from supporting the amendment when he heard the grounds on which it was supported : was there a man who had listened to the speeches supporting the amendment who did not feel that the object of them was to make an alteration in the standard of value, or, at least, in the currency of the country, so as to change these laws which the Parliament had sanctioned after a · most mature and anxious deliberation ? He assured the House that it was the firm determination of His Majesty's Government to adhere to those measures which had that night been so freely discussed.

O'Connell on Irish distress.

O'Connell—whose voice was now heard for the first time on general subjects—asked where the Chancellor of the Exchequer had got his information about Ireland. Were there not 7,000 registered persons in Dublin alone actually living on three half-pence a day—and even this miserable pittance was almost exhausted. Leinster, Connaught, and Munster he knew pretty well, and he knew that the agriculturists in these three provinces at least were suffering the greatest distress. Many causes, no doubt,

[1] *Hansard*, xxii. 4.

contributed, but, unquestionably, the state of the currency was one of these.

Huskisson's appearance on this occasion strikes one as rather petty—certainly not what one would have expected of a minister who had resigned on an unimportant point but had not changed his side. He would support the amendment because, in his opinion, the real facts of the case, as regards the public distress, were more correctly stated there than in the Address. As to the alleged deficiency in the currency—he did not see how that could be when Exchequer Bills at $2\frac{1}{2}$ per cent. were selling at 75/- premium, and interest was at such a low rate: "circumstanced as we were, to propose to increase the currency would be similar to recommending an individual, subject to too great and rapid an action of the blood, to drink a quantity of brandy." If there had been error in the currency settlement—which he did not admit—it would be better to persevere than to unsettle the state of the country by again tampering with the currency.[1] He believed many of the causes of the distress were beyond the power of Parliament to remedy, but it was in their power to satisfy the country as to what the causes were, "and to afford partial relief by giving a better direction to the capital of the country."

Peel defended the statement of the Speech as a truer description of the state of the country than that contained in the amendment. He did not believe that, year after year since 1819—for that was the period from which the distress was dated—the manufacturers of the country had continued manufacturing and exporting at a positive loss. As to the internal consumption, he referred to the number of tons carried on the principal canals for a number of years to disprove the assertion that there had been a serious decline. Referring to O'Connell's statement about Ireland, it was true that distress did exist in the Liberties of Dublin, but, for as long as he had been acquainted with Ireland, he never knew a period when the manufacturers in that irreclaimable part of the city were not in distress—so much so that scarcely a year passed without appeals to the charity of the public. But was there any proof that the agricultural interests of Ireland were suffering under universal distress and depression? Ireland had imported into Liverpool alone, in the past year, agricultural produce to the value of

Peel defends the Speech.

---

[1] But even on this, his own subject, Huskisson did not speak with his old decision. As Greville says, it was a shabby enough speech, and Peel did not spare him in replying.

£1,270,000, exclusive of corn. The same argument applied to Scotland. Moreover, the agricultural interests in other countries had experienced similar depression. In France, and in parts of the United States, the distress was as great as it was with us. In Russia, a proclamation had been issued lowering the rate of interest, with a view to remedy the agricultural distress. And, like Huskisson, he said that, if any error had been committed in establishing the existing system, we should only be exposed to still greater evils by doing anything to unsettle the currency.

As the debate went on, it looked as if the Government would be in a minority. The extreme Tories, Brougham, Althorp, and the moderate Whigs, Huskisson and the remnant of the Canningites were all supporting the amendment. Towards the end, however, Lord Howick turned the tide : while saying that, in his judgment, the Address undervalued the distress, he could not concur in the amendment ; he was anxious to wait and see what would be done or proposed by the Government, and he condemned the system of referring to a Committee consisting of twenty-three members the task of examining into every branch of our enormous establishments, Hume and other Radicals followed him into the lobby, and the Address was passed by 158 to 105.[1] " The result shows," was Greville's comment, " that the Government has not the slightest command over the House of Commons, and that they have nothing but casual support to rely upon, and that, of course, will only be to be had ' dum se bene gesserint ' ; it is pretty clear, however, that they are in no danger of being turned out." " The House is very loose," wrote Ellenborough in his *Diary* ; " in the majority and minority were the most opposite parties."

A second debate,

But, before the Speech was finally disposed of, there were other two debates, and they are, perhaps, more surprising than the first one. On the Report of the Address, on 5th February,[2] Attwood said that, however firmly the Government might hold to its determination to make no alteration in the currency, the currency would be altered, and that before many months ; spoke of the late currency measure as " dishonest legislation," and of " the unwise and improper rejection of silver as a standard "—a clear and explicit statement of intention for which the Chancellor of the Exchequer was not slow ironically to thank him. The Marquis of Blandford thereupon moved an amendment to the effect that " the real cause " of the universal distress was the system by which a few proprietors

[1] *Hansard*, xxii. 59.   [2] *Ibid.* xxii. 137.

of close boroughs, and a few other individuals, by the mere power
of money, had obtained a domination over the representation, by
which the nation was deprived of its natural guardians, with the
result that the taxation had been run up from nine millions to nearly
sixty; the Poor Rates had risen from one and a half to eight millions,
the circulation had been tampered with, etc. O'Connell seconded,
and Burdett, though taken by surprise, supported in one of his
most unfair and extravagant speeches. The amendment, however,
got only 11 votes against 96.

The remaining debate was on the 8th,[1] on the motion that the and a third.
Speech be taken into consideration. Waithman affirmed that the
retail dealers, who had been given as an exception to the universality
of the distress, were suffering greater losses than they had ever
sustained before—that their distress was as great as or greater
than that of the agriculturists—that five out of every six failed in
business. O'Connell said that he had that morning received letters
in which the distress existing in Ireland was painted in the strongest
colours. Fyler gave the case of a district in Warwickshire, where,
out of a population amounting to 7,100 persons on a space of 6,500
acres, 2,000 were receiving parochial relief, 2,100 not receiving
relief but unable to contribute anything to the rates, and the whole
weight of the rates was being borne by 500 heads of families. On
the other hand, the member for Bristol said that a great manufacturing house in Gloucestershire told him that their business
was so good that they could not deliver any further orders for six
months, and that every hand whom they had ever employed was in
full work; that, in Ireland, he was told, on one estate of £30,000
a year, there had not been a single defaulter, and that, altogether,
the agriculturists were flourishing in that country. Sir J. Stewart
said that he certainly had not seen anything in Scotland of the
agricultural distress which some gentlemen talked of; any there
was, arose from the state of the seasons and from other causes
which human foresight could not have prevented: in 1828, the
Scots harvest was so much better than that of England, that Scotland had exported corn to supply the English markets. Maberly
reminded the House that Ricardo had stated that low profits were
proofs not of poverty but of wealth--of redundant capital competing with capital; for himself, he apprehended that the people
would for a long time suffer from low prices, and yet, perhaps,
high prices were the greater evil of the two. Thus statement was

[1] *Hansard*, xxii. 224.

set against statement; the most far-reaching conclusions were
based on the slenderest and most questionable foundations; and
a vast deal of nonsense was talked.

Baring's wise
speech.
The only relieving feature in the debate was an extremely
wise speech by Baring. Fully admitting that the distress was
greater than had been felt for many years, it struck him as
useless to be endeavouring to ascribe it to this or that particular cause. He had his own opinion as to the several causes
suggested, but he could not bring himself to believe that it
was to be attributed to any one of them. Distress so general in
its nature must be ascribed to some general cause. But as to what
that general cause was, he was ready to confess his ignorance. Let
it be recollected that the distress pervaded every country from one
end of Europe to the other, and extended to countries beyond the
Atlantic. But that, in a country like ours, with such vast and
complicated sources of trade and industry, the effects should be more
severely felt than among nations whose mode of trade and commerce
was more simple and less extensive, should not excite surprise.
Who could say, remembering the many committees which had sat
for the last ten or twelve years on every public question, that the
House had not been earnestly enquiring into our condition? In these
circumstances, what was the sense in saying that the Government
must apply the remedy, or, as the farmers said, " Government
must do some'at " ? He would admit that the agricultural interest
was suffering in a greater degree than any other class of the community. Yet it was not to be denied that the distress existed without any very low prices of corn, for corn was not, on the average,
higher for the past five years than it was last year and this. The
difficulty was that there had been two bad years, and that the
farmer, owing to the nature of the Corn Laws, obtained in one year
the high price which would be a compensation to him for low
prices in the preceding. But of these laws the farmer could not
complain, for they were made for his protection. Perhaps he had
not that protection to which he was entitled. But how could he
get a higher rate of protection in a year of scarcity, unless at the
expense of a starving population ? It had always been a doubt
in his mind whether the country could stand that kind of protection
which the agricultural interest required. At the same time, he
would not do away with these Corn Laws, for that would be in
effect to dispossess an immense portion of the landowners—such
were the charges upon land in a variety of shapes that, if protection

were withdrawn, it would leave the present landowners little more than mere nominal proprietorship. Nine-tenths of the property of the country were suffering under mortgage and incumbrance. Still he owned that the question altogether was a problem which had not yet been solved, for he doubted whether the manufacturers could afford the protection required by the agriculturists.

As to the currency, he was one of those who would not easily yield to a restoration of the paper currency as it had existed—he did not think that the distresses generally felt were the effects of its removal. At the same time, he was bound to admit that the withdrawal of the small-note circulation, however much he considered it a measure of sound policy, was still one which had been productive of much suffering. He had concurred in it, because he believed that the continuance of that currency would be productive of evils much worse than its removal. But he did not think that the evil was such as to create a main ingredient in the present general distress. It was said, in answer to the objections against the removal of the small notes, that there was at present a greater money circulation in the country than existed when the notes were issued. That might be true; but then it did not circulate into those minute channels through which the country notes passed, and by which much activity of business was kept up in small towns. It was there that the loss of the small-note circulation pinched most severely. In such places there was usually a small banker whose notes circulated in the town and a little district round it, beyond which they scarcely ever went. Their circulation kept up and gave energy to the small circle in which it moved. He would readily admit that the system, as it was carried on, was open to a thousand objections, and was liable to serious abuses; but the impression on his mind, as to the result of the withdrawal of the paper circulation from such places, was that, though it formed part of a general measure which on the whole was salutary, yet it left to those places no adequate compensation. To the man in middling circumstances, who had long felt the benefit of the small bank in his neighbourhood, and who now deplored the loss of its small-note issues and complained of a want of circulation and accommodation, it was no answer to say " There's plenty of cash to be had in Lombard Street; money never was so plentiful." That might be true; but, in Lombard Street, the credit and connections upon which he could have obtained assistance from the small banker in his own town were wholly unknown.

As to the manufacturers, he admitted their distress to a certain extent, but, compared with the condition of other interests, they were in a state of prosperity. "It was no proof of distress in manufacturing districts to say that business was absorbed by a few large capitalists, for these things should be considered in the general state of the trade. The iron trade and the silk trade were certainly suffering most deeply ; but he believed that the woollen trade of Yorkshire was by no means in a state of distress. Although it, no doubt, did not now enjoy the prosperity which it had enjoyed in former times, he had seen a letter in which it was stated that the manufacturers had nothing to complain of. Great complaints had been made of the distress occasioned by the introduction of machinery. It was certainly true that, to take labour from the hand and to perform it by a steam engine, was the cause of great individual injury, which was much to be lamented. It was like the consolidation of a number of small farms into a large and overgrown one. But it was one of the natural operations of industry and knowledge ; one of those operations which all the best authorities on the subject concurred in declaring ought to be left unshackled by any legislative interference." On the whole, he could discover nothing of an unfortunate character which could with propriety be laid at the door of the Government, and he should on that account be sorry to see the administration embarrassed or disturbed.[1]

The Tory Revolt.

The inner history of the Speech and of the unscrupulous attack upon it, was that two sections of the Tory party, the protectionists and those who wished for the repeal of the Act of 1819, were in revolt against a Government which called itself Tory but had broken with all the traditions of the party. When, for the moment, there was an alliance between extreme Tories, Whigs, and Radicals, and when the weapon used was the " indifference of the Government to the sufferings of the country," we need not look for accurate

---

[1] I have given these somewhat inept debates in some detail, partly to show the strange position of political parties—the House, as Protheroe said, was more like a nursery of young statesmen than a collection of established politicians —but principally as evidence of the prevailing puzzlement as to the distress. To me it is almost inconceivable that, in commenting on Baring's speech, *Blackwood* should say that he was the very top of " the mob of gentlemen who talk with ease," who " could dribble, dribble, dribble, and still continue dribbling from one lunar crescent to the next :

' Globose, a speaker in the House,
Who hems and is delivered of his mouse.' "

statements of these sufferings or rely very much on the picture presented.[1]

For many weeks the struggle went on. Before the end of the month, Stanhope, in his usual exaggerated way, brought up his promised motion for a committee of the whole House " to take into consideration the internal state of the country." He made a weak speech," wrote Ellenborough, " because, to get votes, he abstained from stating the cause of the distress, which, in his opinion, was currency." The principal speech was that of Lord Rosebery—" not a bad speech, but, as usual, pompous." How was it, he asked, that, in fifteen years of profound peace, there should be this frequent distress—in 1815, 1817, 1821, 1822, 1826, 1829— like the return of a wasting disease which undermined the constitution, and at each attack left the body with less strength to resist the next occurrence of the disorder ? The causes, he considered, were : the re-establishment of the currency—which was inevitably painful ; the immense and rapid improvement in machinery ; redundancy of population; influx of Irish labourers; the administration of the Poor Laws—they were no better than a premium on improvident marriages ; heavy taxation ; imperfect banking ; the bad crops of the past two years. While, for many of these, remedy was outside the sphere of the legislature, for some of them, it was not : he mentioned a joint gold and silver currency—which would give all the advantages of small notes ; an Irish poor law, which would check the competition with our labour ; a gradual change in the system of paying wages out of poor rates ; diversion of the surplus meanwhile from a sinking fund to reduction of taxation ; substitution of an Income Tax, on the landed and funded proprietors alone, for various other taxes which bore heavily upon the industry of the country, " leaving out trades and professions which, from the fluctuating nature of their profits, should never be taxed except under the pressure of extreme necessity " ; reduction of the Corn Law sliding scale. In regard to these, he considered an enquiry necessary, but that proposed by Stanhope was, he thought, of all others, the most inexpedient, the most unsatisfactory, and the most unlikely to produce what its proposer was so anxious to effect.

[margin note: Stanhope.]

[margin note: Rosebery.]

---

[1] Walpole seems to overlook this tainted source, and gives the statements of distress made by various speakers as if they were accredited facts. He seems, too, not to notice that even the " facts " relate to agriculture and handloom weaving.

The Duke.

"The Duke, who alone spoke on our side, did not speak well," wrote Ellenborough, "and some of his statements were hazardous." He reiterated his opinion that the intensity and universality of the distress were not proven. The prices of corn had not been lowered beyond what was deemed a remunerating price. The prices of other articles of agricultural produce, such as meat, timber, etc., were fully equal to what they were during the Bank Restriction, when the amount of the taxes was the heaviest. The great fall in prices since 1814 was due to "all the world becoming manufacturers," and was quite beyond the control of Parliament. The shipping tonnage now amounted to more than for many years past, etc. He hinted that the motion was made rather for the purpose of attacking the administration than for anything else; and, in any case, he was sure that relief could not be given by a committee of the whole House which was not to examine into anything, so far as he could understand, by which relief could be achieved.

King.

Lord King put the problem thus : Why did manufactured goods sell at a low rate ? Was it not the case that what limited and settled their price, considering that we made more than we consumed, was the continental market ? How increase the price of our surplus manufactured goods ? By taking that from the Continent which it could give in return for them. "Raise prices and you raise wages ; increase the wages of the manufacturing population, and you benefit the agricultural interests." On this ground, he proposed an amendment for a Select Committee "to enquire into the depressed state of the agricultural and manufacturing interests of the kingdom, for the purpose of ascertaining whether any, and what, relief could be afforded by an extension of foreign trade." On the withdrawal of the amendment, Stanhope's motion was lost by 25 votes to 118.[1]

Still another debate.

Of the further great debate on the distress, which began on 16th March, and was continued with vigour for three days more, it is impossible to treat adequately here. The occasion was a motion by Davenport, for a Committee of the whole House to enquire into and report upon the causes of the distress and the remedy thereof. There were obvious objections to such an enquiry in the form proposed—it was not easy to see, for instance, how the ordinary business was to be continued while a "discussion of opinions" of this extent was going on—but what made the Government

[1] *Hansard*, xxii. 928.

uncompromising in its opposition was that the support of the enquiry was known to be a mere peg on which to hang another determined attack on the currency. In Davenport's speech, as Lord Howick said, currency was the beginning, the middle, and the end. Sadler took up the running, adding to currency, as a principal cause of the distress, the " contemptible delusion " proposed as free trade.[1] Beginning with this, the discussion ranged over every conceivable cause and remedy—to say nothing of the underlying question, strenuously controverted, whether the distress were really so universal and so serious as the petitions made out—till it came to be, on the one side, an attack on everything Ministers had done or homologated, and, on the other, a series of separate replies from supporters of the Government. The notable speeches were a very splendid one by Huskisson—who, this time, dropped his petty carping at the Government—defending both the currency system and the commercial policy ; a fine one by Peel defending the Bill called by his name ; and a wildly extravagant one by Burdett. Finally the motion was negatived without a division, and a modified amendment asking for a Select Committee was lost by 87 to 255.[2]

While this debate on the State of the Nation was proceeding, a similar discussion was raised in the House of Lords by the Duke

---

[1] One feels some sympathy with Courtenay's irritation at Sadler's grandiose verbosity ; "If the honourable gentleman," he said, "continued to blame the Government for the passing of laws in which the great majority of the members had a share as well as many of His Majesty's Ministers, without himself introducing some specific remedy, he would denounce him to the public as a betrayer of his trust—he would call him as a wordy man, without meaning, who did not do his duty to his constituents and his country." The following, for instance, is a specimen of his words without thoughts : " Without pretending to know anything of Political Economy, he believed he might lay it down that capital was a remunerating profit on labour, and that debt was an engagement to pay for so much human labour. The circulating medium was the measure of this labour, and, consequently, whatever affected that circulating medium must deteriorate the measure of labour, and so reduce the amount of the labourer's profit or reward."

[2] *Hansard*, xxiii. 391, 548, 624, 789. In the course of these debates, Sir George Philips confirmed what I have noted in 1826 as regards Glasgow, that, in Lancashire, the merchant had ceased to export at his own risk, and said that the manufacturer, who used, in ordinary times, to give the merchant a credit of eighteen months, and thought himself lucky if he got paid in two years, was now exporting his own goods. This doing away with the middleman he considered a great gain to the manufacturer as well as to the consumer. As for the reiterated statement that such a trade was carried on at a loss, he simply denied it. It had been said that the manufacturers were forced to carry on their export trade because they made more than the country required. But surely it was known that there were manufactures carried on expressly for the foreign markets.

The Distress and its Causes

of Richmond, when asking for a Select Committee to take into consideration the Internal State of the Country, more particularly with respect to the condition of the Working Classes, and the effect of Taxation upon productive industry. Richmond rested his case mostly on Poor Law returns, and the usual broad and divergent statements as to the distress were made by supporters and opponents. The motion was rejected by 141 to 61, on account of the enormous extent of the proposed remit, including, as it did, *inter alia*, such trifling questions as the free trade policy, taxation, Corn Laws, the abuses of the Poor Law, and, particularly currency—and the reason given was amply borne out by the speeches.[1]

After this date, as the indications of reviving trade were too obvious to be ignored, the distress was not much mentioned in Parliament. But those who consistently believed that a contracted currency was the root of all the evil, tried a last fall in June. Attwood,[2] starting with the assertion that the whole of the difficulties of the country were due to the monetary system and to the measures by which it had been established, brought the matter to a head by boldly proposing a Resolution for the establishment of a bimetallic system—" to establish gold and silver coin of the realm, coined in the relative proportions of $15\frac{2850}{13640}$ lbs. weight of sterling silver to 1 lb. of sterling gold"; and Baring supported him, owning, however, that he should prefer to remit the matter to a Committee. The thinness of the House, said Herries, now Master of the Mint, arose from the conviction in the minds of the majority that the question of the Currency was finally set at rest, and not from any want of attention to the wants of the country. Without entering fully on a reply, he pointed out that, on Attwood's own statement, silver was at the moment 5 per cent. less than the proposed ratio. Suppose, then, it became known that the House had now come to a Resolution, the effect of which was that every man who had claims payable upon demand, every man who held notes of small or great value, every man who had debts outstanding, would, if he secured the amount of what was due to him before this Resolution passed into law, get the whole of his money, whereas, if he delayed beyond that period, he could get only £95 for every £100. What would happen? "What would become of the Bank

Attwood proposes a bimetallist resolution.

[1] *Hansard*, xxiii. 476.

[2] Attwood was leader of the Birmingham Political Union, which was founded in 1830 for the repeal of the Act of 1819, and ultimately became an organisation for parliamentary reform.

of England—what would become of every banking house in the kingdom—what would become of all debtors who were liable to pay upon demand all that they owed ? " Huskisson, who agreed with him that, before the end of a week there would not be a sovereign remaining in the country, spoke of the danger arising from an inordinate propensity to voyages of experiment, and gave it as his opinion that there was a general conviction that they were now arrived, after all their sufferings, at a state at which wise men would be willing to stop rather than place the whole system once more in jeopardy by a renewal of unseasonable experiments. In the end, Attwood withdrew his Resolution, and so, one might hope, there was an end to " this wearisome subject," as Peel called it.[1]

One seems to get the impression from this, as from earlier debates, that, if it were to do over again, it was by no means certain that the single gold standard would be adopted. The example of France was not without effect. Peel himself—thanks to his appearances in the agitation against the abolition of the one pound note—was credited in some quarters with a leaning towards bimetallism. But bitter experience was teaching thoughtful men the truth that a settled currency even though pretty far short of perfection was preferable to constant change. And the cause of scientific bimetallism was not advanced by Attwood's praise of the old system before 1797, under which, he contended, debts were paid in whatever happened to be the cheaper metal, and his suggestion that such an option was not undesirable.

But during the autumn session, amid all the excitement of the *Currency again.* " rural war," and under the new Government, still another attempt was made to obtain an enquiry into the State of the Country. This was introduced by Lord Wyndford in a most confused and wandering speech. The distress was caused, he said, by capital being " shut up in strong boxes, and not finding its way into the possession of the producing classes [2]—by the want of a currency sufficient for the wants of the country, the proof offered being that tradesmen were obliged to pay their labourers in goods instead of money— by the use of machinery [3]—by the restriction of small notes. These were fit subjects for an enquiry such as he suggested, to which he

[1] *Hansard*, xxv. 101.

[2] He affirmed that Peel, Huskisson, and Wellington had agreed in this !

[3] What did he mean by " machinery ? " he was asked ; did he include the wheelbarrow, which was only a recent invention dating from the time of Louis XIV. ?

added a few others, such as the absence of seigniorage on the gold coins, the Corn Laws—he had no objection to the repeal of the Corn Laws ; they were of no use to the agricultural interests, although they might be to the speculator—the burdens on land, the Poor Laws, the danger of famine from the abandonment of poor lands, etc.

The proposed enquiry was scornfully ridiculed by Lord King : Earl Grey deprecated it on many grounds ; and it was negatived without division. The only noteworthy thing in the debate, perhaps, was the statement made by Grey that he was entirely convinced that the ultimate interest of the people themselves required that the agriculture of the country should be protected, because, without such a protection, the people could not be assured, in all seasons, of a sufficient, a certain, and, he would add, a cheap supply. He believed this principle was generally acquiesced in, though a few persons yet objected to it. He knew, indeed, that there were some persons who had the courage to recommend the entire abolition of the laws which regulated the trade in corn ; but, for his part, he had not nerves to undertake so hazardous an experiment, knowing well that, if it should fail, the evils which it would occasion could not be remedied. They would lead to the destruction of the country.[1]

Later still, Attwood asked if it was the intention of the Government to propose any enquiry into the distress in connection with the change of currency, reaffirming his conviction that it was to this that the distress was "mainly attributable." Althorp replied that the Government had no such intention, and that personally he would not consent to any further alteration.[2]

Thus the ten years, 1821-1830, ended as they had begun, with distress in agriculture, slow revival of industry, and attacks on the Currency.

[1] *Hansard*, N.S. i. 828.

[2] *Hansard*, N.S. i. 1068. If it were not ascribing too much stupidity, one would be inclined to say that many at this time really thought that there could be no national prosperity without a return to high prices, and that any measure which would raise prices must be good. But how otherwise are we to read this sentence from *Blackwood* of May, in " Hints to the Two Houses of Parliament " : " In the name of commonsense, why do you desire prosperity when you are so violently hostile to high price ? they are one and indivisible." It is interesting to find *Blackwood* holding up Ireland as a refutation of Malthus and his law—and in the by-going as an instance of the folly of Political Economy—because, although its people had "resolutely and fearlessly increased their numbers without regard to consequences," the produce of the country seemed to have at least kept pace with the increase of the population (May, 749).

CHAPTER XLIX

1830. THE BUDGET: REDUCTION OF TAXATION: THEORY OF TAXATION

THE King's Speech in February had promised "a considerable reduction in the amount of the public expenditure, without impairing the efficiency of our naval or military establishments." The Opposition, however, had no mind to let the Government get the credit of any such popular move; and two motions were made within the first fortnight, ostensibly on the plea that the universal distress called for immediate and drastic measures, but, presumably, to take the wind out of the Government's sails, or to suggest·a standard of retrenchment which would reflect on the Government's proposals.

One was by Sir James Graham—who up till now had shown little signs of his future eminence—for a reduction in the salaries of persons employed in the civil and military establishments of the country, on the ground that, as all such salaries had been raised during the Restriction on account of the diminished value of money, it was only just that they should be brought back again now that the metallic standard was restored. Dawson, the Secretary of the Treasury, however, had no difficulty in showing that, since 1797, a great number of offices had been abolished altogether, and that, in those which remained, the principle had already been faithfully followed since 1822 of returning to the scale of 1797, unless where there was some adequate cause, such as the increase of business. Graham withdrew his motion.[1] Retrenchment proposals by Graham.

The other was introduced by Hume in a three hours' speech, in which he urged the reduction of taxation and expenditure to the standard of 1792. He would reduce the Civil List (which Graham had excepted)—"it was absurd to talk of supporting the and by Hume.

[1] *Hansard*, xxii. 438. *Supra*, 127.

dignity of the Crown when rags and tatters covered the land." He would sell the Crown Lands. He would repeal the whole duty on coals, soap, candles, leather, beer, cider, the window duty and the inhabited house duty. He would reduce the duties on tobacco, foreign spirits, sugar, glass, paper, insurance. Thus about £9 millions could be taken off the pecuniary burdens of the country. This was all a wild and extravagant speculation, replied Goulburn. £29 millions of the taxes went to pay the interest of the debt ; when the deadweight and other expenditures to which the national honour was pledged were added, there remained but ten or eleven millions, from which Hume so easily proposed to deduct nine. Considering that the Government had been given no time to disclose the reductions promised, such a motion was out of all order. Then Western turned the debate on to the Currency, and Hume's motion was forgotten, till Peel summed up. He protested strongly against it. What would be the effect produced on the public mind by a resolution promising a reduction of eight or nine millions ? If any member liked to propose the repeal of special taxes, he would be glad to argue the matter, but this motion was not practical politics. As for the Currency, he deprecated the incessant dragging in of the subject without formal notice and without any plan or proposal, and reminded the House of the contracts made within the past thirteen or fourteen years—they surely deserved some consideration. The motion was lost, but Hume got a vote of 69 on his side.[1]

The Government's retrenchment. But all this made it necessary that the Government should lose no time in making public the reduced estimates they proposed, and, four days later, the Chancellor of the Exchequer rose to announce them—premising that, when the claims on account of services long since rendered, that is to say, debts of honour, were satisfied, there was little more than a sum of £12 millions on which reductions could be made.[2] The reductions were :—£453,000 on the Army services, which brought the estimate of the year lower

[1] *Hansard,* xxii. 480.

[2] This was disputed subsequently by Parnell, on the statement of the Fourth Report of the Finance Committee that, out of our gross expenditure of £55 millions, £35 millions only were not susceptible of diminution, namely, the interest on the debt, the Civil List, and the pensions and half pay. But to the £20 millions which, according to this calculation, might be reduced, he would add £3 millions of Sinking Fund and £2 millions which might be saved by converting the four and the three and a half per cents. to three per cents., giving a total of £25 millions instead of Goulburn's £12 millions (*Hansard,* xxii. 801).

than any one estimate of the like kind brought forward for six and twenty years; £29,000 on the Ordnance; £273,000 on the Navy; and £276,000 on the Miscellaneous : in all, something over a million sterling.

Hume was unsparing in his condemnation—Ministers estimated as if they were about to be called on to take the field for another Waterloo. Many dwelt on the prevailing distress, and said that a million was in no wise calculated to give any relief to the labourer and artizan ; nothing was of any avail but a reduction of taxation, or an alteration in the Currency. But, on the whole, the statement was well received—Baring saying that it was more than he had expected—and the critics were more heartily denounced than the Government.[1]

Acknowledging that the position of the country demanded the The Budget. early exposition of the course which the Government intended to pursue as regards the finances, Goulburn brought in the Budget on 15th March. He admitted that his expectations of the early passing away of the distress had not been realised. The revenue for 1829 accordingly had fallen short of the estimates by about £430,000, chiefly in the Malt and Beer Duties, on which the unfavourable weather of the past two years had produced a very considerable effect. The consumption of Tea, however, had not fallen, although the revenue had suffered from the low prices. Happily, the deficiency in the Excise had been to some extent compensated by the augmentation of the Customs—principally, he must say, from the increased receipts on foreign corn. Although the estimated surplus of £3 millions had not been realised, a surplus of revenue of £2,400,000—a real surplus, after making every payment for which the country was justly liable—had been applied to the reduction of debt;[2] and, besides—carrying out the measure of 1828—permanent annuities to the amount of £2,700,000 had been converted into annuities for lives, and, in the course of thirty years, the debt would be reduced by that amount.[3]

As to the future, in the distressed condition of the country, and paying regard to the numerous petitions for reduction of taxation,

[1] *Hansard*, xxii. 743.

[2] " This being the first year since Parliament came to the determination to devote to the payment of the Debt only the surplus revenue."

[3] As we saw, the scheme had been suspended in 1828 to allow of reconsideration of the rate. The granting of annuities was resumed in 1829, on a new scale and with some changes, by c. 24 of that year.

the Government had to choose between two courses ; either the absolute reduction of taxation to the extent to which it was practicable, or the transferring the change, from one set of shoulders to another, by the imposition of a new tax on that portion of the community which was supposed to have suffered the least for the purpose of relieving that which had suffered the most. After giving every consideration to the latter, in the proposed form of a Property Tax [1] they had come to the conclusion—without pronouncing any opinion for or against the abstract principle of such a tax—to adopt the former. On the principle of giving the greatest relief to the most distressed classes at the least cost to the revenue, he would propose to repeal entirely the tax on Beer, which accounted for not much less than three farthings on the quart to the consumer, and had made beer of late rather a luxury than the necessary of life it used to be. As this would get rid of the vexatious restrictions on the manufacture, and of the expenses of collection, the relief to the public would be much greater than that represented by the £3 millions which it would cost the revenue. The remission of the duty would necessarily be attended by the free sale of beer, and both changes would date from the time of the renewal of licenses, 10th October next—thus obviating the necessity of drawbacks on stocks. At the same time, the duty on Cider would be removed. Here also, although the duty amounted only to £25,000 or £30,000, the relief would be much greater from the removal of the oaths, and the vexatious proceedings connected with the manufacture and collection. Similar considerations applied to Leather, and here also he would repeal the whole of the tax remaining since 1822—amounting to a loss to the revenue of £340,000 or £350,000. The repeal of these three duties then would give a positive relief of at least £3,400,000, and a real relief of not less than £5,000,000 a year. This would not be throwing away money with the prodigality of a spendthrift : " We shall not give up anything to speculation and chance, but, as it appears to me, we shall prudently apply the resources of the country to the relief of those particular classes—the agricultural and the manufacturing—which labour under the most distress and have the strongest claim to the sympathy of Parliament."

[1] It seems from Ellenborough's *Diary* that some kind of Property or Income Tax was seriously contemplated by the Cabinet, and was only postponed for a year by the steady opposition of the Duke : " Next year, there must be an Income Tax."

Passing to the Estimates for 1830, he calculated as under :

RECEIPTS.

Customs - - - - - - - -	£17,200,000
Excise - - - - - - - -	19,300,000
Stamps - - - - - - - -	7,100,000
Assessed Taxes - - - - - -	4,900,000
Post Office - - - - - - -	1,500,000
Smaller branches, at the same - - - -	200,000
Miscellaneous - - - - - - -	280,000
	£50,480,000

EXPENDITURE.

Interest and Management of the Debt - -	£25,671,000
Additional charge on Annuities - - -	2,629,000
Interest on Exchequer Bills - - - -	750,000
Pensions, etc. - - - - - - -	2,180,000
Army, Navy, Ordnance, and Miscellaneous -	16,582,000
In all - -	£47,812,000

This would leave a clear surplus of £2,667,000. To bring up the surplus, he would submit two measures ; one, to consolidate all the laws relative to the Stamp duties, which would be a saving of £110,000 ; the other to levy an additional tax on Spirits of all kinds, which would be a saving of £330,000. The House would bear in mind that the great reduction of the duty on Spirits formerly carried into effect was intended to put an end to an extensive system of smuggling, which seriously affected the revenue at the same time that it corrupted the morals of the people. But those who proposed that reduction, as well as the Committee which recommended it, always contemplated, that, as soon as the establishments for illicit distillation were broken up, the duty on Spirits might gradually be raised again, though not to such a degree as to endanger the return of smuggling. In conformity, he would propose an increase in the duty on Scots and Irish spirits, from 2/10 to 3/-,[1] and, on English spirits, from 7/- to 8/-.

These two items would raise the surplus to over £3 millions ; deducting £1 million as the year's proportion of the repeal in beer, cider, and leather, there would remain, he estimated, a clear surplus for the reduction of debt of about £2 millions. But, of course, in 1831, when the whole reduction of £3,400,000 should have full effect, the deficiency in the revenue would be much greater. To

---

[1] It seems that, in 1826, the Scots and Irish Excise had been raised to 2/10 (per imperial gallon) and the English to 7/-.

meet this there were many resources, and in a few days he would propose one ; *viz.* to reduce the four per cents. to a lower rate. The only remaining matter in the speech was the intimation that the Government proposed to empower a Commission to deal with the whole of the colonial expenditure.

Criticism :
Baring,

Baring was severe in his criticism. Apart from sanguine expectations of a future increase of revenue, the Chancellor had, by cutting off £3,400,000 for the succeeding year, laid his hand on the only surplus they had, and taken away all hope of anything applicable to the reduction of debt. He did not mean to say that this need excite the slightest apprehension in the breast of the public creditor —and, be it remembered, there were 247,823 persons of this class— but they need not ever again look to provide for the contingency of war by borrowing. And he was bound to say that the proposed reduction of interest came with a bad grace from a minister who acknowledged that the hope of repaying the debt was abandoned. He recommended Goulburn, before carrying out his promised conversion, to consider the idea, lately ventilated, of converting the four per cents. into five per cents., by giving to the holder of every £100 of stock in the former £70 of stock in the latter, the interest of which would be 3½ per cent. By this means there would be effected a saving of £1,700,000 of interest, and a reduction of forty or fifty millions of capital, the five per cent. stock thus created being made irredeemable for fifty or sixty years.

Althorp,

Althorp differed altogether from Baring, and, repeating his former opinion, only regretted that the Chancellor had not gone further, and reduced some other taxes which bore heavily on the industry of the country, and where repeal would have increased rather than diminished the revenue. " Whatever surplus there might be of income over expenditure ought, in his opinion, to be reduced in taxation. He never approved of the application of such surplus to the reduction of the national debt. He always looked on that debt, not as capital which was to be liquidated, but rather as a perpetual annuity chargeable upon the country ; and he was convinced that if, as he believed, the general wealth of the country would be more increased by repealing taxes than the debt would be diminished by their continuance, good policy dictated that the amount of the taxes should be left in the pockets of the people."

Hume,

Hume, while freely admitting that no taxes could have been more judiciously selected for reduction than those chosen by the Chancellor, agreed with Althorp that he should have gone much further, and used the Sinking Fund for the remission of taxation. Maberly said that the Budget was the best he had ever seen. Huskisson also expressed his gratification with the proposals, while confessing that this gratification was somewhat alloyed by the considerations put forward by Baring. He agreed with the latter as to the advantages which might accrue from converting the permanent four per cents. into five per cent. annuities for a definite number of years.[1] *Huskisson.*

The Conversion scheme met with no difficulties. The dissentients did not represent more than £3 millions out of about £175 millions of stock. The " New Four Per Cents," created by the Act of 1822, irredeemable for seven years from that date, were exchanged, to those who did not signify their dissent, into " New Three and a Half Per Cents," guaranteed for ten years, a stock already standing at 99½ in the open market, with the option of taking instead £70 of a new 5 per cent. stock guaranteed for forty-two years. The Chancellor explained that the reason why he had not preferred converting all the four per cents. into five per cents. was that at least two-fifths of the holders were trustees ; it would, he considered, be an immoral act to compel such trustees, without option, to deteriorate their trust property by one-third. The saving, he calculated, would be £778,000 in the next year, and that without imparing the public credit.[2] *The Conversion.*

Over the Beer Bill there was very considerable discussion. Its object was to promote the more general sale of sound beer—to bring back the consumption of that " good old English beer," which could not be got in any part of the country. Not, it was explained, from any fault of the brewers. It was the publicans who had brought it on themselves by the bad beer they sold ; the many convictions showed that it was by the publicans, not by the brewers, that the beer was adulterated. This object would be obtained by introducing competition instead of the existing monopoly. The throwing open of the trade was a necessary complement to the repeal of the Beer Tax ; otherwise the benefit would be intercepted by the rich brewers. The beer seller, however, though not dependent for his licence on the magistrate, would still be under magisterial control as regarded good conduct. *The Beer Bill.*

---

[1] *Hansard*, xxiii. 301.

[2] *Ibid.* xxiii. 923. A similar mode of conversion to the latter was made in 1818, when 3 per cents. were made into 3½ per cents. (*Economic Annals, 1801-20*, 629).

In its final form, the Bill provided that a licence to sell beer might be obtained, for a payment of two guineas, by any inhabitant householder giving two securities, on application to the Board of Excise in towns and to the excise officers in the country. Of all the proposals put forward in the Budget, this was the only one which met with serious opposition. Not, indeed, for itself. Very few were found to venture the sentiment that beer, being an intoxicating liquor, the encouragement to drink more of it was therefore to be deprecated. On the contrary, the cheapening of beer was at that time looked on as one of the best means of combating the drinking of spirits. Slaney, welcoming the motion, said that " the lower orders looked upon beer as the second necessary of life," and that one of the advantages of the Bill would be that their morals would be improved. A petition from Surrey, asking for the remission of the taxes on beer, malt, and hops, said that the taxation on these was a poll-tax, falling most heavily on the poor labourer, and urged that " the want of these necessaries of existence was shortening the existence of thousands of labourers." Buxton pointed out the injustice of the tax : champagne paid only 27 per cent. duty ; claret, 28 per cent. ; port, 56 per cent. ; while beer paid 165 per cent. The reason of the bitter opposition was its corollary, the throwing open of the trade in beer. Up till now, the sale had been confined to the licensed houses, and these houses were, very largely, either owned by the great brewers or under their thumb. The intimation, accordingly, was followed by the presentation of an immense number of petitions from publicans—and, to a smaller extent from brewers—containing plentiful predictions of ruin to the vast amount of capital involved and protesting the sacredness of vested interests.[1] One alderman calculated that the retailers of beer in the Metropolis numbered 4,300 ; the houses they occupied were worth at the lowest average £250 a piece ; " if the trade in beer was thrown open, they would not be worth anything," and this would mean a loss of over a million sterling. Another alderman put it at two millions, and Maberly claimed that the retailers ought to be allowed five years to retire from the trade. The claim of vested interests was, of course, met by the reply that the licence was an annual one, withdrawable at the decision of the magistrates, and that, in any case, public benefit came before private interests.

[1] It may be granted that the argument of vested interests on the part of the publicans was of less cogency than it would be now, as every industry passing from a regime of Protection to one of Free Trade could, and did, put forward a claim at least as strong.

Apart from opposition on this score, the chief objection urged
was from the temperance side, that the Bill would set up huge
numbers of tippling houses in every quarter : " England, from
one end to the other, would be one great alehouse." As the licensed
victuallers of Nottingham piously protested, " an increase of retail
licences was prejudicial to the public morals." Two attempts were
made at modification, taken from the Scottish system. One was
to prevent the consumption of beer on the premises where it was sold
or brewed—as one member said, "it was the duty of His Majesty's
Government to encourage by every means the poor man to drink
his beer in the bosom of his family "—but this was strongly opposed
by the Chancellor of the Exchequer as inconsistent with the very
principle of the Bill. The other, requiring the beer seller to close
his house at ten, was adopted—Hume objecting on the principle of
free trade. The Act appears as c. 64, " to promote the general
sale of beer and cyder by retail in England." [1]

The " Consolidation of the Stamp Duties " was not such an Stamp Duties.
innocent matter as the title would suggest. The plan proposed
was to consolidate and simplify by levying them on one system
throughout the empire—" to make similar articles everywhere
subject to the same stamp duties." " The measure involved no
augmentation of tax," said the Chancellor of the Exchequer somewhat disingenuously, " yet, in consequence of some stamps being
now lower in Ireland than in England, its effects will be to increase
the revenue." As this, in fact, meant increasing the taxation of
Ireland by about £100,000, it created great excitement in the sister
isle. The gold and silver smiths, " already reduced to the lowest
ebb of distress," represented that their duties would rise from
1/- per oz. to 17/-, and the licence of five guineas for life be changed
into an annual one of five and a half. The increased stamps for
newspapers and advertisements would " annihilate the Irish press,"
said O'Connell—perhaps, he added, that was what was intended.[2]

The proposed increase in the Spirit Duties also gave rise to Spirit Duties.
petitions and remonstrances. The distillers represented that, to
raise spirits by 1/- without putting a similar increase on rum,
was to abandon a protection which had been acknowledged

---

[1] *Hansard*, xxiii. 73, 172 ; xxiv. 15, 323, 387, 401, 446, 951, 1333, 1398 ;
xxv. 573, 862, 990, 1081, 1091, 1158. " The new Beer Bill has begun its operations," wrote Sydney Smith in October. " Everybody is drunk. Those who
are not singing are sprawling. The sovereign people are in a beastly state."

[2] *Hansard*, xxiv. 448, 707, 761.

" necessary," inasmuch as rum might easily be converted into
gin while corn spirits could not be converted into rum. On the
other hand, West Indian interests protested that the 8/6 duty on
rum entirely prevented its introduction into Scotland and Ireland,
and begged for a reduction, and the English distillers in turn protested against the protest.[1] In the end. a compromise was adopted.
A uniform increase of 6d. was put on all spirits, English, Scots,
and Irish, and the same increase was put on rum.

Sugar Duties.   A change in the Sugar Duties was at last made, subsequently to
the introduction of the Budget. Huskisson was said to have given
a pledge in 1827 that they would be reduced. In 1829, Grant moved
the reduction on plantation sugar from 27/- per cwt. to 20/- ; on
East India sugar, from 37/- to 25/- ; and on all other sugars to
28/-, and Huskisson, backing him up, said that, in consequence of
the high price, two-thirds of the poor, he believed, drank their coffee
unsweetened.[2] At that time, Goulburn refused, urging the necessity
of a surplus revenue.[3] But, in February of the current year, came
petitions and deputations from the West India planters pleading
their distress. The price of sugar had never been so low since 1792 ;
it had fallen from 50/- and 60/- to 22/-, and yet not a shilling had
been taken off the 27/- duty imposed as a war tax, at the same
time as the 8/6 duty on rum entirely prevented its introduction into
Scotland and Ireland, where the duty on spirits was only 2/10. They
complained also of the competition of Mauritius—when Mauritius
sugar was first allowed entry, it was represented that the annual
import would never exceed 10,000 hogsheads, whereas it was now
25,000—and of the competition of Cuba and other foreign colonies
which still enjoyed the advantage of the slave trade—700,000 slaves
had been introduced into these colonies since 1815. It was stated
by the supporters of the petition that, great as was the distress at
home, no people were so much depressed as the inhabitants of the
West Indies, and much sympathy was freely expressed. Huskisson

[1] *Hansard*, xxii. 846 ; xxiii. 73, 1418 ; xxiv. 217 ; xxv. 318.
[2] The first of the public coffee houses in London was opened in 1652. In
1675, Charles II. attempted to suppress them as the resort of disaffected
persons—as the judges said, " retailing of coffee might be an innocent trade,
but as it was used to nourish sedition, spread lies, and scandalise great men,
it might also be a common nuisance." The reduction of duty in 1825 and
the low prices at once increased the consumption, and, by 1830, we find the
statement that " Coffee has become universally consumed in countries
(England and America, for instance) where it was but little known or used
only as a luxury " (*State of the Commerce of Great Britain for 1830*, 3).
[3] *Hansard*, xxi. 1578.

said that, by a long course of measures, Parliament had given peculiar claims on protection to the West India proprietors.

The deputation of West Indians which waited on the Government was very roughly received by the Duke, who told them that they were not distressed at all, and that nothing would be done for them. But, later on, the Chancellor of the Exchequer proposed to scale down the duty, retaining the old figure of 27/- for the highest priced sugar, but graduating the duty down to 20/- for the lowest. Huskisson strongly opposed this, partly as opening the door to all manner of fraud and collusion, partly as giving a boon to the newer colonies —from which the coarse sugar mostly came—as against the older ones in which the distress was greatest, and earnestly urged an experiment for one year of reducing the duty on all sugars to 20/-. The Chancellor at the moment adhered to his plan.[1] But, in the end, the duty on " Brown Muscovado " was reduced from 27/- to 24/-, while the duty on East Indian Muscovado was reduced from 37/- to 32/-. Foreign sugars remained unchanged at 63/-.

The taxation of Tobacco came up in a new connection. The discussion began in 1829 when G. R. Dawson, member for Londonderry, brought up the anomalous state of the laws which regulated the growth of tobacco in the United Kingdom. In the days when Virginia and Maryland were British colonies, the cultivation had been forbidden at home with the view of encouraging and protecting them. Previous to this prohibition, a considerable quantity had been grown in Gloucestershire. When these colonies ceased to be part of the empire, the protective motive dropped, but meantime it had been found that indirect taxation, through the consumption of tobacco, was one of the most productive sources of revenue. In 1799, however, the prohibition of growing tobacco in Ireland had been removed, by way of experiment, with the condition, of course, that such tobacco was not allowed entry into Great Britain without paying the usual duties. Hence emerged the grievance in question ; some 700 hogsheads had been smuggled during the past year : and the object of Dawson's Bill was to prevent this smuggling, and safeguard the revenue, by assimilating the laws of the two countries " with respect to the tobacco of domestic growth," *i.e.* prohibiting again the growing of tobacco in Ireland.

Discussion on home-grown Tobacco.

But this raised the related question of why the cultivation of a crop for which the soil and climate of parts of the west of England

[1] *Hansard*, xxii. 848 ; xxv. 314, 525.

were well adapted should not be encouraged, and Grant intimated that he would take another occasion of calling the attention of the House to all the prohibitory duties on the growing of tobacco at home, with a view to their reduction. In the course of the debate, still another question was raised, and an amendment moved, namely, the propriety of encouraging the cultivation in the colonies by lowering the duty on colonial tobacco from 2/9 to 2/- per lb. ; at present, it was said, the whole monopoly of what was " almost a necessity of life " was in the hands of the United States.

Goulburn at that time pointed out that the growing of tobacco in England was prohibited by a penal statute which must be repealed if tobacco was to be grown. He opposed any alteration in the Irish regulations—it would be extremely unjust to persons who had sunk capital in an experiment permitted by Government to stop the cultivation merely for the sake of assimilating the laws of the two countries. As to foreign tobacco, we imported 33½ million lbs. in all during 1828, of which only 64,000 came from the colonies. The cause of this small import was certainly not want of encouragement, as there was already a difference in favour of colonial tobacco of 3d. per lb., which was more than 100 per cent. on the cost of production ; to reduce the duty further as proposed would be to grant a bounty of 9d. per lb., and this was extremely objectionable ; " for, as the effect of bounties was to encourage the investment of capital in the produce of a particular article, when it was found desirable to withdraw the bounty, the man who had embarked his capital could always turn round and say, ' By giving me undue encouragement, you induced me to risk my capital, and now, by withdrawing the bounty, you involve me in ruin.' " The amendment was negatived, but, the opinion of the House being unfavourable, the Bill was withdrawn.[1]

In the current year, however, it came out that 500 acres were under cultivation in Ireland, and that already £750,000 worth was grown annually, paying no duty. Goulburn intimated his intention to remove the existing prohibition as regards England, at the same time as he imposed a uniform duty of 1/8 per lb. on the growing of tobacco in any part of the kingdom. Spring Rice welcomed the proposal as opening a new branch of industry. Hume, on the other hand, strongly opposed. A Chancellor of the Exchequer should be careful how he tampered with his receipts. He was afraid that the proposal would lead to the cultivation of home tobacco to such an

[1] *Hansard*, xx. 1005 ; xxi. 1597.

extent as to be injurious to the revenue. It would be better that the present growers of tobacco should be allowed to carry on their operations for a year or two untaxed, with an understanding that, at the end of that time, they should pay a duty equal to that imposed on foreign tobacco. Goulburn agreed that prohibition would have been the safer course. Meanwhile, the tobacco interests in Bristol petitioned against the measure for " imposing so small a duty as 1/8 a lb. on home-grown tobacco "—it should be made liable to the same duty as foreign ; while Irish tobacco growers petitioned against any duty being imposed—it would amount to a total prohibition of the cultivation, and, moreover, it was a contravention of the Act of Union which prohibited the levying of any duties on the produce of Ireland but such as were " just and reasonable " ! But, apparently, the premature dissolution of Parliament prevented the resolution from being carried into effect.[1]

Great as were the reductions in taxation thus effected, they were not thought sufficient by many who had not the responsibility of keeping up the revenue. As regards the Beer duty, it was urged, by the agricultural interests, that, if the purpose was to increase the consumption of beer among the labourers, it would have been better to repeal the Malt duty, which would allow poor men to brew their own beer at home—the answer, of course, being that this was not possible for the working men in towns.

Many petitions, strongly supported by influential members, urged The taxation on the Exchequer to take up the question of the taxation of Coal, of Coal. setting forth the hardship to the poor consumer, and the inequality of the burden on manufacturers in different parts of the kingdom —London, e.g. paying 6/- a chaldron, Ireland, 1/8, Wales, 1/-, and Scotland nothing at all. Wharncliffe, comparing coast towns like Norwich with towns in Lancashire, pointed out that, just where coal, independently of the tax, must be dear, there it paid the heaviest taxation. Ireland put in a separate claim. She had no coal of her own, and was charged heavily on the coal she had to import if she was to do any manufacturing ; this was a heavy handicap on what everybody wished, the attraction of capital and manufactures to that country. The Chancellor answered that, as England had to pay so much more, surely the greater burden had a greater claim to relief. But, when Alderman Wood asked for a Select Committee to enquire into the Coal Trade at the Port of

[1] *Hansard*, xxiii. 1434 ; xxiv. 26, 34. The course actually taken in 1831 was to extend the prohibition of home growing to Ireland.

London, with the view of determining what restrictions should be attached to the supply of coal, there was no opposition, and the Committee was appointed.[1] The Committee appointed by the Lords in the previous session to consider the State of the Coal Trade in the United Kingdom had already been reappointed.[2]

Taxation of Soap and Candles.

The tax on Soap and Candles, also necessaries of life, was again brought up. The duty on soap was 3d. per lb., or from 110 per cent. to 130 per cent., and pressed heavily on the poor. The 1d. per lb. on candles came to about 18 per cent. on the value. As regards soap, Hume drew attention to the extraordinary increase in the exports of soap to Ireland ; they amounted to 239,000 lbs. in 1827, 859,000 in 1828, and no less than 2,645,000 in 1829—" why, if the Irish used all the soap they imported, they must be the cleanest people under the sun." The fact unfortunately was that the soap was not used in Ireland, but smuggled back to England. There was no duty, either on soap or candles, in Ireland. The duty in England was not payable for two months. But the drawback on soap and candles exported was paid at once. Thus the manufacturers could send them to Ireland three or four times over between the payment of the drawback and the payment of the duty—doing a profitable trade with money borrowed from the Government ! All that the Chancellor of the Exchequer would say was that he had long felt the evil of different duties in the different countries ; he would be glad to see a general scale adopted for all parts of the country, getting rid of drawbacks and at the same time of many frauds ; he had carried this object into effect as regards glass, and he hoped to extend the principle to other things.[3]

The theory of taxation.

It may have been noted that, for some time, little had been said in the House to show that members had any notion that there was a theory of taxation. The burden of the taxes, on the country and on individual interests, was the theme dwelt on, and, indeed, the proper distribution of taxation over the individuals of the community was little more than an academic aspiration so long as that taxation was almost entirely indirect. Occasionally, indeed, we find a passing utterance which showed a recognition of the true

[1] *Hansard*, xxiii. 223, 365, 458 ; xxiv. 696.

[2] *Ibid.* xxii. 92. Its Report was laid on the table shortly before the end of the session. Among other things, it was declared indispensable that coals should be sold by weight instead of by measure, to prevent frauds on the consumer, and called attention to the " extravagant surplus revenue " of £60,000 obtained by the Corporation of London from the port charges (*ibid.* xxv. 1237).

[3] *Ibid.* xxiii. 868 ; xxiv. 1146 ; xxv. 18.

principles. Portman, *e.g.* asked for " the substitution of some one general tax which should fall with proportionate weight on every man," and " from the operation of which even the absentee should be unable to escape." [1] Hume said that he most earnestly wished to see taxation more equalised—taken as much as possible off the working classes upon whom it pressed so hard ; the labouring classes were contributing four-fifths of the taxes, while millions gave, comparatively, nothing ; let the burden of the taxes, he said, be imposed chiefly on property and capital—if the owners were so forward to claim priority in representation, it would be a pity to refuse them precedence in paying. [2] On the other hand, Grey said openly that, if a property tax were brought forward, it would be his duty to give it the most decided opposition.

A notable contribution to the literature of taxation, however, had been made by the appearance, in January, of Parnell's *Treatise on Financial Reform*, a statement, as he said, of opinions formed in consequence of the deliberations of the Finance Committee of which he had been Chairman. Conceiving that the progress of industry and the increase of capital were promoted by " everything that added to the annual amount of imports," the right policy was to remove all obstructions without the slightest reference to what foreign governments might do. His principal recommendations in the *Treatise* were the repeal of all taxes on raw and other materials used in the chief trades ; the removal of taxes which, owing to excise regulations, checked the development of other trades ; reduction of the tobacco and spirit duties to prevent smuggling ; reduction of all duties on agricultural produce to 12 per cent. ; of all the protective duties to 10 per cent., " so as no longer to keep any duties for protection but only for revenue " ; of the export duty on coals to one half—which would yield an extra revenue of three or four hundred thousands ; change of the prohibition of the export of machinery to an export duty of 12 per cent.—again on account of the revenue which would ensue. All this could be secured by the

[margin: Parnell's Treatise.]

---

[1] *Hansard*, xxii. 530.

[2] *Ibid.* 317. " It is questionable, however, whether Hume's endless speeches, addressed either to empty benches or to an impatient audience, and followed by signal defeats, really promoted any useful object. He certainly contributed to make the subject (economical reform) so distasteful and unwelcome to the generality of the members as to render the leading Whigs less zealous in pursuing it " (Le Marchant, *Memoir of Viscount Althorp*, 235). In the present year, he fought the supply, item by item, in a way which Peel called " inflammatory," " an instigation to rebellion," and attributed to " the uneasy character of a disappointed prophet."

imposition of an Income Tax of about 1½ per cent. to 2 per cent. " If once men were allowed to take their own way, they would very soon, to the great advantage of society, undeceive the world of its error in restricting trade, and show that the passage of merchandise from one state to another ought to be as free as air and water. . . . The removal of obstacles is all that is required of the legislature for the success of trade. It asks nothing from Government but equal protection to all subjects, the discouragement of monopoly, and a fixed standard of money." But full consideration should be given to the great importance of making every change in so gradual a manner that nothing would happen to give a shock to trade or reduce the revenue below what was necessary for all the public services. As Mr. Buxton has observed, Parnell, in 1830, laid before the country the financial and fiscal policy which Peel and Gladstone afterwards carried through.[1]

Poulett Thomson asks for Revision of the Taxes.
The influence of Parnell's treatise was manifest in a motion, made a few days after the Chancellor had made his exposition, by Poulett Thomson asking for a Select Committee to enquire into the expediency of making Revision of the Taxes. The Chancellor of the Exchequer, he urged, should have made a more extended view of the whole system instead of contenting himself with a mere reduction. It was not of the amount of the taxation he complained, but of the manner in which it was raised—its effects in checking industry and destroying energy. The incidence of taxation was the important thing, and that was all at fault. He held in his hand a list of no less than 207 taxes imposed on raw materials.[2] To take only the most important.

Raw Materials.
Timber : the net revenue was about half a million. It was a tax on a first necessity of shipbuilding—at the same time as, by prohibiting Baltic timber, we taxed the country half a million more, and, besides, got inferior timber. Hemp : the net revenue was £70,000, the rate 16 per cent. And not only was this another tax on the raw material of shipbuilding, but—most monstrous of all customs—we admitted hemp in the manufactured form free ! Soap : the net revenue was £1,210,000, the rate from 110 per cent. to 130 per cent.—in itself quite a fit object of taxation. But there

---

[1] In 1825, it was stated, by the *Parliamentary Review* of that year, that the principal revenue was raised from scarcely twenty articles, while the list of enumerated commodities which paid duties occupied the space of thirty-four folio pages. One of them—oysters—yielded only 9/- !

[2] *Parl. Pap.* 1829, No. 172. The list is given *in extenso* in Parnell, *Treatise,* appendix i.

was no duty in Ireland, and, notoriously, soap which had got back the duty in drawback was smuggled from Ireland. Barilla : the duty amounted to £59,000, the rate being 100 per cent. It was a tax imposed solely for the benefit of the kelp burners of Scotland, and the kelp burners were ruined all the same by the introduction of a factitious alkali which completely undersold them. Sea-borne Coals : this was no trifle. The net revenue raised was £833,000. It was a tax imposed in times when coal was chiefly used for fuel ; now it weighed heavily on all our manufactures. It was, too, a most unequal tax, burdening the coast and the metropolis and encouraging manufacturers to establish themselves in inland counties. Altogether £6 millions of net revenue were raised on raw materials.

Then as to our own manufactures. Glass : the net revenue Manufactures. was £577,000, while the gross revenue—on which the collection charges depended—was £953,000. Owing to excessive duties, the consumption of glass was now less than it was five and thirty years ago. The rate was at present upwards of 100 per cent., and the numerous regulations and penalties on the manufacture represented something like 25 per cent. more. Thus all improvement was checked—" to improve, experiments must be made, but a man with a duty of 125 per cent. over his head is not very likely to make many experiments." Paper : the net revenue was £700,000, the rate varying from 30 per cent. to 150 per cent. according to the different kinds of paper. Need it be said that this was a tax on science, on knowledge, on education ? And, in the manufacture, the restrictions and penalties were so vexatious as to be almost incredible. Printed Calicoes : the net revenue was £600,000—to raise which a gross tax of over £2 millions was imposed. Here again, the tax was grossly unequal ; the duty was levied on the square yard, and a piece of cloth which sold for 6d., duty paid, contributed equally with that worth 5/-. Altogether, £2 millions were raised on these three manufactures, attended with such obnoxious and harassing and expensive regulations as made the returns not worth collecting.

The removal of these duties, he calculated, would be a gain to the public of at least £3,600,000, whilst the gain from the new employment for capital and skill of these various branches of industry, now languishing, would be infinitely greater. If he were asked how this gap in the revenue was to be filled up, he would suggest the reducing of the expenditure by abolition of the bounties on the fisheries and on linen [1]—both useless and mischievous ; and the applying of the Legacy Duty to real property as well as to personal estate—an item which would represent a million and a half.   Anyhow, he had no doubt that means would be found of supplying whatever might be required without taxing productive industry to the extent done by the taxes enumerated. He thought it only just to himself and fair to the House to say that he personally agreed with Huskisson that the substitution of a direct tax upon income for a large portion of our indirect taxes would be in the highest degree beneficial to the industry and improvement of the country, but the consideration of such a plan formed no part of his present motion.[2]

Taxes for revenue.

Coming to the second, and the more important part of his subject, articles in which a considerable reduction of rates might be effected without producing any falling off in the revenue, the principle on which he went was the established one that, just as there was a point in taxation where, by increasing the amount of your duties, you defeated your own purpose instead of increasing your revenue, so, by lowering duties which have been unduly raised, you not only augmented the means of enjoyment of the consumers, but you increased the actual amount of your revenue.   The five great branches of indirect taxation in 1828 were these :

Sugar (net)	£5,002,000
Tea	3,177,000
Tobacco	2,793,000
Foreign Spirits	2,921,000
Wine	1,699,000
	£15,592,000

Taking these in detail, he had no difficulty in showing historically that, as a general rule, high taxes had reduced consumption and never increased the revenue proportionally, while reductions had had the contrary effect ; that, in the former case, smuggling on an extensive scale inevitably followed [3]—and, in the case of Tea, adulteration, quoting the evidence of a witness before the East India

[1] The bounties on linen were to cease in 1832, and those on fishing in the present year, but, as Parnell said, " putting an end to them had of late years been so often enacted by law, and so often postponed, that it might be set down as certain that every effort would be made to continue them."

[2] Huskisson's opinion was expressed in the course of a very fine speech on 18th March (*Hansard*, xxiii. 580).

[3] Thomson mentioned that it had been established before a Committee of the House that, in one year, seventy cargoes of tobacco, containing 3,644,000

Committee to the effect that he did not believe that what was called
tea in the inns and shops of the interior of the country had the
slightest infusion of the real plant, but was, in fact, all composed of
sloe leaves.

As to Stamps, he asserted that the high rates on sea-policies had Stamps.
driven insurers to make their policies in the United States and
Holland; that those on Fire Insurance prevented many from
insuring who otherwise would insure; that the newspaper stamp
of 4d. kept the number of our newspapers much below that of other
countries, such as America and France; that the advertisement
stamp of 3/6 per advertisement, whether it were one line or fifty,
kept our yearly advertisements under a million, while the United
States had ten times that number.[1]

He was not sanguine enough to expect that the alterations proposed could be made without producing some deficiency in the
revenue in the earlier stages of their operation—perhaps during
the first year. But if his Committee should recommend on the
lines he had indicated, he thought the Government might fairly ask
from Parliament a vote of credit for the purpose.

There could be no doubt that Poulett Thomson had amply Opposition to
proved the expediency of revision, but the objections to remit Committee.
the subject to a Committee were certainly very serious.
Goulburn dwelt upon the interested motives which would influence the witnesses examined; the complete stagnation of
every trade affected when taxes in which it was interested were
being publicly discussed; and, in particular, the taking of
the duty and responsibility of revision out of the hands of
the House and the Government, and practically imposing it
on a Committee of twenty-one. Peel considered the proposal as
no less than an encroachment on the functions and privileges of
His Majesty's Ministers—a superannuation of the Chancellor of the
Exchequer: "if the intention of the vote were to show a distrust
of the Government, it should be expressed in a manner less prejudicial to the public interests." On the other hand, it was maintained that questions of taxation had repeatedly been referred to
Committees; e.g. that on the Salt duty, the Leather duties, on
Foreign Trade, the Bullion Committee, etc.; that, if the Finance

lbs. of tobacco were smuggled on the coast of Ireland, from the port of Water-
ford to the Giant's Causeway alone. Three-fourths of the tobacco consumed
in Ireland was supplied by smugglers, said Parnell (*Financial Reform*, 52).

[1] It was noted that there was not a town in Great Britain that did or could
support a daily paper except London (*New Monthly Magazine*, November).

Committee had been allowed to continue its labours, it would already have done what this Committee was to do. And, of course, the substitutionary taxation suggested was severely criticised—particularly the vote of credit, which was regarded as a recurrence to the wholly discarded idea of borrowing in times of peace. It was noted, too, by Peel, that no person spoke in favour of the motion who did not at the same time profess himself in favour of a Property Tax, and for this the Whigs were not prepared. On a division, the motion was lost by 78 to 167.[1]

All the same, the debate was undoubtedly a useful one as recalling consideration to some at least of the fundamental principles in taxation. In justice to the legislature of these days, however, who, as Thomson complained, seemed to treat taxation as " an amusing game," it should be remembered that the bulk of the taxes was then actually *felt* as a burden—a burden on the present and in times of peace. More than half the taxation went to pay the interest on the Debt, and, roughly, a third was for army and navy services. If we take the modern Budget, and notice that, over a long succession of years, the burden of the debt has decreased both absolutely and relatively, while the expenditure on Civil Services (including Education) has increased from £20 millions in 1896-7 to £52 millions, in 1912-13, we may appreciate better the modern emphasis on taxation as a payment for very definite services rendered. If we add this to the point emphasised by Poulett Thomson, that the indirect taxation was not only a costly way of raising revenue, but was actually hindering the development of industry and the growth of wealth, we may understand the persistence into much later years of the statement that " taxation is an evil "—which seems to the modern economist very much the same, and to have as much truth in it, as saying that payment for one's butcher's bill is a " burden."

Metropolitan Police.

There was a little debate on 15th June on the new Metropolitan Police Strange as it seems, the new institution was most unpopular. The very name was suspect by association with the police of the Continent. Certain sections of the press professed to see in it a design of the Government to hold down the people under military law—even to place the Duke on the throne !—and the baser sort were unsparing in their denunciation of " Peel's Bloody Gang."

[1] *Hansard*, xxiii. 857. Thomson's speech was subsequently published by Ridgway. It deserves the more attention that Althorp's Budget of 1831 was based on it.

But the debate is chiefly interesting as showing how little accustomed many people were to the idea of taxation as a payment for a direct service whose benefits could neither be measured nor allocated. A petition had been presented from a number of working gardeners in parishes round about London, complaining that they had never before paid any watch rate, and were now called on to pay 8d. per £. Peel had to point out that, in the matter of police, those who formerly refused to assess themselves to a watch had been enjoying much of the advantage which other people were paying for; it was but just that those who shared the advantages of living and owning property in the vicinity of a great city should share in its disadvantages. Sir Robert Vyvyan, who had already signified his entire disapproval of this "large organised force entirely moved by the will of the Secretary of State," said that it was evidently the intention of the honourable baronet to supersede all the ancient institutions of the country—his text seemed to be, "the country has outgrown its institutions." He trusted he would never see the police system extended to all parts of the country, and he rejoiced over the tale that the City, as it once stood out against an arbitrary monarch, had now stood against a Home Secretary, and refused to have a police within its area. Alderman Wood quaintly suggested that the best way of demonstrating the efficiency of the old system would be to hold a review at the Guildhall of all the watchmen! Peel was moved to some heat. His remark about the institutions of the country referred to its police institutions; Vyvyan's respect for antiquity carried him too far if he found nothing to admire in institutions unless they were six or seven centuries old. He had told the City that he would not concern himself in any way with its police except by giving it all the documents and papers of the Westminster police which could be of service to the City in forming an improved police. He certainly did wish, however, that all large towns should have their own police, following the plan adopted at Manchester, where an admirable force was entirely under the control of the local authorities. On the whole, the House seemed satisfied with the new system, and even Vyvyan had the grace to say that Peel's statement had obviated many of his objections.[1] In the end of the year, conflicts with the police continued of frequent occurrence, and, although their whole conduct was admirable, several petitions were presented, some complaining of the expense,

---

[1] *Hansard*, xxiv. 1199; xxv. 355. The violent and bitterly hostile article in *Blackwood* must be read to be believed.

others calling for abolition of the new force, and Peel, in the end of the year, gave notice that he would himself ask for a Select Committee to enquire into the whole subject.

In May, Goderich did a good service by calling attention to the facts of the National Debt, the actual pressure it involved, and some of the popular fallacies connected with it. Not less than one half of the current taxation went to pay the charges on the Debt, and, what was worse, the taxes were chiefly taxes raised under the influence of necessity, to supply the immediate wants of the day, and with little consideration of their ultimate consequences. Naturally enough, then, those who groaned under the burden were apt to think that no relief could be obtained unless by laying violent hands on the Debt—a most fatal imagination. Such people pointed to the fact that, in fifteen years, the capital of the debt had been reduced by only £40 millions. As a fact, the reduction was £60 millions, but this was beside the point. There was no such thing as a " capital of the Debt " in the ordinary sense of the term. The public creditor could never claim of right the repayment of a penny of this capital —all he could claim was the payment of an annuity. " The only question for the public was in what degree the pressure occasioned by the charge for this Debt was felt." Now, in 1816, when the charge was highest, it was, including funded and unfunded debt, very nearly £33 millions. In 1829, this had fallen by £3¾ millions, and, if the saving by the coming conversion was added, by £¾ million more : in all £4½ millions, equivalent to a reduction of £150 millions of capital at 3 per cent. If Lord Bexley had pro- phesied in 1816 that the National Debt would be reduced by £150 millions, what a visionary he would have been thought! Others, again, complained that it was wrong to pay in a sound restored currency a debt which had been contracted in a depreciated currency. The whole debt, however, had not been contracted in a depreciated currency. But, as there was no question of paying back of "capital," the only relevant enquiry was how this enhanced the annual charge. Returns showed that the annual charge for the sum borrowed during the depreciation amounted to £17½ millions. Taking 20 per cent. —which was the average rise in prices during that period—to represent the depreciation, 20 per cent. on £17½ millions would be £3½ millions ("that is to say that, but for the war, there would not have been such large loans, and but for the high prices con- sequent upon a depreciated currency, there would not have been this additional charge.") Unless, then, the charge on the debt had been reduced by £3½ millions since the war, the country would, owing to the currency being now restored, be paying a portion of the debt contracted in a depreciated currency. But the reduction, he had just shown, was actually £4½ millions. Thus the "equitable adjustment" had been effected. A third complaint was that the stock holder was now deriving advantages from the general low price of commodities at the expense of the other classes of the community. Now he, personally, believed that no one but sellers disliked low prices, and each seller only so far as his own merchandise was concerned. But the argument was most unfair. Stock holders also had had the evil days while other classes had the sunshine of high prices. It should be remembered that the circumstances which induced the existing low rate of interest were highly favourable also to some other classes, such as landowners, who could now pay off their five per cent. mortgages with money borrowed at 3 per cent. or 3½ per cent. Finally, as to the alleged impossibility of going on under a failing revenue, he simply denied, from figures, that the revenue was failing. He maintained, accordingly, that the energies and the resources of the country were still unimpaired, and were never more equal to any demands which might be made on them for the assertion of national honour.

Goderich was much complimented for his timely reminders, Stanhope alone, as might be expected, ignoring all that had been urged, repeated his gloomy prognostications : we were not able to sustain low prices coupled with high taxation—it was a contradiction in terms ; the dire alternative was either to retrace our steps and restore the currency to the state in which it was immediately after the peace, or to proclaim a national bankruptcy.[1]

It is interesting to find, thus early, a proposal brought forward *Unemployment Insurance.* to insure the working classes against unemployment, when Slaney asked for a Select Committee to consider means to lessen the evils arising from the Fluctuations of Employment in Manufacturing Districts. The evil aimed at was not the general distress, but the fluctuations in the condition of the manufacturing operatives due to fluctuations in trade. These fluctuations, he thought, arose chiefly from three causes : the introduction of machinery in competition with hand labour ; changes in fashion ;[2] and migration of indus-

---

[1] *Hansard*, xxiv. 428.

[2] Older members of the House, he said, might remember the change from shoe-buckles to shoe-strings, when the Birmingham manufacturers remonstrated, and were answered that, if the legislature prevented the use of shoe-strings, it would be injuring Coventry for the sake of Birmingham.

tries to the vicinity of coal (*e.g.* the woollen manufactures which formerly abounded in the south had now found their way to the northern counties). He wished an inquiry made whether it was not practicable to extend the advantages of Benefit Societies from insuring against illness and old age to the contingency of occasional want of employment. He considered that the wage of many classes at least was sufficient to enable them to lay by a provision for this purpose as well as for the others. They had the precedent of the tailors as regards an out-of-work allowance, and the carpet weavers and paper makers of Kidderminster had a system of travelling tickets enabling them to go in search of work. But no others of the manufacturing classes had any such provision, and, in the event of being out of work, unless they had individual savings—which was almost impossible in many trades—they were entirely destitute. While the proposal was favourably received and the Committee appointed, doubts were expressed whether the Committee would do anything more than supply some valuable information : fluctuations of trade were not actuarially calculable ; it would be difficult to tell whether individuals were unwilling to work or really unemployed ; wages were too low to support the heavy weekly subscription that would be required, etc.[1]

---

[1] *Hansard*, xxiv. 682. In the course of his speech, Slaney gave some interesting statistics. In 1801, the manufacturing population of England was to the agricultural as 6 to 5 ; in 1821, as 8 to 5 ; in 1830, it was as 2 to 1. In Scotland, in 1808, the proportion was as 5 to 6 ; in 1821, as 9 to 6 ; in 1830, as 2 to 1. During the past twenty years, while the population had increased 30 per cent., the manufacturing population had increased 40 per cent. (Glasgow 100 per cent.). The average annual import of cotton in 1813 was 79 million lbs. ; in 1829, it was 220 millions. The value of raw cotton imported was £5 millions per annum ; the manufactured article was worth £50 millions, and the quantity of it exported nearly £20 millions. The average import of wool, in 1813, was 7 million lbs. ; in 1829, 27½ millions, while the woollens exported amounted to £5¼ millions. In 1814, we had 11 steam vessels with a tonnage of 540 ; in 1828, 338 vessels, with a tonnage of 30,000—" if he were asked to name the person to whom England was most indebted in bearing up against nearly all Europe, he should say that James Watt was that person." The number of hand-looms now was very much the same as it was in 1820, being about 240,000 in England and Scotland, but the power-looms had increased since that date from 14,000 to 55,000—each power-loom might be calculated equal to three hand-looms. Of cotton workers in Manchester, the best class earned 20/- a week by piecework. In the woollen manufacture at Leeds, spinners and dressers earned 21/-, weavers, 14/-, working twelve hours ; spinners and weavers paid by the day. In Birmingham, still " the toy-shop of Europe," operatives worked ten hours, all by the piece ; the workers there had the reputation of being very independent. In Sheffield, where the finer sorts of cutlery were produced, three classes of workers earned, respectively, 25/-, 20/-, and 16/-. The Benefit Societies had upward of a million members, and had £16 millions invested in the Savings Banks.

CHAPTER L

1830. THE FALL OF THE WELLINGTON ADMINISTRATION

THE confusion of political parties, or rather the breaking down of the old party lines, at the beginning of the year was much com- mented on by contemporaries. The Ministry was presumably a Tory one [1]—at least the avowedly Whig element had been got rid of And yet it had repealed the Test Act and passed Catholic Emancipation against the wishes of the old Tories, and was in- flexibly adhering to the Free Trade policy. "The Whigs," said *Fraser's Magazine*, which started in February, "have been un- whigged, the Tories un-toried."

The position was strikingly put by the Earl of Darlington who had, for the past seventeen years, voted steadily with the Opposition, and now was moving the address to the Throne from the front benches. He found, he said, during these seventeen years many of the topics which had been urged without notice by the Opposition were at last treated with attention by the Ministerial benches, and that many of the measures for which the Whigs had long contended began to be adopted by the other side of the House, and were carried into execution by the Government. He had seen the change gradually approaching. "I felt that the course of events brought with it increased moderation and liberality, and I looked forward

---

[1] " Looking towards the Tories," said the *New Monthly Magazine*, " we are reminded of the sign of the ' Good Woman '—we see a marvellously proper body, but where the devil is the head ? They are the very reflection of a Highland army ; there are men, and arms, and courage enough for conquest, but there are more than enough divisions for defeat. Instead of one captain, they have fifty ; they are all impatience for action, and all confusion when action should begin. They are like the Frenchman's plum pudding ; the ingredients are excellent—there are the citron, the plums, the suet, the sugar, and the brandy—nothing is forgotten but the bag that should have kept them together " (438).

to the day when I might see accomplished that which I now see—namely, the time when Government would be entitled to demand the support of an independent member of Parliament, and when it would be no reflection on his principles to extend that support. . . . I now look upon the distinction of Whig and Tory as empty names, and, equally dreading the violence of both, I can with difficulty say which party I would wish to see predominant. The Government of the present day have shown that, in effect, the sounds of Whig and Tory are synonymous, and we see in them an administration without a party, or rather a Tory administration acting upon Whig principles. I support the administration in which I find a coincidence with those sentiments on which I have hitherto acted, and because I confide in it and in a prime minister who combines promptitude. judgment, and decision equal, if not superior, to any other who has ever been entrusted with power in this kingdom." The frequent applause with which these sentiments were greeted showed how grateful was the expression of what many had felt but no one had hitherto put in so many words.

Growing
weakness
of the
Government.
But it was scarcely to be expected that, in such circumstances, any Ministry could last long. The Duke—and Peel—had gone far beyond the old Tories.[1] They fell short of the wishes of the Whigs. The administration lived so long as it did because neither of the great parties was strong enough to come in alone. As a rule, then, the Government had three parties in opposition : the ultra-Tories who could not forgive the Catholic Emancipation, the Whigs, and Huskisson and his friends, and the Duke depended for the support of any particular measure on those of the three whom it suited, plus the few who were willing to vote according to their reason rather than their traditions.

As for the people outside, for the first part of the year, at any rate, they seemed to have profound confidence in the " strong man." He is the first man in our times, it was said, who has preferred principles to persons. They saw in him a Tory without

---

[1] These, to judge by their Press organs, were quite unable to grasp the new idea that a member who was not professedly a Whig might yet support measures identified with the Whigs. To them such a man was a traitor—not to common sense, not to conscience, but—to party. Hence, I am persuaded, the virulence of their abuse. They could scarcely have used the language they did unless they had believed it, and, to believe it they had to make their party their faith. This may seem far-fetched—it is, however, a choice between giving them this credit, and judging them to be both stupid and foul tongued. Nothing, even in modern politics, is comparable to the expres sions they used about Wellington and Peel.

the traditions ; a Whig without the pledges—one who had no
personal ambition, for there was nothing higher to which he might
attain. As Davenport said, he was " a kind of fourth estate,"
or, rather, he consolidated in his person the other three ; it was
impossible to turn the Ministry out—one might as well say he would
pull the House down.[1] But, later, the four rather absurd libel
suits raised by the Government had made the Duke very unpopular,
at any rate with the press.

Those who imagined that an administration which had
passed Catholic Emancipation would be liberal enough to
follow out the same line of reform were soon disillusioned when
Grant, the member for Fortrose, moved for leave to bring in a
bill for the Repeal of the Civil Disabilities affecting British-born
subjects professing the Jewish religion.[2] The Jews in the metropolis alone numbered about 20,000 and the total number in the
kingdom was 30,000 or 40,000. Their disabilities arose from the
requirement of taking the Oath of Allegiance upon the Evangelists,
and the new test " on the true faith of a Christian." Owing to
this, they could not hold any office, civil or military ; they could
not be schoolmasters or ushers ; they could not be serjeants at
law, barristers, solicitors, pleaders, conveyancers, attorneys, or
clerks ; they could not be members of Parliament, nor could they
vote for return of members if anybody chose to enforce the Oath ;
and, finally, they were excluded from all corporation offices. In
London, indeed, they could not obtain the freedom of the city,
and they could not exercise a retail trade.

One would have thought that the emancipation of the Roman
Catholics in the past year would have made it impossible to refuse
the same to subjects so little aggressive as the Jews, and it would
be waste of time now to repeat the case for their relief as put by
Macaulay—in a short, dignified, and strong maiden speech—and
by Sir James Mackintosh. It is more interesting to sum up the
arguments against the proposal put forward by Sir Robert Inglis,
who, it may be remembered, had ousted Peel for the University
of Oxford.

Jewish Disabilities.

---

[1] *Hansard*, xxiii. 393, 395. " Your great Duke," wrote Sydney Smith,
" seems like my ancle to be getting stronger every day. He is an excellent
Minister, and bids fair to be useful in peace as in war, and to show the utility
of beating swords into pruning hooks."

[2] The case for the Jews had already been temperately and acutely put in
a pamphlet, *Remarks on the Civil Disabilities of the British Jews*, by a well-
known member of their communion, Francis Henry Goldsmid.

(1) None but Christians had ever been admitted to Parliament or to power in this country, whereas Catholic Emancipation restored a right formerly enjoyed.[1]

(2) The Jews were aliens in the true sense—a people, not a sect; their country and their interests were not only different from but hostile to our own. (As another member put it: " No man could be an Englishman so long as he remained a Jew.")

(3) Their command of capital would enable them to obtain seats in Parliament; " the introduction of a Jew ought to be considered direct evidence of bribery, for it was out of the question to suppose that they would ever obtain the unbought suffrages of the people, and certain it was, that, within seven years after the entrance of the first Jew, Parliamentary Reform would be carried: those who were opposed to such reform were therefore bound to vote against the measure." [2]

(4) In France, although the law had given eligibility to the Jews, no Jew had ever been sent to the Chamber of Deputies; the same was the case in the Low Countries and in America.

(5) If the precedent were conceded, it would be difficult to withstand the introduction of any other class.

Goulburn opposed it on more guarded grounds, namely, the expediency of not offending the religious feelings or honest prejudices of the people; a new measure of liberality coming so soon after the other would beget an impression that the House was indifferent altogether to religion. The argument was so overwhelmingly on one side that Grant, in replying, appealed to every unprejudiced person who heard him if any subject had ever been more victoriously argued than the motion had been by those members who supported it. Still the motion was carried only by 115 to 97.

The Bill was supported by a great number of petitions—it was noticed that there was not one against—but, on the second reading, it was met by an extraordinary amount of opposition based almost entirely on religious grounds. Although Russell, Huskisson, Brougham, and O'Connell spoke strongly for it, Peel opposed, although with none of the violence and appeal to passion which distinguished many of the others, and it was thrown out by 228

[1] It did not escape notice that, while the chief objection to the removal of the Catholic disabilities had been political, in the case of the Jews religious persecution was avowed.

[2] As Mackintosh observed, it was a marvellous thing if the need of parliamentary reform which Chatham, Burke, Fox, and Pitt had been unable to persuade them of, should be demonstrated by the intrusion of a single Jew.

to 165. One notes, with some surprise perhaps, that, if the Bill
had admitted the Jews to everything but the right to sit in Parliament, it would almost certainly have passed.[1] When Grant, in
the end of the year, gave notice that, early in the coming session,
he would bring forward a motion on the subject, those who called
the Jews " aliens " were given this problem to think over in the
recess : If a Jew's father, grandfather, and great-grandfather were
born in Monmouth Street, would he be considered a native of this
country ; and, if he were taken with arms in his hands, fighting
against this country in the service of a foreign state, would he be
punished as a native-born subject ? Or would the plea that he
was a Syrian be admitted ? Did it not seem hard to recognize
his birth, only to make it a pretext for punishment ? [2]

As the session advanced, those who wished for a change of administration, but saw that it was hopeless on the old party lines,[3] perceived that there was one measure which the existing Government
was likely to oppose, and on which a strong party might unite.
It was Parliamentary Reform.

On 18th February, the Marquis of Blandford, a fiery and reckless
reformer since the passing of the Catholic Bill—which he considered was done in the teeth of the people's wishes—offered for
the consideration of the House a " practical detailed measure,"
containing, among other things, the transfer of franchises from
places fallen into decay to populous places and towns, and the
payment of members (£2 a day to citizens and burgesses and £4
to knights and county members).[4] The motion was negatived.
In the same month, Russell, in a speech much praised even by its

Anticipations of the Reform Bill.

[1] *Hansard*, xxii. 796, 923, 1308 ; xxiii. 1287 ; xxiv. 784. As *Blackwood*
said, with some point, " It is said the only sure way of making a pig go the
way you wish is to pull him by the tail in an opposite direction. Last year
the tables groaned under the weight of petitions against Catholic Emancipation, and the Bill was passed into law. This year numerous petitions implore
relief for the Jews, and the prayer is rejected ! "

[2] *Ibid.* N.S. i. 1185.

[3] The Whigs, said the *Edinburgh Annual Register* in 1824, " seem to have
lost the hope and almost the idea of occupying the position of their opponents."

[4] *Hansard*, xxii. 672. This latter proposal, as might be expected, met with
a mixed reception. Sir Robert Wilson genially observed that he was most
agreeably surprised at the suggestion that members should have wages, and
certainly could not bring himself to resist what was so pleasantly recommended.
Brougham did not approve. Peel was contemptuous—" they had that night
been occupied in discussing the propriety of reform ; and yet the Bill which
was to effect that reform contained a proposition enabling them to appropriate
to themselves £250,000 annually—a very modest proposal, and one well
calculated to recommend the House to public confidence."

opponents, moved for leave to bring in a Bill to enable Manchester, Leeds, and Birmingham—the capitals of three great manufactures —to have representation apart from the county to which they belonged; but even this very modest proposal was lost.[1] Later on, O'Connell moved for leave to bring in a Bill for an Effectual and Radical Reform of the House of Commons, the three features being triennial parliaments, universal suffrage, and vote by ballot, from all which measures Russell "most decidedly dissented," and the motion was lost by 319 to 13.[2] By all these debates, the policy of Parliamentary Reform was now shaped, and the Whigs only waited to try a fall with the Ministry which they had in the main supported.

Death of the King. On 26th June, George IV. died. It is scarcely surprising that there was little semblance of regret. The best that was said of him was that he was a munificent patron of the fine arts and had the largest collection of pictures by British artists that had ever been brought together : the worst—such as one hopes will never be said of an English king again. The Duke of Clarence succeeded as William IV.[3] and, on 24th July, Parliament was dissolved, not without ample indications that, when it met again, the Duke's Ministry could not count upon the support of the Whigs. With it all, intelligent outsiders could scarcely believe that the Government of the strong man was threatened : "averse from liberal measures, he will be as liberal as the times require," wrote Sydney Smith, "and will listen to instructed men on subjects where he has no opinions or wrong ones."

Independence of Belgium. Meantime came two events which shook the Ministry of the Duke. One was the break away of Belgium from Holland, when Brussels, thinking itself aggrieved by taxation, rose in arms, expelled the royal troops, and declared the Netherlands an independent power. The **Revolution in France.** other was the three days' Revolution in France, when the Duke of Orleans was proclaimed King of the French. It was hailed with uproarious applause in England. Deputations were sent to congratulate the French on the triumph of liberty, and subscriptions opened for those who had suffered. Grey felt strong enough to say that the justice of the cause of the people was proved by the

[1] *Hansard*, xxii. 858.   [2] *Ibid.* xxiv. 1204.

[3] The eccentricities of the new king form many amusing pages in Greville. Now he calls him " at present only a mountebank, but bidding fair to be a maniac "; now, " an incomparable king, as dignified as the homeliness and simplicity of his character will allow him to be."

moderation of their conduct : in the revolution which had been forced upon them, no blood had been shed which the violence of tyrants themselves did not render necessary.

The effect on the Government of the Duke was two-fold. He had been the personal friend of Polignac, the Minister of the fallen King, and it was easy to suggest that the Duke could not be friendly to the new rising against absolutism on the continent. And these two revolutions had shown the power of the people—were the people really represented in the English House of Commons ? Hence Parliamentary Reform, which up till now had excited only languid interest, was thrust to the front in the general election. In these circumstances, despite all the restrictions on popular representation, the Government lost 50 votes on which they had reason to count. As if to emphasise what might have happened under a freer election, Hume was returned for Middlesex and Brougham for York. " The signs of the times," wrote Greville, " are all for reform and retrench- ment, and against slavery." The Duke suddenly became the most unpopular man in the kingdom.

When the King's speech was delivered in person in November, it was bitterly attacked as putting into the King's mouth sentiments which could never be his. Brougham spoke of it as " adopting the principles of the Holy Alliance " ; it was unfriendly to Belgium and to France ;[1] it breathed interference with the affairs of other nations. For a week or so, the House was on edge. Recrimina- tions and personalities flew from side to side. Then the blow fell. Lord Grey, commenting on the danger of being involved in arms with France, said that the way to prepare for defence was to secure the affections of your fellow subjects, and by redressing their grievances, " and—my Lords, I will pronounce the words—by reforming Parliament." Unmoved by, or careless of, public opinion, the Duke said that he had never read or heard of any measure up to the present moment which could in any degree satisfy his mind that the state of the representation could be im- proved, or be rendered more satisfactory to the country at large

Fall of the Government.

---

[1] The passage in the speech ran thus : " The elder branch of the House of Bourbon no longer reigns in France, and the Duke of Orleans has been called to the throne by the title of the King of the French. Having received from the new sovereign a declaration of his earnest desire to cultivate the good under- standing and to maintain inviolate all the engagements subsisting with this country, I did not hesitate to continue my diplomatic relations and friendly intercourse with the French Court "—which does not seem particularly " unfriendly."

than it was at the present moment: he was not only not prepared to bring forward any measure of parliamentary reform, but he would always feel it his duty to resist such a measure when proposed by others.[1]

The challenge was soon taken up. On 12th November, the Chancellor of the Exchequer laid before the House the new proposals for the Civil list, showing a total grant of £970,000 as against £1,221,000 during the late reign. This was objected to by Althorp on the ground that it contained a great many items which were not branches of expenditure relative to the Monarchy itself; what was the use of his Majesty having monies paid to him—such as the salaries of ambassadors, the Lords of the Treasury, etc.— for the mere purpose of paying them out again, instead of these charges being annually brought under the view of parliament, and Parnell carried his motion for a Select Committee against the Government by 233 to 204. On 16th November, Wellington resigned.

The Whigs at last in power.

The King sent for Earl Grey, who accepted office on the understanding that Parliamentary Reform would be a Cabinet measure. The new Ministry included Lansdowne, Durham, Holland, Althorp (Chancellor of the Exchequer and Leader of the House of Commons), Melbourne (Home Secretary), Palmerston (Foreign Secretary), Goderich (Colonial Secretary), Howick (Under Secretary), Charles Grant (President of the Board of Control), Auckland (President of the Board of Trade), Poulett Thomson (Vice-President),[2] Sir James Graham (First Lord of the Admiralty), Duke of Richmond (Postmaster General), Lord John Russell (Paymaster General), and Mr. Stanley (Secretary for Ireland). To the surprise and indignation of many, Brougham, who had signified that he would take no part in the new Government, accepted the office of Lord

[1] " A violent and uncalled for declaration against reform which no doubt sealed his fate," said Greville. A statement so unlike his usual cautious habits, said the *New Monthly Magazine*, as to suggest that he wanted to " go out." Even before the dissolution, he seemed thoroughly unhappy, and would have retired gladly in favour of Peel—never did a man suffer so much and for so little purpose, he wrote Knighton. " One man wants one thing and one another," he wrote of his Cabinet; " they agree to what I say in the morning, and then in the evening up they start with some crotchet which deranges the whole plan. I have not been used to that in all the early part of my life. I assembled my officers and laid down my plan, and it was carried into effect without any more words."

[2] " There never was a more rapid rise than this: a young merchant, after two or three years of Parliament, and two or three speeches, is made Vice-President of the Board of Trade and a Privy Councillor " (*Greville*).

Chancellor.[1] So the Whigs came back after an absence from power of three and twenty years. The new Parliament assembled on 2nd November, and the remainder of the session was occupied by the Government staving off insistent demands upon them to justify their office.

The discussion in Parliament during the year was out of all proportion to the legislative issue—if, indeed, legislation be regarded as the issue. The debates extend over five large volumes instead of two as in former years. And yet the General Acts put on the Statute Book by the end numbered only 85. One explanation is the enormous place which petitions now took in the daily routine. Every now and then Ministers had to complain that they could not get through the public business on account of the time occupied by presenting petitions and making speeches on them.[2] Another explanation was advanced by the Peers. It was, shortly, that there was not a fair division of labour between the two Houses. It was not only that, owing to congestion, Bills did not come to the Upper House till late in the session, but that the Commons had limited the business of the Lords by their extreme doctrine relative to money clauses in Bills. They insisted that a clause imposing penalties was a money clause, because possibly money might be levied under it. The result was that no Bill containing such a clause could originate in the House of Lords, although it was a place peculiarly fit for the consideration of measures connected with penalties, such as Bills for the regulation of police, or for the regulation of law proceedings, and so all such Bills began in the Lower House, which was overlaid with business and with hundreds of accumulated orders, and reached the Lords at a period of the session when it was utterly impossible to consider them properly. Nay, the Commons had gone further. For two or three years, they had thrown out the Lords' Game Bill, not because it imposed any penalties, but because it remitted some. If persevered in, the practice must

A small legislative output.

---

[1] " The joy is universal ; once in the House of Lords, there is an end of him, and he may shout and storm and thunder without hurting anybody " (*Greville*).

[2] The petitions sometimes came from single individuals, and, once at least, Peel indignantly complained of the necessity of printing " any nonsense which an individual might choose to call a petition." Of another such, M. A. Taylor said that it was neither more nor less than a dissertation on the state of the country, and he must object to the expense of recording these lucubrations upon the Journals. It is gratifying to find that the prayer of many of these petitions was met by an order issued by Lord Wm. Bentinck in January, forbidding " suttee " in the East Indies.

prevent the Lords from originating any measure which either imposed or removed a pecuniary penalty. Was it not absurd that the House of Lords might inflict a punishment of death or imprisonment, but could not inflict a penalty of 40/- or £5 ? [1]

Repeal.   In the early part of the session, it may be noted, we hear the first expression in Parliament of the new agitation on which O'Connell now entered. It was on the occasion of a petition being presented from Drogheda, alleging that Ireland was suffering incalculable mischief from the Act of Union and praying for Repeal. O'Connell frankly and openly supported the petition, charging Parliament with utter disregard of the local interests of Ireland. The Sub-letting Act, the Vestries Act, the disfranchising of the Forty Shilling Free-holders, were all passed in contempt of Irish interests. He did not see any reason for depriving Ireland of a separate legislature any more than Canada, Halifax, or Jamaica, where independent representation was permitted to deliberate on the local interests of the people. He believed the day was not far distant when the friends of Ireland and England would unite in giving their consent to the repeal of the Union as an advantage to both countries. This was somewhat of a bombshell. Wetherell and others said that the petition was so clearly an attack on the Constitution —so little short of treason—that they would call for its rejection. Peel, though he did not feel much surprise at the doubts expressed regarding the propriety of receiving a petition in support of a proposal "so mad and so absurd," while deprecating in the strongest way the doctrines put forward, and declaring that he could not find language strong enough to express his disapprobation of the doctrines set forth, saw no reason why the petition should not be received, seeing that it did not propose separation and dismemberment, and the petition accordingly was laid on the table. [2]

But during the summer, the agitation, which had not been even mentioned at the last election, spread so fast that, in November, it was made the subject of a special clause in the new King's Speech : " I cannot view without grief and indignation the efforts which are industriously made to excite among my people a spirit of discontent and disaffection, and to disturb the concord which happily prevails between those parts of my dominions, the union of which is essential to their common strength and common happiness." " There is no

---

[1] *Hansard*, xxiv. 1346 ; xxv. 415.   [2] *Ibid.* xxiii. 701.

doubt that repeal is making rapid advances," wrote Greville in the end of December.

It is, perhaps, worth noting that, in these early days, O'Connell defined Repeal, though in words that themselves needed defining. It was a false and villainous assertion, he said, that Ireland wanted, or ever wanted, to be separated from England except so far as related to the Protestant Established Church. " Never was there a greater mistake than to suppose that we wish to dissolve the connection. No, but we want a connection of authority, not of subserviency—of equality, not of submission. Ireland must be equal, not inferior—she must be a kingdom, not a province." Whatever it meant, petitions began to pour in from Ireland claiming Repeal. Repeal was no whim of his, said O'Connell, but the ardent desire of 99 persons out of every 100 in Ireland—although he subsequently changed the statement to " in three of the provinces 99 per cent. were in favour of Repeal." But, by this time, England had good reason to think that O'Connell had one voice in Ireland, another in Parliament.

The obituary of the year is very heavy. Besides George IV., it Obituary. includes Sir Thomas Lawrence, President of the Royal Academy, Lord Redesdale, George Tierney,[1] and Sir Robert Peel, in his 80th year.[2]

But a greater man died before Parliament met again. The Death of Liverpool and Manchester Railway was opened on 15th September [3] Huskisson. amid great rejoicings. Immense crowds—a million and a half of people, it was said—made the passage of the train a triumphal progress. The Duke was in a special carriage, and the famous " Rocket " driven by George Stephenson himself, seems to have been giving exhibition trials on the other line. At one point,

[1] See *Economic Annals*, *1801-20*, 360. There is a good memoir in the *Gentleman's* for March.

[2] His personalty was sworn above £900,000, on which the modern observer notes with interest that the death duties (probate, and stamp, and legacy duty) amounted to no more than £25,000.

[3] The opening was recognised as an event of national importance. In 1829, the directors had almost given up the idea of a travelling engine, till Stephenson induced them to offer a prize of £500 for the best locomotive, which was won by his own " Rocket," moving at the rate of 35 miles an hour. Creevey had gone a trial trip in November, and describes the speed (sometimes 23 miles an hour) as " frightful; it is really flying, and it is impossible to divest oneself of the notion of instant death to all upon the least accident happening. . . . It gave me a headache which has not left me yet." Some interesting particulars as to the marvellous work at Chat Moss in 1828 are given in the *New Monthly Magazine* of that year, p. 228.

Huskisson had got out to shake hands with the Duke, whom probably he had not met since his resignation, and was standing on the foot-way when the cry arose that the " Rocket " was coming. Before Huskisson could get in, the door of the carriage was caught by the passing locomotive, and Huskisson was thrown across the rails, to die—" the death of a great man "—in a few hours after. Seldom has a day of rejoicing closed in deeper gloom.

Much might be said of Huskisson, but the story told in these pages of what he had done since 1824 is his best monument. Greville's words, however, may be quoted :

" Huskisson was about sixty years old, tall, slouching, and ignoble-looking. In society he was extremely agreeable, without much animation, generally cheerful, with a great deal of humour, information, and anecdote, gentlemanlike, unassuming, slow in speech, and with a downcast look, as if he avoided meeting anybody's gaze. . . . It is probably true that there is no man in Parliament, or perhaps out of it, so well versed in finance, commerce, trade, and colonial matters and that he is therefore a very real and irreparable loss. It is nevertheless remarkable that it is only within the last five or six years that he acquired the great reputation which he latterly enjoyed. I do not think he was looked upon as more than a second-rate man till his speeches on the silk trade and the shipping interest ; but, when he became President of the Board of Trade, he devoted himself with indefatigable application to the maturing and reducing to practice those commercial improvements with which his name is associated, and to which he owes all his glory and most of his unpopularity. It is equally true that all the ablest men in the country coincide with him, and that the mass of the community are persuaded that his plans are mischievous to the last degree."

Economic literature.

The following appear among publications of the year : *Essays on Political Economy, in which are illustrated the principal causes of the present national distress with appropriate remedies ;* Western's *Letter on the Present Distress of the Country ; The Present Distress in relation to the Theory of Money,* by Edward Solly ; Sadler's *The Law of Population, a treatise in disproof of super-fecundity of human beings and developing the real principles of their increase ;* Jacob's *Inquiry into the production and consumption of the Precious Metals, and on the influence of their augmentation or diminution on the commerce of the world ;* Senior's *Three Lectures on the Cost of obtaining*

Money ; Senior's *Three Lectures on the Rate of Wages ;* Sir Henry Parnell's *On Financial Reform.*

MISCELLANEA.

In *Fraser's Magazine,* which started in February, the eye is caught by the arrogant, challenging style, soon to be identified with Carlyle, and by the famous Goethe rendering :

> " In Existence' floods, in Action's storm,
> I walk and work, above, beneath,
> Work and weave, in endless motion,
> Birth and death,
> An infinite ocean,
> A seizing and giving,
> The fire of living :
> Thus at the roaring Loom of Time I ply,
> And weave for God the Garment thou seest him by."

NOTE ON THE CYCLICAL MOVEMENT.[1]

The characteristics of the decade may be tabulated thus :

	Industry.	*Agriculture.*
1821.	Slow revival.	Deep gloom.
1822.	Confirmed revival.	Settled gloom.
1823.	Prosperity.	Revival.
1824.	Flourishing beyond example.	No distress.
1825.	Climax of prosperity.	Prosperity.
1826.	Commercial crisis and collapse.	No complaints.
1827.	Revival.	No complaints.
1828.	Steady progression.	Bad harvest.
1829.	Sudden relapse.	Bad harvest.
1830.	Depression and quick recovery.	Poor harvest : settled gloom.

[1] Cf. *Economic Annals, 1801-20,* 606, and *supra.*

INDEX OF PERSONS

Cobbett, 2, 14, 51, 52, 57, 82, 92, 114, 116, 136, 137, 154, 172, 173, 179, 183, 186, 207, 244, 257, 317, 370, 401, 417, 515, 516.
Cockburn, 361.
Coffin, 33, 202, 397.
Cohen, 181.
Coke, 59, 136.
Colchester, 509.
Coleridge, 54.
Collins, 54.
Constable, 332, 391.
Cooper, Fenimore, 54.
Cooper, Thomas, 509.
Copley (Lyndhurst), 419, 438.
Corbaux, 246.
Courtenay, 248, 458, 531.
Craig, 55.
Creevey, 61, 67, 128, 132, 149, 154, 301, 317, 321, 389, 396, 407, 417, 419, 429, 430, 467, 569.
Croker, 49, 122, 129, 132, 254, 317, 328, 419, 444, 504.
Cruickshank, 179.
Cruttwell, 55.
Cumberland, 502.
Curteis, 185.
Curwen, 4, 6, 7, 40, 68, 81, 107, 122, 143, 151, 384, 385, 447.

Darlington, 558.
Davenport, 530, 561.
Davies, 128, 218.
Davy, Humphry, 54, 509.
Dawson, 535.
Dawson (Londonderry), 545.
Denman, 395.
De Quincey, 54, 246.
Derby, 321.
Disraeli, 406.
Doubleday, 452.
Dowell, 215, 268, 425.
Droz, 509.
Drummond, 400.
Dudley and Ward, 438.
Dunlop, 114.
Durham (Lambton), 566.

Edwards, 436.
Eldon, 406, 418, 420, 429, 438, 443.
Ellenborough, 31, 166, 175, 388, 429, 437, 439, 444, 457, 524, 529, 530, 538.
Ellice, 200, 207, 237, 351, 365, 369, 370.
Elliston, 54.
Emperor of Austria, 192, 193, 201.
Enniskillen, 418.
Ensor, 181.
Erskine, 131, 174, 179, 182.
Etty, 54.
Everett, 181.

Farren, 54.
Ferdinand VII., 175.
Ferguson, 409, 443.
Finlay, Kirkman, 282.
Fitzgerald (Kerryshire), 393.
Fitzgerald, Vesey, 169, 445, 448, 458, 479, 485, 487, 488, 495.
Fitzwilliam, 93.
Flaxman, 54.
Fox, 562.
Francis, 188.
Franklin, 194.
Fry, Mrs., 54.
Fyler, 478, 484, 488, 491, 525.

George IV., 48, 52, 125, 131, 402, 407, 419, 430, 437, 502, 512, 564, 569.
Galt, 54, 179.
Ganilh, 111, 400.
Gascoyne, 424, 427, 458.
Giffen, 72.
Gladstone, 550.
Goderich, Robinson, 538, 566.
Goethe, 571.
Goldschmidt, 324.
Goldsmid, 561.
Gooch, 3, 6, 14, 67, 68, 413, 416.
Gordon, 436.
Goulburn, 68, **169**, 259, 437, 448, 449, 450, 452, 458, 475, 495, 497, 521, 522, 524, 536, 537, 540, 541, 543, 544, 545, 546, 547, 548, 562, 566.
Graham, 334, 400, 494, 535, 566.
Grant, Chas., 227, 285, 371, 439, 440, 441, 442, 458, 460, 466, 544, 545, 562, 566.
Grant (Fortrose), 561.
Grattan, 317.
Gray, Simon, 391, 513.
Grenfell, 36, 83, 84, 152, 236, 296, 353, 377.
Grenville, 447, 448.
Greville, 49, 122, 324, 347, 348, 419, 421, 488, 513, 514, 523, 524, 564, 565, 566, 569.
Grey, 76, 175, 419, 420, 514, 534, 564, 565, 566.
Griffith, 124.
Grimaldi, 54.
Grosvenor, 243, 297, 352.
Gurney, 90, 299, 347, 348, 351.

Hale, 210.
Hall, Geo. Webb, 14, 93, 117, 246, 386, 407.
Hamilton (Lord Archibald), 99, 100, 103, 106, 178, 334, 353.
Hannay, 181.
Hardinge, 226.
Harrowby, 167, 239.
Harvey, 459, 471, 476.
Haworth, 509.

SUBJECT INDEX

Absentees, 89, 254 ; M'Culloch on, 370.

Adams (President) on U.S. tariff, 463 ; on Balance of Trade, 464.

Agricultural Committee's Report, of 1821, 6 ; Ricardo's opinion of, 16 ; the author of, 67 ; of 1822, 75.

Agriculture, annual phenomena, 1821, 18 ; 1822, 113 ; 1823, 144 ; 1824, 184 ; 1825, 301 ; 1826, 389 ; 1827, 434 ; 1828, 454 ; 1829, 473 ; 1830, 513.

Agriculture, puzzling condition in 1821, 1 ; distress ascribed to Peel's Act, 2 ; to taxation, 58 ; depression of 1821, 18 ; of 1822, 58, 115 ; still the chief industry, 113 ; distress passes in 1823, 134, 143 ; disappears in 1824 and 1825, 183, 291, 301 ; despair of, in 1830, 513 ; wages in 1821, 20 ; in 1824, 185.

Aliens Act recast, 394.

Althorp, would divert the Sinking Fund, 69 ; on the distress of 1822, 69 ; on the Debt as a perpetual annuity, 270.

Annuities (National Debt), 216, 362, 428, 451, 537.

Apprenticeship on merchant vessels, 167.

Artizans, emigration of, 229.

Assessed taxes, reduced, 150, 151 ; Maberly moves repeal, 221 ; reduced again, 268.

Attwood, on diminishing returns, 79 ; on Peel's Bill, 99 ; on protection, 493 ; on bimetallism, 532.

Austrian loan, 193, 201.

Balance of Power redressed by Canning, 405.

Balance of Trade (President Adams), 464.

Banking, crisis in 1825, 298 ; six partners' restriction, 350 ; backwardness of France and other countries in note issue, 340 ; county, 345 ; Scots, 353 ; Irish, 350, 353, 356. (*See also* Small Notes.)

Bank of England, restriction ends, 42 ; criticism of its conduct, 83, 236 ; run on, 299 ; advances to landowners in 1824, 237 ; advances on goods, 327.

Baring, on the timber duties, 30 ; the double standard, 140 ; silk protection, 205, 212, 370 ; crisis of 1825, 300 ; small notes, 341, 344 ; treaties, 404 ; philosophic doubts on Free Trade, 485 ; wise speech on distress of 1830, 526.

Barrack system, 225.

Bathurst's circular to slave colonies, 178.

Beer, intermediate, 155 ; tax repealed, 538, 541, 542, 547 ; free sale of, 538, 541.

Bethnal Green a hereditary group, 488.

Bimetallism, 44, 46, 140, 519, 529, 532.

Blandford's Reform proposals, 563.

Bonded corn released, 1825, 303 ; 1826, 387 ; 1827, 422, 441.

Bounties (whale, herring, linen) reduced, 194 ; on exported silks repealed, 199 ; on sugar, 217 ; on fisheries, 552 ; on linen, 213, 552.

Brandy, smuggling of, 218.

Brassage, 43.

Bread, white supplants brown, 1823, 142.

Brougham on distress of 1822, 59.

Budget, 1821, 38 ; 1822, 77, 80, 88 ; 1823, 149 ; 1824, 192 ; 1825, 264 ; 1826, 358 ; 1827 (Canning's), 427 ; 1828, 449 ; 1829, 475 ; 1830, 537.

Burgh Electoral Reform (Scotland), 178, 392.

Caledonian Canal, 202.

Canadian wheat to enter at 5/-, 274, 304.

Candles, tax, 143, 154, 548.

Canning, retires from Cabinet in 1821, 49 ; opposes parliamentary reform, 130 ; succeeds Castlereagh, 132 ; restores the Balance of Power, 405 ; introduces 1827 Corn Bill, 407 ; on a fixed duty, 408 ; Premier and Chancellor of the Exchequer, 419 ; death, 429.